The
L.L. Bean
Game and Fish
Cookbook

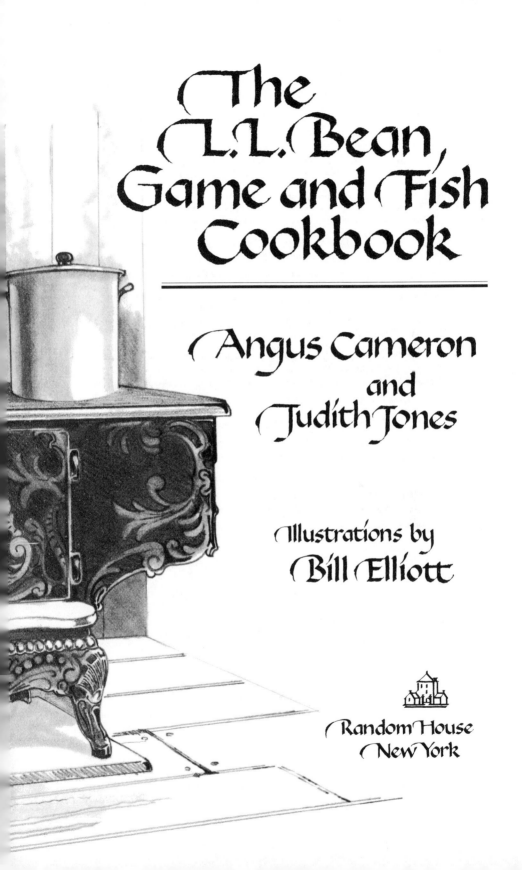

The L.L. Bean Game and Fish Cookbook

Angus Cameron
and
Judith Jones

Illustrations by
Bill Elliott

Random House
New York

*Grateful acknowledgment is made to the following for permission to reprint
previously published material:*

Alfred A. Knopf, Inc.: Recipes from four sources. "Fish, Veracruz Style" and
"Rabbit in Coconut Milk" from *The Book of Latin American Cooking* by
Elisabeth Lambert Ortiz. Copyright © 1979 by Elisabeth Lambert Ortiz. "Baked Rigatoni
with Meat Sauce" from *The Classic Italian Cook Book* by Marcella Hazan, trans-
lated by Victor Hazan. Copyright © 1973 by Marcella Hazan and Victor
Hazan. "Swordfish Stimpirata" from *More Classic Italian Cooking* by Marcella
Hazan, illustrated by Marisabina Russo. Copyright © 1978 by Marcella Hazan
and Victor Hazan. "Baked Parsnips with Fruit" from *The Victory Garden
Cookbook* by Marian Morash. Copyright © 1982 by Marian Morash and
WGBH Educational Foundation. Reprinted by permission of Alfred A. Knopf, Inc.

Atheneum Publishers: "Cameron Bread Sauce" from *The Highland Fling Cookbook* by Sara Walker. Copyright © 1971 by Sara Walker. Reprinted with the
permission of Atheneum Publishers.

Robert Cornfield Literary Agency: Recipe from *Feasts for All Seasons* by Roy
de Groot. "Roast Leg of Venison with Chocolate Sauce," Copyright © 1966
by Roy Andries de Groot.

Farrar, Straus and Giroux, Inc.: "Roast Haunch of Venison" from *With a Jug
of Wine* by Morrison Wood. Copyright 1949 by Morrison Wood. Renewed
© 1977 by Beatrice Wood. Reprinted by permission of Farrar, Straus and Giroux, Inc.

Gourmet: Recipe from *The Gourmet Cookbook*, volume 1. Reprinted by permission of the Editors of *Gourmet* Magazine.

Library of Congress Cataloging in Publication Data

Cameron, Angus.
The L.L. Bean game and fish cookbook.

Includes index.
1. Cookery (Game)   2. Cookery (Fish)
I. Jones, Judith.   II. Title.
TX751.C27   1982   641.6'91   82-15089
ISBN 0-394-51191-3

Manufactured in the United States of America

10

Book design and calligraphy by Carole Lowenstein

Acknowledgments and Dedication

For the help given to us by the various friends who cook game we extend our thanks twice over, for each is acknowledged in the recipe's introduction, but others contributed to this book various services that were much appreciated. Kate Hargrave Smith, late mother-in-law of the senior author, was helpful in many ways, including the typing of first drafts of many of the recipes. Joseph Conte, angling and fishing partner and wingshot nonpareil, supplied game on many occasions when the author's supplies became exhausted through the testing of recipes.

Carol Atkinson, who typed the manuscript, deserves special credit, for she learned to read our handwriting better than the authors could manage it themselves.

We are particularly indebted to our copy editor, Millie Owen, for her sharp eyes, common sense and unfailing good humor.

Our thanks also go to Carole Lowenstein, the book's designer, who, even though herself a vegetarian, brought a meateater's enthusiasm to the creative task. We also wish to thank Bill Elliott for the magnificent pencil drawings of game, game birds and fish that adorn and illuminate this book.

Without our inspired editor Jason Epstein this marriage between the authors and L. L. Bean might never have been consummated, and we are grateful, too, to his editorial assistant Beverly Haviland for her patience, perseverance, and good judgment as she saw the manuscript through.

The senior author would like to thank Sheila K. Cameron, his wife and favorite hunting and fishing partner for a thousand contributions, including culinary, to this book, and to dedicate his part of the book to her.

The junior author dedicates her share to her husband, Evan Jones, an inexhaustible source of information and of inspiration.

My grandfather was the first person in Freeport to own a freezer. Back in the forties when they first came on the market, he quickly recognized the freezer's value in preserving deer meat, salmon, and other fish and game for future consumption. "L.L." was as enthusiastic about eating his catch as he was in hunting or fishing for it. He even put various freezer accessory items in his catalog to share his discovery with other sportsmen.

Yet for all his success with rod and gun and his well-known gusto at the dinner table, L.L. wasn't much of a hand in the kitchen. His brother, Otho, did the cooking at their hunting camp, and his other hunting and fishing companions learned with bitter experience to keep L.L. away from the stove. It's not known where his notoriety as a camp cook began, but his sautéed black duck and fried potato dinner was certainly one of the reasons it persisted.

Just before the Second World War, L.L. went duck hunting for the day with two or three friends off Lane's Island near Freeport. It was a successful outing and he volunteered to work up dinner that evening for the group. While L.L. was sautéing the black duck breasts, the group got talking about duck calls. George Soule, a good friend of L.L.'s, had developed a special type of duck call which he had been testing throughout the day. Whenever he called, the whole sky seemed to light up with ducks. Everyone, especially L.L., had been impressed. On occasion L.L. would interrupt the conversation and ask how people liked the duck cooked. Each person gave the usual response, rare. L.L. would turn the breasts and the conversation would resume. After a dozen such breaks, he turned the duck once again, asked each person how he liked it cooked, and served up something that looked more like well-done liver than waterfowl. The potatoes were a new type of dehydrated potato that had just become available for campers. They came in one-quarter-inch cubes and you soaked them overnight before frying. L.L. had soaked them only half an hour. They had barely swollen up at all and his friends described them as fried bullets with bacon-fat flavoring.

Most of L.L.'s game dinners turned out better, thanks to talented friends, and they were all good fun. Eating in camp or along the trail is always a time for reliving the day's adventures. When the meal is fresh duck breasts or newly caught trout, the bond with the outdoors is that much greater. Get-togethers at home featuring fish or game extend to the indoors the joys of the outdoor life. The tales grow taller and the friendships fonder, and the better the meal, the better the memories.

Most of us at L.L. Bean enjoy hunting, fishing, or other outdoor sports. We also enjoy the times in camp and the anticipation of dinnertime. Over the years several first-rate cooks have emerged, and their special recipes have been much in demand. Other sportsmen friends of ours have developed worthy cooking specialties that deserve to be shared. We started offering clinics at our retail store in the preparation and cooking of wild game. These proved exceptionally popular and convinced us there was a real need for a full-scale L.L. Bean book on cooking wild game.

Since we didn't know anything about publishing a cookbook, it was quite fortunate that Angus Cameron showed up one day with the same idea. Angus is a long-time Bean friend who's hunted, fished, and cooked game on wood ranges and sheet-metal stoves from Maine to Alaska. In 1946 while he was editor-in-chief of Little, Brown in Boston, he was the one who first tried to persuade L.L. to write a book about outdoor gear, and his persistence ultimately proved instrumental in the publication of our *L.L. Bean Guide to the Outdoors* (Random House, 1981). No newcomer to the book-publishing business, Angus was senior editor at Alfred A. Knopf for many years and has written a number of articles for *Field and Stream, Fly Fisherman,* and *Sports Afield.* He also edited such well-known outdoor books as *The Complete Wilderness Paddler, The Complete Walker,* and all of Jack O'Connor's hunting books.

Angus has also accumulated hundreds of outstanding recipes of wild game cooking. Being a serious student of eating wild game as well as of preparing it, Angus tested all his recipes and his enthusiasm for our project was unbounded. He invited his long-time colleague Judith Jones to join in. Judith comes from the Northeast Kingdom of Vermont and is currently vice-president and senior editor for Alfred A. Knopf. She has worked there for twenty-five years and has been involved in a wide variety of different books, including cookbooks with such author-cooks as Julia Child and James Beard. She edited the twelfth and revised version of *The Fannie Farmer Cookbook,* and most recently was author with her husband Evan Jones of *The World of Bread,* published by Harper and Row.

We now had Angus's great collection of recipes along with those of our staff. We collected more from our many sportsmen friends and solicited others from hunting and fishing guides, game wardens, outdoor writers, and sporting camp owners. Angus and Judith gave us one of the best editorial teams that ever went into a cookbook. They went through the prodigious task of sorting out all of the recipes, testing those that showed promise, and putting the final selections together in this book. Interesting and appropriate editorial material based on first-hand experience precedes each section. Many helpful hints are included. The result is, in our opinion, the finest cookbook yet on the preparation and cooking of wild game.

—LEON GORMAN

Contents

Introduction

The cooking of game and game fish has always been an important part of the American cuisine; if anything, it is more American than apple pie and more indigenous. Game and fish have supplied an important part of the American diet for at least two centuries and are still important in many areas of our country today. When the frontier was on the Eastern Seaboard the use of game was often crucial and continued to be an important part of the diet as the frontier moved on across the continent—to the middle frontier, to the Old West, and finally to Alaska.

To hunt and fish and to eat game and fish came naturally to Americans, and no wonder—our ancestors in Europe were either enthusiastic hunters or poachers and savored game meats of all kinds. Of course if we wished to go back far enough, all the familiar meats—beef, pork, mutton and goat—were once game. Our remotest Stone Age forebears hunted the wild ancestors of all of our domestic critters long before they settled down as herders and farmers.

It is perhaps not at all surprising, then, that this game cookbook should have originated with an institution like L. L. Bean; what better origin for a game and fish cookbook than with an outfitter of people who love the out-of-doors. The people at Bean had long had the idea of such a cookbook simmering on the back of the wood range, as it were. Bean had long wanted a game cookbook to house their own and to add other good game recipes—a book that would be useful to the twenty-five million men and women, many of them Bean customers, who hunt and fish and are always on the lookout for good recipes.

Similarly, the authors, long-time colleagues in book publishing at Alfred A. Knopf, had been talking for several years about a fish and game cookbook. Indeed, the junior author* had tried in her role as cookbook editor at Knopf to get the senior author to write just such a book. When Bean heard of this potential team through Jason Epstein of Random House, the project was soon launched.

From the outset a very large number of tested recipes were already available from the card files of both authors, from the files of the cooking clinics at L. L. Bean, from numerous Bean staff members, and from many friends of all three of the principals. The senior author had been cooking game and game fish in his own kitchen and in a host of hunting and fishing camps from Maine to Alaska for forty years. The other author—and her husband, Evan, himself an author-cook—had cooked game in France as well as in their own homes in New York City and Vermont. Since 1959 the senior author had often supplied venison, game birds, wild fowl, and salmon and trout for his colleague's kitchen. At the publishing office of Knopf the two often swapped stories of new fish and game dishes and methods of handling and preparing game.

We have tried to produce a book whose recipes for each animal, bird, or fish will range from the simplest broiling, stewing, sautéing, or roasting recipes to those somewhat more elaborate. More elaborate, yes, but not more complicated;

*Judith Jones is referred to as the "junior author" only because she is the younger of the two.

everyone connected with this cookbook believes that it can be easily used by anyone who can read and has a zest for eating. Recipes that include a longish list of ingredients are not necessarily difficult recipes. Every recipe in this book can be prepared in the average American kitchen. You don't have to be a practiced cook to use this cookbook.

The person who periodically serves game knows that most people tend to consider game a special delicacy. They can generally count on the fact that the prospect of a game dinner arouses in most guests a hint of primitive anticipation.

The "ancient humours of the chase" still have the power to stir the hearts and palates of most modern men and women, and the cook can usually count on the fact that game, if properly cooked, seldom disappoints. The flavors of most game birds, animals and fish are distinctive; subtly distinctive with grouse, rabbit or salmon, more strongly so with goose, woodcock or bluefish. Though in a casserole or stew moose meat will fool some people, passing easily for the very finest of prime beef, a broiled venison chop does not taste like either beef or lamb. It is different, that is certain. It is also delicious. Whether that taste of game can be called a wild or gamey taste is a matter of semantics.

However, a most important factor that the users of this cookbook will quickly discover is that any game meat, like domestic meats, depends partly for its flavor on how it was handled in the woods or fields, how it was transported home, and how and when it was butchered and stored. Many a guest who claims that he or she does not like venison because it is too gamey is usually really commenting on the taste of the meat from a deer poorly field-dressed, transported in the trunk of a car (or in the old days, draped over a car fender), and carelessly butchered. In this book—sometimes in the introductions to the game animals, birds, or fish, sometimes in special appendixes—we have tried to lard the recipes, as it were, with useful information about proper handling. Too many game cookbooks ignore this kind of essential detail. We have also sought to give suggestions about the selection of recipes based on foreknowledge of the condition of the game—i.e., its age, size, relative tenderness or toughness, nature of the cuts, etc.

Even many experienced cooks are not sufficiently aware that good game dishes often depend on knowing as much as possible about the game in question. For example, the cook who comes by a Canada goose that weighs 6½ pounds dressed should know that that bird is mature and probably old and tough, and should be braised under a lid rather than roasted dry and uncovered. Similarly where age determines tenderness; often, it is useful for the cook to know the age of the game or determine it himself or herself.

In the text and in the appendixes we have given information not only on the handling of game and fish but on the tricks of the trade for determining age and the likelihood of toughness in certain instances. Throughout the book we have also suggested useful ways of tenderizing tough game or reducing toughness by the particular cooking method selected.

Each species of game has its virtues, its own particular character, and we have tried with each entry to present recipes that seem peculiarly suited to that animal, bird, or fish, offering a wider range of selection for those species that are the most common in America. Yet many recipes serve more than one species deliciously. So in each recipe that can be used for game other than that for which it was specifically created, this fact is noted in the introduction to that recipe. In the case of game birds, where size determines amount, the cook is given quantities for each bird to which the recipe might apply. A recipe for one pheasant, yet which can be used for grouse, partridge, or ptarmigan, would call for two grouse, and perhaps for three partridges.

Recipes are listed in the index under the name of the game animal or bird or fish, but if you find yourself with moose stew meat, for instance, you may discover that a stew listed under venison or elk or caribou is the one you would prefer to make, so browse around in the book and your repertoire will be greatly increased. The truth is that the differences in taste and texture of the meats of big-game animals is not so great. I have seen many diners over the years who were quite unable to detect the difference between a moose and a beef stew. To many eaters, venison tastes quite different from moose or elk, yet the latter two are sometimes mistaken for each other, and moose could easily be taken for musk ox. Both in my opinion taste like beef—with one difference: they are far tastier than the beef we get today.

Dall sheep is a particularly delicious big-game meat: it does not taste like mutton. It does, however, taste a good deal like the lamb one gets in Iceland, where the sheep flocks are nearly wild on the high moors there.

Bear meat is distinctive. It tastes like a meld of pork with beef—as fat as pork yet with a color and texture more like beef.

For the increasing numbers of cooks who do not shoot but who love the taste of game, and buy it in the market for preparation at home, let us recommend ourselves by saying that we are not game wasters, and where big game is concerned, the people who hunt at L. L. Bean and the authors are not trophy hunters who take the head and the loins of an animal and leave the rest of the meat to scavengers. The senior author can say that he has never killed a big-game animal that has not been wholly used as meat. This always entails hard work and often hard packing back to camp. But the record is unblemished; as an old Indiana farm boy I would no more waste the meat of a big-game animal than I would that of a carefully boned and fattened farm hog or steer. Most hunters that I know feel and act the same way.

As for fishing, all connected with this book—L. L. Bean, Random House, and the authors—are strong adherents to the "catch and release" programs of most states. When we do keep fish, we keep enough for one meal; most of the fish taken are carefully returned to the water.

We hope we have produced a book that the late Leon L. Bean would have approved of; and it is equally our hope that this book reflects in some general way that mix of the traditional and the modern that characterizes L. L. Bean in the last quarter of this century. Here are recipes whose origins date back to the early days of the republic, and in some instances beyond; at the same time many of these recipes belong to a more modern cuisine. None, as we have said, is really complicated. We believe that anyone who can read *and who likes to eat* can become a good cook.

There are many basic recipes throughout the book that are well suited to camp cooking (marked with this symbol ⊟) as well as those that can be easily prepared under canvas (marked ◿△◺). There is also a special section on some of the strategies for successful camp cookery based on the senior author's experience of being chief camp cook on hunting trips over a period of more than forty years, preparing meals for hungry hunters and fishermen both on ancient wood ranges in remote cabins from New Brunswick to Alaska and on sheet-metal Yukon stoves in tent camps on many a lake and stream.

It is our hope that this book will stimulate all who love to hunt and fish to use their game well, never to waste a morsel (for recipes using leftovers, see pages 337–350), and to relish the fine taste of the wild in a variety of new ways, some simple and relatively unadorned, others more challenging and innovative.

Angus Cameron
Judith Jones

Red Meat

WHITETAIL DEER

All Meat Is Game

It is well to remember that *all* meat is game in a sense; for millennia man hunted all the animals we now eat before he domesticated them. In this sense the flavor of beef or lamb has "gamy" flavor, i.e., that animal's distinctive flavor, and the distinctive flavor of game is no different from the distinctive flavor of beef or mutton.

The person unfamiliar with the eating of game should consider that in a sense the difference, say, between veal and beef—meat from the same animal—is that the latter is "gamier" than the former.

The person who prefers the lustiness of a rare rack of mutton on occasion to the delicacy of spring lamb is in fact preferring the "gaminess" of the former.

Unhappily in our times the husbandry of beef culture has reduced the gaminess of the beef we eat and in the process has reduced its deliciousness: the sometimes insipidity of the beef we buy is to be explained by the fact that we are now eating "baby beef." For reasons of profit (and price) it is simply no longer possible to buy beef whose flavor has matured to its ultimate excellence. Beeves are now killed at sixteen months instead of speed-fattened twenty-four or more; it just isn't economical to feed the critters long enough to produce the real flavor of beef. As a result there are literally millions of Americans who do not know what truly fine beef tastes like.

The Eskimos, who until recently were still living the hunting and fishing life, know that the mature caribou, the old mature bull taken when he has a thick layer of fat over his loins, is far finer eating than the young animal.

Nothing could be further from the truth than the old saw one hears around the hunting camp from the hunter who has bagged a spike horn. He is apt to say, perhaps partly to compensate for his envy of his partner's ten-pointer, "Well, he may not have a trophy head but he's real 'eatin' venison.'" The truth is the meat from the younger deer, though delicious, as veal is delicious, is not generally as good eatin' meat as that from a bigger animal.

Like beef, the fat of a three- or-four-year-old animal invariably has a better flavor than the gilpin's or calf's of the same species.

We will have a few remarks to make specifically about the meat of deer, antelope, moose, elk, caribou, etc., as we go along, but here suffice it to say that most deer and antelope recipes are completely interchangeable. Moose, elk, and caribou recipes are mostly interchangeable, and a great many deer recipes are excellent for the meat of larger animals too.

And now, a final word about gaminess: the strong gamy taste that some people speak of seldom describes the real taste of big game meat; more often it is a flavor caused by improper handling of the game animal when it was dressed, butchered, or transported. We have some comments to make on the handling of game in the Appendix, but here let us say that while a bull moose that has run all of his fat off during the rut may not be prime, so neither would a skinny, stringy beef steer be prime eating.

Determining Age in Large-Horned Game

Twenty-five years ago when the Eskimo culture was intact and the people were still living the hunting and fishing life, the caribou was one of two chief mainstays for food. Like most of the rest of us, Eskimos are very taste-conscious.

They say that the fat mature animal, which generally means an old bull taken when he has a thick layer of suet over his loins, is far finer eating than the meat from a young animal. Equally good among antlered or horned animals is the dry meat from a cow—the female that has not suckled young that year.

Deer

Fat meat with some marbling in the tissue tends to be tenderer than the meat from a thin, slab-sided animal, and for this reason the meat from an old and active buck, say an old Roman-nosed ten-pointer, may be tougher than the meat from a fork horn. However, this is not true if the old trophy-head is fat. Sometimes late in or after the rut, an active, mature buck may have lost his fat during the "running" period when he eats little and chases much, but some late rut bucks are still fat, especially if it's been a good beechnut year. An old dry doe will also be fat and tender. But marinating will tenderize meat tending to be tough, especially if the hog-dressed animal has hung with the skin on for a week in a cold-to-cool, airy place to allow the tissue to break down. All big game is tough if it is eaten just after it has cooled out, but then so is beef. Such meat eaten even three or four days later will usually be quite tender.

Some of the tastiest and most tender venison I ever ate came from a huge late-November twelve-point buck. Conversely, the only venison I ever used that *had* to be marinated to tenderize was from an even bigger *slab-sided* ten-point post-rut buck that had hardly an ounce of suet over his loins. The meat, however, was delicious.

Moose and Other Antlered Game

I once ate the meat from a four- or five-year-old bull that had run off almost all of its fat. This was a post-rut bull, and the meat was both tough and "strong," i.e., it seemed to have a slight metallic taste, perhaps a by-product of the changed metabolism of the rutting animal. A three- or four-year-old fat bull provides meat of the greatest excellence, and so does that from a dry cow. The last bull I killed was a young bull whose antlers showed their first palmation. It was a fat, probably three-year-old animal, whose meat was both tender and delicious. We both grilled and made moose bourguignon from the loins of that animal and the meat was wonderful and so were the steaks.

Spike horn bulls are both tender and tasty.

Aging Game Meat in the Freezer

In these days when most every hunter owns a deep freezer, the handling and storage of game meats has not only changed in practice but, unbeknownst to many of us, it has been revolutionized in theory as well. Until recently, most of us stuck pretty much to the practice of our ancestors and hung our game "in a cool airy place" for a number of days to age before butchering. We knew that aging not only made the meat more tender but more flavorful as well, and we had all heard that hanging the game tenderized the meat by "breaking down the meat cells." Some hung the meat for three or four days; others, when the night and day temperatures were low enough, might leave the game hanging for a week, or ten days, or even more. Let me say at once that there is nothing wrong with this time-tried procedure.

And let me add that there are now two other ways to age meat.

Many deer, especially whitetails, are killed in areas close to the hunter's home on hunts that begin with a predawn trip by car to the cover and end by a hike back to the car or truck after the last drive. Deer killed on such hunts do not have to be hung at all; if such deer are skinned, cut up, and the meat packaged for the freezer immediately after the deer has been brought home, *they "age" beautifully right in your deep-freeze!*

If the reader-hunter is like this writer-hunter, he will scorn such advice out of hand. I did too until our friend, the wildlife artist Peter Parnall, finally persuaded us to try the method. My wife Sheila shot a six-point buck at 8:10 A.M. on a crisp, cold opening day in New Jersey. Out to our platform stands at first light, we had agreed to come in for breakfast at 9:30, and by that time Pete had Sheila's deer hanging on the game stick in his front yard. At 4:00 P.M. Pete and I skinned the deer, took the meat into Pete's kitchen (where he had a professional butcher's block), cut it up, and packaged it for the freezer. By 11:00 P.M. my wife and I were back home in Connecticut and had stowed the meat packages into our freezer, fifteen hours after the deer had been killed. The meat from this deer was not only tender but especially flavorsome. Two of our friends, both aficionados of game and one a hunter-cook as well, commented later: "We both agreed that the venison you gave us was the best we have ever eaten." The hunter of the pair asked specifically how long the deer had hung and was of course astonished to discover that it had not hung at all but had "aged" right in the freezer.

Not three months after our experience I read an article on the very subject based on specific experiments with quick freezing without hanging. Immediate freezing was found to break down the cells and age the meat as a perfect substitute for several days of hanging.

While it is true that the meat from my wife's deer came from a prime animal, the fact remains that the meat would have been tough had we eaten it the same day it was killed. Pete Parnall claims that the quick-freeze aging works just as well for lean old bucks shot well into the rut as it does for younger animals.

Here is Ginny Parnall's method: "Place a solidly frozen 6–7 lb. leg of venison on a rack in a shallow pan. Turn oven to 250° and roast for about 2 hours. Make a small slit to the bone and check to be sure it is thawed. Then roast another hour or so (checking occasionally). If a crust is desired, roast at 450° for the last 20 minutes. Meat is done when it appears very rare, as it will keep on cooking (from its own inner heat)."

A friend of mine does the reverse with frozen roasts. Roast at 450° for 30 minutes; then at 250° until desired doneness (about 2 hours).

Marinades and Marinating

I have never relied on marinating to tenderize meat, preferring to let the cooking method, usually braising, achieve that condition. But marinating will tenderize if the process is extended. Twenty-four hours won't do it; about four days or more (under refrigeration) are required. Marinades that do double duty—used for tenderizing and for flavoring the meat—become part of the sauce or gravy at the end of the cooking.

Bear in mind that when you marinate two things happen: The meat takes up some of the flavor of the marinade, and the marinade takes on some of the flavor of the meat. The liquid always contains an acid—vinegar, wine, or lemon juice—for it is the acid that tenderizes the meat.

Because of this acid content use only crockery (ceramics), glass, or porcelain for marinating. Avoid aluminum especially.

For big roasts, especially when the marinade calls for wine, you may find that your container requires more liquid than is practical (or affordable) to cover the meat completely. In such cases, let the liquid come up as far as the amount of wine you can afford permits, but remember to turn the meat many times during the process.

If the meat is dry be sure to include cooking oil in the marinade.

Now as to the variety of marinades: their names are legion, indeed infinite, and you should not hesitate to experiment. I usually have the following ingredients in all marinades.

wine, vinegar, or lemon juice	garlic
onions or shallots or scallions	bay leaf
carrots	sauce: Worcestershire or Harvey's
celery with tops	sauce, or walnut or mushroom
coarsely crushed peppercorns	catsup

It is best to slice the vegetables very thin—as thin as your knife permits—and when vinegar (or vinegar and water) makes up the liquid, bring it to a boil, then simmer, for 5–10 minutes; cool the marinade before use. For sauerbratens or other sweet-sour dishes I use vinegar and apple juice, for the latter employing the frozen concentrate (6-ounce cans to be mixed with 3 cans of water). When this is used, note whether the label indicates that sugar has been added. If it has, then don't use as much sweetening (sugar or honey) in the recipe itself.

Herbs in the Marinade

In addition to the basic ingredients listed above, herbs and/or spices come into their own in a marinade. Again your preferences should rule, but I have listed below some herb combinations especially good for various meats.

Venison and other red meat game: I always use thyme, rosemary, and savory, and sometimes basil and/or oregano, more often, combinations as the mood dictates.

Game birds: basil, marjoram, rosemary, savory, thyme, tarragon, juniper berries.

Wild fowl: same as above.

Fish: tarragon, chervil.

NOTES: To my taste most recipes recommending juniper berries do not call for enough crushed berries for a good flavor. In cooking from recipes in other cookbooks I always double or treble the quantities called for (see notes on juniper berries, p. 218). The same goes for bay leaf.

Remember when marinades are used later in the sauce or gravy, the herb combination you used will dictate the flavor. This is a happy fact, for one can make a different dish out of a basically identical recipe by varying the herbs (see p. 42).

Spices in Marinades

For sauerbratens, à la mode, and similar dishes, I use cinnamon, cloves, nutmeg, allspice, *and* ginger. But remember both cloves and ginger are dragons (like tarragon among herbs).

Meat Roasting Methods and Cooking Temperatures for Big-Game Roasts

All of the big-game meats are best when cooked rare, although nowadays one never dares to cook bear meat in this fashion because of trichinosis—and even some North Slope caribou have been found to carry this parasite.

Use a good meat thermometer, one that can be depended on; don't buy a cheap one. Some people swear by an instant thermometer that is inserted quickly so that you take the meat's temperature in various places in the roast.

Below are thermometer readings for various states of doneness of game meats from venison to musk ox.

DEGREE OF DONENESS	INTERNAL TEMPERATURE
Rare	120°
Medium rare	130°
Medium	135° to 145°
Medium well	150° to 155°
Well done	160° to 170°

ROASTING METHODS

I used to use the searing method exclusively on roasts (see below) but of late seem to be able to control the cooking better by putting the roast into a 325° oven and allowing about 16 minutes to the pound before I check the meat thermometer to see if it is the right degree of rareness. When the thermometer registers the internal temperature at 120° or a bit more it is about right for those who like rare meat. To achieve a medium-rare roast takes roughly 18–20 minutes to the pound. The medium-rare internal temperature should be about 130°. Some people like their roasts medium and achieve this at about 140°, a bit more or less, but in my judgment anything much over 145° is well done.

The Searing Method Some recipes in this book call for use of the searing method. If the roast is first put in an oven at 450°–475° and kept at this temperature for 30 minutes, then if the oven is turned down to 325° the roast will be rare when the overall roasting time comes to about 12–13 minutes to the pound.

But use these minutes per pound figures roughly: depend on the meat thermometer to tell you when it's rare, 120° more or less.

When using the searing method 18–20 minutes per pound will produce about 140° on the meat thermometer, or what I would call medium.

The 200° Method This method is in a sense the very opposite of the searing method, but if you have a tight, well-insulated oven it works remarkably well. Place a roast, fat side up, in a 200° oven and roast the meat for about 25 minutes per pound. This will bring the internal temperature to the 120° for rare meat, but check after 20 minutes to the pound on the meat thermometer.

When you roast by either the searing or low-temperature methods, normally allow the game to stand outside the refrigerator for 4–5 hours before roasting. If you use either of the above methods with frozen game, let it thaw out overnight in the refrigerator and then let it stand outside the refrigerator for the 4–5 hours.

Remember that when you let a game roast "rest" for a half hour before serving, it will continue to cook some after removal from the oven.

Broiling Game Steaks

To bring out the excellence of game steaks they should be cut thick, 1 to 2 inches preferably, and they should be basted with butter. For a basic broiling technique over charcoal see page 63 for a method that I notice is being practiced by more and more charcoal broilers who are sick and tired of fighting flame.

As for broiling time, it depends to some extent on the heat, but the following chart provides a few rules of thumb. And remember you can check for doneness with a sharp knife. These times are all for 2-inch steaks.

Very rare	15–18 minutes
	(7–9 minutes to a side)
Rare	20–25 minutes
Medium	25–35 minutes
Well done	40 minutes

Game Ribs

Those who stay at home while the hunter is in the hills seldom savor certain choice parts of the game; hearts, livers, kidneys, and brains don't usually survive camp consumption. With the larger game animals this is also true of the fat ribs. Even with big game like deer, that are frequently brought home whole, the rib meat is often discarded or trimmed for burger by meat processors unless you specify that you *want* the ribs intact. Yet as mentioned earlier, hunters, whether they be Eskimos or the run-of-the-mill-once-a-year huntsmen, know that some of the most toothsome meat on the animal lies between the ribs. Braised or barbecued game ribs are simply delicious. A general recipe for barbecuing ribs follows; for braising, see p. 84. I never freeze the ribs but cook them immediately after butchering.

Barbecued Game Ribs

Fat ribs may be at their best when barbecued (with or without sauce) over willow, alder, or charcoal, but they can also be "barbecued" in the oven basted with your favorite sauce. Venison ribs take 1–1¼ hours, but the ribs from heavier game like moose will take a bit longer in a 350° oven.

I happen to have a roaster with a recessed bottom that I use for this purpose, but with the average roaster it is best to place the ribs on a rack. I sometimes brown the ribs first, but always roast them covered. When using sauce in oven-barbecuing, coat the ribs at once and then turn and baste them several times with the sauce. Be careful you don't burn your knuckles in removing the lid for basting.

It may be a private prejudice, but I use lots of pepper on game ribs.

Use your favorite barbecue sauce, commercial or homemade. My own homemade sauce will be found on page 360.

Note on symbols accompanying some recipes Many of these recipes can be prepared conveniently in camp as well as at home. Such recipes are labeled with either or both of these symbols:

Venison

MULE DEER

Venison fanciers relish the distinctive flavor of the deer's fine-grained flesh, finding it as distinctive in its own way as mutton, and even lamb, are positive and definitive in theirs. But as with beef, certain cuts of venison (the same cuts as with beef), are more tender than others. The meat from shoulder, neck, and shank, while succulent, should be braised or prepared in savory stews. Roasts should be confined to the loin, rump, or leg, and in lean, old bucks, run-down from the rut, the latter two cuts might best reward the fancier in stews.

But one should not get the notion that old animals must be tough. On the contrary, old bucks when they are hog fat before the rut may be tender as well as delicious. Young bucks and dry does, that is, does that have had no fawns that season, will be both fat and tender well into the fall.

In preparing venison, bear in mind that the texture of venison is dry, i.e., without notable marbling; that is true of fat animals with a layer of suet over the loins. For this reason when you cook heavy, roast-size cuts, the meat should be larded with strips of salt pork (marinated in brandy gives a nice touch). If you do not have a larding tool you really should get one if you are expecting to serve game roasts (see page 18).

While fat venison is both more tender and tastier than meat from skinny animals, the cook should trim off venison fat from steaks or chops, as venison fat becomes strong (even when frozen). This is not true of fat from the larger game animals like moose. Moose fat or caribou fat, well browned and crispy, is as delicious as beef fat.

Many cooks use marinades for tenderizing meat that is on the tough side. But I have found that marinating doesn't help much unless the meat has soaked in it for a minimum of forty-eight hours. More is better, of course, since marinating is also done to impart different flavors to meat. I myself seldom marinate game, preferring to put the added flavor in the gravy or sauce.

Aging Venison

If the weather is consistently cold to cool (ideal temperature range is 36°–40°) one can age the deer still in the skin in a shed, barn, or even an outdoor garage. How long to hang a deer to break down the muscle cells (and thus both tenderize the meat *and* improve flavor) depends entirely on the individual animal. For a buck that is prime and fat—one with his kidneys encased in solid lumps of white suet, with the entrails webbed with a veil of fat—the process takes no longer than a week including the time the deer hung in the woods. But if the deer is shot after the rut, or if for other reasons it is lean and fatless, three weeks is not too long. However, hanging a deer that long should be done under controlled conditions; locker plants or butchers will sometimes hang a whole deer in the skin for you. Don't get the notion that a young buck provides tender meat superior to a mature buster-of-a-buck. A *fat* old-timer in prime condition is just as tender *and tastes much better* than the "veal" of young "eatin' deer." The same goes for any old "dry" doe.

If you go bag a huge old buck that has run off most of its fat during the rut, and thus have to hang him two or three weeks to age the meat, don't be dismayed if a fuzz of mold forms inside the body cavity. This can be scraped off, just as one scrapes off the mold of a well-aged smoked ham; the meat underneath will be sweet and tasty.

For notes on hog-dressing, butchering deer, and carving, see the Appendix, and for estimating the age of venison, see page 4.

Hog-Dressed and Dressed Weights

Although there are regional differences in nomenclature, generally speaking, in the U.S., a "hog-dressed" game animal is one that has been bled and gralloched, i.e., gutted, period.

In some areas the term "dressed" is used to mean a hog-dressed animal that has also been skinned and from which the head and antlers and hooves and lower legs (from the "knees" down) and damaged meat have been removed.

Among hoofed game a hog-dressed animal weighs about 80 percent of what it weighed on the hoof; a dressed animal weighs about 80 percent of its hog-dressed weight and about 60 to 70 percent of its weight on the hoof.

Two small deer that weighed 100 and 116 pounds hog-dressed (say 120 and 145 pounds on the hoof) produced 76 pounds of steaks, chops, roasts, and burger. This weight did not include the ribs, and presumably the butcher was honest. But the loss from two deer might be expected to be greater proportionately than from one, i.e., I would expect that a big buck weighing 265 pounds having only one head and one hide would produce a greater percentage of freezer meat than two deer whose combined weights equaled his.

Venison from Grill to Table

Venison tallow, like that of domestic lamb, congeals rapidly; therefore the timing of a venison dinner is extremely important. You *must* "come out even." Rather that the mashed potatoes keep cooking and be a bit on the dense side than that the steaks or chops cool and the fat congeal on teeth and utensils.

STEAKS AND ROASTS

A venison entrée must not only come to the table piping hot but both platter and dinner plate must come in the same condition. If your kitchen has a dish-washer, put both the plates and the platter through the drying (and heating) phase of the cycle so they come to your guests hot. If the phrase "good manners spoils good food" ever applies it is here. Serve steaks or chops right from the grill and insist that those guests who come from the school that waits until everyone is served should not do so on this occasion.

If your entrée is a roast leg or haunch do not "rest" the meat as you would ribs of beef unless you have a warming table but bring it from the oven hot and commandeer assistance in serving the vegetables and pouring the wine. Your task is to carve and serve with dispatch hot meat on hot plates.

The same applies to the sauce or gravy and the more fat you can skim from the sauce, the better, for venison fat when cooled is as rigid as pan ice on an autumn pond and just about as appetizing.

ROAST LEG OF VENISON, UNMARINATED

SERVES 10

10 larding strips, 1½–2″ long
(about ¼–½ lb. salt pork)
6-lb. leg of venison
2 cloves garlic, sliced thin
¼ lb. butter, softened
1 Tb. powdered thyme (or thyme
mixed with rosemary)

3 Tb. flour seasoned with salt and
pepper
2¼ cups stock or beef broth (or
water with bouillon cube)

NOTE: For those who don't have larding needles: When a larding needle is used the cook can insert the garlic slices right along with the lardoons (larding strips); otherwise stick a sharp-pointed small knife into the meat and, prying the slit open, slip a slice of garlic along the flat of the knife, withdraw knife, and with finger punch garlic slice all the way in. Do this around the leg in 8–10 places. Put slices of salt pork under the meat and, affixed with wooden toothpicks, place other slices on top of leg.

Rub all surfaces of the leg with soft butter and dust the powdered herb or herb mixture over all. Also, if you wish, dust with one tablespoon of the seasoned flour.

Put roast in uncovered roasting pan, add ½ cup liquid, and roast at 325° for about 2 hours. If you use a meat thermometer, make sure that it does not touch the bone. Venison should be served rare, but not bloody, so figure on 16 minutes to the pound.

Watch the meat and add liquid from time to time. Because the venison has been roasted with some liquid you may wish to turn the oven to 450°–500° for the last 10 minutes to brown the roast.

Turn off the oven, open the door, and wave it open and shut a few times to reduce the heat. Then place the leg on a metal pan and keep it hot in the oven. Just hot—don't roast it more.

In the roasting pan, after removing the crackling on and under the roast, make the gravy. By this stage, if all has gone well, the dredgings in the bottom of the roasting pan will be chiefly essence of venison and fat from the salt pork.

Take the pan off the heat and stir in the remaining 2 tablespoons of flour, mixing it thoroughly with the fat and dredgings. Then place the pan over the heat and brown the flour and dredging mixture. Stir in stock in sufficient quantity to make the gravy to your preferred consistency, adding liquid (water if you've run out of stock) when it threatens to thicken too much. Add salt and pepper to taste. (I usually add a tablespoon of mushroom catsup or a dash of Worcestershire sauce and a dash of Kitchen Bouquet.)

Serve gravy in a sauceboat. Carve and transfer meat to your guests on warmed plates and serve at once so that what venison fat there is won't congeal. Tell your guests to eat at once, that "good" manners spoil good food when venison is the dish.

SADDLE OF VENISON MT. DESERT

This recipe can be used for a leg of venison, a rump roast, or any red meat roast. I seldom roast a saddle in spite of the fact that it is of the very finest; trouble is it is too much like putting all of your eggs in one basket—I hate to give up those loin and rib chops. The saddle is, of course, a noble roast; again, if you prepare it make sure *all* of your guests deserve it.

PRELIMINARY NOTE: With a piece of prime aged venison I often do *not* put the meat down in the marinade at all, but roast it straight (for those who like it better that way) and use the marinade to make the sauce. Here I give the recipe including the marinating. If you have a favorite marinade of your own by all means use it, but remember if yours calls for vinegar plus several spices (not herbs) you'll get something closer to sauerbraten than to the results of this recipe. Remember, also, when you make enough marinade to cover the meat, you'll have some left over after making the sauce; freeze this and use again for some other red meat gravy. Or cut this marinade recipe in half.

SERVES ABOUT 8

THE MARINADE

1 bottle *good* burgundy (splurge with a saddle)
¼ cup oil, olive preferred
1 onion, sliced as thin as your knife will permit
2 carrots, sliced the same way
1 stalk celery, with leaves, chopped fine
12 juniper berries, crushed
3 cloves garlic, crushed

1 tsp. thyme
½ tsp. savory
3 bay leaves
3 sprigs parsley, cut fine
1 tsp. freshly ground pepper
1 Tb. Harvey's sauce } or 2 Tb. Worcester-
1 Tb. mushroom catsup } shire

THE SADDLE

1 venison saddle (if using rump or leg, lard the roast)
1 cup broth
flour and water

¼ cup beach plum or red currant jelly
½ cup sour cream

Combine marinade ingredients. Put the saddle down in the marinade—if you wish adding half water/half wine if the marinade doesn't cover the saddle in the marinating vessel you use. Refrigerate and marinate it for 4 days, turning it as often as you can think of it.

Dry off the saddle (reserving the marinade), place on a rack in a regular shallow roasting pan, and roast it at 450° for 20 minutes or so. Turn down to 375° and, with a saddle, do use a meat thermometer, for it should be rare—and you should watch it like a hawk—for when it registers 125°–130° it is done. With a saddle this usually can be judged *roughly* ahead of time by giving it about 12 minutes to the pound for rare. (If the roast is a big rump or leg, roasting time for rare is *about* 16–18 minutes to the pound.)

During the roasting of the saddle (give yourself 40 minutes or so for this), put the marinade in a skillet (to give more evaporating surface), bring it to a boil, and continuing the high heat, reduce it to about 2 cups. Strain the marinade.

Simmer 1 cup of the marinade and 1 cup broth over low flame for 15–20 minutes. Thicken with a mixture of 1–2 tablespoons flour mixed with twice the amount of water, stirring and watching to see to it that it doesn't stick. If it threatens to get too thick, add water.

When you remove the saddle to a *hot* platter salt it, then check to see if there are drippings under the rack that you might wish to add to the sauce.

Stir in and melt the jelly, and just before you serve stir in the sour cream, making sure to blend it uniformly. Heat but do not bubble. Check the seasoning.

ROAST HAUNCH OR ROUND OF VENISON

This wonderful recipe comes from Morrison Wood's *With a Jug of Wine*, which is one of the very best cookbooks I know of, especially for meat, poultry, and game. I use this recipe when I prepare a marinated venison roast. One comment: Mr. Wood's 6–7-pound haunch is unusually small for a haunch; a like amount of round roast would do as well. I'd use a meat thermometer to be sure the roast comes out pink, about 125°.

Mashed potatoes, baked Hubbard squash, and old-fashioned coleslaw are perfect accompaniments to roast venison, and don't stint on the gravy!

SERVES 10–12

1 large mild onion, chopped	freshly ground pepper
2 Tb. chopped scallions	salt
2 large carrots, chopped	½ lb. salt pork
5 Tb. butter	2 cloves garlic
4 whole cloves	1 cup red currant jelly
½ tsp. thyme	powdered ginger
½ tsp. marjoram	powdered cloves
½ tsp. tarragon	1 tsp. lemon juice
½ tsp. basil	¼ cup sour cream, at room
½ tsp. rosemary	temperature
2 cups dry red wine	granulated flour, if necessary
olive oil	1 Tb. brandy
6–7-lb. venison roast	

First, marinate the meat. The standard marinade at many hunt clubs is two-thirds red wine and one-third cup water, to which generous seasonings of pepper, bay leaves, thyme, tarragon, and mustard seed have been added. But there's a better one that dates back to the 17th century. Fry the onion, the scallions,

Knives

In the appendix section "Carving Game" are comments and recommendations on carving knives. But in addition to the two carving knives there are two or three that ought to be in the knife rack of any household where game may be prepared and cooked.

If your household also occasionally butchers game, there ought to be three basic knives available: a big butcher knife, a smaller Russell Green River–type butcher knife (unchanged in design, by the way, since becoming famous as the knife used by the buffalo hide hunters in the sixties and seventies), and a boning knife. My big butcher knife shown here has a 10¼-inch blade; my smaller Green River butcher has a 6-inch blade, while the boning knife has a blade of 5 inches.

big butcher knife

Green River butcher knife

boning knife

As far as kitchen knives are concerned, one also ought to have a filleting knife for fish. This knife should be flexible with a fairly thin narrow blade.

I personally use only carbon steel knives, but there are stainless steel knives now available, such as those sold by L.L. Bean, that are not too hard to be sharpened. Old-style stainless knives were useless once dulled, for they were so hard that they could only be crudely sharpened on one of those draw-gouges. No stone would touch them.

I keep a small metal file in my kitchen (for thinning blades of knives that when new are too thick at the blade edge), a couple of stones, including an Arkansas hard stone for final touching up, and a steel for the same purpose.

But recently I acquired a belt-sheathed sharpener that is close to all-purpose. This is the sharpener to end sharpeners, with a dowel-shaped blade that is impregnated with thousands of tiny particles of diamonds. It comes also shaped like a regular stone and will put an edge on the stainless knives that are manufactured of steel that is not too hard for sharpening.

Use this diamond sharpener judiciously, for it cuts metal quickly. A few strokes are sufficient to sharpen any knife that is not so thick at the edge as to require a file.

and the carrots in the butter. Add the cloves, thyme, marjoram, tarragon, basil, and rosemary. Add 1 cup of the wine. Then put everything through a coarse sieve. Now brush the venison with olive oil, dust with plenty of freshly ground pepper and salt, pour the marinade over the venison, and let it soak for about 8 hours.

To cook, lard the venison generously with salt pork and insert slivers of garlic into the meat. Roast in a 450° oven, 20–30 minutes* to the pound, basting frequently with the drippings and the marinade. When the meat is tender, remove from the roasting pan but keep in warm oven while making the gravy.

And now the gravy! In the roasting pan slowly melt the red currant jelly with the drippings and the marinade; add remaining cup of wine. While this is sim-mering, add a pinch of powdered ginger, a pinch of powdered cloves, and the lemon juice. When the gravy has thickened and reduced a little, slowly add the sour cream and blend everything thoroughly. If you prefer the gravy a little thicker, sprinkle in a little granulated flour, being sure no lumps form. Just before serving, add 1 tablespoon of good brandy, and pour into gravy boat.

* When I made this recipe, I found it more to my liking turning down the oven to 325° after 15 minutes and roasting 16 minutes to the pound.

ROAST LEG OF VENISON
WITH CHOCOLATE SAUCE

With appreciation to Roy de Groot, here is a recipe from his fine book *Feasts for All Seasons*. I have made my own adaptations, so any shortcomings are mine.

Before you reject this recipe as just too difficult, read it through, notice its step-by-step sequence, and I think you will see that the steps are feasible for you and that the whole dish is not difficult at all.

Don't let the name of this superb meat sauce put you off: "Venison with chocolate?" you might ask. The answer is "yes," but this sauce tastes nothing like a chocolate sundae; indeed this delicious meat sauce does not taste like chocolate at all. As in so many sauces, one ingredient is a catalyst for another or helps to produce a meld that tastes like no one of its *several* ingredients but partakes for its final excellence from them *all*. (See also Tuscan Hare, page 104.)

Although this is a venison roast that will be a long-time conversation piece for your guests it is not really a difficult dish to prepare.

Lard or bard two or three days before you plan to serve the roast (see page 18).

SERVES 12 OR MORE

THE MARINADE
1/4 cup oil
2 onions, chopped fine
2 carrots, sliced very fine
2 ribs celery with leaves, chopped
  fine
2 garlic cloves, minced or put
  through garlic press
THE VENISON
1 leg of venison (about 7–12 lb.)
salt and pepper
1/4 lb. (1 stick) butter

6–8 cloves
1/2 tsp. cinnamon
several parsley sprigs, minced
1/2 tsp. fresh thyme leaves
  (or 1/4 tsp. powdered)
1/2 tsp. crumbled rosemary
1 bottle some lusty red wine

2 carrots, sliced
2 onions, sliced
1 rib celery with leaves, sliced

THE CHOCOLATE SAUCE

2 Tb. sugar
½ cup vinegar
4 oz. chocolate, grated

Optional:

2 Tb. pine nuts
2 Tb. each candied orange and lemon peel
¼ cup currants
¼ cup yellow raisins

Bring marinade ingredients to a boil and simmer for 5 minutes, cool, and put into bowl that will just hold the roast and the marinade. Cover and refrigerate for 48–72 hours, turning the roast 2–3 times a day.

On the morning of the day you roast the venison, remove it from refrigerator and allow it to continue to marinate until it loses its chill. It should be at room temperature by the time you are ready to roast it.

Preheat oven to 350°. Remove roast from marinade, dry it, salt and pepper it, and put it on a rack in a shallow roasting pan. Ideally you should use a meat thermometer, inserting it halfway through the roast if it is a rolled roast; if it has the bone in it, insert so it does not touch bone. You want the roast rare, and the rare reading should be 120°–125°. Begin to watch the roast carefully after about 10 minutes to the pound, i.e., if it is a 7-lb. roast after an hour and 10 minutes. (It will usually take 12 minutes to the pound to bring the roast to a rare reading of 120°.)

Let it roast for 30 minutes at 350° and during this period, strain the marinade, bring it to a boil, and stir in the butter. Let the marinade and butter boil for 3–4 minutes, then turn down to a low simmer. Begin to baste the roast with this at once and continue to do so every 15 minutes.

After the roast has been in 30 minutes, turn heat up to 400° and add the carrots, onion, and celery.

After you take the roast out and it is resting, make the sauce. Put the sugar into a heavy sauepan and place over quite high heat to melt. As soon as it becomes caramel-colored, remove at once from the heat, let it cool a bit, then pour in the vinegar. Stir and simmer for a few minutes.

Using a bulb baster, draw off 1½ cups of meat juices from the roasting pan. Add half of this gravy to the caramel, then half the chocolate, stirring over low heat to blend. Continue adding the two alternately, but taste before you've used them up to make sure you have a pleasing blend (you may not want to use quite all the chocolate; you may need a touch more vinegar).

Baron de Groot adds pine nuts, candied orange and lemon peel, currants, and raisins to this sauce as well. Include some or all of his prescription, as meets your fancy. Frankly in my opinion the sauce doesn't need any of this embellishment.

ROLLED ROAST LEG OF VENISON
À LA DOTTIE D'AVANZO

Dottie D'Avanzo, sprightly chatelaine of Vic D'Avanzo's well-run shooting reserve (East Mountain Shooting Preserve in Dutchess County, Dover Plains, New York) and "house mother" over the years to a host of fine bird dogs retired to the house for their honorable achievements afield, is a versatile lady. Winemaker and fine cook (she taught us how to make dandelion wine), she has generously shared her favorite recipes with us. The D'Avanzos' larder always includes quail, pheasant, chukar partridge, wild fowl, and venison; and sometimes grouse, woodcock, rabbits, squirrels, and woodchuck. Vic and Dottie eat well and probably eat more game each 365 days than most households eat in the gunner's entire shooting career.

SERVES 6

boned 3–3½-lb. leg of venison
pepper
salt pork (or pigskins) in thin
  slabs, each at large in area as
  possible
2–3 cloves garlic, sliced thin
1 Tb. marjoram

1 cup chopped onion
1 cup chopped carrots
1 cup chopped celery
½ cup beef or venison broth
  (optional)
⅓ cup red wine
2 Tb. red currant jelly

Preheat oven to 350°.

If the deer is a large one the leg may be cut in half before boning out the section to be used.

Pepper the roast before rolling and tying. Lay thin pieces of salt pork into cavity or on flattened roast and distribute thin slices of garlic on tops of salt pork pieces.

Roll leg and wrap top and bottom or rolled leg with thin slabs of salt pork (under which you have distributed thin slices of garlic) and tie in 8 places with string, binding the pork slices to the roll.

Sprinkle marjoram on bottom of shallow roasting pan, add rolled roast, and bake for 20 minutes.

Put the chopped vegetables around roast and if you feel liquid is needed add beef or venison broth. Roast an additional 30 minutes or until meat thermometer registers 120° in center of roast.

Remove roast to very hot platter and allow to rest for 5–10 minutes. Remove vegetables to hot gravy boat.

Remove fat from roasting pan, add the wine and currant jelly, and stir goodies while bringing to quick boil, then add to vegetables in hot gravy boat.

═══ BROILED TENDERLOIN OF VENISON, ═══
HUGH FOSBURGH

My late friend Hugh Fosburgh believed, and rightly so, that it was a crime against nature to do anything with a tenderloin of venison but to quick-roast it, or broil thick "steaks" cut from it. He would tolerate a bit of garlic rubbed on it and he admitted that thyme sprinkled on it sparingly "didn't hurt it," but to marinate was anathema. He had an old, beaten-up electric broiler in the kitchen of his lodge at the North Woods Club, and he used it a lot on venison steaks and chops.

With broiled venison I usually serve "fried" potatoes and a sauce on the side. Or sometimes I will indulge in making a skillet of buttery, crisp Potatoes Anna (see page 382).

SERVES 5–8 DEPENDING ON SIZE

A tenderloin of venison, cut in
  thick steaks
1 garlic bulb, sliced in half and
  crisscrossed with cuts
Oil or melted butter (or both)

¼ tsp. powdered thyme (sometimes
  I use rosemary too with venison)
freshly ground pepper
salt

In broiling, whether it be on an open charcoal grill or in an inside broiler, the game is to do it fast over (or under) high heat so it comes out rare. Rub both sides of the steaks with the garlic halves and with oil or butter, sprinkle a scant dusting of thyme and pepper, and broil, basting some with the oil or butter during the short time it takes to cook this small bit of meat rare.

Broiling time depends on how high the heat and the thickness of steaks cut from the tenderloin. Just hover over it and be sure it is pink and moist in the middle. Salt it when you serve it.

Larding and Barding

Because venison tends to be quite lean—and because other red meats may often be lean—larding is a useful technique in cookery. By inserting strips of fat deep into the interior of the meat, you provide a form of internal basting which is especially helpful in roasting.

The two types of larding needles pictured on this page are, first, one with multiple splayed ends that will grip the tip of the lardoon (as the strips of fat are called), allowing you to pull the strip through. I have always found it necessary to use a pair of pliers to pull the needle through.

The second type of larding needle I have found requires a knife to make the first stab into the meat. This type is loaded with a lardoon, then is pushed in and withdrawn—the person doing the larding using a finger of his other hand to keep the lardoon from coming out as the tool is withdrawn. There is also a model now available that has a pointed end (not pictured here), which would take care of the problem.

If you do not have a larding tool, you can make do with a longish tapering knife. Once you have made a slot in the meat, the strip of fat can be forced in with the point of a knife or an ice pick.

Lardoon for roasts may be 3 inches or so long and ¼ inch thick and are invariably made of pork fat—sometimes salt pork. For added flavor, occasionally they are marinated beforehand in brandy, and I sometimes slip a sliver of garlic in with each lardoon.

Round roasts and rump roasts particularly are much tastier if larded.

Barding means draping thin sheets of fat over and sometimes all around the meat in order to lubricate while cooking any game meat or birds that tend to be dry.

VENISON STEAK L.L. BEAN

Mr. Bean himself gave his camp recipe for pan-broiled venison steak in his book *Hunting, Fishing, and Camping.* I myself pan-broil this way, except that I dust the skillet with salt (coarse if I have it).

"Cut steak about 1½ inches thick. Remove excess fat and wipe clean and dry. Have a very hot fire and when frying pan is smoking hot, drop steak into the pan and allow to sear quickly on one side. Then turn.

"If you like steak medium or well done, reduce the heat of the fire and turn occasionally until at desired stage. If you prefer a rare steak, it will require 10–12 minutes; if medium, 15–20 minutes.

"Serve on hot platter. Spread steak with butter and add salt and pepper to taste."

PAULINE SMITH'S SOUTHERN FRIED VENISON

Pauline Smith of Greensboro, North Carolina, whose recipe this is, writes: "Venison loin is preferred for this recipe, though tender round may also be used. The whole loin should be peeled away from the bones, which gives a small but long, tender strip of meat. Cut this loin strip (or choice round) into slices about ½ inch thick. The boneless loin will produce rather small pieces; from the ends the slices are hardly more than 2 inches in diameter (some just bite size, but they are tender and good).

"Place sliced meat on chopping board and with a heavy, but dull, kitchen knife pound or chop each piece as for chopped steak, crosswise and lengthwise.

"Salt and pepper each slice, and dip lightly in flour.

"Peel and slice one medium onion.

"Heat about ½ inch of vegetable shortening in frying pan over medium heat, just hot enough to begin cooking the meat as put in, but not too hot. The pieces, being very thin and small, begin cooking very fast. Stand by with fork in hand, and as browning begins (2–3 minutes), turn meat and cook on other side. Place sliced onions on top of meat in pan; turn once more, allowing onions to sauté. As soon as onions are sautéed, remove meat and onions and drain lightly. Serve hot."

BRACIOLE OF VENISON ROUND OR TENDERLOIN
(also from either moose or elk)

Again, the courtesy of Dottie D'Avanzo. Serve this dish with *diced* potatoes. It can be handily prepared in a wok.

SERVES 4–5

2½ lb. braciole (round or tenderloin in slices ¼" thick)*	2 Tb. butter or margarine
1 cup chopped and sautéed onions	1 Tb. oil
1 cup chopped and sautéed carrots	¼ cup water
1 cup chopped celery (with leaves)	½ cup red wine
	2 Tb. currant jelly

In a *large* skillet sauté the vegetables until soft and *lightly* browned in butter and oil. Remove to warm dish.

Turn up heat, put braciole into hot skillet a few at a time, and sear and turn and sear (this is a matter of seconds, surely less than a minute). Remove to heated platter.

Sprinkle vegetables over meat slices.

To skillet add the water, wine, and currant jelly. Bring to quick boil and pour over venison and vegetables.

*If meat slices are thicker than ¼ inch, pound with wooden mallet to ¼-inch thickness.

VENISON STEAKS WITH MUSHROOMS AND GREEN PEPPERCORN BUTTER

The aromatic and pungent flavor of green peppercorns* mashed into butter is just the right complement for quickly sautéed, tender venison steaks surrounded with browned mushrooms with a hint of garlic. Serve these with crisp pan-fried sliced potatoes and a green vegetable or just a sprig of watercress.

SERVES 4

¼ pound butter	salt and pepper
6 Tb. green peppercorns	8 tender venison steaks
2 Tb. vegetable oil	(2–3 ounces each and about
2 garlic cloves	¼ inch thick)
½ pound mushrooms	3 Tb. red wine

Soften 6 tablespoons of the butter and then mash in the green peppercorns.

Melt the remaining butter in a good-sized skillet along with the oil and when sizzling toss in the 2 garlic cloves, just crushed with the flat of a knife. Add the mushrooms, quartered if they are large, halved if smallish. Sauté over moderate heat, seasoning with salt and pepper and tossing occasionally for 5 minutes. Remove with a slotted spoon and keep warm.

Now sauté the steaks in the same skillet, 4 at a time if necessary, so the pan isn't crowded. Have the heat quite high and cook only a minute on each side. Salt and pepper well and remove to a warm platter.

When the last steak is done, toss in the wine, scrape up all the pan juices, and pour this little bit over the steaks. Top them with the green peppercorn butter and surround them with the mushrooms.

*You'll find green peppercorns preserved in small jars are available at almost any fancy food shop today.

VENISON STEAKS WITH DRIED WILD MUSHROOMS

Use tender steaks cut from the leg about ¾ inch thick so they may be sautéed quickly, browned on the outside, rare in the middle. We first tasted this dish in Tuscany during the hunting season when literally the entire male population takes to the woods, gun in hand; the beautiful large wild mushrooms known there as porcini or little pigs (here as cèpes) are plentiful in the woods at about the same time, so the two flavors have a natural affinity. You can buy dried porcini or cèpes here, and they give the same flavor if not quite the same texture. Or if you are a wild mushroom hunter, dry out your *boletuses, chanterelles, morels*—all excellent in this dish.

SERVES 4

1 oz. dried porcini or cèpes	¼ cup red wine
5 Tb. butter	¼ cup strong beef stock
2 Tb. vegetable oil	freshly ground black pepper
4 venison steaks, ¾ inch thick	salt
4 shallots, minced	

Cover the dried mushrooms with warm water and let stand for 30 minutes.

Heat 2 tablespoons each of the butter and the oil in a large skillet until the foam subsides, then put in the steaks. Fry them 3–4 minutes on each side, depending on how rare you like them. Remove to a warm platter.

Add the remaining butter to the skillet and toss in the shallots. Sauté quickly for a minute, stirring, then splash in the wine, letting it boil and scraping up any browned bits. Add the beef stock, the mushrooms, and their soaking liquid. Let cook over quite high heat for a minute, tossing and stirring. Season to taste. Pour the sauce and mushrooms over the steaks and serve immediately.

VENISON SKILLET-STEAK MEXICAINE

This is a hearty camp dish that you'll never go wrong on. If you've made up a proper grub list you'll have everything perhaps but the pimento. But when you make this one-dish meal at home you can easily get the pimento. Serve this with mashed potatoes.

SERVES 4–6

2 lb. venison steak	1½ tsp. salt
5 Tb. flour	½ tsp. pepper
2 Tb. bacon fat, oil, or butter	½ tsp. thyme
1 large or 2 medium onions	½ tsp. cumin and/or 1 Tb. chili
1 green pepper	powder
5 Tb. tomato sauce or catsup	1 package frozen green beans
1 Tb. Worcestershire sauce	or peas (or in camp, one can
3 tsp. red chili flakes	of either drained)
1½ cups beef broth or 1½ cups	4 oz. (2 small jars) sliced
water and 2 bouillon cubes	pimento

Dredge the steak in the flour and then with the edge of a plate pound and press in as much flour as the meat will hold.

Over a medium fire brown the meat on both sides in the fat. Do a conscientious job of this. While the second side is still browning, sauté the onions and green pepper around the meat.

Add all the rest of the ingredients save the beans and pimento. Cover and simmer for about 2 hours. As the liquids absorb the browned flour off the meat the mix will thicken. If it cooks down too much, add more liquid.

About 10 minutes before serving, add the beans and pimento.

Game Carcass Nomenclature

The terms loin, rack, saddle, baron, brisket, haunch, chuck, etc., are variously used to indicate parts of a carcass, depending on the country or even particular areas within countries, but generally speaking the following definitions are all serviceable and generally agreed upon in both British and American usage.

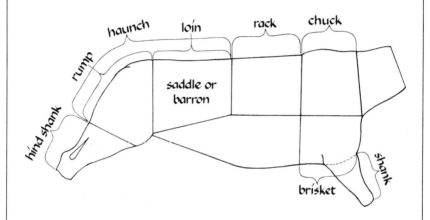

Haunch: This is a heroic piece of meat even on deer-size animals. It consists of the leg (minus the shank), the rump, and the loin, all in one piece from one side of the animal.

Saddle: Here usage differs somewhat: (a) some consider the saddle to be the rack and the loin in one piece from one side of the animal, but (b) technically, the saddle is both loins in one piece (see *baron* below).

Loin: Usually the back section behind the ribs and in front of the rump from one side of the carcass. Loin chops are cut from this section.

Rack: The section of back in front of the loin and behind the shoulder from one side of the animal. Rib chops are cut from this section.

Baron: Technically the loin of a beef- or moose-size animal, both sides in one piece. Same as saddle. Also used for either side of this section.

Brisket: The breast or the lower part of the breast lying next to the ribs.

Chuck: The cut on top of the forequarter between the neck and the shoulder blade.

Shank: The lower end of either the fore or hind leg.

Rump: The big section above the hind leg hip joint and behind the loin end from one "side."

JOE MURRAY'S VENISON OR MOOSE STEAK

Serve with mashed potatoes, mixed vegetables, and "red wine and two candles," Joe Murray of L.L. Bean suggests.

SERVES 6–8

4–5 onions
3 green peppers
18–20 mushrooms
¼ lb. butter
2 bay leaves

3–4 lb. venison or moose steaks,
   1½"–2" thick
salt and pepper
4 garlic cloves, smashed

Dice onions, green peppers, and mushrooms. Take a cast-iron fry-pan and fry these up in the butter with the bay leaves.

Then take the steak and rub salt, pepper, and smashed garlic cloves into the meat on both sides.

Fry with onions and peppers. Do not overcook the meat, as this will make it tough.

SCALOPPINE OF VENISON
WITH WINE AND CHESTNUT SAUCE

SERVES 4

8–12 thin slices venison, cut
   from leg
flour
salt and freshly ground pepper
5 Tb. clarified butter or equal
   parts butter and vegetable
   oil
¾ cup fruity white wine

¾ cup heavy cream
½ cup chestnut purée (page 386)
1–2 Tb. chopped dill or Chinese
   parsley
garnish: triangles of toast
   spread with foie gras or
   liver pâté

Pound the slices of venison between pieces of waxed paper (count 2–3 slices per person depending on the size of the pieces). Dust with flour and salt and pepper.

Heat a couple of tablespoons of butter (or the butter and oil combination) in a large heavy skillet to medium hot, then put in enough of the venison scaloppine so the pieces don't overlap. Sauté about 2 minutes on each side, then remove to a warm platter. Sauté the rest, adding more butter as necessary.

When all are done, splash the wine into the skillet, let it boil down a bit, then pour in the cream, stirring as you bring it to a boil. Now add the chestnut purée, mashing with a fork to break up any lumps, until you have a smooth sauce. If it's too thick, add just a little more wine and cream.

Return the scaloppine to the skillet to heat through, spooning the sauce over them. Correct seasoning. Arrange on hot platter, sprinkle with dill or Chinese parsley, and surround with toast garnish.

BROILED VENISON CHOPS WITH CURRANT OR BEACH PLUM JELLY SAUCE

Broiled venison chops are a king's fare provided you get them off the grill *rare and hot* and have the sauce ready and waiting. Also, always be sure to trim the fat off the chops and to have them cut at least an inch thick.

I serve venison chops with a spaetzle (flavored with thyme) and with sliced zucchini sautéed in garlic butter.

This dish is best when one person makes the sauce and another puts the chops under the broiler just 4 or 5 minutes before the sour cream and jelly are stirred into the sauce.

SERVES 6–8

6–8 venison loin chops, 1"–1½" thick
4 Tb. softened butter
salt and pepper
1 small onion, finely minced
2 Tb. butter

½ cup consommé or stock
¼ cup tawny port
1½ Tb. beach plum or red currant jelly
2 cups sour cream, at room temperature

Preheat broiler. Spread chops with softened butter and broil, 4–6 minutes for each side. Salt and pepper to taste.

Sauté the minced onion in the 2 tablespoons butter for a couple of minutes, then add the stock and wine. Cook over high heat to reduce by half.

Stir the jelly into the sour cream until blended and then stir the mix into the onions and reduced liquid. Do not boil.

BREADED VENISON CHOPS FOR FOUR

Here is a recipe from Alex Delicata, resident chef from L. L. Bean's staff who, with Joe Murray, presides over Bean's annual game dinner.

Serve this with boiled parsley potatoes and pickle spears. A hearty burgundy is a good wine to serve with it. Wine should be slightly cooler than room temperature.

SERVES 4

6–8 venison chops, ½"–¾" thick
¼ cup vegetable oil
2 eggs
2 Tb. milk
2 cups crushed Saltine crackers

1 finely minced garlic clove or ¼ tsp. garlic powder
¼ tsp. dried basil
dash of pepper

Wipe off chops with a damp towel, making sure no bone dust from butchering remains.

Heat oil in large skillet at medium heat. Beat eggs and add milk. Dip chops into milk and egg mix, then into crumbs to which you have added the garlic, basil, and pepper, making sure they are mixed well.

Fry chops at medium heat until coating is medium brown. When coating is medium brown, the chops are cooked, but still moist.

VENISON CHOPS WITH WINE, CHEESE, AND SOUR CREAM

Serve with noodles, rice, or riced potatoes, or even with Potatoes Anna or potato cakes. Sliced zucchini sautéed in butter (or garlic butter) under a lid makes a good second side dish. In preparing the zucchini in this fashion you need no moisture; the butter and the juices of the vegetable itself are sufficient. The wine should be a hearty red that will fight back, for this is a lusty dish.

SERVES 4

THE MARINADE
1 cup vinegar
1 cup red wine
4 Tb. crushed juniper berries
2 cloves garlic, minced
¼ tsp. thyme

¼ tsp. basil
1 Tb. mushroom catsup or Worcestershire sauce
1 tsp. honey or brown sugar

THE CHOPS
4 venison chops, trimmed of fat
flour
salt and pepper
2 Tb. lard or oil
1 onion, chopped, or 3 shallots, chopped
½ green pepper, chopped
½ lb. mushrooms

2 Tb. butter
1 Tb. catsup or 1 tsp. tomato paste
¼ cup freshly grated Parmesan or Romano cheese
½ cup sour cream
2 Tb. dry Marsala or Madeira
3 sprigs parsley, cut fine with scissors

Combine marinade ingredients. Bring marinade to boil, then cool, and marinate the chops for 12–24 hours. (Unless you know the meat is tough, you can marinate only for an hour or two, or not at all.)

Dry the chops thoroughly and roll in flour seasoned with salt and pepper to take up moisture and help brown the meat. Sauté the chops in lard or oil until brown on both sides, and when you turn to brown the second side put onion and green pepper in to sauté also. Add about ¾ cup of the marinade (set aside the rest) and the catsup, cover, and simmer for about 40 minutes.

Ten minutes before the end of the simmering sauté the mushrooms in the butter, then add to the chops. During the process you may wish to add liquid (the marinade) and when you do so taste the sauce to be sure it does not need more honey or sugar. You be the judge of how much you want the vinegar to dominate the taste.

Remove chops, and keep them warm off heat. Melt in the cheese, then stir in the sour cream and Marsala or Madeira. Return chops to skillet and warm all over low heat. Do not allow to boil. Serve chops on a chop plate with a spoon of sauce and the parsley over each; serve the rest of the sauce in a sauceboat.

NOTE: If you want the chops rare, don't braise them at all but rather after sautéing the onions and pepper proceed with all the steps without the venison. It will take only 15 minutes or so to cook the sauce. When you put in the mushrooms, broil the chops until rare. Add them for a minute or two to the sauce and serve.

VENISON LOIN CHOPS ARDENNES

This recipe, an adaptation from Elizabeth David's *French Provincial Cooking*, will introduce you to the wonderful flavor combination of juniper berries (for more about them see page 218) and venison. The slow baking of the chops gives you a chance to tenderize a tougher chop, if such may be the case; if it is tender, cut the cooking time as indicated.

SERVES 4

12 crushed juniper berries
   (or more)
¼ tsp. dried thyme
about ½ tsp. salt
freshly ground black pepper
juice of ½ lemon
4 thick loin venison chops
5 Tb. butter
1 small onion, chopped

3 carrots, diced
½ cup dry white wine or
   vermouth
½ cup water
about ¼ cup diced cooked ham
⅓ cup fresh bread crumbs
¼ cup chopped parsley
2 tsp. red currant jelly
1 tsp. bitter marmalade

Mash the juniper berries with the thyme, salt, and pepper.

Rub the lemon, squeezing the juice out, over both sides of the chops, then rub the juniper mixture over them. Let sit for an hour to absorb the flavors.

Melt 4 tablespoons of the butter in a skillet large enough to accommodate the chops. Sauté the onion and carrots until light brown, then add the meat and brown lightly on both sides, too. Pour in the wine or vermouth and boil to reduce a little. Add the water.

Distribute the chopped ham on top of the chops, then some bread crumbs mixed with parsley. Dot butter on top.

Bake in a 325° oven, uncovered. The cooking will take anywhere from 1 to 2 hours, depending on the tenderness of the venison. Prick with a skewer after about 50 minutes to see how much more baking may be needed.

When tender, pour off the juices into a wide pan, keeping the chops warm. Boil to reduce somewhat, then add the currant jelly and marmalade. Pour the sauce over the chops and serve hot with boiled new potatoes.

The Use of Kidneys in Red Meat Stews

Kidneys are, to our view, culinary catalysts nonpareil. Added to stews they give a distinction, an effect of heightening the meat taste, without giving a kidney taste to the dish. Don't talk about it at the table, lest one of your guests "can't abide kidneys." Just do it, and remove the evidence before you serve the entrée. In cases where you suspect a guest is a kidney hater, or one who is known to dislike all inside meats (known as innards), cut the kidneys into large enough chunks to identify and just remove them before serving. (Reserve for yourself or for the cat who knows what's good.)

STOVE-LID STEW

This stew is really a basic camp stew, and I've made a lot of them on an old lumber camp stove on Horseshoe Lake in the Ontario bush. A nice thing about a wood range is that you can be boiling something over one stove lid, simmering something over another, and keeping something warm over still another, all at the same time and with the same fire. It's just as good at home, where I usually use half beef broth and half red wine for the liquid.

This is a one-dish meal in camp with a large can of peaches for dessert; at home serve with a salad and French bread. Beaujolais goes well with this dish.

SERVES 6

3½ lb. venison, moose, elk, or whatever stew meat, cut into 1½-inch cubes
flour
5 Tb. lard or oil
2 large onions, chopped
1 rib celery with leaves, chopped
1 green pepper, chopped
2 cloves garlic, crushed or thinly sliced (or 5 cloves garlic, unpeeled, to be taken out later)
1½ cup game or beef broth (canned will do)
1 cup tomato sauce, canned or homemade*
1 tsp. Worcestershire sauce

2 sprigs parsley, chopped (or 1 Tb. dried)
1 tsp. thyme
½ tsp. savory
4–5 bay leaves
2 tsp. salt, at least
pepper
vegetables: Use potatoes (5 quartered), carrots (4 scraped and cut into thick slices), onions (2–3 small ones), 1 turnip (diced)
1 Tb. blackstrap molasses
½ lb. kidney of game, veal, or lamb, cubed (optional)
1 dill pickle, chopped (optional)

Roll the meat cubes in flour and brown them in lard or oil in a Dutch oven, deep metal casserole, or electric skillet. Don't crowd the cubes but rather brown them in relays so that they do not touch each other in the pan. When one batch is browned, take it out and set aside, while you do next batch. This will take 20–25 minutes.

Add chopped onions, celery, and green pepper, and sauté until tender (not brown), 6 minutes or so.

Return the meat, add whole garlic cloves,† broth, tomato sauce (or tomatoes), Worcestershire, parsley, thyme, savory, bay leaves, salt, and pepper and bring to a quick boil. Cover, turn down heat, and simmer (if you use electric skillet, simmer at 250°) for about an hour. Stir occasionally.

Add vegetables, molasses, and kidney cubes (optional), cover again and continue to simmer for another 1–1¼ hours.

If the flour on the browned meat has not thickened the stew sufficiently, mix 1 tablespoon flour with a little water and stir into stew gradually. Let it simmer (along with the optional chopped pickle) a bit longer to thicken.

* In camp, maybe 1 small can (11 oz.) tomatoes
† If you use crushed garlic add it when you add the vegetables.

VENISON À LA HARRY GROESCHEL
or Game Meat Sauerbraten

My uncle, who was a very good German-style cook, said the way to make a sauerbraten marinade was to use the same spices you would use for pumpkin pie. This recipe makes a delicious sauerbraten, and if anything, it is better with moose than it is with venison. As with most pot roast recipes, however listed, it serves any red meat well: elk, caribou, sheep, etc.

My uncle used cider in his marinade, but I use frozen concentrated apple juice, which comes rather sweet. If cider is used, the stew must be sweetened a bit with honey, maple syrup, or brown sugar.

Serve with noodles, spaetzle, or, preferably (I think), potato pancakes.

SERVES 8–10

THE MARINADE
1½ cups vinegar
6-oz. can frozen apple concentrate
three 6-oz. cans water
3 onions, chopped fine
3 bay leaves
1 tsp. powdered cloves

1 tsp. powdered cinnamon
1 tsp. powdered ginger
½ tsp. allspice
½ tsp. nutmeg
1 tsp. pepper

THE VENISON
5 lb. round, rump, or brisket of
　venison
3 Tb. oil
2 onions, chopped
1 green pepper, sliced
1½ cup strained marinade
1 cup broth
1 cup tomato juice or V-8 juice

⅔ cup red wine
3 cloves garlic, sliced
½ tsp. oregano
1 tsp. ginger
¼ cup maple syrup, honey, or
　brown sugar, if needed
½ cup sour cream

Mix the marinade ingredients and let meat stand in it, covered, for 2–3 days. If the above mix won't cover the meat in the container you use, add more liquid (½ vinegar, ½ water).

When ready to make the sauerbraten remove the meat, dry it, and sear it in a Dutch oven or casserole in the oil or lard, adding the onions and pepper to sauté when meat is half seared.

At the same time bring the marinade to a quick boil and bubble it for 10 minutes. Add 1½ cups, strained, to the meat, onions, and green pepper. Add the rest of the ingredients (except sour cream) and simmer, covered, for about 3 hours. When I use a deepish electric skillet I simmer at 250°.

Just before serving stir and blend in the sour cream.

VENISON SWISS STEAK

This is a simple but utterly delicious way to prepare any thick steak of red game meat. This recipe is for a big venison steak of, say, 1-inch thickness. I prepare it in an electric skillet, but it can just as well be at a simmer in an iron skillet with a lid.

⌒ ⌒

salt
pepper
1 venison steak, 1½" thick
flour
3 Tb. bacon fat
1 medium onion, chopped
½ green pepper, chopped
1 small rib celery with leaves,
   chopped

½ cup red wine
½ cup water (with dissolved
   bouillon cube if you wish)
8-oz. can tomato sauce
1 tsp. marjoram
½ tsp. thyme
½ tsp. savory

Salt and pepper each side of the steak.

Dust the surface of the steak heavily with flour, then press it in with the nub face of a meat mallet. Turn steak over, and flour other side.

Repeat the flouring a second time (this is to thicken the gravy so that it needn't be done later).

Sauté each side of steak in the hot fat until golden brown.

When second side is half-browned, turn heat to medium. Add around the edges the chopped onion, pepper, and celery.

When onions are soft add wine, water, and tomato sauce. Stir in the three herbs.

If you are using an electric skillet, simmer at 250° covered for 1½–2 hours or until steak feels done to your fork; or simmer covered over low heat.

Turn the steak once or twice and watch it, for the heavily floured steak will thicken the gravy. Just add water when it bubbles heavily and threatens to stick.

═══════ VENISON STEW PAPRIKA D. D'A. ═══════

Serve with egg noodles or spaetzle, salad, and hot Italian bread.

2½–3 lb. venison stew cut into
   1½" cubes
½ cup flour
3 Tb. paprika
salt and pepper
2 Tb. butter or margarine
2 medium onions, chopped

2 cloves garlic
1 tsp. marjoram
1 small can (11 oz.) tomatoes
   (or 1 can tomato sauce)
½ cup wine
½ cup sour cream (optional),
   at room temperature

Shake meat cubes in paper bag with the flour, 1 tablespoon paprika, salt, and pepper.

In Dutch oven or fireproof casserole melt butter and sauté the coated venison cubes until nicely browned. (You may have to brown the cubes in stages; do not crowd them but leave space between them; otherwise they will steam, not brown).

Remove cubes to warm dish and in same casserole sauté until soft the onions and garlic with 2 tablespoons paprika, then add marjoram and tomatoes, and wine. Cover, and cook under medium heat for 20 minutes.

Add browned venison cubes and simmer over low heat for 1½–2 hours or until meat is tender.

Just before ready to serve stir in, if you wish, ½ cup sour cream.

TEN-POINTER POT ROAST OF VENISON

This big venison roast for eight people is most handily prepared with a boned and rolled leg of venison, for you can lard the venison by wrapping up slices of salt pork inside the roll and you can flavor it by interspersing sliced garlic cloves with the salt pork. To do this, roll up the meat and tie it tightly in 7–8 places.

Like all stews, this one is a good dish to prepare from venison that is on the tough side, that of an old mossy-horned ten-pointer, for example. If you wish, you can put in quartered potatoes about 45 minutes before the roast is done. I prefer however to serve mashed potatoes or boiled noodles with the roast.

SERVES 8

THE MARINADE
3/4 cup finely chopped onion
1 white of leek (optional)
2 medium to small carrots, thinly sliced
2 Tb. vegetable oil
2 1/2–3 cups red wine (a new Beaujolais is good for this)
1/2 cup vinegar

THE VENISON
1 boned and rolled leg of venison (6–8 lb.)
1/4 lb. sliced salt pork (inside roll)
2 cloves garlic, sliced thin (inside roll)

1 rib celery with leaves, finely chopped
3 bay leaves, broken in halves
2–3 sprigs parsley, minced
10 juniper berries, crushed
1/2 tsp. thyme
1/2 tsp. oregano
8 peppercorns, crushed

salt and pepper
flour
2 Tb. lard or oil
1 Tb. flour (in some water)
1/2 cup sour cream

Sauté the onion, leek, and carrots in oil for 3–4 minutes, add all of remaining marinade ingredients, bring to a boil, then lower heat and simmer for 10 minutes. Cool the marinade, then put it in a large bowl with the rolled roast, cover with plastic wrap, and store in refrigerator for 24 hours. Turn roast 3–4 times.

About 4 1/2–5 hours before you wish to serve the meat, remove roast but reserve the marinade.

Dry the roast, salt and pepper all around, roll well in flour, and sauté it in lard or oil in the big casserole or Dutch oven you expect to use. Slow-brown the meat on all sides and don't stint on the time. See to it that it is appetizingly browned. This should take about 20–25 minutes over medium to low heat.

While the meat is browning, heat the marinade (don't strain), then put 1 1/2 cups of the marinade in Dutch oven with the roast, cover, and simmer in a 300° oven for 3 1/2–4 hours.

Baste occasionally with the oven liquids and add marinade as needed. *

When roast is done let it breathe on a very hot platter while you thicken the gravy if necessary on top of the stove. I swirl a tablespoon of flour in some water, stir it into thicken over low heat, then add 1/2 cup or more of sour cream and stir this in last (but do not boil). Serve the gravy in a gravy boat.

This pot roast will even convert doubting Thomases not used to game, and it's easy to carve.

* After the roast has been in the oven for a couple of hours or on one of the later occasions when you check for liquid, taste it. You may wish to modify the roasting liquid by adding water or the marinade diluted with water or with beef broth. Just depends on how flavorful you want the gravy, but make sure you have plenty.

══ BUCK AND BOURBON ══

If you have both a buck and a bottle of bourbon in camp, this is a nice change-of-pace stew. Good with moose or any other red meat.

SERVES 6

2–2½ lb. venison, cut in 1½"
   cubes
5 Tb. flour
1 tsp. salt
¼ tsp. pepper
2½ Tb. oil or lard
2 medium onions, diced
½ cup chopped green pepper

2 cloves garlic, diced
1 cup tomato sauce, canned or
   homemade
½ tsp. thyme or crushed rosemary
   (or both)
3 oz. bourbon
½ cup water with bouillon cube

In a skillet (with a lid for later use) brown over slow to medium fire the meat cubes shaken or rolled in flour, salt, and pepper. Don't crowd the meat pieces, but brown in the oil or lard and remove as they are ready, then set aside.

Sauté the onions, green pepper, and garlic in same skillet until soft.

Add browned meat cubes and remaining ingredients, cover, and simmer slowly for about 1½ hours. Check for liquid two or three times.

NOTE: If the meat cubes are well floured the stew will be properly thickened when finished.

══ VENISON SHANKS VIENNOISE ══

Serve these shanks with buttered noodles and cooked cranberries.

SERVES 4

6–8 juniper berries
salt and pepper
1 tsp. nutmeg
4 foreshanks, with fell removed
2 Tb. cooking oil
1 onion, sliced
4 carrots, sliced
1 large celery root, sliced
1 tsp. Dijon mustard

bay leaf
½ tsp. thyme
2 cloves
½ cup red wine
1 cup chicken stock
1 pint sour cream
1 tsp. grated lemon rind
1 Tb. capers

Preheat oven to 325°.

Crush the juniper berries and mix with salt, pepper, and nutmeg, then rub the meat with this mixture.

Heat oil in skillet and in it brown the shanks lightly but thoroughly. Add the sliced vegetables and sauté 5 minutes.

Add mustard, bay leaf, thyme, cloves, wine, and stock. Bring to simmer, cover, and bake 1½–2 hours.

When meat is tender, slice it and keep it hot on a platter. Stir sour cream into the vegetables and sauce, mixing until smooth. Pour the sauce over the meat, and sprinkle with grated lemon rind and capers.

SMOTHERED VENISON CUBES
WITH BARBECUE SAUCE

Mrs. Edward Nadeau of Casco, Maine, adds cheese to her barbecue sauce, a nice addition to the stew. Use your own favorite barbecue sauce or see page 360. Serve over rice or noodles.

SERVES 4–6

2 lb. venison stewing meat
flour for dredging
fat
2 medium onions, cut up
2 cloves garlic, cut fine
2 tsp. grated Cheddar cheese

2 tsp. salt
½ tsp. pepper
2 cups water
5 tsp. barbecue sauce
1 small can mushrooms or ¼ lb. sliced mushrooms (optional)

Remove any visible fat from meat. Cut meat into 1-inch cubes; dredge in flour, and brown in hot fat. Add onions and garlic; brown lightly. Add cheese, salt, pepper, water, and barbecue sauce. Cover and simmer about 1 hour and 30 minutes; stir occasionally to prevent sticking. Add mushrooms before thickening gravy.

VENISON CHILI

Serve this in good-size soup bowls, adding hot steamed rice for those who need to cushion the tantalizing assault of chili on the palate. Tenderfeet and others will appreciate beer as an accompaniment.

SERVES 8

½ lb. pinto or red beans
4 lb. coarsely chopped venison (neck, flank, plate, brisket, round, hind shank)
1½ tsp. cumin seed
½ cup chopped suet or sowbelly cut in julienne strips
6 good-size onions, chopped
2–4 cloves garlic, minced

1 tsp. oregano
3 Tb. fresh chili powder
1 large can Italian peeled tomatoes
1 small can green chilies
salt and pepper
dash of Tabasco sauce (optional)
2 Tb. instant masa harina or cornmeal

Wash the beans, cover with fresh cold water, bring to boil, and simmer 2 minutes; let stand, tightly covered, 1 hour.

Prepare meat (stewing cuts are best if fat-free) by cutting into ½-inch cubes.

Put cumin seeds in a skillet over medium heat and keep them moving until they smoke and turn toast-colored; then spread them on a flat surface and crush with a rolling pin.

Now melt the suet or sowbelly in a large skillet; you may substitute enough vegetable oil or other shortening to coat the bottom of the pan, but you'll lose meaty flavor. As soon as the fat is rendered or begins to sizzle add pieces of meat a few at a time and sear, turning cubes to seal all sides. Lower heat and add onions and garlic, stirring occasionally until onions are translucent. Add parched cumin seed, oregano, and the freshest chili powder you can get, preferably from a Spanish-American grocer; stir to coat meat with seasonings, add tomatoes and green chilies, and bring to boiling point, then reduce heat to simmer.

Bring the soaking beans to a boil again and allow to bubble almost imperceptibly until they are tender—30 minutes to an hour, depending upon beans.

Meanwhile watch the meat mixture to see that it is not getting too dry, adding water or stock as necessary to maintain a rather fluid consistency. Taste for seasoning, adding salt and pepper if necessary, and a dash of Tabasco as your taste buds decree.

After about 1½ hours (time will depend upon quality and toughness of venison cuts) sample the meat; if tender skim off the excess grease—or refrigerate overnight to let the fat coagulate for easy removal. Add masa harina for thickening. Then combine chili with cooked beans, bring back to simmering point, and allow flavors to meld for another 30 minutes.

═══ DEVIL'S RIVER (TEXAS) VENISON ═══ IN BEER AND BEANS

The late J. Frank Dobie, that wonderful writer and naturalist from Texas, gave me this dish. Mine is a reconstruction from memory, but I am sure of the basic ingredients. Mister Frank did not give me quantities, so in working this out I have added a touch or two.

Any piece of thick chuck or thick round of moose or elk or other big game is equally fine for this Mexican-influenced game dish.

Mister Frank once had this dish or its near equivalent made with a round steak of desert sheep.

SERVES 8 WITH LEFTOVERS

1 lb. dry frijoles or red kidney
   beans
6 unpeeled garlic cloves
¼ lb. salt pork
2 large onions, chopped
1 small rib celery, with leaves
2 cups chopped carrots
2 Tb. lard or other fat
1 tsp. salt
pepper
1 bouillon cube
3 Tb. Guajilla honey or blackstrap
   molasses

2 to 2½" thick venison steak, round or
   chuck
1 cup beer
1 Tb. Worcestershire sauce
2 Tb. tomato paste (or catsup)
1 hot green pepper, diced
   (or ½ tsp. crushed red pepper)
2 Tb. chili powder
parsley
1 tsp. dry mustard

Wash the beans and soak them overnight in a quart or so of water. In the morning add enough fresh water to cover the swelled beans, add the unpeeled garlic cloves and the chunk of salt pork, and simmer for 45 minutes to an hour. Drain the bean liquor in another saucepan and save it. Remove unpeeled garlic cloves and squeeze pulp into the reserved bean liquor. Remove, dry, and cube the salt pork.

In a casserole make a bed of about half the onions, celery, and carrots, and over this put half the beans. In a skillet fry the diced salt pork in fat until cubes are browned. Remove cubes and sprinkle them over beans. Add salt and pepper.

In the remaining fat squash and melt the bouillon cube and the honey or molasses and sauté the meat in it over a very low fire until both sides have been glazed and the meat richly colored. Watch out you don't turn the glaze into taffy. You are not trying to sauté the meat, just glaze it.

Put the meat over the bean layer, then the rest of the onions, celery, and carrots, and last the rest of the beans. Season again.

Pour into glazing skillet the beer, Worcestershire, 1 tablespoon tomato paste, chopped pepper (or crushed red pepper), the chili powder, parsley and dry mustard, and stir around to dissolve as much of the remaining glaze as possible and to meld the tomato paste and mustard. Pour over beans, then cover the beans with as much of the bean liquor as required. Cover the casserole and bake in a slow oven, perhaps 300°–325°, for 2½–3 hours.

Check every so often lest the beans absorb all of the liquor; if they get too dry add bean liquor which you have fortified by stirring in the second tablespoon of tomato paste.

═══ MRS. LESLIE'S VENISON PIE ═══

James Beard turned up this recipe during his research for his fine book *James Beard's American Cookery*. Between 1832 and 1851 Elizabeth Leslie wrote five cookbooks, and this recipe for venison pie has been adapted from Mrs. Leslie twice, once by Jim Beard and once by me. For Eliza's own words see p. 235 of Mr. Beard's book.

Buttered Brussels sprouts go well with a meat pie. A hearty red wine and a last course of fruit and cheese are consistent with tradition.

SERVES 4–6

1½ lb. cubed venison steak or stew
    meat
4 Tb. flour
salt
4 Tb. butter-oil mixture
1 medium onion, chopped
1 bay leaf
¼ tsp. mace
¼ tsp. nutmeg

parsley
½ tsp. thyme
¼ cup Madeira*
3 tsp. flour
3 Tb. black currant jelly (or beach
    plum jelly)
salt and pepper
4 eggs
dough for two crusts (see p. 433)

Preheat oven to 375°.

Roll the meat cubes twice in flour that has been salted. Sauté them in the butter and oil until nearly browned.

When meat is two-thirds browned also sauté onion.

Put meat, onion, bay, mace, nutmeg, parsley, and thyme in casserole and cover with hot water. Bring to boil, cover, then simmer for about an hour. If sauce is not thick enough, make a paste of the wine and 3 teaspoons flour, stir into stew, then stir in the jelly, simmer until thickened to right consistency, season with salt and pepper, and set aside to cool.

Make dough and place in refrigerator and put on eggs to boil for 20 minutes (according to Mrs. Leslie; we could cook them only 12 minutes). Remove eggs, run cold water over them, peel, and set yolks aside. (Discard whites.)

When ready to assemble divide dough in half and roll out (about ⅜ inch thick) to make shell and cover to fit a deep ovenproof glass pie pan. Line bottom for one crust.

Pour in cooled venison and sauce mix, crumble the egg yolks over, cover with remaining dough lid, and bake in 375° oven for 45–60 minutes, until crust is browned.

* Mrs. Leslie calls for "a glass," which then was 3 oz.

The Errant Lilies—Garlic, Onions, Leeks, Shallots, and Chives

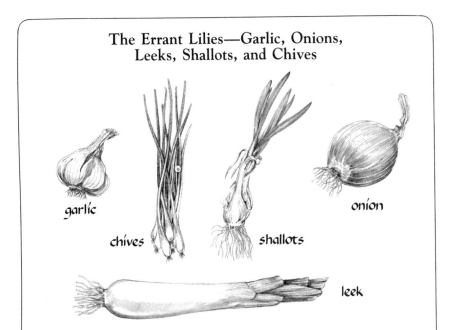

garlic

chives

shallots

onion

leek

What would cookery do without the errant lily,* garlic, and its cousins, onions, leeks, shallots, and chives?

In this book we will often distinguish among members in this lineage and recommend gentler cousins in one kind of dish and lustier ones in another. For example, the leek or shallot often imparts a more delicate savor to game bird recipes than onions or garlic, while the latter are surely the proper flavors for a hearty red meat stew.

Incidentally, it is interesting to discover how the flavor of garlic changes according to the way it is cooked. Chopped and fried, it is very volatile, whereas whole cloves cooked gently for a long time become mild and buttery. Sometimes with a stew, if you want a more pronounced flavor, it's a good idea to add crushed garlic near the end of the cooking along with the additional vegetables. The easy way to chop or mince a clove of garlic is to smash it first with the flat of a large knife so that the skin slips off easily, then just chop.

Above all, we recommend using all members of this family *fresh* whenever possible, not in powdered or salt form. Garlic particularly leaves an unpleasant aftertaste for most discriminating cooks when it has been dehydrated. Always look for bulbs that have plump, firm cloves.

* So called by Irma Goodrich Mazza in her treasure of a book, *Herbs for the Kitchen.* All the above are members of the lily family.

ED WUORI'S DEER RIB BARBECUE

Ed Wuori of Ellsworth, Maine, begins his recipe with a note that shows him to be a man after my own heart. Furthermore, he stands in the great tradition of hunters the world over who consider the fat ribs of game the best-tasting meat on the carcass. One of the tastiest parts of a deer is usually thrown away or fed to the dogs. People who have learned to barbecue deer ribs would prefer if a deer were all ribs. Don't scoff until you have tried this recipe.

SERVES 2–3

1 tsp. salt
1 tsp. pepper
1 Tb. sugar
1 Tb. ground horseradish
1 Tb. prepared mustard
1 clove garlic, minced (optional)
2 onions, chopped fine

1 cup water
1 cup tomato sauce or catsup
¼ cup lemon juice or vinegar
2 Tb. butter
1 tsp. paprika or 2 tsp. chopped parsley
1 side of ribs (about 3 lb.)

Mix salt, pepper, sugar, horseradish, mustard, garlic, onions, water, and tomato sauce or catsup, and simmer, uncovered, for 20 minutes. Remove from heat and add lemon juice or vinegar and butter; mix well. You may also add paprika or chopped parsley. Cut deer ribs in serving-size pieces. Place meat in baking sheet and smear generously with sauce. Bake at 350°–375° about 2 hours or until done. During baking, turn ribs over and baste, adding more sauce if needed.

NOTE: Cooking time will depend on how well done *you* like your deer meat. Moose or elk can also be barbecued with this sauce (or your own favorite barbecue sauce); I usually cook one side for 8 minutes, turn the ribs for another 8, then turn back and smear the first side with the sauce and continue barbecuing until the sauce is browned. Then do the same with the second side. This may prevent the sauce from carbonizing. Time depends on the heat of the coals, how far the meat is from the coals, etc. I test with a sharp knife and I like the rib meat pink.

Innards

When I first began to hunt big game I was appalled to find that few guides in bush camps ever saved the brains, sweetbreads, kidneys, hearts, and tongues. Indeed, few knew how to obtain or prepare them. Here are some of our favorite ways, and we hope you'll be tempted to forget any prejudices.

VENISON OR OTHER BIG GAME
TONGUE, BOILED

Venison tongue should be thoroughly washed, then parboiled until it can be skinned. The water is then discarded, new boiling water substituted, and the skinned tongue treated exactly as in the recipe for boiled moose heart (see page 54).

Sliced cold tongue makes delicious sandwiches for the noon tea-fire or served with catsup or mustard is equally welcomed as a stormy-day snack in camp. To me, it is especially good with hot mustard made by mixing powdered mustard with water and a dash of vinegar until it makes a paste of the right consistency. If you like mustard hot, try to find time to make it up about a half hour before serving it.

Any tongue should be extracted from a cut at the base of the throat and cut loose from the bony root; a meat saw and certain technique are required to extract the brains.

Fresh tongue is perishable—it really should be eaten within a few days after the animal is killed. Any tongue—fresh, smoked, or pickled—can be simply boiled until tender in an aromatic liquid such as that below, then skinned and served as is with some horseradish or Dijon mustard or a mushroom sauce. To intensify the flavor of a fresh tongue, an additional braising on a bed of vegetables is highly recommended, and then the braising liquid becomes the basis for a tasty sauce. This recipe is for a tongue of about 2–3 pounds but can be used for much smaller—or even larger—tongues; simply prick to see when tender and shorten—or lengthen—the cooking times accordingly.

SERVES 2–3

1 venison tongue
BOILING LIQUID
1 onion stuck with 3 cloves
1 carrot
2 cloves garlic
5–6 parsley sprigs
FOR BRAISING
1 carrot, diced
1 rib celery, diced
4 shallots or 1 small onion, minced
2 Tb. butter
1 cup tongue boiling liquid, strained

1 bay leaf
¼ tsp. thyme
2 tsp. salt
4–5 peppercorns

½ cup beef bouillon
½ cup white wine or vermouth
2–3 slices country ham or prosciutto, diced
¼ tsp. thyme
soft butter and flour (optional)

Put the tongue in a large enough pot so that it can sit comfortably, cover with water, and add all boiling liquid ingredients. Bring to a boil, then lower heat and simmer, covered, for about 2 hours. The flesh should be quite tender when you prick it with a fork; smaller tongues will take less time.

Remove the tongue and when cool enough to handle peel off the tough skin all around. Trim the root end of any fat.

In a casserole large enough to hold the tongue flat, sauté the carrot, celery, and shallots or onion in the butter until beginning to turn limp. Place the skinned tongue on top, add the liquids, ham, and thyme, cover, and braise in a preheated 325° oven or on top of the stove over very low heat—the liquid should be barely simmering—for about 2 hours, turning once.

Remove the tongue to a warm platter. Either strain the braising liquid or spin quickly in a food processor or blender to retain the puréed vegetables (frankly we prefer it that way) and thicken, if necessary, with a mixture of equal parts of softened butter and flour, stirred ¼ teaspoon at a time into the boiling braising liquid. Serve in a sauceboat.

The Use of Anchovies in Stews and Braises

Any red meat stew or braise is improved by adding minced anchovies or, more conveniently, by a 2-inch squeeze of anchovy paste. Watkins, the English firm, makes an excellent anchovy sauce that can be used in place of either. The authors urge you to try it in big meat stews and braises whether called for in our recipes or not. It is also a welcome ingredient in most sauces for fish.

════════ BRAINS AND SWEETBREADS ════════

In camp I've found that there is apt to be only one other member of the party who is eager to eat brains and sweetbreads. I have been able to make some converts—after these morsels have been appetizingly cooked—but you don't want to make too many enthusiasts. After all, each animal has only one brain and one pair of sweetbreads. Usually if cooking them in camp, we would do things casually, just running the brains and sweetbreads under cold water, rather than soaking them, then trimming off the membranes. If we didn't get to them the first night, we'd put them in a bread box outside to keep cool and firm up. The recipe and variations that follow are perhaps for more civilized circumstances, but feel free to cut corners if necessary. One pair of sweetbreads of a big animal would serve 2–3; the brain 2 at best. But you can combine them for a larger yield.

SERVES 2–3

1 pair sweetbreads and/or 1 brain	flour for dredging
2 Tb. lemon juice	salt and freshly ground pepper
4 cups water	8 Tb. butter
1 tsp. salt	1–2 Tb. capers

Soak the sweetbreads and brain in cold water for an hour, changing the water a few times.

Pick off exterior membrane and any bits of blood; this is best done with your hands.

Place the sweetbreads and/or brain in a pot with a mixture of lemon juice and cold water. Add 1 tsp. salt, bring to a boil, then immediately lower the heat and simmer ever so gently for 20 minutes.

Drain and plunge into cold water. If time allows, refrigerate the meats, placing them on a plate with another plate on top to allow them to firm up.

Roll the pieces, broken up into large bite-size morsels if you wish, in flour seasoned with salt and pepper. Sauté in 3 tablespoons of the butter over medium heat, turning to brown lightly on each side—it should take only 2–3 minutes. Remove to a warm plate.

Now add the remaining butter to the pan and cook until it turns brown—but not black. Remove immediately and toss in the capers with a little of their preserving juice. Pour this sauce over the meats, or if they have cooled, return them to the pan and heat in the brown butter sauce.

Variations: Omit the browning of the butter and the capers and simply sauté the sweetbreads and brains in 4 tablespoons butter. Add sliced or quartered mushrooms, if you like. Sprinkle with chopped parsley and serve with lemon wedges.

For brains, mustard-coated: After blanching and chilling, paint the brains all over with a generous amount of Dijon mustard. Then roll lightly in flour, dip into a beaten egg, and finally roll in bread crumbs. Fry in equal parts butter and oil.

For sweetbreads, braised: Sauté 1 small chopped onion, 1 chopped carrot, and 1 rib chopped celery in 3 tablespoons butter for 2–3 minutes. Add an optional tablespoon or two of chopped country ham or prosciutto. Dust blanched sweetbreads with flour and place on top of the vegetable mixture. Add 3 tablespoons Madeira, Marsala, or dry white wine and ½ cup beef broth and simmer, covered, in 325° oven for 40 minutes.

VENISON STEAK AND KIDNEY PIE
Venison in a Short Crust

Somehow I always feel this dish should be served when snow is on the ground. Guests should have shed heavy coats and perhaps left galoshes on your doorstep before sitting down to this meal. Leftover Christmas decorations (maybe a centerpiece of pine cones and hemlock sprigs) seem about right. Perhaps it's a Twelfth Night dinner.

In any case, venison pie is a festive winter dish with a slightly old-fashioned feel to it. It is of course as old as the hills of Northumberland. Serve this with broccoli and/or a salad and a good burgundy.

SERVES 4–6

2½ lb. 1¼″ cubes of venison round
4–5 Tb. flour
1 tsp. thyme
½ tsp. cloves
1 pinch nutmeg
salt and pepper
3 onions, chopped very, very fine
1 carrot, chopped fine
1 Tb. Worcestershire sauce

1 bay leaf
½ cup claret or burgundy
3 cups rich beef consommé
3–4 deer kidneys or 2 veal kidneys
4 lamb kidneys
cornstarch or mixture of butter and
  flour (optional)
1 recipe pastry, page 433

Roll the venison chunks in flour into which has been mixed the thyme, cloves, nutmeg, salt, and pepper. Sauté in a little fat until meat is browned. Add the onions, carrot, Worcestershire sauce, bay leaf, wine, and consommé. In a covered saucepan simmer gently until the venison is tender—about 50 minutes to an hour and 10 minutes. Watch out that the floured mix doesn't stick.

While the stew is simmering, trim the kidneys of fat and gristle tissue, cut in ¼-inch cubes, and simmer during the last 10–15 minutes with the stewing venison.

Grease a casserole and put in it the meat and kidneys. Add 2–2½ cups of the sauce. If the vegetables or the flour or meat chunks have not thickened it, stir in cornstarch dissolved in water or a mixture of soft butter and flour. Make a short pastry and cover the meat, kidneys, and sauce with the dough. If you are a bit of an artist, decorate the top of the pastry with a set of pastry deer antlers. Bake in a 400° oven for 30 minutes.

VENISON LIVER À LA MARIO

The famous game restaurateur Mario prepared the venison liver I presented him with in the following fashion; he took over the camp kitchen that morning to make certain he had the liver the way he wanted it.

SERVES 6

2½ lb. venison liver, sliced ½″ thick	salt and pepper
½ cup flour	6 Tb. butter
	2 Tb. lemon juice

Mario, all 300 pounds of him, dipped the liver in flour, salt, and pepper and sautéed it over a fairly high heat in the hot butter, turning it once. (He liked it rare and we ate it rare, about 4 minutes to each side.) He then stirred in the lemon juice, loosening the browned particles in the process, poured the lemon butter over the liver and, on his way into the camp dining room, commandeered a tin plate of crisp bacon that had already been prepared by the regular camp cook. "Better with sautéed onions," he said, "but I didn't have time."

HEARTS BRAISED WITH ROOT VEGETABLES

SERVES 4

2 hearts, halved (2 deer or 1 moose)	2 large parsnips, peeled and diced
flour	½ large rutabaga, peeled and diced
2 onions, chopped	3 Tb. butter
3 Tb. lard or oil	(or part ham fat if available)
½ cup red wine	1½ tsp. sugar
1 cup game or beef bouillon	¼ cup diced ham
½ tsp. savory	(preferably country ham)
¼ tsp. thyme	2 Tb. chopped parsley
salt and freshly ground pepper	

Dredge the halves of heart in flour. Shake off excess.

In a large skillet (with a top) sauté the onions in the lard or oil until beginning to brown. Push aside and add the meat pieces. Brown lightly on each side.

Add the red wine, bouillon, and herbs, and salt and pepper lightly. Cover and simmer very gently 1¼ hours for the deer hearts, 1½ or more for the moose.

Sauté the parsnips and rutabaga in the butter (to which you've added a little ham fat if you're using a country ham). Sprinkle sugar on top and toss to glaze lightly, then add the vegetables to the meat, and cook, covered, another 30–40 minutes or until hearts are just tender.

Toss the diced ham into the skillet for the last 5 minutes of cooking. If the liquid gets too thick add just a little more bouillon or water, if necessary. Sprinkle with chopped parsley and serve with mashed potatoes.

STUFFED HEARTS

The Welsh call this delicious heart dish "love in disguise."

SERVES 4–6

2–3 deer hearts, depending on size,
  or 1 moose heart
1 cup fresh bread crumbs
1 cup minced ham
1 cup finely chopped suet
1 egg, lightly beaten
¼ cup chopped parsley
1 sprig marjoram, chopped,
  or ¼ tsp. dried

1 sprig rosemary, chopped,
  or ¼ tsp. dried
1 tsp. grated lemon peel
salt and freshly ground pepper
3 strips bacon
2 Tb. flour
2 cups boiling water
2 tsp. tomato paste

Soak the hearts in cold water for 1 hour.

Remove the veins and arteries with a sharp knife, then wash out and dry hearts.

Prepare the stuffing by mixing the bread crumbs, ham, suet, egg, herbs, and lemon peel together. Taste and salt and pepper as desired.

Make a 2–3-inch slash on one side of each heart and fill with the stuffing. Wrap each stuffed heart with a strip of bacon and secure it with a skewer.

Place hearts upright in an earthenware casserole and bake in a 350° oven for 2–3 hours, until meat is tender.

Remove the hearts to a heated platter. To the pan drippings add the flour, stir, and cook a minute or so. Off heat pour in the boiling water and tomato paste, then return to the heat and stir as the sauce thickens. Simmer a few minutes, then serve in a sauceboat along with the hearts.

ALEX DELICATA'S VENISON JERKY

Jerky can be cured with no salt or brine mix at all. It can be dried plain, only it will just take longer to be dry enough. The salt brine will allow the jerky to keep longer.

2 lbs. lean venison, trimmed
  of all fat
½ cup pickling salt

¼ cup brown sugar
½ tsp. black pepper
½ tsp. garlic powder

Cut strips of meat as thin as possible; ⅛ inch or less by 4–6 inches long. Combine remaining ingredients to make a dry brine. Roll pieces quickly in dry brine solution and place on rack in smoker. The temperature in the smoker should stay between 75° and 95°, for 10–12 hours or until jerky strips snap when bent.

Varying Herbs in Game Cookery

The recipes in this book calling for herbs or herb combinations should be taken with a grain of salt. The good cooks I know are all experimenters both in selection and in quantities and use recipes as counselors rather than as tyrants. They vary herb selection and combinations according to their own palates. However, good cooks who wish to repeat good recipes know that a different herb combination will of course result in a different dish even when all other ingredients are precisely the same.

But do not allow this to deter you in making your own combinations. Just be sure you keep a record in memory or on a card file of just which and how much of each herb you used for that venison stew that made such a hit on a certain occasion. Perhaps "a rose is a rose is a rose," but the same cannot be said for a bouquet garni.

Remember also, however, that some herbs make especially happy marriages together. Marjoram and summer savory, and thyme with parsley and marjoram or both, happen to be happy blends, but there are many others that you can discover for yourself—for example, tarragon and chervil for fish.

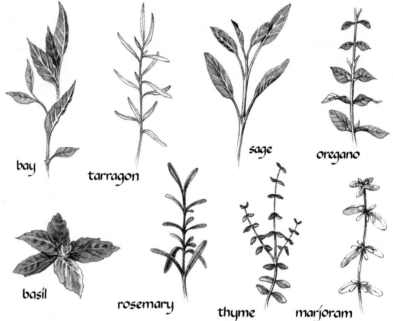

bay

tarragon

sage

oregano

basil

rosemary

thyme

marjoram

If I personally were selecting eight basic dried herbs, I would select thyme, bay, sage, oregano, marjoram, rosemary, tarragon, and basil. But if I were to do so I would sorely miss savory, fennel, chervil, and cumin. (I have left out the so-called aromatics I invariably use fresh—celery, parsley, shallots, scallions, onions, garlic.)

Remember, tarragon and oregano are strongly flavored and tend to dominate herb combinations if not used sparingly.

═══ AU SABLE VALLEY VENISON MINCEMEAT ═══

This is a rewarding way to use some of the meat you might have ground as venisonburger, and when made in a large batch can be divided into presized portions in glass jars or plastic containers tied round with a red ribbon and given as Christmas presents. The bulk recipe given below will make enough for 8 pies; the shorter version is sufficient for 2 pies. The larger recipe was given to me by the late Hubert Burrell, "Captain of the Hunt," in the Au Sable Valley of the Adirondack Mountains of New York. It is a reduced version from his sister, Carrie Pelkey, who was one of the ladies in a group that made venison mincemeat each fall as a community operation. Meat was pooled from several hunters, the cost of the other ingredients shared, and a great batch prepared and then divided.

Mincemeat pie is virtually a medieval dish, a little-changed descendant from the sweet, spicy meat and fruit dishes of the Middle Ages. Indeed, it is a scarcely altered version of the Grete Pye of the fifteenth century, and if one wanted to come even closer to the medieval Grete Pye, part of the ground cooked meat should come from cooked pheasant or other game birds.

The Au Sable Valley Eight-Pie Recipe

8 cups venison meat, cooked, then ground
12 cups diced tart apples
1½ cups raisins
1½ cups currants
1 pint apple jelly
4 cups ground suet
3 cups stock*

2 cups apple cider†
4 Tb. ground cloves
4 Tb. ground cinnamon
4 Tb. nutmeg
2 cups sugar
  (or to taste; I'd use more)
1 tsp. salt
brandy

Combine all ingredients except brandy and simmer for 1 hour, stirring often. When cool stir in brandy to taste.

*The meat stock can be venison stock in which the meat is boiled when you start the recipe from scratch.
†Frozen apple juice diluted as can directions indicate can be substituted for cider.

Our Two-Pie Adaptation

MAKES 2 PIES

2 cups ground cooked venison
  (leftover roast perhaps)
3 cups chopped tart apples
1 cup chopped beef suet
¾ cup chopped seedless raisins
¾ cup currants
¾–1 cup stock
½ cup chopped dried apricots
  (optional)
4 Tb. apple or beach plum jelly
2 Tb. blackstrap molasses

1½ cups light brown sugar,
  tightly packed
2 tsp. cinnamon
1 tsp. cloves
½ tsp. ginger
½ tsp. nutmeg (or mace)
¼ tsp. allspice
¼ cup chopped citron
cider
brandy

Combine all ingredients except cider and brandy and simmer in saucepan for an hour, stirring often. During simmering add cider if additional liquid is needed. Stir in brandy to taste when the batch has somewhat cooled.

See page 433 for recipe for double crust pie.

Moose

The Moose and Its Delicious "Beef"

Most moose meat is *better than the beef that one can now buy,* and the reason for this we've given on page 3.

Moose meat, say from a three- or four-year-old bull with two inches of suet on its loins, tastes like the *mature* beef that was available before it became too expensive to raise beef to an age when the full succulence and taste of beef had developed. Moose meat is a bit coarser-grained than the beef from a "baby beef" available in today's shops, but only a few would notice this. Moose meat is the meat to serve those who think they don't like game; I have never yet after forty years of serving moose meat found one single person who did not consider it a superb delicacy. A common remark has been "If anything, it's better than beef."

Any man who, with his partner (in my case once, just my wife and I), has ever gone through the hard, back-breaking work of butchering a moose in the woods knows that his incentive for this cruel labor is the delicious packages of meat that will eventually come out of his deep freeze. Moose meat will last, if properly wrapped, a year or even more in the deep freeze. With an animal as large as a moose, it sometimes takes this long to eat it all.

While it is true that moose is never as marbled with fat as good beef is, it is not always necessary to lard moose roasts. But if you have meat from an old bull skinny from the rut, by all means lard roasts off the rump or roasts off the round top or bottom. I sometimes lard the tenderloin, as it is a strip of pure muscle with virtually no larding of its own.

ROAST MOOSE FILLET

My wife and I once had all to ourselves while camping in a tent on the Alaskan tundra a whole tenderloin of a three-year-old moose that I had shot in the willow flats of an oxbow of the Colville River. Although I did not weigh it, that great length of solid meat must have weighed 10 to 20 pounds and it was the finest fillet I ever tasted, infinitely better than the best fillet of beef that one can get these days.

We roasted the chateaubriand section, cut 2-inch steaks from the filet mignon section (see below), and used the flat "tail" portion of the tenderloin for bourguignon and moose stroganoff. But ideally the sapid chateaubriand section (see below) should be roasted at home where better oven control is also accompanied by a meat thermometer. Roast fillet should be served rare; overcooking is truly lese majesty.

If you have guests who like a sauce with their meat, make it either Béarnaise or Bordelaise. I serve roast fillet with Potatoes Anna (plus a green vegetable) or with a casserole of mashed potatoes and sour cream and cheese.

SERVES AT LEAST 12

1 moose or elk chateaubriand roast (approximately 7 lb.), brought to room temperature
¼ lb. salt pork, cut into 3" × ¼" strips (see note)

¼ cup brandy (optional)
1 clove garlic, slivered (optional)
salt and pepper
bacon slices (optional)
parsley

Lard the fillet by inserting strips of salt pork (see page 18) and place meat thermometer precisely halfway through the fillet.

In preparing roast tenderloin remember that this is a fast operation; you must time the rest of the meal to accommodate.

Bring oven to 475°. Place larded, salted, and peppered fillet uncovered on a rack or on a bed of bacon slices in a flat shallow roasting pan. When you put the fillet in, turn the heat down immediately to 325° and, watching the meat thermometer like a hawk, roast until it registers 120°–125°. This can take from 18 or 20 minutes to 30 minutes. The dense, tender, fast-roasting fillet should be pink-rare at this reading. Don't invite guests who like well-done meat, but don't worry either that the fillet will be too rare; it won't.

Put the fillet on a hot platter, garnish with parsley and let it rest 2–3 minutes, then slice it fairly thin.

NOTE: If you want to be a bit fancy, marinate the salt pork lardoons in brandy for a couple of hours and slip a sliver of garlic clove in with each lardoon. Or you can roll the lardoons in the juices and pulp of crushed garlic cloves or cloves put through a garlic press.

Notes on Marinating Game Steaks

Don't feel bound by the recipes in this book or in any other book for marinades for broiled steaks. Experiment yourself with herbs and flavors. And remember, if you have some guests who prefer their steaks broiled *au naturel* and some who like the marinated flavor, you can prepare your favorite marinade, make it into a sauce, and serve separately—without ever putting the steak into it at all.

Let us say, but for the preference of one or two of your guests, you would have put down the steak in the following simple marinade.

MAKES ABOUT ¾ CUP

2 cups red wine	½ tsp. marjoram
1 onion, minced	½ tsp. Worcestershire sauce
1 clove garlic, smashed	3 Tb. soft butter
½ tsp. pepper	

Instead of marinating the steak in it, put the marinade (all the above ingredients except butter) on the stove, bring it to a boil, lower the heat, and simmer until the 2 cups are reduced to a half or ⅔ cup. Just before you serve the steak, warm the reduced marinade, take it off the stove and stir in the soft butter until it melts. Serve this in a sauceboat for your guests who would relish it with the plain broiled steak.

Or consider either as a marinade or a marinade sauce the following alternatives. Substitute thyme and/or rosemary for the marjoram and soy sauce (into which you have stirred ½ teaspoon dry mustard) for the Worcestershire. Incidentally whenever a marinade calls for Worcestershire you may use, if you wish, Harvey's sauce, walnut sauce, or mushroom catsup.

As with a belfry full of bells, you can "ring changes" on a marinade or sauce as well, and with the same harmonies.

MARINATED FILLET OF MOOSE OR ELK

This dish will taste quite different from the preceding recipe because the fillet is marinated first and picks up the savory flavor of the marinade. I would be more apt to do this with tougher, older meat that's been in a freezer a long time. As in the last recipe use a meat thermometer for best results, for a fillet should really be pink inside. But giving roasting times for a roast fillet is difficult. Roughly for a 5–6-pound fillet it should take about 30–35 minutes in a 450° oven, but with a meat thermometer you know when the meat is the way you prefer it. The thermometer should be inserted to a midpoint in the fillet. When it registers 125° the meat will be rare. The cook can work from there. Rare (or pink) fillet of moose is noble fare.

Roast fillet can be served with home-fried potatoes or, if there is room in your oven, with Potatoes Anna.

5- to 6-lb. moose or elk fillet
about ¼ lb. salt pork, cut in
  ¼" strips
2 carrots, very thinly sliced
1 large onion, very thinly sliced
1 lemon with peel removed and
  discarded, thinly sliced
2 bay leaves, crumbled
2 sprigs parsley, minced
½ tsp. powdered thyme

¼ tsp. savory
½ cup oil
1 tsp. La Choy brown gravy sauce
  (or glace de viande)
4 cups beef or moose stock
  (bouillon cubes will do)
¼ cup butter
salt
½ cup dry Marsala or Madeira

Trim and lard the fillet, and if it includes the thin tapering end, fold this back and tie (a full moose fillet is too long for any normal kitchen roasting pan).

Lay the fillet in deep glass dish, cover with vegetable and lemon slices, sprinkle with herbs, and pour the oil over all. Marinate the fillet for 5–6 hours, turning it often, at least a half dozen times.

Meantime add brown gravy sauce to stock and simmer it until it becomes thickish and syrupy—that is, until it is reduced to about ⅔ cup. Reserve.

When almost ready to serve bring oven to 450°, place fillet on a rack and set into a buttered roasting pan.

Baste it often with the butter but for the last 7–8 minutes, 10 or more degrees before the thermometer reaches 125°, paint it 3–4 times with the stock glaze. (As you see, this will keep you busy.) Baste and paint quickly so oven heat stays high. Watch the thermometer.

Turn off oven, salt the fillet, remove it to an ovenproof platter, and set it back into the cooled-down oven with the door open to rest for about 10 minutes.

If you have any remaining glaze add it, along with the wine, to the roasting pan; stir and simmer 3–4 minutes. Serve the sauce separately in a sauceboat.

MOOSE TENDERLOIN STEAKS
CHATEAUBRIAND

Because of the embarrassment of riches I mentioned (see page 45), we used an abundance of moose fillets three ways—as a moose bourguignon, in a lesser stew, and as 1½-inch steaks (cut from the chateaubriand or the thickest part). Cooking on a sheet-metal Yukon stove, I didn't risk that stove's detachable and hellishly hot oven, but sautéed those steaks instead. Result: I will never, never broil another tenderloin steak. The procedure was simple, but the secret was that the fat used was kidney suet from the moose itself.

At home I would serve such heavenly fare with a béarnaise sauce, Potatoes Anna, hot French bread, and a salad.

1 Tb. butter
1 chunk moose kidney suet, diced

four 1½" moose fillet steaks

In our case, I wet the skillet with butter and tried out the suet until there was enough fat for sautéing.

With dry willow sticks making that little stove hump with heat, I sautéed the steaks in that tasty fat just until brown on the outside and rare within.

═══════ MARROW SAUCE FOR MOOSE STEAK ═══════

Marrow sauce is an ancient one and an elegant accompaniment for thick steaks from game moose, elk deer, or caribou. This dish can be made in the roughest bush cabin, indeed perhaps better made there, for usually such camps have a great skillet left over from some lumber camp. The large bottom area of such skillets (the one I used each fall for nine years in an Ontario trapping cabin was a 24-inch skillet) can be accommodated of course on a four- or six-lidded wood stove's spacious hot surfaces and can hold 3- or 4-pound large game steak moose (or elk) round steak about 2–2½ inches thick.

Few guests will ever forget either the steak or the sauce in this scrumptious entrée. Don't forget that, as with most red-meat recipes in this book, this is a fine sauce for pan-broiled beef steaks as well as game steaks.

⊿⊾ ⊟ᐅ   SERVES 6 WITH SECONDS

MARROW SAUCE

5 or 6 large marrow bones
  (beef marrow bones are fine)*
6 shallots, chopped, or 4 cloves
  garlic, chopped
3 Tb. butter or lard or rendered
  marrow bone fat
2 Tb. flour
2 cups red wine
½ tsp. powdered thyme

FOR SAUTÉING STEAKS

2 shallots, chopped, or 1 clove
  garlic
2 Tb. butter or spare lard
  or moose suet
1 tsp. chopped parsley (see above)

½ tsp. crumbled rosemary
¼ tsp. savory
½ Tb. dried parsley (if in camp,
  otherwise fresh sprigs chopped)
½ tsp. salt
¼ tsp. pepper
2 tsp. Worcestershire sauce or
  mushroom catsup

3–4-lb. moose steak, 2–2½″ thick
salt
3 sprigs parsley or watercress
  for garnishing

Put marrow bones in a pie pan in a very hot oven and brown. Reserve the rendered liquid marrow fat and extract the marrow itself. Chop and squash.

Sauté the shallots or garlic in butter, lard, or marrow fat until soft and, off heat, stir in flour. Brown over low heat for a couple of minutes, then off heat add the wine, stirring continuously. Add herbs, salt, pepper, Worcestershire or catsup, and simmer for 7–8 minutes, then stir in the marrow and keep warm at a simmer.

Sauté shallots or garlic in butter or lard, then, with fire up to medium, sauté the steak, turning once, for 10 minutes. All chopped parsley. With a steak this thick the meat will be rare. If medium rare is preferred, sauté 5–6 minutes longer. Salt and hold in a hot platter.

Stir sauce into meat skillet and stir and scrape in shallot and browned meat essences. Pour some sauce over steak, garnish with parsley, and carve on the diagonal in thin slices. Add the rest of the sauce to the sauceboat.

NOTE: If you wish, instead of using the liquid, rendered-out marrow fat in the sauce, you can fry slices of bread in it and serve the steak on the crisp fried bread slices.

  * Try to buy marrow bones that show the marrow at both sawn ends.

═══════ BARBECUED MOOSE, LIBBY KUHN ═══════

Libby Kuhn is surrounded with the paintings by her husband (Bob Kuhn) of big mammals—and she knows what to do with their meat, too.

SERVES 6

1½"-thick slice of moose haunch (round or rump)

THE MARINADE

2 Tb. vinegar
½ cup olive oil
1 clove garlic, crushed

1 tsp. salt
½ tsp. freshly ground pepper

Marinate the haunch for at least 2 hours in the marinade.

Meanwhile prepare the sauce by mixing together all of the sauce ingredients below and bring to a boil.

THE SAUCE

2½ Tb. chili sauce
1 tsp. chili powder
¾ cup olive oil
⅓ cup lemon juice
1 Tb. brown sugar
1 bay leaf

2 dashes Tabasco sauce
1 tsp. dry mustard
⅓ cup water
2 cups finely chopped onion
2 cloves garlic, crushed
1 tsp. salt

Broil marinated steak over charcoal embers (7 minutes on one side, 5 on the other) and baste with the sauce.

Glazing Vegetables for Stews

If you want to get that authentic French taste in bourguignon, meat à la mode, and other stews, you should glaze the vegetables before adding them to the casserole. It is a simple process.

In a small skillet crush three moistened (if dry) beef bouillon cubes, add 1 tablespoon brown sugar, 2 dashes of Worcestershire, and a couple tablespoons of jelly. Currant jelly is fine, but beach plum jelly is better.

Put over a low fire and, stirring and mixing, melt and blend the mixture while it is growing sticky. Watch it, for it can quickly become taffy.

Add pearl onions (or coarsely chopped regular onions) and thick, chunky slices of carrots and stir and mix until the vegetables have been coated. Try to use the heat so the thickening glaze is used up completely as it coats the vegetables.

When the vegetables are added to the casserole or Dutch oven, if there is a touch of glaze clinging to the pan, scrape it out, providing it is not too taffylike, and add to the stew sauce.

My junior partner recommends simply sautéing the vegetables in a few tablespoons of butter, then sprinkling sugar over them—just enough to lightly coat all over; shake the pan and let the vegetables brown and glaze, then add them and scrapings from the pan to your stew.

It is important not to let these vegetables cook too long. Add them only about the last half hour of cooking so that they are just tender, not soft and mushy.

═══ MOOSE (ELK, CARIBOU, OR VENISON) ═══ BOURGUIGNON

This is the game stew deluxe and deserves its reputation as queen among stews. I believe the glazed vegetables and the kidney endow this stew with its especially marvelous flavor. When made this way, it has that "best of French restaurants" taste.

Serve with noodles, homemade spaetzle, or rice.

SERVES 6

¼ lb. salt pork, diced
½-lb. slice of ham, diced
  (or 3 strips bacon, diced)
flour
salt and pepper
3 lb. round or rump, cut in 2″ cubes
1 game kidney, sliced
  (if moose or elk, both if deer)
  or beef kidney
1 Tb. brown sugar
1 Tb. currant or beach plum jelly
1 tsp. Kitchen Bouquet
2 bouillon cubes
24 small or pearl onions
  (if unavailable, quarter 3 medium
  onions)

5 carrots, sliced
3 cloves garlic, sliced
2 cups red wine
1 can cream of mushroom soup*
  or 1 cup beef broth
1 Tb. Worcestershire or Harvey's
  sauce
3 bay leaves
2 tsp. thyme (or 1 tsp. thyme
  and 1 tsp. of crumbled rosemary)
½ lb. mushrooms, sliced
butter
¾ cup cream
3 Tb. chopped parsley

In a skillet try out the salt pork and frizzle the ham cubes (or bacon). Reserve cracklings and ham.

Roll or shake the meat chunks in salted and peppered flour. Same for the kidney slices. Brown the meats in the salt pork fat on all sides, making sure you do not crowd the pieces, i.e., brown one batch of pieces, remove to casserole, then brown the next batch.

Stir sugar, jelly, and Kitchen Bouquet into skillet, then smash in the 2 bouillon cubes and melt, stirring to blend over low flame. Glaze the onions, carrots, and garlic slices until sticky with glaze but not caramelized. Remove to casserole. Stir in red wine, then the can of mushroom soup, if you are using it; otherwise add beef broth. Stir in bay leaves and thyme and smooth out the liquid. Set aside.

Cover and simmer for 2–2½ hours, adding water if stew thickens too much. Add vegetables to casserole for the last 30–40 minutes of cooking. If you didn't use canned mushroom soup, sauté the mushrooms in butter for 2–3 minutes, then add the cream. Cook down until the cream has thickened—about 5 minutes. Add cracklings and ham to the mushroom mixture just long enough to warm them, and add to stew along with parsley.

*Use the canned mushroom soup if you're in camp or anywhere that fresh mushrooms are not available.

═══════════ MOOSE À LA MODE ═══════════

This is an elegant game dish and, along with its peers game bourguignon and sauerbraten, is the preeminent braise for red meat. There are as many variations of à la mode as there are cooks, and you should add your own variation if you wish to join the company. But there are four indisputable rules: (1) do lard the meat, (2) do try to include the two split calves' feet, (3) do coat the roast with flour before you slow-brown it, and (4) do cook it slowly, if in the oven or in an electric skillet at 250–275°; if in a Dutch oven on top of the stove at the slowest simmer you can manage, always tightly covered, of course. Either thick game steak or round or rump roast may be used. I serve this pot roast with whipped potatoes.

NOTE: Any red game meat can be prepared à la mode, but moose, elk, or musk ox (like beef) takes somewhat longer to cook than venison or antelope. Proceed confidently no matter which meat you use, and this includes bear meat.* This dish delights everyone except dyed-in-the-wool vegetarians. Make no retort if one of your guests, new to game dishes, says, "Why, I couldn't tell it from beef à la mode." This is not true, but then who would denigrate beef?

¼ lb. salt pork, cut in 3″ strips ¼″ wide
¼ cup brandy
4 to 6-lb. top or bottom round or rump
2 cloves garlic, sliced
3 Tb. cooking oil
salt and freshly ground pepper
4 Tb. flour
4 Tb. lard
3 onions, sliced
1 calf's foot, split
3 cloves
½ tsp. mace

1 rib celery with leaves, chopped
½ tsp. thyme
½ tsp. rosemary
½ tsp. marjoram
2 bay leaves
1 cup red wine
1 Tb. Harvey's or Worcestershrie sauce
3 cups beef broth or consommé
¼ cup Madeira
4 carrots, sliced
4–5 white turnips, cubed
½ cup sour cream, at room temperature

Marinate the salt pork strips in brandy for an hour.

With a larding needle or a long, sharp-pointed knife make 3-inch incisions into the meat. Slip first a sliver of garlic in along the flat of the blade and then the marinated pork strips. Lard in several rows with incisions about 2 inches apart.

Rub the roast with the oil, salt and pepper it, then flour it well. Make as much flour adhere as you can.

In a big casserole, electric skillet, or Dutch oven melt the lard and brown the roast on all sides. Do this over medium to low heat and take 25 minutes or so to do it.

Sauté the onions in the pot during the last 5 minutes of the browning, then add all of the rest of the ingredients save the carrots, turnips, and sour cream.

Bring to a boil, cover, turn down heat, and simmer as slowly as possible for 3 hours. In an electric skillet set the heat for 250°.

After 3 hours or a bit less, add the carrots and turnips and simmer another 30–40 minutes.

Remove roast and vegetables to a hot platter and stir in the sour cream. Do not boil the gravy.

*You won't have to lard bear meat.

QUICK À LA MODE

Each cook sometimes must face a situation where a late decision about "what to have" leaves him wishing he had the time to marinate and then braise a fine cut of game meat. Don't despair, for while I agree that long simmering adds to the joy in a braised dish, I also argue from experience that the pressure cooker can be a life saver in a pinch. And the result can be so good that you need not apologize (or ever even confess) that it was pressure cooked.

As with regular à la mode it can be prepared without first marinating the meat, although you must be sure the contents of the normal marinade are also in the pressure cooker. This recipe for quick game à la mode is a slight variation of the preceding recipe.

A good rule of thumb for solid pieces of meat like a rump roast is 11–12 minutes to the pound at 15 pounds pressure. The thickness of the piece and whether or not there is a bone in it are factors that control cooking time with a pressure cooker. In any case, when it should be done, reduce pressure immediately by cooling the cooker under the faucet (not by removing at first the pressure gauge head) and check for doneness. If doubtful, return cooker to stove, bring to 15 lb., and continue cooking. Then reduce pressure immediately as above.

POT ROAST OF MOOSE

(or Venison, or Caribou, or Whatever)

This is a plain old pot roast that every wilderness camper is familiar with in one guise or another. It is another "poker game" dish that can be prepared between supper and the last hand for tomorrow's evening meal, for it simmers on a back lid of the same wood range that keeps the card players warm. If the weather is hot and humid, the skillet or Dutch oven should be placed in an ice box or cooler overnight.

SERVES 6–8

3½–4 lb. rump, round, or
  shoulder
2 cloves garlic
flour
salt and pepper
4 Tb. lard (or bacon fat if you
  have accumulated enough)
3 carrots, sliced
1 rib celery, leaves and all, diced
6 onions, sliced
2 white turnips or 1 small
  rutabaga, sliced

1 large can tomatoes
1 cup beer (wine is okay too)
3 bay leaves
½ tsp. cinnamon
¼ tsp. powdered cloves
1 tsp. thyme
½ tsp. oregano
pasta (noodles, spaghetti,
  or macaroni)

With a small paring knife or your jackknife stick 7–8 punctures in the meat and slip a sliver of garlic along the blade down into the meat.

Pound in as much flour, salt, and pepper as you can. In a deep skillet or Dutch oven brown the roast in the lard or bacon fat on all sides.

Add all the rest of the ingredients except pasta, cover, and simmer from 9

P.M. to 1 A.M. or whenever the poker game degenerates into cutting cards. Check liquid, and if more is needed, pour in what's left in somebody's can of flat beer. If the game breaks up early, continue simmering the next day, but figure to simmer this dish a total of 3½–4 hours overall.

About a half hour before you are ready to serve the pot roast, put it on to reheat. While it's heating put on a kettle of water and boil some pasta.

Take out the roast and set it on a pie pan or some such on the open oven door to keep warm.

If your camp has a colander or sieve pour the sauce through it and work and press the vegetables through to thicken the sauce.

Slice the pot roast onto a platter, pour on some of the sauce, and serve the rest in a "sauceboat" (some small saucepan with a handle).

BARBECUED MOOSE RIBS
À LA PALFREY LAKE LODGE

There are very few meals that can top roast fat moose ribs. Here is Jean Day's recipe for roast ribs barbecued. Larry Day and she run a hunting and fishing lodge situated less than a quarter mile from some of the best landlocked salmon fishing in the Northeast. The smallmouth bass fishing in nearby Spednik is as good as can be found anywhere. Address: McAdam, New Brunswick. Serve these ribs with favorite vegetables and a nice red wine.

SERVES 6

BARBECUE SAUCE
½ cup magarine
¾ cup brown sugar
1 cup catsup
⅓ cup Worcestershire sauce

2 Tb. soy sauce
dash Tabasco
salt and pepper to taste

Melt the margarine in a saucepan. Add the remaining ingredients, bring to a boil, and simmer 10 minutes.

MOOSE RIBS
4–5 lb. moose ribs cut in 3" strips.   1 large onion, sliced

Place ribs in a roasting pan with onion slices. Pour hot barbecue sauce over the ribs. Cover and cook in 325° oven for 2 hours.

MOOSE OR ELK OR VENISON OR CARIBOU
STROGANOFF

This is the classic way to make the dish, and its distinction lies in the fact that its ingredients are cooked separately and are not simmered for any length of time in the sour cream. Smuggling a pint of sour cream into the grub list seemed a bit odd to our young Piper Cub pilot who put us down on a gravel bar 60 miles south of the Arctic Ocean.

When you yourself are slicing the meat you can assure yourself that it is sliced thin enough. No butcher worth his salt will slice beef a scant quarter-inch thick as you should slice your elk or moose meat. After the thin slicing, cut it in strips 3″ × 1″ size.

This delicious dish is good with rice or, preferably for me, riced potatoes.

⌂ ⌂   SERVES 6

1½ cups thinly sliced onions
butter
1½ cups mushrooms, thinly sliced
(in camp half as much dried
mushrooms)
2½ lb. moose or elk (or venison
or caribou) round steak, sliced
in strips (see above)
1 cup sour cream, at room
temperature

2 tsp. Dijon or any other prepared
mustard
1½ tsp. tomato paste or catsup
1 pinch thyme
salt and pepper (white pepper if
you want to be a purist)
¼ cup Madeira
(or sherry or dry Marsala)
chopped parsley

Putting this dish together reminds one of Chinese methodology. First sauté the onions in butter until translucent and set aside. In another small skillet, sauté the mushrooms in butter. (Or you can use the same skillet.) Then, again in hot butter, quickly sear the thin strips of meat—just until the redness colors; the meat should be rare.

Ideally the sour cream that comes next should not be right out of the refrigerator but at room temperature. Meld into the sour cream the mustard, tomato paste or catsup, and thyme.

Now salt and pepper the meat, mix in the onions and mushrooms, stir in the wine, and stir together with the sour cream mixture. Sprinkle parsley over the top. Heat without bubbling.

MOOSE HEART BARLEY SOUP
WITH ONIONS AND BAY LEAVES

Perhaps this is really a camp soup, but it is delicious prepared in camp or kitchen.

Any heart of big game is good in this simple soup. The heart can be stuffed and baked as well.

⌂ ⌂   SERVES 4

1 moose heart, washed, cut in two
after ventricle linings have been
removed
3 onions, sliced
5–6 bay leaves

½ tsp. thyme
salt and pepper
8 cups boiling water
½ cup barley

Put all, save the barley, in a big kettle, set on the wood stove, bring to boil, and let it simmer as long as you are in camp. When you return, put it on a hot simmering section of the stove again, add hot water, if needed, and simmer soup more at same stage. Maybe the next evening, add barley a half hour before you serve it and continue the simmer until grain is done, adding hot water as needed for quantity. Place a slice of heart in each bowl, retaining the rest to slice cold for sandwiches or to serve sliced cold with catsup as a rainy day snack.

Use of Marrow Bones, in Stews and Braises

Marrow bones improve any stew or braised dish and, happily, they freeze well. Often a deer—and occasionally a larger animal—is brought in whole, i.e., hog-dressed. Hunters, both in the East and in the West, occasionally drive a truck into or near the hunting area and can thus bring out a whole moose or elk. In such cases, the lower legs, normally abandoned, should be skinned out, sawed up into marrow bone size (3- or 4-inch pieces), packaged, and frozen at the time the meat is frozen. Similarly save the bones after boning-out meat.

If this is not possible, beef or veal marrow bones and knuckles may be purchased in the market and substituted. Sometimes they come frozen. Consider that any of the stews or braises will be enhanced if marrow bones are used in the cooking of them. Also see page 48 for marrow bone sauce for game steaks and for the technique of browning marrow bones.

(Caribou marrow is eaten raw by our Arctic friends and called "Eskimo butter.")

MOOSE STEW

I have made this stew with venison, caribou, moose, and beef; its chief distinction lies in the simple but happy herb mix, thyme and marjoram. For a basic stew that uses a little molasses and pickle and tomato sauce to enhance the flavor, see page 27.

Serve with riced or mashed or boiled potatoes.

SERVES 6

3½ lb. stew meat, cubed (I sometimes use the eyes of venison chops)
salt and pepper
½ tsp. powdered thyme
3–4 Tb. flour
2–3 Tb. lard or oil or bacon fat
1 large onion, diced
½ green pepper, diced
3 carrots, sliced

2 celery tops with leaves
½ tsp. marjoram
2–3 big shakes of Worcestershire sauce
2 cups red wine or enough to cover
1 clove garlic, smashed
2 tsp. beef bouillon powder (or 2 cubes)

Sprinkle meat cubes with salt, pepper, and half the thyme, then coat heavily with flour.

In Dutch oven or electric skillet melt fat and sauté the meat cubes on all sides in several batches so the pieces are not crowding, removing those that are nice and brown to make way for more.

When all the meat is browned, sauté onion, green pepper, carrots, and celery in the same pan, adding more fat if necessary until onions are barely translucent.

Return the meat to the pan, add the rest of the ingredients, cover, and simmer for about 1½ hours. Add water as the liquid absorbs the flour from the meat cubes. You may have to do this several times.

Antelope

PRONGHORN ANTELOPE

Although one writer-cook considers antelope "slightly gamier than venison," I think of it, at least in texture, as more tastily flavored veal. I once partook of a haunch spit-roasted over open coals and steaks similarly grilled and thought it delicious. Friends of mine in the West say that any recipe for venison will be fine for antelope, and I have found this to be true at the board of a friend who prepared it in the same ways that we prepared the various cuts of whitetail deer. He sometimes larded the roasts.

The antelope is a small animal, dressing out at about half the weight of a good big deer, but though it comes in small packages it is very tasty. I think sage is one herb that ought to be in an antelope stew, perhaps to celebrate the brushy terrain he sometimes frequents.

ANTELOPE OR VENISON TRANSMONTANA

This is Peggie Lunt's recipe for veal, but I have made it often using antelope or venison for the roulade. You could also use thinnish round steaks instead of breast meat.

SERVES 4–6

1 breast antelope, boned
4 Tb. lard
3 oz. prosciutto (or smoked ham), minced
6 Tb. finely minced parsley

1 clove garlic, smashed
1 tsp. salt
¼ tsp. freshly ground pepper
½ cup white wine

With a sharp knife score a crisscross of ⅛-inch-deep lines on one side of the breast.

Make a paste of 2 tablespoons of the lard, the prosciutto, 4 tablespoons of the parsley, garlic, salt, and pepper, and spread it over the cut surface of the breast.

Beginning at the narrow end, roll up the breast, paste inside, and tie in 6–7 places with string.

Brown the roulade on all sides in the remaining lard. Take the time to brown thoroughly over medium heat; don't rush it.

Add the wine, cover, and simmer for about an hour or until the meat is tender.

Remove the roulade and let stand for 10 minutes before slicing in ¼-inch slices. Taste the juices for salt, add 2 tablespoons minced parsley, and a bit more wine if too reduced, heat, and serve as a sauce with boiled potatoes.

ANTELOPE MARSALA PARMESAN

Immodestly, perhaps, but exuberantly I wrote on the back of the card I made up for this recipe "(This is a super-delicious dish!!!)." The first time I prepared it I used veal, for I was trying to reproduce an entrée I had immensely enjoyed in a New York restaurant. Since that time I have used antelope (given to me by the late Larry Koller) and venison. The steak (or steaks) for this dish should be sliced quite thin.

SERVES 2

1 antelope round steak, sliced ⅛" thick	1 Tb. chopped parsley
	¼ tsp. oregano
3 Tb. butter	¼ tsp. powdered thyme
1 small onion, finely chopped	¼ tsp. marjoram
½ green pepper, cut in thin strips	1 clove garlic, mashed
½ cup chicken broth	¼ cup *dry* Marsala
½ cup white wine or vermouth	2 Tb. sour cream
1 cup fresh or canned tomato sauce	¼ cup freshly grated Parmesan

With a mallet pound the steaks thin and then sauté them in the butter until lightly brown. Set aside.

In the same pan sauté the onion and green pepper until just soft. Add the steaks and the remaining ingredients, save the Marsala, sour cream, and Parmesan. Simmer, covered, until the liquid has almost boiled away.

Lift the steaks out onto a hot platter.

Stir the Marsala and sour cream into the pan, heat through, then pour over the steaks. Serve the cheese in a bowl with a spoon or dust over the steaks yourself.

OSSO BUCO
(Antelope Marrow Bone Shank with Herbs)

If you have butchered your own antelope, don't relegate the meat on the shanks to burger meat (above knee or lower hind leg) but rather saw shanks with meat on them into 2-inch lengths. Shank meat close to the bone is very flavorful.

SERVES 4–5

4 shanks of antelope, sawed into
  2″ chunks
5 Tb. flour
salt and pepper
4 Tb. lard, butter, or oil
2 medium onions
2 cloves garlic, minced
2 carrots, sliced across in chunks
1 rib celery with leaves

1 Tb. tomato paste or 2 Tb. catsup
1 cup dry red wine
1 Tb. sage, crumbled between
  thumb and fingers
¼ tsp. savory
¼ tsp. thyme
1 cup boiling beef broth or water
2 Tb. chopped parsley

Roll shanks in flour, salt, and pepper, and brown them in hot fat in an electric skillet, Dutch oven, or heavy casserole.

    Remove meat and sauté onions, garlic, carrots, and celery in same pot for 5–6 minutes; add a bit more butter and stir in flour to make a *roux*. Cook 4–5 minutes, then add tomato paste or catsup, wine, rosemary, savory, and thyme and simmer 5 minutes. Put shanks in, add enough hot broth or water to come up two-thirds way on shanks and simmer, closely covered, for 2½–3 hours. If an electric skillet is used, simmer as with Swiss steak at 225°–250°. Check a couple of times to see if more wine and/or broth is needed. Before serving season to taste with salt and pepper and sprinkle chopped parsley on top.

═══════ FLEMISH-STYLE ANTELOPE STEW ═══════
WITH BEER

A Flemish stew known as a carbonnade uses dark beer as a braising liquid and lots of onions. The same savory treatment can be given to any red game meat; only the cooking time will vary, depending on the toughness of the meat. So be sure to start testing after 1½ hours of cooking.

SERVES 6

3 lb. antelope stewing meat
4 Tb. pork fat
6 medium onions, sliced
4 large cloves garlic, smashed
  and chopped
salt and freshly ground pepper
2 cups dark beer or 1 cup regular
  beer and 1 cup stout

1 cup game or beef stock
½ tsp. thyme
2 Tb. brown sugar
2 bay leaves
about 8 sprigs parsley
2 Tb. arrowroot or potato
  or cornstarch
2 Tb. red wine vinegar

Cut the antelope meat into pieces approximately 1½–2 inches square and ½ inch thick.

    Heat 2 tablespoons of the fat in a large, heavy skillet. Pat the pieces of meat dry and brown them, not too many at a time so they don't crowd each other, over high heat, turning until all sides are seared. Remove pieces as they are done and continue with the rest.

    Add remaining fat to the skillet and sauté the onions until they are lightly browned all over. Add the garlic and sauté gently, stirring, for a minute more.

    In a casserole of about 2-quart capacity and not more than 3 inches deep, arrange a layer of the meat, salt and pepper well, spread half the onion mixture over, add another layer of meat, season, and finish with onions.

Heat the beer and stock in the skillet, scraping up any good browned bits, stir in the thyme and brown sugar, then pour this over the meat and onions. Lay bay leaves and parsley sprigs on top. Cover with foil and the casserole cover, and bake in a preheated 325° oven anywhere from 1½ hours to as much as 2½. Check carefully and remove when tender; don't overcook so that meat gets stringy.

Mix the arrowroot with the vinegar and a little cold water to get a smooth paste. Pour the liquid out of the casserole into a saucepan, stir in the paste, and bring to a boil, whisking to make smooth. If the sauce seems a bit thin, let it boil down for a few minutes.

Remove the bay leaves and parsley sprigs and pour the thickened sauce over the meat. Reheat if necessary.

BLANQUETTE OF ANTELOPE

A "blanquette" is the French term for a delicate stew, usually made of veal, that is enriched with a cream and egg sauce, garnished with mushrooms and little white onions. It's every bit as delicious—and certainly more exotic—made with antelope. Serve it with rice.

SERVES 4

2 lb. antelope stew meat, cut in cubes
1½–2 cups chicken or game broth
1 medium onion stuck with 2 cloves
1 carrot
1 bay leaf
1 rib celery

½ tsp. thyme
12–18 small onions
salt and freshly ground pepper
12 oz. mushrooms
2 Tb. butter
2 egg yolks
⅓ cup heavy cream
1–2 Tb. fresh lemon juice

Put the meat in a stew pot and add enough broth to just cover it. Bring to a boil and skim off any scum that rises to the surface. Add the onion with cloves, carrot, bay leaf, celery, and thyme, reduce the heat, cover, and let simmer for about 1 hour.

Peel the onions and make a shallow cross in the root ends. Add to the pot when the meat is almost tender but still somewhat resistant when pricked, and let cook slowly until onions and meat are both tender—20–30 minutes more. Add salt and pepper to taste.

If the mushrooms are very large, cut in quarters; otherwise leave whole or just halve them. Sauté them in the butter quickly for 3–4 minutes, then add them to the stew.

Beat the egg yolks with the cream. Ladle up about ½ cup of the hot stew broth and slowly add to the egg-cream mixture, beating; then stir in with the rest of the stew. Heat just to warm, making sure the liquid doesn't boil now. Stir in lemon juice to taste and correct salt and pepper seasoning if necessary.

BREADED PRONGHORN CUTLET

This is Wiener schnitzel with antelope cutlets. Serve it with spaghetti and a sage butter sauce.

SERVES 6

six 6-oz. antelope cutlets
4 Tb. bread crumbs
3 Tb. grated Parmesan
½ tsp. crumbled rosemary
1 egg
salt and pepper

1 tsp. minced parsley
¼ tsp. grated nutmeg
½ cup cream
6 Tb. butter
1 Tb. lemon juice
parsley sprigs

Pound the cutlets with a wooden mallet until they are very thin—¼ inch or less.

Mix the bread crumbs, cheese, and rosemary and put in plate or pie pan.

Beat the egg, then add the salt, pepper, minced parsley, nutmeg, and cream, and beat again until smooth.

Melt 4 tablespoons of the butter in a heavy skillet. Dip the cutlets first in the egg-cream mix, then in the crumb-cheese mix, then back in the egg-cream mix. Sauté until golden on both sides. Set cutlets aside on a warmed platter.

Melt the rest of the butter in the pan and cook until it shows color. Add the lemon juice, pour over the cutlets, and garnish with parsley sprigs.

ROLLED ROAST OF MARINATED ANTELOPE
WITH SOUR CREAM SAUCE

This recipe calls for a buttermilk marinade, and the game is to get the flavor of the marinade into the meat before you roll and tie the roast. Use boned rump or shoulder.

When you roll and tie, be sure to tie at least 8 places to ensure a neat roll. This recipe is fine for a rolled roast of sheep or venison.

SERVES 6

THE MARINADE
1 qt. buttermilk
2 onions, chopped
1 clove garlic, smashed
THE ROAST
3-lb. roast of antelope
2 Tb. capers, with their juice
THE SAUCE
4 shallots, chopped
4 Tb. butter
2 Tb. flour
1½ cups beef broth

2 bay leaves
½ tsp. rosemary, crumbled

1 clove garlic, sliced
¼ lb. salt pork, sliced

½ cup white wine
¾ cup sour cream
1 Tb. paprika

Combine all marinade ingredients. Lay the meat in the marinade and leave it for 48 hours.

Crush the capers and rub the caper pulp with juice on the meat's inside side. Distribute garlic slices over the same side.

Roll the roast and tie.

Lay salt pork in the roaster, set in the rolled roast, and roast for 15 minutes in a preheated 400° oven.

Meanwhile, make the sauce: sauté the shallots in the butter for 3–4 minutes, then stir in the flour and cook for 2 minutes more. Off heat add the broth and wine and, back on the heat, cook over a low fire, stirring, until the sauce thickens. Stir in the sour cream and then the paprika.

Pour half the sour cream sauce over the roast and turn the oven down to low, about 300°. Continue cooking until overall time comes to about 20 minutes to the pound.

When roast is done, add the rest of the sour cream sauce and bring just to hot.

Elk

Bob Kuhn, the great mammal painter, who has eaten the meats of the hoofed game of both North America and Africa, considers elk the best meat of all, better than sheep—"and, yes, I'd include beef in that estimate," he says.

All agree, of course, that superb meat rewards the diner when prepared as the meat in any of the red meat recipes offered in this book. The following specific recipes for elk come from friends.

The best sausages I ever ate were those (both hot and "sweet") made by an old German butcher in Miles City, Montana, from elk meat supplied by Larry Koller. Larry used elk sausage in his superb game bird cassoulet (see page 337)—that much-missed trencherman-chef sometimes had his sausages made with a mix of elk and antelope meat.

BROILED ELK STEAK
MARINATED IN BRANDY

This is plain fare with just a touch of elegance before you take it off to the charcoal grill.

SERVES 6

4- to 5-lb. elk (or moose, or caribou) steak, 2" thick
¾ cup cognac or any decent brandy

3 Tb. butter, melted
salt and freshly ground pepper

Marinate the steak in the brandy for about 45 minutes, turning it a couple of times.

Drain and pat steak with a paper towel (yes, reserve the expensive marinade). Broil steak over hot coals, basting a few times with melted butter. Salt and pepper it.

Serve steak on a garnished hot platter after you have *warmed* the reserved cognac marinade in a saucepan.

Just before you bring in the platter light the warmed brandy and pour just enough of it onto the steak to make the blue flames dance (and to make you feel better about using so much expensive brandy for the marinade).

GREAT FALLS ELK STEAK WITH HERBS

This recipe is an adaptation from a friend's method of broiling beef sirloin steak. For the herbs she used Zachary's Game seasoning, a very happy herb mixture. I have substituted some of the herbs in the seasoning in case Zachary's mix is unavailable. Also good with moose, caribou, venison, and bear.

SERVES 8–10

4 Tb. butter, soft
1 tsp. marjoram
1 tsp. thyme
1 tsp. tarragon
⅛ tsp. powdered cloves
4–5-lb. elk steak, 1½" thick
2 cloves garlic, sliced

5 Tb. dry mustard
1 tsp. black pepper
3 Tb. red wine
2 Tb. red currant or beach plum jelly
2 Tb. chopped parsley

Combine the soft butter with the three herbs and the cloves.

Cut a series of ½-inch-deep cuts in the steak about 1½–2 inches apart and insert a garlic slice and ¼ teaspoon of herb butter in each incision. Keep remaining herb butter for later use.

Make a paste of the mustard, pepper, wine, and jelly, and spread it on both sides of the steak. It is best, but not imperative, to do this about 2 hours before broiling.

Charcoal Grilling

Everyone who grills over charcoal has been plagued by the persistent flaming of the coals. The apprehensive griller, standing ready with a water spray to suppress the flames, suffers much wear on his nerves at every grilling. Happily there is a solution, one given to me by an old friend who once watched me fight flames with a spray gun. Make the fire as usual and let it build to the point where you would normally begin to grill. Then scrape back the coals to the edges of the grill, leaving space in the middle to accommodate the size of the steak, fowl, or fish. Do not leave any coals directly beneath the meat, but arrange them with your fork or poker so they lie around and just outside the silhouette of your meat. The fat that normally leaps into flame, when it falls onto coals, will now fall into nothing but hot ashes under your meat. If it occasionally flames up it can usually be blown out or subdued early with a squirt of water.

This method, widely used by expert grillers, requires a bit more time but not much more; however, game or fish grilled this way will be the jucier and tastier for broiling more slowly.

Broil the steak herb-butter side up for about 9 minutes; turn and broil 3–4 minutes more.

Take steak from broiler and spread the half-broiled side with the rest of the herb butter and with the chopped parsley and broil another 3–4 minutes.

Slice steak on the slant in ¼-inch slices and serve with a sauce if you wish—hollandaise or béarnaise.

═══ ROLLED STUFFED ELK OR MOOSE STEAK ═══

This adapted Colonial recipe, at least in the stuffing, goes right back to medieval times in the use of forcemeat, spices, and herbs to make a bread "sauce." It can be prepared with venison steaks, but I use steaks of the bigger animals merely because they are bigger. If round steaks of deer are used, make two roulades—or rolls.

SERVES 4–6

THE STUFFING
1 onion, chopped very fine
1 Tb. bacon fat
¼–½ lb. pork sausage
3 slices bread, moistened with
    red wine and crumbled
pepper
THE ROULADE
2 lb. elk steak cut ½″ thick
flour
3 Tb. butter

½ tsp. salt
½ tsp. nutmeg
¼ tsp. ground cloves
¼ tsp. cinnamon
½ tsp. mixed marjoram, basil,
    and thyme

½ cup Madeira
1 Tb. flour mixed with water

In a casserole or Dutch oven sauté onions in bacon fat until soft, then brown sausage, smashing and breaking with a wooden spoon.

Mix the sausage and onions with the rest of the stuffing ingredients in a bowl, using your fingers.

With mallet pound steak thin, and then cover with the bread sauce or stuffing and roll, tying with string in 6–7 places.

Flour the roulade all over and in a Dutch oven brown it in butter.

Add the wine, cover, and simmer over low heat for about an hour. Add water if the pan liquid cooks down too much.

Remove the roulade. Add as much of the flour paste to thicken as desired, stirring it into the juices, and simmer for 3–4 minutes.

Serve gravy in sauceboat with sliced roulade.

HEARTY ELK OR MOOSE BROWN STEW

SERVES 5–6

½ lb. suet, preferably beef
2½ lb. elk stew meat, cut up
   in 2″ cubes
½ cup flour
salt and pepper
2 cloves garlic, minced
2 medium onions, chopped
1 bay leaf
½ tsp. marjoram

½ tsp. thyme
2 Tb. chopped parsley
1 cup red wine
1½ cups boiling water or broth
2 carrots, in thick slices
4 potatoes, quartered
2 Tb. flour dissolved to paste
   in water

In electric skillet or Dutch oven or heavy casserole try out cubed suet.

Take out the suet cracklings. Roll meat cubes in flour, salt, and pepper; then brown the meat in the remaining fat.

Add garlic and chopped onions and cook until soft. Add the cracklings, herbs, wine, and water or broth, cover, and simmer over low heat for 1½–2 hours, checking liquid from time to time and stirring the stew.

About 45 minutes before the meat is done, add the carrots and potatoes. When the meat is done, if sauce is thin, add enough of the flour and water, stirring it slowly into the stew and simmering a bit until thickened to the consistency you want.

ELK STEW, PERUVIAN STYLE

For the cook who might wish to give a Latin American touch to a game stew, here is a recipe converted from Elisabeth Ortiz for beef (Seco de Carne) in her *Book of Latin American Cooking.*

SERVES 6

4 Tb. lard or vegetable oil
4 cloves garlic, finely chopped
1 medium onion, finely chopped
1 tsp. hot ground pepper* or cayenne
3 lb. elk or moose, etc., cut
   into 1″ cubes
2 cups beef stock

salt and freshly ground pepper
2 Tb. chopped fresh coriander
   (cilantro or Chinese parsley)
   or 2 tsp. ground coriander
juice of 1 lemon
2 lb. potatoes, boiled and halved

Heat the lard or oil in a casserole and sauté the garlic, onion, hot pepper, and meat cubes until latter are lightly brown.

Add the beef stock, salt and pepper to taste, and the coriander. Cook partially covered over low heat until the beef is tender, 1½–2 hours. The liquid should be reduced so that the sauce is quite thick and not very abundant.

Just before serving, stir in the lemon juice and cook a minute or two longer. Heap the stew on a warmed serving platter and surround with freshly cooked, hot potato halves.

* If you are able to buy small hot dried chilies, just crumble in fingers to get the "ground" pepper called for in the recipe. But if you do crumble chilies so, be sure to wash your hands in warm soapy water lest you accidentally rub chili in your eyes.

Vary the Liquids in Stews, Braises, and Sauces

Wine is a standard ingredient, but other liquids also can be used as flavorings for stews, braises, and sauces. The use of cognac and other brandies is familiar to most cooks, but beer, whiskey, rum, gin, and many of the other liquors are less widely used. They do not deserve to be overlooked in this fashion, especially in game cookery.

As the late Jack O'Connor, *Outdoor Life*'s longtime shooting editor, taught me, gin has a wonderful affinity for game birds. And why not? I had long used juniper berries as the essential flavoring of such dishes.

But it wasn't until ten years ago that Emanuel and Madeline Greenberg educated me through their excellent book *Whiskey in the Kitchen* about the use of whiskeys, rums, and other spirits in meat and bird dishes. Since adding their book to my culinary library I have not only used their recipes but have taken their hint by using a variety of spirits in my own recipes.

ELK OR GAME MEAT GOULASH WITH NOODLES OR SPAETZLE

Since stew meat makes up a fair proportion of butchered game, the cook with game in the larder will want to vary its use. Game Hungarian style is a tasty variation. Round of game can be used too. This dish is made in Hungary with red deer as the meat. Elk meat would be the New World version. Try to use real, sweet Hungarian paprika.

SERVES 6

3 lb. stew meat or round cut
   in 1½" cubes
flour
4 Tb. lard or butter and oil
2 large onions, chopped
2 cloves garlic, smashed
2½ Tb. sweet Hungarian paprika
1 rib celery with leaves, chopped
½ tsp. thumb-and-finger-crumbled
   savory

¾ cup red wine
1 cup game or beef broth
salt and pepper
1 cup tomato sauce or purée or
   4 tomatoes from a can
1 cup sour cream*
noodles or spaetzle

Roll the meat cubes in flour and brown in lard as in Stove-Lid Stew, page 27.

Add and sauté onions and garlic and when soft add paprika, mix it thoroughly, and cook for another minute or so.

Return all the meat to the pan and add the celery, savory, wine, broth, salt, pepper, and tomatoes, cover, and simmer over low heat for 1½ hours or until meat cubes are done (taste one). If you use electric skillet simmer at 250°.

When the meat is tender, check to see if flour on the meat cubes has given you the right consistency for the sauce. If too thin, mix flour and a little water and stir in, simmering 3–4 minutes longer to thicken.

Stir in the sour cream and serve with noodles or spaetzle.

* If made in camp where sour cream is scarce, don't worry; it will be good without it.

══════ POT ROAST OF ELK ══════
WITH DUMPLINGS, GERMAN STYLE

The red deer (or hirsch) of the German forests is basically the same animal (same genus *Cervus*) as our elk or wapiti, and in some park forests almost as big. This recipe is fine for moose, caribou, venison, or sheep, too.

Serve with red cabbage or with Steamed Cabbage Ben More.

SERVES 8

THE MARINADE
1½ cup beef broth or water and
  bouillon cubes
½ cup Rhine wine or any other
  white wine
¼ cup vinegar
1 tsp. powdered cloves
½ tsp. thyme
1 tsp. sage

¼ tsp. cinnamon
¼ tsp. ginger
½ tsp. crumbled rosemary
½ tsp. pepper
4 bay leaves
3 Tb. lemon juice
1 Tb. grated lemon rind

THE ROAST
3½–4-lb. pot roast of elk
2 cloves garlic, sliced
½ cup flour
3 Tb. lard or other fat
2 onions, diced

1 carrot, diced
1 stalk celery, diced
Dumpling batter (page 391)
1 cup sour cream, at room
  temperature

Mix marinade ingredients and just bring to a boil, then cool.

Put elk roast in bowl or crock, pour the marinade over, and let it marinate in a cool place or, if the weather is hot, in the refrigerator overnight and next morning, turning it as often as you think of it.

Remove meat from marinade, dry it with paper towels, cut slits in 7–8 places, and insert slivers of garlic.

Roll roast in flour and brown in the fat all over in heavy casserole or Dutch oven.

Add marinade and the onions, carrot, and celery, cover, and simmer until meat is tender (about 2½ hours).

Remove roast and if gravy has not thickened, add 1 tablespoon flour dissolved in ¼ cup of water. Stir smooth.

Return meat to Dutch oven and drop in dumpling batter, cover, and continue to simmer until dumplings have raised (about 15 minutes).

Stir in the sour cream and let it just heat.

DEVILED RIBS OF ELK, CARIBOU, OR MOOSE

This recipe is written for camp use, but it would serve for a feast out of your kitchen.

SERVES 6

4–5 lb. ribs in 4″ lengths	vinegar
1 bay leaf	Dijon mustard
½ tsp. powdered thyme	bread crumbs
1 onion stuck with 2 cloves	1 tsp. marjoram
salt and pepper	½ cup butter, melted

Simmer the ribs in a big kettle in water to cover along with the bay leaf, thyme, and onion for 2 hours. Set aside ribs to cool. If using short ribs from a rib roast dispense with this step.

Fire up the wood range to produce a very hot oven (500° at home).

Salt and pepper the ribs, then paint well all over with vinegar and let stand for a few minutes and paint again.

Smear ribs all around with mustard, then dust them thickly with the bread crumbs mixed with marjoram.

Pour melted butter over the ribs and roast in the hot oven for 15 minutes until brown.

NOTE: If you've neglected to bring the herbs to camp, don't worry; the deviled ribs will be a great hit anyway. Provide two sections of paper towels for each hungry eater. Further note: This recipe is good when made with game shanks.

The Elk of the Highlands

Here we have included a few recipes for stag, i.e., the Highland red deer, for that great quarry is a brother of our own elk.

In the past, red deer meat was a staple in the Highlands, but Nickey MacNicol, head stalker at the famous stalking lodge at Ben More, contended that he seldom ate deer meat (he prefers, he said, the meat from a full-year-old wether) because as a boy "all we had was red deer and salmon and I got fed up with it." Poor Nicky. But the stag's venison is delicious to most of us who do not have it often enough to be cloyed with it.

In many restaurants in the U.S. the venison served in the fall is red deer—from the herds in the highlands of New Zealand, where the species was introduced and where it thrives, producing venison in exportable quantities. It is not surprising that red deer tastes like elk, for red deer and elk are circumboreal brothers. Indeed, had our forebears been better taxonomists they would have called our elk or wapiti the red deer instead of misnaming it elk, which was their European name for the animal we call moose.

The Highlander's hearty if simple cuisine has a number of recipes for red deer that can be used for our own venisons, especially for elk, our own red deer.

SUTHERLAND STAG IN BROTH
OR BOILED ELK DINNER

This hearty Scottish dish is in a way the Highland version of a New England boiled dinner except that the peas and barley give it a thicker consistency.

SERVES 8

⅓ cup dried peas or lentils
4 lb. 1″ cubes elk stew meat
½ cup barley
salt and pepper
8 cups water
½ tsp. thyme
½ tsp. rosemary

2 sprigs parsley
2 carrots, cut into chunks
2 onions, chopped
1 turnip, diced
2–3 leeks
1 rib celery, with leaves, chopped
½ small head of cabbage, shredded

Wash peas, then soak overnight in water to cover. If using lentils, this preliminary step is not necessary.

In a stewing kettle combine drained peas, meat, barley, salt, and pepper with water and bring to a boil, skimming it a couple of times in the process.

Make a bundle out of thyme, rosemary, and parsley and add it to the stew. Add carrots, onions, turnip, leeks, and celery and simmer for 2½–3 hours depending on how tender the meat is.

About half an hour before the meat is done, add the cabbage.

STEAK AND A DRAM

Here is a Scottish sauce served in the Highlands with red deer steaks. It goes well with any game steaks from our side.

SERVES 4

4 red deer or elk steaks
4 Tb. butter
3 Tb. heavy cream
2 Tb. whiskey
    (we'd call it Scotch)

½ tsp. thyme
grated Cheddar cheese*
minced parsley

Grill or broil the steaks on one side.

Meanwhile melt butter in a skillet and add the cream, scotch, and thyme.

When done on both sides pour some of the sauce over each steak, grate on some cheese, and sprinkle with minced parsley.

NOTE: If you pan-broil the steaks mix the sauce ingredients into the pan drippings.

After this meal, if you want to stick to a Highland practice, serve as a cordial a small glass of "Athol Porridge"—2 parts scotch, one part honey. Sam Johnson would have approved of this.

*When I ate it, the cheese was crumbled Stilton.

══ A HIGHLAND HAGGIS (RED DEER OR ELK) ══

Our Scottish brothers and sisters under the skin, those who stalk the red deer, surely subscribe to the adage "Waste not, want not." Here's how they use everything from the deer (preferably a hind) in their "national dish."

Note for elk hunters: Don't knock it until you try it, but try it with Athol Brose, the Highland punch served traditionally with haggis. See recipe below.

Incidentally, a lowland haggis, say the Highlanders, is made from *sheep* meat and innards.

This recipe comes by courtesy of Marjory Macleod, coauthor with Mabel Mackie of *Bothy Brew.* This delightful book is what we would call a camp fish and game cookbook, simple but delicious game and fish recipes that can be prepared in a bothy, i.e., a shack in the high moors.

SERVES 8

1 whole red deer or elk tripe
1 heart, halved with artery gristle cut away
1 liver
2 "lights," i.e., the lungs (optional)
2 kidneys, trimmed
2 lb. red deer or elk, diced in ½" cubes or ground
1 lb. rolled oats
¼ lb. suet
1 lb. onions, minced
½ tsp. nutmeg

½ tsp. cloves
½ tsp. dry mustard
½ tsp. powdered thyme
½ tsp. sage
½ tsp. basil
½ tsp. rosemary
½ tsp. celery salt
½ tsp. salt
½ tsp. black pepper
½ tsp. cayenne
2 oz. scotch whiskey
1 cup venison or beef stock

Empty the stomach bag (paunch) and wash thoroughly, then turn inside out and wash. Then while turned, scald in boiling water and scrape with a dull knife. Rinse.

Put aside in cold, salted water overnight, smooth side out now.

Cover with water the heart, liver, lungs (if you use them), kidneys, and meat cubes, bring to a boil, and simmer for 45 minutes. Let cool.

Toast the oats on a cookie sheet in the oven.

Chop the innards, the meat chunks, and grate the liver coarsely. Mince the suet and add to the onions. (If you have a food processor you can reduce the time necessary for chopping and mincing.)

Put meats, oats, suet, and onions in whatever large bowl or pan will hold them, add the battery of herbs and spices, whiskey, and stock, and mix it all thoroughly with your ten fingers.

Drain and dry the tripe bag and fill partially with the mixture. There should be plenty of room with this quantity for the oats to swell.

Press out the air, sew up the bag securely, and put it in a big pot of boiling water. It will begin to swell shortly and when it does just prick it ("with a hatpin," says one of the recipes I consulted) in a dozen places so it will not burst.

Boil, uncovered for about 2 hours, adding more boiling water when needed.

Place the haggis on a hot platter, remove the stitches, and serve with a big wooden spoon.

If the traditional haggis intimidates you, then dispense with the paunch and put the haggis filling in an oven-proof bowl, cover bowl with foil, and place it on a rack in a shallow baking pan of boiling water; cook for 2 hours in a 350° oven, adding boiling water as needed.

Haggis is traditionally served with "neeps and tatties"—that is, with turnips and potatoes. Sometimes the two vegetables are mashed together.

The Athol Brose? Here it is:

1 cup oat brie (see below)	1 cup thin honey
1 egg	2 cups whiskey
1 cup thick cream	pinch of nutmeg

To make oat brie: soak overnight ¼ pound oats in 2 cups of water.

Beat the egg and stir it into the cream and honey.

Strain out the oat liquid and add a cup of it to the mix. Then stir in the whiskey. Grind or sprinkle nutmeg over the top and chill.

One recipe adds slyly, "If too thick, thin with whiskey."

Two Bothy Warmers

When Scottish stalkers hie to the hills they sometimes stay over in a bothy, a sometimes stone, sometimes wattle and wythe, sometimes lean-to, home away from home. Bothys are usually left over from the sheep tending and are seldom (never?) comfortable.

A Highlander or a Sassenach helps make the poorest bothy habitable.

Highlander: 3 parts whiskey, 1 part sloe gin
Sassenach: 3 parts sloe gin, 1 part whiskey

════ CASSEROLE OF HIRSCH ════
An Elkburger Dish from a German Kitchen

I owe this tasty dish to a friend whom, alas, I cannot credit, for though I have the card written for my files, I cannot remember who was my benefactor. If the cook remembers to include caraway seeds in his grubbox, this makes a hearty dish for the hunting camp.

SERVES 4 (IN CAMP) OR 6 (AT HOME)

1½ lb. elkburger	salt and pepper
2 Tb. butter or oil	3 cups thinly sliced potatoes
1½ cups beef gravy (see below)	1 cup evaporated milk
2 cloves garlic, smashed	4 cups shredded cabbage
¾ tsp. crushed caraway seeds	4 oz. (1 cup) grated sharp Cheddar

While sautéing the burger in a skillet in the butter or oil (just enough to turn the red color to gray) make up the gravy by mixing 4 teaspoons of instant beef gravy with 1½ cups water.

Stir into the meat the gravy, garlic, caraway, salt, pepper, and potatoes. Cover, bring to a boil, then simmer for 20 minutes or until the potatoes are tender.

Stir in the evaporated milk and bring just to a bubble.

With a slotted spoon, lift out the meat and potatoes and place them in a casserole.

Add the shredded cabbage to the sauce in the skillet and cook 5–6 minutes until cabbage is just crisply tender, then pour mixture over the burger and potatoes.

Add the grated cheese, cover, and, in oven or on top of the stove, heat until the cheese has melted.

Caribou

All of us recall those meals that somehow managed to become the essence of gustatory delight. One of these for me was a wilderness brunch near the end of a four-day backpack hunt in the mountains west of the Alatna River in the Brooks Range of Alaska. Bud Helmericks, that master guide and wilderness man, and I had left his Takahula Lake cabin traveling light. For grub we had 8 pounds of moose jerky (equivalent of 32 pounds of meat), tea, sugar, and salt, period. Jerky is sustaining for a short period eaten either as shavings whittled off with a sheath knife, or boiled up and softened in a kettle of simmering water. We were hunting grizzly (no, we did not kill one) and had decided to eschew any other game until we were close enough to camp to pack in the boned-out meat of a caribou. Bud wanted one for part of his winter's meat.

At the end of an exhausting fourth day of hiking and climbing, when about six miles from the cabin, we killed a bull caribou, hog-dressed it, rolled it up on some poles to cool out, rigged a tarp for shelter, and hit the sacks. I, at least, was too tired even to cook the liver for supper; we gathered two tin cups full of absolutely delicious blueberries, sugared them, and made do with nothing more than hot tea. I was asleep by the time I had zippered up my sleeping bag. My next conscious impression was olfactory, an aroma of surpassing savoriness, the lusty aroma of grilled meat and browned fat, spitting luscious essences in the alder coals. Bud had fetched in a side of ribs, spitted it on a green pole across two Y-sticks, and now hunkered down was turning it over the glowing coals. That meal of caribou ribs with just our fingers and a belt knife for implements was an experience never, never to be forgotten. I didn't even feel guilty for sleeping through that onerous preparation.

Caribou meat is delicious whether prepared à la Helmericks as our Stone Age ancestors did or with benefit of a civilized kitchen and its utensils and ingredients.

Some discriminating eaters of big game prefer caribou to any other. The meat is somewhat more finer grained than moose, and the animal, of course, is a much smaller deer than either moose or elk, although when you first see caribou and note the size of the stately antlers you tend to think the beast is larger than it is. Some mountain caribou get to 600 pounds on the hoof but a 300-pound bull hog-dressed is a big bull. Our *Rangifer tarandus* is the same beast as the European reindeer.

BRAISED CARIBOU IN SOUR CREAM

SERVES 6

4–5-lb. 2½″ thick rump or bottom round of caribou

3 Tb. lard or bacon fat or tried-out salt pork

2 onions, chopped

3–4 carrots, sliced thick

2 cloves garlic, sliced

2 cups red wine

1 cup bouillon (water and bouillon cubes in camp)

2 bay leaves

1 tsp. rosemary

½ tsp. savory

½ tsp. thyme

8–10 juniper berries, crushed

2 Tb. catsup

2 Tb. butter

2 Tb. flour

2 cups sour cream, at room temperature

salt and pepper

Brown the caribou well in the fat on both sides over medium heat in a Dutch oven or casserole.

When second side is nearly browned, add the onions, carrots, and garlic and sauté until onions are soft.

Add the liquids, the herbs, juniper berries, and catsup, and bring to a boil. Turn down the fire and simmer for 1½ hours or until meat is done. Add water if it cooks down too much.

In a skillet melt butter, stir in the flour, and cook gently a minute or two. Pour off the liquid from the casserole, and off heat stir into the butter-flour mixture. Return to a medium flame, let it slowly thicken, stirring all the while. Stir in the sour cream and heat but do not allow the sauce to boil. Season with salt and pepper. Serve the sauce or gravy in a sauceboat.

NOTE: In camp, substitute 1 cup of sour milk (made up from dried milk and water) which you have clabbered by adding 1 tablespoon of vinegar and allowing the milk to stand for 2–3 hours.

SWISS STEAK OF CARIBOU OR OTHER GAME

Thick steaks of caribou, moose, elk, or venison prepared in this fashion are delicious even if the meat be a bit on the tough side to begin with. Besides, this stew gives the host a sense of being a dispenser of good things, since the steak cooked in one piece affords the added pleasure of being sliced at the table. As with most dishes of this kind, suet from the game animal (same with venison) improves the dish. Beef suet will do handily, however.

Serve these steaks with riced or mashed potatoes and a light vegetable like zucchini.

SERVES 6

3–3½-lb. caribou steak 2½" thick
½–⅔ cup flour
chunk of game or beef suet (lard
   or vegetable shortening will do)
¼–½ tsp. cayenne pepper
1 tsp. marjoram
½ tsp. savory
1 onion, sliced

1 green pepper, cut in strips
½ rib celery with leaves, diced
2 cloves garlic
½ tsp. salt
⅛–¼ tsp. freshly ground pepper
½ cup dry red wine
1 cup boiling game or beef stock
   or canned beef broth

Take a bit of time to pound into the steak as much of the flour as possible, for it not only draws and absorbs meat flavor but thickens the gravy to the right consistency. Many cooks use the edge of an old white ironstone plate for this process, but I have found the wooden meat mallet better, the kind that has sharp ridges on one face and pointed nubs on the other. I find pressing the flour into the meat (with the nubbed face of the mallet) first, then pounding afterward, then pressing in more flour, less messy.

Wipe the steak with a damp cloth first, then in stages (while you are trying out the diced suet in a skillet) press and pound in the flour; get in as much flour as possible, then wait 15 minutes or so and press and pound in as much more of the flour as the meat will take.

Remove suet cubes from skillet (or you can use a Dutch oven or an electric skillet), heat remaining fat, and brown the floured meat on both sides. Do this over a steady medium heat but brown it well—it may take 20–30 minutes to get properly done. Dust the cayenne pepper and the herbs over the meat. Scatter sliced onion, pepper slices, and diced celery around the meat. Add garlic, salt and pepper, and carefully pour the red wine and boiling broth on, around, and under the steak. Cover closely and simmer over low heat (225°–250° if you use an electric skillet) for about 2 hours or until meat tests tender with a fork.

Baste the meat as often as convenient, turning the steak two or three times in the process and scraping up and stirring in the browned flour under the meat in process. Add liquid (hot water or a mix of hot broth and wine) if need be so the gravy ends up with the right consistency.

CARIBOU NORSKE STYLE
WITH DILL AND SOUR CREAM

The European reindeer is a smaller version of our own *Rangifer*, the caribou, and this recipe is an adaptation of a Norwegian recipe for reindeer. It is simply boiled caribou with a dill and sour cream sauce.

Red cabbage, boiled diced turnips, or Harvard beets go well with this dish, and maybe home-fried potatoes or potato cakes.

The use of dill in Scandinavian cookery is not confined to red meats. See page 242 for dill-pickled salmon, the justly famous *gravlax*.

SERVES 8

4-lb. shoulder, rump, or round roast of caribou
salted water to cover (2 tsp. salt to each quart of water)
1 bay leaf
1 onion, sliced
1 carrot, sliced
6 sprigs of fresh dill or 2 tsp. dill seed
2 Tb. butter
2 Tb. flour

2 Tb. lemon juice or white vinegar
1 Tb. sugar
3 Tb. finely minced dill or 1 Tb. crushed dill seed and a pinch of powder or 1 Tb. dried dillweed
1 tsp. mushroom catsup or Worcestershire sauce
½ cup sour cream, at room temperature
dill sprigs or parsley for garnish

In a large kettle combine meat, salted water, bay leaf, onion, carrot, and dill sprigs or dill seed, and bring to a rolling boil. Reduce heat, cover, and simmer over low heat until the meat is tender, 3–4 hours.

Remove meat to a hot serving platter. Strain and reserve the broth.

Melt the butter, stir in the flour, and cook over gentle heat 2–3 minutes. Then off heat whisk in 1 cup of the strained caribou and vegetable stock; simmer for 5 minutes. Add the lemon juice or vinegar, sugar, minced dill, and mushroom catsup or Worcestershire. Last, stir in the sour cream, heat and blend, but do not boil.

Slice the roast in thin slices and overlay them around a platter. Garnish with dill sprigs or parsley and cover thinly with the sauce.

Serve remainder of sauce in a sauceboat.

Caribou Non-Norske Style

The above dish can be made using marjoram and rosemary instead of dill with a horseradish sour cream sauce. Like beef, caribou seems especially delicious boiled.

Caribou Recipes à l'Iliaska

Mary Gerken, angler, chef, and with her husband, Ted, co-proprietor of Iliaska Lodge in Iliamna Village, Alaska, has made available the next two recipes direct from the land of the caribou. The big board at Iliaska provides the same excellence and amplitude as the numerous rivers provide sensational rainbow and salmon fishing. Visiting fishermen find it difficult to say whether the meal or the fishing is more memorable at Iliaska.

MARY GERKEN'S CORNED CARIBOU

Mrs. Gerken produced slices of this superdelicious appetizer for ten greedy anglers in the fall of 1980. The corned caribou came from the first batch Mary had ever produced, and three plates of it disappeared in a trice. Postmortems months later among these happy anglers always included praise for Mary's corned caribou to match superlatives about the fishing itself. Mary made it in a heroic quantity—and this is her recipe—but you can cut it in half.

2–4 gallons water
1½ lb. brown sugar
2½ lb. salt
¼ lb. baking soda

1 oz. saltpeter
50 lb. caribou meat
   (in sliceable pieces)

Heat water in a large iron kettle. Add sugar, salt, soda, and saltpeter. Allow to cool, then skim. Put meat in a large crock or keg, pour the brine solution over, and let stand. Keep covered tightly in a cool place, with meat weighted down to ensure total immersion. Can be used after one week.

After I asked Mary for the recipe, she said, "Don't let the *appearance* of what's in the crock *repel* you. It won't *look* edible." But drained, rinsed, and patted dry it produces heavenly slices of meat. I intend to corn some venison next chance I get.

Use the meat as you would corned beef—in a New England boiled dinner with leftovers for corned beef or red flannel hash.

MARY GERKEN'S CARIBOU POT ROAST

SERVES 6–8

3–4 lb. caribou roast
flour for dusting
2 Tb. shortening
salt and pepper
1 clove garlic, minced, or
   ½ tsp. garlic salt

2 small onions, sliced
2 bay leaves
1 cup water
½ cup vinegar

Coat the caribou roast with flour. In heavy pan, heat the shortening and slowly brown the meat on all sides.

Season with salt and pepper and sprinkle minced garlic over or a generous amount of garlic salt. Add onions, bay leaves, water, and vinegar. Cover tightly and cook slowly 2½ hours or until tender. Add water if needed to prevent sticking. Thicken juices for gravy.

CARIBOU BROTH AND VEGETABLES

Soup is heartily welcomed in any hunting camp (or any nonhunting "camp" for that matter). This simple soup recipe is one I've used with both moose and caribou. The last time I made it the meat was from a caribou shoulder, but the shank meat and shank bone from any big game animal is fine. It can be a one-dish meal served with bread slices fried brown in bacon fat or with dumplings (see page 391) floating on top during the final cooking.

SERVES 4–6

3 qt. water
2–3 lb. shank meat
  (or any stew meat)
1 shank bone sawed in pieces
  (at home use beef marrow bone)
2 beef bouillon cubes (optional)
3 carrots, cut up in chunks
1 onion, sliced

3 potatoes, diced
2 ribs celery with leaves
29-oz. can tomatoes
salt and pepper to taste
½ cup chopped parsley
½ tsp. thyme (optional)
2 bay leaves (optional)
¼ tsp. savory (optional)

If you are in camp, put on a stewing kettle as soon as you have a fire up, put in meat, bone, and bouillon cubes. Bring to a boil, and set back to simmer for a couple of hours. Before you go to bed, set the kettle with its lid askew where it will cool.

Next morning remove and discard the "pan" of congealed fat.

That night rally your "cookees" to prepare the vegetables. While they are peeling, scraping, and dicing put the kettle of broth and meat on the wood range or sheet-iron stove and bring to a boil.

Add the vegetables, salt, pepper, and the herbs and simmer covered for 20–30 minutes depending on how large the carrot and/or potato chunks have been cut.

Campers have always welcomed bread slices browned on both sides in hot bacon fat.

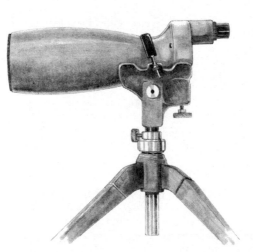

sheep

DALL SHEEP

Many hunters who have eaten a variety of big game consider wild mutton the best of all red meat. I believe I agree with this: at least the meal from the fat ribs of a Dall ram broiled over the embers of a willow fire was perhaps the most memorable game meal I ever enjoyed.

Mountain sheep does not taste like domestic mutton or lamb, but then neither does it taste like venison. It has its own succulent red meat flavor and it is relatively fine in texture. One thing is certain: it is surpassingly good.

When a hunter gets up to the rock-topped alpine pastures, above or north of the timber line, he is apt to be in the wildest, most remote regions of North America. There the open tundra slopes, crossed and crisscrossed with the traceries of sheep trails, offer the grandest scenery and the most romantic of all hunting experiences. To eat sheep meat one must have good legs, sound wind, and, sometimes, the patience of Job.

ROAST SADDLE OF WILD MUTTON

The saddle of a wild sheep, like that of domestic mutton that has been raised for meat, is of surpassing savoriness. To serve a heroic saddle you must, of course, sacrifice having the chops separately, which are delicious, but since sheep meat doesn't come regularly into most households, perhaps it is best to celebrate prodigally when such meat is available.

SERVES 6–8

1 saddle of mountain sheep	4 Tb. flour
2 cloves garlic, sliced thin	1½ cups pan juices, plus broth
6 slices bacon	1 tsp. thyme
salt and pepper	¼ tsp. oregano
1 medium onion, diced	2 tsp. sage

With a sharp pointed knife punch 8–12 slits into the saddle and slip in along the flat of the knife a garlic slice into each slit.

Place the bacon in the bottom of a shallow roasting pan, then put meat over the bed of bacon and roast in a preheated 400° oven for about 50 minutes to an hour or to an internal temperature of 145°. It is best, of course, to use a meat thermometer (insert to the middle of the thickest part, but do not touch bone).

Salt and pepper the roast and set it aside to breathe while you make the gravy.

Leave about 3–4 tablespoons of the fat in with the dredgings and over heat stir in the diced onion and sauté for 3 minutes. Then stir in the flour. Blend and brown.

Stir in the liquid and the herbs off heat. Then over a low-to-medium heat simmer the gravy, stirring, until it thickens.

NOTE: You can, of course, serve other sauces with the roast.

═ MOUNTAIN MUTTON CHOPS BRAISED IN BEER ═ WITH ONIONS AND POTATOES

This is a hearty one-dish meal that always seems to please everyone at the board whether in camp or in my own dining room.

SERVES 6

six 1½" sheep chops, with fat trimmed off	3 large onions, sliced
salt and pepper	6 potatoes, sliced
3–4 Tb. flour	1 tsp. thyme
3 Tb. lard or oil	1 can beer, or enough to show itself under the onions and potatoes

Trim the chops of their fat, salt and pepper them, and coat them with flour.

In a skillet with a lid, melt the fat and sauté the chops swiftly on both sides (2 minutes to each side).

In alternating layers of onions and potatoes, each salted and peppered and sprinkled with a bit of thyme, cover the chops.

Add the beer, cover, and simmer for about 30 minutes over medium heat.

═ BOILED SHEEP WITH SPAETZLE (OR NOODLES) ═ AND HORSERADISH SAUCE

Ideally this dish should be made with game brisket, but rump or a big piece of the bottom of the round is fine. I've eaten this dish (actually it was a simplified version) more often with caribou than with sheep, and I remember vividly how glad we were that we had brought along a pressure cooker on that busy summer-long stay on the Arctic coast. The dish is fine when pressure cooked, but better perhaps when simmered in the normal way.

SERVES 6

6 cups salted water or bouillon
3 lb. rump, or bottom round
   of sheep or moose
1 onion stuck with 2–3 cloves
½ cup sliced carrots
½ cup sliced celery with leaves
1 turnip or ¼ rutabaga, sliced

1½ tsp. salt
8 peppercorns
2 bay leaves
1 tsp. thyme
¼ tsp. savory
½ tsp. rosemary

THE HORSERADISH SAUCE
4 Tb. butter
1 small chopped onion
2–2½ Tb. flour
2 cups sheep broth
¼ cup cream (or evaporated milk)

1 dash Worcestershire
3 Tb. horseradish
1 Tb. sugar
2 Tb. dry mustard
2 Tb. vinegar

Bring the water to a rolling boil, then add the meat and bring to a boil again (this seems to set the blood "whey").

Skim, add all the rest of the ingredients (except those for the horseradish sauce), cover with a lid, and simmer for 3–4 hours. Sheep cooks somewhat more quickly than moose.

Drain off and reserve the stock (I always drink a half cup of it at this point) and set meat aside.

More or less simultaneously with the next step prepare or have someone put on the spaetzle or noodles. Use the broth from the boiled sheep or moose to boil the noodles but first reserve 2 cups for the sauce (for spaetzle see page 391).

Melt the butter and sauté the onion in it until soft. Add the flour and cook over low heat, stirring, for 2–3 minutes. Off heat stir in the 2 cups of sheep stock and then cook over low heat, stirring until the sauce thickens some, then add the cream.

Add remaining sauce ingredients and heat, but do not boil.

Serve sauce in sauceboat or slice the boiled meat and heat slices in with the sauce.

ROLLED ROAST OF BIG HORN
WITH HERBS IN WINE

A friend who appreciates sheep meat says that this roast will compensate the hunter who had to settle for a ram under 35 inches.

SERVES 8–10

6- or 7-lb. boned leg of sheep roast
¼ lb. salt pork
2 cloves garlic, sliced
½ tsp. rosemary, crumbled fine
salt and pepper
1 medium onion, diced
1 cup beef broth

1 cup red wine
1 Tb. Worcestershire sauce
1 tsp. anchovy sauce (optional)
½ tsp. thyme
flour and water, mixed to a paste
¼ cup red currant or beach plum
   jelly

Before rolling, lay out the boned meat and cover the surface with six 1″ × 3″ thin slices of salt pork. Also distribute evenly over the surface slices of garlic and dust the rosemary over all. Salt and pepper the meat and roll the roast by tying it in 7–8 pieces. If you have one, stick in a meat thermometer.

Lay several slices of salt pork on secured toothpicks, place on rack in shallow roasting pan. Roast in a preheated 475° oven for 30 minutes.

Remove roast from oven and put in the onion, broth, wine, the two sauces, and the thyme.

Reduce oven temperature to 400° and return the roast to the oven. Roast for an hour more, basting occasionally, and test with a meat thermometer. When it comes to 125° the roast is done rare. Roast longer for other degrees of doneness.

At these temperatures the roast should take 12 minutes per pound.

Remove sheep roast to a hot platter, spoon off most of the fat, and stir in enough paste of water and flour to thicken when simmered on top of the stove. Stir in and melt the jelly and serve in a sauceboat.

═══ BRAISED BIGHORN OR OTHER BIG GAME ═══

This to me is a most appetizing game recipe. It was developed over the years by putting a bit here and taking a bit there. It is a favorite of mine because it is twice the beneficiary of the flavorsome fat of marrow bones. I use it interchangeably for all cloven-hoofed game meats, but it is wonderful with sheep meat.

SERVES 6–8

5–6 marrow bone (I use beef marrow bones)
4 Tb. flour
3–4 lb. rump or top round of sheep
lard, oil, or bacon fat
3 onions, diced
1 green pepper, sliced, then chopped
1 rib celery with leaves
1 cup red wine
1 tsp. Worcestershire sauce
1½ Tb. catsup
3 sprigs parsley, minced

½ tsp. thyme
½ tsp. ground or crushed fennel seeds
3 bay leaves
¼ tsp. summer savory
3–4 garlic cloves
½ lb. mushrooms
3 Tb. butter
salt and pepper
4 slices white bread
1–2 Tb. flour mixed to a paste with water

Put marrow bone sections in a pie pan and brown in a 400° oven. Set bones aside and save the dried-out marrow fat.

Flour, then brown the meat in fat of your choice in an electric skillet or a deep heavy iron skillet (with a lid).

When meat is browning on a second side, put the onions, pepper, and celery around the sides and sauté until onions are soft.

Add the wine, Worcestershire, catsup, and enough water (or broth) to bring liquid halfway up on the side of the meat. Add the herbs and garlic and the browned bones.

Simmer over low heat, covered, for 2½–3 hours. If using electric skillet simmer at 250°F.

During the last half hour of cooking sauté the mushrooms in the butter for 2–3 minutes. Add to the meat about 20 minutes before it is done.

Just before you serve, dice the bread in ½-inch cubes and brown in hot marrow-bone fat.

Remove the marrow bones and the meat and keep meat warm while you thicken the gravy if need be with a flour-water mix.

Serve the gravy in a boat with a dish of the croutons.

═══ DALL SHEEP SHANKS WITH LENTILS ═══

If there were whitetails or antelope in Alaska, I am sure Martha Helmericks would use this recipe for shanks of those animals as well. In such substitution I'd use three shanks.

SERVES 4–6

2 Dall sheep shanks, cut and sawed
  in pieces
flour for dredging
salt and pepper

2 cloves garlic, minced
½–1 cup dried lentils
1 large carrot, grated
1 onion, sliced

Dredge shanks in flour and brown on both sides in Dutch oven. Add salt and pepper and garlic to taste; add lentils, grated carrot, sliced onion, and enough water to cover. Cover and simmer until lentils and meat are done, stirring occasionally. Add more liquid as necessary if lentils absorb it all.

The ultimate quarry of the highest and most remote parts of our continent is the fine animal we North Americans call the mountain goat. To taxonomists he is not a goat (*Capra*) but belongs to a separate genus (*Oreamnos*), an animal that might better be called a goat-antelope. But the word "mountain" in his name is most apt, for he *is* a creature of the most inaccessible peaks and ledges, perhaps the most sure-footed mountain animal of them all. A big billy is handsome as a trophy not chiefly for his black, scimitarlike horns, but for his white coat, which makes such a luxurious rug. He is not usually hunted primarily for his meat; perhaps the claim that his flesh is not special for the board is merely a rationalization of those who find it too much of a chore to tote down his meat from such remote and difficult places.

I have never hunted, cooked, or eaten goat, although twice I have been fortunate enough to see him in his natural habitat. Some hunters say the meat of a young billy is quite palatable. When guides do use his meat in high alpine tent camps they prepare it much as they would sheep.

ROAST MOUNTAIN GOAT

The two recipes for sheep roast—Roast Saddle of Wild Mutton and Rolled Roast of Big Horn—may be used for mountain goat as well, but my informants tell me that it is a good idea to marinate goat. See the introductory note to Billy Bones and Beans, following recipe, for the marinade ratio.

BILLY BONES AND BEANS:

A Savory Dish of Mountain Goat Shanks and Neck Chunks with Beans

I have never "given the black spot" to a Rocky Mountain billy nor have I ever tasted wild goat meat, but an outfitter friend says that his wife cooks mountain goat as she does big-horn sheep except that she always marinates roast of goat, whereas she seldom marinates sheep. In using any of the sheep recipes for goat, I would first put it overnight in a strong marinade with a 1:½:½ ratio of wine, water, and vinegar respectively.

SERVES 6–8

2 cups "navy" beans	6 Tb. butter
(pea beans or Great Northern)	4 Tb. oil
1 onion, stuck with 2 cloves	salt and pepper
2 bay leaves	1 cup red wine
½ tsp. thyme	1½ cups broth
1 tsp. crumbled rosemary	1 Tb. tomato paste or catsup
10 garlic cloves	1 tsp. horseradish
4 goat shanks, each cut and sawed	2 onions, diced
in half	1 Tb. brandy
½ lb. 1½" goat neck chunks	6 slices bacon or salt pork
2 Tb. flour	

Soak the beans overnight. But if you forget to do this, put beans in a saucepan, just cover with water, bring to a quick boil, and boil furiously for 3 minutes. Remove from heat and let them stand, still covered, for about 45 minutes.

Add the onion with cloves, bay leaves, ½ teaspoon of the thyme, the rosemary, half of the garlic cloves, and more water if needed. Bring to boil, cover, and simmer over low to medium heat for one hour.

Make several slits in the shank pieces and the neck chunks, roll them in flour and brown them in half the butter and all of the oil. Salt and pepper them.

When nicely brown, put shank bones and meat and the neck cubes in a saucepan, add the wine, broth, tomato paste or catsup, and horseradish, and cover. Bring to a boil, then reduce heat to simmer, and cook for about 1 hour. Add liquid if too thick.

Sauté the onions in the remaining butter until soft.

Drain the beans, but reserve the bean liquid.

Assemble as follows: Put a layer of beans in an 8-quart casserole, then the shank pieces and neck cubes.

Cover the meat with the sautéed onions and the remaining garlic, finely minced. Now the rest of the beans.

Put the brandy into the liquid in which the meat was simmered and pour over all. Lay the bacon slices or slices of salt port over the beans and cook in a preheated 350° oven for about 45 minutes. If it cooks down too much, add some of the reserved bean liquid.

=== GROUND BILLY WITH PEPPERS, ZUCCHINI, === AND EGGPLANT PARMIGIANA

Don't be intimidated by the long list of ingredients, for here is an easy-to-make, delicious dish that uses any kind of gameburger. Here it is given for the strongly flavored mountain billy. Also because the goat lives a strenuous and athletic life amid those high rocky ledges, his meat can become quite tough.

SERVES 4

1 large onion, diced
2 cloves garlic, smashed
4 Tb. oil
4 Tb. butter
2 green peppers, sliced
4 zucchini, cut into 1/4" slices
1 1/2 lbs. ground goat
16-oz. can tomatoes, undrained
6-oz. can tomato sauce
2 tsp. tomato paste
1 1/2 tsp. dried oregano
1 1/2 tsp. dried basil

1 tsp. salt
1/4 tsp. pepper
1 Tb. brown sugar
1/4 cup water
1/4 cup white wine
1 large eggplant, about 1 1/2–2 lbs.
2 eggs, beaten
1/2 cup bread crumbs
1 cup grated Parmesan
1/3 cup oil
1/2 lb. mozzarella, sliced

Sauté the onions and garlic for a couple of minutes in the oil and butter. Add the peppers and zucchini and continue to cook over medium heat until the vegetables are soft.

Add the meat, mix, and continue to cook just until the meat loses its pink color.

Add the tomatoes, sauce, and paste, the two herbs, salt, pepper, brown sugar, water, and wine and bring to a boil. Reduce heat and simmer for 25 minutes.

Cut the unpeeled eggplant into 1/2-inch slices and prepare for sautéing by putting the beaten eggs into a pie pan and the bread crumbs and half the Parmesan, mixed, onto a plate.

Get the oil hot in a skillet. Dip the eggplant slices into the egg and then the crumb-cheese mix. Brown 2–3 eggplant slices at a time, turning to brown the other side.

Butter a large, shallow baking dish, then lay in half the eggplant slices and cover with ¼ cup of Parmesan and half the mozzarella slices.

Cover with half of your meat and tomato sauce and repeat with another layer of eggplant, the rest of the two cheeses, and the rest of the sauce.

Bake in a preheated 400° oven for about 20 minutes or until you see that the mozzarella is just browned.

Musk Ox

In this section are two recipes for the meat of that delicious creature, the musk ox. Musk oxen are rare now and may not be found in their high Arctic open range. In Alaska a few culling permits are issued each year to keep the herd on Nunivak Island to its proper size. Surely musk ox rates with the very, very best of game meals.

═══ BRAISED RIBS OF MUSK OX À LA MARTHA ═══

This recipe may seem exotic, for few ever have the chance to eat musk ox, but Martha Helmericks's recipe is also delicious when made with the ribs of *any* big game animal. Incidentally, although I have eaten musk ox only twice, I will assert on the basis of this small sample that the musk ox carries almost the best-tasting meat found on four legs. Well, at least, one of the three best-tasting.

SERVES 3 OR 4

3–4 musk ox ribs, cut and sawed
   in serving pieces
flour for dredging
3–4 Tb. lard, oil, or shortening
2 cloves garlic, minced

salt and pepper
2 onions, sliced
1 can sauerkraut
11-oz. can stewed tomatoes
flour and water for thickening

Cut ribs in serving pieces, flour on all sides, and brown lightly in fat in Dutch oven or roasting pan. Season with garlic, salt, and pepper. Put sliced onions, sauerkraut, and stewed tomatoes over ribs, cover, and bake at 325°–350° until meat is fork-tender (about 2 hours), adding water if necessary. Remove meat, add flour and water for gravy, and enjoy.

═══════════ BARBECUED MUSK OX RIBS ═══════════

Fat ribs may be at their best when barbecued (with or without sauce) over willow, alder, or charcoal (see page 63), but they can also be "barbecued" in the oven, basted with your favorite sauce. Musk ox ribs should cook about 2 hours; venison ribs take an hour to an hour and a half, but the ribs from heavier game like moose will take a bit longer (350° oven).

I happen to have a roaster with a recessed bottom that I use for this purpose, but with the average roaster it is best to place the ribs on a rack. I sometimes brown the convex side first, but always roast them covered. When using sauce in oven-barbecuing, coat the ribs at once and then turn and baste them several times with the sauce. Be careful you don't burn your knuckles in removing the lid for basting.

It may be a private prejudice but I use lots of pepper on game ribs.

Use your favorite barbecue sauce, commercial or homemade. My own home-made sauce will be found on page 360.

Unhappily this great traditional European game animal cannot be widely hunted in the United States. North Carolina and Tennessee have open seasons for boar, but the animal's appearance in a few other states like California and New Hampshire is confined to reserves.

Boar is, however, to be found in the game markets on occasion; it is delicious fare and has a flavor beyond pork. Like bear, it is a trichinosis carrier, so the meat must be well done; when it is, of course, there is no danger whatever.

ROAST BOAR (OR BEAR) LOIN IN MUSTARD AND HERB SAUCE

If you can't get the boar, here is a recipe that I evolved from scratch on pork loin. I have never had boar meat in my freezer, alas, but I know it would be good this way, for I *have* eaten this wild porker. Practice on a loin of pork for your boar meat to come someday, but use it on bear loin with confidence.

SERVES 8–12

THE CRUST SPREAD
3 Tb. flour
2 Tb. brown sugar
2 tsp. dry mustard
2 tsp. powdered thyme
THE LOIN
4–6-lb. loin
3 cloves garlic, slivered
  lengthwise
THE BASTING SAUCE
1½ Tb. flour
2 Tb. brown sugar
2 tsp. dry mustard
2 tsp. powdered thyme

1 tsp. powdered sage
¼ cup liquid: half vinegar, half
  white wine

salt
pepper

1 tsp. powdered sage
½ cup liquid: half vinegar,
  half white wine

Thoroughly mix the dry ingredients of the crust spread, then stir in gradually the wine and vinegar to make a paste.

With a sharp pointed knife puncture the loin, pry flat of knife blade to one side, and slip slivers of garlic along the knife blade well down into the meat. Distributing your punctures evenly, use up the garlic slivers. Salt and pepper the loin.

In a roaster with a lid lay down a thin layer of crust spread paste and set the loin on it. Smear remaining paste over the roast.

Place roaster, uncovered, in a 450° oven and roast for 10 minutes to set the crust a bit.

Mix the basting sauce ingredients and set aside.

Turn oven down to 325°, cover, and roast loin for 45 minutes to the pound, basting often.

When the roast is done and you have set it aside, you will have to inspect the "greables"* to decide about the gravy. If the liquid has been much reduced, there will yet be a good deal of fat accumulated. Spoon off excess fat, leaving 3 tablespoons. Tip up the pan and stir 2 tablespoons of flour into the fat, then back on the stove add water to make a gravy. Taste the gravy and if it needs a bit more vinegar, pour a bit in with circumspection. Stir the gravy to assimilate all of the flavor of the basting sauce. Sometimes there will be a thickish sauce in the pan and only liquid need be added (no flour) to make the gravy.

---

* I am going to adopt Martha's "greables" (agreeable) instead of dredgings from now on. O.E.D. lists first usage in 1410.

══════════ WILD BOAR CHOPS ══════════
BLACK FOREST STYLE

I have eaten boar chops, but I have never prepared this recipe with them. However, I know how good this dish is when made with thick domestic chops, and I know also that if someone gave me some thick wild boar chops, this is the way I'd prepare them.

Baked yams and coleslaw go well with this dish.

SERVES 4–5

4 Tb. flour	1 cup strong beef stock
¼ tsp. ground thyme	2 bay leaves
3 Tb. salt	½ tsp. summer savory
3 Tb. freshly ground pepper	2 Tb. vinegar
4–5 thick chops	2 tsp. sugar
4–5 whole cloves	¾ cup sour cream
2 Tb. lard	

Preheat oven to 325°. Mix flour, thyme, salt, and pepper and dredge slightly moistened chops two or three times to get as much of the mix as possible to adhere.

Stick a clove in the center of each chop so both ends are buried.

In the casserole you plan to use sauté the floured chops in the lard until they are nicely browned.

Heat the remaining ingredients in a saucepan and stir with a whisk until the liquid is uniform, i.e., until the sour cream is assimilated.

Pour over chops in casserole, cover with the lid, and bake for an hour.

Check once or twice to be sure there is enough liquid; if not, add a bit of milk.

WILD BOAR CUTLETS

SERVES 4

2 lb. wild boar cutlets
1 cup buttermilk
1 tsp. salt

3 juniper berries, crushed
1 Tb. soft butter
1 Tb. flour

Submerge cutlets for 3 days in buttermilk in refrigerator.

Drain and dry, then rub with salt and crushed juniper. Preheat oven to 350°. Cover bottom of roasting pan with ¼ inch of boiling water and place meat on rack grazing water. Roast 1 hour, basting occasionally with buttermilk.

Meanwhile blend together the butter and flour with your fingertips. When the meat is tender and does not bleed when pierced, stir the butter-flour paste into the liquid in the roasting pan. Stir until thick and smooth and adjust seasoning.

BROWN BEAR
(COASTAL GRIZZLY)

Whenever I hear dire maledictions leveled against bear meat as so strong and rank a meat as to be unfit for human consumption, I know that either the meat came from an ancient, skinny, slab-sided bear or that it came from an animal that would have been delicious had it been butchered and handled and respected as meat rather than maltreated and spoiled because it was first valued only for its glossy pelt.

Our family of four is unanimous in saying that the most delicious meat and attendant gravy we ever ate was from the loin and rump roast of a three-year-old bear shot by my wife in Alaska.

First it may be worthwhile to mention that though almost as omnivorous as man, the bear, as mammalogists know, is at least 80 percent a vegetarian. Anyone who has seen the claw marks of a bear shinnying up a beech tree to shake off nuts or a patch of scrub oak where branches have been broken down by an acorn-hungry bear, or anyone who has watched a bear comb out blueberries or graze like a cow on the succulent grass of an Alpine meadow—anyone who has seen these things knows the succulent diet from which the meat and fat of a bear comes.

The result? A delicious red meat as fat as pork; indeed, bear can be prepared as you would prepare pork—i.e., no larding and basting. Further, as our frontier forebears knew, the fat of a bear renders out into a pure white lard that is just as good as pork lard, and just as delicately flavored. I once rendered out and used 40 pounds of it for cooking. We discovered one fall (when our son provided us with a bear in the same season we butchered two hogs) that the hams and shoulders of a bear respond to sugar and smoke curing exactly as those of a fat porker. Roast smoked ham of bear is a delicacy.

Size is about the only method of determining the age of a bear and to the inexperienced eye *all* bears seem big with the possible exception of one huge old black bear, a grizzled veteran whose skull measurements missed the Boone & Crocket Club Record book by a scant ⅛ inch and which was a tatter-eared aged animal so skinny that it probably would not have survived its next hibernation. All bear meat I have eaten has been not only delicious but as tender as aged beef. An animal that weighs 125 pounds bag-dressed will be a fairly young bear. A prime bear is big and fat and can weigh up to 650 pounds or more, although average weight is usually 200–300 pounds.

Do not merely gut and hang a bear but skin it out as soon as you possibly can and remove the fat from the carcass that lies immediately beneath the skin. If time seems a consideration, then rough-skin the animal in the woods, i.e., skin it completely to the paws, wrists, and head, leaving these on the skin to be finished in camp. Most of the time skinning a bear is spent skinning the feet and the head (lips and ears take time) and this can be done at camp before you flense and salt and peg down the skin.

A bear should cool out quickly and under no circumstance should you hang a bear in the hide, especially if the sun can get to it; the fat holds heat and, worse, the black fur absorbs heat from the sun like an Arab's tent.

To repeat: Think of the meat first and the eventual bear rug second.

WARNING: Owing to the danger of trichinosis, bear meat, alas, must be cooked until well done. This is a pity, for bear roasted pink is delicious: I know, for once in my innocence (thirty years ago in Alaska) I roasted rare the loin and rump of a fine young Brooks Range bear bagged by my wife—it was scrumptious, but having got away with it, I wouldn't do it again.

ROAST BEAR

Bear loin or rump is surely one of the finest game roasts of all when prepared as one would roast a pork loin. As I've noted, it's as fat as pork and the fat should be thinned, i.e., the excess sliced off, leaving only about a quarter of an inch on the meat. If the roast is the rump cut, put it on a rack in a shallow roasting pan; otherwise stand the roast on the bones—fat side up, in either case.

Mashed potatoes, Brussels sprouts, and jellied cranberry sauce go well with this rich roast. Or applesauce instead of cranberry if you prefer.

SERVES 6–8

3–4-lb. bear roast, loin or rump, fat thinned to ½" thick
2 cloves garlic, sliced
salt and pepper
1 small onion, chopped fine
½ rib celery with leaves, chopped fine
3 Tb. flour

1½ tsp. dried, pulverized sage leaves*
¼ tsp. thyme
¼ tsp. savory
2 cups water or beef stock
1 tsp. Worcestershire sauce or mushroom catsup

Cut deep knife-width slits in top of roast and insert garlic slices.

Salt and pepper the meat well. Lay a few fat slices under the roast, put it in a preheated 500° oven, and roast 20 minutes or so until you hear the sputtering of browning fat. Reduce heat to 300°–325° and roast about 2½ hours.

Look at the roast a few times and if the juices do not seem to be cooking out sufficiently stick with a knife the lower edge of the meat in a few places—you want browned dredgings in the fat later when you prepare the gravy.

When done, remove roast and the fat cracklings to a hot pan or platter and leave it on edge of oven on its open door to keep warm.

Retain 2–3 tablespoons of fat in the roasting pan with the drippings and in it sauté the chopped onion and celery until onion is translucent. Stir in the flour and meld it with the fat. Cook a couple of minutes, then stir in the herbs.

Add the liquid and Worcestershire or catsup a little at a time, stirring until it bubbles, then lower fire and simmer for 5 minutes. Stir occasionally.

NOTE: Bear meat is delicious rare, but you had better not chance it, for even in the Arctic, where you would think the animal would be immune, there have been cases of trichinosis. Treat bear as you would pork.

*Sage loses its potency if you keep it too long. Taste the sage you have on hand before it's too late (the day before so there's still time to replenish if stale) to be sure it has retained its pungency.

BEAR FILLET IN BURGUNDY

Serve this roast with sauerkraut and mashed potatoes.

SERVES 12

THE MARINADE
4 cups chopped mixed onions and shallots
1½ cups chopped carrots
2 cloves garlic, minced
THE BEAR
1 fillet of bear, 6–7 lb.
10 juniper berries
salt
6–8 medium onions, peeled
3–4 large parsnips, peeled

⅔ cup chopped celery
2 bay leaves
1 tsp. tarragon
6 cups dry white wine

1 dozen medium carrots, scraped
1 cup sliced celery
6 cups burgundy
2 cups beef stock

Combine all marinade ingredients. Handle the well-hung bear meat gently, carefully cutting out all sinews and nerves, and—unless you have reason not to—marinate it in a cool place 3–4 days.

When preparing to cook, pat the meat dry with paper towels. Preheat oven to 325°. Pound the juniper berries into tiny fragments and firmly rub into the meat; salt well. Place the fillet in an ample roasting pan and surround it with the vegetables.

Pour wine and stock over all and put roast in oven uncovered. Baste frequently for 3½–4 hours, or until center of roast does not bleed when pierced with two-tined fork.

Remove the meat and keep warm. Lift out vegetables and spin in a food processor to a coarse pulp or put through a strainer or vegetable mill; reduce wine sauce to about 1½ cups, then add vegetable mixture. Stir and serve as gravy.

BEAR LOIN BARBECUE STYLE

This recipe comes from Mary Wade, wife of Sonny Wade of Bingham, Maine, who was until recently only Maine's most famous bear-hunting guide and outfitter but who after 1983 has added New Brunswick to his domain as well.

SERVES 6

3 lb. bear tenderloin
BARBECUE SAUCE
¾ cup vinegar
¾ cup catsup
1 cup water
1 onion, chopped
1 clove garlic, minced
2 tsp. salt

¼ tsp. pepper
1 Tb. Worcestershire sauce
¼ tsp. Tabasco
3 Tb. brown sugar
1 tsp. dry mustard

Slice meat in ½-inch pieces and cook 30 minutes in oven at 350°.

Meanwhile, mix the sauce ingredients together in a pan and cook 20 minutes over moderate heat.

Pour off liquid from meat, cover with barbecue sauce, and cook 1 hour.

BEAR NORTHERN STYLE

If the bear is old, scar-faced, and skinny, and possibly stronger than a young bear fat on mast, you'll certainly want to marinate. Here is a recipe from northern Minnesota that uses either the whole fillet or loin, to be marinated first for 3 or 4 days, cut into steaks or chops, which are then fried and simmered in a pungent sauce.

SERVES 8–10

1 fillet or whole loin bear (6 to 7 pounds)

2–3 Tbs. vegetable oil

THE MARINADE
3 medium onions, chopped
12–15 shallots or scallions, chopped
3–4 carrots, chopped
¾ cup vinegar
2 tsp. salt
4 cups dry white wine or 3 cups
    vermouth mixed with 1 cup
    water

2 cloves garlic, minced
1 tsp. coarsely ground black pepper
4 bay leaves
2 tsp. fresh tarragon, chopped, or
    ½ tsp. dried
3 ribs celery, chopped

SAUCE
½ tsp. minced garlic
1 tsp. minced pickled onions
2 tsp. chopped capers
2 tsp. chopped shallots or scallions
1 Tb. chopped parsley
¼ cup chopped mushrooms

¾ tsp. salt
¼ tsp. black pepper
3 Tbs. butter
3 Tbs. flour
1 clove, crushed

Cut out any sinews and nerves from the meat.

Put all the marinade ingredients in a saucepan, bring to a boil, and cook 5 minutes, covered. Let cool and then pour the marinade over the meat, which should be placed in a crock or large ceramic bowl—any nonmetallic container. Keep in a cool place, covered, for 3 to 4 days, turning the meat over daily. Refrigerate only if the weather is warm.

When ready to cook, remove the meat, reserving the marinade, and wipe dry. Cut the fillet into ¾-inch pieces or the loin into chops.

Heat enough oil to coat the bottom of a large skillet, then brown the meat, several pieces at a time, about 1 minute on each side. Remove and brown remaining pieces, adding more oil as necessary.

To prepare the sauce, pound the garlic, pickled onions, capers, shallots or scallions, parsley, mushrooms, salt and pepper together or puree in a food processor. When mixed to a paste, strain 2 cups of the reserved marinade into it and blend.

Now melt the butter in the skillet, stir in the flour, and cook slowly a few minutes to brown lightly. Add the clove and, off the heat, stir in the above marinade sauce. Return to the heat and stir until thickened, then add the browned steaks or chops, and slowly simmer for 6 to 8 minutes. Stir frequently and watch to see that the bottom doesn't burn; the sauce should be thick and highly flavored.

Serve with baked or boiled potatoes and stewed dried apricots or cranberries.

══ MARINADE FOR BEAR CHUNKS ON A SKEWER ══

½ cup soy sauce
1 Tb. honey
¼ cup peanut oil
¼ cup lemon juice
1 tsp. curry powder

1 tsp. chili powder
1 cup finely chopped onions
2 cloves garlic, finely chopped
Salt, pepper, and ground ginger
    to taste

Mix all the ingredients together and marinate bear before grilling.

Small Furred Game

COTTONTAIL RABBIT

Everyone knows, of course, that rabbits and squirrels are widely eaten as favored fare in the United States, but most people would be surprised perhaps to find that there are five more small furred animals that are equally delicious. They are muskrat, beaver, woodchuck, raccoon, and opossum.

I have eaten all five with relish and have often prepared in camp or in my own kitchen the first three on the list. It is well to bear in mind that older animals among all furred game save possibly cottontail can be tough. What follows here has chiefly to do with how to judge possible toughness among the seven small furred-game animals commonly eaten.

Determining Age in Small Game

The average cottontail lives usually less than a year and in areas where protected from man's incursions something less than two years. Personally I have never paid much attention to age where this delicious animal is concerned; indeed I cannot remember, boy or man, eating a tough one, even when "chicken-fried," my favorite way of preparing rabbit. Part of the reason for this is that rabbit, as compared to the hares, tends to have more fat on it. But cottontails do come tough on occasion.

By reverse token, the snowshoe "rabbit" (varying hare) is lean and stringy and often tough. After a few tries I never again prepared this game in any way except as hasenpfeffer or in other stews. Although I have never prepared any of the jackrabbits (also hares), I gather that one cooks these western hares as one does the snowshoe, and for the same reason.

Size is one indicator of age. Though not always a reliable criterion, if you find yourself with a cottontail that weighs between 4 and 4½ pounds in the fur, you have got yourself a very big one and an old one and might wish to prepare it in a burgoo, stew, braised—anyway but fried. Cottontails average between 2 and 3½ pounds.

Similarly, a 4-pound-plus snowshoe will likely be even tougher than a smaller hare. Snowshoes under 3 pounds are apt to be young hares. I did notice, educated on the point by Frank G. Ashbrook in Cooking Wild Game (New York, 1945, with Edna N. Sater), that the bigger and presumably older snowshoes had shortish, blunt, rough claws, while smaller snowshoes had long claws like those of a pet dog kept too long in a city apartment.

Most recipes for squirrel—the tastiest of the furred game, in my judgment—call for preparing them in stew or for braising because they can be tough in their old age. I have bagged and eaten a great number of squirrels, but have never kept a record of their weights. I have, I suppose, handled enough of them to estimate age roughly by size and weight. Old ones are delicious in stews and pies, but young ones, like cottontails, are fine chicken-fried. Older and large squirrels always seem more difficult to skin, because the hide adheres tightly to the carcass. Grays weigh from 1 to 1½ pounds; fox squirrels from 1½ to 2½ pounds.

The eastern woodchuck when young is as good (almost) as squirrel, and a spring woodchuck taken in the late summer or early fall can be recognized by size. Chucks of the year look smaller than mature animals. Undressed woodchuck run in weight between 5 and 10 pounds, with an extreme of about 14. The heaviest one I ever weighed pulled the scales at 8 pounds 9 ounces. Its size and the extra grizzled mask marked this big old chuck as a stewer. But young chucks can be chicken-fried like squirrel.

Although I have eaten both opossum and raccoon a number of times and hunted the latter with hounds, I have never personally weighed either. The latter roasted is delicious, and Ashbrook says the young of the species can be marked by the fact that they do not have a full set of teeth. Again weight is some indication: possum may be between 8 and 15 pounds, while raccoon range normally from 10 to 25 pounds, but sometimes big boars can weigh up to 45 pounds, or even a bit more.

The muskrats I have prepared in an Ontario trapping camp were all braised or stewed, and I never noticed that any of them was tough. And the same applied to the beaver eaten in the same camp. Roast beaver with a bread-sage-onion stuffing is excellent fare. All of the beaver meat I have eaten has come from younger animals that weighed from 20 to 25 pounds undressed. Beaver weigh from 40 to 50 pounds up to a normal maximum of 70 pounds. Roy Smith, an Ontario trapper friend, once caught a beaver himself that weighed 88 pounds and saw one caught by a fellow trapper that weighed 101 pounds.

Arctic ground squirrel is another delicious meat that comes from an animal whose age seems to have little bearing on tenderness. The first I tasted was braised on a driftwood-fueled Yukon stove in the late summer tent camp of an Eskimo family.

Hare and Rabbit

The snowshoe rabbit, smallest of the hares native to the contiguous forty-eight states, is probably the hare most often encountered in the kitchen. However, the whitetail jackrabbit is fancied as the favorite game among the four species of jackrabbit found in this country. All are hares.

The largest native North American hare is the Arctic hare (weight 6 to 15 pounds); the largest in Continental U.S. is the northern hare of Alaska (weight 7 to 10 pounds).

The largest hare to be found in the Lower Forty-eight of our country is an introduced species (Dutchess County, New York, in 1893), the European hare. This hare found now in the Great Lakes region and east to New York, Vermont, New Jersey, Delaware, and Maryland is the biggest of all, weighing from 6½ to 20 pounds.

Weight of Snowshoe Rabbits (Varying Hare)

Over a period of ten years, I weighed and kept a record of 38 snowshoe rabbits trapped or shot in front of trailing hounds in the Adirondacks. Curiously, these 38 hares, all weighed before gralloching, averaged precisely 3.5 pounds in dividing the total weight by 38. There was not even a single hundredth decimal to carry. The largest of the 38 animals weighed 4 pounds 4 ounces. To my knowledge I never weighed any of these after they were dressed.

Unhappily little of that 3.5 pounds is fat, and the meat takes a lot of braising or stewing. One dare not chicken-fry snowshoe rabbit as one can so successfully do with the cottontail. Indeed this hare should be marinated and in this case the chief purpose of the marinade is to tenderize the meat, for the snowshoe is apt to be tough. Marinating isn't necessary, of course, if rabbit is stewed slowly.

Snowshoe rabbit meat is dark and is strongly flavored. Jugged hare made from snowshoe rabbit (this animal is, of course, a hare) is a fine dish. Hasenpfeffer is basically the same dish in German.

Cottontails

This little animal of the brushy edges, hedgerows, and fields provides good sport for the shotgunner loaded with 6's, especially when posted in front of a good beagle. The alertness of riflemen, walking the hedge and fence rows, is well tested by the cottontail "frozen" in his form. My father, it seemed to me as a boy, was unconscionably skilled in spotting the bright eye of the otherwise camouflaged rabbit.

Rabbit can be substituted in many, indeed most, pheasant, grouse, and other game bird dishes. Cottontails provide literally millions of American meals each year.

In offering these recipes for rabbit, I should in all honesty say to the users of this book: have confidence that rabbit can be prepared with *any recipe* that you use for chicken. In my humble opinion there is only one difference: rabbit is better than chicken. And I love chicken.

═══ ROAST RABBIT OR HARE ═══

Rabbits and especially the large hares look appetizing roasted whole. The old-country way of doing it was to skin out not only the head but also the hind legs down to the claws so the animal could be trussed. Trussing now involves only tying the front legs back against the body; the head is no longer cooked in most kitchens.

Most any recipe for pheasant will be equally good for roast hare; for that matter any recipe for chicken will be good for roast hare.

In this recipe one may marinate hare for two or three days with your favorite marinade. If you do marinate, use the strained marinade instead of the wine and the vinegar.

SERVES 4

1 tsp. salt
1 tsp. pepper
½ tsp. thyme
1 tsp. marjoram
4–5-lb. dressed hare or
   2 cottontails
¼ lb. salt pork, sliced
¾ cup dry red wine
1 Tb. vinegar

1 small onion, chopped
½ cup beef or chicken stock
1 Tb. beach plum or red currant
   jelly
½ cup heavy cream
pepper
1 tsp. flour stirred with
   2 Tb. water

Mix the salt, pepper, and the two herbs and rub it all on and inside the hare. Truss the front legs and in doing so, tie on slabs of salt pork over the saddle.

In a shallow roasting pan, roast the hare uncovered for about 30 minutes in a 450° oven. Turn the oven down to 350° and roast another 45 minutes to 1 hour. Remove and keep warm.

Place the roast pan and contents over a medium heat. Add the wine, vinegar, onion, and stock and simmer over low heat for 10 to 12 minutes. Add the jelly, cream, pepper (taste for salt) and quickly dissolve jelly. Stir in the flour and water paste and let it thicken a bit before serving it in a sauceboat.

Quantities and Servings of Furred Game

One "fried" rabbit prepared as a Middle Western country woman "fries" chicken is a delicacy that will, with the fixin's, usually appease two guests. To be on the safe side three will amply serve four. The same can be said for squirrel. Rabbits come more easily to the kitchen than grouse or woodcock, and one seldom has to worry about quantity. When prepared in casserole dishes one can make do with slightly less quantity of either of these two delicacies.

For those who like the meat (and we do) a kit beaver will serve four and a "blanket" will serve eight.

A young woodchuck will serve two or three depending on food prejudices.

Figure a rabbit or squirrel to produce three initial servings in the two legs and the saddle and one serving from the two rather skimpy forequarters, four portions in all, enough for "seconds" for two.

═ CHICKEN-FRIED RABBIT WITH CREAM GRAVY ═

This is as delicious a way to prepare rabbit as there is, I suspect, and is the way both chicken and rabbit are fried in rural Indiana. It is equally delicious with young squirrel. Serve with hot biscuits.

SERVES 4

2 cottontail rabbits, cut into
  serving pieces
4 Tb. flour
salt and freshly ground pepper

5 Tb. lard, for starters
2 Tb. flour
¾ cup milk
½ cup heavy cream

Shake the rabbit in a paper bag with the flour, salt, and pepper. Pick a heavy skillet (which some lid will fit) that, crowded, will just hold the rabbit pieces. Melt the lard in it until hot, then turn heat to medium, crowd in the rabbit pieces, and for the next 10–12 minutes stand over the skillet, turning and adjusting the pieces until all sides are golden brown.

As you brown the pieces, their floured surfaces may absorb enough fat to require more lard; add as needed.

Now, turn heat to low, cover the skillet, and simmer for 12 minutes or so. Turn the pieces, if need be, during this process.

Turn heat to medium or medium high, remove lid, and turning the pieces when needed, evaporate the moisture for another 10 minutes or so.

Remove rabbit to a hot platter, pour off all but 3 tablespoons or so of fat, stir the flour into the fat and "greables" (or dredgings) and cook over low heat for 2 minutes or so.

Off heat, stir in the milk, then back on low heat cook until it starts to thicken. Stir in the cream and continue to heat but do not boil.

NOTE: For a variation, stir in with the cream 1 teaspoon of Dijon mustard and ¼ cup of grated Parmesan.

HARE OR RABBIT IN A SOUR CREAM AND MUSTARD SAUCE

Rabbit—and squirrel, too, for that matter—is good when flavored with a touch of mustard. Serve with boiled potatoes and green peas.

SERVES 6–8

2 hares (3 lb. each, dressed)
  or 3 cottontails, cut into serving
  pieces
5–6 Tb. flour
salt
½ tsp. freshly ground pepper
4 Tb. lard or cooking oil
4 shallots, or a medium onion,
  diced
2 cloves garlic, minced
2 bay leaves

1 tsp. marjoram
½ tsp. powdered thyme
1½ tsp. dry mustard
2 tsp. Harvey's or Worcestershire
  sauce
1 cup chicken broth
½ cup dry vermouth
½ lb. mushrooms, sliced and
  sautéed in 2 Tb. butter
1 cup sour cream
2 Tb. chopped parsley

Shake the rabbit pieces with the flour, 1 teaspoon salt, and pepper until each piece is well coated.

In a large casserole or Dutch oven sauté the rabbit in lard or oil over medium heat, turning often until pieces are nicely browned. This should take 10 minutes.

After 7 minutes or so add the shallots or onion and garlic and sauté until soft.

Stir in all the rest of the ingredients save the mushrooms, sour cream, and parsley, cover the casserole, and simmer until the rabbit is tender—20–30 minutes for rabbit and 30–40 minutes for hare.

Remove rabbit pieces to a hot platter, then stir in the sautéed mushrooms, sour cream, and parsley, and taste for salt. Heat but do not boil.

Pour some of the sauce over the rabbit pieces, and serve the rest in a gravy boat.

NOTE: If you wish, the cream added can be heavy sweet cream instead of sour cream.

RABBIT BAKED IN TARRAGON MUSTARD, GARLIC, AND CREAM

Again, the happy combination of rabbit and mustard—but this time it is a French tarragon mustard. If that is not easily available (it's usually found in gourmet shops) use a Dijon mustard to which you add ½ teaspoon of dried tarragon per 3 tablespoons mustard.

SERVES 6

2 rabbits, cut in serving pieces
3 Tb. tarragon mustard
  (or above substitute)
2 Tb. minced garlic
⅓ cup minced parsley
salt

3 Tb. red wine vinegar
1 cup chicken broth
¾ cup heavy cream
freshly ground pepper
1–2 Tb. chopped parsley

Coat the rabbit pieces with the mustard. Mix the minced garlic and minced parsley together with a little salt, and sprinkle half over the rabbit.

Combine the vinegar and broth and pour into a large baking dish. Sprinkle the remaining garlic and minced parsley over, then put the rabbit pieces on top.

Bring to a boil, then cover the baking dish and bake in a preheated 350° oven for an hour. Check after 45 minutes to see if tender and turn the pieces of rabbit. When tender throughout, remove rabbit and keep warm.

Pour the cream into the juices in the casserole and boil to reduce the liquid by half or more—it should have the consistency of a light cream sauce.

Salt and pepper the rabbit pieces and return them to the casserole. Spoon sauce over and taste to correct seasoning if necessary. Sprinkle chopped parsley on top and serve.

BRANDIED RABBIT OR HARE WITH MUSHROOMS AND CREAM

This is a deluxe casserole that is one of my own favorites, and of course it is delicious with any small game, furred or feathered. Two hen pheasants, or three partridges, or a brace of grouse can be handily substituted for rabbit or hare. Rice and peas go well with this dish.

SERVES 4–6

2 cottontail rabbits, or a
  4-lb. hare, cut into serving pieces
6 Tb. butter
4 shallots or 2 cloves garlic,
  sliced thin
1½ oz. brandy
½ cup chicken stock
½ cup dry vermouth

2 tsp. mushroom catsup (optional)
1 herb bouquet
  (parsley, tarragon, and basil)
salt and pepper
½ lb. mushrooms
3 egg yolks
1½ cups heavy cream
1 Tb. Madeira

In a shallow casserole sauté the rabbit pieces in 4 tablespoons of the butter. Let them brown just a bit.

After you turn the pieces, put in the shallots or garlic and let the slices soften while the second side of the rabbit is becoming golden.

Pour in the brandy, put a match to it, and let it flame.

Add the stock and vermouth, and mushroom catsup if you have it, herb bouquet, salt and pepper to taste, cover, and simmer for 30 minutes or so until the pieces are tender.

While the simmering is going on, sauté the mushrooms in 2 tablespoons of the butter, and add them to the casserole for the last 5 minutes or so.

Beat the egg yolks in a bowl, and in a small saucepan *warm* the cream. Do not boil.

Just before serving, remove rabbit pieces to a warm platter, pour ¼ cup of the warm cream into the bowl with the beaten yolks, then stir this into the warm cream.

Stir cream and egg yolks into the juices in the casserole, add the Madeira, return rabbit pieces, and heat. Again reheat gently; do not bubble.

SNOWSHOE RABBIT WITH APPLEJACK

This is a recipe from Vermont, where both snowshoes and applejack are not uncommon.

SERVES 4–6

2 snowshoe rabbits, cut into serving pieces
8 Tb. flour
6–8 Tb. bacon fat or lard
salt and pepper
½ tsp. thyme
½ tsp. basil
2 cloves garlic

1 cup or more white wine or dry vermouth
1 cup applejack
1 bay leaf
1 tsp. Worcestershire sauce or mushroom catsup
½ lb. mushrooms, sliced
2 Tb. butter
1 Tb. flour (optional)

Roll serving pieces in flour or shake in paper bag and sauté in fat or lard in skillet or electric skillet, turning often, until browned (about 15 minutes on medium heat).

Add remaining ingredients, save the mushrooms and butter, cover, and simmer for 1–1½ hours.

After an hour sauté the mushrooms in the butter for 5 minutes, then add them to the skillet.

Timing instructions cannot be exact, so you must test the thickest pieces of hare from time to time.

If sauce thickens too much, add more white wine; if after, say, 1½ hours it is not thick enough, make a paste of 1 tablespoon flour and liquid and stir into sauce.

ENGLISH JUGGED HARE À LA CAROL JANEWAY

Boiled potatoes or spaetzle is the best accompaniment to this, along with broccoli.

SERVES 5

1 jointed hare (cut into serving
  pieces), approximately 5 lb.
1 cup red wine vinegar
3 Tb. butter
½ lb. finely chopped bacon
1 celery rib, finely chopped
1 cup peeled and minced onions
¼ lb. chopped mushrooms
2½ cups good beef stock
¼ tsp. powdered mace
¼ tsp. powdered cloves

bouquet garni of bay leaf, thyme,
  and parsley sprigs
1 clove garlic, peeled and crushed
juice and thinly pared rind of
  1 lemon
1 ½ Tb. soft butter mixed with
  1 ½ Tb. flour
hare's blood (optional)
¼ cup port
2 Tb. red currant jelly
parsley to garnish

Marinate the hare in the wine vinegar for 24 hours.

Drain, dry, and fry the pieces in butter until well browned, then pack them into a casserole.

Simmer the bacon in 2 quarts water to blanch—about 5 minutes. Drain, pat dry, then fry in a clean frying pan until the fat runs. Add the celery and onions and sauté until soft but not colored, then add the mushrooms for a few minutes more.

Drain the vegetables on absorbent paper, then add them to the casserole with the hare.

Heat the stock in a saucepan, add the mace and cloves, the bouquet garni tied in muslin, the garlic, lemon juice, and two strips of lemon rind finely shredded. Stir, and pour the stock over the hare.

Cover the casserole tightly and cook in the oven at 350° for 2 hours. Then reduce the temperature to 300° and cook for another hour.

Remove the hare and keep it warm. Discard the bouquet garni.

To thicken the juices, add the soft butter-flour mixture to the liquor a little at a time, whisking, and bring to a boil for a moment. Add a few spoonfuls of liquid to the blood if you have it (the blood isn't crucial, but does act as a thickener), stir, and pour back into the pan. Add the port and the red currant jelly. Reheat but do not allow the liquid to boil. Pour over the hare in a serving dish and garnish with parsley.

JAN HERBERT'S RABBIT STEW, MAINE STYLE

Jan Herbert, a Bean staff member, likes the way her sister, Helen MacDonald, makes a rabbit stew. "Good with dumplings," she writes.

SERVES 6

1–2 rabbits
8 carrots
2 large onions, cut up
6 ribs celery and leaves, cut up

6–8 boiled potatoes, cut up
1 Tb. salt
pepper to taste
Flour

Dress rabbit and wash. Put in a kettle with lightly salted water to cover, and cook until just tender.

Remove rabbit, take meat from bones, and put back in the cooking water.

Add the carrots, onions, and celery. Add the potatoes last when the other vegetables are tender. Season with salt and pepper. Thicken stock with a thin paste of flour and water.

"ROAST" RABBIT

This Early Republic method of roasting rabbit (on a spit, of course) is easily adapted for the oven, the rotisserie, or a flat grill. It is quite likely that another Virginian, Mr. Washington, ate stuffed roast rabbit prepared in this classic Virginia fashion.

It is interesting to note that early American cooks achieved the fine succulent brown crust on their meats by alternately basting with cold lard and then dusting with flour while the spit turned. We can do the same.

Mrs. Randolph's stuffing, or pudding as she calls it (given below), is the basic bread stuffing used today—crumbs, butter, cream, eggs, and herbs. The only things I'd add to this stuffing would be sautéed onions and celery.

One thing for sure, the next time I grill a rabbit on the rotisserie I am going to truss it as Mrs. Randolph recommends—just for old times' sake.

To Roast Rabbits (Mrs. Randolph's recipe)

"When you have cased* the rabbits, skewer their heads with their mouths upon their backs, stick their forelegs into their ribs, skewer the hind legs doubled, then make a pudding for them of the crumb of half a loaf of bread, a little parsley, sweet marjoram and thyme, all shred fine, nutmeg, salt and pepper to your taste, mix them up into a light stuffing, with a quarter of a pound of butter, a little good cream, and two eggs, put it into the body and sew them up; dredge and baste them well with lard, roast them near an hour, serve them up with parsley and butter for sauce, chop the livers† and lay them in lumps round the edge of the dish."

Note Mrs. Randolph's time for grilling a rabbit before an open fire is about right when the rabbit is spitted on a rotisserie.

---

* That is to say, skinned.

† The livers should be lightly cooked in butter first—about 5 minutes, turning, until brown on the outside but still rosy inside. Season with salt and pepper.

RABBIT IN COCONUT MILK

This recipe is from Colombia, and Elisabeth Ortiz points out in her fascinating *Book of Latin American Cooking* that the common game there would be the *neque* or *paca*, an animal more like hare, but either hare or rabbit will do nicely. Serve with rice.

SERVES 4

6 cloves garlic
1 tsp. salt
¼ tsp. cayenne pepper
½ tsp. cumin
freshly ground pepper
3 Tb. white vinegar
2½–3-lb. hare or rabbit,
   cut into 8 serving pieces
1½ Tb. oil

1 Tb. annatto
   (if unavailable, use sweet
   paprika)
1 medium onion, chopped
1 large tomato, peeled, seeded,
   and chopped
1 Tb. tomato paste
½ cup thick coconut milk*

Mash the garlic with the salt, cayenne, cumin, and a dozen turns or so of the pepper grinder. Stir in the vinegar.

Spread this mixture over the pieces of hare or rabbit in the casserole in which they'll be cooked and let marinate at room temperature about 4 hours, turning the pieces once or twice.

In a small pan heat the oil with the annatto over moderate heat until the seeds give up their color and the oil turns a deep orangey red—in about 1 minute.

Strain the annatto oil into a skillet, discarding the seeds, and sauté the onion in it until soft and well colored. Scrape all this into the casserole and add the chopped tomato and the tomato paste. Add enough water to barely cover and bring to a boil. Cover and cook over low heat until the hare or rabbit is tender, about 1½ hours.

Lift out the rabbit pieces with a slotted spoon to a serving dish and keep warm.

Reduce the liquid over brisk heat to about 1 cup, stirring frequently. Stir in the coconut milk and heat through, but don't let it boil. Pour this sauce over the hare or rabbit.

* To make thick coconut milk: Choose a fresh coconut that has plenty of liquid in it—shake it to find out. Pierce the three eyes with an ice pick or similar sharp implement and drain out the liquid (this is *not* the milk). Bake the coconut in a preheated 400° oven for 15 minutes. Then put it on a hard surface and whack it until it breaks open, or you can take it outdoors and drop it with force against a stone. Once it's cracked open, pry out all the white flesh and cut away the brown skin. Chop the coconut into rough pieces and grate—a food processor does this job easily. Pour 1 cup boiling water over the grated coconut and let stand 1 hour, then squeeze the grated coconut through a damp cloth, squeezing the cloth and twisting it to extract as much liquid as possible. This is your thick coconut milk.

TUSCAN HARE

There's not too much meat on a hare, and frankly this dish will just barely serve four. A better idea is to serve two the first time around and then shred all the remaining meat from the bones to add to the remaining sauce to make a wonderful hare pasta. This is a dish that one of us once tasted in a small trattoria in a hill town in Tuscany and the pasta sauce made thus is as close as we've come to duplicating that memorable treat.

SERVES 4, OR 2 WITH LEFTOVERS

6 Tb. red wine vinegar
1 hare, cut into 8 pieces
3 Tb. butter
1 large onion, sliced
2 oz. ham, chopped
1 Tb. sugar
¼ cup red wine

1¼ cups rich poultry or game stock
salt and freshly ground pepper
1 tsp. chopped fresh rosemary or
    ½ tsp. dried
1 Tb. shaved bitter chocolate
3 Tb. raisins
3 Tb. slivered almonds

Use about 2 tablespoons of the vinegar to rinse the pieces of hare.

Melt the butter in a large skillet, add the sliced onion, the hare, and the ham. Sauté gently about 5 minutes on each side.

Dissolve the sugar in the remaining vinegar and then add that to the skillet along with the wine and the stock. Salt and pepper well and sprinkle on rosemary. Cover and simmer slowly for 40 minutes.

Mix in the shaved chocolate and raisins and simmer another 15–20 minutes or until tender.

Stir well, and add the almonds. If the sauce seems too thin, remove the hare to a warm platter, boil down the juices for a minute, then pour over the meat to serve.

Hare Sauce for Pasta

Discard any raisins that may be left in the above leftover sauce. Remove the remaining pieces of hare and shred every scrap of meat from the bones. Heat the sauce, add 1 mashed chicken liver to give it body, sprinkle a pinch of sage over, and add enough rich stock to make about 1 cup. Stir in the hare meat. Serve over fettuccine boiled until just al dente. Serves two.

CURRY OF RABBIT OR HARE

SERVES 4

2 lb. rabbit or hare, cut in
    serving pieces
2 medium onions, chopped
4 cloves garlic, crushed and
    chopped
2 tsp. minced ginger
1½ Tb. butter
1½ tsp. garam masala (page 323) ⎫
1 tsp. turmeric ⎭ or 2 tsp. or more curry powder

1 tsp. chili powder (optional)
2–2½ tsp. salt
2 Tb. chopped fresh sage or
    2 tsp. dried
3 medium tomatoes
2 Tb. yogurt
2 tsp. lemon juice

Soak meat in salted cold water 30 minutes or longer. Wash well, and while the pieces are draining sauté the onion, garlic, and ginger in butter in a large skillet 2–3 minutes. Add garam masala and tumeric or curry powder, plus optional chili powder, salt, and sage. Taste and decide whether you want more curry powder.

In about a minute add tomatoes and sauté before stirring in the yogurt. Continue cooking, giving this sauce a chance to lose some of its moisture before adding meat; coat each piece well with the rather dry sauce and stir over medium heat for 5 minutes. Cover and simmer over low heat—thus the meat juices will ooze out and prevent burning, at the same time providing a natural gravy. Add no water or other liquid unless you want a particularly thin sauce.

Keeping the pan well covered, simmer for 1½–2 hours; stir in lemon juice 5 minutes before cooking ends.

HARE OR RABBIT BELGIAN STYLE

This is really an adaptation of my recipe for sauerbraten, save that the liquid is beer instead of wine. One could, of course, also think of it as still another recipe for hasenpfeffer. Again, it is good either with hare or rabbit, of course, or squirrel for that matter. Try this with muskrat, also.

SERVES 6

2 snowshoe rabbits or
   2–3 cottontails
3 cups strong ale
2 tsp. Worcestershire sauce
4 shallots or 2 cloves
   garlic, minced
2 bay leaves
¼ tsp. each of powdered cloves,
   ginger, nutmeg, and cinnamon

½ tsp. marjoram
3 onions, sliced thin
1 carrot, sliced thin
6 Tb. flour
salt and pepper
6 Tb. butter or bacon fat
5 medium-sized potatoes, sliced
   (optional), or noodles

Cut the hares into serving pieces and put down overnight in a marinade made of the ale, Worcestershire, shallots or garlic, bay leaves, spices, marjoram, onions, and carrot.

When ready to prepare remove and place rabbit sections on paper toweling and pat almost dry. Roll them twice in flour, salt, and pepper (or shake in a paper bag) until sections are heavily coated with the flour mixture.

In a heavy skillet that has a lid or in an electric skillet heat the fat and sauté the rabbit pieces, turning often over medium-high heat until brown. This should be about a 15-minute process.

Add all of the marinade vegetables, herbs, etc., and half of the marinade liquid, cover, and simmer over low heat (if you use electric skillet simmer at 225°–250°) for 1–1½ hours. Check occasionally and if and when more liquid is required, add a bit of the reserved marinade liquid.

After an hour or so, check the thickest rabbit pieces with a fork for doneness, especially if you use snowshoe rabbits in this recipe, for sometimes they can be tough.

The sauce should not be watery but should have thickened some; if it seems too watery, mix a bit of marinade with flour into a paste and stir into the sauce.

Serve with noodles, or, if you prefer, potatoes. You can add sliced potatoes to the skillet for the last 40 minutes of the simmering.

HARE ILIAMNA

It took Ted Gerken and his three beagles plus Mary to produce this recipe. The northern hare of the Alaska Peninsula (*Lepus timidus*) are big animals (7–10 pounds plus), but do not usually weigh as much as the Arctic hare (*Lepus arcticus*) of Greenland, Ellesmere, and the Northern Baffin Islands. The latter may weigh up to 15 pounds. Our *Lepus timidus* is the same species as the blue hare of the Scottish Highlands and Scandinavia.

This recipe would produce a fine dish if 2 snowshoe rabbits were substituted for the northern hare.

SERVES 10–12

10-lb. hare (winter phase)	1 qt. fresh Alaskan low-bush
vinegar	cranberries, picked after first
salt and pepper	frost
flour	2 cups pineapple
4 Tb. lard or oil	1 apple
4 onions	1 orange, unpeeled
6 potatoes	sugar
8 carrots	

Cut hare into ½-pound serving pieces. Soak 24 hours in lightly vinegared water. Wipe dry. Salt and pepper the pieces, roll them in flour and brown in fat or oil in a Dutch oven, then bake at 350°, covered, until tender.

Add vegetables when meat is half done (perhaps after 45 minutes to an hour). Remove to platter and prepare gravy from drippings.

To make sauce, grind cranberries, pineapple, apple, and orange together. Sweeten to taste. Serve on the side.

BARBECUED RABBIT OR SQUIRREL

When I was a youth in Indiana, pork barbecue sandwiches were the rage for a snack after a movie. Later and for years, I experimented until I produced a recipe to duplicate that taste. Then I found that it was equally good for rabbit, squirrel, and young woodchucks. Although I have not prepared it with muskrat, beaver, or raccoon, I would bet it would be equally good with any of the meats of these three tasty animals. Here I give it for 3 rabbits but 3½ to 4 pounds of other meats on the bone would make a similar blend.

SERVES 6–8

3 cottontails, dressed	salt
water to cover	8 peppercorns
2 onions, sliced	1 bay leaf

Bring above ingredients to a boil, then simmer for 1½–2 hours or until meat can be shredded (2½–3½ hours for beaver or raccoon) from the bones with a fork. Remove rabbits and shred off the meat. Reserve the stock.

BARBECUE SAUCE

2 onions, diced	3 garlic cloves, smashed
3 cups or one #2½ can tomatoes	2 bay leaves
3 cups reserved stock	1 Tb. Worcestershire sauce
½ cup catsup	3 dashes Tabasco or a pinch of
1 small can tomato paste	cayenne
¼ cup vinegar	1 tsp. dry mustard
1½ tsp. salt	¼–½ tsp. powdered cloves
12 peppercorns	¼–½ tsp. cinnamon
2 tsp. light brown sugar	

Combine above ingredients, bring to a boil, then simmer covered for 15 minutes or so.

Taste to suit your own palate to get the proper sweet-sour blend and for the spice blend. If too sweet, add vinegar discreetly. Do the same for the spice blend.

Add the shredded meat and continue to simmer until it is not watery but thickened a bit.

Serve as an open sandwhich on two halves of hamburger buns that have been buttered and browned, butter side down, in a skillet.

NOTE: If your game meat is skimpy, supplement with pork shoulder meat or pork loin.

Squirrel

GRAY SQUIRREL

Squirrel hunting with a .22 is for me one of the most rewarding of the rifle sports, and for two reasons: one, the wary squirrel, gray or fox, is not an easy quarry and, two, I believe, squirrel meat is the most delicious of all small game meats. Chicken-fried young squirrel is better than rabbit or chicken, two of my favorite meats; in addition, the squirrel lends itself to most savory stews and braises.

A good point to bear in mind is that like rabbit, squirrel meat is equally good in most any recipe for pheasant, grouse, partridge, etc.

Fox squirrels weigh from a shade over 1 pound to 2¼ pounds or a bit more; the smaller gray squirrel from a couple of ounces under a pound to 1½ or a bit more. The western gray may weigh up to 2 pounds. Abert's, or the tassel-eared squirrel, weighs from 1½ to 2 pounds.

Squirrel meat is succulent fare. Here are ten recipes, but do remember that when you have a brace of bushytails take a look at the recipes for a rabbit, hare, muskrat (particularly if you want a roast squirrel) or even pheasant or grouse for other ways to prepare squirrel.

BRUNSWICK STEW

Technically this stew is always made with squirrel, but it can be made with other meats—rabbit, muskrat, beaver, or combinations. Here's the stew for four made from one squirrel. Very slow simmering is the trick. Serve this stew in soup bowls with corn pone or hush puppies.

SERVES 4

1 squirrel, cut into 6–7 pieces	1 cup fresh corn
flour	1 cup lima beans
salt and pepper	3 potatoes, quartered
3 Tb. butter	¼ tsp. cayenne
8 cups boiling water	2 onions, sliced
1 tsp. thyme	2 cups canned tomatoes with juice

Roll the squirrel pieces in flour, salt, and pepper. Brown in butter. Add squirrel and all other ingredients, save the tomatoes, to the boiling water, cover, and simmer for 1½ to 2 hours.

Add the tomatoes and continue to simmer another hour.

BARBECUED SQUIRREL

The recipe for barbecue sauce on page 360 will serve for all barbecued small game—hare, rabbit, beaver, muskrat, woodchuck, but with squirrel I think a little variation is called for. Instead of the 2½ tablespoons of Worcestershire, and the tablespoon each of Harvey's sauce and walnut sauce, reduce the Worcestershire here to 1 tablespoon, omit the other two (even if you can find them in the stores), and substitute 3 tablespoons mint sauce. If you can't find mint sauce you have two alternatives: (1) substitute 3 tablespoons of mint jelly for the brown sugar in the recipe or (2) add ¼ cup, packed, of minced mint leaves to the sauce before you begin to simmer it.

SERVES 4–6

2 dressed squirrels, cut in serving pieces	1 large onion, chopped
¾ cup red wine	2 carrots, sliced
1 cup water	1½–2 cups barbecue sauce (page 360 with adjustments noted above)
salt and pepper	
2 bay leaves	

In a kettle boil, then simmer, the squirrel pieces in the wine and water with the rest of the ingredients except the barbecue sauce.

Cook covered for about an hour. Remove pieces, place in a baking dish, and cover with the sauce. Bake in a preheated 300° oven for another 45 minutes.

SQUIRREL STROGANOFF WITH MUSHROOMS, ONIONS, AND SOUR CREAM

I learned from Jim Beard and from my late hunting partner Leonard Pelky that mustard goes well in any rabbit or squirrel recipe. This can also be prepared with rabbit or even pheasant. Serve with boiled or mashed potatoes.

SERVES 4–6

¼ lb. diced salt pork or
  6–7 slices bacon, diced
2 squirrels, cut into serving pieces
¾ cup flour
2½ tsp. dry mustard
1½ tsp. thyme
½ tsp. pepper
1½ tsp. salt

¾ cup chicken broth
1 large onion, diced
¼ lb. mushrooms, sliced
3 tsp. butter
2 cups sour cream
¼ cup sherry
minced parsley

Fry out the salt pork or bacon until the chitlins (the bits of meat) are crisp; remove them and set aside.

Roll the squirrel pieces in the flour mixed with mustard, thyme, pepper, and salt, using all of the flour mixture if possible, and brown the pieces over medium heat. Take 15 minutes to do this.

Add the chicken broth, cover, and simmer until the saddle pieces seem tender, about 15 minutes.

While the squirrel is simmering, sauté first the onion, then the mushrooms, in butter and set aside.

When done, remove the squirrel pieces temporarily and stir in the sour cream, onion, and mushrooms. Make sure the sour cream melds with the other ingredients, and if necessary add a bit of hot water. Simmer for 5 minutes, but don't let it boil.

Now stir in the sherry, add the chitlins and the squirrel pieces, and simmer just until the squirrel is heated again. Garnish with minced parsley.

SQUIRREL IN A CLAY POT

SERVES 4–6

1 tsp. savory
1 tsp. marjoram
1 tsp. thyme
coarse salt and freshly ground
  pepper
2 squirrels, about 1 pound each,
  cut into 8–10 pieces

2 large onions, chopped
3 oz. country ham with some fat,
  cut into strips
1 Tb. sweet butter
⅓ cup red wine

Crush the herbs together with some salt and pepper and rub the pieces of squirrel thoroughly with the herbs.

Place the chopped onions in the bottom of a presoaked Roemer-Topf clay pot, put the squirrel on top, and then strew ham strips over. Dot with butter and cover with the clay top.

Bake in a 450° oven for 1 hour and 40 minutes.

Remove and add the wine, then bake, covered, for a final 20 minutes. Serve with spoon bread.

═══════ SQUIRREL STEW WITH BLACK OLIVES ═══════

Ripe olives, especially if they are those wrinkled, ill-tempered-looking oil-cured olives from France or Greece, have an affinity for game. Any black olives will do, but if they are unpitted you must pare off the flesh ahead of time to extract the pits. And there is time for this, for the olives are added to this sauté-stew after the dish is cooked.

Of course you can also use this recipe for rabbit, two pheasants, four grouse or four or five partridges. All gallinaceous game birds are delicious prepared this way.

SERVES 6

1 Tb. oil or lard
¼ salt pork or enough cubed
　to make ⅔ cup
2 squirrels, cut up as you would
　a frying chicken
juice of 1 lemon
¾ cup flour
1 tsp. thyme
1 tsp. rosemary
salt and pepper
3 onions, minced

1 small carrot, sliced very thin
½ cup dry white wine or
　dry vermouth
½ cup giblet stock or
　chicken broth*
3 cloves garlic
3 bay leaves
2 Tb. tomato paste
½ cup pitted black olives
chopped parsley

In a big skillet or casserole put a tablespoon or so of oil or lard and when hot try out the salt pork cubes in it until they are crisp. Remove and reserve these delicious cracklings.

Moisten the squirrel pieces with lemon juice and then roll or shake in a paper bag with enough flour mixed with the thyme, rosemary, salt, and pepper to use up all of this flour-herb mixture. If you can't use it all, reserve remainder.

Next sauté the floured pieces in the fat. Do this over a medium heat and try to stand over the skillet or casserole with a fork or kitchen tongs, turning the pieces until they are golden brown. Add lard or butter if need be; the browning should take 10–12 minutes.

Remove squirrel pieces and sauté the onions and sliced carrot slowly for 8–10 minutes. Now add the wine, the stock, garlic cloves, and bay leaves and meld in the tomato paste. Simmer together for 5 minutes.

Put the squirrel pieces and the salt pork cracklings in and cover. Cook at a simmer for 30 minutes or so or until the fattest piece tests "done" to the fork.

During the latter process you may need to check for moisture. If needed, add stock or half stock and half white wine. The browned flour pieces should cook off enough flour to thicken the sauce some. If in your ministrations it becomes too thin, swirl some of the reserved flour-herb mix in a little water and stir into the sauce. Simmer a few minutes more to phase out the raw flour taste.

A few minutes before serving, fish out the gum-cutting bay leaves and stir and work in the olives. Garnish with parsley.

* If you have made the giblet stock yourself, dice the cooked squirrel livers, then squash and add to the ingredients later.

SQUIRREL OR RABBIT WITH HAM IN WINE

My grandmother knew that squirrel and rabbit were delicious with ham. She cooked "fried" ham cubes in the gravy made from chicken-fried squirrel or rabbit.

SERVES 4–6

½-lb. ham slice, diced and browned
2 squirrels or 2 cottontail rabbits,
    cut into serving pieces
flour
salt and pepper
3 Tb. butter
2 Tb. oil

1 cup dry white wine
½ tsp. marjoram
½ tsp. rosemary, crumbled
3 cloves garlic, finely diced
1 dash Tabasco
½ tsp. Worcestershire sauce
    or mushroom catsup

Dice and brown the ham pieces until crispy.

Shake the squirrel or rabbit pieces in flour, salt, and pepper and sauté until brown in butter and oil, turning often in a skillet that crowds them, about 10–12 minutes.

Add remaining ingredients, cover, and cook over fast simmer for 20–25 minutes more.

The flour coating should thicken the sauce some; if not enough add flour and water shaken or smoothed into paste.

SQUIRREL BRAISED IN
JAMES BEARD SAUERKRAUT

This recipe is based on the redoubtable talent for discovery that is uniquely Jim Beard's (see page 201 for Roast Duck with Sauerkraut Stuffing) and it can also be used for rabbit or any upland bird. See page 137 for cooking times for grouse, partridge, quail, dove, etc. I like to serve this with whipped potatoes.

SERVES 6

2 squirrels, cut into serving
    pieces
3–4 Tb. butter or lard
1-lb.11-oz. can sauerkraut
6 slices bacon, thick if you can
    get them
1 lb. hot (or sweet) Italian
    sausage, sliced (you can use little
    pig sausages)

4 cloves garlic, sliced
24 juniper berries, crushed
1 tsp. crushed caraway seeds
2 cups good beer or ale
    (not "light and tasteless")
salt and pepper

Sauté the squirrel pieces in butter or lard until nicely browned. Set aside.

Drain the sauerkraut, pressing out the juices, but retain this liquid.

In a deep skillet fry the bacon until it is half done. Set aside.

Brown the sausage in the bacon fat. Add the sauerkraut, bacon, garlic, juniper berries, caraway seeds, and beer and with two forks mix thoroughly. Simmer for 10 minutes.

Put half of this in a casserole, lay in the browned squirrel pieces, then cover with the remaining sauerkraut.

Simmer, covered (or bake in a 325° oven), for about an hour, adding beer (or beer and kraut juice) if it cooks down too much.

SQUIRREL COBBLER

Believe it or not, this is sometimes served in the Middle West as a breakfast dish; the squirrel, however, was stewed the night before.

SERVES 6

2 squirrels, cut into pieces
liquid to cover (half water, half
  dry white wine)
2 bay leaves
2 carrots, each cut into 4 chunks
2 leeks, sliced, or 1 onion
2 parsnips, sliced
3 cloves
2⅓ cups Bisquick

6 Tb. butter
6 Tb. flour
½ cup milk
1 tsp. Worcestershire sauce
salt and pepper
thyme
1 cup heavy cream
15 small white onions, cooked
1–2 Tb. melted butter

Put the squirrel pieces, liquid, bay leaves, carrots, leeks or onion, parsnips, and cloves in a big saucepan. Bring to a boil, partially cover, and simmer for about an hour.

Remove the squirrel pieces and set aside to cool. Strain and retain the liquid. Also retain the vegetables but fish out and discard the cloves and the bay leaves.

Remove the meat from the squirrel pieces and cut up in 1–1½-inch chunks.

Using the Bisquick box instructions, make up a shortcake dough ball, but without the sugar.

In a saucepan combine the 6 tablespoons each of butter and flour; cook over a low fire for a minute or two. Off heat, stir in the milk and the squirrel broth and Worcestershire, then cook over low to medium heat until it thickens. Stir in salt, pepper, and thyme, and then the cream. Just heat through, but do not boil.

In a straight-sided casserole, spoon in a bit of the sauce, then lay in the squirrel pieces and mix in the carrots, leeks, and parsnips, and scatter the small cooked onions around. Add the remaining sauce.

Knead your crust dough seven or eight times and pat it out on a floured board until it is just a bit greater in diameter than your casserole.

Lay it out on top of the sauce, squirrel, and vegetables. Brush with melted butter. Crimp the edges just for looks.

Bake in a preheated 425° oven for about 30 minutes or until crust is browned.

SQUIRREL CACCIATORE

This dish when made with chicken is prepared in a thousand different ways, but here is how I prepared it with squirrel. Grouse, partridge, pheasant, and rabbit are also good in the dish. In Italian the name means "hunter's" squirrel.

SERVES 6

2 squirrels, cut up in serving
   pieces
flour
salt and pepper
2 Tb. lard or oil
3 shallots or 1 onion, chopped
½ green pepper, chopped
1 rib celery with leaves, chopped
2 Tb. chopped parsley
½ cup dry white wine

½ tsp. oregano
¼ tsp. mace
¼ tsp. powdered cloves
2 tsp. anchovy paste
½ lb. mushrooms
2 Tb. butter
½ cup tomato sauce
12–15 small stuffed olives,
   sliced

Shake the squirrel pieces in a bag with flour, salt, and pepper. In a casserole sauté the pieces in the lard or oil until golden brown. Take 12–15 minutes to do this over medium heat.

Add the shallots, green pepper, celery, and parsley to the pan and sauté with squirrel pieces a few minutes. Add the wine, oregano, mace, cloves, and anchovy paste, cover, and simmer for 10–15 minutes—until meat is tender.

While this is cooking, in a separate pan sauté the mushrooms 3–4 minutes in the butter, then add tomato sauce. When hot, stir together with the sliced olives. Add this mixture to the squirrel pan and serve.

CASSEROLE OF SQUIRREL IN CREAM

This recipe may be used interchangeably with rabbits (2), hare (1), muskrats (3), or a young woodchuck (1). I have never used it with, say, pheasant, but how could it fail to be good?

SERVES 4–6

6 Tb. butter
2 squirrels, cut into serving pieces
1½ cups thick cream
¼ cup vinegar
2 shallots, or 5–6 scallions,
   diced fine

½ tsp. salt
½ tsp. pepper
½ tsp. thyme or rosemary, or
   ¼ tsp. of each

Melt 3 tablespoons of butter in casserole and brown the squirrel pieces lightly in it.

Mix the cream, vinegar, shallots or scallions, salt, pepper, and herbs.

Dot squirrel pieces with remaining bits of butter. Pour half the cream mixture over the squirrels.

Cover casserole and simmer over very low heat (perhaps use asbestos pad) for an hour. Baste several times and watch it, for you want the cream sauce to cook down, but not, of course, stick.

Skim off the butter and add remaining cream mixture.

Heat and cook for 10 minutes, uncovered, until sauce thickens somewhat.

Muskrat

In New Orleans and other eastern cities whose restaurants serve muskrat in season, this delicious meat is often listed as "marsh rabbit," to avoid the stigma attached to the word "rat." It is a pity that the name puts off some people, for the tender, fine-grained meat is excellent fare. This little denizen of the marshes, whose live weight ranges about that of the eastern cottontail rabbit, 2 to 4 pounds, is chiefly vegetarian, feeding on aquatic plants, indeed making its "push-up," or lodge, from some of the same marsh vegetation it feeds on.

Some palates find muskrat similar in taste to wild duck; others fancy that its flavor is similar to terrapin. The first time I tried muskrat was in a trapping camp in the Ontario bush. The meaty, savory-looking carcasses of two rats that had just been skinned tempted me to chicken-fry them as I would squirrel. I dressed them, removed, at my trapper friend's instruction, the two glands under the front legs and the two in the small of the back, cut the muskrats into serving pieces, and put them down overnight in salted water. The recipe I used was precisely the same one used for country-fried chicken, and the results made a believer of me on the subject of the excellence of muskrat meat. See page 98 for the simple recipe.

ROAST MUSKRAT
(OR RABBIT OR SQUIRREL)

When roasting small furred game, it is best to tie the front legs back and the hind legs forward, so both sit snug against the body. Put a few slices of onions and celery in the cavity before tying up the legs.

Lay muskrats in a shallow uncovered baking dish, breast down, and pin a couple of strips of bacon over the back of each.

Roast at 325° for 50–60 minutes. When done, remove to a pie pan and set on the open oven door to keep warm.

Depending on the amount of fat in the drippings, stir in flour and heat on top of the stove. Stir in a cup of milk and continue stirring while it simmers and thickens, about 3–5 minutes.

"MARSH RABBIT" NEW ORLEANS STYLE

The euphemism for muskrat stew is pertinent, for rabbit also is served in this fashion in Cajun country. Indeed, this recipe will serve rabbit, squirrel, woodchuck, and beaver equally well.

SERVES 4

2 muskrats, "deglanded,"
   disjointed and floured
6 Tb. oil or lard, or combination
2 medium onions, chopped
1 green pepper, chopped
3 carrots, sliced
2 cloves garlic, sliced
¼ lb. diced ham
1 rib celery, diced
¼ tsp. crushed red pepper seeds
¼ tsp. cayenne

1 cup red wine
1½ cups homemade or canned
   tomato sauce
3 bay leaves
½ tsp. thyme
½ tsp. marjoram
2 tsp. lemon juice
3 Tb. chopped parsley
1 Tb. Harvey's or Worcestershire
   sauce
salt and pepper

In a Dutch oven or heavy casserole sauté the floured muskrat pieces in fat until brown.

Add onions, green pepper, carrots, and garlic when you have almost finished browning the meat and cook until onions are soft.

Add all remaining ingredients and simmer covered, for 1½ hours or until the muskrat meat is tender.

If the flour on the muskrat pieces has not thickened the sauce do so with a flour and water paste. If liquid is required during the simmering, add water.

BRAISED MUSKRAT

Jack Duke, who each year "farms" hundreds of muskrats off his 400-acre salt marsh in Delaware, enjoys muskrat the way his mother prepared it. The secret, says Jack, is long, slow cooking. I added a touch of thyme as I give the recipe here, but in its pure form it is not called for.

Boiled potatoes and steamed kale (served with a cruet of vinegar on the side) go well with this dish.

SERVES 8

4 muskrats, cleaned and "deglanded"
5 Tb. salted and peppered flour
½ lb. salt pork, diced and tried
   out in a Dutch oven

8 onions, sliced
1 tsp. thyme

Cut the muskrat into hindquarters, saddle, and forequarters. Dust with seasoned flour and brown in the fat.

Add as many of the onions as possible and soften as the meat browns.

Add remainder of onions, the thyme, and enough water just to cover. Cover, bring to boil, turn down heat, and simmer as slowly as you can for at least 4 hours.

As the delicious broth cooks down, add more water sparingly, for, when finished, the Dutch oven should hold little more than muskrat meat, ready to fall off the bones, and a moist onion purée.

Just before serving add the cracklings. Sometimes I remove the meat and stir ½ cup of sour cream into the onion purée.

NOTE: Wild-fowl shooters who journey each November to Delaware or Maryland can often find muskrats for sale at roadside stands; sometimes raccoon is also offered.

BASIC SWEET-SOUR RECIPE FOR
BRAISED MUSKRAT OR OTHER FURRED GAME

The rich red flesh that is typical of the muskrat, beaver, squirrel, woodchuck, and raccoon lends itself to so-called sweet-sour dishes. I say so-called because I believe the intent of such dishes is to provide acidic tartness—i.e., sourness balanced by sugar, not sweetness as a thing-in-itself.

SERVES 4

2 lb. serving pieces muskrat
   ("deglanded")
flour
salt and pepper
4 Tb. lard or butter
1 onion, chopped fine
½ green pepper, chopped fine

½ tsp. powdered thyme
¼ cup sugar, preferably brown
2 tsp. dry mustard
1 cup cream
½ cup red wine
¼ cup vinegar

Roll or shake the muskrat pieces in seasoned flour and sauté in lard or butter until brown. Just before the meat pieces are browned, sauté the onion and green pepper in with them until soft.

Put in casserole with the other ingredients and bake at 325° for about 1½ hours or until meat is tender.

Beaver

This animal, whose pursuits accounted for so much of the exploration by voyageurs and mountain men of North America, should be as well regarded for the taste of its flesh as for the value of its dense, soft underfur. Its dark red meat, fine in texture and "spoon meat" tender in younger animals, seldom fails to please even the most sophisticated palate.

The meat of the beaver is more apt to find its way into a wilderness cabin than into the average kitchen, but in either case its preparation involves a bit of doing. While not an onerous chore, it requires overnight soaking, especially if it has been taken dead from a trap. It is also essential to remove the glands in the armpits under the front legs, in the small of the back, and sometimes along the inside of the thigh. And there is also the castor to be removed, a gland that lies like a pad just under the skin in front of the genital organs of both sexes. If this sounds complicated it really isn't; the castor or musk gland is quite identifiable (don't cut it by mistake), and other glands come off when you remove all excess fat (leave a thin layer only) inside and out from the carcass, even if you are vague about what is a gland and what a fat tissue globule.

To draw excess blood, the beaver should be soaked in salt water with 2 or 3 tablespoons of vinegar added. Remove the fat first and then let the beaver stand overnight. Then rinse and dry.

The beaver is a large, robust beast ranging from 20 to 30 pounds for yearlings, to 50 to 70 pounds for mature adults. My old friend the trapper Roy Smith weighed one "superblanket" beaver from his trap that tipped the scales at 88 pounds, and saw one weighed in Spanish Ontario, on a reliable scale, that came in at 102 pounds.

A skinned and dressed beaver will weigh out at about 55 percent of its live weight. I have found that two-year-old beavers of 35 to 40 pounds or so are as tender as yearlings but seem, to me at least, better flavored, but a yearling is nonetheless delicious. Beavers are vegetarians, like domestic stock, fattening on tender bark, grasses, buds, lily-pad roots, and other plants.

Beavers, incidentally, are graded in the fur market by both the density of the underfur and by size. The latter is determined by adding the length and width measurements of the stretched skin. (A beaver skins out and stretches almost round.) In the early days of the Hudson's Bay Company it is alleged that a "blanket" beaver, one that measures 60 inches by the above determination, was taken in trade for a single Hudson's Bay woolen blanket. I once taped one of Roy's "superblankets," a skin that measured out at 72 inches.

Some people swear by beaver tail, contending that the fatty, soft-gristly meat is delicious. I have never tried it, chiefly because Roy Smith, who liked beaver meat very much, said, "Whoever tells you that beaver tail is good is trying to get the best of you with an old trapper's joke." Whether or not this be true, I can vouch for the fact that beaver liver is very fine. I used it in place of the kidney in my beaver and "kidney" pie.

Closing the belly opening of a stuffed beaver can be done with string and the assistance of either small skewers or toothpicks (I remember I used kitchen matches with the heads cut off in preparing the last beaver in camp). Insert the skewer or pick through both sides of the skin at the cut and lace alternately with string. The legs, front and back, should be laid back against the belly and secured by tying into the laced skewers or picks. Roast the beaver on its side, turning when half-done.

The last beaver I roasted whole in 1960, in the oven of Roy Smith's trapping cabin, was a yearling. I roasted that beaver, stuffed with sage dressing, and then used the leftover meat to make a beaver pie.

ROAST BEAVER

I roast a beaver just as I would a wild goose, i.e., I actually braise it or roast it, covered, in liquid and aromatic vegetables. The first time I roasted one of these delicious critters, I stuffed it with a regular bread, onion, and sage dressing. A young beaver weighing 8 to 10 pounds dressed is ideal.

Remove the glands and all of the fat you can trim off (see opposite). If the beaver was trapped, soak it overnight in a bucket of clean water and ¼ cup of vinegar. I, personally, leave the head on, but cut off the great paddle of a tail, of course.

⬡ SERVES 8

8–10-lb. beaver, ready for the oven
a stuffing (if you wish)
salt and pepper
3 onions, sliced
2 carrots, sliced
1 rib celery, sliced

1 turnip, sliced
½ cup red wine
½ cup water
½ cup beach plum or currant jelly
½ tsp. thyme (optional)
½ tsp. rosemary (optional)
flour

Stuff the beaver, if you wish, and salt and pepper it all over.

Place beaver in uncovered roasting pan and bake for 15 minutes at 450° (in camp you'll have to guess).

Add the vegetables, wine, water, jelly, and herbs (optional), cover, and continue roasting at 325°. The total roasting time will be 3–3½ hours.

As the beaver bakes, skim off the fat from time to time. No matter how much exterior and cavity fat you have removed, a lot more will accumulate.

Check the liquid, adding a wine-water mix when needed.

When the roast is done, remove and make a gravy by stirring in a mixture of flour and water and whisking until the liquid comes to a boil and thickens.

Simmer on top of stove for 5 minutes.

═══ BEAVER STEW ═══

The savory dark meat of a young (kit) beaver makes a fine camp stew. In fact, any red meat stew recipe in this book will be good when made with beaver meat. After dressing, removing glands and fat, debone about 3 pounds best parts of beaver, cut into 1-inch cubes, flour and brown, then proceed as with any stew with this quantity of meat. Rosemary, thyme, and savory are good with beaver.

In camp, I usually serve beaver stew with boiled noodles (or spaghetti), drained, then tossed with garlic butter.

⬡ SERVES 6–8

15-lb. kit beaver
1½ lb. pork skins
2 onions, chopped
3 carrots, sliced
3 turnips, sliced
3 cloves garlic, smashed
1 tsp. thyme
½ tsp. savory
2 bay leaves, crumbled

½ tsp. cloves
2 Tb. chopped parsley
½ cup dry red wine
4 oz. brandy
1 egg yolk
½ cup heavy cream or milk
5 tsp. Dijon mustard
salt and pepper to taste

The legs and loin of even a small beaver are big enough for minor carving, so in this recipe just use the saddle and the legs (see page 118 for dressing beaver). If you wish you can bone out the leg meat and the loin beforehand.

In a casserole lay out a layer of pork skins on the bottom, then half the sliced vegetables, then the beaver meat. Sprinkle with thyme, savory, bay leaves, cloves, and parsley.

Now another layer of the other half of the vegetables, then another layer of pork skins. Add the wine and brandy.

Cover the casserole and simmer on top of the stove for 2 hours or roast at 325° for 2½ hours.

When the meat is done remove it to a serving platter, surround it with the vegetables, and keep warm.

Place the casserole over low heat and skim off the fat.

Beat the egg yolk, then beat in the cream. Spoon out 2–3 tablespoons of the casserole juices and stir into the egg and cream mix. Then stir this into the casserole juices.

Simmer without boiling until it thickens a bit, then stir and blend in the mustard, salt, and pepper. Serve in a sauceboat.

CRUMBED AND FRIED BEAVER TAIL

Despite Ray Smith's derogatory remark about beaver tail—see introduction to this section—this recipe comes to us highly recommended by Evan Jones, the author of *American Food: The Gastronomic Story.*

SERVES 2–3 (DEPENDING ON SIZE OF BEAVER)

1 beaver tail	1 egg, beaten
1 cup water	bread crumbs
1 cup vinegar	butter, oil, or fat for frying

Skin the tail, wash it well, then cover it in a pot with water and vinegar. Simmer about 1½ hours, or until tender.

Drain the meat, which will resemble pork, and cut it into slices as one would for London broil. Dip the slices in beaten egg and roll in bread crumbs. Fry until golden brown.

CHICKEN-FRIED KIT BEAVER

If the trapline produces a kit beaver, dress it, remove fat, and soak it overnight in salted water. (In a kit beaver the glands may be hard to find, or even nonexistent. Just remove *any* fatty tissue under forelegs and small of back.) Cut the beaver into serving pieces (you can manage even though the parts will not be as familiar as those of a frying chicken), rinse, and dry.

SERVES 6–8

salt and pepper	flour
1 small beaver, cut into serving pieces	4–6 Tb. lard or oil
	milk or water, or both

Salt and pepper the pieces, roll them in flour, and crowding them closely brown them, uncovered, on all sides in the hot fat in a large skillet that comes with a lid. You have to stand over this preparation, turning and adjusting the tightly crowded pieces. It will take 15–20 minutes over medium heat to brown the pieces.

As the floured meat takes up fat, add more fat if needed.

When the pieces are nicely browned, turn down the heat (in camp, move the skillet to a lid that is less hot), cover tightly, and cook for another 15–20 minutes. Turn and adjust the pieces two or three times, for they will continue to brown as they steam a bit under the lid.

Now remove the lid, turn up heat, and brown the steamed pieces again. This may take another 15 minutes.

Remove pieces, pour off all save 3 tablespoons of the fat, stir in 3 tablespoons of flour, and cook gently a minute or two. Off heat, stir in 2 cups or so of water or water-and-milk mixture, then return to heat, stirring until sauce bubbles and thickens. Simmer for 5 minutes.

In camp serve the gravy over hot biscuit halves.

Woodchuck

When one considers the number of woodchucks shot each year as varmints it is a pity that so few of them are eaten. The meat of a young woodchuck is as delicious as squirrel (and can be "chicken-fried" also) and the flesh of more mature animals makes savory stews.

Woodchucks weigh from 4½ to 14 or 15 pounds. A 4½- to 6-pound animal is likely to be young and tender.

Woodchucks are fat, and like certain other game they have small-of-the-back and under-forearm glands. Both fat and glands should be removed.

Older animals that are headed for the stew pot, I usually put down in water with 2 or 3 tablespoons of vinegar overnight.

Some people parboil animals whose weights mark them as "old and likely tough," before stewing or braising.

BAKED YOUNG WOODCHUCK
IN SOUR CREAM AND MUSTARD

The first time I used sour cream and mustard for furred game was with woodchuck, but this dish is equally good with squirrel, rabbit, or muskrat. Refer to page 121 for preparing woodchucks for cooking.

SERVES 4

6-lb. woodchuck, cut into serving
  pieces
flour
salt and freshly ground pepper
5 Tb. lard or butter
Dijon mustard
3 slices bacon
1 onion, diced

¼ cup thinly sliced carrots
½ cup sliced mushrooms
3 Tb. chopped parsley
1 tsp. Harvey's sauce or Kitchen
  Bouquet
1 cup sour cream
½ cup sweet cream

Soak the woodchuck pieces in salted water overnight or for several hours, then rinse dry, roll in flour, salt, and pepper, and sauté in fat until nicely browned.

When cool enough to handle spread the pieces generously on all sides with Dijon mustard.

Place on strips of bacon in shallow baking dish.

Sauté the onion, carrots, and finally the mushrooms, add the parsley and Harvey's sauce, check for salt and pepper, then, over low heat, stir in the sour cream and the sweet cream, melding the two creams.

Pour over meat pieces and bake in a 350° oven 40–50 minutes or until meat is tender (bake rabbit, squirrel, or muskrat 30–40 minutes). Check the dish once or twice and if it seems to need moisture add cream.

OVEN-BARBECUED WOODCHUCK OR MUSKRAT

A young woodchuck (size itself is the best determinant of age) is delicious when barbecued in the oven, and the same goes for muskrat. Both animals can be stuffed with your favorite dressing.

SERVES 3–4

1 young woodchuck, dressed (see page 121) and stuffed
1 cup barbecue sauce, your own favorite or my favorite (see page 360)

Roast the chuck on a rack in a low roasting pan at 350° for 1½–2 hours or until tender, basting regularly with the barbecue sauce. When two muskrats are used in this recipe roast approximately 1½ hours.

Raccoon

I have never cooked a raccoon, but I have eaten it with relish a number of times. The last time I had it in 1979 at a game dinner in Delaware, it never tasted better, and I have participated twice in dressing them. The recipe for that roast raccoon is the first one in the following collection. All of these recipes have been tested by raccoon aficionados. I think raccoon is just as tasty as squirrel, and better than rabbit. As a delicious meat it is much neglected save by a few country people, especially in the Midwest and South.

This nocturnal black-masked and ringtailed animal, widely hunted with hounds at night and trapped for its fur (now going at premium prices) is indigenous throughout the U.S. save for portions of a tier of Rocky Mountain states. The coon is as omnivorous as a black bear (or as man), prowling stream and pond edges for frogs, crayfish, and fish, and gleaning fields and woods for small mammals, birds, eggs, nuts, and a variety of fruits, both wild and domestic. Anyone who has put in a truck garden knows that the coon loves corn at the very same stage of succulence that man prefers it.

Raccoons weigh from 12 to 35 pounds and will dress out at a bit more than half that weight depending partly on whether or not you leave on the head. An old boar coon can be tough and before roasting should be put down in salt water for 10 or 12 hours and then parboiled for 30 minutes to 1 hour through at least one change of water (to the first of which may be added 2 teaspoons of pepper and 1 tablespoon of soda) before rinsing and drying for the roasting pan.

A coon that weighs around 6 to 8 pounds dressed is ideal. An animal of this size should also be put down in salt water after it is dressed. Whatever the size of the coon, its inside and outside layers of fat should be removed and the single gland under each foreleg near the body and the gland lying on each side of the spine in the small of the back should also be removed. These waxy kernels are brownish in color and about the size of a kidney bean. When you defat the coon you'll get these kernels willy-nilly, so don't worry about them. A coon of 5 to 8 pounds dressed is best roasted, but heavier animals are best braised after parboiling.

Dress a coon for roasting as you would a beaver (see page 118).

ROAST RACCOON, HOOSIER STYLE

John Stuart was a tobacco salesman who was the mentor of the boys in our neighborhood, for he was a great bird shooter, squirrel hunter, and general outdoorsman. He and his wife Mary invited me once while I was home on vacation from college to a raccoon dinner. Miz Mary had stuffed it—the dressing was bread, sage, and liver—and roasted it. This recipe will come close to hers, but I remember that she said she had parboiled the raccoon in two waters before roasting. Beaver would also be good stuffed with this dressing and roasted.

Serve with baked yams and kale or Brussels sprouts.

SERVES 6

6–8-lb. raccoon, glands removed, and all possible fat trimmed away
water to cover (salted, 1 tsp. to quart)
pepper
the raccoon liver, or 2–3 chicken livers
4 Tb. butter or lard
2 medium onions, diced
1 stalk celery with leaves, diced

4 cups commercial bread stuffing or white bread, diced
1 egg, beaten
salt
4 tsp. sage
1 tsp. marjoram
hot milk
flour
1 cup beef broth

In a deep roaster, preferably long enough to hold raccoon without curling him, bring cold water to a boil and simmer covered for 15 minutes.

Pour off fatty water and repeat. Drain, wash under faucet, and pat dry. Grind plenty of pepper in the cavity.

Sauté the livers in butter or lard until color is gone. Set aside.

Sauté onions and celery until onions are just soft, then smash up the livers with the onions and celery. Mix with bread, egg, salt, sage, and marjoram, moistening with a bit of hot milk.

Stuff the coon and sew up. Grind plenty of black pepper on the outside and dust with flour.

Place in a shallow roasting pan on a rack, add beef broth, and roast at 350°, basting five or six times for 2½–3 hours. Add more broth if necessary.

Make a gravy of the pan drippings by stirring in and blending a couple tablespoons of the dressing and adding milk to get the proper consistency.

═══ ROAST RACCOON WITH SWEET POTATO, ═══ SAUSAGE, AND CORN BREAD STUFFING

Here is another recipe from the Stuarts who first introduced me to raccoon (see preceding recipe).

This dressing is good for roast wild turkey, and I am sure it would stuff a kit beaver handsomely, too.

SERVES 6

4–5 yams or large sweet potatoes
6 Tb. soft butter
2 tsp. salt
½ tsp. pepper
5–7-lb. dressed raccoon (see page 118)
½ lb. sausage meat
1 medium onion, chopped
1 cup chopped celery

¼ cup cream
1½–2 cups corn bread crumbs
2 tsp. Dalmation rubbed sage
3 Tb. chopped parsley
1 tsp. marjoram
½ tsp. mace
1 Tb. Grand Marnier or ¼ cup orange juice
1 cup red wine

Boil yams in their jackets for 35–40 minutes, skin, mash, and whip with 3 tablespoons of the butter.

Salt and pepper the raccoon inside and out.

In the remaining butter cook the sausage meat until it is brown, then sauté the onion and celery.

In a bowl thoroughly mix the mashed yams, sausage, and vegetables with all of the remaining ingredients except wine.

Stuff the coon and sew up the belly vent, place on rack, and roast uncovered in a 300° oven for 45 minutes to the pound.

Turn the animal when half done and baste frequently with wine and, later, with wine and the pan juices.

═ ROAST MARINATED RACCOON WITH LIVER, ═ ONION, AND BREAD STUFFING

Like the possum, the raccoon "likes" sage; this dressing is a good one, so don't be afraid of the sage quantity.

SERVES 5–6

5–6-lb. raccoon, dressed (see page 118)
THE MARINADE

1½ cups vinegar	½ tsp. powdered ginger
1½ cups water	¼ tsp. powdered cloves
½ tsp. basil	½ tsp. sugar
½ tsp. tarragon	1 Tb. salt
½ tsp. powdered cinnamon	freshly ground pepper

Be sure to trim off, inside and out, most of the raccoon's fat. Mix together all the ingredients for the marinade and put the raccoon down in it overnight.

Many cooks leave the head on.

THE STUFFING

1 large onion, diced	1 tsp. salt
8 Tb. butter	freshly ground pepper
1 rib celery, diced	1 Tb. plus 1 tsp. rubbed sage
5–6 chicken livers	½ cup Madeira or Marsala
5 cups bread crumbs	

Sauté the onion in the butter, and when just beginning to soften, add the celery. When the celery becomes soft, add the chicken livers. Cook until the livers are just pink.

With a heavy fork mash the livers with the vegetables, then mix with the bread crumbs. Stir and mix in thoroughly the salt, pepper to taste, and sage. Then moisten the stuffing, stirring the while with the wine.

Rinse, dry, and stuff the coon. Close the vent by sticking deheaded and sharpened kitchen matches through each edge of skin and then lacing crisscross around them.

Tie the front legs back along the belly and the hind legs forward, if you can.

Place the stuffed coon on a rack in a shallow roaster and roast in a preheated 325° oven for about 35 minutes to the pound. Roast a raccoon under 5 pounds dressed weight 45 minutes to the pound.

If you wish gravy, pour off all but 3 tablespoons of fat, stir flour into the dredgings, and add liquid that is made up of half the drained marinade and half beef broth. Cook over low heat until it begins to thicken.

BARBECUED RACCOON

This dish can be made with any barbecue sauce of your choice. My recipe for Game Meat Barbecue Sauce is a good one, but if you want a higher tomato content than that sauce provides, add, as we do here, one 8-ounce can of tomato sauce. Serve with corn bread, kale, and potatoes.

SERVES 4–6

4–6-lb. raccoon, dressed (see
   page 118) and cut into serving pieces
1 cup red wine
2 carrots, sliced
2 onions, sliced
3 bay leaves
1 Tb. salt

pepper
3 cloves garlic, sliced
1 cup Barbecue Sauce (page 360)
1 cup tomato sauce, fresh or canned
1 Tb. sweet paprika (in addition to
   that in barbecue sauce)

Place the raccoon pieces in a large kettle. Add wine, enough water barely to cover, and the vegetables, bay leaves, salt and pepper, and garlic. Bring to a boil and simmer, covered, for about 1 hour.

Remove, drain, and place in a big buttered casserole or baking dish, cover with the barbecue sauce and the tomato sauce with paprika mixed into it. Bake in a preheated 325° oven for another 45–60 minutes.

NOTE The raccoon pieces may be quickly prepared in a pressure cooker for 20–30 minutes at 15 pounds pressure.

RACCOON PIE

Raccoon pie is an old country dish in the Midwest and the South and can be made in the same way as Squirrel Cobbler. To prepare this meat pie, cut up the coon in pieces (discarding the head and rib cage) after you have removed the glands and defatted the meat.

In preparing the cooked meat and the pie, proceed as in the squirrel recipe (page 113), but with raccoon it would be better to simmer it for 1½ hours before cooling and removing meat from the bones.

Opossum

The reason one hears so often about "roast possum" as a southern dish is because the opossum originally was a southern animal. But the old sleepyhead has been extending his range north for many years now, and today he appears in the upper peninsula of Michigan and, in the East, at least as far north as Saratoga, New York. The possum is good fare, North or South, but preparing it for the kitchen is a bit more complicated than for other furred game.

Remove the foreleg and small-of-the-back glands, but do this without skinning the animal, for possums should be handled like hogs—scalded first and then the fur scraped off. In roasting possums it is the practice to parboil for about an hour if the animal is to be roasted uncovered; parboiling is not required for covered roasting. However, most possum aficionados skin the animal and thus are able to trim off most of the outside as well as the cavity fat. Don't leave much fat on the dressed animal. It is a good idea to soak a possum overnight in salt water.

ROAST POSSUM WITH YAMS

Remember a possum should be handled first to last just as you would handle a suckling pig. First, it should be scraped, not skinned, and the hair is removed as follows: bring a bucket or big pot of water to a boil, adding a cup of wood ashes. Wet the possum down under the hot water faucet, then soak him in the boiling water for a minute or two. His fur can now be scraped off with a dull knife. Now, having given traditional advice, let me repeat: you can skin the animal if you wish.

Next slit from throat to vent and clean out viscera, then remove reddish gland kernels under forelegs and in small of back. Cut off head and tail. Remove all of the fat you can find inside the animal and put the possum down in salted water overnight.

When ready to roast, rinse thoroughly and dry.

SERVES 4

1 young opossum, prepared as above	1 cup beef broth
1 clove garlic, sliced	2 Tb. vinegar
3 Tb. flour	1 Tb. Worcestershire or Harvey's
1 tsp. thyme	sauce
salt and pepper to taste	4 yams, peeled and quartered

With a thin, sharp pointed knife cut into skin of the possum's legs, saddle, etc., and slip into each a sliver of garlic.

With trussing string tie front legs back and hind legs forward and dust with a mixture of flour, thyme, salt, and pepper.

Roast on a rack with the broth, vinegar, and sauce in a shallow pan as you would a loin of pork, basting often. Allow about 40 minutes to the pound.

About an hour before the possum is done, parboil the yams for 15 minutes or so, then arrange them around the meat to roast.

ROAST POSSUM WITH SPICED APPLES AND SWEET POTATOES

This dish is from Tennessee; tradition has it that it comes from the kitchen of Sam Houston. Serve it with hush puppies and a tossed salad.

SERVES 3–4

flour	4 sweet potatoes, pared and split
salt and freshly ground pepper	lengthwise
1 tsp. thyme	4 apples, pared, cored, and halved
1 opossum, dressed, washed, and	1 cup brown sugar
patted dry (see page 127)	½ tsp. allspice
½ cup red wine	¾ tsp. ground cinnamon
1¼ cups water	½ tsp. nutmeg

Mix flour, salt, pepper, and thyme and rub inside and outside the animal. Place on rack in roasting pan. Add the wine and water, cover tightly, and roast in a preheated 350° oven for about an hour.

Pour off all but a cup of the liquid. Lay the sweet potatoes in the pan, cover, and continue roasting for 45 minutes. Now lay in the cored and halved apples amid the sweet potatoes and sprinkle both fruit and vegetables with a mixture of the sugar and the spices.

Continue to roast, with the roaster now uncovered, for another 30 minutes, or until the possum is tender.

ROAST POSSUM AND KRAUT

Sauerkraut is an excellent antidote to fatty meats, and the opossum qualifies here in spades.

This country dish of possum and sauerkraut can be prepared in two ways: the kraut can be used either as a stuffing or as an accompaniment. Here it is offered in the latter role. This possum recipe calls for no parboiling.

SERVES 3–4

1 dressed opossum, trussed
  (see page 127)
salt and pepper
1 tsp. rosemary, crumbled
½ cup water with ½ cup white wine
  (optional)
3 lb. sauerkraut

1 onion, quartered
1 cup beer
2 cups chicken broth
¼ lb. salt pork
20 juniper berries, crushed
1 tsp. freshly ground pepper
1 tsp. caraway seeds

Rub possum inside and out with salt, pepper, and the rosemary. Place it on a rack in a shallow roasting pan, and roast until tender in a preheated 325° oven for about 2–2½ hours.

If you wish, you can put ½ cup water and ½ cup white wine in the pan and baste the animal occasionally.

Meanwhile, wash thoroughly and drain the kraut. Place it in a kettle with the remaining ingredients and bring to a boil. Turn down heat, cover, and simmer for about an hour.

Place drained sauerkraut around the roast possum on a platter and serve with boiled or mashed potatoes.

Game Birds

RUFFED GROUSE

In traditional American parlance "quail on toast" has become a generic term for the supreme epicurean treat, but quail while food for the gods is only one of the delicious game birds available in our country. Originally handsomely endowed with winged treats from doves, snipes, and woodcock to the lordly wild turkeys, we have added to this cornucopia by naturalizing the ring-necked pheasant and two partridges.

Happily, several birds are now available in some markets; most large cities at least have one or two shops that can supply pheasant, quail, partridge, and sometimes other birds as well. Some of these places ship game by mail for those who cannot find them within shopping distance by car. But most winged game eaten in the United States, including ducks and geese, is bagged by hunters; millions of upland birds and waterfowl are shot each year to add to the excellence and variety of American cooking.

In this section are seventy recipes for nine species of game birds; later on in the book, additional recipes for using leftover cooked meat from these birds will be given on pages 337–350 as well. The rest of these preliminary remarks will offer general information useful to the cook.

Handling birds afield and dressing wild birds are discussed in the Appendix, pages 448–449.

How to Determine Age of Game Birds

A good general rule to follow is this: braise rather than roast an old bird. This applies especially to the goose among waterfowl and to the pheasant among the gallinaceous birds. Ducks and the smaller chickenlike birds are usually tender enough to make age determination unnecessary when deciding how to cook them. But it goes without saying that no old bird should be chicken-fried or broiled—so determining the age can be important to the cook.

GALLINACEOUS BIRDS, ESPECIALLY TURKEYS AND PHEASANTS

One fairly reliable way to establish age among these birds is to note the shape of the tip ends of the first two or three primary wing feathers: if they are rounded, the bird is apt to be at least a second-year bird; if definitely pointed they indicate a young bird, probably a bird of that year.

With pheasants and turkeys, which can be tough when old, age determination is important. In the cock bird the length of the spur is a good indicator. A young cock hardly shows more than a nub, whereas the longer spur indicates a somewhat older bird. Beware: don't roast without first parboiling a cock bird with a long spur that is actually upcurved.

Some test for age by holding the bird by the lower mandible and then with a dropping and jerking-up movement test whether the lower beak breaks in the action. In a very old bird it will not break.

If a friend gives you a brace of pheasants bagged on a shooting preserve you can be reasonably sure they are, in wildfowl parlance, "birds of the year," i.e., young birds, for almost all birds released on shooting preserves in the fall were raised from chicks hatched in the spring of that same year. The same goes for chukar partridges. A pheasant that weighs from 2 to 2½ pounds *dressed* is apt to be a young bird. These very young birds will have short tail feathers and a lot of pin feathers on their backs just in front of the "preacher's (or parson's) nose." A young tom turkey won't weigh much over 10 pounds in the feather.

Handling and Hanging Game Birds

As with chickens, the cook faces a certain contradiction when considering the age of game birds. There is such a fetish about tenderness—as if the ability to eat meat with a spoon were the only consideration. After all, flavor is involved in our appreciation of food, too. It is nice to serve tender meats, but it isn't nice to serve *tasteless* tender meats. It is possible to serve young pheasants—birds, say, under fourteen weeks of age—that are less tasty and flavorful than chicken. This comment applies primarily to gallinaceous birds. Such birds hung a few days definitely improve in taste.

Ducks and geese (and woodcock) have ample flavor when young, although we happen to hold to the view that all game birds, upland or waterfowl, profit in taste by being hung for a few days with feathers.

But, and this but is *very* important, do not hang undrawn birds in warm weather, and do not ever hang undrawn birds that have been too badly shot up.

In warm weather, those suddenly unseasonably warm days in the fall, birds should really be drawn in the field and then carried on a strap carrier, not stuffed into a hunting coat or game pouch where they will "heat," i.e., will not cool out. And when driven home they should not be crowded together in a trunk, but laid out where the air can get at them, e.g., on the floor of a station wagon with the window cracked.

Hanging birds in the feather for four or five days in the fall, when it drops into the 30s or low 40s at night and doesn't get up higher than 50 or so in the daytime, does, we believe, improve the bird's taste: this applies, as we have said, especially to young birds. And hanging tenderizes any meat by breaking down the cells some. In the fall, when I was a boy in Indiana, practically every farm's latticed-in back porch or summer kitchen overhang had a string of quail (undrawn) and a rabbit or two (still in the fur, but gutted) hanging in the open breezes. The sight of such hanging game always delighted me, even before I realized that aesthetically I was looking at a bucolic still life or that hanging game improved the taste.

Every wildfowler has experienced November days so unseasonably warm that fly dope was welcome to keep away the mosquitoes. On such days when you lay out the ducks or geese in the shade of the blind, draw them first. And don't pile them up, either, if the shooting has been good.

As every shooter knows, how to hang game birds and how long to hang them are perennial questions for hot debate when discussion of what shot size to use on various game has subsided. The late Ray P. Holland, editor of *Field and Stream* for eighteen years, wrote very amusingly in his book *Scattergunning* about a poll he conducted on the former subject among twenty leading countrywide shooters. Does one hang birds by the head or by the feet? Only one or two were neutral; the remainder split about evenly and each school rallied a variety of reasons and/or rationalizations supporting their views. Mr. Holland concluded with these words, "As for me, I will go on as I always have, hanging them by the feet, unless the birds have been drawn, in which case I reserve the privilege of reversing both myself and the birds and hanging them by the head."

We vote with Mr. Holland.

But in a sense, the latter question—how long to hang them—is probably the more important. The French school hangs undrawn game birds so long (by the head, incidentally) that they drop of their own weight (see Box, page 138). Such birds *seem* spoiled, if the odor and green color of the flanks be taken as the criterion. I will conclude these remarks by saying that on two occasions I ate meat from pheasants that had hung that long. I have to admit that I thought those birds the tastiest I had ever partaken of, yet I myself do not dare hang birds that long by any means. If the weather is cool we hang them three to five days, undrawn unless the bird is badly shot up.

In drawing birds in the field we dry out the cavity with a bunch of grass or sometimes, if we have counted our chickens before they've hatched, with paper towels brought along for the purpose. Never wash out cavities with water if you are going to hang the birds; water, they say, introduces bacteria that hastens spoilage. *Dry* them out.

QUANTITIES AND SERVINGS

It is my theory that one must have a touch of the prodigal if he is to be a good host. A memorable meal must always produce seconds and maybe even thirds, and when it is set forth it must quite obviously appear capable of such extra helpings. There is nothing more pitiable than the server or carver reducing successive servings lest there not be enough to go around. No amount of "fluffing up" the quantities of the servings will truly succeed either. Sharp-eyed guests will estimate with computerlike accuracy just how much is left at each stage of serving and will therefore respond eagerly to offers to another helping only if they see that everyone else could respond similarly without straining the quantity left.

Do not be beguiled by your spouse's comment, "You see, there was plenty for all; all this was left over."

Many a meal will end with food left over, yet with several unappeased guests, for guests will refuse further helpings unless there appears to be a real surfeit. The entrée should appear from the first to be more than enough. To accomplish this you must be wary in reading any recipe. The phrase "Serves 6" should be taken with a grain of salt from most cookbooks, and this is curious, too, for most cookbook writers are themselves hearty eaters and should know better.

Of course, the question of quantity is affected by several factors. An elaborate hors d'oeuvre course (especially if late guests extend the process) can considerably dampen big appetites. The quantity of grouse on hand can be stretched by a hearty hors d'oeuvre tray, and grouse often do not come in prodigal numbers from the game host. Accompanying dishes will also stretch the quantity of the entrée. For example, if the amount of braised goose is borderline, one can stretch it a bit by serving, instead of a lightly curried rice, a lusty barley and red bean dish to accompany the Brussels sprouts or braised celery.

But such tricks are for crisis situations only; the better alternative is to have plenty in the first place. (In passing it may be noted that if one finds himself with a mixed but limited bag of a grouse or two, one pheasant, and perhaps a single wild duck he can still serve eight by producing that grand concoction the game bird cassoulet.) Or more simply a tasty hotchpotch.

Often game comes to households in spurts as it were from the mixed bags (or of accumulation from more than one shoot). Odd quantities of game are common occurrences. One can, of course, rectify skimpy quantities of wild game by purchasing additional birds or one can combine game birds. Three quail cannot make an occasion, but served as a garnish around the platter holding a pheasant or two they can give the host the pleasure of serving this lovely bird as more than a gesture. And there is something Lucullan about a mixed bag anyway once it gets to the table.

Two birds to each guest will suffice perhaps, and most guests will relax if they know they can have two birds. Ideally, though, fifteen birds will seem right to an average board seating six.

Grouse

Although this delicious game bird is as large as a quail, it is the rare occasion that one ever has on hand at one time enough ruffed grouse to make a dinner party, even for six. If a shooter is fortunate enough to have six grouse at one time, he can serve six guests and not feel too guilty about it. Anyone lucky enough to be served a whole grouse will feel compensated amply by quality even though he might eat more.

In a hunting camp in the bush where occasionally the party will kill a limit, I have found that 1½ roast grouse are about right for one person with an appetite sharpened by the elements and the terrain.

Pheasant

Normally a mature cock bird will serve two people, but four lusty diners can often make inroads on a third bird. No one feels really cheated, however, when the host splits a pheasant down the middle and serves him half.

Guests who appreciate game also realize that a sufficiency is not always possible. (Guests of this kind know that it must sometimes be potluck.) A pheasant and two grouse will serve four. A platter laden with three such delicious fowls will be more pleasing, actually, than two pheasants. For one thing grouse is the more delicious of the two.

Partridge

There were originally no native partridges in North America, but two have been introduced, the Hun and the chukar, and I have found that one bird per person is about right. You might get by with three birds for 4 people, although this latter portion makes me nervous.

Quail

Unless your guests themselves "eat like birds," at least two quail per person.

Woodcock

This bird is so rich and well flavored that one bird will serve most any guest. Personally, I can eat two woodcocks, but when I do I feel truly sated. Besides, knowledgeable guests will consider just having woodcock at all a memorable treat.

Wild Turkey

Those fortunate enough to grace their boards with wild turkeys can estimate servings by weight just as with domestic birds. Don't expect the wild variety to provide the proportion of breast meat that the roly-poly domestic birds produce, however. But it will taste better than birds raised on chicken wire.

What does wild turkey taste like? Like domestic turkey, only more so.

Guide to Game Bird Servings and Cooking Times

GAME	AMOUNT PER PERSON	METHOD		TEMP/TIME
Dove	1–1½ birds	Roast	400°	18–22 minutes
		Braise (oven)	325°	30 minutes
		Braise (over fire)		30–35 minutes
		Broil		12–15 minutes
Grouse	1 bird	Roast	350°	20–30 minutes
		On spit		30–35 minutes
		Broiled, in halves		15–20 minutes
		Braise (oven)	325°	60–70 minutes
Partridge	1 bird	Same as grouse		
Pheasant	1 bird will	Roast	350°	35–40 minutes
	serve 2–3	Roast, stuffed	350°	1½ hours
		On spit		45–50 minutes
Ptarmigan	1 bird	Same as grouse		
Quail	2 birds	Roast	400°	20–30 minutes
		Braise (oven)	375°	30–40 minutes
		Broil		10–15 minutes
Snipe	2 birds	Roast	400°	30–35 minutes
		Braise (oven)	350°	35 minutes
		Broil		7–8 minutes
Wild Turkey	1–1½ lb.	Roast, stuffed:		
		8 lb.	350°	2½ hours
		10 lb.		2¾ hours
		12 lb.		3¼ hours
		15 lb.		3½ hours
		20 lb.		3¾–4 hours
Woodcock	1 bird	Roast	350°	20–30 minutes
		Braise		45 minutes
		Broil		8–10 minutes

Time Table for Game Birds on the Rotisserie

This table is intended to be helpful for timing game birds spit-roasted on a rotisserie. The timing assumes the rotisserie is glowing before the spit is inserted, but you must always check for doneness, as size, temperature, etc., of birds can vary.

Before you spit the birds, truss them well in such a way as to bind the drumstick joints to the "preacher's nose" and thus close the vent. Before trussing put a lump of butter in the cavity with a slice or two of onions, herbs if you wish, salt, and pepper. *Be prepared to baste.* A roasting chicken's fat will baste itself, but game birds need help. Try to spit the birds from rear through breast opening so the weight will be distributed evenly around the spit.

Pheasants	40 minutes
Grouse	30 minutes
Chukar	30 minutes
Teal	10–15 minutes
Woodcock	10–15 minutes
Quail	10 minutes
Dove	10 minutes

Hanging Game Birds, French-Style

Every game cook owes it to himself to at least try the French method of hanging game birds. My reason for this recommendation is simple: the best roast pheasant I ever tasted, prepared by a French lady, the late Helene D'Agostino, had been hung by the head, in the feathers, in the French manner. I saw the bird when Helene's novelist husband, Guido, took it down; if he had left it another day it would, indeed, have fallen by its own weight. It had been hanging, "Oh, eight, maybe, ten days, or maybe more," said Guido and it looked it. To be sure it had been hanging in an airy, dry place in November, but I remember well that the flanks of the bird next to the second joints, and the second joints themselves, were of a sickly green color. It had not been drawn, and it was limp as a rag. *But*—it was delicious.

I do hang game birds, especially pheasants, but I just have never had the nerve to hang it as long as French cooks hang it.

Removing Shot Pellets from Game Birds

Even though lead shot is relatively soft, it can be dismaying to bite down on a pellet. Happily, and often to the surprise of the shooter, who likes to think he centered each bird in the pattern, most birds don't receive many pellets. The pellet whose deep penetration bagged the bird usually comes out when the bird is drawn, but sometimes shallowly penetrating pellets may still be in the breast or drumstick. These, as well as other pellets that did penetrate deeply, will leave a dark-colored hole by driving into the entry strands of feathers. Such feathers should be removed by knife point or better by a pair of tweezers. If the pellet is embedded with the feather strands bunched around it, it will come out with the feathers as you probe. If not the knife or tweezer point will "feel" the pellet and you can remove it after you have drawn out the balled feather flues.

Shooters cleaning a number of birds get careless about this sometimes, so the cook may have to exert quality control.

Smoked Game Birds

If you have, or have access to, a smoker, don't neglect smoked pheasant, partridge, quail, duck, and goose, to say nothing of wild turkey. I think any game cook ought to invest in a smoker. I myself swear by the excellent and inexpensive Little Chief Smoker, which L. L. Bean carries in stock.

You can total-smoke birds, but I always part-roast them and finish them in the smoker. Allow 2½–4 hours for total baking, plus smoking, time (see recipes). Whole game cook reputations have been based on serving smoked game birds, for no guest ever forgets his pleasure and never ceases to talk about it.

SMOKED PHEASANT

Truss the bird after seasoning it with salt, pepper, and a dusting of dry tarragon and stuffing it with your favorite stuffing.

Lay it on a rack on a roasting pan, cover with foil, and roast for 45–60 minutes in a 325°–350° oven.

Get your smoker going when the birds are halfway through the roasting process, using hickory chips if you can get them.

When you take the bird out of the oven, paint it well with melted butter and put it immediately into the smoker.

Smoke for 1½–2 hours, checking it for the wonderfully appetizing golden-cinnamon color that the smoking imparts.

Serve as you would any roasted bird.

SMOKED GROUSE, PARTRIDGE, DOVE, OR QUAIL

Sometimes I baste pheasant while it's roasting, but for some reason I always baste chukars using Madeira and butter (see also basting liquid for broiled game meat, page 359). The two biggest birds can be stuffed if you wish, with sliced shallots or scallions and diced celery. Paint each bird with melted butter before smoking.

ROASTING AND SMOKING TIMES

	Roast (325°)	*Smoke*
Grouse	30 minutes	1½ hours
Partridge	25 minutes	1–1½ hours
Dove and Quail	15 minutes	1 hour

For smoked turkey, see page 187.

Preparing Gamebird Giblets

Cooks who have never dressed a chicken from scratch but get their giblets from a small paper bag stuffed in the dressed chicken's cavity, may need a word of advice on preparation of the giblets of gamebirds. The heart is no problem and can be used as is, but the liver and gizzard are something else again.

The Liver: Embedded in an edge of the organ is a visible green sac, and its green liquid content is, indeed, "as bitter as gall." This sac must be cut away, and in doing so, you should take a bit of liver tissue with it to make sure you don't puncture it. If the gall sac appears to have been broken before you cut it away, you can check this by touching your tongue to the liver itself. If it tastes bitter, throw the liver away. Note: You don't need to look for a gall sac on a deer liver; deer have no gall.

The Gizzard: This tough muscle, the "stomach" of gallinaceous birds, contains the gravel ingested by the bird to grind up its food. The gizzard achieves this first stage of digestion by slow contortion and writhing, thus rubbing the gravel against the seeds, corn, and other solid food matter. Cut into the gizzard so that it lies open like a bivalve. Empty out the gravel and food matter. The lining of the gizzard is a corrugated, yellowish layer that can be skinned out. A knife edge can start the process; then this inner skin can be pulled off easily by the fingers, usually all in one piece. When the corrugated lining has been removed, wash the gizzard under the faucet.

Remember, the heart and gizzard take five or six times as long to cook as the liver, whether you are sautéeing or stewing.

Pheasant

This gaudy naturalized citizen has become so thoroughly "native" since the 1880s as to be a standard American game bird. When the cock goes up out of some brushy fence row, his cackle is superfluous; we don't need it to be properly impressed with this fine bird's showy beauty. Nor do we need word from him to remind us how delicious he is on the family board. Pheasants from the wild are delectable fare, bringing to the table a kind of wild chicken flavor that all diners find pleasing. Preserve pheasants—usually young birds of the year—need to be hung a few days when the temperature permits to bring up their latent flavor. Mature birds from the open range can be tough, so see page 133 for a few words on how to determine age in older birds. See the Appendix for other pertinent comments on handling game birds. Pheasants normally weigh: males, 2 pounds 11 ounces; females, 2 pounds 1 ounce; up to 4 pounds for males and 3 pounds 4 ounces for hens at extremes.

ROAST PHEASANT WITH HERBS—
UNDER THE SKIN

My late fishing partner, the wildlife artist Lou Henderson, described this recipe to me, or rather described the method; the stuffing is my own. The method is simply an extension of the technique described in the box on larding and barding, page 18.

The underskin "stuffing" can be made in a trice with a food processor or blender, but a mortar and pestle will serve too.

4 shallots, quartered
6 medium-size mushrooms, sliced
1 tsp. basil
2 tsp. tarragon
8 Tb. chopped parsley

1 Tb. brandy
4 Tb. butter, at room temperature
2 pheasants
salt and pepper

Put the shallots, mushrooms, basil, tarragon, parsley, and brandy in the food processor and, turning on and off for short "takes," mince to a fine texture, then strain off excess liquid.

Now add the butter and swiftly by the on-and-off routine make a paste. Set it in the refrigerator.

As in the recipe on page 165 loosen the skin from the breast meat, beginning at the neck end. This time continue until you have also loosened the skin from the thighs. This sounds difficult but it really isn't. Use only your fingers.

Salt and pepper the birds inside and out. With a knife or spreader insert the paste on the meat under the skin. If you have some of the paste left over, put it inside the birds. Rearrange the skin to normal.

Truss the birds (see page 449) and roast in a 350° oven for an hour or until thigh is tender.

Remove birds to a hot platter and snip off trussings.

NOTE: You can stir flour into the fat in the bottom of the roasting pan to mix, cooking a minute while you scrape up all the browned bits. Add half water (or chicken stock) and half cream and stir well to make a delicious gravy.

═══════ PHEASANT FLAMED WITH APPLES ═══════

This recipe comes from Gerard-Denis-Marie Lanceveau of Ambrosia in New York. It is a dish typical of his birthplace in the Auge Valley in France.

SERVES 2–3

salt and freshly ground black
  pepper
1 pheasant
3 Tb. butter
4 small tart apples
4 slices dense white bread, crusts
  removed

4 tsp. gooseberry jam
⅓ cup Calvados or applejack
½ cup crème fraîche or half heavy
  cream and half sour cream left
  at room temperature 4–5 hours

Salt and pepper the pheasant inside and out, then put 1 tablespoon of the butter in the cavity. Place in a small roasting pan with ½ cup water.

Roast in a preheated 350° oven 1 hour.

Meanwhile peel and core the apples, leaving them whole. Sauté them in 2 tablespoons butter, turning and basting them until they are just tender; don't let them become mushy.

Toast the bread and butter it.

When the pheasant is done, put it on a warm platter. Surround it with the apples placed on the toast. Fill the cavity of each apple with a teaspoonful of gooseberry jam. Keep warm.

Warm the Calvados or applejack and pour it over the pheasant. Set aflame.

Pour the cream into the roasting pan juices, scraping up all the good brown bits. Serve this on the side.

══ ROAST STUFFED PHEASANT WITH SORREL ══

SERVES 4

2 pheasants
1 cup cold water
1 cup chicken or duck stock
1 small onion
¼ lb. mushrooms, chopped
4 scallions or shallots, minced
6 Tb. butter

1 cup cooked rice
salt and freshly ground pepper
⅓ cup puréed cooked sorrel*
strips of pork fatback or cooking oil
1 cup heavy cream

Cover the necks and gizzards of the birds with 1 cup cold water and 1 cup chicken or duck stock and let simmer with the onion.

Prepare the stuffing by sautéing the chopped mushrooms and scallions or shallots in 3 tablespoons of the butter for about 5 minutes, then add the rice to warm through and season well with salt, pepper, and 2 tablespoons of the sorrel.

Wipe out the cavity of the birds with a damp cloth, salt lightly, then fill them with the mushroom-rice stuffing. Truss the birds (see page 449) and rub them with the rest of the butter. Either place pieces of pork fat on the breasts or saturate a piece of cheesecloth with oil and cover the breasts. Roast in a preheated 425° oven for 50 minutes, basting frequently.

Remove birds and pour off excess fat. Add to the roasting pan the broth, which should have reduced to 1 cup or less (if not, boil down rapidly), plus the cream. Boil hard, scraping up the brown from the pan and, when thickened, swirl in the remaining sorrel. Test seasoning, and salt and pepper if necessary.

To serve, split the pheasants, distributing stuffing evenly, and pour the sauce over.

*Sorrel can be purchased puréed and packed in jars imported from Europe. It is seen more frequently now in farmers' markets, and it is easy to grow your own—it's just sourgrass. If using fresh, remove stems and center rib if stringy. Sauté a big bunch in 2 Tb. butter; it will wilt and turn greenish-gray. Cook, stirring, until water has evaporated—it is then ready to use or freeze for future use.

══ ROAST PHEASANT WITH ══
WILD RICE AND MUSHROOMS

SERVES 6

½ cup wild rice
½ cup butter
2 lb. mushrooms, sliced
7 shallots, chopped
2 pheasants
4 strips bacon

4–5 chicken livers or pheasant livers and 3 chicken livers
2 Tb. flour
1½–2 cups chicken broth
½ tsp. tarragon

Prepare and cook the wild rice (see page 381) and set aside in a bowl.

Sauté the mushrooms in the butter until most of the juices have been reduced; add 3 of the chopped shallots and sauté a minute or so longer.

Mix the cooked wild rice, the mushrooms, and the 3 shallots and stuff the birds with it. Then truss the pheasants and skewer the vents (or sew).

With toothpicks pin a strip of bacon along each side of the breast of each stuffed, trussed bird or insert it under the breast skin (see page 165).

Roast birds in a preheated 375° oven in shallow roaster with a foil tent laid over the birds for 40 minutes, basting often with butter.

Remove the foil tent and continue roasting for 30 minutes, basting 4 or 5 times with the pan's juices.

During the last 10 minutes put livers in roasting pan, turning once.

Remove the birds and livers, and keep them warm. Skim off all but 2 tablespoons of the fat in the roasting pan, add remaining shallots, and cook a few minutes. Sprinkle in flour, stir over low heat, scraping up all brown bits, then add chicken broth slowly, stirring constantly. Add tarragon. Cook down until you have a sauce the thickness of cream. Chop up reserved livers and stir or mash them into the sauce.

ROAST PHEASANT STUFFED WITH GRUYÈRE AND NOODLES

This recipe is an adaptation of Evan Jones's recipe for roast chicken to be found in his wonderful book *The World of Cheese*. The recipe could be adapted for partridge and grouse, of course, with four partridge or three ruffed grouse providing the rough equivalent of two medium-size pheasants.

SERVES 6

3 pheasants	½ cup heavy cream
salt	freshly ground pepper
8-oz. package wide noodles	½ tsp. dried sage
1 qt. chicken broth	1 carrot, cut in ¼″ slices
¼ lb. mushrooms	1 onion, coarsely chopped
¼ lb. butter	Mornay sauce (see page 364)
½ cup freshly grated Gruyère	

Wipe the pheasants with a damp cloth and sprinkle a little salt inside.

Cook the noodles 4–5 minutes in broth, until half done.

Wipe mushrooms with a damp cloth, trim ends, and mince stems with a sharp knife; slice caps thinly. Sauté both in 4 tablespoons butter in a large saucepan.

Drain noodles well (reserving broth), and stir into mushrooms. Mix in Gruyère and 4 tablespoons of the cream, adding salt and pepper to taste and the sage.

Stuff the pheasants with the noodle mixture, scraping juices from the pan; skewer openings and truss legs and wings.

Put remaining butter in a roasting pan with the carrot and the onion, and heat until the butter melts. Roll the pheasant in the butter until it is well coated, then put the roasting pan in the oven at 450°, adding from time to time a little hot broth from the drained noodles.

When the pheasant begins to brown—after about 15 minutes—in the oven, turn it breast side down and cover the roasting pan. Reduce heat to 325° and

Stock from Roast Game Bird Carcasses

Since game birds are not as common in most kitchens as chicken, the cook should make sure to get all the good out of each of them. Frozen stock from the carcasses of carved roast pheasants is handy for future use.

MAKES ABOUT 3 CUPS

1–2 carved pheasant carcasses, plus giblets and neck if you haven't used them
1 onion, chopped (or an equivalent of dried onion flakes)

1 carrot, sliced thin
1 celery top, with leaves scissored small
5 bay leaves
¼ tsp. thyme and/or tarragon
salt and pepper

In a stew pot (with lid) bring to boil the above with enough water to cover by an inch or so, then simmer for 2 hours, salting only slightly in the beginning. Taste to determine strength; sometimes one can add hot water and still have a strong broth. Correct seasoning. Strain, cool, and store in freezer in a plastic container with a lid. Be sure to label the container and date it, e.g., Pheasant broth, 11/15/83.

When you need it, run hot water over container held upside down under faucet until whole contents drop out. Put frozen block in stew pan, melt quantity you need, then put unthawed remainder back in container and return to freezer.

Gruyère-Stuffed Pheasant (continued)
continue roasting 25–35 minutes, basting frequently with more hot broth and pan juices. Remove cover from the pan, salt and pepper the pheasant lightly, and cook about 10 minutes longer. Serve with Mornay sauce made with the reserved broth, thinned with remaining cream.

PHEASANT SOUVAROFF

Pheasant with Liver and Mushroom Stuffing

Each fall I take my goose kills to a dressing establishment near the blinds. Here I not only get the giblets from my own geese, but usually come away with two or three pounds of livers given to me as a gift, since many shooters do not bother to keep the giblets (such establishments are licensed to sell only their plucking and cleaning services). After such a windfall I make this dish, but of course the recipe is almost as good when made with pheasant livers plus chicken livers. The authentic dish is not only made with fresh foie gras but with fresh truffles; I have never managed the truffles. Grouse or chukars can be prepared this way, too.

The recipe is adapted from an old book, *Paris Cuisine*, now out of print, by James Beard and Alexander Watt.

SERVES 4

8 mushrooms, sliced
1 garlic clove, sliced
2 Tb. butter
½ cup cognac
½ cup port wine
½ tsp. tarragon
1 tsp. mushroom catsup or
  Kitchen Bouquet

½ lb. foie gras or pheasant liver
  plus chicken livers
2 pheasants, dressed
salt and pepper
8 slices bacon
1 cup chicken broth

Sauté the mushrooms and garlic in the butter for 2–3 minutes. Add the cognac, half the port, the tarragon, and the mushroom catsup or Kitchen Bouquet and cook for a minute together, then add the livers and cook 2–3 minutes more.

Stuff the birds with the mixture, salt and pepper lightly, truss lightly, and pin a bacon slice along each side of each breast.

In a shallow baking pan, in which you have laid down a bedding of 4 bacon slices, roast the birds for 40 minutes at 375°, basting often.

While the birds are roasting reduce the cup of chicken broth by half, add the remaining port, and reserve.

Remove bacon slices and trussing string when birds have roasted, and place pheasants in a casserole. Leave the oven on.

From roasting pan remove bacon and pour off fat. Stir the broth and wine mixture into the dredgings, then bring to a boil and hold it there for a minute or two. Pour it over the pheasants.

Lay a piece of heavy foil over the casserole, set on lid to make a tight fit, and return to the oven for 15 minutes more.

═══════════ PHEASANT MARENGO ═══════════

This recipe can be prepared with any of the gallinaceous game birds, but if used with grouse, partridge, or quail do not disjoint the smaller birds, but rather truss them closely and cook whole.

The dish is an adaptation of chicken Marengo, said to have been served to Napoleon after his hard-won victory over the Austrians at Marengo, Italy. His chef prepared a quick pickup improvised dinner using what he had available. To the chicken simmered with tomatoes, he added, not shrimp, but crayfish, and a fried egg. Here we make do with shrimp and a boiled egg to keep the dish as traditional as may be.

SERVES 6

2 pheasants, cut into serving pieces
salt and pepper
3 tablespoons flour
2 Tb. butter
2 Tb. lard or cooking oil
1 medium onion, chopped fine
2 shallots or 1 garlic clove, minced
½ lb. mushrooms, sliced
2 bay leaves
½ tsp. thyme
½ tsp. marjoram

1 cup drained canned tomatoes
  (or fresh peeled)
½ cup dry white wine
1 Tb. tomato paste
½ cup chicken broth
¼ cup ripe olives
⅓ pound cooked shelled small
  shrimp or 1 5-oz. can cocktail
  shrimp
1 egg, hard-boiled and sliced
2 sprigs parsley

Shake the pheasant pieces in a paper bag with salt, pepper, and flour to coat. In a skillet sauté the pieces in melted butter and lard until chicken pieces are nicely browned—about 15 minutes over medium heat.

Remove pieces to a casserole and sauté the onion, shallots or garlic, and mushrooms. Add to casserole. Do not brown. Add the remaining ingredients, save for the olives, shrimp, egg, and parsley, cover the casserole, and simmer until done. Another 20–25 minutes should suffice.

About 5 minutes before the pheasant is done, add the olives and the shrimp.

When serving, slice the egg on top of the sauce in the sauceboat or garnish the edge of the serving platter with egg slices and sprigs of parsley.

Removing Pheasant or Turkey Leg Tendon

On biggish gallinaceous game birds the drumstick becomes a chore to eat because of the strong tendons in it. These can be removed if you obtain your bird with the scaly part of the leg and the feet still on it. I always freeze game birds with lower leg and feet intact in order later to pull out the tendons.

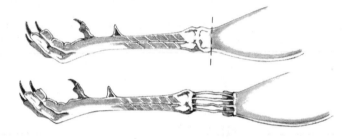

To do this (it is not always 100 percent possible) cut around the skin above the "knee" joint and snap the knee joint against the bend. You can use the edge of your meat block or work table if you find you can't do it with your hands. Jiggle the leg to loosen the joint fully and then pull on the foot. The tendons, or most of them, will pull out. If you can see or locate the ends of remaining tendons, just seize each with a pair of pliers and finish the job.

═ BAKED PHEASANT BREASTS IN ORANGE SAUCE ═
—A QUICK DISH

When you have promised a game dinner, then find yourself trapped for time, here is an astonishingly fine dish that comes right out of three commercial packages; you need do nothing but assemble it and turn on the oven. If you wish you can use the drumsticks and second joints as well as the breasts of *two* pheasants. In this case, you should take the time to sauté in oil and brown the dark meat pieces.

This dish is courtesy of my friend Adele Fruiterman of Maryland. Serve it with brown rice and broccoli.

SERVES 4–6

THE SAUCE
⅓ of a 1 lb. 2 oz. jar
  orange marmalade
1 bottle French dressing

½ cup water
1 package Lipton's
  onion soup

THE PHEASANT
4 pheasant breasts as 8
  supremes, or 2 pheasants,
  using dark meat as well

About 2 hours before you intend to serve, mix and stir all sauce ingredients into a shallow baking dish.

Lay in the pheasant pieces.

Preheat the oven to 350°.

When the guests arrive for cocktails, set the pan in the oven and bake for about an hour, turning the pieces a time or two in the process.

When your guests compliment you—as they will—keep your own counsel. What they don't know won't hurt them.

NOTE: If you use quail, partridge, doves, or woodcock for this dish, you may wish to use the whole birds split down the back with your poultry shears and flattened with the heel of your hand. A bit less oven time for smaller birds. See chart, page 137.

STEWED PHEASANT WITH SAGE DUMPLINGS

When you have a brace of long-spurred, tough old cock pheasants consider this old-fashioned stew, and give the dish a lift with sage dumplings.

SERVES 6–8

THE PHEASANTS
2 large pheasants, cut up as for
  frying
2 carrots, thinly sliced
2 medium onions, thinly sliced
1 rib celery with leaves, chopped
½ tsp. savory
½ tsp. marjoram

1½ tsp. salt
½ tsp. pepper
½ tsp. mace
2 tsp. mushroom catsup or
  Worcestershire sauce
½ cup white wine

THE DUMPLINGS
2 cups flour
3 tsp. baking powder
1 tsp. salt

3 tsp. rubbed Dalmatian sage
2 eggs
⅔ cup milk

Place pheasant pieces and the remaining pheasant ingredients in a casserole and add just enough boiling water to cover. Bring to a boil, cover, and simmer for 1–1½ hours.

When pheasant pieces are tender, remove them but keep warm in a pot with a little sauce. Make the dumplings while the broth continues to bubble. Thicken broth, if you have decided it needs thickening, with flour and cold water paste.

Sift the flour, baking powder, and salt, then stir in the sage, being sure to distribute it evenly.

Beat the eggs with the milk and stir into the flour mixture. Drop spoonfuls of the dough into the boiling broth. Cover and cook gently for 15 minutes. Do not lift lid to peek.

Arrange pheasant pieces on a platter, surround with the dumplings, pour over some of the sauce, and serve remainder in a sauceboat.

===== HANK WALKER'S OVEN-FRIED PHEASANT =====

This recipe is by courtesy of Henry Walker via Ben Pearson via Bill End of L.L. Bean. "Done this way the pheasant remains very moist—excellent," he writes.

SERVES 2–3

flour
salt and pepper
1 pheasant, cut into serving pieces
   (see page 150)
2 eggs beaten with 1 Tb. water

36 Ritz crackers, rolled medium
   fine
oil or lard for deep frying
½ cup melted butter

Mix flour with salt and pepper in a bag. Add the pheasant pieces and shake to dust them all over.

Dip the pheasant pieces in the egg mixture, then roll in cracker crumbs.

Deep-fry for 15 minutes in oil heated to 350°. Remove and dry on paper towels.

Now roll the fried pieces in the melted butter and spread on a baking sheet. Bake 30 minutes in a preheated 350° oven.

===== PHEASANT COQ AU VIN =====

This is a delicious way to serve pheasant; braised thus in burgundy it is an appetizing-looking dish as well as a richly flavorful one. Even an old cock with spurs will be good in this dish. Save giblets and lower backs if you intend to make your own stock.

Boiled potatoes sprinkled with parsley, green peas, and red wine are traditionally served with coq au vin.

SERVES 4–6

2 pheasants, cut into frying pieces
   (see page 150)
¼ lb. salt pork diced into ½"
   cubes
flour
3 Tb. brandy
1 cup sliced scallions or scallions
   plus a leek or two
12–15 whole mushrooms
12–15 small pearl onions

2 cloves garlic, smashed
½ tsp. marjoram
½ tsp. thyme
1 bay leaf
1 tsp. salt
¼ tsp. white or black pepper
2½ cups burgundy
1 cup chicken broth (or your own
   pheasant stock)
2 tsp. tomato paste or catsup

Unless you decided to use canned chicken broth, put 1½ cups salted water on to boil, then add the giblets and the rear back pieces, and let simmer.

Wash the bird pieces and pat dry.

In a metal casserole or Dutch oven try out the salt pork until the cracklings are brown. Remove to a paper towel to drain.

Coat the pheasant pieces in flour and brown them slowly in the fat (add butter if needed) over medium heat, turning and readjusting the pieces. This will take 10–12 minutes. Don't rush it.

Spoon the brandy over the bird pieces and flame it, then set aside the pieces.

Spoon off all but 3 tablespoons of fat and add the scallions, mushrooms, onions, and garlic cloves. Cover and braise the vegetables over a low heat in the fat and their own liquids—10–12 minutes.

Remove from heat and stir in 2½ tablespoons flour, marjoram, thyme, bay leaf, salt, and pepper, distributing evenly among the vegetables. Now gradually add the burgundy and stock (either chicken or your own that has been simmering). Stir in the tomato paste or catsup, bring to a bubble, lower the heat, and simmer for 3–4 minutes.

Add the pheasant pieces and the cracklings. Cover and bake in a 350° oven for about an hour.

SMOTHERED PHEASANT

This recipe is from Mrs. Elaine G. Kinney of Phillips, Maine. She says the dish is good with grouse or quail, too. Of course, smaller birds cook in less time.

SERVES 2–3

1 pheasant, cut in serving pieces
 (see page 150)
flour for dredging
salt and pepper (to season flour)

½ cup lard or shortening
2 cups sliced onions
1 cup water, milk, or light cream

Roll the pheasant pieces in seasoned flour.

In a Dutch oven, brown meat slowly on both sides in hot fat, turning once. Top with the sliced onions; pour in the water, milk, or light cream. Cover tightly and cook on top of range over low heat or bake at 325° until tender, about 1 hour.

THELMA CLARK'S STEWED FRICASSEE OF PHEASANT

Thelma Clark, a Bean retiree, contributed this recipe.

SERVES 4

2 pheasants, cut in 4–6 pieces
flour
salt and pepper

3 Tb. butter
2 cups thin cream

Roll pheasants in flour seasoned with salt and pepper. Brown thoroughly in the butter in a large skillet. Add the cream. Set on back of stove, covered, to simmer for about 1 hour. Check seasoning.

Cutting up a Pheasant for Sautéing or Other Dishes

In Indiana, home of the best "fried" chicken, the bird is traditionally cut up into 10 pieces: 2 wings, 2 drumsticks, 2 thighs (or second joints), 1 pulley bone or wishbone, 1 breast (2 pieces can be made of it), the forward back and ribs, the nether back.

The job is done in the following sequence and manner:

Lay the bird on its side, feet toward you; lift leg and slice close to body and down to hip joint. Break it loose at the joint and finish slicing through. Bend the "knee" joint and slice through from on top until you find joint; continue between the joint once joint is severed; cut up from underneath to complete production of drumstick and thigh.

To remove the wing, lift it by the elbow and cutting close to the body, find the joint and slice it through the socket.

Repeat process on other side.

To produce the wishbone, cut across in front of breastbone, continuing ing the slice down each side; with three fingers pull the loose meat away: This piece of white meat will contain the pulley bone (*furcula* to the biologist).

Place bird neckside down, tail up, and cut down until you can finish by breaking the breast away.

Divide remainder of bird in half by breaking it in two at the small of the back.

PHEASANT POT PIE

There are many ways to make a bird pie, but I like to give this ancient dish just a touch of the blend of flavors that characterized such pies in the Middle Ages when they were standard fare. Our Continental forebears used saffron for color as well as taste, but it's not necessary if you find it too costly today (you can even color the pie with a few drops of yellow vegetable coloring).

SERVES 4

1 pheasant (or 2 grouse or 3 chukars)
½ water and ½ white wine to cover
1 small onion, stuck with 3 cloves
1 rib celery with leaves, sliced
8 peppercorns
1 tsp. salt
½ tsp. thyme or tarragon (or ¼ tsp. of each)
1 bay leaf
3 medium potatoes, cubed
1 medium onion, diced, or 4 shallots, minced

2 carrots, sliced
1 rib celery, sliced
4 Tb. butter
3 Tb. flour
3 cups broth
1 pinch saffron, or see above suggestion
¼ tsp. cinnamon
¼ tsp. nutmeg
½ Tb. Worcestershire or Harvey's sauce
cream (optional)
pie crust or biscuit dough (Bisquick can be used)

Simmer the bird in a kettle in wine-water to cover, along with clove-studded onion, celery with leaves, peppercorns, salt, thyme or tarragon, and bay leaf until pheasant leg is tender, perhaps 1–1½ hours. Remove the bird to cool.

Cook the potatoes in the same stock until they are tender (you can put the potatoes in for the last 20 minutes of step 1 or you can cook them separately). Retain 3 cups of the stock.

Bone and dice the bird.

Prepare dough for the crust.

Sauté onion or shallots, carrots, and celery in the butter until carrot is soft. Stir in the flour, cook a minute or so, and then off heat stir in the broth, saffron, cinnamon, nutmeg, and sauce. Return to the heat and simmer this gravy for 3–4 minutes, correcting for thickness with cream.

Put diced pheasant, potatoes, and other vegetables in the sauce in a casserole, cover with crust, and bake in a 500° oven for about 15 minutes or until crust is brown.

BRAISED PHEASANT MARSALA

I am indebted to *The Gourmet Cookbook* for this notable recipe for pheasant. If I were allowed only one way to prepare pheasant this would be my choice. The recipe here is my adaptation for the purposes of this book. Two grouse or three chukars may be substituted, but if smaller birds are used, cut sautéing time to 8–9 minutes and baking time to 30–40 minutes.

SERVES 2

1 pheasant	1 clove garlic, sliced
the pheasant liver	1 Tb. flour
1 tangerine, peeled	2 Tb. dry Marsala
4 Tb. lard	¼ cup pheasant or chicken broth
12 medium to large mushrooms	½ tsp. crushed fennel seed
3 Tb. butter	6 juniper berries, crushed
4 shallots or scallions, finely chopped	

Stuff pheasant with the liver and tangerine and truss tightly.

Melt the lard in a deep skillet (to reduce spatter) and brown the bird for 15 minutes, turning it on all sides and basting the upper side all the while with the hot fat. Put pheasant in casserole (I use a white glazed duck's head lid casserole) and keep warm.

In same fat sauté the mushrooms until moisture is almost gone. Remove mushrooms to the casserole.

Add butter to the fat remaining and sauté the shallots and garlic.

Add flour and cook lightly (but do not brown), stirring for a minute or so. Off heat add Marsala and broth. Return to heat, stirring as the sauce thickens; if more liquid is needed to make a viable sauce to pour, add it.

Add fennel seed and juniper berries.

Pour all over pheasant and mushrooms and bake in a preheated 450° oven for 40–50 minutes.

PHEASANT TIKKA

This recipe, being Asiatic, is appropriate for pheasant, the Asian bird. It is a spicy pheasant dish from Pakistan and most delicious. Serve it with plain or saffron rice or with rice mixed with green peas.

SERVES 4–6

1 cup yogurt
½ tsp. ground coriander seeds
1 Tb. chili powder
¼ tsp. freshly ground pepper
½ tsp. salt

1 tsp. sugar
1–4 cloves garlic, crushed
2 pheasants, cut up as described
  on page 150

Combine all ingredients except the pheasants. Pierce pheasant pieces thoroughly all around with a fork. Brush generously with the yogurt mixture and let stand 30 minutes, during which time repeat the brushing process. Place pheasant pieces on foil-lined broiler and roast slowly in oven at 350° for 30–40 minutes.

PHEASANT OR GAME BIRD
COCK-A-LEEKIE

The leek was once as ubiquitous in cookery as the onion; indeed in the Middle Ages the little garden plot of each cottager was called a "leekie." In this Scottish dish the leek's bouquet, gentler than the onion's, melds beautifully with the light flavors of pheasant or grouse. The dish serves a game dinner well, too, for it provides a bird or poultry "course" and a soup course in the same dish; and it serves easily and can be prepared while a venison roast is in the oven.

It has a special function, too, when your larder is limited to a lone pheasant or a grouse or a brace of partridge insufficient for a full poultry course.

SERVES 8

8 cups water
1 pheasant (or 2 chukars), trussed
the giblets
3 sprigs parsley
¼ tsp. tarragon or thyme
2 bay leaves

8 leeks, with most of green cut off
  and cut in two and each piece
  cut in half lengthwise
salt
white peppercorns, crushed

Place water, bird, giblets, parsley, tarragon or thyme, bay leaves, 3 of the leeks, salt, and white pepper in a deep pot. Bring to a boil and simmer for 1–1½ hours.

Remove bird, and set aside to cool so you can handle.

Strain the broth and put back in the pot, along with the rest of the leeks. Simmer for 30 minutes.

While the leeks are softening, remove meat from the birds, dice it small, and add it to the hot broth.

NOTE: In Scotland, they add 8–10 prunes to the broth when the final leeks go in, but I never do. However, I sometimes add a tablespoon or so of barley to cook for the final 30 minutes.

Game Birds and Lemon Juice

Sometimes game birds and poultry that have been refrigerated for a day or two in the market or that have taken on a slight "icebox odor" can be freshened by squeezing on a few drops of lemon juice and spreading the juice over the surfaces with your fingertips. Also, on occasions, the second joint and/or cavity has some lingering odor of the innards. Lemon juice "sweetens" the bird in such cases.

When supremes are to be made of breast meat of birds and poultry, it's good to smear a sprinkle of lemon juice over them and then leave them covered in a dish for later preparation that day or the next.

Lemon juice, or even a diluted mild vinegar, can also have a tenderizing function on old birds, say an old cock pheasant. After all, it is the acids in marinades (lemon juice, vinegar, or wine) that are the tenderizing agents for meats less than tender.

We always use lemon juice in this fashion on fish fillets. Both supremes and fish fillets can be frozen (the latter for shorter periods) after lemon juice has been used to lightly rub their surfaces.

═════ CASSEROLE OF GAME BIRD MARSALA ═════

This recipe, which can be fixed on top of the stove in a skillet or in the oven in a casserole, reveals why I am partial to dry Marsala. It is a peer of both sherry and Madeira. Either of the latter can be substituted for Marsala in this recipe. See page 159 for a similar casserole, using whole birds trussed.

SERVES 4–6

2 pheasants, cut up as you would a frying chicken
2 sets giblets
4 Tb. flour, salted and peppered
1 tsp. thyme
4 Tb. lard or a mixture of 2 Tb. oil and 2 Tb. butter
1 cup Marsala

3 cloves garlic or 3 cloves shallots, minced
3 bay leaves
½ lb. mushrooms, sliced
2 Tb. butter
½ tsp. rosemary or ¼ tsp. tarragon
¼ cup warm brandy

Shake the pheasant pieces along with the giblets in the salted and peppered flour mixed with half the thyme.

Heat a big skillet of a size to crowd the pheasant pieces. Melt the lard and when sizzling put in the pheasant pieces and giblets and, turning often, sauté them until they are golden brown, about 10–15 minutes.

Add about 3 tablespoons of the Marsala, the garlic or shallots, and bay leaves. Cover and simmer for 5 minutes more.

Sauté the sliced mushrooms in a separate skillet in the butter for about three minutes until the liquid has evaporated. Add these to the pheasant pan, add rosemary or tarragon, then cover and cook at a strong simmer for 10 minutes. After that remove the lid and continue simmering for another 10 minutes.

Serve in a deep platter. At table pour the brandy over the pheasant and flame it.

Grouse

I love *all* game birds, but if pressed I would have to say that ruffed grouse is first among equals when taste is the criterion. Whether it be labeled partridge in Maine or ruffy in Michigan, it is found in the toughest cover of any game bird. Surely there are more flushed-but-unshot-at grouse than any other game bird, for the grouse is a bird of the heavy woods. It is a hard, hard bird to hit, and the shotgunner who learns to begin to mount the gun when he first *hears* the whirry throb of the flush is the man who may have a possible target when he first *sees* the bird. It is usually a matter of two or three seconds.

It is because the bird is hard to come by that my cousin-in-law, Kay Bailey, excellent cook and aficionada of game dishes, said once, "I want grice not grouse." Alas, I fear I have never served her more than one bird at a time.

A Note on Spruce Grouse

The dark flesh of this bird of the deep evergreen northern woods, inordinately tame in the woods compared to its cousin, the ruffed grouse, has been denigrated by those who have only tasted it after it has become "sprucey." The bird does feed heavily on the needles and buds of the spruce and during the winter months perhaps almost exclusively on such a diet. But before the snows of winter close in on its northern range the spruce grouse varies its diet considerably.

I have eaten spruce grouse in late November that were sprucey indeed, but I have also eaten the bird in September in Alaska when its dark flesh was not sprucey at all, but tasted very much like the delicious ptarmigan.

Any recipe for ptarmigan (or any other grouse or partridge for that matter) will serve well for early-season spruce grouse. Actually, though I seldom seek out the spruce grouse as a shooter, I rather like it even when on the sprucey side.

Weights of Grouse

Ruffed grouse weigh from a pound to 1¾ pounds or a bit more; blue grouse from 2 pounds for hens to 2 pounds 9 ounces for cocks; spruce grouse 1 to 1½ pounds. Sharp-tailed grouse, farthest east ranger of the western grouse, weigh for males 2 pounds 2 ounces to 2 pounds 6 ounces, females from 1 pound 13 ounces to 2 pounds 3 ounces. The greater prairie chicken is about the same size as the sharp-tailed; the lesser prairie chicken usually 1¾ to just under 2 pounds.

Sage grouse are our largest grouse, by far, with considerable sexual dimorphism as to size; males weigh almost twice as much as females—males 5½ to 6 pounds or so; females 2 pounds 10 ounces to 3 pounds, 3 ounces.

═══════ GRILLED GROUSE OR PARTRIDGE ═══════
STUFFED WITH OYSTERS À LA ROCKEFELLER

This dish can be prepared by roasting the birds in the oven instead of grilling them on a grill or spit—and it can only be called Lucullan. The idea for it came up while the late Larry Koller and I were eating Baked Clams Martha* during a Catskill trout fishing trip. Whether Larry ever tried to duplicate it, I do not know, but I worked out this recipe, later tried it on chicken, and still later on chukar partridges. It's as good as it sounds. It usually becomes a conversation piece with guests for months afterward.

SERVES 4–6

4 tsp. butter
5 Tb. chopped shallots or scallions
4 Tb. chopped celery
4 Tb. chopped parsley
2 cloves garlic, minced
½ cup chopped raw spinach
about ½ cup bread crumbs
½ tsp. chervil or ¼ tsp. tarragon

¼ scant tsp. cayenne
salt and pepper
20 small oysters, drained
   (retain oyster liquor)
4 partridges or grouse, or
   2 pheasants
½ cup basting liquid: dry white
   wine with 4 Tb. melted butter

Sauté in skillet, using half the butter, the shallots or scallions, celery, parsley, and garlic until shallots are light golden and celery is tender (4–6 minutes). Add the chopped spinach and more butter if needed and cook and stir-fry (Chinese fashion) for a minute or so. Now, off heat, stir and mix in the bread crumbs, chervil, and cayenne. You want to have a moist but not runny stuffing. If too dry, moisten with oyster liquor; if too moist, add more bread crumbs. Salt and pepper.

Stuff raw oysters (10 for each of 2 pheasants, 5 for each partridge or grouse) and a portion of the dressing in each bird, and sew up cavity.

Roast or grill, basting with wine-and-butter mix. Stuffed birds take one-fourth longer than unstuffed.

*Whether that lady still runs a summer restaurant in the Catskills now or not I do not know, but her baked clams on the half shell were glorious.

ALEX DELICATA'S GROUSE CACCIATORE STYLE

Here's a touch of Italian cuisine from one of L.L. Bean's resident chefs. See pages 24, 41, 212, and 236 for other Delicata recipes.

Serve with broiled green peppers dressed with oil and vinegar along with a room-temperature rosé.

SERVES 2–4

¼ cup olive oil
1 clove garlic, crushed
1 medium onion, chopped
1 medium green pepper, chopped
2–4 grouse, quartered

16-oz. can tomatoes
dash of oregano
¼ tsp. dried basil
½ tsp. dried parsley
dash of pepper

In a Dutch oven or heavy deep pot heat olive oil to medium-high heat. Brown the garlic in the hot oil. Remove before the garlic begins to burn. Add the onion and green pepper. Cook for several minutes, then brown the grouse in the mixture until the surfaces are seared. Add the can of slightly mashed tomatoes (do not drain liquid out of tomato can) and the oregano, basil, parsley, and pepper. Cook uncovered until tender. Simmer for about 45 minutes, turning grouse several times.

GROUSE WITH MUSHROOMS ON LIVER-SPREAD TOAST

SERVES 4–6

THE TOAST
1 stick butter or 8 Tb. bacon fat

4–6 slices of bread

THE LIVER SPREAD
8 chicken livers plus the grouse
    livers, diced
1" square salt pork, diced

salt and pepper
½ tsp. tarragon
1½ Tb. dry Marsala

THE GROUSE
4 grouse or 6 chukar partridges or
    12 quail
6 Tb. minced shallots or scallions
½ tsp. thyme or marjoram
4–6 orange wedges, punctured with
    a fork

salt and pepper
4 strips of bacon
4 Tb. butter, melted
2 Tb. white wine

THE MUSHROOMS
1 lb. mushrooms, sliced
3 Tb. butter

2 Tb. minced shallots

THE SAUCE
1 Tb. minced shallots or scallions
1 cup chicken broth
1 Tb. Harvey's or Worcestershire
    sauce

⅓ cup dry Marsala
parsley (for garnish)

In a skillet melt the butter or bacon fat and fry the bread slices until they have absorbed the butter and are a golden brown color.

For liver spread, chop the livers and salt pork fine or whirl into a near puréed form in a food processor with the salt, pepper, tarragon, and Marsala to make a paste.

Spread the fried bread trenchers with the paste; place the slices on a broiling tray for later.

For the grouse, mix the minced shallots or scallions with the thyme or marjoram and put some into each bird along with 1 wedge of orange. Salt and pepper the birds.

Truss the birds, pin a strip of bacon over each bird, and roast them in a 450° oven for 25 minutes. Combine the melted butter and wine and baste the birds. While the birds are roasting sauté the mushrooms and shallots in butter, 2–3 minutes. Set aside.

Remove birds to a hot platter and cut off trussing strings. Stir all of the sauce ingredients except parsley into roasting pan and boil furiously over top of stove until liquid is reduced by half. At same time put the spread trenchers under broiler for 1½ minutes.

Put mushrooms and shallots upon each trencher, top with a bird, spoon a bit of sauce over each bird, and garnish with parsley.

NOTE: From the time you begin to prepare the birds themselves this roast game bird dish can be prepared easily in an hour and a half or less the first time you try the recipe.

═══ GROUSE SMOTHERED IN SOUR CREAM ═══

This is a delicious dish and justifies wild rice as accompaniment. Use this recipe with chukars or with pheasant (cut into frying pieces).

SERVES 4

4 ruffed grouse, halved
flour
salt and pepper
1 tsp. thyme or ½ tsp. rosemary
¼ lb. butter
4 shallots or scallions

½ lb. sliced mushrooms
2 cups sour cream, at room
 temperature
½ cup chicken broth
1 tsp. beach plum jelly

Roll the grouse halves in flour, salt, pepper, and herbs.

In a casserole or skillet sauté the grouse halves in 6 tablespoons of the butter.

Remove grouse pieces and sauté the shallots or scallions and mushrooms in same casserole or skillet, using the remaining butter.

Return grouse to casserole, add sour cream into which has been stirred the chicken broth and beach plum jelly.

Cover and bake in 350° oven for about an hour.

═══ BROILED GROUSE ON GIBLET TOAST ═══

My late friend Larry Koller put me onto this way of serving grouse (or quail, or partridge or woodcock) on toast. Somehow broiled game birds served on toast spread with this liver paste are especially delicious. This recipe has the virtue of providing you with a basting liquid while you prepare the liver spread for the toast. The liver paste is my variation of the paste Larry described on the phone.

SERVES 6

THE LIVER PASTE
8 Tb. butter
¼ lb. livers (3 *whole* chicken livers
 plus the giblets of the grouse)
3 shallots or 2 cloves garlic,
 minced
1 cup white wine
¼ tsp. chervil
THE TOAST CANAPÉS
6 bread slices
¼ cup butter
THE GROUSE
3 grouse
salt

¼ tsp. savory
1 chicken bouillon cube
1 sprig parsley
1 bay leaf
¼ tsp. tarragon
¼ tsp. thyme
1 Tb. lemon juice

¼ cup bacon fat

white pepper
6 Tb. soft butter

Melt half the butter in a saucepan and sauté the grouse giblets, chicken livers, and shallots or garlic over low heat until the chicken livers are cooked through but still pink in the middle (4–5 minutes).

Add the wine, chervil, savory, bouillon cube, parsley, and bay leaf, bring to a boil, and simmer for 15 minutes.

Take out and set aside the livers and giblets.

Strain the stock and set aside (you will use this stock to baste the grouse). You should have about ¾ cup.

Mince the grouse gizzards and hearts. Add the livers, tarragon, thyme, and 1 tablespoon lemon juice and put all, or livers only (smash with fork), into blender or food processor. Turning the machine in quick on-off succession, render into thick paste by mixing in remaining 4 tablespoons butter.

For the toast canapés, melt the butter and bacon fat and sauté the bread slices until golden brown on both sides.

With poultry shears or knife split the grouse down the backbone and along one side of the breastbone, rub with salt and pepper, and spread the soft butter on skin side.

Place 6 grouse halves in shallow broiling pan, skin side up, and broil about 3 inches from the heat for about 18 minutes on each side, basting often with the stock and the melted butter drippings from the pan.

Spread the toast with the liver paste, put a grouse half on each slice of toast, place on hot platter, and keep warm.

Put broiling pan and its contents over high heat on top of stove. Add more stock (or water if you are out of stock) and boil furiously until it reduces to form a gravy.

Pour over grouse halves and serve.

NOTE: Can't you tell by merely *reading* it here that this is a fantastic treat?

═══ GROUSE OR CHUKARS WITH GARLIC ═══

When you come to the garlic in the list of ingredients, do not flinch, but proceed with confidence; although the flavor of the dish will be deliciously unique, *it will not taste garlicky.*

SERVES 2

4 grouse or chukars
3 chicken livers or 2 chicken livers
   and the grouse liver
2 Tb. butter
¼ cup bacon fat

25 cloves garlic, skins removed*
2 sprigs parsley, minced
½ cup white wine
½ cup tomato sauce or purée
juice of 1 lemon

In a fairly snug casserole sauté the grouse or chukars and the livers slowly in 1 tablespoon butter and the bacon fat until nicely browned.

Add the garlic and parsley and continue sautéing gently for 3 minutes or so more.

Remove the livers and set aside. Add the wine and the tomato sauce to the casserole.

Cover and simmer gently for 1 hour and 15 minutes or until grouse or chukars are tender. Add more white wine if liquid cooks down.

Remove birds to a hot platter or pie pan and strain the sauce through a fine sieve, using a spoon to squash through the garlic pulp.

Smash the cooked livers into a paste and add to the sauce, along with the juice of the lemon. Reheat.

You can, if you wish, warm the birds again in the sauce as it is reheating. Just before serving stir a tablespoon of butter into the hot sauce until melted.

˙ An easy way to remove skins is to drop the cloves first into boiling water for a minute.

BRAISED RUFFED GROUSE OR CHUKAR PARTRIDGES WITH MUSHROOMS

I use canned or prepared ingredients sparingly, but I find one of the canned soups is a boon to cookery, cream of mushroom soup, particularly in camp when you cannot get fresh mushrooms and cream. It makes the sauce for Sheila's Venison Meatloaf (see page 323) and serves this dish well too.

SERVES 4

3 grouse or 4 chukars, trussed
  tightly to make a ball
½ cup butter or margarine
½ cup diced shallots or scallions
  or even onion
15 small mushroom caps (optional,
  chiefly for appearance)

20 juniper berries, crushed
1 cup vermouth or dry white wine
2 cans cream of mushroom soup
  (do not dilute)

Sauté the birds in the butter over low to medium heat, taking 15 minutes or so to brown them on all sides.

When almost done sauté the shallots, mushrooms (if used), and juniper berries in with the birds.

Stir the wine and cream of mushroom soup to a uniform texture and pour over birds and vegetables.

Cover and simmer for another 20–30 minutes, checking a few times for liquid. You want the mix to cook down to concentrate the flavor without sticking (*but* it should *almost* stick for the richest flavor).

CASSEROLE OF GAME BIRD MARSALA II

When I prepare this or similar dishes with grouse or chukar, I use 3 birds; 8 birds when quail are used, but instead of cutting up the smaller birds, I truss them into a "ball" and sauté them whole in a heavy skillet on top of the stove before putting them in the casserole.

SERVES 6

3 grouse or chukars or 8 quail
¼ cup flour seasoned with salt,
  pepper, and ¼ tsp. thyme
3 Tb. lard or butter and oil
1 cup Marsala
3 shallots, or scallions, minced

3 bay leaves
¾ tsp. thyme
¼ tsp. tarragon
½ lb. mushrooms, sliced
2 Tb. butter
¼ cup brandy

Dust the birds with seasoned flour. Brown them in the fat all over, then put them into a casserole with the Marsala, shallots or scallions, bay leaves, thyme, and tarragon, cover, and braise in a 350° oven for about 30 minutes for grouse and chukars, 15 minutes for quail.

Sauté the mushrooms in the butter for 3–4 minutes, then add them to the casserole for the last 5 minutes of cooking.

Just before serving pour brandy over and set aflame.

═══════ DEVILED GROUSE OR CHUKARS ═══════

This dish can be prepared with any of the upland birds and in a variety of ways, beginning, as here, with poaching the whole bird first or dispensing with the poaching process in favor of broiling on a rotisserie for the full process. The times given here are for grouse or partridge; for quail, doves, or woodcock, poach 10–12 minutes. For pheasant, poach the bird whole until tender (about 35 minutes), then cut it in half down the backbone and grill flat in a broiler until crumbs are brown.

SERVES 2–3

2 grouse (with giblets), trussed into a tight "ball"	½ tsp. marjoram
1 medium onion stuck with 2 cloves	2 sprigs parsley
1 carrot, sliced	1 Tb. salt
2 bay leaves	6 peppercorns
1 rib celery	4 Tb. melted butter
2 shallots or whites of scallions, sliced (optional)	¾ cup bread crumbs

Put the grouse, giblets, and all of the ingredients save the butter and crumbs in a pot, just cover with water, bring to a high boil, then turn down heat and simmer for about 20 minutes. Strain the broth and freeze it for future use.

Drain the birds, then dry them with a paper towel, and cover them thoroughly with melted butter.

Roll them in the crumbs, patting and pressing to be sure they are well covered everywhere. Broil on rotisserie (or on grill, turning them) until the crumbs are nicely browned, about 20 minutes.

Serve with the Sauce Diable.

Sauce Diable

There are a number of ways to prepare this sauce, and you can make it as devilish (hot) as you yourself wish, but this sauce is so delicious with broiled meats that it ought to be in every saucier's repertoire.

6 shallots or scallions, finely chopped	¼ tsp. Tabasco
3 Tb. butter	1 tsp. Worcestershire or Harvey's sauce
8 crushed peppercorns	1 tsp. red currant or beach plum jelly
¼ cup white wine or vinegar	2 livers
1 cup brown sauce (see page 354)	
1 tsp. dry mustard or Dijon	

Sauté the shallots or scallions in the butter, then add the peppercorns and the wine or vinegar and simmer until soft and the liquid is reduced.

Stir in the brown sauce, mustard, Tabasco, Worcestershire, and jelly and simmer for 3 minutes or so to meld the flavors. If it's not devilish enough for your palate add another ¼ teaspoon Tabasco. At the end, smash and stir into the sauce the livers of the birds, cooking them just a minute or so. Serve in a sauceboat.

═══ GROUSE OR PARTRIDGE AU GRATIN SAVOIE ═══
(adapted from Michael Field)

Serve this with rice and a salad and speak a word of admiration for the late Michael Field.

SERVES 2 OR 3

2 roasted or spit-broiled grouse or partridge, cooled	½ tsp. tarragon
6 Tb. butter	½ tsp. chervil
6 Tb. flour	¼ tsp. cayenne
1 cup chicken stock	2 tsp. Dijon mustard
½ cup dry white wine or vermouth	4 Tb. grated Swiss cheese
1–1¼ cups heavy cream	salt and white pepper
	½ cup bread crumbs

Remove legs and wings and cut breasts in half, so you have 6 pieces from each bird.

Melt 4 tablespoons butter in a stainless steel or enamel skillet, and stir in the flour and cook gently a minute, stirring until you have a smooth roux. Remove from heat, pour in the chicken stock and the wine, and whisk it smooth, then return pan to the heat and cook until the sauce begins to thicken; turn heat down to the very slowest simmer and cook for 4–5 minutes, stirring occasionally. Do not be alarmed if it is the thickest white sauce you have ever dealt with, for you *are* now going to thin it *some* with the heavy cream. Using half the cream, stir it in and then add little by little enough of the rest of the cream just so the sauce, as Mr. Field put it, "runs sluggishly off the spoon when it is lifted from the pan."

Now quickly add tarragon, chervil, cayenne, mustard, Swiss cheese, salt, and pepper. Simmer and stir just long enough for the cheese to melt.

Put a thin layer of the sauce on the bottom of a shallow ovenproof baking dish (glass or enamel) and place the grouse or partridge pieces on top. Cover with remaining sauce, then sprinkle bread crumbs over all, dot with remaining butter, and put into a preheated 375°–400° oven until the sauce begins to bubble—about 25 minutes.

If handy, put under broiler just long enough to brown the surface.

══════ COLD BIRDS AND A BOTTLE ══════

If on occasion you want to impress a friend with a cold but elegant lunch and would like a conversation piece to go with it (or if you wanted to serve a hot poultry course of pheasant, grouse, or partridge), here's one with a 600-year tradition behind it. Serve the birds cold (or hot) with a bottle of chablis.

SERVES 3–4

3 grouse or chukars, trussed
4 Tb. or more of lard or oil
2 medium onions, chopped
1 cup white wine
¼ tsp. cinnamon
⅛ tsp. powdered cloves or 3 whole cloves
¼ tsp. nutmeg
5 white or black peppercorns, crushed
1 tsp. sugar
¼ tsp. powdered ginger
¼ tsp. saffron (optional)
salt

In a heavy stewing pot or Dutch oven brown the trussed birds on all sides, ladling the hot fat on the upper sides during the process, about 10 minutes. Drain on paper towels.

Sauté the onions in the fat until soft.

Return birds to the pot and add remaining ingredients and just enough water barely to cover the birds. Bring to a boil, then turn down heat and simmer covered for about 15 minutes.

BOBWHITE QUAIL

When I was a boy, most country households in the Middle West had throughout the fall a string of bobwhites hanging in the feathers outside the summer kitchen door or behind the green-painted lattice that screened the back porch. "Birds," as they are still called in many parts of the country, were a part of fall fare.

This tiny butterball of toothsome bird weighs an average of 5.7 ounces in the extreme southern part of its range, to 7 ounces average in Wisconsin, thus again bearing out Bergmann's Rule that the same species weighs more in the northern edge of its range than in the southern. At these live weights the dressed birds will weigh a bit on either side of a quarter of a pound. Again when a cookbook tells you that 4 bobwhites will serve four, take a good look at your guests. I think two quail are a minimum serving.

The other quails of the southwestern and western United States are of similar size: Gambel's quail, males 6 to 7½ ounces, females 5¾ to 6⅞ ounces; California quail, 6¼ to 7⅛ ounces; mountain quail, the largest and some think the handsomest of American quails, average for both males and females 8½ ounces, a large male up to 10 ounces; scaled quail, 6⅞ ounces average for both sexes.

Quail on Toast

When you serve "quail on toast" you are perpetuating an ancient practice common at medieval boards. Food was often served on trenchers, a term applied later to wood boards or plates, but originally to a great slab of bread that served as a plate. Trenchermen literally did eat the plate as well as the food, for bread trenchers sopped up the juices, sauces, and gravies of the meat that was served on them. A trencherman is a gourmand who would, if he could, eat the plate itself. Yes, there were trencherwomen in those days, too.

STUFFED ROAST QUAIL ON SCRAPPLE
WITH LIVER AND WINE SAUCE

SERVES 2–3

3 slices bacon
6 quail
½ lb. mushrooms, sliced
6 Tb. butter
½ cup bread crumbs
2 Tb. Madeira

3–4 thickish slices scrapple
6 quail livers
2 chicken livers
½ cup white wine
½ cup chicken stock

Cut the bacon slices in half and work each half back under breast skins of the dressed birds.

Sauté the mushrooms in half the butter, stir in bread crumbs and Madeira, and stuff each bird.

In separate skillet brown the scrapple slices.

In a 450° oven roast the quail (on a rack) for about 25 minutes, basting the birds often with the pan juices and fat.

During last 5–6 minutes of the roasting, in a skillet sauté the livers in the remaining butter for just a few minutes. Chop and squash the livers, then mix with the wine and stock.

Remove rack of birds from the oven and keep warm on a platter on oven door.

Pour livers, stock, and wine into roasting pan and bring to a boil over high heat. Reduce while stirring up "greables" from pan.

Lay out scrapple, pour sauce over each slice, and top with the quail.

VIOLA HAMILTON'S PAN-FRIED QUAIL (OR DOVES)
(for indoor or outdoor cooking)

"This recipe is for 10 to 12 birds in a large 15- or 16-inch skillet," writes Viola Hamilton of Green Pond, South Carolina. "If fewer birds are used and smaller pan, less bacon should be used."

SERVES 5–6

10–12 quail (or doves)
salt and pepper

1 lb. good breakfast bacon

Wash cleaned birds and season with salt and pepper.

Place the bacon in large skillet or frying pay, over medium heat, separating slices with long-handled fork as cooking begins; brown bacon until done and crispy.

Remove bacon from pan, but keep in warm place.

Put birds in bacon grease and cook 4–5 minutes, turning continuously to cook evenly and prevent burning. Remove from pan, drain on paper towel, and serve immediately with warm breakfast bacon.

STUFFED QUAIL DOTTIE D'AVANZO

SERVES 3–4

1 cup cracker crumbs
2 strips bacon, sautéed crisp and
   crumbled
2 Tb. chopped celery
1 cup chicken broth (bouillon
   broth will do)

1 strip bacon for each quail
6–8 quail
butter
½ cup white wine or vermouth

Preheat oven to 350°.

Mix crumbs, crumbled bacon, and celery with ½ cup chicken broth for stuffing (or use stuffings; see pages 377 to 380 for our suggestions).

Wrap 1 slice bacon around each quail and hold in place with toothpicks. Place in a buttered, ovenproof casserole.

Add wine and roast uncovered for 30 minutes. Add liquid from remaining ½ cup broth if more liquid is needed.

QUAIL ON A BED OF LEEKS

SERVES 4

8 quail
4 Tb. butter
1 Tb. vegetable oil
6–8 leeks, about 2 cups, cut into
   1" slices

salt and freshly ground pepper
⅓ cup heavy cream
2 Tb. chopped parsley

In a large skillet or a wok sauté the quail in 1 tablespoon butter and the oil, browning quickly on all sides. Remove.

Sauté the leeks in the same pan in the remaining butter. Add just a little water to them—no more than 2 tablespoons—cover, and cook slowly for about 10 minutes until the leeks have begun to soften and have absorbed the liquid.

Place the quail on top of the leeks, salt and pepper them, then add the cream all around. Cover and cook slowly for 20 minutes. Sprinkle parsley on top when serving.

ROAST QUAIL WITH TARRAGON AND CHERVIL BUTTER

This method (which works with chukars or grouse as well) doubles in brass as it were: it bards the bird and flavors it well.

SERVES 2

½ stick butter
salt and pepper
½ tsp. tarragon
½ tsp. chervil

4 quail
2 onions, halved, each half stuck
   with a clove
½ cup chicken stock

Let the butter soften some, then thoroughly mix with salt, pepper, tarragon, and chervil. Shape into a roll, cover, and return to refrigerator.

Loosen skin at neck of each bird and continue to loosen until breast skin has been pulled loose from breast meat on both sides.

Put ½ pat of butter on each supreme (breast meat) and pull skin back and cover naturally.

Put a half onion with clove in each bird, set birds on rack in a shallow roasting pan with the stock, and roast in a 450° oven for 20–30 minutes, basting with the pan juices.

NOTE: For grouse, roast in a casserole at 450° for 10–15 minutes, then turn down to 300° and continue roasting for another 30 minutes, covered.

QUAIL OVER VEGETABLE AND HAM STRIPS

SERVES 2–3

4 Tb. vegetable oil
1 tsp. minced fresh ginger
3 quail, split
salt and pepper
3–4 Tb. chicken broth
1 medium zucchini, cut in thin
   strips

1 carrot, scraped and cut in thin
   strips
4 whole scallions, cut in thin strips
2 large broccoli stalks, peeled and
   cut in thin strips
2 oz. country ham or prosciutto,
   cut in thin strips

In a large skillet or wok heat 2 tablespoons of the oil with the ginger. Brown the quail on all sides. Salt and pepper them. Add a little broth, cover, and steam-braise slowly for 15 minutes.

Remove the quail with their juices and keep warm.

Add the remaining oil to the pan, then the vegetables. Stir-fry them 2–3 minutes over medium-high heat, tossing constantly.

Stir the ham into the vegetables, then place the quail and their juices on top. Cover and steam 4–5 minutes. Check seasonings and add additional salt and pepper if necessary.

══ QUAIL, SPLIT, MARINATED, AND ROASTED ══

By splitting and marinating some of the smaller game birds, such as quail, partridge, and dove (you can use a combination of these birds if you don't have enough of one kind), not only does the flavor of the marinade permeate both inside and out more readily but the birds can be then done very quickly in a hot oven. If you have a large, shallow earthenware casserole, the birds can marinate, then roast, and come to the table right in the same dish. Serve them with a potato and vegetable purée or on top of a potato pancake.

SERVES 4–6

8 quail, 3 partridge, or 6–8 doves
3–4 Tb. olive oil
4 cloves garlic
1 Tb. coarse salt or 2 tsp. table salt
2 Tb. chopped fresh tarragon or
　about 1½ tsp. dried tarragon
freshly ground pepper

juice of 2 limes
3 Tb. soft butter
2 tsp. fennel seeds
½ cup dry white wine
½ cup game bird or chicken broth
½ lb. mushrooms, quartered

Split the birds on the back sides lengthwise, open them up to lie flat, and rub them inside and out with olive oil. Crush the garlic cloves and mash them into the salt. Rub this all over the birds and sprinkle on tarragon and pepper. Spread birds out in a large dish (they should just about fit snugly in one layer) and squeeze the lime juice over them. Let marinate overnight in the refrigerator, if the weather is warm.

Rub soft butter over birds, toss fennel seeds on top, pour the wine and broth around the birds, and roast skin side up in a preheated 450° oven for 15 minutes. Then scatter the mushrooms around the dish, baste with the juices, and roast another 10 minutes for small birds, 15–25 minutes for larger, basting again and adding a little more broth if needed. Serve immediately.

══ GRILLED OR BROILED QUAIL ══
À LA GRECQUE

During hunting season in Greece restaurants will display whatever game they have to offer, whether it be a tiny quail nestled among other meats in the display case or a wild boar hung outside the restaurant still dripping blood. Birds are invariably grilled over hot coals, rubbed first with a little oil, some garlic if wanted, salt and pepper—a technique that can be easily adapted to the backyard barbecue or to the oven broiler, provided you get it good and hot.

2 Tb. olive oil
½ tsp. coarse salt
freshly ground pepper

1–2 cloves garlic, mashed
½ tsp. thyme (optional)
3 quail per person

Mash the olive oil, salt, pepper, garlic, and thyme, if used, together in a mortar and pestle. Rub the mixture over the quail inside and out.

Set the birds on the grill or the rack of a preheated broiler, and grill or broil them 5 minutes on each side.

═══════ QUAIL ROASTED IN VINE LEAVES ═══════

SERVES 6

6 quail
olive oil
salt and freshly ground pepper
6 thin good-size pieces fresh
  pork fat
about 18 grape leaves, fresh or
  preserved

the quail giblets
1½ cups chicken broth
2 oz. cognac
2 Tb. soft butter
2 Tb. flour
6 squares fried cornmeal mush
  (page 430)

Rub the quail all over with olive oil. Salt and pepper them inside and out. Wrap each bird in pork fat, making sure to cover the breast, then wrap in 2–3 vine leaves. Tie up firmly to hold the leaves in place, then wrap in foil.

Roast the quail in a 375° preheated oven for 45 minutes.

Meanwhile prepare the sauce. Cook the giblets in the chicken broth until tender. Remove the giblets and chop them up. Add the cognac to the broth. Mix the soft butter and flour together thoroughly, then, bit by bit whisk enough of this paste into the boiling sauce to thicken it lightly. Taste and add salt and pepper as necessary. Stir in the giblets and keep warm in a sauceboat.

When the quail are done remove the foil and the strings and serve the birds in vine leaves on squares of fried cornmeal mush. Serve sauce separately.

Partridge

HUNGARIAN PARTRIDGE

As we have pointed out, there are no native partridges in North America; our partridges are, of course, both introduced species: the "Hun," or "Hungarian partridge," is the common gray partridge of Europe and the British Isles, the most common and widespread European partridge (*Perdix perdix*). It has been widely introduced in the U.S. and Canada, but though locally persistent has not done well in the East; its most successful incidence has been in the prairie states and provinces, where it has done very well, indeed.

The chukar (*Alectoris chukar*), similar in size and shape to the Hun but of the same genus as the red-legged partridge of Europe, has done very well in arid mountainous areas, canyons, and grassy slopes with rock outcrops of both the United States (mainly the Great Basin) and southwest Canada from British Columbia, south to Baja California, and east to Colorado. Happily for eastern tables, this fine bird is widely raised on game preserves from whence it supplies both sport and a delectable flesh for the board. All of these recipes for partridge may also be used to prepare grouse.

Huns run from 12 to 14 inches in length; chukars, 13–15½ inches, are smaller than either our ruffed grouse (16–19 inches) or our sharp-tailed grouse (15–20 inches), or the lesser prairie chicken (16–18 inches) or greater prairie chicken (17–19 inches). Our biggest grouse, the sage grouse, is a much bigger bird—26–30 inches.

When preparing chukars judge your quantity by the knowledge that the average partridge dressed to cook, plus its neck and giblets, will weigh just about a pound.

Any of the grouse or partridge recipes in this book will serve partridge equally well.

Picking Chukars

Recently I have been wet-picking my chukars. These have been birds undrawn and frozen in the feathers picked after thawing for six hours or so. Using 180° water and dipping birds (already thoroughly wetted under the faucet) seven or eight times, I found the feathers came off easily, yet the skin did not cook and tear. By the time I was halfway through picking, the bird's skin was again cold to the touch. The innards on the other hand, still frozen, came out in one easy lump. It is also easy to remove a crop still partly frozen. I timed myself and found that it took me an average of eight minutes to wet-pick, singe, and draw each bird.

I concluded that I would never again dry-pluck a partridge, pheasant, or grouse that had been frozen, undrawn, in the feathers. When I freeze chukars in the feathers, I freezer-wrap the birds in packages of two.

═ LINDA WOLVERTON'S PARTRIDGE CASHEW ═

We are indebted to *The Maine Way* for the following recipe. Partridge is, of course, a ruffed grouse recipe in Maine.

SERVES 6

oil
6 partridge breasts
¼ cup milk
½ cup flour
1 chicken bouillon cube (optional)

3 scallions, including tops, chopped
4 ounces cashews
salt to taste
cooked rice

Heat ¼ inch oil in skillet.

Cut meat from breasts. Cut into bite-size pieces. Dip pieces in milk, then dip in flour.

Boil partridge bones in water to cover to make 3 cups broth; after 30 minutes, salt lightly and taste—if broth is not strong enough, add a chicken bouillon cube.

Fry partridge in oil until lightly browned.

Add broth to partridge. Let simmer until thickened and meat is tender. Add scallions and cashews. Season with salt. Stir; do not cook further. Serve over rice.

═ CORA LONGLEY'S BAKED PARTRIDGE IN FOIL ═

Again, partridge is ruffed grouse in this recipe from Maine.

SERVES 2

1 partridge
about ½ cup bread stuffing
   (your own, or use one of
   the stuffings, pages 377–378)

6–8 strips salt pork or bacon

Clean bird, leaving legs and wings on.

Make bread stuffing, same as for chicken. Stuff partridge with stuffing. Cut pieces of foil large enough to seal bird in. Place stuffed bird on foil, breast side up. Place salt pork and/or bacon strips all over the bird. Seal the partridge tightly in foil.

Place on rack in roasting pan with just enough water in bottom of pan to cover but not come up over rack and touch bird. Cover roaster. Bake at 325° for

2 hours or until meat falls off bone. Remove from oven. Do not allow to dry out before eating.

PARTRIDGE SCAPRIELLO

Here is another recipe from Evelyn Soriano's kitchen at Quimby Pond Camps on Rangeley Lake. See page 236 for Mrs. Soriano's recipe for trout crêpes. This recipe, here given for ruffed grouse, is of course just as good with chukar or pheasant breasts. Serve with tossed salad and garlic bread.

SERVES 4

4 boneless partridge breasts
½ cup flour
½ tsp. parslied garlic salt
¼ tsp. paprika
¼ tsp. salt

⅛ tsp. pepper
¼ tsp. rosemary, crushed
⅓ cup olive oil
3 Tb. butter
2 cloves garlic, minced

Cut breasts into 1-inch chunks. Mix flour, garlic salt, paprika, salt, pepper, and rosemary and dredge partridge pieces with this mixture. Heat olive oil, butter, and fresh garlic in large skillet. Sauté partridge chunks over medium heat, stirring constantly, until golden brown. Cooking time is approximately 7 minutes.

CHUKAR (OR GROUSE) PAPRIKA

In preparing any dish where paprika is intended to flavor rather than merely color the dish, it is worthwhile to try to find sweet Hungarian paprika. Some paprikas on the market are as tasteless as vegetable coloring. If your paprika is bland use more. Dottie D'Avanzo's recipe follows: Serve it with egg noodles and tossed salad. Try halved butternut squash baked with butter and a sprinkling of nutmeg if you want a vegetable.

SERVES 3–4

3 chukars, disjointed (leave drumstick and thigh as one piece)
4 Tb. flour
2 Tb. paprika
salt and white pepper
2 Tb. butter or margarine
2 Tb. cooking oil
1 clove garlic, chopped
1 medium onion or 4 shallots, chopped

1 Tb. chopped parsley
1 tsp. marjoram
½ cup chicken broth (or use chukar bouillon cubes)
½ cup orange juice
½ cup white wine or vermouth (Ms. D'Avanzo uses her own dandelion wine)
2 Tb. sour cream

Shake chukar pieces in paper bag with flour, half of the paprika, salt, and pepper.

In heavy casserole, cook chukar pieces in butter and oil over low to medium heat until very light brown (about 5 minutes to a side).

Add garlic, onion or shallots, parsley, the second tablespoon of paprika, marjoram, and chicken broth. Cover and cook over medium heat for 30 minutes.

Add orange juice and cook covered about 10 minutes more.
Add wine and cook until fork-tender, about 10 minutes more.
Stir in and warm the sour cream.

PARTRIDGE IN GREEN ALMOND SAUCE

Elisabeth Ortiz gives this recipe for chicken, but when I've made it I've used both partridge and grouse halved. I agree with Mrs. Ortiz, who says of this dish, "I find all Mexican green chicken dishes delicious; this one is enchanting." I give it here with her kind permission as it appears in her *Book of Latin American Cooking.* When I made the dish I used an equivalent amount of fresh spinach, having no romaine at hand. I used 2 canned jalapeño peppers and ¾ teaspoon ground coriander for the fresh sprigs but, of course, the fresh is better, if you can get it. This dish would also serve 2 pheasants or 3 grouse.

SERVES 2–3

2 partridges, cut into serving
  pieces
2 cups chicken stock
1 medium onion, chopped
1 clove garlic, chopped
1 cup parsley sprigs, coarsely
  chopped
1 cup coriander (cilantro) sprigs,
  coarsely chopped
1 heart of romaine lettuce,
  coarsely chopped

1–2 fresh hot green peppers,
  seeded and chopped, or
  2 canned jalapeño
  or 3 canned serrano chilies,
  seeded and chopped
4 oz. ground almonds (about ¾
  cup)
3 Tb. vegetable oil or lard
salt

Put the partridge pieces into a heavy casserole with the stock, bring to a boil, reduce the heat, and simmer gently, covered, for 45 minutes, or until tender. Lift the partridge out onto a platter and set aside. Pour the stock into a jug. Rinse out and dry the casserole.

In a blender or food processor combine the onion, garlic, parsley, coriander, lettuce, hot peppers, and almonds, and reduce to a coarse purée. Do not overblend, as the finished sauce should have some texture, not be entirely smooth. Heat the oil or lard in a large, heavy skillet and pour in the purée, which will be almost pastelike because of the almonds. Cook the mixture, stirring constantly with a wooden spoon, for 3–4 minutes over moderate heat. Transfer it to a casserole. Stir in 2 cups of the stock and season to taste with salt. Add the partridge pieces, cover, and simmer just long enough to heat the chicken through.

PARTRIDGES IN PAPER

Not in a pear tree, but in buttered paper (or foil); better that way.

SERVES 2–3

2 chukars, with giblets
juice of ½ lemon
small pinch of tarragon

big pinch of sage
1 small onion, halved
2 strips thick bacon

Rub inside and out of birds with lemon juice, and while still wet, sprinkle inside and out with sage and tarragon.

Put giblets and half an onion in the cavities, place bacon along the breast, and wrap each bird in buttered brown paper (or foil).

Put into lidded casserole and roast in a slow oven (about 300°) for an hour.

═ BRAISED CHUKARS SMOTHERED IN CABBAGE ═

Game birds have been cooked with cabbage for a very long time. Three partridges, two grouse, or a pheasant can be used in this dish, which is a composite from an eighteenth-century recipe. It is recommended for an old cock bird whose tenderness may be suspect.

SERVES 4

4 slices bacon, dried
  (or equivalent of salt pork)
¼ lb. proscuitto or other ham,
  diced
1 medium onion, diced
2 carrots, sliced thin
½ tsp. crushed rosemary
¼ tsp. tarragon

2 bay leaves
salt and pepper
1 large head of cabbage, quartered
3 chukars, dressed, each stuffed
  with a small onion stuck with a
  clove, and then trussed
1 cup game bird or chicken stock
½ cup white wine

In the casserole you expect to use, try out the bacon until you accumulate some fat, then add the proscuitto and cook until both begin to brown.

Add the onion and carrots and cook 2–3 minutes, then add the herbs and the salt and pepper.

In a kettleful of boiling, salted water blanch the cabbage sections for 5 minutes. Drain and dismantle one quarter to make a bed of its leaves on top of the vegetables, herbs, etc.

Lay in the trussed birds, fit in the remaining three cabbage sections, and pour in the stock and the wine.

Bring to a boil, then simmer, covered, for 1–1½ hours.

NOTE: You can add livers to this dish: sauté 4–5 chicken livers with the onion and carrots, then when livers have lost their pinkness, smash and stir them into the bacon, ham, and vegetables before you lay in the cabbage leaves.

═ CHUKAR CUTLETS WITH SAGE SPAETZLE ═

This dish can as well be made with pheasant as with partridge. It has an added virtue: the birds used can be skinned instead of plucked. This recipe and Chukar Paprika on page 170 and Chukar Soup on page 174 are Dottie D'Avanzo's. Chukar cutlets are nice with Sage Spaetzle (page 392) and a salad.

SERVES 2–3

2 partridges, skinned
½ cup cracker crumbs
2 or more Tb. butter

1 clove garlic, crushed
salt
white pepper

Bone the breasts and legs, lay pieces between two layers of waxed paper, and pound lightly with flat head of a mallet or side of cleaver until thin. Set cutlets aside.

Roll out on waxed paper enough crackers to make ½ cup or so of crumbs. (You may use prepared cracker or bread crumbs, of course.)

In a skillet melt butter with the crushed garlic. Set aside.

Dip chukar pieces in garlic butter, then in crumbs, and set aside until you have crumbed all of the pieces. Turn heat under skillet up to medium. Add more butter if necessary and brown cutlets quickly, perhaps 2 minutes to the side. Do not overcook. Season to taste.

CHUKAR PARTRIDGES, SPLIT, BAKED, AND BROILED

If you're a little short on the game you brought home, this is a good way to make one partridge do for two, particularly if you serve each half on a potato pancake (see page 381) with a good helping of red cabbage alongside. Of course, if you have plenty of partridges, be generous and offer both halves per serving.

SERVES 2–4

2 chukar partridges
softened butter
salt and freshly ground pepper
½–¾ cup Madeira

4 thin slices fatback
1 dozen or so cloves garlic, unpeeled
½ pound mushrooms, roughly chopped

Cut through the bird's backbone, using poultry shears or a sharp knife, and slice each partridge open from neck to tail. Flatten out and place in a baking pan just large enough to hold the two birds. Rub them well on both sides with butter, salt, and pepper.

Pour in enough Madeira so the pan is filled by ¼ inch. Put the birds in, skin side up, cover the breasts with fatback slices, and scatter unpeeled garlic cloves around. Bake in a 400° oven for 30 minutes, basting every 5 minutes.

Add the chopped mushrooms, tossing them well in the basting juices, and bake about 10 more minutes or until the juices at the leg joints run clear when pricked. Then quickly brown under a very hot broiler just long enough for the skin to get crackly and darken slightly. If making potato pancakes, have them ready just before you slip the birds under the broiler.

Cut the birds in half if serving only half per person. Garlic lovers can squeeze the cloves over crusty bread and eat.

CHUKAR SOUP

SERVES 4–6

2 or more chukar carcasses
and bones
2 chicken bouillon cubes
2 large carrots, cut in chunks
1 large onion, chopped
3 sprigs parsley, chopped

2 ribs celery with leaves, sliced
1 medium potato, cubed
½ tsp. your favorite herb
(if you wish)
¼ cup white wine
¼ cup sour cream

Place carcass and bones in stew pot, add remaining ingredients (except wine and cream), add water almost to cover, and bring to boil. Turn down heat and simmer for 1 hour.

Strain the liquid into another pan. Remove carcass and bones and set aside.

With spoon work the vegetables through the sieve into the broth.

When ready to serve soup, heat and add wine (Dottie D'Avanzo uses her own delicious dandelion wine) and sour cream.

Chukar Spread

Pick remaining meat off chukar bones (there will be more than you think), chop it fine, and do the same with celery, parsley, and a few pieces of nuts. Stir in 1 tablespoon mayonnaise and serve as a dip or spread with crackers.

PARTRIDGE OR GROUSE PIE
WITH OYSTERS

This was originally an English pie, but it was also a popular Colonial dish. I give it here for 3–4 chukar partridges, but it is delicious made with 2 pheasants or 2–3 ruffed grouse.

SERVES 4

3–4 chukars
(or 2 pheasants or grouse)
24 oysters with their liquor
½ cup chopped shallots
½ cup chopped celery
12 Tb. (1½ sticks) butter
6 Tb. flour
1 cup heavy cream
2 Tb. sherry (originally claret)

salt and white pepper
¼ tsp. tarragon
½ tsp. nutmeg
1 Tb. lemon juice
1 tsp. grated lemon rind
pie crust dough (or you can
use Bisquick)
1 egg, beaten

In a stew pot cover chukars with water and stew over low heat until tender (about 30 minutes). Save broth but remove partridges to cool.

Now, or later, drain oysters and save the liquor.

Sauté shallots and celery in butter until soft, then stir in flour. Add 1 cup chukar broth, 1 cup oyster liquor, and cream and, whisking, simmer until it thickens a bit. Stir in sherry, salt, pepper, tarragon, nutmeg, lemon juice, and rind.

Remove meat from stewed chukar and put in buttered 3-quart casserole with the oysters.

Pour the sauce over and cover with the rolled pie dough.
Brush top of crust with beaten egg and puncture "lid" with a fork.
Bake in 400° oven for 30–40 minutes, or until crust is nicely browned.

NOTE: If you are artistic, save a bit of dough, roll it thin, cut out a partridge, and place in center of pie.

In Great Britain, August 12, the opening day of the grouse season, is so important in that culture that it is marked on their calendars with the legend: "The Glorious Twelfth." This impressive title reflects the long anticipation for the awaited day not only by British shooters but by those who take an inordinate delight in preparing and eating this delicious bird. Englishmen and Scotsmen call this bird the red grouse. There it is *the* game bird among game birds, as the salmon is *the* game fish among game fish.

Most sportsmen on this side of the Atlantic (and, I suspect, on the far side too) are not aware that it is the same bird that we Americans in U.S. and Canada call the willow ptarmigan. The red grouse to the taxonomist, who is not interested in political boundaries or local nomenclature, is *Lagopus lagopus*. The bird we call the willow ptarmigan is also *Lagopus lagopus*, same genus, same species, the self-same bird. The bird the British specifically call the ptarmigan, *Lagopus mutus*, is the bird we call the rock ptarmigan, also *Lagopus mutus*.

Most people, even game fanciers, have little opportunity to sample the dark red, juicy breast of the willow ptarmigan unless as shooters they encounter the bird on a tundra or northern mountain hunting trip. If you are a shooter who has eaten willow ptarmigan, you know why such a premium is put on this same bird at, say, Wheeler's in London, where it is listed on the menu simply as grouse. To an Englishman or Scotsman of course there is only *one* grouse.

The recipe that follows was first prepared on a Yukon stove in a tent on the Alaskan tundra.

Any recipe for woodcock will be equally delicious made with ptarmigan.

════════ PTARMIGAN IN TARRAGON CREAM ════════

In 1976 I prepared this dish in a cast-iron skillet on a sheet-metal Yukon stove while camped on the tundra. On that occasion I thinned the mushroom soup with water and wine rather than cream and wine; I had no parsley, and I used minced onion rather than shallots.

SERVES 3–4

3–4 ptarmigan
flour
salt and pepper
1 tsp. dried tarragon
   or ½ tsp. chervil
6 Tb. butter or oil

3 shallots, minced
1 can cream of mushroom soup
½ cup dry white wine
½ cup heavy cream
chopped parsley

Truss the birds into little bundles and after rolling in flour, salt, pepper, and tarragon or chervil, brown in the butter or oil, turning them on all sides.

Toward end of browning add the minced shallots and sauté them.

Add the rest of the ingredients, save the parsley, cover, and simmer over low, low heat for 35–45 minutes.

Garnish with parsley and serve with rice.

═══ PTARMIGAN CASSEROLE WITH MUSHROOMS ═══ AND ARTICHOKE HEARTS

This recipe is scrumptious with any of the white-meat or other game birds.

SERVES 4

4 ptarmigan
juice of ½ lemon
4 Tb. butter
3 Tb. oil
salt
½ lb. mushrooms, sliced
3–4 shallots, or white of
  scallions, or 1 clove garlic,
  minced

2 Tb. flour
¾–1 cup chicken broth
3 Tb. dry Marsala
½ tsp. tarragon
1 bay leaf
14-oz. can artichoke hearts,
  drained

Rub the birds inside and out with lemon juice. Truss them and brown them in 2 tablespoons each of butter and oil. Dust with salt and remove to a casserole, preferably one that they will just fit into.

Add remaining butter and oil to the pan and sauté the mushrooms and shallots (or scallions or garlic) until the liquid is almost gone.

Stir the flour into the pan, cook over low heat 2–3 minutes, stirring, then add the broth. Simmer, stirring until sauce thickens, for 4–5 minutes. Off heat add the Marsala and herbs.

Place artichokes around and between the birds, pour the mushroom sauce over all, cover, and bake for 50–70 minutes in a 325° oven.

Check a couple of times to see if more liquid is needed; if so, stir in a little more chicken broth. The liquid should be just simmering.

═══════════════ PTARMIGAN! ═══════════════

This recipe evidently so delights Martha Helmericks (and this goes for me, too) that *she* put the exclamation mark after her title. This recipe (and this method of larding) will work also, of course, for chukars, ruffed grouse, pintail grouse, and in a deeper casserole for pheasant.

Serve with lingonberries and boiled potatoes, and let guests pick up ptarmigan with their fingers. Also let them crush the potatoes to clean up every last drop of the delicious gravy.

SERVES I

1 ptarmigan, dressed, per person
2 strips bacon
¼ tsp. salt
butter
giblets, diced (add 6 chicken
  livers for additional
  richness)

1 slice white bread
¾ cup milk
¾ cup water
½ cup sour cream

Pluck bird and clean; save giblets. Carefully loosen breast skin and insert 2 strips of bacon between skin and body. Pull skin back in place. Put salt into body and fry bird on all sides in butter in a heavy deep skillet until browned. Fry the diced giblets along with the bread.

   Boil milk and water, pour gradually into skillet—but not over bird—and let simmer for 45 minutes, basting frequently. Now add the sour cream and simmer 1 hour. Remove ptarmigan, cut in two, and season gravy with salt if needed.

Woodcock

Most of us feel grateful—indeed, even blessed—by two brace of woodcock after a weekend's shoot. Those four birds are usually a fortunate remainder of four times as many chances in the field; they are residue of missed shots and missed chances while "we stood in bed" and didn't even manage the concatenation of reflexes to produce a shot at all. Memory of birds bagged is always sicklied o'er by the recall of disgust on the dog's face as he looked back at you after a flubbed chance.

The woodcock is a fragile bird that succumbs often from a scant few pellets of 9's from the edge of your pattern. But he is not fragile when it comes to *flavor*. Here he is *big* game, for the dense, dark rich meat from this 8- to 10-ounce bird concentrates as much flavor as a pheasant, say, six times his size. Happily the woodcock is so protein-nutritious that one bird per person is enough, and besides, how often can a bird shooter supply more than one to a dinner table of six (or even four)?

Take care about serving woodcock to "picky" eaters; woodcock is for woodcock fanciers who delight in its strongly flavored flesh. Everyone has much-loved friends who do not deserve woodcock. Invite such friends as guests when you are serving grouse or pheasant.

CHARLES KESSLER'S WOODCOCK HOR D'OEUVRE

Here is an impressive way to launch a game dinner when you don't have enough woodcock in your larder for a full course. It comes from Charles Kessler of L.L. Bean's promotion department.

SERVES 8

4 woodcock breasts	1 egg yolk, beaten
3–4 shallots	1 Tb. Madeira or
3–4 sprigs parsley	Harvey's Shooting sherry
4 Tb. butter	8 slices white bread
1 Tb. flour	(crusts removed), buttered

Finely chop the woodcock breasts, shallots, and parsley. Sauté all in the butter. Then mix with the flour, egg yolk, and Madeira or sherry. Let stand overnight.

Toast the bread. Spread the paste on the toast and bake in a 350° oven for 10 minutes.

"ROAST" WOODCOCK À LA MARY RANDOLPH OR ISABELLA BEETON

Thirty-three years before Mrs. Isabella Beeton's famous book was published in London (1861), Mary Randolph's *The Virginia Housewife or Methodical Cook* was published in its third edition in Washington, D.C. (1828). Mrs. Randolph also had a recipe for roast (i.e., spitted before "a clear fire") woodcock. Both ladies knew better than to draw a woodcock, and both knew also that you must catch the juices on toast. Any cook with a rotisserie can reproduce Mrs. Randolph's dish, toast, juices, and all, given below.

Until you have tasted broiled, *undrawn* woodcock, don't knock the dish, but don't tell a guest that the birds retained the trails.

To Roast Woodcocks or Snipes

"Pluck, but don't draw them, put them on a small spit, dredge and baste them well with lard, toast a few slices of bread, put them on a clean plate, and set it under the birds while they are roasting; if the fire be good, they will take about ten minutes; when you take them from the spit, lay them upon the toasts on the dish, pour melted butter round them, and serve them up."

WOODCOCK ROASTED WITH CREAM

To roast woodcock you have to be on your toes, for it is a quick and busy process. Served on toast "buttered," as the English do, with a liver paste, it is lovely fare indeed.

SERVES 4

4 woodcock with livers, salted
   and peppered inside and out
4 Tb. butter
3–4 chicken livers
½ tsp. tarragon (optional)
salt

¼ cup white wine
4 slices bread
2 Tb. bacon fat
¾ cup sour cream thinned with
   ½ cup sweet cream

Stuff each woodcock with its own liver and a chunk of butter (about 2 tablespoons for all 4 birds).

Sauté the chicken livers in 1 tablespoon butter until soft but preferably still pink in the middle. With a spoon or fork smash the livers, add tarragon (if you like) and salt, and moisten with wine until you have a spreadable paste. Set aside.

Brown both sides of bread slices in bacon fat.

Put birds in a shallow roasting pan and into a preheated 400° oven.

In a saucepan warm the two creams with a tablespoon of butter to make a baste and stir to a uniform consistency.

After 8–10 minutes pour half the cream mix over the birds. Ten minutes later pour remaining cream mix over birds and baste with the whole mixture. The birds will roast to a proper doneness in 30 minutes at the most.

Spread fried bread slices with liver paste and serve the birds on them. Pour the cream sauce into a sauceboat.

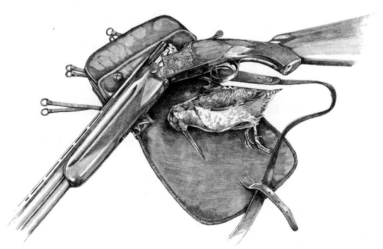

WOODCOCK ON A SPIT

Remember that this chunky, toothsome bird can be ruined by overcooking; furthermore, the natural, distinctive flavor of woodcock requires little or no enhancement from the cook. When spitted on a rotisserie, 15–20 minutes usually do the job, and the rotisserie is an excellent method, for the drain pan can catch the basting juices from the bird to the pan or even directly onto the toast on which the bird will be served.

Before spitting, put into the cavity the liver and a lump of butter ("the size of a walnut" seems appropriate here).

Melt some butter in a saucepan, put in a few tablespoons of white wine or vermouth, and use this to baste the birds, catching the internal and external basting juices directly on the toast.

JANE GUSMANO'S WOODCOCK WITH CREAM

Another recipe from *The Maine Way*, contributed by Jane Gusmano of Medford. Especially good with wild rice.

SERVES 1–2

2 woodcock	Several gratings fresh nutmeg
3–4 Tb. butter	4 Tb. heavy cream
salt and pepper	

Carefully dry pluck birds to prevent loss of juices. Put the liver, heart, and 1 tablespoon of butter inside the bird, then skewer it shut. Rub birds well with butter, salt, pepper, and nutmeg.

Place in a low baking dish and pour 2 tablespoons heavy cream on each bird. Bake in a 375° oven for about 25 minutes until tanned and tender. Baste every 5 minutes. Spoon hot cream and juices over each serving.

WOODCOCK KENNEBUNK (OR DOVES)

In the days when the spits of Colonial kitchens were festooned with game birds, the cooks basted their birds, just as we do, with wine, butter, and various sauces. This recipe, which comes to me indirectly from Kennebunk through friends in Kittery, Maine, calls for whole birds on a rotisserie; if done over coals or a top-heat broiler split each bird in half and broil flat.

Serve with rice, stewed cranberries, and Brussels sprouts.

SERVES 4

4 woodcock, with giblets	¾ cup port wine (or dry Marsala)
6–8 slices bacon	anchovy paste
3 Tb. mushroom catsup	(a couple of 1″ squeezes)
salt and pepper	beach plum or currant jelly
1 medium onion, diced fine	(optional)
6 Tb. butter	

Loosen woodcock skin near neck, work it loose from breast with fingers, insert bacon strip on each side, and pull skin back in place. Moisten birds inside and out with half of the mushroom catsup. Salt and pepper bird inside and out and stuff each with giblets and its share of the diced onion.

In a small saucepan melt butter, add wine, the remaining mushroom catsup, and anchovy paste, and just bubble. Use this to baste. If you wish to serve some of the sauce separately, you can increase the quantity by adding a tablespoon or two of either of the jellies to the sauce; stir and heat.

Spit and broil the birds about 15 minutes, depending on size of bird, basting often.

I believe I have a right to a brag and the duty of a confession when it comes to snipe: the only time I ever fired a shot (not in anger but in hope) at jacksnipe I made an outlandishly lucky double, a classic right-and-left that I have never forgotten. The confession? I have never cooked snipe; this recipe came from my friend Charles Bolton, a shore-runner of wide experience who doubles as a cook. He says, "Don't get complicated when you cook snipe. Salt, pepper, butter, and maybe a touch of Madeira are all you need." He does agree, however, that snipe can be substituted in woodcock recipes. Charles uses a rotisserie usually, but also braises the little birds. "Don't overdo with snipe. Get 'em to and away from the high heat fast!"

My expert puts a chunk of butter into the cavity with the liver, then melts butter into which he stirs a bit of Madeira. He uses the butter and Madeira blend to baste the birds and lets the juices drip onto slices of toast placed under each bird in the drip pan. Sometimes, he says, he sautés garlic slices (shallots are fine, too) in the butter before he adds the wine. Fifteen minutes on the spit is about right.

An English touch: When you pick the bird, pick the head and neck too, and then truss them against the bird's side so the long bill points toward the tail. Lusty aficionados will relish this touch, but don't do it if you suspect that you may have a queasy or melancholy guest at your board. (You may do the same with woodcock.)

SNIPE IN A SKILLET

SERVES 3–4

4 snipe, with their livers	½ cup Madeira or
juice of ½ lemon	very dry Marsala or vermouth
salt and pepper	½ cup strong or
4 kumquats or 1 tangerine	reduced chicken stock
2 shallots, sliced	⅛ tsp. tarragon (optional)
2 Tb. lard	¼ tsp. chervil (optional)

Rub the birds inside and out with lemon juice, salt and pepper them, then place a kumquat or a section of tangerine and the liver in each bird. Truss. Sauté the shallots in lard, then slowly brown the birds all around. For best results use a heavy skillet of a size to crowd the birds both when browning and when cooking in the liquids.

Add Madeira and chicken broth, cover, and simmer for 15 minutes or so. To vary, add tarragon and/or chervil to the liquids.

This recipe can be used for woodcock as readily as for snipe. See page 153 for the use of Marsala (or Madeira) with pheasant.

MOURNING DOVE

The dove, a tender and toothsome fine-grained and dark-meat bird, is a challenge to the scatter-gunner, for it is a fast and difficult target. However, it is a blessing to the chef: it is more delicious than squab, and surely more tender than our adult domestic pigeon (actually the rock dove).

The dove lends itself to many recipes listed for other game birds; most of the woodcock recipes, those for quail, etc., are excellent when prepared with doves.

There are three species of doves in the United States, but the mourning dove is perhaps the most widely hunted in spite of the fact that in most of the Northeast this dove is protected as a song bird.

Remember the dove is a very small game bird weighing only a bit over a quarter pound in the feathers and undrawn! I've gone hungry at boards where the cook heeded a game recipe for four doves that read "serves 4." One dove won't serve this hunter, for 2¾ ounces of bones and meat are scarcely an entrée serving.

Doves are best when braised or broiled (and basted), for they are quite lean; roasted they tend to dry out.

GRILLED DOVES

Serve these with Potatoes Anna.

SERVES 2

¼ cup oil
2 cloves garlic, or shallots,
  minced
1 tsp. dried rosemary, crumbled

salt and pepper
6 doves, split down back
  and flattened

Mix the oil, garlic or shallots, rosemary, and salt and pepper and brush over both sides of the birds.

Grill or broil 4–5 inches from heat 7–8 minutes to the side, basting several times with the oil mixture.

BRAISED DOVE IN VEGETABLES

This recipe can be used with any of the small game birds. The food processor makes the preparation easy.

SERVES 2–3

6 doves
3 Tb. butter
4 shallots or 6 scallions,
  roughly sliced
1 carrot, roughly sliced
1 rib celery with leaves
  roughly sliced
½ green pepper, seeded and
  roughly sliced

2 bay leaves
1 tsp. marjoram (or thyme,
  tarragon, or rosemary)
½ cup boiling liquid, half
  chicken broth, half white wine
¼ cup sour cream
  at room temperature

Sauté the doves in butter until lightly browned in the casserole you intend to use. Set birds aside.

In processor or blender reduce the 4 sliced vegetables to a fine mince, but not quite to a purée. Drain, then sauté the minced vegetables in the casserole.

Add herbs, the boiling liquid, and the birds. Cover and bake at 350° for 15–25 minutes.

Remove doves. Stir the sour cream into the vegetables and serve as sauce. If it is not thin enough add sweet cream.

BRAISED DOVES IN MADEIRA SAUCE

This recipe, says my friend John Wilson, is equally good with woodcock. Also he says he varies the dish by sometimes using dry Marsala or sherry instead of Madeira. This recipe serves older birds well.

SERVES 2

4 doves
lemon juice
salt and pepper
7 Tb. butter
3 Tb. chopped onion

2 Tb. flour
½ cup Madeira
½ chicken stock
¼ cup heavy cream

Rub doves inside and out with lemon juice, salt, and pepper. Brown them in 3 tablespoons butter right in a casserole dish, then sauté the onions in 2 tablespoons butter.

In a small skillet, melt 2 tablespoons butter, stir in flour, and cook a minute or two. Off heat, stir in the wine, stock, and cream. Return to heat, stirring until sauce thickens. Pour sauce over the birds, then cover and bake at 350° for about 40 minutes.

DOVES WITH RICE IN MARSALA

Woodcock can be prepared with both this and the following recipe. The result is delicious, but the time required is minimum.

SERVES 2

1 cup uncooked rice
3 Tb. butter
4 doves
lemon juice
salt and pepper

½ tsp. rosemary, crumbled
8 small white onions
½ lb. mushrooms
1 cup chicken broth
1 cup Madeira

Sauté the rice in the butter, allowing it to brown but not to burn. Place in the bottom of a casserole.

Rub the doves inside and out with lemon juice, then with salt, pepper, and rosemary. Place doves on the rice and surround with the onions and mushrooms.

Pour broth and Madeira over the doves, cover, and simmer in a 350° oven for 30–40 minutes.

BRAISED DOVE WITH WILD RICE

This recipe can also be prepared with woodcock.

SERVES 6

⅔ cup wild rice, washed
10 dove breasts
juice of ½ lemon
salt and pepper
3 Tb. butter
4 shallots or scallions,
  minced

1 rib celery, chopped
½ lb. mushrooms
½ tsp. tarragon
½ cup dry vermouth
  or white wine
1½ cups chicken broth

Wash the wild rice until water runs clear. Drain.

Skin the dove breasts, rub with lemon juice, and salt and pepper them.

In the butter, sauté the shallots or scallions, celery, and mushrooms lightly.

Place rice on bottom of casserole, lay in the dove breasts, and add the rest of the ingredients.

Cover and bake in a 325° oven for 1½–1¾ hours.

DOVES DELAWARE—SAUTÉED WITH BACON CREAM SAUCE

Here's a country-style dove dish from Delaware. It is also good with woodcock or quail.

SERVES 2–3

12 slices bacon
6–8 doves
salt and pepper

3 egg yolks
1½ cups heavy cream
1 tsp. sweet Hungarian paprika

In a skillet large enough to accommodate the doves, sauté the bacon until just crisp. Drain on paper towels.

Sauté the birds over medium heat in the bacon fat, making sure you do it on all sides. Salt and pepper the birds. This should take 10–15 minutes. Take out doves and keep warm. Pour off all but 3 tablespoons of the hot fat.

Beat the egg yolks with the cream, add the 3 tablespoons of fat, then put cream-egg-fat mixture back in skillet and cook over low heat just to thicken, stirring constantly, and *making sure mixture does not boil.* Stir in paprika and serve sauce in a boat. Garnish the doves with the crisp bacon.

Wild Turkey

This grand bird is not the king of upland birds but rather the emperor. Beautiful beyond compare, wily in his native haunts, and savory on the table, the wild turkey is also *more* American than apple pie. Thoughtful conservation policies in many states have resulted in a spectacular comeback for the turkey after this noble bird was extinct in many areas and greatly reduced in numbers in most others. The wild turkey's flavor is one that can be described—like domestic turkey, only more so! Smoked, then roasted, wild turkey may be the finest-tasting bird that flies.

In preparing wild turkey, you may pay heed to the bird's age, especially if you plan on chicken-frying the bird (yes, young toms or hens are delicious fried). A fall gobbler with a long beard that weighs 15 pounds in the feather should be smoked or roasted; young fall gobblers weigh about 10 pounds. An adult hen weighs about 7½ pounds and a young hen about 6. Spring gobblers weigh more, about 17 pounds for an adult and 12 for a young tom.

Lovett E. Williams, Jr., chief of the Florida Bureau of Wildlife Research, who was good enough to supply the information given here through the good offices of my friend James Campbell, M.D., says that about half of the turkey population in Florida, a fine state for this game bird, are "birds of the year," i.e., young turkeys. Mr. Williams estimates that "on the average 50 percent of the kill is only six months old and about 25 percent of the kill is 1½ years old and the rest of the kill older. A turkey over 7 years old is rare, and a 10-year-old is something like 1 in 2,000."

Jim Campbell, the most successful turkey hunter I know, wet-picks his gobblers. See page 449 for his excellent advice on this subject.

I have never shot a wild turkey and have never prepared one, but I know—and envy—a lot of gobbler hunters. I *have* eaten this glorious bird on a number of occasions. These general comments are courtesy of my good angler friend in Florida, Jim Campbell, and of his friend of the Florida Bureau of Wildlife Research. The recipes come from my betters who have both hunted and cooked the wild turkey.

SMOKING WILD TURKEY

My Florida shooting friends smoke most of the wild turkey they bag. They and most other people I know who have tasted it consider smoked wild turkey, hot or cold, as one of the premier taste treats. Turkey can be smoked and cooked in two ways: (1) it can be brined, then smoked, and finally finished in the oven, or (2) it can first be roasted for ⅔ or ¾ of the time you would normally roast a turkey and then smoked.

I usually employ the former method and as often as not wrap and freeze the bird after it has been smoked; then later I thaw it out and finish it in a 300° oven.

Smoked turkey is delicious, hot or cold. The carcass makes a wonderful smoked turkey soup.

Method I
Prepare a brine in a large stock pot that will hold the turkey, for it should be totally submerged.

THE BRINE

4 qt. water	2 whole cloves
1½ cups curing salt	2 onions, chopped fine
(or regular salt)	4 Tb. black pepper
½ cup brown sugar	½ cup lemon juice
3 cups cider (see Note)	½ tsp. mace
½ tsp. powdered ginger	2 tsp. Worcestershire sauce

THE TURKEY

1 turkey	⅓ cup melted butter
¼ cup brown sugar	¼ cup port wine

Combine the brine ingredients. Immerse the turkey, bring to a bubble, and barely simmer for 3–5 minutes per pound of turkey.

Remove the bird from the brine. Wipe as dry as possible with paper towels, then let it dry further for at least an hour. I usually dig up a small electric fan and let it play air over the bird for an hour.

Before hanging in the smoker, rub bird with brown sugar and smoke for 1 hour per pound. To catch the roasting juices make an aluminum foil lining for the drip pan and baste or brush the bird every 1–1½ hours with a mix of the melted butter and port.

If you mean to serve the bird immediately or the next day, after smoking finish it in a preheated 300° oven until the legs and second joint move loosely in the hip socket when jiggled.

If, after smoking, you want to store the turkey, let it cool, then wrap and freeze. When ready to use, thaw, then finish in the oven.

NOTE: If you can't get cider, substitute a 6-ounce can of frozen concentrated apple juice diluted in 3 cans of water.

Method II
This method involves no brining and a shorter smoking time. When smoking in this way roast the turkey just you normally would except keep it in the oven about ⅔ to ¾ of the time you would normally roast it. Then smoke, after removing from oven, only 6–8 hours. Baste with juices from roasting pan mixed with melted butter.

═ VIRGIL THOMPSON'S ROASTED WILD TURKEY ═

SERVES 8–10

8 ribs celery with leaves
7–8-lb. wild turkey,
  barded with salt pork
1 medium onion, halved
  (reserve skin)
1 medium carrot, halved
2 cloves
1 bay leaf

1 tsp. thyme
1 bunch Italian parsley,
  coarsely chopped
juice of 1 lemon
outer leaves of a
  head of lettuce
salt and freshly ground pepper
½ cup brandy

Cut leaves from celery and reserve. Remove neck, giblets, and last two wing joints from the turkey. Put these in 2 cups of water with the onion, carrot, 4 celery ribs cut in chunks, cloves, bay leaf, thyme, and parsley, and bring to a boil. Reduce heat to simmer and cook 1 hour uncovered. Strain broth; there should be 1½ cups for basting and gravy.

Wash turkey inside and out with lemon juice; put remaining celery ribs inside.

Put turkey in an open roasting pan and surround it with onion skins, celery leaves, and lettuce leaves. Roast for 1¼ hours in a preheated 400° oven undisturbed.

Remove salt pork, strings, and surrounding leaves. Reduce heat to 350° and cook for another hour or until juices run clear and yellow around the thigh joints. Baste frequently this last hour with the basting stock.

Remove the turkey to a heated platter and keep warm while making gravy.

Skim off excess fat from the pan, add remaining broth, and bring to a boil. Season with salt and pepper and add brandy. No flour is used to thicken this sauce.

════ ROAST WILD TURKEY ════
WITH FRUIT AND CHESTNUT STUFFING

If you are fortunate enough to obtain wild turkey, you don't want to make any mistakes about preparing so rare a bird. Since this game bird is not fat like a domestic "butterball" turkey, you will want to guard against overcooking lest you dry it out. Use a meat thermometer and consider it done at 180°. For timing the roasting, consider that about 18–20 minutes to the pound represents the time you'll have on hand to do other things. Here's a recipe from Thomasville, Georgia, that I once enjoyed. The silver platter on which it was served was "garnished" with roast quail.

The great Thomasville tom was stuffed with the chestnut-fruit dressing that I give here, but your favorite stuffing will be fine, too.

If the feet and lower legs are on your bird pull the tendons (see page 146).

SERVES 6–8

THE STUFFING
12 prunes, pitted
½ cup diced celery
2 Tb. butter
3 cups cooked chestnuts,
  (see page 386)
3 cups pared, cored,
  and chopped apples
½ cup raisins
THE TURKEY
1 big tom turkey
½ cup lemon
salt and pepper

4 cups white bread,
  cubed and moistened in
  ¼ cup (or more) of port
1 tsp. salt
1 tsp. ground cinnamon
¼ tsp. ground cloves
¼ tsp. nutmeg or mace

softened butter
½ cup white wine (optional)

Prepare the stuffing: Bring the prunes just to a boil and while doing this sauté the celery in butter until soft.

Chop the chestnuts and then the softened pitted prunes.

In a large bowl mix all of the stuffing ingredients thoroughly, being sure the spices are uniformly mixed.

Rub the turkey inside and out with lemon juice, then salt and pepper it.

Stuff the bird, both cavity and neck-breast area, sew up the cavity, and rub the turkey all over with softened butter.

Put turkey on a rack in a shallow roasting pan, cover with a loose foil tent, and roast at 350°, basting with the pan fat and juices and/or with pan juices and wine.

Remove foil tent for last 30 minutes of roasting.

ROAST WILD TURKEY WITH
A CHESTNUT, SAGE, AND SAUSAGE STUFFING

A nonfruit chestnut stuffing that is good with turkey gravy.

SERVES 6–8

THE STOCK
wild turkey giblets and the neck
THE STUFFING
½ lb. sausage meat, broken up
1 large onion, chopped
2 ribs celery and leaves,
  diced
½ green pepper, chopped
4 Tb. butter
3 cups white bread cubed
  or commercial stuffing cubes
THE TURKEY
1 big tom turkey
½ cup lemon
salt and pepper

1 bay leaf

2 cups chestnuts, peeled and
  cooked
½ tsp. thyme
4 tsp. sage
¾ tsp. salt
freshly ground pepper

softened butter
½ cup white wine
  (optional)

Make a stock first by putting on the giblets and neck to boil with bay leaf, then simmer for 20 minutes.

Meanwhile sauté the crumbled sausage. Add the three vegetables and sauté in butter until onions and pepper are soft and the sausage crumbles are brown.

In a bowl mix the remaining stuffing ingredients with the sautéed ingredients, and when the stock has flavor moisten the dressing with it. Do not make too moist, for the bird should be stuffed loosely; if too moist it will pack like cement. Taste for sage flavor.

Stuff and roast the bird as in preceding recipe.

When ready to serve make gravy of dredgings, 2 tablespoons of the fat, and 3 teaspoons of flour. Use about 1 cup of stock plus a few tablespoons of cream for the liquid.

BRAISED WILD TURKEY

This is a good way to prepare any wild turkey but is imperative with an old tom. This is a simple recipe but delicious.

SERVES 6

salt and pepper
8–10-lb. tom turkey
½ apple, peeled and cored
1 onion, quartered
3 ribs celery, cut in chunks
⅛ lb. salt pork, sliced
2 carrots, sliced
4 shallots or 1 onion, sliced

2 bay leaves
1 tsp. basil
1 tsp. thyme
3 sprigs parsley
2 cups chicken or beef broth
1 cup dry white wine
1½ Tb. flour

Salt and pepper the dressed bird inside and out and stuff with the apple, onion, and 1 rib of celery. Lay slices of salt pork alongside breast and inside thighs. Tie legs to the "parson's nose" or tail, then continue back to bind salt pork slices by a couple of turns of string around body at thighs. Tie off.

Place uncovered on a rack in a roasting pan that has a lid and brown about 15 minutes in a 450° oven. Spoon out fat.

Reduce the oven heat to 325°. Add remaining celery, carrots, shallots, bay leaves, basil, thyme, parsley, and the broth and wine, cover, and continue roasting in the oven for about 2 hours if you have an 8-pound bird, longer for larger birds.

When the bird is done, remove it to a hot platter, remove rack, and put roaster over medium heat.

Mix the flour with ¼ cup cold water and stir into contents of the roaster. Simmer until thickened.

Birds braised under a lid cook in somewhat less time than open-roasted birds.

Braised Wild Turkey in a Roemer-Topf or Wet Clay Pot

The clay pot produces the best braised turkey ever. Follow the previous recipe except for the quantities of liquids. Reduce each to *half* the previous quantities.

After the pot and lid have soaked add the stuffed turkey and remaining ingredients to the pot as in the previous recipe. Cover, put into a cold oven, then turn heat up to 475° and roast for about 1½–1¾ hours. Remove lid, paint bird with La Choy brown gravy sauce, and brown bird another 10 minutes or so.

WILD TURKEY GUMBO

You can also use wild goose or duck to make a similar gumbo. It is often served with a spoonful of cooked rice in each soup plate.

SERVES 6–8

2 Tb. butter
2 lb. fresh okra,
    trimmed and sliced
1 Tb. flour
½ cup chopped celery
2 cloves garlic, minced
1 green pepper, chopped

2 qt. water
3 bay leaves
about 1 Tb. salt
dash of cayenne or Tabasco
⅓ cup tomato paste
5–6-lb. wild turkey,
    cut in pieces

Heat the butter in a large soup kettle and sauté the okra. Add the flour and cook a few minutes until it begins to turn brown.

Stir the celery, garlic, and green pepper into the pot and cook, stirring, another minute or so.

Add the water, bay leaves, 1 teaspoon of the salt, cayenne, and tomato paste. Bring to a boil and let simmer 15 minutes.

Add the turkey pieces to the pot and continue to cook at a simmer for 1½ to 2 hours or until tender.

Remove the turkey and extract all the meat from the bones. Cut in fairly small pieces and return the meat to the gumbo.

Let the gumbo simmer for 5 minutes. Taste and correct the seasoning, adding more salt if necessary.

Waterfowl

CANADA GOOSE

The waterfowl shooter and the waterfowl cook is a creature apart. The man, for instance, strong-minded enough to put up with rain, wind, sleet, and snow, the pitch-dark arrivals, and the long cold vigils in pit or blind might be expected to hold strong opinions. He'll either have mallard roasted rare or he will scorn it. He hangs his ducks and geese either by the feet or by the head and holds those who do the opposite with something near contempt. He will be certain to have a favorable recipe that is "the only way to roast a duck."

Here is a collection of recipes for wild ducks and geese that cover most prejudices, we hope. Both are dark-meat birds whose flesh has a definite flavor. They'll stand up to big hearty red wines and strongly flavored accompanying side dishes. They are best when slightly underdone, for unlike that of domestic ducks and geese, their flesh carries little fat. They are almost always barded with bacon or slabs of sliced salt pork before cooking.

Servings from Waterfowl

Most recipes give the number of persons that various game birds will serve, but the writers of cookbooks are quite inconsistent among themselves and sometimes among recipes in the same book. It is true that the recipes themselves will provide more servings when, for example, the bird is braised with vegetables or, more certainly, when prepared as a meat pie, but nevertheless there is often disparity within the same book for the same bird in similar dishes. I have also noticed that the servings indicated *may* reflect the size and appetite of the writer.

In the attempt to be useful we have based the following servings on roasted or grilled birds (stuffed or unstuffed). The weights indicated are of course for birds prepared for cooking, not undrawn and in the feathers.

"Big" Ducks — cans, mallards, blacks, etc.

These ducks weigh from 1¼ to 1¾ pounds dressed, and most people consider that one duck will serve two people. This is a fair assumption, although I have felt stinted on occasions when I shared a bird with another who had an appetite comparable to my own. But, like goose, the flesh of the wild duck is protein-rich (not fat-rich, mind you), and one is appeased with less of it than, say, of the lighter flesh of a gallinaceous bird. Three ducks *are* ample, however, for four diners with big appetites.

Small Ducks, e.g., teal

One bird to one guest, since teal weigh less than ½ pound dressed as against 1¼ to 1¾ for a dressed "big" duck. On the other hand, I share the view of scores of fellow shooters that teal is the tastiest of all waterfowl.

WILD GEESE

For realistic weights of dressed geese see page 213. If you have several game cookbooks in your kitchen library you may be wildly misled by serving quantities predicted in the recipes. When a recipe begins with the notation "one 10- to 12-pound wild goose" you may be absolutely certain that the weight given is for an undrawn bird in the feathers, or that the weight is for a domestic goose dressed, for a 12-pound wild goose dressed would be a 20-pound live goose, and even giant Canadas are gigantic when they weigh even 16 pounds (as rare as, say, a 6-pound broiling chicken). The mystical "10- to 12-pound" goose referred to above is supposed to serve fifteen people!

Realistically, you had better use the weights given below for estimating the number of servings to be expected from wild geese. Ninety percent of the dressed geese you will have available will weigh between 4 and 6 pounds dressed (i.e., from 6½ to 10 pounds in the feathers, undrawn). A big goose, i.e., one that dresses out as much as 6 pounds, might serve six; one that dresses out at 4 pounds will make skimpy servings for six people, but it will serve four handily.

If only the two supremes of a goose are served, one goose breast will serve three in a pinch.

GUIDE TO WILD FOWL SERVINGS AND COOKING TIME

Coot	1 lb.	Stew	1½ hours
Duck, large e.g. mallards blacks, cans, etc.	1 to a person	Roast, rare Roast Broil on spit Braise	400° 20 minutes 400° 30 minutes 26 minutes 1½ hours
Duck, Teal	1 to 1½ birds per person	Roast, rare Roast Broil on spit Braise	400° 12 minutes 400° 20 minutes 18 minutes 40 minutes
Goose	4½ lb. (dressed) goose will serve 4 in a pinch	Roast Braise	375° 2½ hours 350° 2 hours

AVERAGE WEIGHTS OF DUCKS AND GEESE IN THE FEATHERS[*]

Species	Males	Females
DUCK ·		
Bufflehead	13 oz.–1 lb. 4 oz.	8 oz.–1 lb. 5 oz.
Canvasback	Av. 2.76 lb.	2.55 lb.
Block	2.76 lb.	2.45 lb.
Ring-necked	Av. 1¾ lb.	Av. 1½ lb.
Ruddy	Av. 1 lb. 2 oz.	Av. 1.19 lb.
Wood	Av. 1½ lb.	Av. 1.48 lb.
Eider, King	Av. 3.68 lb.	3.45 lb.
Eider, Spectacled	3 lb. 3 oz.–3 lb. 12 oz.	3 lb. 6 oz.–3 lb. 14 oz.
Gadwall	1 lb. 9 oz. to 2 lb. 8 oz.	1 lb. 5 oz. to 2 lb.
Goldeneye	Av. 2½ lb.	Av 1¾ lb.
Mallard	Av. 2.75 lb.	Av. 2.44 lb.
Old Squaw	2 to 2.22 lb.	1.65–1.82 lb.
Pintail	Av. 2.26 lb.	Av. 1.91 lb.
Redhead	Av. 2½ lb.	Av. 2¼ lb.

[*]From *The Audubon Society Encyclopedia of North American Birds* by John K. Terres

Scoup, Greater	1 lb. 5 oz.–2 lb. 10 oz.	1 lb. 5 oz.–2 lb. 1 oz.
Scoup, Lesser	Av. 1.82 lb.	Av. 1.65 lb.
Scoter, Surf	Av. 2¼ lb.	Av. 2 lb.
Scoter, White Winged	Av. 3½ lb.	Av. 2½ lb.
Shoveler	Av. 1½ lb.	Av. 1¼ lb.
Teal, Green Winged	Av. .71 lb.	Av. .68 lb.
Teal, Black Winged	Av. 1.02 lb.	Av. .83 lb.
Teal, Cinnamon	Av. 1 lb.	Av. 13 oz.
Pigeon, American	Av. 1.81 lb.	Av. 1.69 lb.

GEESE

Brant	2 lb. 10 oz.–3 lb. 10 oz.	2 lb. 10 oz.–3 lbs. 10 oz.
Goose, Blue	Av. 6.06 lb.	Av. 5.5 lb.
Canada, Interior	Av. 9.2 lb.	Av. 7.7 lb.
Canada, Giant	Av. 12.5 lb.	Av. 11.1 lb.
Canada, Lesser	Av. 6 lb.	
Canada, Cackling	Av. 3–4 lb.	
Goose, Snow	Av. 6.06 lb.	Av. 5.5 lb.
Goose, White Fronted	Av. 6.29 lb.	Av. 5.53 lb.

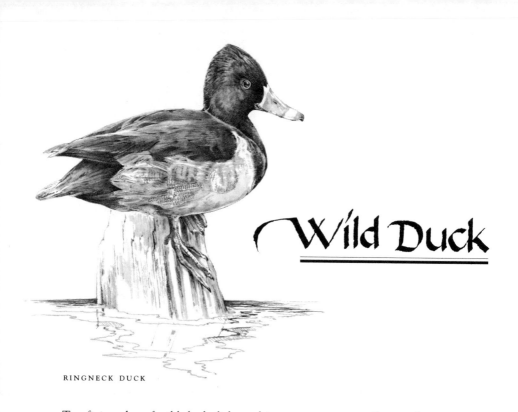

Wild Duck

RINGNECK DUCK

To aficionados of wild-duck dishes, this next comment will seem deprecatory, but the truth of it is that, for some, wild duck is an acquired taste like olives. The generalization is by no means always applicable, but it is often enough true to take a word of warning: some of your guests, coming the first time to the taste of wild duck, may not relish it. Undoubtedly wild duck is a highly sapid, full-flavored meat. The reader can see that I am purposely avoiding the word "strong," because so often a flavor that is dubbed strong is thought of too readily as unsavory. But often the negative response to wild duck is the result of first tasting it blood rare, as many people prefer it. I am one of the lucky ones who likes it both ways, but most newcomers to this delicious fowl will be apt to respond more readily to duck that is well done, i.e., roasted for 30–40 minutes (never more) in a 500° oven rather than one roasted 15–20 minutes.

The person who is lucky enough to be exposed to wild duck regularly will usually end by considering it one of the most delicious of birds.

I consider it a good tactic to introduce somewhat picky eaters to duck by first serving them teal. Many fanciers consider teal the ultimate. As much as I relish all wild duck, I believe I prefer teal as the first among equals. This little duck, whose flashing speed over decoys caused my friend Jerry Mason to call them "fast butterflies," weighs but a third as much as a mallard or a black, and for that reason cooks done sooner than one of the big ducks.

I, personally, cannot remember eating a tough wild duck, while I *have* eaten wild goose that was tough. "Big" ducks—mallards, blacks, cans, sprig—that weigh 1¼ to 1½ pounds dressed can be safely used, as far as tenderness is concerned, in any of the roast or grilled recipes given in this book. Small ducks like teal have also always been tender in the experience of this writer.

Three hundred and fifty-five years ago (in *Via recta ad vitum longam*, London, 1628) Thomas Venner wrote: "Teal, for pleasantnesse and wholesomenesse of meat excelleth all other water-fowle." Many writer-shooters (and other fanciers of game since then), including Ernest Hemingway, have considered teal the king of wild fowl when it comes to taste. I, neither the writer nor the shooter that Hemingway was, concur enthusiastically.

Although each of us knows that it is impossible to describe a flavor, I will venture here a comparison that describes the taste of the toothsome little duck for me. It tastes like a blend of the flavor of ruffed grouse with the flavor of wild duck. It is the most delicately flavored of all the wild fowl and is even delicious when served cold.

Which duck recipe to try first on doubting Thomases? I'd say broiled or roast mallard with Colonel Hawker's sauce. But first, some comments about roasting duck.

General Comments on Roasting Wild Ducks

However you and/or your guests may like wild duck it is important to remember that the texture of the flesh and the paucity of fat is such that overcooking is anathema. Wild ducks also must be considered as small birds—the larger ones weigh about 1½ pounds dressed, and they will cook well done in much less time than a domestic duckling which may weigh four times as much as a good-sized mallard. In general all wild duck roasted should be started in a very hot oven, even when cooked well done. Wild ducks that are to be served rare should be rubbed with butter or olive oil, draped with bacon or salt pork over the breast, or otherwise barded (see page 18 for underskin barding), then put on a rack, and roasted in a very hot, 450°–500° oven for 18–20 minutes. They may be basted a couple of times with a mixture of red wine and butter, flambéed for the fun of it, and served whole or split with some of the pan juices ladled over them.

If you like your wild duck well done or at least less rare then proceed as above and roast for 18–20 minutes in the 450° oven, then cool the oven to 350° and roast, basting frequently with the butter-wine mixture, until the bird is the way you like it.

But don't roast an unstuffed duck for more than a total of 40–45 minutes in any case unless you want a mummy instead of a palatable wild fowl.

If you roast the bird with a stuffing that is moistened you may roast a wild duck up to an hour or even a bit more.

You may wish not to stuff with a dressing but want to put a few flavors inside even a rare-done bird. Use celery, onion, a sliver of orange peel, a couple of cloves of garlic crushed with either (1) a mixture of thyme and parsley or (2) the above items mixed with 7–8 crushed juniper berries instead of the thyme-parsley mix. When roasting for any period you should put a strip of salt pork over the breast of each bird or otherwise bard the bird. See page 18 for underskin barding.

Smoked Duck

When I smoke ducks I baste them often with Colonel Hawker's sauce while they are preroasting and stuff them first with their livers and a tangerine or half of an orange, sticking the fruit sections with a fork so the juices will run out.

I roast mallards or blacks in a hot oven 450° for about 10–15 minutes and smoke them for 1½–2 hours.

GALA ROAST MALLARD

Since this is a gala way to prepare wild duck be sure you know your own preference about just how rare you want your birds to be. You certainly don't want to waste your efforts, so please read the discussion on this subject on page 199. As written, this recipe is for fairly rare ducks; otherwise roast 25–35 minutes. You may wish to make the Madeira sauce the day before.

Wild rice and a green vegetable with a good, hefty red wine make this a notable meal.

SERVES 6

3 wild ducks, oven-ready
1 apple, cored and quartered
6 sprigs of parsley
4 ribs celery with leaves
4 shallots
12 juniper berries, crushed
  (see page 218)
4 Tb. soft butter
¾ cup white wine

2 bay leaves
2 whole cloves
¼ tsp. powdered thyme
3 cups hot Madeira sauce
  (see page 183)
6 slices bread fried in butter
  (or fried and then spread with
  liver paste, page 156)

Preheat oven to 450°.

In each bird stuff its share of the apple, parsley, celery, shallots, and juniper berries. Sew up cavity.

Spread soft butter over each bird and in a shallow roasting pan place ducks breast down on shallow rack.

Add the wine, bay leaves, cloves, and thyme to roasting pan and roast 18–20 minutes, turning the birds and basting twice.

Set the ducks aside to cool enough so you can handle them, and strain the wine and dredgings, reserving this sauce.

In a saucepan put the Madeira sauce on to heat over a low fire.

Here you have an option: you can either remove the supremes from each breast (so you have two solid pieces) or you can cut the ducks in two halves (down the backbone and along the belly-breast line). Discard stuffing.

Return the strained sauce in which the ducks were roasted to the roasting pan, add and combine boiling Madeira sauce, lay the breasts (or halves) in, cover with foil, and keep warm.

When ready to eat, place one of the six servings on each of the fried bread slices, pour some of the sauce over each, and serve the remainder in a sauceboat.

ROAST TEAL

This delicious little duck is good cold prepared in any way but seems especially good prepared in this fashion. Here it is intended to be served hot.

SERVES 2–4

salt and pepper
4 teal
2 tangerines, peeled, halved,
  and stuck in several places
  with a fork
8 strips bacon

½ cup port wine
1 Tb. lemon juice
1 cup beach plum jelly
  (or plain plum or red currant)
½ Tb. flour

Salt and pepper the birds inside and out and place half a well-punctured tangerine in each bird. Truss the bird so as to bind down the 2 slices of bacon that you wrap around each teal. Place in roasting pan.

In a small skillet heat the wine and lemon juice, then stir in and dissolve the jelly. Ladle it over the birds and roast in a 400° oven for 18–25 minutes, depending on how rare you like your duck.

Remove the little ducks to a platter and make the sauce by first skimming off the bacon fat, then stirring in over a simmering flame the ½ tablespoon of flour stirred into 2 tablespoons of water. Simmer until the sauce is somewhat thickened, pour it over the birds, and serve.

MALLARD MILLINOCKET

Roast Duck With Mushroom-Madeira Sauce

SERVES 2

1 mallard duck	2 strips bacon
½ chopped, peeled sour apple	½ cup Madeira
½ rib celery, chopped	½ cup boiling water
½ small onion, chopped	¼ lb. mushrooms, sliced
salt and freshly ground pepper	1 tsp. cornstarch

Wipe out the cavity of the duck with a damp cloth and fill it with the apple, celery, and onion. Salt and pepper inside and out. Lay strips of bacon over the breast.

Place the bird on a rack and roast in a preheated 475° oven for 10 minutes, then reduce the heat to 350° and continue roasting another 20–30 minutes, basting every 10 minutes with most of the Madeira (reserving 2 tablespoons for the sauce) and the boiling water. During the last 10 minutes of roasting scatter the sliced mushrooms into the roasting pan.

When done, remove the bird and swirl the cornstarch mixed with the remaining Madeira into the pan juices. Bring to a boil to thicken, and spoon over the duck.

ROAST DUCK WITH SAUERKRAUT STUFFING

Jim Beard makes an impassioned plea for sauerkraut in his *Beard on Food*, and I am with him in this. Although I had used sauerkraut as a delightful stuffing for wild duck and goose, I realized that Jim had discovered something about affinitives for the great cabbage dish that I was ignorant of—how it blends with beer, garlic, and juniper berries. I already knew it was enhanced by caraway seeds. This recipe for roast duck is pieced together out of what Jim discovered in using sauerkraut with pork chops.

SERVES 4

4 mallards, blocks, or sprigs	1 lb. 11 oz. can sauerkraut*
12 or so thick slices of bacon	24 juniper berries, crushed
(4 of them soaked first	1 tsp. caraway seeds, crushed
in brandy)	or put through a peppermill
salt and pepper	1 cup ale or good beer
4 cloves garlic, sliced	(not "light" and tasteless)

From the neck of the ducks loosen the skin of both sides of the breast and insert a half slice of brandied bacon over each supreme. Pull skin back to normal. Salt and pepper each duck inside and out.

In a skillet sauté all but 4 slices of the remaining bacon, diced, until it is half cooked; add the garlic and sauté a bit longer.

Add sauerkraut, the crushed juniper berries, the caraway seeds, and the ale or beer, and spend some time distributing the ingredients uniformly throughout.

Cook gently for 15 minutes, then drain through a sieve, pressing the kraut as dry as you can. Reserve the liquid and keep warm.

Spoon the kraut into the ducks and secure cavities, then lay the ducks on a bed of the remaining bacon strips or on a rack in a shallow baking pan, pour in a cup or so of the liquid, and bake uncovered for 30 minutes in a 450° oven. (Some may wish to roast the ducks longer than 30 minutes.) Baste them quickly three or four times with the liquid.

Same Recipe for Wild Goose

When using this stuffing with wild goose I lay the stuffed goose on a bed of sliced onions and carrots, add 1½ cups of liquid, and braise-roast the goose under a lid, basting regularly and adding more liquid if necessary.

The only time I have prepared goose in this way, I mashed the onions and carrots, added a bit of blend of flour and water, and stirred a little in to thicken the sauce. If you find that too much of the liquid has been used up in the basting, control the thickness of the sauce by adding beer as it simmers on top of the stove. Serve the sauce in a gravy boat or top the stuffing servings with a ladle of sauce.

---

* Out of an authentic keg or crock if you can get it; if not Shopwell's in my area is outstandingly superior to any other canned variety.

══════ MRS. RANDOLPH'S "ROAST" ══════ WILD DUCKS OR TEAL

Mrs. Randolph's way with wild duck produces a dish as delicious now as it was 200 years ago (Mary Randolph was an eighteenth-century lady, for she was a mature woman when the third edition of her cookbook was published in 1828). Here again Mrs. R. roasted on a spit before an open fire. Alas, we have to use a rotisserie.

To Roast Wild Ducks or Teal

"When the ducks are ready dressed, put in them a small onion, pepper, salt and a spoonful of red wine; if the fire be good, they will roast in twenty minutes; make gravy of the necks and gizzards, a spoonful of red wine, half an anchovy, a blade or two of mace, one onion, and a little cayenne pepper; boil it 'till it is wasted to half a pint, strain it through a hair sieve, and pour it on the ducks; serve them up with onion sauce in a boat; garnish the dish with raspings of bread."

NOTE 1: "If the fire be good," as it always is on a rotisserie, it will take about 23 minutes to broil a mallard to the doneness I prefer.

NOTE 2: In Mrs. R.'s day "gizzards" was a generic term, like our giblets, and included, of course, heart, liver, and gizzard.

Timetable for Game Birds on the Rotisserie

This table is intended to be helpful for timing game birds spit-roasted on a rotisserie. The timing assumes the rotisserie is glowing before the spit is inserted, but you must always check for doneness, as size, temperature, etc., of birds can vary.

Before you spit the birds, truss them well in such a way as to bind the drumstick joints to the "preacher's nose" and thus close the vent. Before trussing put a lump of butter in the cavity with a slice or two of onions, herbs if you wish, salt, and pepper. *Be prepared to baste.* A roasting chicken's fat will baste itself, but game birds need help. Try to spit the birds from rear through breast opening so the weight will be distributed evenly around the spit.

Pheasants	45–50 minutes
Mallard or black duck	25 minutes (*slightly rare*)
Grouse	30–35 minutes
Chukar	30–35 minutes
Teal	12–15 minutes
Woodcock	10–15 minutes
Quail	10 minutes
Dove	12–15 minutes

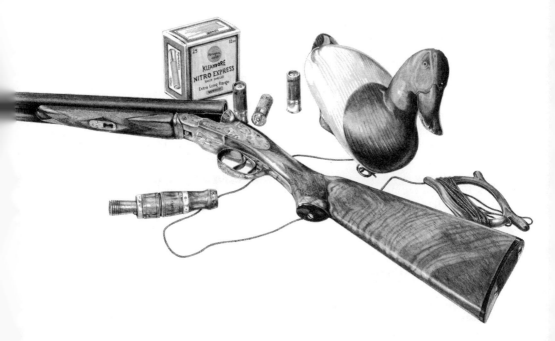

ROAST WILD DUCK WITH ORANGE SAUCE

Wild ducks as well as domestic go well in an orange sauce. This recipe calls for marinating the ducks ahead of time in a cooked, then cooled marinade. The rich flavor of wild duck (or goose) makes it feasible to use red meat marinade recipes if you wish (see page 5). Here is another good marinade.

Wild rice with mushrooms or polenta go well with this dish.

A DUCK MARINADE

1 small onion, diced	½ tsp. crumbled rosemary
½ rib celery, with leaves	6 peppercorns, coarsely crushed
2 cloves	12 juniper berries, smashed
½ tsp. mace	¼ cup oil
2 bay leaves	¼ cup wine vinegar
½ tsp. thyme	3 cups red wine

Put marinade ingredients in a saucepan, bring to a boil, then turn down the heat and simmer for 15 minutes.

Strain and set aside to cool, and when cool, marinate the ducks in it for 6 hours before roasting.

SERVES 6–8

4 ducks, previously marinated	2 oranges, unpeeled and quartered
1½ Tb. Kitchen Bouquet	24 juniper berries, smashed
2 Tb. brown sugar	¼ lb. salt pork, sliced thin
1 tsp. powdered ginger	1½ cups marinade (see above)
½ tsp. thyme	½ cup Grand Marnier
½ tsp. crumbled rosemary	1 tsp. Harvey's or
salt and pepper	Worcestershire sauce
juice of ½ lemon	

In a small skillet, mix the Kitchen Bouquet, sugar, ginger, thyme, rosemary, salt, pepper, and lemon juice. Just heat to melt and blend.

Put two quarters of an orange plus 6 smashed juniper berries in each duck, paint with the Kitchen Bouquet mixture, and affix salt pork strips over duck breasts with toothpicks.

Put ducks in shallow roasting pan, add the marinade, Grand Marnier, and sauce, and roast in an oven preheated to 400° for 25–30 minutes, or until the ducks are done to your liking.

Put the ducks on a hot platter, garnish, and serve sauce in roasting pan in a sauceboat.

NOTE: If you wish, you can thicken the sauce by stirring in a tablespoon of softened butter mixed with 1 tablespoon of flour. Add in small bits, stirring the simmering sauce until thickened.

WILD DUCK WITH COLONEL HAWKER'S SAUCE

This recipe is without doubt the most legendary of waterfowl sauces, if not for taste (although it is quite good) then as a historic survival. The old soldier, whose shooting journals are to the gun sport what *The Compleat Angler* is to angling, was the lusty enthusiast nonpareil of the fowling piece and the water-fowl marshes. His passion for all kinds of duck and goose shooting was a mono-mania, but his prose, as hearty and bright as his squire's eighteenth-century visage, is classic.

Here is the recipe, as best recovered now, years after the Colonel last tasted it.

SERVES 2–3

THE SAUCE

1 Tb. Harvey's sauce
1 Tb. mushroom catsup
1 Tb. lemon juice
3 shallots or scallions, chopped
2 cloves
½ tsp. mace

Pinch cayenne pepper
1½ cups chicken stock
2 glasses port wine
(you figure out what an
18th-century glass holds)*

THE DUCKS

2 mallard ducks
1 onion, halved
12 juniper berries, crushed

¼ cup melted butter
1 tsp. grated orange rind
¼ cup red wine

Put all the sauce ingredients save the wine in a saucepan, bring to a boil, and simmer 10 minutes. Add the wine and bubble again. Set aside. Melt 3 table-spoons butter and stir in 2 tablespoons flour. Cook a minute or two. Off heat, stir in the liquid. Return to heat and stirring, bring to boil, then simmer for 5 minutes.

Stuff the cavities of each duck with ½ onion and 6 crushed juniper berries. Put ducks on spit of rotisserie and broil for 20–25 minutes, basting often with a mixture of the melted butter, grated orange, and red wine.

Serve with the colonel's sauce.

* I have since learned that an eighteenth-century wine glass usually held 3 ounces.

ROAST DUCK WITH GIN AND JUNIPER SAUCE

I once decided to take a leaf out of Colonel Hawker's notebook and substitute gin for port in his famous sauce. The duck is roasted and the sauce served separately.

SERVES 4–5

THE GIN AND JUNIPER SAUCE

1 Tb. Harvey's sauce
1 Tb. mushroom catsup
1 Tb. lemon juice
3 shallots or scallions, chopped
2 whole cloves
10 juniper berries, smashed
½ Tb. mace

⅛ tsp. cayenne
1½ cups chicken stock
¼ cup gin
½ cup red wine
3 Tb. butter
2 Tb. flour

THE DUCKS

3–4 ducks
2 tart apples, quartered
2 onions, quartered
3–4 celery tops

¼ cup gin
¼ cup water
4 Tb. butter, melted

Put all of the sauce ingredients save the gin, wine, butter, and flour in a sauce-pan. Bring to a boil, then, on low heat, simmer for 15 minutes.

Add gin and wine and bring to a bubble. Set aside.

Stuff the ducks with the apples, onions, and celery. Place on a rack over a shallow baking pan and roast in a preheated 425° oven for 20 minutes (for rare; more if you prefer medium), basting with the ¼ cup of gin, ¼ cup of water, and the melted butter.

While the ducks are roasting, melt the 3 tablespoons of butter for the sauce, and, stirring constantly, add the flour. Cook over low heat until the flour colors, then, off heat, stir in and blend the sauce liquid. Place back over medium heat and simmer, stirring, until the sauce thickens.

Pour a bit of sauce over each bird and serve the rest in a sauceboat.

═══════ BREAST OF TEAL, BROILED ═══════

This is a very good way to prepare this toothsome bird if it is not overcooked. I like teal just barely done but not rare, and the time given below is just right for my broiler with the breasts about 2½ inches from the element.

SERVES 2—4

4 teal breasts
6 Tb. butter
1½ tsp. lemon juice

white pepper
¼ lb. mushrooms, sliced
¼ cup port wine

Remove breasts of the ducks, then flatten them as much as you can by pressing with the heel of your hand.

Melt 4 tablespoons of the butter and add the lemon juice and white pepper. Place where handy for basting.

Broil the breasts 8–10 minutes to the side, basting until you have used up the mix. Then continue to baste from the pan dredgings.

While breasts are broiling, sauté the mushrooms in 2 tablespoons of the butter and when the liquid from the mushrooms has evaporated, add the port and cook that down, too.

When the breasts are done remove to hot platter and pour the pan drippings onto the mushrooms and then the combined mushrooms and drippings over the teal breasts. If there are not enough basting drippings left, melt another 2–3 tablespoons of butter and add to mushroom sauce.

═══════ BLACK DUCK À LA BANGOR: ═══════
BRAISED WITH TURNIPS AND ONIONS

Serve this with green peas and crusty bread.

SERVES 2

1½ tsp. rosemary, savory, and
   thyme, crushed
1 black duck
salt and freshly ground pepper
4 Tb. butter
5 small white turnips, peeled and
   halved

10 small white onions, peeled
½ tsp. sugar
¼ cup bourbon
¾ cup duck or chicken stock

Sprinkle half the herbs into the duck cavity. Rub the inside and outside of the bird with salt and pepper.

In a flameproof casserole, just large enough to accommodate the duck with the vegetables around it, melt the butter over medium heat. When foaming, skim off the froth. Now brown the duck on all sides.

Add the turnips and onions and brown them, sprinkling the sugar over and turning until glazed.

Warm the bourbon, pour it over the duck, and set aflame, basting the bird.

Add the stock and sprinkle the remaining herbs over all. Bring to a boil, then cover and place in a 325° oven for 20–30 minutes. Uncover, baste, and raise the heat to 375° for a final 10 minutes to brown the skin a little.

Remove the duck and split in half. Set on a platter, then scoop up the vegetables and arrange around the bird. Keep warm. Skim off excess fat and boil down the pan juices until amost syrupy. Pour over the duck halves.

MALLARD

═ MRS. MARY RANDOLPH'S BRAISED WILD DUCK ═

This recipe came from the third edition of Mrs. Randolph's book, published early in the year of Andrew Jackson's first election as president, 1828.

Rice pilaf and braised celery go handsomely with this dish, as does a good claret or a California Cabernet Sauvignon.

SERVES 3–5

4 wild ducks (with giblets)
salt and pepper
1 tsp. powdered cloves
8 shallots (or scallion or onion equivalent)
butter or 4 bacon strips
½ cup wine
⅓ cup vinegar

½ tsp. honey or brown sugar
½ lemon peel, grated
1 bouquet "sweet herbs" (bay, chervil, parsley, tarragon, or rosemary)
½ tsp. cornstarch dissolved in 1 Tb. water (optional)
croutons (optional)

While simmering duck giblets and necks in 1½ cups water, rub the insides of the ducks with salt, pepper, and ¼ tsp. cloves each. Place in the cavity of each bird its own giblets, two peeled shallots, and a tablespoon of butter. Cover each bird's breast with butter (or with a strip of bacon held in place with wooden toothpicks) and sew up cavity.

Place fowls in casserole, preferably in one that will just hold them snugly, and add the remainder of the ingredients (except for cornstarch and croutons). Put in 500° oven for 15 minutes uncovered, then turn down heat to 300° and continue braising (now covered) for about 25 minutes more. (See page 199 for a discussion of cooking times for wild ducks.)

Baste occasionally (half broth, half wine) and each time you baste press herb bouquet with bowl of spoon to release herb essence.

You may thicken the pan juices, after the birds are removed, with cornstarch dissolved in water.

Near the end of the braising you may wish to fry 2–3 pieces of bread in bacon fat, or in garlic butter, cube into croutons, and place a few on the top of the sauce in the boat and the remainder in a bowl beside the sauceboat.

═══════ WOODBRIDGE ISLAND DUCK ═══════

This recipe is a favorite of Bill End, senior vice-president of L. L. Bean. It comes from his friend Ben Pearson, owner of the Byfield Snuff Company of Byfield, Massachusetts, manufacturers and importers of fine snuffs. Serve these duck breasts with wild rice.

SERVES 6–8

8 slices bacon
2 large onions
4 black ducks, breasted
flour, salt, and pepper mixed
  together in paper bag

½ cup red wine (or any dry wine)
½ cup orange marmalade

Cook the bacon until crisp. Remove from the pan and reserve fat and bacon.

In a large fry pan sauté sliced onions in the bacon fat until soft. Remove them and set aside.

Dredge the duck breasts in the flour, salt, and pepper mixture. Sauté them in bacon fat until lightly brown on both sides.

Return onions and crumbled bacon to pan, covering the duck. Pour wine and marmalade mixture over all, cover, and simmer on medium heat 15–20 minutes. The duck should be pink in the middle.

Put the duck breasts on a warm platter and pour sauce over top.

BRAISED DUCK IN CREOLE SAUCE

There are so many Creole sauces that one can take his pick from almost any cookbook. They range from the simple to the "complex," but complexity consists merely of a lengthy list of ingredients. Here is a very serviceable one that goes well with wild duck. Serve with rice pilaf or wild rice.

SERVES 4

1 onion, diced	½ tsp. thyme
1 green pepper, diced	½ tsp. cumin
6 Tb. butter	¼ tsp. red pepper flakes
12 mushrooms, sliced	4 Tb. Madeira
2 garlic cloves, smashed and peeled	1 tsp. chili powder
16-oz. can of tomato purée or	¼ tsp. allspice
tomatoes in purée	salt and pepper to taste
1 cup stock	3–4 ducks, cut into serving pieces
2 bay leaves	

Sauté the onion and pepper in 3 tablespoons of the butter. Then after 3–4 minutes add the mushrooms. Add the rest of the ingredients (except ducks) and simmer, uncovered, for 30–40 minutes. The sauce should be thickish.

While the sauce is simmering, sauté the duck pieces in remaining 3 tablespoons of butter in a deep casserole or Dutch oven until nicely browned.

Add the sauce, cover, and braise at a simmer for about 30 minutes or until duck is done to your taste.

NOTE: You can coat the duck pieces with flour before browning if you wish.

BRAISED DUCK WITH MADEIRA
AND HERB GRAVY

This adapted Colonial recipe betrays its British origin by its use of mushroom catsup. Wild rice is traditional with this dish.

SERVES 2–3

6 slices bacon	½ tsp. thyme
1 carrot, sliced thin	¼ tsp. tarragon
1 large onion, chopped	3 Tb. orange juice
2 mallards, sprig, black duck,	½ tsp. grated orange rind
or any other "large" duck,	1 Tb. mushroom catsup
salted and peppered inside and	or mushroom sauce
out	1½ tsp. cornstarch dissolved
1 cup chicken broth or water	in ⅓ cup water or broth
2 bay leaves	½ cup Madeira (or dry Marsala
½ tsp. chervil	or sherry)

Place 4 strips of bacon on bottom of roasting pan and cover with sliced carrot and chopped onion.

Cut 2 strips of bacon in halves and affix half a strip on each side of duck's breasts with toothpicks.

Roast the seasoned ducks in 450° oven for 18–20 minutes, then cool to 350°

and continue until done (see page 199), basting (and perhaps adding broth if required) as often as other chores permit.

Turn off oven, remove ducks, and set in pan on oven's open door to keep warm.

Skim off fat and add herbs (as a bouquet if you wish), orange juice, grated rind, and mushroom catsup. Put roasting pan on top of stove and simmer for 10–12 minutes.

Remove herb bouquet (if not in bouquet, remove bay leaves) and stir in thin paste made of cornstarch and the Madeira and water or broth. Bring to a bubble.

Cut ducks in half and serve each on a piece of toast (or fried bread, see "The Toast" section of Grouse with Mushrooms on Liver-Spread Toast, page 156) with the gravy poured over.

CASSEROLE OF WILD DUCK AND ERRANT LILIES

This dish celebrates *all* of the "Lilies" (see p. 35).

SERVES 4–6

4 white parts of leeks, chopped	½ cup chicken broth
3 shallots, minced	½ cup red wine
1 clove garlic, minced	6–8 chicken livers
4 scallions, diced	3 Tb. butter
12 small pearl onions	2 Tb. bread crumbs
1 rib celery, with leaves	¼ tsp. nutmeg
½ lb. small mushrooms, sliced	1½ Tb. Madeira or Marsala
1 carrot, sliced thin	4 ducks, salted and peppered
12 juniper berries, crushed	inside and out

1 sprig parsley
6–8 chives } tied together in a cheesecloth bundle
1 sprig thyme or ¼ tsp. dried

Put all of the vegetables, juniper berries, herb bundle, chicken broth, and wine in a big casserole and bring just to boil on top of the stove.

Sauté the chicken livers in butter until just pink inside. Mash with a fork, then stir in and mix the bread crumbs, nutmeg, and Madeira. Stuff the ducks with this mixture, then truss and sew up or tie the ducks.

Lay them in the casserole atop the hot vegetable and liquid mix, cover, and roast in a preheated 400° oven 20–30 minutes, 40 if you want the ducks well done.

DUCK À LA MARMALADE

Here is L. L. Bean annual game dinner chef Joseph Murray, Sr.'s recipe for preparing coot and other diving ducks. He serves it with wild rice and white wine.

SERVES 4–6

6–8 ducks, cut up (parts of sea ducks, eider, coot, or any diver duck)

Make a brine of wine, vinegar, and lemon; soak overnight in a large pan, making sure that the duck is completely submerged in brine. For proportions, see his brine for spiced smoked goose, page 221.

1 garlic, minced	6 Tb. butter
6–8 onions, chopped	marinated duck pieces (above)
4 green peppers, seeded and chopped	2 cups flour; more if needed
1 lb. mushrooms, chopped	1 large bottle A-1 Sauce
1 tsp. salt	2 cups red table wine
1/2 tsp. pepper	2 cups red wine vinegar
1 tsp. sage	10 oz. or largest size orange marmalade

In a large oval frying pan (cast iron), sauté in butter the garlic, onions, green peppers, mushrooms, half the salt, pepper, and sage.

Take ducks out of brine and wipe them off with paper towels. Put flour, remaining salt, pepper, and sage into a large bag with the duck parts and shake so that the flour mixture will coat them.

Add duck parts to frying pan with onion-pepper-mushroom mixture, and cook until blood comes to the top of meat; turn then to cook other side. Do not overcook; when almost done pour A-1 sauce over ducks. Let sit for a few minutes, then mix into the meat. Pour wine and vinegar over duck, then add orange marmalade; spread it over the mixture. Take off stove and let sit 10 minutes before serving.

JUDY MARSH'S COOT STEW

The American coot, often scorned as food, is actually quite tasty if the shooter handles the bird properly. This bird eats very much the same food as ducks do, but is not of the duck-goose-swan family but rather of *Rallidae*, the rails, gallinules, and coots. The bird should not be plucked but skinned, for the fat lining of the skin, what there is of it, can be quite strong. Some shooter-cooks not only remove skin and fat but soak the bird in salt solution with a couple of tablespoons of vinegar added. We have here two versions of coot stew—one from Judy Marsh of West Gardiner, Maine, and one from L. L. Bean's Alex Delicata, who uses buttermilk for his marinade.

SERVES 4–6

5 egg-size onions	1 large bay leaf
5 large carrots, in chunks	1 qt. water
1 good qt. tomatoes	3 Tb. cider vinegar
1 pinch marjoram	3 Tb. wine
1 heaping tsp. parsley	2–4 beef bouillon cubes
1 Tb. salt	3–4 coots
1/4 tsp. pepper	1/8–1/4 lb. butter

In a large iron pot, simmer all the ingredients but the coots.

Cut the breast of several coots (scoter) into bite-size pieces. Roll them in well-seasoned flour and brown in a large heavy skillet in 1/8 to 1/4 pound butter. Thin carefully with water to make a smooth gravy. Tilt into the pot with the vegetables. Simmer very slowly in covered pot at least 2 hours. Almost any other meat can be substituted for coot.

ALEX DELICATA'S COOT STEW

"Use buttermilk as a tenderizer or marinade for strong-flavored game or water-fowl, especially for badly blood-shot birds and small game such as ducks, bluebills, coot, old squaw, etc.," Alex Delicata advises.

Serve this stew over a bed of steamed wild rice and offer a room-temperature hearty burgundy.

SERVES 2

1½ lb. breasts (and legs,
   if desired) coot, or other game
   (see above)
2 cups buttermilk
½ lb. bacon
2 cloves garlic, smashed

1 medium onion, chopped
2 ribs celery, diced
½ tsp. dried basil
about ¼ cup red wine
about ¼ cup water

Place the meat in a glass or crockery container (stainless is okay; never use aluminum). Cover with buttermilk and marinate for 48 hours or more in a cool place.

Remove meat and wipe off excess buttermilk. Reserve the buttermilk for thickening gravy or sauce.

Over medium heat fry bacon in a large skillet. Remove when crisp. Brown the garlic in the hot bacon fat; remove before garlic browns. Add the onion, celery, and basil. Cook until onions are soft.

Add the coot portions and cook quickly to seal in the juices, turning once. Add water and/or red wine. (I prefer to use a mix of half water and half wine.)

Cook for 15–20 minutes at medium heat. The liquid in the skillet can be thickened with the reserved buttermilk.

Geese

SNOW GOOSE

Like turkey, the big game of upland birds, the goose is the big game of the waterfowl. All goose shooters agree with the late author of *Scattergunning*, Ray Holland, when he wrote. "If there is anything with more thrill in it than seeing a flock of Canada geese with set wings coming straight at you I wouldn't know what it is. I haven't found it." The dyed-in-the-wool goose shooter is usually one of strong opinions. He will have his own theories about setting out decoys, about the virtues of 2's over 4's or vice versa, and of pump guns vs. autoloaders. He'll be hard to please when it comes to goose calls of just the right timbre. Similarly, he won't experiment much with the way he or his spouse prepares a goose. Here are a number of goose recipes that we have found rewarding.

Weights of Geese

For a guide to servings from wild geese, see page 196. With proper barding you can roast a wild goose that is a "bird of the year," a bird that was hatched during the spring of the same year that it was bagged in the fall. C. S. Williams of the then Bureau of Sport Fisheries and Wildlife of the Department of the Interior wrote, "Any goose weighing much over 8 pounds (in the feathers, that is, undrawn) in October or November can hardly be a honker of the year, but this does not preclude the existence of small adults below 8 pounds."

If the dressed weight ready for cooking is much over 4 pounds 8 ounces, it is unlikely to be a young bird.

The chart below gives a fair sampling from the geese that I have actually weighed in the feathers and after dressing; those with asterisks are certainly not "birds of the year." You can be sure I braised those birds.

WEIGHT IN FEATHERS UNDRAWN	WEIGHT DRESSED FOR COOKING	PERCENT OF DRESSED WEIGHTS TO BIRD IN FEATHER
*11 lb. 2 oz.	6 lb. 5 oz.	57%
*10 lb. 3 oz.	6 lb.	59%
*9 lb. 4 oz.	5 lb. 10 oz.	60.8%

WEIGHT IN FEATHERS UNDRAWN	WEIGHT DRESSED FOR COOKING	PERCENT OF DRESSED WEIGHTS TO BIRD IN FEATHER
*9 lb. 1 oz.	5 lb. 8 oz.	60.7%
*9 lb.	5 lb. 8 oz.	61.1%
*8 lb. 4 oz.	5 lb. 1 oz.	61.3%
7 lb. 8 oz.	4 lb. 5 oz.	57.5%
7 lb. 1 oz.	4 lb. 3 oz.	59.3%
6 lb. 6 oz.	4 lb.	62.7%
6 lb. 1 oz.	3 lb. 10 oz.	59.8%

So the rule of thumb is that when your dressed bird weighs 4½ pounds or under it is apt to be a young bird.

NOTE: When you receive a goose in the feathers and undrawn, you can come very close to its eventual dressed weight if you multiply its dressed weight by .60. Conversely, if you received the bird dressed and weigh it thus and a guest wants to know out of curiosity how much the bird weighed alive you can come close by dividing its dressed weight by 3 and then multiplying by 5.

Smoked Wild Goose

This delectable bird ought to be put down in brine overnight, totally immersed, then washed in clear water, drained, and dried. I pick a bird of 4 pounds dressed (or less), tuck bacon slices under the skin of the breast, and put a quartered onion and half an apple in the cavity. A 4-pound bird dressed should roast 1¾–2 hours. I baste him often, again with Colonel Hawker's sauce (page 205), and smoke him a full 2 hours. I sometimes baste a goose while it's in the smoker.

Roast Wild Goose

Roast wild goose is a great delicacy, but, as noted earlier, the cook should beware of the old bird. It may be useful to read the information above to get some idea of the age of your wild goose. It is best to braise an old goose, but if you insist on roasting, then roast it, uncovered, with liquid in the roasting pan. Geese that weigh 5 pounds or more dressed are almost certainly not "birds of the year." So consider a 4- to 5-pound goose dressed about the right size for roasting.

═══ ROASTING GOOSE WITH ONION STUFFING ═══ IN JUNIPER AND GIN

Before preparing this recipe have a look at page 218 and note suggestion about juniper infusion.

SERVES 4

THE DRESSING
6 Tb. butter
2 onions, chopped
1 rib celery, diced
3 cloves garlic, sliced
3 cups bread crumbs

¾ tsp. salt
1–1½ Tb. rubbed sage
½ tsp. thyme
1 egg, beaten
¼–½ cup chicken broth or water

THE GOOSE
salt and freshly ground pepper
4- to 5-lb. goose, dressed weight
¼–½ lb. salt pork; sliced thin
3 cups chicken broth
½ cup gin

2 bay leaves
12 juniper berries, smashed
2 onions, chopped
1 Tb. flour mixed with 3 Tb. water

Melt the butter and sauté the onions, celery, and garlic until onions are soft.

In a bowl mix the bread crumbs, salt, sage, and thyme, then mix in the vegetables and butter. Stir in the beaten egg, then if necessary stir in enough broth or water to give the right degree of moisture. The stuffing should not be wet, for if it is, it will set like a plum pudding inside the bird.

Salt and pepper the goose inside and out and stuff loosely.

Now either slip pork slabs under breast skin or lay alongside breast, and when trussing the legs together whip back with the string and tie salt pork slabs down securely.

Put the liquids and all other ingedients except the flour in a shallow roasting pan. Then put the goose breast side up on a rack set in the pan and roast in a 375° oven for an hour. Baste the bird often with the pan juices, at least five or six times.

I sometimes make a foil tent over the bird; I take it off after an hour and roast the goose uncovered about 1 hour more.

When done, remove bird and keep warm while you stir into the roasting pan liquid 1 tablespoon of flour mixed with 3 tablespoons of water. Put roasting pan on top of stove and simmer until gravy has thickened.

I got good murmurs around my board once when I garnished the goose on its platter with pickled peach halves.

NOTE: Wild goose and ducks roasted over liquid and under a lid or foil tent need glazing at the end of the roasting to replace their moist gray look with an appetizingly brown one. I do this by brushing the bird with 1–1½ tablespoons La Choy brown gravy sauce and then turning the oven up to 500° for the last 15 minutes of the uncovered roasting.

═══════ ROAST GOOSE ═══════
WITH APRICOT AND APPLE STUFFING

Here's a stuffing for those who like a fruit filling and a tart taste of fruit in the stuffing liquid.

SERVES 2–3

THE STUFFING
1 tsp. pickling spices
½ cup red wine
1 cup water
1 Tb. blackstrap molasses
2 apples, peeled, cored, and diced
THE GOOSE
3–4 lb. goose, dressed
½ cup lemon juice

1 cup dried apricots
½ cup raisins
½ cup bread crumbs
¼ lb. salt pork, sliced thin

salt and pepper

The night before you plan to roast the goose, prepare the stuffing as follows: Simmer the pickling spices in the wine, water, and molasses for 10 minutes or so. Then strain and add the apples, apricots, and raisins. Simmer for 5 minutes, cover, and set outside overnight, on a cool porch if you have one.

When ready to roast, rub inside and outside of goose with lemon juice; salt and pepper the bird inside and out.

Strain the liquid out of the stuffing and reserve liquid. Stir bread crumbs into the fruit.

Stuff, truss, and close goose vent by sewing or by skewering. Place slices of salt pork over the breast.

Place goose in a rack over a shallow roasting pan and roast in a preheated 350° oven for 2 hours or so, basting frequently with the strained liquid.

ROAST GOOSE STUFFED WITH POTATOES AND PARMESAN

This stuffing is fine for wild goose, but it is also good in roast duck or pheasant.

SERVES 2–3

THE STUFFING
2 cups mashed potatoes	½ tsp. thyme
½ cup sour cream	2 tsp. rubbed sage
5 Tb. grated Parmesan	1 egg, beaten
½ tsp. chervil	1 cup or more bread crumbs

THE GOOSE
2 tsp. lemon juice	1 onion, sliced
salt and pepper	2 garlic cloves, sliced
1 dressed honker	½ cup chicken broth
½ lb. salt pork, sliced	½ cup red wine
1 carrot, sliced	

To make the stuffing, add bread crumbs last. Mix all the other ingredients thoroughly first. Then add 1 cup bread crumbs or enough more to give a proper stuffing consistency.

Rub lemon juice, salt, and pepper on the goose inside and out, add stuffing, and sew up cavity.

Lay salt pork slices on goose breast and secure with two toothpicks. Strew into the roasting pan the carrot, onion, and garlic, and place goose over the vegetable layer.

Add the liquids. Cover with a loose foil tent after you have roasted it for about 20 minutes in a preheated 450° oven. Continue roasting for another 1¾–2 hours until done, basting often with the pan liquid.

ROAST GOOSE BUDAPEST

This is a covered roast with red cabbage flavored with sweet Hungarian paprika, sage, and marjoram as a stuffing.

3–4 lb. goose, dressed for roasting
juice of ½ lemon
salt and pepper
¼ lb. salt pork, cubed
2 onions, sliced
2 cloves garlic, sliced
1 goose liver
2 Tb. sweet Hungarian paprika
½ tsp. marjoram

1 Tb. rubbed Dalmatian sage
½ medium-size red cabbage,
   shredded
2 medium-size white turnips,
   sliced thin
1 Tb. vinegar
¾ cup red wine
1 tsp. brown sugar
5 bacon slices

Rub the goose inside and out with lemon juice; salt and pepper it in the same fashion.

In a large skillet try out the salt pork cubes. Remove the cracklings and reserve.

Sauté the onions and garlic and then the goose liver in the salt pork fat, and when liver is almost soft, stir in the paprika, marjoram, and sage, mixing thoroughly. Mash the liver.

Add the shredded cabbage, sliced turnips, salt pork cracklings, vinegar, wine, and sugar. Cover, bring to a boil, then turn down heat and simmer for 15 minutes or so until the turnips are soft and the cabbage just short of done.

Drain the cooked cabbage mixture thoroughly, reserving the liquid. Stuff the goose with cabbage mixture, sew up the cavity, and place bacon strips over the breast.

Roast the goose in a preheated 450° oven for 15–20 minutes. Then reduce heat to 325° or so, cover the goose loosely with a foil tent, add a bit of the cabbage liquid to the pan, and roast for about 1½ hours, or until the goose is tender. Baste often with the cabbage liquid.

CANADA GOOSE, ROTISSERIE

This is a relatively easy way to cook wild goose, although during the hour and a half that the bird is on the spit you will (or ought) to baste fairly continuously. The point is to use the fat and juices from the bird and the stuffing to flavor the bird from the outside as well as inside. A 4- to 4½-pound dressed Canada should be used here; when you have 5½- to 6½-pound (or more) dressed birds they are apt to be old and should be braised. See page 213 for dressed and live weights of Canadas and the recipes that follow for braised goose.

½ cup butter, creamed until soft
2 tsp. anchovy paste
   or anchovy sauce
½ tsp. onion juice
¼ tsp. lemon juice

1 dash hot sauce (e.g., Tabasco)
2 sticks or 1 cup of butter
   (½ lb.)
1 young Canada goose, with liver*

Mix all ingredients except goose together.

Place goose on the spit of the rotisserie and broil for 1½ hours, basting as often as possible with anchovy butter.

* If you drop off your geese with one of the outfits that pick and dress geese, never fail to ask that your birds be dressed with the giblets.

How to Get the Most out of Juniper Berries

Juniper flavor goes so well with game birds and especially roasted, braised, or spit-broiled wild fowl, that I did some experiments to see if I couldn't impart more juniper flavor to such dishes and/or to the sauces served with them than a few crushed juniper berries would permit. I discovered that 2 ounces of gin (itself, of course, juniper flavored), first warmed, then poured over eight or ten thoroughly crushed juniper berries and then flamed produced an infusion most redolent of juniper. The residue of liquid after the flickering blue flames burn out (or after you have blown them out) when added to a sauce imparts a wonderful juniper bouquet. In making this game-bird sauce ingredient with 2 ounces gin and eight or ten berries you will have enough liquid after the fire goes out to flavor a sauce, a braised dish (in which case pour the juniper berries with the infusion into the braise liquid), or a stuffing. Vary the amount of gin and berries you use to fit the quality of the dish. If you have flamed it down so far that the remaining gin-and-juniper liquid tastes a bit bitter, add a quarter teaspoon of sugar and/or dilute it with a bit more gin.

    Most recipe books recommending the use of juniper berries in various dishes and sauces are too skimpy in their quantities. When I use a recipe that calls for "6 juniper berries, crushed" I almost invariably use a dozen or even fifteen.

═══════════ WILD GOOSE ═══════════

BRAISED IN SAUERKRAUT AND ALE

The hearty flavor of wild goose competes and blends well with other equally hearty flavors. The result here is delicious. Wild ducks may be substituted.

SERVES 3–4

4–5 slices bacon, preferably thick	1 28 oz. can sauerkraut, drained
1 small onion, finely chopped	12 juniper berries, crushed
1 clove garlic, chopped	1 tsp. caraway seed
4- to 5-lb. goose, dressed, with giblets	½ tsp. pepper
	2 cups ale
	2 Tb. red currant jelly, melted

Sauté the bacon lightly—until cooked through but still soft. Remove to plate.

    Sauté onion and garlic and goose giblets in bacon fat until onion is soft. Add kraut, reserved bacon, and other ingredients (except goose), plus one cup of the ale. Simmer for 3–4 minutes.

    Put the contents of the skillet into baking pan, set goose, salted and peppered inside and out, atop, and braise, covered, in a 350° oven, until goose is done (about 1½–2 hours).

Use reserved ale if more liquid is needed while goose is braising.

About 20 minutes before goose is done, remove lid and paint the bird with the currant jelly to glaze it; turn heat up to 450° to do this.

══ BRAISED GOOSE À LA COLONEL HAWKER ══

This recipe is a derivative of the wild duck recipe on page 205, for I found that a variation of the doughty colonel's sauce formed a fine base for the liquid needed in braising wild goose and for the eventual gravy.

This dish is good served with whipped potatoes (or with grits or hominy) and red cabbage. Of course, it is also good served with wild rice, but then, what isn't? I like a big, hearty Beaujolais with this meal.

SERVES 2–3

THE GOOSE
4–5-lb. goose, dressed,
   with giblets
1 apple, pared and sliced
THE BRAISING SAUCE
1½ cups chicken or duck broth
1 Tb. Harvey's or
   Worcestershire sauce
1 Tb. mushroom catsup
   or mushroom sauce
1 Tb. lemon juice
3 shallots or scallions, chopped
2 carrots, sliced

1 onion, sliced
salt and pepper
4–5 slices bacon

2 cloves
½ tsp. mace
½ tsp. dried marjoram
½ tsp. crumbled dried rosemary
1 small pinch cayenne
¾ cup port wine
3 Tb. butter
1 Tb. flour

Stuff the goose with the apple and onion, salt and pepper it inside and out, and save giblets for the sauce.

Put giblets and all of the sauce ingredients, save the wine, butter, and flour, in a saucepan, bring to a boil, and simmer for 10 minutes. Add the wine.

Place bacon strips on bottom of lidded roaster or casserole, lay the goose on it, and place uncovered in 400° oven for 15 minutes.

Turn oven down to 325°, add the braising sauce, giblets, vegetables, and all, cover, and roast for 1½–2 hours.

When the goose is done, strain the sauce and skim off fat. In a skillet melt the butter and add the flour, cooking for a minute or so. Take off heat and stir in sauce. Return to a low heat, stirring to thicken. Chop the gizzard and heart fine, mash the liver, and stir them into the gravy. Sometimes the braising liquid is thick enough so you might not need the butter-and-flour mixture.

══ BROILED BREAST OF GOOSE ══
À LA DUDLEY LUNT

The late Dudley C. Lunt was a dyed-in-the-wool Maine man who moved to Delaware. To compensate for the loss of his native wilderness, he spent as much time as his native journalism, book writing, and conservation activities permitted in a goose blind. He taught me whatever I know about goose shooting, and now that I have inherited his famous favorite goose call he might even approve my calling. This recipe was his favorite goose recipe.

Serve this with celery braised in butter and chicken stock, and rice, either white or wild. Dudley always served a fine Cabernet Sauvignon with his broiled goose breast.

SERVES 3–4

¼ cup white wine
½ stick butter, melted
4 supremes: the 2 sides of
  2 goose breasts

salt and pepper
parsley

Stir the wine into the melted butter and use for the basting liquid.

Coat supremes on both sides with the baste and broil about 3 inches from the flame or broiling element for about 3–4 minutes to the side, basting often. The supremes should be rare—i.e., they should if you like your steaks rare. Broil longer if you like them less rare. Salt and pepper, and garnish with parsley.

══ BROILED MARINATED GOOSE BREASTS ══

Serve these breasts with braised celery and lightly curried rice.

SERVES 2–3

½ cup teriyaki or soy sauce
½ cup tawny port
  (sherry will do too)
½ cup olive oil
1 medium onion, finely sliced
3 cloves garlic, sliced

15 juniper berries,
  crushed in mortar and pestle
2 tsp. powdered ginger
1 tsp. grated orange rind
salt and pepper
1 wild goose

Mix all the ingredients except goose.

Split goose down back, spread flat, and marinate 6–12 hours, turning as often as possible, or put ribs up and fill cavities.

Broil 8–10 minutes to side or according to preference for doneness, basting two or three times with marinade.

══ BRAISED BREAST OF WILD GOOSE ══

Rice and braised celery go well with this dish, a hearty red wine with this meal.

1 goose breast (i.e., 2 supremes)
flour for dusting
2 medium to large white onions
4 Tb. butter
3 Tb. flour
bouquet garni

1½ cups good red wine
¾ cup canned consommé
  (undiluted)
¼ cup water
peppercorns (6 or so)
salt

Dust the goose supremes with flour.

Brown onions lightly in butter. Remove onions.

Brown goose supremes in same butter, and remove them.

Add 3 tablespoons flour to butter in pan. Add bouquet garni, stir, and cook a minute or so.

Add slowly, while stirring, the wine, consommé, water, and peppercorns, and simmer over low heat for 10 minutes to thicken and reduce some.

Add goose supremes and onions, cover, and simmer about 20 minutes, more or less, depending on size of breasts, for rare but not purple breast halves.

Don't salt the goose breast until after it has browned.

SPICED SMOKED GOOSE

Joe Murray, Sr., is a Bean staff man who acts as co-chef with Alex Delicata at L.L. Bean's annual game dinner. Joe gives you his proportions for a presmoking "brine"; you can vary the total amount of liquid, using enough to cover the goose in the container you use.

Joe uses one of Bean's Little Chief Smokers; I also swear by his handy device. Serve this with wild rice, red wine, and mixed vegetables.

SERVES 4–6

4–5-lb. goose	2 Tb. allspice
½ cup lemon juice	apple chips
1 cup A-1 sauce	oranges
3 cups wine	apples
1 qt. vinegar	onions
salt and pepper	

Soak goose in brine made of lemon juice, A-1 sauce, wine, vinegar, salt, pepper, and allspice. Make sure goose is submerged in brine; if there is not enough to cover, add water until covered. Let set 24 hours, covered.

I fill the pan with apple chips and light them. I use about 3 pans of chips altogether. Put goose into smoker and smoke until all the chips are used up. After the goose is smoked, put apples, onions, and oranges into cavity and bake in oven at 350°–400° for 3 hours or more. Slice onto a hot platter.

Fish

BROWN TROUT

American anglers in general tend to take their catch too much for granted when it comes to cooking the fish. Perhaps it's the routine cuisine of American "seafood" restaurants that limits the imagination of too many angler-cooks, who too often confine their cookery to deep-fried, sautéed, or baked fish dishes. On the other hand, the French, English, Italian, and other European cuisines offer a whole tradition of fish cookery too often unheeded by American cooks. There is no reason why American angler-cooks should confine their cookery to fried fish *cum* tartar sauce.

In this section the intention is to give a few conventional recipes but at the same time to offer some recipes that take advantage of other cuisines. By that we do not mean to stress "fancy cookery." Many fish recipes that have been adapted from foreign cuisines are delicious, perhaps innovative to some, *but no more difficult to produce in an American kitchen* than deep-fried fish; in fact less difficult, for it is an art to deep-fry a thing as delicate as a trout.

The observant cook will notice that the use of herbs in fish cookery is performed with a lighter hand than in preparing a red meat dish from other game. For example, in poaching, the court bouillon while flavored with herbs and vegetables is more lightly flavored than, say, a moose stew, because the flesh of fish, especially fresh-water fish, is usually delicately flavored and its cookery should take this into consideration.

The greatest sin in cooking any kind of fish is overcooking. Because of its very delicacy fish dries out quickly when exposed to heat too long—and when the juice goes, flavor is greatly reduced, to say nothing of texture. Most recipes use the gauge "cook until flaky"; usually that's too long (except when smoking). A better measure is to cook until the flesh turns opaque—and the place to test is around the bone; when opaque, the flesh will come away from the bone, not stick to it.

In this section, we have given some dishes their French names, but the practiced cook will know that dishes under a traditional name are prepared in a wide variety of ways. Our recipes for such dishes represent *our* ways of preparing such traditional dishes. Indeed, we hope that this section will send American cooks to other cookbooks on their shelves, for a French recipe, say, for fillet of flounder will be just as good and perhaps even better when made with a fillet of walleyed pike or lake trout or channel catfish.

Remember, many—indeed, most—of the recipes listed for specific fish may be used for other species as well. For this reason we have indexed many recipes under several kinds of fish, e.g., Baked Redfish Fillets (page 304) is also indexed under baked snook, pompano, walleye, trout, and salmon fillets.

Also remember that you yourself may wish to combine recipes using some ingredients found in one recipe in another recipe of somewhat different type—e.g., most fillet recipes will apply to fish steaks, and vice versa.

It is also helpful to bear in mind that a recipe calling for 5 or 6 quarter-pound fillets can be adapted to whole fish of smaller size, i.e., to whole fish weighing perhaps a half pound each.

General Notes on Cleaning, Handling, Filleting, and Cooking Fish

Everyone who has eaten his own catch knows that fish are best when cooked and eaten right off the hook, as it were. Like asparagus and corn, the sooner killed (or picked) and cooked the better. Barring streamside campfire cooking, the game is to come as close to this freshness as possible in the handling of fish.

TREATMENT OF FISH TO BE EATEN THE SAME DAY CAUGHT OR THE DAY AFTER

I de-gill and gut fish to be eaten soon after they are caught (the same day or the next) and after thumbing out the kidney (the soft, dark, bloodlike vein under the backbone) and washing out the cavity and thoroughly drying it, I put it in a creel lined with dampened ferns (and add more ferns between succeeding fish—i.e., if there are any!). It is amazing how cool evaporation will keep the contents of a wicker creel.

If the fish are larger—like salmon, steelhead, or trophy-sized trout—I bleed them by sticking them just behind the gill cover and tie them, air free, in a plastic tube cut off a roll of a length to accommodate the fish plus two knots. I then lay the fish in the stream to keep cool.

I do not gut and gill such fish or any smaller fish that I intend to ship, and if I'm doing the "shipping"—i.e., driving home by car—I put the fish down in ice cubes in a Styrofoam cooler (pouring off or draining off the water often, for water is a notorious carrier of the bacteria that spoil flesh). Fish to be kept on ice or fish eventually to be frozen should not be cleaned, old-time advice notwithstanding.

FREEZING FISH

Fish kept on ice will remain reasonably flavorful for two days or a bit more, but I do not keep fish longer than 4–8 hours in the refrigerator before freezing. All fishes deteriorate in flavor after they are frozen, but you can reduce this deterioration markedly by freezing the fish in a block of ice or with a skim of ice over its surface.

I follow the Icelanders, or rather had already adopted the freezing technique recommended by their fisheries people, namely, to freeze the fish without dressing them beyond bleeding. See Box, page 246.

FILLETING FISH

In filleting fish, try to start the process by using a filleting knife. It should be as flexible as possible and have a narrow blade curving to a sharp point. It should also be razor sharp.

The process of filleting fish like pike, bluefish, walleyes, bass, snook, etc., is really a simple one. Lay the fish on a board and cut down to the spine and around the sides. Do not cut the spine in two.

Cut into fish behind the transverse cut and slice toward the tail, cutting down to, but not through, the ribcage.

When you have sliced down two-thirds of the length of the fish where it begins to taper, push the point clear through, keeping the flat of the blade close along the backbone.

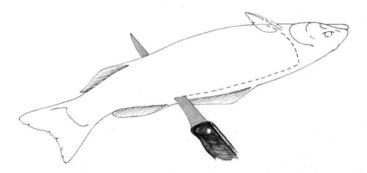

Holding the fish with the left hand, continue the cut close against the backbone all the way to the tail.

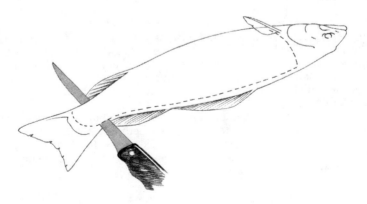

Now lay the fillet open and finish cutting the flesh away from the ribcage.

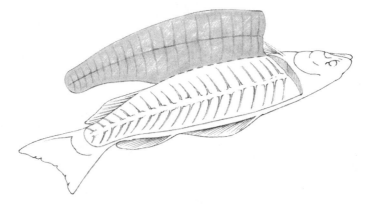

Slice it loose along the belly line, turn the fish over, and duplicate process on the other side.

To remove skin, place the fillet on the board, skin side down, and take hold of the tip of the fillet with the left hand. Cut in between skin and flesh, then change your grip with the left hand and hold tight onto the skin tip while you slice forward, pressing the flat of the knife blade down as you slice forward.

CHARCOAL-GRILLING FISH

Anyone who has ever experienced the succulent delight of a trout spitted on a green stick and broiled over the graying coals of a noon tea-fire needs no encouragement to grill game fish over charcoal at home. But if you haven't done it, you might bear in mind a few points relating *in general* to fish cookery and *specifically* to the grilling of fish.

First, always bear in mind that fish grilling, like sautéing, should not involve high heat. Fish should be cooked slowly. When you grill fish you should do so over subsiding coals and you should have the fish 5–6 inches above the heat. Indeed it is better to consider the suggestions on page 63 about grilling in general and not grill your fish directly over the coals at all. When coals leap into hellish flame you are not only blackening the fish but are cooking it too fast to boot.

Second, I prefer to sauté small fish in butter to grilling. Best results over charcoal come when the fish is of fair size, at least 1½ pounds in weight.

Turn the fish but once (you may have to use two utensils to keep from breaking it in two); with a fish of 1½ to 2 pounds, I have found that 7–8 minutes to a side is about right, but of course timing depends on the variable of the heat of your coals. Don't hesitate to cut along the spine into the thickest part of the back to check for doneness. There should be just a hint of translucence in the appearance of the fish. Don't overgrill.

Aesthetically, fish should be cleaned, then grilled whole; don't cut off the heads and tails.

See individual recipes about preparing fish for broiling and for basting liquids and sauces especially suitable for fish. As for herbs, nearly all of them have an affinity for fish—but don't be heavy-handed; some fish, such as trout and salmon, are distinctly, if delicately, flavored but can be overwhelmed by too much seasoning.

Salt and pepper grilled fish after they are done.

On the other hand some species, notably certain salt-water fish, are so weakly flavored that when served alone they may account for the many people who say they "don't really care much for fish." French cookery, however, takes this into account and has produced many fish dishes in which the texture and flavor of fish is enhanced by a congenial sauce.

Smoking Fish

One of the finest rewards of owning a smoker is that it enables you to smoke fish. The smoking process seems to do more for fish than for any other meat; smoking not only adds the bouquet and flavor of hickory or of other wood flavors but, much more important, heightens the fish flavor itself. Smoked salmon, for example, has a stronger *salmon* taste than fresh salmon.

I have smoked the following fish: salmon, trout, Arctic char, catfish, and bluefish, and each species responds wonderfully to the smoking process.

There are a number of manuals and books on smoking fish, poultry, and other meats. A good one is Jack Sleight's *The Home Book of Smoke-Cooking Meat, Fish and Game* (he has also written *The Smoked Foods Recipe Book*). The cook who buys a smoker will receive with the smoker itself a pamphlet of instructions and recipes; those who want to go beyond the basics will turn to Jack Sleight and other smoker-writers.

The basic method I use for smoking fish comes straight from the pamphlet written by Dan Stair for Luhr Jensen & Sons, Inc., manufacturers of the Little Chief Smoker. I have found that Dan Stair's advice is sound on all aspects of smoking and preserving fish.

Put the dressed fish (fillets or whole) down in the brine and sugar solution (see below) for 5–6 hours. For smoking do not skin or scale fish.

Remove fish from brine solution, thoroughly rinse out the brine, then roll and pat dry inside and out. Let it dry in the air for an hour or so, or if you are in a hurry place fish so you can blow it dry with an electric fan. Preheat the smoker about a half hour before you put in the fish.

When the fish is dry is the time to rub in other flavorings if you wish. I sometimes dust with garlic powder and tarragon.

Place fish or fillets on the racks, putting the largest fish (or thickest fillets) on the lower racks, and begin smoking.

After about 6–7 hours you should begin to test for doneness. You'll learn to do this by color eventually, but at first you should do it with a fork: probe a thickish section and see if it's done and if it flakes.

When you remove fish from the smoker, allow it to cool to room temperature, then refrigerate in airtight containers.

NOTE: Smoked fish will keep very well indeed in a freezer. Don't pay any attention to those who say you can only hold frozen smoked fish for a month or so. First smoked, then put in airtight plastic bags from which all air has been "exhaled" before closing, and then frozen, smoked fish will keep for a solid year, at least.

TWO BRINES FOR SMOKING FISH

I

4 cups water
½ cup salt
½ cup sugar

plus your choice of flavorings,
    if you wish (see note below)

II

4 cups water
2 cups brown sugar
1 cup salt, regular or curing

1 cup rock salt
plus your choice of flavorings,
    if you wish (see note below)

NOTE: Although I recommended rubbing in flavorings just before putting the fish into the smoker, it is well to remember that you can also put flavorings into either of the above brines; in other words you can prepare a brine marinade flavored with garlic, shallots, tarragon, dill, thyme, or whatever you fancy. After brining in flavored brine, fish should also be washed off and dried before smoking.

Fresh Water Fish

Trout

RAINBOW TROUT

Izaak Walton spoke for all anglers when he quoted a brother fancier on the subject of trout: "—he is a fish that feeds cleanly & purely, in the swiftest streams, and on the hardest gravel; and that he may justly contend with all fresh-water fish, as the mullet may with all sea fishes, for precedency and daintiness of taste; and that being in the right season, the most dainty palates have allowed precedency to him."

Walton placed this premier game fish solidly in the sporting tradition when he wrote, "It may be justly said, as the old poet said of wine, and we English say of venison, to be a generous fish, a fish that is so like the buck, that he also has his seasons, for it is observed that he comes in and goes out of season with the stag & buck."

Trout have delighted the palate of *Homo* since long before the hook was invented. As a stream-side delicacy it is of course famous. Most anglers have in their print and slide files of bygone fishing junkets scores of shots of the noon tea-fire, the blackened skillet, and delicately browned trout sautéing in butter. But there are many ways of preparing, and we give here only a sampling.

BROOK AND BROWN TROUT WEIGHT-FOR-LENGTH CHART
(from Bud Leavitt, Outdoor Editor, *Bangor Daily News*)

INCHES	WEIGHT	
	lb.	oz.
9	0	5
10	0	7
11	0	9
12	0	12
13	0	15
14	1	3
15	1	7
16	1	12
17	2	2
18	2	8
19	2	15
20	3	7
21	4	0
22	4	9
23	5	3
24	5	15
25	6	11
26	7	8

RAINBOW WEIGHTS
(from Ted Gerkin, Iliamna, Alaska, 1979)

27	8–9 lb.
28	9 10 lb.
29	10–11 lb.
30	11–12 lb.
31	12–14 lb.

TROUT SAUTÉED IN BUTTER

As every angler knows, skillet-size brook, brown, and rainbow trout are never more tasty than when prepared in this way. Can there by any tastier dish than the one that comes from this happy marriage of fresh trout and butter? But for best results, a few words of warning: a basic rule of fish cookery is that fish, unless deep fried, should be cooked slowly. Yet, at the same time, one wants the flesh moist *but with the outside golden brown.* Furthermore, one wants to be able to serve trout whole, not in broken chunks, the result of sticking. One other word: since trout are delicately flavored, I do not "flour" trout with cornmeal but with flour. However, either way, the trout will be delicious.

SERVES 4

salt and pepper
4 fresh trout, dressed but with
    heads and tails left on
a few Tb. flour
6 Tb. unsalted butter (if in camp
    where you may not have
    unsalted butter, but do have
    cooking oil, add a tsp. or so
    to reduce sticking)

parsley sprigs
lemon wedges

Salt, pepper, and coat the trout by rolling them in the flour.

Melt the butter in a big iron skillet (if your Teflon-coated skillet is still operative, use it).

When the butter is hot (over a medium heat) but has not yet shown color, lay in the trout and turn the fire low. A steady, low heat will do two things: cook the trout slowly, and at the same time *brown* the trout.

You must police this process continuously, and it will take about 15–20 minutes, depending somewhat on the size of the trout. A pliable spatula and a spoon or fork are the utensils.

Just as soon as the flour coating has set on the down side, loosen each trout from the skillet, employing a light hand with the spatula. Repeat this process occasionally, shaking the skillet gently to keep the slowly browning trout free. Add a bit of oil and butter if necessary.

After 10 minutes of slow browning and using two utensils, turn each trout carefully and repeat the above process.

When you serve the trout, pour a bit of the butter over each and garnish with a sprig of parsley and a wedge of lemon.

Sautéed Quick Meunière

If you wish, add a couple of pats of butter to the skillet after the trout have been served, melt them, squeeze in a tablespoon of lemon juice, turn up heat, and stir. Then pour this lemon-butter sauce over each trout.

For some reason, if this is a breakfast dish, I serve plain old bread and butter, not toast, with sautéed trout.

NOTE: Sauté thick fillets of larger fish this very same way.

TRUITE AU BLEU (BLUE TROUT)

French chefs prepare truite au bleu with *live* trout at hand, to achieve the glassy blue coloration of the skin, but it will work with very fresh trout as well. If the skin doesn't turn to the authentic brilliant blue hue, don't worry—it will be delicious anyway. In either case just eviscerate the trout; do not wash it, for the natural surface of the skin makes the "bleu" possible. However, you may blue *fresh* trout by dousing them in boiling vinegar, then quickly rinsing before putting them into the bouillon.

This dish is prepared in a score of ways, but is basically trout poached in a vegetable court bouillon flavored with a cut-up trout. It is a lovely way to offer the delicacy of trout, and can be either a fish course, if the trout are 6–8-inchers, or a main course if the trout are 10–11 inchers. As a fish course for a game dinner serve the trout cold (in an aspic if you wish—see below). Either way, serve the trout whole, i.e., do not cut off the heads or tails.

SERVES 4–5

2 Tb. butter
1 shallot or scallion, minced
1 rib celery with leaves, chopped
1 carrot, thinly sliced
1 dressed trout, head and all,
  but cut into chunks
1 tsp. salt
6 peppercorns
½ tsp. thyme
2 Tb. minced fresh parsley
1 bay leaf

3 cups water
1 cup white wine or dry vermouth
3 Tb. tarragon vinegar or white
  vinegar with ¼ tsp. dried
  tarragon
four or five whole 10″ trout for
  main course or four to six
  whole 7″ trout if for fish
  course, dressed, head and tails
  still on

In a big saucepan or deep skillet with lid melt the butter and sauté the vegetables until shallot is just soft.

Add the single cut-up trout and the remaining ingredients (except whole trout), bring to a bubble, and simmer for 10 minutes or so.

Add the dressed whole trout (heads and tails still on), cover, and simmer very slowly for about 20 minutes.

If the dish is a main course, remove the fish, drain, and serve immediately with melted butter and lemon juice or herb butter.

If the dish is just a fish course, allow the fish to cool in the liquor and serve the drained trout with a slice of lemon.

Trout Served Cold in an Aspic

The above poached trout
1 cup tomato sauce, homemade or
  canned

4 tsp. gelatin
parsley
lemon slices

If you'd like to serve the trout as a fish course in aspic, let the trout cool in the liquor, then remove and drain trout.

Strain the liquor the trout were simmered in, add to it the tomato sauce, and over fire stir in the gelatin. Stir over low heat just until the gelatin melts. Set gelatin liquid in refrigerator (or in freezer) until it cools but is not as yet "set."

Arrange trout in a flat dish, pour over them the aspic, and allow to set.

Arrange parsley and then lemon slices around trout and serve.

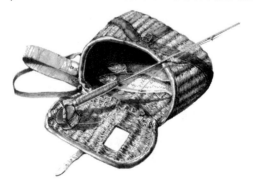

STEELHEAD TROUT

═══════ TROUT AND VEGETABLES IN FOIL ═══════

This delicious dish can be prepared for a noon campfire if the camp itself has a blender or food processor in its kitchen. If the fish is to be a sizable one, be sure to take enough foil in one piece; if the servings are to be individual for each guest, then cut foil accordingly.

SERVES 4

four 10″ trout
juice of ½ lemon
salt and pepper
½ tsp. thyme (or ¼ tsp. thyme,
　¼ tsp. tarragon)

2 carrots
2 small onions
3 ribs celery
4 Tb. butter

Clean the trout, leaving on the heads and tails, and sprinkle inside and out with lemon juice, salt, pepper, and herbs.
　Put vegetables through food processor, mix well, and strain.
　Sauté vegetables in butter until they are soft, and stuff each fish before wrapping it loosely in foil.
　Place in ashes or on cookie sheet in 450° oven for 15–20 minutes.

═══ FILLETED TROUT WITH MACADAMIA NUTS ═══
AND FRIED CAPERS

A very special way of doing trout fillets, inspired by a dish created by chef Seppi Renngli at the Four Seasons.

SERVES 2

3–4 Tb. butter
2 trout, filleted
salt and freshly ground pepper
¼ cup macadamia nuts, sliced
oil for deep frying
2 Tb. capers

splash of dry white wine
¼ cup fish stock, or half clam
　juice, half water
3 Tb. heavy cream
⅛ tsp. tomato paste

In a skillet large enough to hold the fillets melt about 3 tablespoons butter and, when almost sizzling, add trout. Sauté on one side for about 3 minutes, turn, cover for a minute, and then sauté the other side. A total of 6–7 minutes should do it.

Salt and pepper the fish and remove to a warm place, add nuts for a moment to the pan to toast, then toss over the trout fillets.

Meanwhile, in a separate small, sturdy pan, heat enough oil so that a small strainer can be lowered into it.

Let capers drain in the strainer.

Returning to the trout pan, splash in a tablespoon or two of wine, then add stock and cream and boil down rapidly, stirring in just a taste of tomato paste and a little more butter. When reduced and slightly thickened, spoon this little bit of pan sauce over the fillets.

Now quickly lower the capers into the almost smoking oil. Let them splutter and sizzle a few seconds, then remove the strainer and shake free of oil. Distribute fried capers in neat piles at either end of the fillets and serve immediately.

====== SPRING TROUT AND FIDDLEHEAD ======
SPECIAL FOR TWO

From Chef Delicata's (of Bean's retail store) repertoire comes this recipe for sautéed trout. It is a part of the menu as characteristic of Maine as a pair of Mr. Bean's hunting shoes. As you read the recipe just listen to the overtones of culinary enthusiasm. Serve this with sourdough toast and sparkling white wine, chilled.

SERVES 4

four 10″ freshly caught trout	¼ cup salad oil
¼ cup white flour	fiddlehead ferns
¼ cup cornmeal	4 qt. boiling water
salt and pepper	butter
dash of garlic powder	

Clean the fish well in cold water. Dredge in both flours to which salt, pepper, and garlic powder have been added. Fry in hot oil, turning once when skin is crisp.

Cook the fiddleheads in the boiling water. Boil for 3 minutes only. Fiddleheads will be cooked, yet very crisp. Remove from water and drain. Dot with pats of butter.

NOTE: Fresh fiddlehead ferns are a real delicacy, but, happily, canned fiddleheads are also good—if you can find them.

====== QUIMBY POND TROUT CRÊPES ======

The reader can easily see one reason why Roy and Evelyn's fishing and hunting camps at Rangeley, Maine, are popular with people at L. L. Bean: the food there is notable. For another of Mrs. Soriano's recipes see page 170 for her Partridge Scapriello.

In cooking the crêpes, before filling and rolling up with the trout mixture, a 6-inch skillet is handy.

MAKES TWENTY 6-INCH CRÊPES

CRÊPES
4 eggs   1 cup water
1 cup flour
FILLING
⅓ cup minced onion   ¼ tsp. pepper
1 clove garlic, minced   1⅓ cups milk
⅓ cup butter   ⅔ cup sauterne
¼ cup flour   4 cups cooked, skinned, and
½ tsp. salt   deboned trout

NOTE: To make crêpes, mix the ingredients for the batter together thoroughly (it can be done in a blender or food processor) and let rest at least 1 hour. Make individual crêpes, following the method in the recipe for cornmeal pancakes, page 346.

Cook and stir onion and garlic in butter until onion is tender. Remove from heat. Blend in flour, salt, and pepper. Cook over low heat, stirring, until mixture is bubbly. Remove from heat. Stir in milk and wine. Heat to boiling, stirring constantly. Boil and stir 1 minute. Stir in trout. Fill each crêpe with 2 tablespoons filling. Heat crêpes in 350° oven for 10 minutes. Serve crêpes topped with remaining filling. This is an excellent luncheon dish.

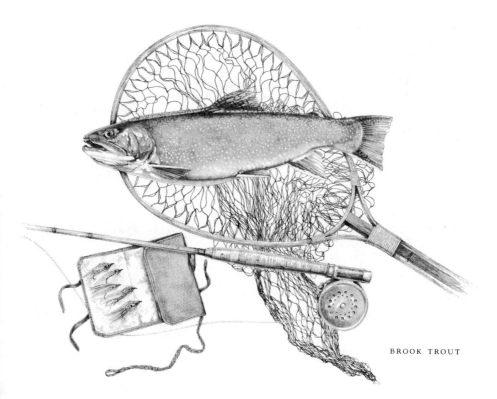

BROOK TROUT

BROOK TROUT L.L. BEAN

Mr. Bean's personal recipe for brook trout shows that he knew the secret of slow cookery for fish.

"Cut heads off, clean and wipe dry. Fry out liberal amount of pork fat. Roll in flour with a little salt added. Drop in fry-pan when fat comes to a boil. Turn often to avoid burning. *Fry slowly* until every trout is crisp and well browned.

"Place in hot platter on clean paper to absorb fat. Have cut lemon on table for those who want it.

"Pork fat is much better than bacon fat or butter, and flour is much better than meal."

FILLET OF STEELHEAD BONNE FEMME

This lordly French dish is prepared in a variety of ways, but basically it is fish fillets served with two sauces and mushrooms in between. The fillets from small-ish salmon, walleye, lake trout, and channel cat are all superb prepared in this fashion.

If the *two* sauces seem too time-consuming just note that this dish is excellent if only the *wine* sauce is used.

SERVES 4

head, tail, backbone of the fish	4 Tb. butter
6 peppercorns	1 cup Hollandaise Sauce
2 shallots, sliced	(see page 362)
1 cup water	1½ Tb. flour
⅓ cup white wine	4 Tb. milk
2 lb. fillets of steelhead	salt and pepper
1 bouquet garni	cucumber and lemon slices or
(¼ tsp. thyme, ½ tsp. tarragon)	watercress
½ lb. mushrooms	

Put the fish head, etc., peppercorns, and shallots into the water and wine, bring to a boil, then simmer gently for 30 minutes. Strain and set aside.

Arrange the fillets in a shallow glass or earthenware fireproof dish that has been liberally buttered. Add the bouquet garni.

Pour in the reserved fish stock and poach in a 325° oven for 20 minutes.

Sauté the sliced mushrooms in 2 tablespoons of butter for 5 minutes, coating and stirring a couple of times. Reserve.

Prepare the hollandaise and hold it by covering with a lid or dish.

Make the wine sauce by melting 2 tablespoons butter in pan, then stir in the flour and cook a few minutes. Off heat, pour in the liquor from the poached fillets, then stir and thicken over the fire. Add the milk, then stir until it bubbles. Season to taste.

To assemble: lay the fillets on a fireproof dish and cover with the wine sauce. Now dot the top with the mushrooms. Ladle the hollandaise over all and glaze under the broiler.

Garnish with cucumber and lemon slices or with watercress.

TROUT STUFFED JAPANESE STYLE

SERVES 4

¼ lb. mushrooms, sliced
1 cup seeded, sliced in ¼" strips,
  red or green pepper
  (or mixture of both)
3 scallions, cut in 1½" slices,
  including green
1 cup bean sprouts
2 ribs celery, sliced at angle
  ¼" thick

2 Tb. vegetable oil
4 eggs, lightly beaten
2 tsp. soy sauce
4 trout, 8–10 oz., boned with skin,
  head, and tail on
8 strips bacon

Mix the vegetables together. In a large skillet or wok heat oil, then toss in the vegetables and stir-fry for 2 minutes. Add the eggs and soy sauce and continue to toss and cook for another minute until eggs begin to coagulate.

Stuff each of the 4 trout with one-fourth of the vegetable mixture—the filling will expand the opening by about an inch. Wrap 2 slices of bacon around each trout, tucking the ends under the trout.

Bake in a large baking pan so trout are not touching in preheated 500° oven about 15 minutes, until skin is crisp and the fish is opaque to the bone (time will vary according to the heat of the oven and temperature of fish and filling). Test after 12 minutes. Vegetables will remain crisp.

Terms Used for Carving Various Fishes

You barb a lobster.
You chynne a salmon.
You culpon a trout.
You sauce a tench, plaice, or flounder.
You trance a sturgeon.
You side a haddock.
You splay a bream.
You splat a pike.
You tayme a crab.
You trassene an eel.
You tusk a barbel (and, presumably, a catfish).

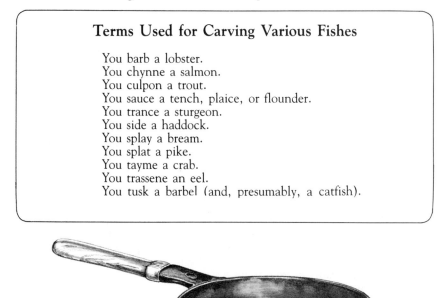

ATLANTIC SALMON

Salmon

Until a very few years ago eastern and western salmon anglers sought entirely different species, even genera, of these delicious game fish. Easterners angled only for *Salmo salar*, the famed gamester, the Atlantic salmon, while westerners with a wide choice sought kings, cohoes, reds, and others. Now eastern fishermen in the Great Lakes area and in waters even farther east may try their hands at coho fishing (as well as steelhead trout). Both species have been introduced successfully.

All salmon are excellent fare. Some, like the sockeye or red salmon, return each year to the rivers of their origin in prodigious numbers; others, like the Atlantic salmon, return, alas, in ever dwindling numbers to rivers on both sides of the Atlantic. The latter salmon is a delicately flavored fish much sought after as both fresh and smoked fish. Smoked Scottish salmon in the summer of 1981 commanded a price of $36 a pound; New Brunswick smoked salmon came at a bargain price—$7 for ¼ pound.

Salmon are delicious poached, baked, or grilled, but are most rewarding to the palate when they are *not* overcooked. This, of course, is true of all fish.

In the East, you know it's summer when you can get in a restaurant cold, poached salmon with green mayonnaise, fresh garden peas, and cucumbers. None of the other three seasons is more appropriately (or deliciously) ushered in by such a timely repast.

About Poaching Salmon or Other Large Fishes

Atlantic salmon, or any salmonoid like Alaska trophy-size rainbows—or, for that matter, silver salmon, lake trout, or big Arctic char—are rare treats when poached. Served hot with hollandaise they are fit for a king, but to my taste they are best when poached, then served cold with rémoulade sauce, green mayonnaise, salsa verde, sauce verte, or any favorite fish sauce. Cucumbers and green peas (and boiled potatoes if the fish is served hot) seem to go with salmon or any of the fishes poached.

If you have a fish poacher use it by all means, for the poaching tray in this elongated "kettle" is a great asset and nothing graces a big garnished platter or board more elegantly than a whole fish served with the head and tail on au naturel. The largest fish poacher available these days is 30 inches in length. Such a poacher will accommodate an 8–10-pound whole salmon and will cost a small fortune. Salmon or other large fishes may be cut in two. The heroic effect of the whole fish may be achieved later by simply placing the head and tail ends together on the serving board before you serve.

I manage a 6–7-pound salmon by poaching over two burners in an old enameled refrigerator vegetable crisper. I have poached 10-pounders in it by cutting the fish in half and then rejoining the halves. In any case use your longest baking pan.

A whole fish of 5–7 pounds or a big half fish should be wrapped in a piece of cheesecloth first so it can be handled. Leave enough length of cheesecloth beyond the head and tail to provide hand holds (or holds for two pliers) for lifting the fish out of the liquid.

Now a trick or two: for big whole fish start the fish in cold liquid (either salted water or court bouillon: see below), bring rapidly to a boil, then turn down immediately to a *low* simmer. You can determine doneness by inspection, i.e., lifting a piece of the heavy flesh on the back near the dorsal fin with a thin-tined fork. There is a guide to poaching time that is, however, quite precise. My New Brunswick friends allot poaching time by the thickness of the fish and they swear by the method. Lay the salmon on the counter; set a ruler end on counter and measure thickness at the thickest place, say, just forward of the dorsal fin. Poach 10 minutes per inch of thickness or part of an inch. Example, 35 minutes for a salmon 3½ inches thick. Ms. Dorothy Coulter of East Eddington, Maine, uses a liquid thermometer to determine poaching time (*The Maine Way*, p. 79). She contends that the size of a salmon makes little difference, but I assume her salmon don't vary much in size. Ms. Coulter poaches by keeping the water (she poaches in water and vinegar, 1½ teaspoons vinegar to each quart of water) at 185° for 45 minutes. She then turns off the fire and lets the temperature come down to 140° before removing a salmon to be served hot.

═══════════ POACHED ATLANTIC SALMON ═══════════

Read the foregoing notes on poaching.

MAKES 2 QUARTS

THE COURT BOUILLON

2 qt. water
1 medium onion, sliced very thin
1 carrot, sliced very thin
6 peppercorns
¼ cup vinegar
¼ cup dry vermouth or dry white wine
1 tsp. salt

1 bouquet garni (using a piece of cheesecloth, enclose 3 sprigs of parsley, the leaves of a celery rib, 2 bay leaves, ½ teaspoon dried thyme leaves, not powdered, and 3 cloves)
fish heads and frames (optional)

Bring the water to a boil in a big saucepan.

Add the remaining ingredients, including any fish heads and frames that you may have on hand, and simmer for 5 minutes.

Set aside to cool.

THE SALMON

Dress the salmon, removing gills and entrails, leaving on the skin, head, and tail, or cut out section of a large salmon for the purpose. Do not scale.

Using your hands, rub salmon outside and in with a couple tablespoons of lemon juice.

Lay the salmon onto a piece of cheesecloth large enough to accommodate length of fish plus a hand-hold length of cloth in addition and wide enough to enclose the salmon.

Put the cooled court bouillon into your poaching roaster, lift in the salmon, which the water should just cover, and, even if your receptacle has a lid, make a foil tent over the fish.

Bring to a boil, then turn down heat and poach the fish at a low simmer. Time it from the moment you turn down heat to simmer, timing by one of the methods on page 248.

Lift out the salmon gingerly to avoid breaking, lay on draining board to drain with the cheesecloth still on it, then roll it onto platter or serving board.

ICELANDIC GRAVLAX

Whenever you are blessed with an Atlantic salmon and are tempted to smoke it (a very happy thing to do, of course), consider this unbelievably delicious Scandinavian recipe instead. If *anything* is better than smoked Atlantic salmon, this just may be it. I first tasted it on a salmon fishing junket in Iceland, and I am indebted for this recipe to the chef of the Laxa i Kjos' lodge on the river by that name. Icelanders serve it with a mustard sauce, also given here, and unleavened hard bread.

If you *buy* fresh salmon at current prices this delicious appetizer will almost make you forget the cost.

One more note: Lake trout or any other big trout or char is just as good when pickled à la Icelandia.

SERVES 6

1 dressed but unskinned salmon, head and tail removed if necessary, and split in half*	2 tsp. crushed or coarsely ground peppercorns
2½ Tb. coarse salt (kosher is fine)	¼–½ cup dried dill weed or about 10 sprigs fresh dill
1½ Tb. sugar	

Remove the backbone and whatever bones you can get with it. Pulling them out with a tweezer is a good idea.

Put the two salmon halves in a shallow glass or earthenware baking dish and on both surfaces, skin sides up, rub in half of a mix of the salt, sugar, and peppercorns.

Now sprinkle both halves with dill weed. *Important:* make certain that each side is covered so that all you see is a solid coating of dill weed.

Cover the salmon halves, now skin side down, with foil; then, if you're lucky, you'll have a plastic or wooden dicing board to fit over the foil. If not, cut a piece of corrugated box to fit.

Weight this down with anything weighty enough to press heavily on the salmon—an array of big cans of tomatoes or a couple of sash weights, or even building bricks will do.

Refrigerate with weights 24–36 hours, drain, and slice at an angle, as you would smoked salmon.

The Mustard Sauce

3 Tb. prepared mustard†
5 tsp. sugar
3 Tb. vinegar (wine vinegar if you have it)

2 cloves garlic, crushed
8–10 Tb. oil (with the princely salmon it ought to be olive oil)
dill weed to taste

Make a thin paste of the sauce ingredients by blending and stirring.

* This recipe is for a grilse of 4 to 5 pounds. If the salmon is "braggin" size, use a portion, perhaps the tail third or half.

†Icelanders make their own mustard from Fiskesennep Danish mustard (directions on box), but Dijon or English mustard or the Sage Mustard on page 359 will do nicely.

SALMON SEBAGO

I first tasted fresh-caught Maine landlocks at a noon lunch at East Grand Lake; they were grilled over hot coals and they were delicious. Since then (1940) I try to fish in Maine or New Brunswick for landlocks every year, most often trolling old stand-by tandem hook streamers straight from the counters of Mr. Bean at Freeport. Favorite patterns: Gray Ghost, Supervisor, and Nine Three. In our house we serve broiled landlocks with green mayonnaise.

SERVES 4

2½ lb. landlocked salmon fillets
4 Tb. butter, softened

2 Tb. chopped parsley
salt and pepper

Brush each side of the fillets with combined butter-parsley mixture. Sprinkle with salt and pepper. In a preheated broiler whose pan or rack has been greased with cooking oil, broil fillets about 3 inches from the flame or filament for about 4 minutes for the first side. Broil second side about 5 minutes more.

Meanwhile make a quick Green Mayonnaise, which I make variously, using almost anything green—parsley, tarragon, spinach, chives, or the green tops of scallions. I "chop" the greens in a blender.

Green Mayonnaise

1 Tb. lemon juice
2–3 sprigs spinach, trimmed from stems
1 tsp. dried or 2 Tb. fresh tarragon leaves

2 Tb. chives or tops of scallions
2 Tb. capers
1½ cups mayonnaise

Put the lemon juice, spinach, tarragon, chives or scallions, and capers in the blender and make a quick purée.

Mix into the mayonnaise with a spoon.

BAKED STUFFED SALMON—
DOWN HOME STYLE

Joe Murray of L.L. Bean gave us this recipe referring to landlocked salmon. Serve it with boiled potatoes and raw onions and lemon wedges, white wine, and 2 candles, he advises.

SERVES 3–4

1 large salmon, 2–3 lb.
1 Tb. butter
salt and pepper
1–1½ cups bread crumbs
1 clove garlic, minced

1 orange
1 lemon
1 cup milk
6 strips bacon

Clean salmon; cut off head and tail and fins. Wash clean and dry with paper towels. Rub butter inside cavity and on outside of salmon.

Mix salt, pepper, bread crumbs, garlic, and the juice of the orange and the lemon; add milk. Stuff fish and lay in baking pan; put strips of bacon on top of fish. Bake 30–40 minutes in a preheated 350° oven.

Variation: Mix ½ pound crabmeat with a little horseradish, ½ cup salad dressing, 3 diced onions, salt, pepper, and diced pickles. Serve over salmon as a sauce.

KING SALMON (CHINOOK)

KEDGEREE (SALMON AND RICE)

The chef at Ben More Lodge in Sutherland, Scotland, made a kedgeree that was simple and delicious. The salmon came from leftover poached salmon. Cooked lake trout can be substituted for the salmon.

SERVES 6

1 large onion, chopped	2 cups flaked cooked salmon
1 Tb. butter	2 tsp. curry powder
1½ cups cooked rice	3 Tb. milk or cream

Sauté the onion in the butter until soft.

Combine all ingredients in a casserole and heat in a hot oven. The heating can be done over water in a double boiler, but it looks better served in an earthen casserole.

Variation: Some cooks add another ingredient: 2 chopped hard-boiled eggs.

STREAM- OR LAKE-SIDE BAKED FISH DELUXE
(Salmon, Lake Trout, Steelhead, Char, Large Trout)

Roger Jorstad, one of Alaska's finest young angling guides (and one of the most amiable and entertaining), produced this lunch on the Iliamna River. Perhaps, I should say, he executed this sumptuous lunch handsomely from Mary Gerken's recipe (see pages 75 and 106 for other Iliaska Lodge recipes). The recipe not only produces a luscious lunch but is the easiest of all waterside lunches to prepare.

Before leaving in the morning cut off a piece of aluminum foil of a size to hold the fish you expect to catch so that you can make a "boat" with enough foil to fold over and turn up at the ends. Wrap in this a stick of butter cut into pats and a large onion, finely chopped, with plenty of salt and freshly ground pepper.

When you have a good bed of coals in your tea-fire (in our case Roger had to cut off the tail and head of Joe Bates's handsome 7-pound whole char to fit the foil boat), lay the dressed fish in the foil, double-fold the foil on top, and do the same for the turned-up ends. Bake-steam the fish right on the coals for about 20 minutes. Move the boat around in the coals until it lies on ashes with coals all around. If you don't agree that this makes one of the best and easiest "fish fries" you ever tasted, I'll be much surprised.

To vary, dust ½ teaspoon of tarragon or marjoram in with the butter and onions before you leave camp; half tarragon and half chervil will produce "Fish Béarnaise."

Notice: No utensils needed; a can of fruit juice, a loaf of bread, and some cookies to go with your second cup of tea will put you in a frame of mind to forgive the river if the afternoon fishing slacks off.

At home? Just prepare as above and bake in a 400° oven for about 20–30 minutes, depending on the size of the fish. You can grill the foil boat over coals at home, too, if you wish.

Handling and Freezing Salmon
and Other Game Fish

The Icelanders have learned, with a little trial and error in the process, that the best way to handle salmon is not to gill and gut the fish, then lay it in a little pebble corral built in the river's shallows to keep cool, but rather to bleed the fish by sticking it just behind the gills and package it right at streamside. To achieve this, the gillies carry flat rolls of heavy plastic tubing which they measure against the fish, leaving enough extra for two knots, then cutting off the proper length. After a knot is tied in the bottom, the fish is dropped in, the air pressed out by hand, and a knot tied in the open end. This is laid in the cooling current and that night placed in the cold room, where it is kept until the angler reluctantly must leave.

This angler on arriving home takes the packaged fish out of the heavily insulated boxes in which these modern Vikings have put them, unties one end of each tube, runs in some water from the tap, reties the knot, and places the fish on the freezer's shelf. Before the water has entirely frozen, he turns the fish so as to coat the other side with ice. Salmon frozen in this fashion, ungutted and ungilled, thaw out *months* later smelling and tasting, believe it or not, as if they had been butchered streamside and grilled a half hour later. When the fish thaws, the angler butchers and cleans the fish just as he would have had it been unfrozen.

Most anglers have handled trout in a similar manner using a washed-out two-quart milk carton, dropping in the fish and filling with water and freezing.

This angler may be kidding himself just the least little bit when he says the fish is as good as when fresh, but the fact is that palates used to fresh fish are astonished at the flavor of fish frozen in this fashion. One of course should not keep fish frozen for months, but if one does, the result is anything but catastrophic. Even with fatty fish, like the incomparable salmon, the fats seem most reluctant to take on any rancidity.

═ BROILED SALMON (OR LAKE TROUT) STEAKS ═
WITH SHALLOTS AND TARRAGON

I seriously doubt that Atlantic salmon steaks (or fillets) can ever taste any better than those grilled over coals, basted with butter, as done by the guides on Labrador's Forteau River, but here's a recipe that may be as good. I have never made a direct comparison, for to do so I would have to accompany the steaks in this recipe with home-baked bread, still warm, that went with the Forteau lunches.

SERVES 4

⅓ cup olive oil
2 Tb. lemon juice
2 Tb. finely chopped shallots or
  scallions
½ tsp. dried tarragon, crumbled to
  powder

salt and pepper
4 salmon steaks about 1½″ thick
4 Tb. butter, melted
black olives
parsley
lemon wedges

Combine the oil, lemon juice, shallots or scallions, tarragon, salt, and pepper and beat or shake to uniformity as you would French dressing.

Coat each side of the steaks with the dressing, lay the steaks on a greased broiler grill over a tray, pour remainder of the dressing over the steaks, and broil about 4 inches under the heat for 7–8 minutes for each side.

Baste often with the melted butter during the broiling process. (If fillets are used, broil for a shorter time, depending on thickness of the fillets.)

If you can recover it, retrieve some of the hot basted liquor and pour over each steak.

Garnish with black olives, parsley, and lemon wedges.

NOTE: Other herbs can be used; for example, I like a mix of half tarragon and half chervil.

BAKED SALMON FILLETS
LAPLAND STYLE

This dish, prepared with Atlantic salmon in Finland, can, of course, be prepared with the fillets of any salmon, or, for that matter, with the fillets of lake trout, steelhead, or any big trout. Serve with a rémoulade sauce or any other fish sauce.

SERVES 4

2½ lb. salmon fillets
3 Tb. butter, softened
2 Tb. cooking oil
salt and pepper
½ tsp. celery seed

1 tsp. dill seed*
minced parsley
½ cup vermouth or dry white
wine

Spread the fillets with the butter and pour the oil in a shallow baking dish.

Put half the salt, pepper, celery seed, dill seed, and parsley on the oiled bottom of the dish, lay in the fillets, and season their top sides with the rest of the seasonings. Bake in a 375° oven for 10 minutes.

Pour in the wine and bake another 10 minutes, basting the fillets a couple of times, until the fillets show they are done by flaking to the prod of a fork.

* When using dill seeds, I empty a pepper grinder momentarily, add the dill seeds, and grind them onto the fillets.

A LONDON STUFFING

FOR SALMON BAKED WHOLE, CIRCA 1710

The author of *The Accomplisht Lady's Delight* suggests that the salmon be drawn from the head after the gills have been removed and that it be stuffed from the gill end.

"Take about a pint of oysters parboyled,* put to these a few sweet herbs,† some grated bread, about a half dozen hard eggs, with 2 onions, shred all these very small, and put to it ginger, nutmeg, salt, pepper, cloves, and mace; mix these together and put 'em all within the salmon at the gills."

* Presumably for a minute or so in their own liquor.
† Thyme, marjoram, and parsley would be one "sweet herb" combination.

A Quick Rule of Thumb
for Timing the Cooking of Fish

I first heard of this system from a chef in a Labrador salmon camp. Later I found out that my discovering this method in Canada was not happenstance. According to Jim Beard, the Canadian Department of Fisheries and their Home Service Bureau have made exhaustive tests with all types of fresh- and salt-water fish and with the various methods of cooking fish and have discovered an astonishing uniformity: whatever the method of cooking and whether the fish be whole or in fillets, cook 10 minutes for every inch of thickness or part thereof. Jim Beard has used the method regularly in his cooking classes and demonstrations and has found it to be "infallible."

Thickness is measured through the body side to side, not from dorsal to ventral.

Since first hearing of the system, I have used it to determine cooking time for baking fish and for poaching and found that it works. Jim Beard says it works for broiling when the fish is cooked 2–3 inches from the flame and for sautéing as well (when sautéed "over a hot but not smoking" heat in ¼ inch of fat).

When employing the system in poaching over a fire, the measurement of time is taken when it comes to a gentle simmer. The last salmon I poached was 3½ inches thick, thus I poached it for 35 minutes and it was done perfectly to my taste.

When baking fish and using the 10 minutes per inch of thickness rule, the cooking is done in a hot oven, 450°. Cooking times given for baking at lower temperatures in most cookbooks, including this one, are always approximate.

The system also applies for fish thicknesses of less than one inch; e.g., ¾-inch-thick fillets broiled 3 inches from the flame take 7½ minutes to cook, say 4½ minutes for the first side and 3 for the second.

The 10 minutes to the inch time is given for fish at room temperature. Fish very cold takes longer to cook; and according to Jim Beard, frozen fish take twice as long, i.e., 20 minutes to the inch.

SALMON STEAKS, HIGHLAND BROILED

In her *Highlander's Cookbook,* Sheila MacNiven Cameron says with pardonable Gaelic pride, "With the best salmon in the world being caught in Scottish waters, who but the Scot would know best how to cook a salmon?" Here is her recipe for broiled salmon steaks.

Take salmon steaks, 1 inch thick, and sprinkle with salt and pepper. Set steaks on pieces of parchment or foil. Dot with butter. Seal steaks in the foil or paper. Broil under medium-low heat for 10–12 minutes, turning frequently. Remove foil or parchment, and serve immediately with curl of butter. Allow one or two steaks per person.

NOTE: When broiling under electric heat, I'd place the steak about 4 inches below the hot element. I sometimes broil thick fillets in foil in the above manner. A pat of herb butter (see page 357) could provide the "curl" if you wish.

FILLET OF COHO NORMANDE

I once took the late, great angler Roderick Haeg-Brown to the old Louis & Armande restaurant in New York City and recommended this dish to him (I had it, too). Delighted with the fare, we tried to get the recipe, but had to be satisfied with a very general description of how the dish was prepared. Here's how my wife and I worked it out. It may not be authentic, but it is good.

SERVES 4

1½ lb. mussels
⅓ cup water
⅓ cup white wine
5–6 shallots or scallions, minced
1 bay leaf
6 fillets (trout, salmon, walleye), heads and tails kept for making stock
½ tsp. thyme

½ lb. mushrooms, sliced
4 Tb. butter
2 Tb. flour
½ cup white wine
⅔ cup cream
3 egg yolks, beaten
salt and white pepper

COHO (SILVER) SALMON

With a brush, scour the mussels well and scrape off beards, then in a steaming basket steam them over boiling water until they come open. Remove mussels and set them aside (reserve their delicious liquid for another use).

In a saucepan combine the ⅓ cup water, wine, shallots, bay leaf, fish heads and tails, and thyme, bring to boil, and simmer for 5 minutes. Strain and save this stock.

In a shallow ovenproof glass baking dish, or any other dish suitable for eventual serving, lay in the fillets, pour in the stock, and bake in a 400° oven for 10–15 minutes.

Meanwhile in a skillet sauté the mushrooms in the butter, and when done, stir in the flour; off heat, drain and stir in the fish broth when ready, leaving the fillets in the baking dish.

Back on the fire, simmer the drained-off sauce and as it thickens control by adding the ½ cup of wine.

Now stir the cream into the beaten eggs. Mix 2 or 3 tablespoons of the hot sauce with the beaten yolks and cream, and stir this mix back into the sauce.

Add the mussels. Add salt and white pepper and just heat (but do not boil).

Pour hot sauce over the fillets and serve.

NOTE: When you add the mussels you may if you wish add also a handful of cooked shrimp.

══════════ BRAISED COHO SALMON ══════════

This method of braising a whole fish can be used for Arctic char, Atlantic salmon, lake trout, etc. Herbs other than fennel can be used, of course; for example, tarragon and chervil or thyme and rosemary.

SERVES 6

6 Tb. butter	1 tsp. fennel seeds, crushed in
2 large onions, chopped	mortar or put through a
3 carrots, chopped	peppermill
2 ribs celery, chopped	6- or 7-pound silver salmon
3 bay leaves	1½ cups white wine
3 sprigs parsley	1 tsp. anchovy sauce

Melt the butter in the roasting pan on top of the stove and sauté the onions, carrots, and celery until onions are soft.

Add bay leaves, parsley, and fennel with ½ cup water, bring to a quick boil, and boil away most of the water. Off heat, lay in the fish, add the wine, and stir in the anchovy sauce.

Cover and cook in 350° oven for 25–30 minutes.

⌠Arctic char

When well into the spawning run from the sea this delectable fish, silvery when it leaves the salt, is gloriously transformed. The skin and flesh take on a rubescent blush, a bloody-golden hue that seems to promise excellence. It does not disappoint. Filleted and sautéed in butter over the coals of a noon tea-fire of dry willow sticks, on some Arctic or sub-Arctic shore, it vies with the best of the trouts or salmons. Sea-run char often, as in the mighty Payne found in the Ungava Peninsula of Nouveau Québec, reach 12, 15, or even more pounds. Large char brought back from such a fishing junket should be treated just as you would an Atlantic salmon. Smoked, they are superb, as good as lox.

See below for one way to prepare a big char for a noontime lunch over your tea-fire.

═══ BRAISED ARCTIC CHAR OR COHO SALMON ═══

This recipe is a basic braising recipe for fish. The fish and wine make a lovely fish broth with which to finish the sauce. The first time I prepared this dish I did it with a 5-pound sea-run Arctic char from Nouveau Québec. See page 245 for one way to prepare a big char over your noon tea-fire.   SERVES 6

3 carrots, very thinly sliced	4–5-lb. Arctic char
2 medium onions, thinly sliced	¼ lb. mushrooms, sliced
1 rib celery, chopped	1 Tb. lemon juice
4 Tb. butter	⅓ cup heavy cream
1 bay leaf	salt and pepper
2 Tb. minced parsley	lemon wedges
½ tsp. rosemary	chopped parsley
1½ cups dry white wine	

Sauté the vegetables in 2 tablespoons of the butter until just soft, then use them to cover bottom of a buttered baking dish big enough to hold the fish.

Add the bay leaf, minced parsley, rosemary, and white wine (or wine and enough water to come up between a quarter and halfway on the char). Add fish to dish, cover with foil, and bake at 325° for about 35–40 minutes, basting 4–5 times.

Remove fish to warm platter and reduce the braising liquid in the pan by half; strain.

Sauté the mushrooms in the remaining butter and stir into the strained liquid.

Now stir in the lemon juice and cream; reheat but do not bubble. Season with salt and pepper.

Pour over fish and serve with lemon wedges and chopped parsley as garnish.

ARCTIC GRAYLING

This handsome fish memorializes a common herb in its name, *Thymallus arcticus;* freshly caught it is said to give off a bouquet of fresh thyme. I have never noticed this, but agree that, freshly caught, its blend of lovely hues of blues, lavenders, and pinks earns the species name, *arcticus,* for it is as varied, subtle, and evanescent as the Northern Lights. Distinguished alike by its huge, sail-like dorsal fin and its willingness to take any kind of fly—dry, wet, nymph, or streamer—the grayling adds a unique note of adventure to any far northern angling junket.

═══════ SAUTÉED GRAYLING ═══════

I have never prepared grayling in my home kitchen, but I have cooked a lot of them in a host of Arctic camps. I always scale or skin grayling, for I find that even in the dew-drop clear water of Arctic streams, grayling vary considerably in taste. I figure the variation in flavor is, somehow, skin deep. Besides, I consider the big scales on grayling the only flaw in the beauty of this fish of the Aurora.

SERVES 4 (IN CAMP)

six 10″–13″ grayling, heads and tails removed	2 Tb. very finely diced onion
½ cup yellow cornmeal	¼ tsp. tarragon
6–8 Tb. butter	¼ tsp. chervil
parsley for garnish	4 Tb. lemon juice
	salt and pepper

After dredging the fish in the meal, sauté them in butter in a big skillet until done, about 20 minutes total over a slow fire.

Remove fish to a warm platter garnished with parsley. Add onion, tarragon, and chervil to the dredgings and butter (add more butter if necessary), and cook quickly until onion is soft. Stir in the lemon juice, loosening the dredgings the while, season to taste, and pour butter and lemon sauce over the fish.

Lake Trout

In 1974, I discovered two things about the lake trout, one having to do with his sporting qualities, the other with his quality as a food fish. I had eaten lake trout before and found it good, but I had not yet discovered that the flesh from a 15-pound laker compared to that of a 3–4-pounder of the same species was like beef compared with veal. Both are delicious, of course, but the flesh from the mature fish is far better even than that from a smaller fish. The scene was a trapper's cabin in the Brooks Range of Alaska; the stove was a little sheet-metal rig set atop a 55-gallon drum which served as a veritable furnace to heat the camp. Our skillet accommodated two steaks, center cut, from a 12-pound cock fish. My wife and I agreed—then at least—that those steaks were the best fish we had ever eaten.

We poached the tail half of that trout in a court bouillon; cooled and served with Hellmann's mayonnaise it was as good as salmon. Here is perhaps as good a place as any to suggest that any *big* trout, whether a lunker brook or one of those huge Alaskan rainbows of 8–12 pounds, should be prepared with the same recipes offered here for Atlantic salmon.

What did I learn about the sporting qualities of the togue, as he is sometimes called? Previous to that occasion I had fished for lakers only during the summer, trolling deep, deep down with a copperline and a big spoon to reach the deep-lying fish. It was not much fun. Here out of a canoe I was trolling the shoal edges with an unweighted streamer fly on a 5-ounce fly rod. In the cooling waters of Alaska's late September, these great trout follow the spawning ciscoes to the surface and feed voraciously on their favorite prey. I found it high drama to watch for the wall of water pushed ahead of the great heads of 15–30-pound lakers as they pursued the fly. It will scarcely come as a surprise to any togue angler to say, "Yes, those big Alaskan lakers showed a three-to-one preference for a Gray Ghost."

POACHED LAKE TROUT OR STEELHEAD IN CAMP OR AT HOME

Even though the recipe for poached Atlantic salmon can be followed in detail for poached lake trout, I give this separate entry to make sure that cooks who have lake trout available far more often than they have salmon will not miss this method of preparing trout. This is the way I poached a 5-pound chunk from the 12-pound lake trout I've just described, using a big deep kettle but dispensing with the cheesecloth. I had all of the ingredients save fresh parsley (see page 396 for cooking preparations before leaving on a camping trip) and vermouth, but I did have white wine.

BAKED STUFFED LAKE TROUT, SALMON, OR WALLEYED PIKE

I think marjoram goes well with fish, and here's a recipe that uses it both in and on the fish. Neither lake trout nor salmon need be scaled, but do scale the pike. A whole baked fish on a garnished platter always looks good to guests.

SERVES 6–8

1 tsp. salt
white pepper
4–6-lb. fish, dressed, with head
  and tail left on
your favorite stuffing or see
  stuffings, pages 377–380
1 lemon, sliced as thin as you can
  manage
2 shallots, thinly sliced
  (or 1 small onion is fine)

1 carrot, thinly sliced
1 rib celery, thinly sliced
¾ tsp. dried marjoram
1 bay leaf
1½ cups white wine, or ½ wine,
  ½ stock
4 Tb. butter, melted

Salt and pepper the fish inside and out, then stuff it and sew up or skewer the opening.

Place in a buttered baking pan and lay lemon slices along its length. Stick a toothpick in each slice.

Add the vegetables, marjoram, bay leaf, and wine and bake, uncovered, for about 35 minutes in a 400° oven, basting first with the melted butter and then with the liquid in the pan.

FRIED LAKE TROUT WALKER LAKE

On the south slope of Alaska's Brooks Range, a hundred miles north of the Arctic Circle, lies Walker Lake, one of the headwaters of the Kobuk. On an island in this 15-mile-long wilderness lake, Bud and Martha Helmericks have a fine log lodge and a guest cabin. The choice of fish there is lake trout, Arctic char, and grayling. Here is one of Martha's recipes for dealing with this bounty.

SERVES 6

1 laker or char or several grayling
½ tsp. salt
¼ tsp. pepper or lemon pepper
cornmeal enough for dredging

shortening enough for frying
2 Tb. butter
1 cup sour cream
½ tsp. lemon juice

Clean and wash the fish and cut into serving pieces, leaving skin on. Salt and pepper and coat thoroughly with cornmeal.

In a fry-pan bring ¼–½ inch of shortening to high heat, add fish, and fry for approximately 4 minutes; turn, and cook for 3 minutes more. Fish should be nicely browned. Put cooked fish on hot serving platter.

Pour off fat from pan and replace with the butter, add the sour cream, and stir with a spoon to loosen any greables. Cook for several minutes, but do not boil.

Remove from heat, add lemon juice, stir, and pour over trout.

Fishing through the ice for smelts when a mean north wind has scoured the ice clear of the last snowfall can be among the coldest of sports, but the tiny fish is its own reward—when there are enough of them. I like to pan-fry them in butter and ring a few changes with minor variations.

SAUTÉED SMELTS AND A SAUCE

SERVES 4

5 Tb. flour
2½ lb. smelts, gutted but with
  heads left on
salt and pepper
12 Tb. (1½ sticks) butter
3 Tb. oil
2 Tb. finely chopped shallots
½ tsp. chervil

2 Tb. finely chopped parsley
1 tsp. walnut sauce or
  Worcestershire sauce
1 tsp. anchovy sauce or
  2″ anchovy paste
2 Tb. capers (with liquid),
  chopped

Flour the smelts, salt and pepper them, and sauté them in a mix of 6 tablespoons of the butter and the oil. Don't try to sauté them all at once, for you want them nicely browned, not steamed. Do as many as you can at a time without crowding them in the skillet.

Sauté them about 1½ minutes on each side over fairly high heat. Put the browned smelts on a warm platter as you finish each batch.

Melt the rest of the butter in the same skillet, then stir into the skillet the shallots, the chervil, parsley, walnut sauce, anchovy sauce, and capers. Let sauce heat a minute.

Pour the sauce over the smelts and serve.

shad

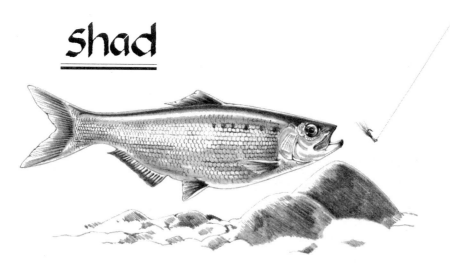

I am one of those who loves shad roe, but who feels that the ideal dish in season is "Shad *and* Roe." I think the flesh of this traveler from the sea is very fine, a delicious accompaniment of the savory roe.

The Conservation Department of the State of California in Sacramento has favored shad fishermen everywhere by publishing an instructive pamphlet "How to Catch, Bone, and Cook a Shad" by John Radovitch, but there is a way of preparing shad *without* boning (see opposite).

When the roe and buck fish come into the rivers of their birth to spawn they provide lively sport. Some anglers dub shad "the poor man's salmon."

═══════════ SHAD ROE AND BACON ═══════════

Joseph D. Bates, Jr., famous as author of numerous books on angling and of a big bestseller on outdoor cookery, has favored me with this delicious dish at his board and now makes it available for this book. When asked for it, he protested that preparing shad roe was too simple a process to require a recipe, but Joe's avoids pitfalls that can catch the unpracticed in preparing shad roe.

2 strips bacon for each roe	parsley for garnish
shad roe	lemon juice
1 lemon wedge for each roe	salt and pepper

"Fry bacon in heavy skillet until there is enough grease to cover bottom. Reduce to low heat and add the roe with the bacon around it. Cover skillet, turning over the roe every few minutes until they are a rich golden brown, about 10 minutes. If the bacon becomes done before the roe is, put the bacon slices on top of the roe. Drain bacon and roe on absorbent paper and serve immediately with lemon wedges. Garnish with fresh parsley if desired.

"If shad roe is fried over high heat the eggs will pop excessively. A few will pop anyway, so a covered skillet is necessary. Reduce heat if popping is rapid.

"When you first try this and think the roe is done, partly slice a roe length-wise to be sure it is not pink inside. It should cook long enough to be an even grayish-tan inside. At table each person slices his roe lengthwise, spreading the two halves open like a book. Then add lemon juice, salt, and pepper to taste. One roe per person usually is enough."

NOTE: Joe freezes his roes individually packaged, and shad roe freezes beautifully without losing any of its delicately delicious flavor.

BAKED STUFFED SHAD, "DEBONED"

If you love the taste of shad but refuse to learn how to bone this fish, take heart. This *is* the way: you "melt" away the labyrinth of tiny Y bones by long cooking. If you want to learn to bone one, you'll have to ask my wife or write to Sacramento (see the introduction to this section on shad).

SERVES 6

4-lb. shad, buck or roe fish, dressed
1 tsp. lemon juice
salt and pepper
your favorite bread stuffing
(I use both sage and rosemary when I make stuffing for baked fish)

2 Tb. melted butter or oil
finely chopped scallions or shallot (optional)
4 strips of bacon

Rub inside and out of shad with lemon juice.
Salt and pepper the fish, stuff it, and sew or skewer the cavity.
Coat fish with melted butter or oil and lay on a sheet of foil large enough to enfold the fish. If you wish you can sprinkle the shad with finely dried scallions or shallot.
Lay over the fish the bacon strips and enfold the shad securely.
Place the foiled shad in a shallow baking dish and *bake at the lowest temperature your oven can achieve (225°) for 5–6 hours.*

NOTE: Don't be in the least dismayed at the seemingly exorbitant baking time; the shad will come to the table moist, succulent, and "boneless."

SHAD STUFFED WITH ROE IN SORREL SAUCE

SERVES 4–6

2 pairs shad roe
2 Tb. butter
2 Tb. chopped scallions or shallots
3/4 cup dry white wine or vermouth
salt and pepper
2 sides boned shad, about 3/4–1 lb. each

1 tsp. cornstarch
1 1/4 cups heavy cream
1/3 cup cooked, tightly packed puréed sorrel (page 142) or use same amount from a can or jar of imported sorrel

Preheat oven to 375°.

Prepare roe first by sautéing them, briefly, in butter with scallions or shallots in an enameled frying pan or saucepan, turning them once. Pour the wine over and simmer 10 minutes.

Remove the roe with a slotted spoon, break up with a fork, salt and pepper liberally, and stuff into the cavities of the two boned sides of shad.

Bake in a generously buttered pan or shallow dish (just large enough to hold two fish) covered loosely with foil.

While the shad is baking prepare the sauce by boiling down the pan juices from the roe, reducing by a third. Dissolve the cornstarch in a little of the cream and add along with the rest of the cream to the boiling juice. Simmer until it is the consistency of a thin cream sauce. Add the sorrel, mix well, and heat long enough to exchange flavors.

After 30 minutes test the shad to see if it flakes easily. If so, it is done (if you like it a little drier, bake another 5 minutes). Remove to a platter, pour some of the hot sorrel sauce over the fish, and serve the rest in a sauceboat.

Black Basses

LARGEMOUTH BLACK BASS

The largemouth and smallmouth bass, both doughty and pugnacious battlers on appropriate tackle, are sometimes downgraded by epicures. "Okay for a chowder" is the way one friend of mine rather loftily described the white flaky meat of these fishes. I myself used to hold similar views until another friend educated me. His rule was: "Always skin bass, never scale them," and this, he said, applied even to smallmouth bass taken from the cold, clear waters of a northern lake. I believe that even though the lack of skin on a sautéing fish tends to make the fish break up in the skillet, skinning rather than scaling is the way to prepare bass for the kitchen. It is then quite delicious.

In objecting to the denigration of the bass as suitable only for a chowder, I am not suggesting that it should not be used in fish chowders. On the contrary, it is ideal for chowder, as anyone who has tasted the famous chowder as prepared at Fraser Mason's camp on Spednik Lake in New Brunswick knows very well indeed. Ethel Mason's recipe for her memorable chowder is on page 310. (I wish I had her recipes for the breads, rolls, five cakes, cookies, and pies she baked for that beautifully run fishing and hunting camp.)

FILLET OF BLACK BASS
WITH ANCHOVY AND CAPER BUTTER

For years I have skinned bass, either largemouth or smallmouth, and I would do so for this dish before filleting. If the bass is small, skin and use whole.

SERVES 5–6

5–6 fillets of bass
2 Tb. anchovy sauce or 2¼ inches anchovy paste
1 Tb. capers, mashed
1 shallot, minced

4 Tb. softened butter
bread crumbs
¼ cup dry vermouth
3 sprigs parsley, minced
lemon wedges

Preheat oven to 375°.

Mix the anchovy sauce or paste, the capers, and the shallot with the softened butter and spread on the bass fillets.

Roll fillets in crumbs, lay them into a buttered shallow baking dish, pour in the wine, and bake for 20 minutes.

Sprinkle fillets with parsley and serve with lemon wedges.

PAN-FRIED BLACK BASS
WITH MAÎTRE D'HÔTEL SAUCE

This recipe includes a very simple sauce that enhances sautéed, broiled, or baked fish. It can be made in camp if you have brought parsley and usually impresses any old "fried fish angler."

SERVES 4

THE MAÎTRE D'HÔTEL SAUCE
¼ cup butter
½ tsp. salt
⅛ tsp. pepper
THE FISH
four 1-lb. bass, dressed and skinned
salt and pepper

½ clove garlic, smashed
1 Tb. lemon juice
1 Tb. finely minced parsley

¼ cup yellow cornmeal
¼ cup flour
4 Tb. butter

Make the sauce first.

In a bowl set the butter out to soften. Then cream it with a fork and then a spoon until it is light and fluffy. Work in the salt and pepper.

Mix the smashed garlic and the lemon juice, then work this liquid into the butter. Take a bit of time to do this.

Mix in the parsley and serve in a gravy boat with a spoon.

Pan-fry the bass by following the general instructions for pan-frying perch on page 269. Again, the trick is to brown the fish on both sides but not to overcook.

Serve hot on *hot* plates and pass the sauce.

FILLET OF BLACK BASS
WITH ASPARAGUS AND CREAM SAUCE

When the bass are in the shallows aggressively taking big hair bugs, the asparagus is in season and, along some bass waters, is just coming up wild. Here's a dish for both; just as good with whitefish, walleye, or snook.

SERVES 3

1½ lb. bass fillets	12 spears of asparagus
⅓ cup white wine	3 Tb. butter
⅓ cup water	2 Tb. flour
5 peppercorns	¼ cup heavy cream
2 shallots or scallions, minced	salt and pepper
1 garlic clove, sliced	2 Tb. grated Parmesan
1 bay leaf	

Place the bass fillets in a buttered baking dish and add the wine, water, peppercorns, shallots or scallions, garlic, and bay leaf. Poach in a preheated 325° oven for 15 minutes. (If you have dressed the bass and filleted them yourself, save the backbones, ribs, and tails and lay them in with the fillets. They will add to the flavor of the liquid while poaching.)

Steam the asparagus for 7–8 minutes, and reserve.

Melt the butter and then add the flour, stirring constantly over low heat for 2–3 minutes. Off heat, stir in about ¾ cup of the fish liquor and cook over medium heat, stirring, until it thickens. Add the cream, a bit at a time. Do not boil. Salt and pepper to taste.

Cut the asparagus stalks into ½-inch slices, leaving tips whole. Stir both into the sauce. Pour the sauce over the fillets and sprinkle over all the Parmesan. Put under a broiler for a minute or two and serve.

SMALLMOUTH À LA SPEDNIK,
SAUTÉED BASS MEUNIÈRE

Plain old "fried" style is the way I usually cook smallmouth bass, and it's a method that's hard to improve on. This one comes from Vanceboro, Maine.

two 1½-lb. bass, dressed, heads and tail removed, and skinned or with big bass, 2 lb. bass fillets	salt and pepper
	5 Tb. butter (or 3 Tb. butter and 2 Tb. oil)
⅓ cup yellow cornmeal	parsley for garnish
⅓ cup flour	1 Tb. vinegar

Dredge the whole bass or fillets in a mix of cornmeal, flour, salt, and pepper, and sauté slowly in the melted butter over medium heat until well browned.

Turn carefully with a spatula and brown the other side. When the flesh has turned opaque, remove to a warm platter and garnish with parsley.

Stir vinegar into the fat and "greables." Heat and pour over fish.

Walleyed Pike

In taste this is the "English sole" of the fresh water, yet a great many good eaters have never sampled it. Not that it is rare as a game fish; in fact, that's how it usually comes to the table. Fish markets do offer it at times, and some of those times under the name of "blue pike." In lower Canada it is locally dubbed "pickerel"; the actual fish by that common name is thought of by some of our northern cousins as a small great northern pike. But by any name the walleye is one of the most delicious of fresh-water fishes. Its snow-white flesh is both delicately and distinctively flavored, and it invariably comes as a delightful surprise to a diner who tastes it for the first time.

Most states and provinces have a lower limit law of 14 inches, so 3–5-pounders are fairly common. This sizable fish is often filleted or baked. The record walleye weighed 16 pounds. Although a deep feeder and a fish that does battle down under, the walleye is a strong, determined fighter. Sometimes, as in pockets below a falls in a lake chain, the walleye schools in large numbers. Fishing for walleyes can be fast and furious under some conditions. Walleye fillets sautéed over a campfire on some wild shore are seldom forgotten by the appreciative angler. The walleye can be scaled, as its skin does not seem to carry a strong displeasing flavor.

BAKED WALLEYE IN SOUR CREAM

Scale but don't skin the walleye and pick a 3–3½-pounder. With the walleye I cut off the head and tail, but I'd leave on a lake trout's head and tail or that of a fat coho salmon, or char, prepared with this same recipe. In any case, serve with baked potato and tossed salad.

SERVES 4–5

salt and pepper
3-lb. walleye, scaled and dressed
2 Tb. finely minced shallots
   (or scallions or even onion)
2 Tb. soft butter
5 strips bacon

1 cup sour cream
¼ tsp. thyme
½ cup grated Parmesan cheese
½ cup bread crumbs
2 Tb. lemon juice

Salt and pepper the fish. Mix the minced shallots with the soft butter and spread it inside and out of the fish.

Lay the bacon strips on the bottom of a shallow baking dish and lay in the fish.

In a bowl mix the sour cream, thyme, grated cheese, bread crumbs, and lemon juice and spread the mixture over the fish. Bake at 325° for about 30 minutes.

═══ FILLETS (OR STEAKS) OF WALLEYE MORNAY ═══

I put this recipe under walleyed pike, but I might just as well have called it Fillet Mornay of any fish, for it is delicious when made with the fillets or steaks of any large game fish, even great northern pike. It is also most toothsome when the steaks are cut from a sizable lake trout.

SERVES 4–5

2½ lb. fish fillets or steaks
salt
juice from ½ lemon
small pinch cayenne or dash of
   hot sauce
1 cup cream

4 Tb. butter
1 shallot or scallion, minced
½ tsp. tarragon or marjoram
2 Tb. flour
2 egg yolks, beaten
6 Tb. grated cheese

Place fillets or steaks in a saucepan, just cover with cold water, add salt, lemon juice, and cayenne, bring to a bubble, then turn down heat and simmer for 10–12 minutes. Remove fish, but retain the fish broth. Place fillets or steaks in a buttered baking dish.

Stir together 1 cup fish broth and the cream.

Melt 3 tablespoons of the butter and add minced shallot or scallion, tarragon or marjoram. Cook just until shallots are soft. Stir in the flour and cook a minute or two. Then, off heat, stir in 2 cups of the fish broth until smooth. Return to low heat, stirring until sauce begins to thicken.

Spoon 2–3 tablespoons of sauce into beaten eggs, then stir beaten eggs slowly into sauce. Add the cheese, stirring the while, and cook until uniform.

Pour the sauce over the fish, dot with remaining butter, and bake in preheated oven at 375° for about 10 minutes to brown the sauce.

WALLEYED PIKE · 263

WALLEYES IN RED WINE SAUCE

If you hook small walleyes—¾ pound to a pound—this is a good way to prepare them, leaving heads on or off as you like. Their delicate flesh readily absorbs this lusty Provençale sauce and tastes delicious.

SERVES 4

salt and freshly ground pepper
4 walleyes, ¾–1 lb. each, cleaned
2 Tb. flour plus more for dredging
1 onion, minced
6 Tb. olive oil
2 cloves garlic, minced
1 cup red wine

1 cup boiling water
2 bay leaves
½ tsp. thyme
1 Tb. tomato purée
2 Tb. capers
3 Tb. chopped parsley

Salt and pepper the fish and dredge in flour. Shake off excess.

In a heavy saucepan sauté the onion in 2 tablespoons of the olive oil. When translucent, add the garlic and sauté slowly another minute. Stir in 2 table-spoons flour, blend well, and cook, stirring for a minute or two. Off heat pour in the wine and boiling water; whisk thoroughly. Return to the heat, whisking as the sauce thickens. Add bay leaves, thyme, and tomato purée. Let simmer while you sear the fish.

In a pan large enough to hold the 4 walleyes in one layer, heat the remaining oil and when hot, but not smoking, sear the fish quickly on each side.

Now pour the red wine sauce over the fish. Bring to a boil, then quickly lower the heat. Cover and let simmer 15 minutes.

Just before serving remove the bay leaves, adjust seasoning (the sauce will probably need salt and pepper), toss in the capers, and sprinkle chopped parsley on top.

BAKED FILLETS OF WALLEYE
IN CAPER SAUCE

This recipe produces a delicious dish with the fillets of most any fish—whitefish, pompano, pike—especially pike.

SERVES 4–6

4–6-lb. walleyed pike, dressed and
    skinned, with the head and
    5 inches of the tail reserved
3 cups water
1 carrot, sliced
1 medium onion, stuck with 2 cloves
1 rib celery, sliced
½ tsp. thyme
2 bay leaves
2 cloves garlic, sliced

3 Tb. butter
3 Tb. flour
salt and pepper
¼ tsp. nutmeg
1 Tb. capers, minced, with their
    juice
1 Tb. minced parsley
¾ cups heavy cream
bread crumbs

To make the fish stock put the fish head and tail, water, carrot, onion, celery, thyme, bay leaves, and garlic in a saucepan and bring to a boil.

Then simmer uncovered for 30 minutes or until liquid has boiled down to 1½–2 cups. Drain and reserve.

Now melt the butter in a skillet or saucepan, stir in the flour, and cook a few seconds while blending. Off heat, stir in about a cup of the fish stock, and back on a low heat cook for 2–3 minutes, stirring occasionally. Add salt, pepper, nutmeg, capers, and parsley, then stir in the cream.

Lay the pike fillets in a buttered shallow glass or porcelain baking dish, cover with the caper sauce, sprinkle with bread crumbs, and bake in a preheated 400° oven for 10–15 minutes.

DEVILED WALLEYE FILLETS

This is a delicious way of broiling *any* kind of fish fillets, as well as walleyes.

SERVES 6

1 small onion or 2 shallots, very
  finely diced
½ small green pepper, very finely
  chopped
¼ lb. (1 stick) butter
1½ Tb. Dijon mustard
1 tsp. Harvey's sauce or soy sauce
1 pinch cayenne or dash of
  Tabasco

3 Tb. lemon juice
½ cup bread crumbs
½ cup grated provolone or
  Parmesan
salt and pepper
2 lb. walleye fillets
  (or snook, redfish, etc.)

Sauté the onion and pepper in the butter until soft, then add mustard, sauce, cayenne, and lemon juice. Stir in crumbs and cheese.

Salt and pepper the fillets, lay them on foil broiler liner, and broil for 5 minutes about 4 inches from the flame.

Turn fish, cover evenly with bread-vegetable-cheese mixture, and broil another 6–8 minutes.

GRATIN OF WALLEYE

As with the recipe on page 294, roasted peppers lend a wonderful flavor to fish dishes. This dish, which can be prepared in a shallow baking dish, seems better when cooked in small individual gratin dishes. Serve with baked potatoes and a green salad.

Fillets of whitefish, bass, pike, or pickerel can be substituted for walleye.

SERVES 4

2 lb. walleye fillets
salt and pepper
2 green peppers
4–5 Tb. oil
2 cloves garlic, chopped fine

2 Tb. parsley, minced
2 Tb. capers (with their juice),
  minced
½ cup bread crumbs
½ tsp. powdered thyme

Wash and pat the fillets dry, then dice into 1-inch squares. Season with salt and pepper.

Wash, then dry the peppers and roast them under a broiler, turning them as the skin blackens. Place the peppers in a paper bag, seal by twisting the top, and set aside for 5 minutes or so. Then remove and, with the fingers, push and pinch off most of the blackened skin. Cut in half, remove the seeds and stem sepals, and slice into thin strips.

Put the oil in a big skillet and sauté the garlic until it barely colors. Then scrape in the fillet squares from your cutting board, turn up the heat, and cook, stirring constantly, for about 5 minutes.

Off heat, add and mix thoroughly the peppers, parsley, capers, and half the bread crumbs into which you have mixed the thyme.

Divide the mix into four gratin dishes, sprinkle the rest of the crumb-thyme mixture over all, and place under the broiler for a minute or so to brown.

Whitefish

I have never caught a whitefish on rod and reel, but once during the early fifties I did catch 12,300 pounds of them in gill nets. Bud Helmericks and his wife and my wife and I spent a summer fishing for Arctic whitefish in the Colville River in Alaska. We encamped at its mouth, where it debouches into the Arctic Ocean. Sheila and I caught the fish, and Bud flew them to the market in Barrow, where the Eskimos had gathered to work for the civilian contractors building the Navy's research base there. Tired of eating out of Spam cans and yearning for their delicious *anaklik*, the Eskimos provided an eager and appreciative market.

Whether they were smoked or poached or "fried," we found that we simply didn't tire of whitefish on a daily fare during that Arctic summer.

Smoked whitefish, like salmon, today is almost priced out of market—ounce for ounce almost as expensive as anything that swims—and just as good.

STUFFED FILLETS OF WHITEFISH

This method of preparing whitefish is also a good way to prepare fillets of any fish. It is particularly delicious with whitefish because whitefish is particularly delicious.

SERVES 4

4 whitefish fillets
juice of 1 lemon
salt and pepper
¼ cup bread crumbs
¼ cup grated cheese
½ tsp. tarragon
5 Tb. butter plus 4 pats
1 small onion, finely minced

3 tomatoes, peeled and quartered
½ lb. mushrooms, sliced
½ cup dry vermouth or dry white
  wine
½ cup water
2 Tb. flour
2 sprigs parsley, chopped

Wash the fillets, pat dry, and lay on oiled paper. Squeeze and pat lemon juice on each fillet, then add salt and pepper.

Mix the bread crumbs, cheese, and tarragon and spread a fourth of the mixture over each fillet. Lay a pat of butter in several lumps on each fillet.

Roll up the fillets as you would French pancakes, and secure with toothpicks.

Heat 2 tablespoons of the butter in a big iron skillet, add the onion, and sauté until soft.

Lay in the fillet rolls, then add the tomato chunks and the mushrooms.

Pour in the vermouth or white wine and the water, and cover. Simmer for 8 minutes, timing from the time it begins to bubble.

Butter a baking dish and lay in the rolls of stuffed fillet, which you remove from the liquid carefully with a slotted spoon.

Over a highish flame reduce the fish liquor to about a cup.

In a saucepan or another skillet, melt remaining 3 tablespoons of butter, stir in the flour, and cook a minute or so. Then, off heat, stir in the liquid. Simmer and stir until the sauce thickens. Check seasonings, stir in parsley, and pour sauce over the fillet rolls.

Bake in a preheated 375° oven for 10–12 minutes, until golden on top.

BAKED WHITEFISH

Here again is a recipe that does nicely for whole fish of 3 to 5 pounds, with red fish, lake trout, char, or steelhead. Use the head and a section from the tail to make the fish stock (page 241).

SERVES 3–4

salt and pepper
1 whitefish, dressed and scaled
3 Tb. butter or oil
2 shallots, sliced
2 medium carrots, thinly sliced
1 rib celery, sliced
½ lb. mushrooms, sliced
2 Tb. flour

¾ cup fish stock
¾ cup light cream or milk
2 Tb. mushroom catsup or
  Worcestershire sauce
3 Tb. grated Parmesan
½ cup bread crumbs
3 Tb. chopped parsley

Butter a shallow baking dish. Salt and pepper the whitefish inside and out and lay it in the dish.

Melt the 3 tablespoons of butter or oil and sauté the shallots, carrots, and celery for 3 minutes or so; then put in the mushrooms and cook another 2 minutes.

Blend in the flour and cook, stirring, a minute or so. Then, off heat, stir in the fish stock. Cook over low heat until it thickens, then stir in the cream or milk, the mushroom catsup, and half the grated cheese.

Pour the sauce over the whitefish.

Mix the remainder of the cheese with the crumbs and sprinkle on top of the sauced fish.

Bake in a preheated 350° oven for about 30 minutes.

Garnish with parsley and serve.

BAKED WHITEFISH FILLETS

My wife never fails to delight me with this recipe. It makes no difference whether the fillets be whitefish, trout, walleye, salmon, char, or sole. This simply made dish is delicious.

2–2½-lb. whitefish fillets	½ cup bread crumbs mixed with
1 Tb. lemon juice	¼ cup grated Parmesan
salt and white pepper	butter
2–3 thinly sliced shallots	white wine
(or 4 scallions, or, even,	
minced onion)	

Moisten the fillets with lemon juice.

Place them in a shallow, buttered glass baking dish. Salt and pepper them, cover with the sliced shallots, then add the crumb and cheese mixture.

Dot with butter, then pour in white wine until it is about a third of the way up on the fillets.

Bake, uncovered, in a 450° oven for 25 minutes or until flesh is opaque.

Camp Cooler Practice with Fish

If you take a cooler to camp in order to bring back a few fish, here is the advice a Maine camp owner used to give: "Take a leaf out of your experience with the use of your ice cream freezer if you want to keep your fish; and don't clean them before you put them in to chill.

"Lay in a layer of crushed ice, then lay in your fish. Then mix about a half pound of rock salt to ten pounds of crushed ice and lay this over the fish. You can do this in layers if you need to."

In the days before the Second World War, and for a very few after, camp proprietors would build sturdy wooden boxes for taking home a day's limit or so. The ice? It came in 50-pound cakes out of sawdust in the ice house, put down there the winter before.

Panfish

Panfish is not a scientific name but one that arose in the kitchen; it is a measure of length referring to size of fish in their adult stage, a size that can be accommodated, presumably, in a skillet. For our purposes, it includes the various sunfishes, the perches, rock bass, crappie, and the bullhead catfish. Small individuals from species that normally grow beyond pan size are called just that— *pan-size* bass, or *pan-size* trout.

Although many, many fish recipes are interchangeable among species, this is particularly true for the panfish. Panfish are generally scaled (save for the catfish), as the skin crisps deliciously in these smallish fish.

A generalization about cooking panfish: when sautéing them I as often as not use bacon fat, the fat left over from frying bacon, which I find goes particularly well with fish—just as bacon "goes with" calves' liver. My reason is probably compounded from boyhood experiences: my mother and grandmother usually served the fish I'd caught the day before at the next day's breakfast.

Note the recipe for sautéeing perch below (Pan-Fried or Sautéed Yellow Perch) as an all-purpose recipe for all "fried" panfish. I dip panfish in yellow cornmeal (or a combination of ⅔ meal and ⅓ white flour), but with pan-size trout I use all flour. So much for cooking prejudices. My junior partner sometimes uses rye flour—a technique she picked up from good Danish cooks.

Perches

YELLOW PERCH

For me, the yellow and white perches crowd close behind the catfish, salmon, trout, and walleye (I am listing them alphabetically in order not to show a preference) as the most delicious of fresh-water game fish. I had fished for, cooked, and relished yellow perch since boyhood, but had never tasted white perch until I caught my first of the species while trolling for landlocked salmon in New Brunswick in the 1950s. While both are commonly called perch, the white variety is actually a member of the bass family, indeed is closely related to the striper. The yellow perch is a true perch. Both are scrumptious fare.

Happily for the angler-gastronome both are schooling fish, and usually where you catch one you can catch a mess.

══════ WHITE PERCH IN BEER BATTER ══════

Several of my friends spoke so enthusiastically of trout dipped in a batter (using beer as the liquid) and then sautéed that I tried it, first with white perch, then with bullhead catfish. Here is my version, but the fish can also be fried in deep fat if you prefer.

SERVES 4

6 Tb. flour	¼ can (3 ounces) beer
2 Tb. yellow cornmeal	4 white perch, scaled and
½ tsp. dill weed or tarragon	sprinkled inside and out
1 tsp. salt	with lemon juice
1 Tb. paprika	4 Tb. lard or cooking oil

Mix the flour, cornmeal, dill or tarragon, salt, and paprika in a bowl, then add the beer and beat until smooth.

Dip the fish in the beer batter one at a time.

Heat the lard in an iron skillet and sauté the fish 8–9 minutes to the side.

══════ PAN-FRIED OR SAUTÉED YELLOW PERCH ══════

My grandmother used to put down cleaned panfish in a mild salt-water solution overnight, but I have stopped that tradition. I usually wash the dressed, scaled, beheaded, and de-tailed perch, pat almost dry, and then roll them in the meal. Some cooks pat them dry, then dip them in milk or beaten egg, before dredging with meal or flour.

SERVES 2–3

6 small yellow perch,	4 Tb. bacon fat, lard,
7–9″ long	or butter and oil
salt and pepper	4 Tb. butter
cornmeal (or combined with flour)	1 lemon (optional)

Dress, scale, and wash the fish, pat dry, salt and pepper, and then dredge them in the meal or meal-and-flour combination.

Heat the fat until it is hot enough to cook at once, but not burning, sputtering hot. Lay in the fish, turn heat down to a barely medium flame, and begin to brown the fish. At the same time begin the process of loosening the fish from the pan bottom with a thin metal spatula.

Taking 8–10 minutes to a side (turn heat to low if it seems to "fry" too fast), brown the fish slowly until crisp. Do not overcook.

Sometimes it is a bit tricky to brown without overcooking. When the flesh is opaque the fish is done; one hopes it's all browned by then.

Add 4 tablespoons butter to the skillet after removing fish and, if you like, squeeze in the juice of a lemon, stir the fat and juices to loosen the dredgings, and pour over the browned fish.

Variation: After removing fish from the skillet, toss in about ⅓ cup chopped black walnuts. Brown lightly with the remaining butter and sprinkle over the fish before serving. The lemon should be served separately in wedges so you can appreciate the special taste of the black walnuts.

PALFREY PERCH:
BROILED WHITE PERCH

Among the panfish, or pan-size fish, the white bass, big rock bass, and crappie all brown well.

SERVES 2–4

4–5 white perch
salt and pepper
6 Tb. butter, melted

3 Tb. chopped parsley
1 Tb. lemon juice

Dress, scale, and wash the fish, pat dry, and season inside and out with salt and pepper. Preheat broiler.

Spoon some of the butter over each fish after they are laid onto the broiler, and broil about 3 inches from the heat or element. Broil about 10 minutes on the first side, then turn and brown the skin on the off side, 4–5 minutes more perhaps.

Put fish on a warm serving platter and set aside.

Cook the parsley in the remaining butter while the butter browns a bit. Squeeze in the lemon juice and pour all over the fish.

Variation: Sometimes I spoon out a tablespoon of capers with whatever juice comes with them, squashing and smashing them, then adding the capers and their juice to the butter-parsley mix.

PERCH BAKED WITH SHALLOTS AND MUSHROOMS

Either of the two perches, the white bass, or the rockbass ("red-eye" or "goggle-eye" in the Midwest) is fine for this dish. Indeed the recipe is excellent for any panfish, including very large sunfish and the crappies. Fillets of larger fish may be substituted.

SERVES 4

five or six 8″–10″ perch,
   scaled and dressed with
   heads and tails removed
¼ cup yellow cornmeal
¼ cup flour
salt and freshly ground pepper
6 Tb. butter
¾ lb. mushrooms, sliced thin

1 Tb. capers, crushed,
   with 1 tsp. of their juice
6 shallots or scallions, sliced
2 garlic cloves, sliced
¼ cup bread crumbs
½ tsp. dried tarragon
2 Tb. minced chives

Dredge the perch in a mix of the cornmeal, flour, salt, and pepper.

Sauté the fish in a couple of tablespoons of the butter, browning each side (see page 269 under Pan-Fried or Sautéed Yellow Perch).

Transfer the perch to a pie plate or dish. In another skillet and with 2 more tablespoons butter sauté the mushrooms, mashed capers, and their juice for 2–3 minutes. Stir constantly to blend the capers and caper liquid. Remove mushrooms to a lightly buttered shallow baking dish.

Add remaining butter to the mushroom skillet and sauté the shallots and garlic for a minute or two.

Now lay the perch on an even bed of mushrooms, sprinkle with the bread crumbs mixed with tarragon, then spread the shallots, garlic, and chives on top. Bake in a preheated 400° oven for 10–12 minutes.

DEEP-FRIED YELLOW PERCH

Like the bullhead catfish, this succulent panfish deep-fries very well. Smallish yellow perch, those three-quarters of a pound and under, should be selected for deep-frying. I scale yellow perch rather than skin them whether I deep-fry or pan-fry.

The recipe for deep-frying catfish, page 273, is excellent for yellow perch. Also, see page 269 for a beer batter for use in deep-frying or pan-frying perch.

"Sunnies"

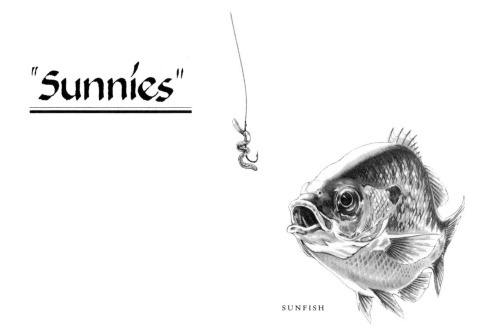

SUNFISH

The average angler, boy and man, seldom has identified the various kinds of sunfish that have come to his worm or fly, but, for most of us, whose first "trophy" was a 7-inch "sunny," it matters little. Rolled in flour or cornmeal and sautéed slowly but finally to a crisp brown, the tidbit is excellent fare, say, as a breakfast fish course before the eggs and bacon.

Bony? Yes, but one should be venturesome when eating these browned, crisp morsels. When sautéed slowly the little panfish may be eaten bones and all by the experienced. Ten fingers and at least three paper napkins are all you need. An old hand either eats, or eats around, the bones, but for your young you had better "carve" until your child later masters the technique.

An appreciative friend of mine once said, after taking a dozen "red-ears" on a tiny dry fly and noting their sporty antics, "Ounce for ounce, the fighten'est fish alive. Why, if those sunnies weighed ten pounds apiece a man wouldn't dare take a canoe onto the same lake with 'em."

═══ PANFISH SUNNIES WITH MARJORAM ═══
AND LEMON BUTTER

This recipe can be employed with any of the panfish from sunnies to crappies. It is super with white perch, and is simple to make with any panfish.

SERVES 4

6 Tb. butter
4 shallots or 3 cloves garlic,
  chopped
½ tsp. dried marjoram

4 sunnies, cleaned and scaled
salt and white pepper
flour
1½ Tb. lemon juice

Melt the butter in a skillet (that has a lid for later use) and add the shallots or garlic, marjoram, and sunnies that have been salted, peppered, and floured. Brown both sides of the fish, about 5 minutes.

Add the lemon juice, cover, and over medium to low heat cook the fish another 10 minutes or so.

When you serve the fish pour some of the lemon butter from the pan over each fish.

Catfish

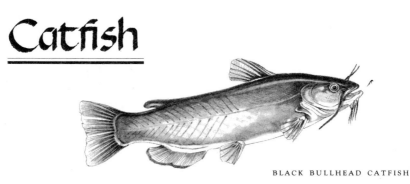

BLACK BULLHEAD CATFISH

I was appalled when I first moved from the Middle West to the East Coast to discover how few people ate the delicious catfish. Many New Englanders considered the "mud pout," as they dubbed the bullhead catfish, an inedible if not disgusting trash fish. Yet those same people often considered eel a delicacy, which it surely is. But then so is the catfish. My pursuit of this fish began as a boy with a bamboo pole, a can of worms, and a "coal-oil" lantern, for this ready biter is even a more willing taker after dark. Later, on the Embarrass River in Illinois, I caught and ate the racy channel cat. To this day, when I find myself driving in the South or Midwest, I seek out the restaurants en route that serve catfish. Nowadays, what with the large-scale commercial "farming" of catfish, one finds it more widely offered by restaurants. And even today there are still "as much as you can eat" places in the Midwest and South specializing in "Fried Catfish Today" where this delicious fish is served by the platterful.

It can indeed be fried in deep fat and is delicious that way, but I believe I prefer it rolled in yellow cornmeal and sautéed in butter, or half butter and half bacon fat.

The flesh of the catfish is pinkish white and of more uniform homogeneous and fleshy texture than the flaky textures of most fresh-water fishes. In my view it has only three peers (and no superiors) for flavor—salmon, trout, and walleyed pike.

Most anglers skin the catfish, handling small fish charily, to escape the barbs, both lateral and dorsal, but I usually scald and scrape the fish (to remove its viscous skin covering). Catfish are scaleless.

My own preference (it is actually an addiction) is for sautéing when the fish is small (larger catfish like the channel cat are filleted). As with very small trout, I simply don't consider alternate ways of cooking these two delicious fishes.

DEEP-FRIED CATFISH

This recipe can be used for other fish, such as yellow or white perch, rock bass, etc., and for fish chunks from larger fish. If you have an oil thermometer, you can check to see when you have reached proper deep-frying heat of about 375°. If you do not have a thermometer, the rule of thumb is to test for temperature with an inch-square cube of white bread; the oil is hot enough when it will color the cube a golden brown after one minute.

Don't try to fry more than a couple bullhead-size fish at a time, and try to have the fish at room temperature when you begin the deep-frying. Serve with rémoulade or with tartar sauce.

SERVES 5–6

lard or oil for frying*
5–6 bullheads, skinned
  with heads and tail cut off
¼ cup yellow cornmeal

¼ cup flour seasoned with salt
  and pepper
1 egg, beaten

Heat enough oil in a saucepan (to cover fish by at least 1 inch) to frying heat of 375° or use my method, if you prefer. Because I am stingy with lard I usually simply fry bullhead catfish and other small fish in about ½ inch fat in a skillet. This takes a bit longer than deep-fat frying, but it saves fat and achieves virtually the same result.

Meanwhile dip fish in a mix of cornmeal and seasoned flour, then in the egg, and then again in the meal and flour.

Fry for 3–6 minutes, depending on fish size.

* Nowadays most people use vegetable oil or Crisco-type solidified oils for deep-frying. I, personally, stick to lard.

Pickerel

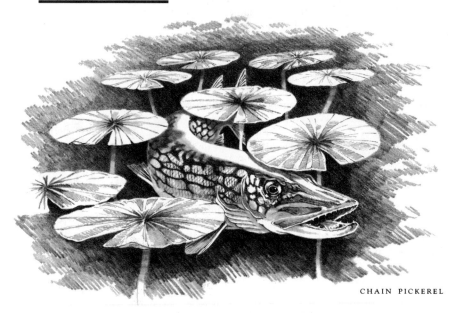

CHAIN PICKEREL

The genus *Esox* provides three of the most savagely predaceous of fresh-water fish: the musky, the great northern pike, and the pickerel. A friend once said of them: "They are all three gangsters of the lily-pods; and if the musky is the Godfather and great northern a Capo, then the lurking pickerel is at least a minor hit man."

I can agree; on two occasions I have taken pickerel with my own spinning spoons in their lips that they had broken off earlier on the same day.

But the pickerel is also good eating; those who scorn the pickerel are missing a tasty fish.

A word of warning: Pan-frying and broiling are not recommended as ways of preparing this rather dry fish.

BAKED PICKEREL IN A MUSHROOM SAUCE

I usually skin this fish no matter how I plan to prepare it, and with this recipe I make a fish stock as a base for a sauce.

The so-called lowly "snake" is not lowly at all prepared in this way.

SERVES 6

3 pickerel, dressed, skinned,
   but with heads and tails saved
1 onion, stuck with 2 cloves
1½ cups water
1 cup white wine
¼ tsp. cumin
¼ tsp. basil
2 Tb. minced parsley

2 bay leaves
salt and pepper
2 Tb. butter
½ lb. fresh mushrooms, sliced
2 Tb. flour
1 cup fish stock
1 Tb. mushroom catsup
   or Worcestershire sauce

Put fish heads and tails, onion with cloves, water, wine, cumin, basil, parsley and bay leaves in a kettle and bring to a boil. Continue to cook at a high simmer until the liquid is reduced by half. Add salt and pepper. Strain and set aside the stock.

In a saucepan melt the butter and sauté the mushrooms for 2–3 minutes, then stir in the flour. Mix well with the butter and mushrooms, and cook for 2–3 minutes longer.

Off heat, pour in a cup of the fish stock and then cook, stirring, at a simmer for 4–5 minutes. Season with mushroom catsup or Worcestershire.

Lay the pickerel in a buttered baking dish, pour the sauce over them, and bake in a preheated 350° oven for 25–30 minutes.

PICKEREL AND POTATOES

Here is a camp dish that is just as good at home. Like his big cousin, the great northern pike, the pickerel is a bit bony and tends to dryness, but the flesh is very tasty and responds to poaching.

SERVES 4–6

2 pickerel, scaled or skinned	6 Tb. butter, melted
6 potatoes, sliced thin	½ cup white wine
salt and pepper	juice of 1 lemon
6 cloves garlic, finely minced	2 Tb. chopped parsley

Lay the fish in a lidded casserole and arrange the potato slices over them. Salt and pepper over all, then add the garlic and the melted butter.

Pour in the wine, then add enough water to come up to the potatoes. Cover, and cook over a low flame until the liquid has all but evaporated and potatoes are cooked—about 20 minutes.

Squeeze in the lemon, then sprinkle the parsley over all and serve.

POACHED PICKEREL WITH
A CHILI AND HORSERADISH SAUCE

This is a delicious way to prepare a couple of 1½–2-pound pickerel or a larger 3–3½-pound chunk of its cousin, the great northern pike.

I skin pickerel and pike.

SERVES 4–6

fish stock (see page 241)	2 Tb. chili sauce
2 pickerel, dressed and skinned	4 Tb. horseradish
2 Tb. butter	3 Tb. grated cheese mixed with 1
2 Tb. flour	Tb. bread crumbs

Bring the fish stock to a boil, lay in the fish, and cook at a steady simmer for about 20 minutes or until the meat on the thickest part of the back is opaque.

Remove fish to a shallow baking dish and strain the stock, reserving 2 cups.

In a skillet or saucepan melt the butter, then stir in the flour. Cook for a minute, then take off heat and pour in 1½ cups of the fish stock.

Cook the sauce over medium heat, stirring until it thickens, and then stir in the chili sauce and horseradish. Pour sauce over the fish, cover with the cheese-crumb mixture and brown in a 400° oven.

Muskellunge

This largest member of the genus *Esox*, "the tiger of fresh water," say its passionate pursuers, is better known for its size, savage strike, and thrashing power than for its excellence as table fare. In this the musky is as unfairly maligned, as are its cousins, the great northern pike and pickerel, for poached or stuffed and baked these fishes have a fine flavor.

See pages 277 and 278 for two great northern pike recipes that may be used with equal excellence for muskies, and for one striped bass recipe also excellent for musky.

POACHED MUSKY L'INDIENNE

I have found that some of the herbs that go to make curry powder have a most affectionate affinity for fish. This recipe would do for great northern pike, pickerel, striped bass, or any of the salmon or large trout like the steelhead where a whole fish of 4–6 pounds or a section cut from an even larger fish is available.

SERVES 6

1 small onion or 3 shallots, thinly sliced	¼ tsp. cumin
3–4 bay leaves	¼ tsp. fenugreek
salt and pepper	¼ tsp. turmeric
3-lb. section of musky, scaled	¼ tsp. mace
1½ cups dry white wine	2 Tb. flour
⅓ cup heavy cream	2 Tb. dry Marsala

Put the onion, bay leaves, salt, and pepper in an enamel roast pan or fish poacher, if you have one. Lay the fish onto two thicknesses of heavy foil that is longer than the pan, set it inside, and add the wine and enough water to come up three-fourths of the way on the fish.

Simmer for about 15 minutes, then turn the fish over and simmer another 10–12 minutes.

Let the fish cool in the stock, then remove the fish and skin it. Keep warm.

Pour off ¾ to 1 cup of the broth for later use, leaving the remaining broth in the pan to heat the fish in.

In a small saucepan mix the cream with ¾ cup of the fish broth. Add the spices and bring to a simmer. Remove from the heat. Stir the flour with the Marsala to make a thickening paste. Whisk this into the cream broth mixture. Back on very low heat let it cook for 3 minutes while you are reheating the musky.

Serve the sauce over the fish.

Great Northern Pike

Don't scorn this somewhat bony fish. True, the meat is drier than that of certain other fishes and it *is* bony, but this is a problem with small pike and its close relative, the pickerel; with fish of 6–8 pounds (or more) the bones are larger and findable. The taste of pike is excellent, and bacon or salt pork and/or basting with butter and wine will solve dryness.

BAKED STUFFED GREAT NORTHERN PIKE

This recipe can be used to bake any largish fish—walleye, lake trout, char, and trophy-size rainbows, steelhead, and various Pacific salmon. I leave heads and tails on with all fish, save pikes. Somehow the wicked shovel-jawed head of a pike seems unappetizing.

SERVES 6

5–6-lb. pike
Stuffing*
6 strips of bacon or salt pork
    equivalent
1 small onion, finely chopped

4 Tb. butter, melted
¼ cup white wine
watercress
lemon slices

Fill the dressed and scaled pike with the stuffing and sew up the opening (or use small skewers).

In a shallow baking dish or pan lay down a base of bacon strips and place the fish upon them, fastening with toothpicks. Fasten 2–3 strips of bacon or salt pork on top of the fish. Sprinkle the finely chopped onion over all.

Melt the butter and stir in the wine and keep warm.

Bake the fish in a 325° oven for 30–40 minutes, depending on size, but be sure to baste often with the butter and wine.

Garnish the fish with watercress and slices of lemon.

NOTE: If you wish, add oysters, canned shrimp, or canned minced clams to your own favorite stuffing.

*Use your favorite sage and bread stuffing, or one of those on pages 377–380.

════════ BRAISED GREAT NORTHERN PIKE ════════

While it is true that this fish is rather dry, it is also true that its flesh is quite tasty. Braising is the rule when this fish is baked.

SERVES 8

1½ cups water
1 onion, sliced
1 carrot, sliced
1 rib celery with leaves, chopped
½ tsp. tarragon
6–7-lb. dressed pike (head and
   tail removed, but reserve)

4 shallots or scallions, diced
3 tomatoes, diced, or 3 canned
   tomatoes, squashed
½ cup dry white wine
salt and pepper (to taste)
lemon wedges

Boil the water, then simmer the onion, carrot, celery, tarragon, and the fish head and tail until you have ½ cup of liquid. Strain and set aside.

Sprinkle the shallots and tomatoes over a buttered shallow baking dish large enough to hold the fish.

Lay the fish in; pour over it the fish stock and the white wine. (The fish should lie in liquid about halfway up its side.)

Bake 25–30 minutes in a 400° preheated oven, basting often. When done, remove the pike to a serving platter. Purée the sauce in a food processor, if you have one; otherwise push through a strainer, then check the seasoning.

Pour sauce over the fish and serve garnished with lemon wedges.

QUENELLES

In our parlance these are little fish dumplings, but let us add that they are surely one of the lightest and most delicate creations of France. There they are made with pike *Esox,* the same fish we call the great northern, but you can also use fillets of sole, halibut, or flounder, even though the flesh of the latter is a bit more coarse. Using some lettuce in the dumpling dough keeps the quenelles particularly light, a trick we learned from Albert Stockli, the original chef of New York's Four Seasons. He was a Swiss who was most creative about using fresh fish and combining classic recipes with indigenous American products. The accompanying avocado sauce is an example of his inventiveness and it is delicious, but if ripe avocados are not readily available, you could serve the quenelles with a hollandaise thinned with some cream (see page 362).

SERVES 4

½ head Boston lettuce	¼ cup melted butter
1 lb. pike (or sole, flounder, halibut), skinned and boned	½ tsp. salt
	¼ tsp. pepper
1 egg	¼ tsp. dried savory
3 egg yolks	¼ cup heavy cream

Boil the lettuce in water for just 1 minute. Drain and pat dry on paper towels.

Dry the fish thoroughly on paper towels.

Put the fish and the lettuce into the food processor and process until smooth, then add the egg and egg yolks, butter, salt, pepper, savory, and cream. Scrape down the sides and be sure that you get all of the mixture smooth. Refrigerate for 1 hour or more, covered.

Bring a large pot of salted water to a boil, then reduce to a simmer. Wet 2 tablespoons in warm water, then with one of them scoop up enough of the chilled dough to mound well over the spoon. Shape with the other spoon into a neatly rounded oval, then scrape it off into the simmering water with the tip of the spoon. Repeat with the rest.

Let the quenelles simmer very gently for 10 minutes—they will all rise to the top. When done, turn off the heat and let sit in the hot water while you make the sauce.

AVOCADO SAUCE

⅓ cup dry white wine	1 Tb. lemon juice
1½ cups white sauce (page 364)	½ cup heavy cream
1 ripe avocado	

Boil the wine down until it is reduced by half, then whisk it into the white sauce.

Peel the avocado and remove the pit. Cut in chunks and put into the food processor along with the sauce, lemon juice, and cream, and blend until smooth.

Remove the quenelles from the water with a slotted spoon and blot dry around the edges if still wet. Arrange on a warm platter and pour the sauce around.

Eel

Like the bullhead, the eel is sometimes more difficult to get *off* the hook than *onto* it, but once off it and onto a platter it is a fish for a king. In his *Fresh Water Fishes as Food*, E. G. Boulanger said, "A humorist has observed that eel might be much more popular if it looked less like an eel," and perhaps a friend of mine sought to palliate the snakelike appearance of this delicious fish when he referred to it as the Serpent from Heaven.

Ways to cook eel are infinite, but since it qualifies dubiously as a game fish, we may be excused for including only two recipes here.

STEWED EEL IN CREAM SAUCE

This recipe is wonderful with eel chunks, but it can also be used when you have a mess of small bullhead catfish. I think of it as a country version of the famous French dish Eels en Matelote.

SERVES 6

¼ lb. salt pork,
  cut into ½" cubes
3 lb. eels, cut into 3" pieces
1 Tb. chopped shallots
  or scallions (white part)
1 carrot, sliced
1 rib celery, diced
1½ cups dry white wine
¼ cup applejack or brandy
1 tsp. salt
6 peppercorns

1 bay leaf
¼ tsp. powdered thyme
¼ tsp. tarragon
¼ tsp marjoram
½ tsp. sage
3 Tb. butter or 2 Tb. salt pork fat
1½ Tb. flour
2 egg yolks, beaten
½ cup heavy cream
juice of ½ lemon

Try out the salt pork cubes in a saucepan. Remove and reserve the cracklings and all but 2–3 tablespoons of the fat. Add eel pieces and brown on all sides, then add the shallots, carrot, and celery, and cook for 3–4 minutes more over low to medium heat.

Add the wine and applejack or brandy, the salt, peppercorns, and the five herbs, and simmer until eel pieces are just done—about 20 minutes.

Remove eel pieces to a hot serving dish and strain the stock in which the eels simmered. Return to the heat and boil to reduce to 1 cup.

Melt the butter in a separate saucepan or use all or part of the remaining salt pork fat to make 2 tablespoons, stir in the flour and cook, stirring, a minute or two. Off heat add the eel stock. Cook over low heat, stirring, until sauce begins to thicken.

In a bowl mix the beaten egg yolks with the cream and spoon in several tablespoons of the hot sauce. Then slowly stir this egg mixture back into the sauce, add lemon juice, and cook over very low heat until the finished sauce is thick and smooth; do not allow it to boil. Pour the sauce over the eel and sprinkle cracklings on as a garnish.

NOTE: If 8–10-inch catfish are used instead of eel pieces, cut the catfish into two equal pieces after they have been skinned and the heads and tails cut off.

IZAAK WALTON'S SPITTED EEL

A small eel or a long spit make this recipe of Izaak Walton's quite feasible today. Of course, an eel so prepared can be tied head to tail and broiled on a modern grill. The "sweet herbs" mentioned by Master Walton could be thyme, basil, and tarragon.

"First, wash him in water and salt; then pull off his skin* below his vent—, and not much further; having done that, take out his guts as clean as you can, but wash him not: Then give him three or four scotches [slashes] with a knife; and then put into his belly and those scotches sweet herbs, an anchovy, and a little nutmeg grated or cut very small; and your herbs and anchovies must also be cut very small, and mixed with good butter and salt: having done this, then pull his skin back over him all but his head, which you are to cut off, to the end you may tie his skin about that part where his head grew, and it must be so tied as to keep all his moisture within his skin: and having done this, tie him with tape and pack-thread to a spit, and roast him leisurely, and baste him with water and salt till his skin breaks, and then with butter: and having roasted him enough, let what was put into his belly, and what he drips, be his sauce."

---

*The skinning process might be better explained: slice just through the skin around the eel just back of the eyes, then, without slitting the belly, skin the eel back as far as the vent. Cut a slit into the belly cavity and take out the entrails. Cut two or three gashes lengthwise in the flesh. Stuff the body cavity and the open slashes with the herbs and anchovy butter.

Now pull the skin back over the body, cut off the head far enough back so the skin can be tied off to seal the eel's body, which is once again in its own skin.

Salt Water Fish

Striped Bass

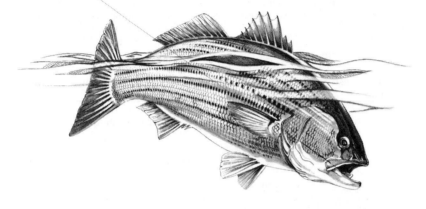

This grand fish of the beach and inlets is so formidable and so temperamental (a combination that anglers both love and hate) that he creates a unique company of devotees who pursue him. Like Atlantic salmon fishermen, striper fishermen are a breed apart. Used to the mysterious vagaries of their quarry, they invariably show the patience of Job. Strung along a stretch of white beach they seem sometimes almost automatons casting, reeling, casting again, their long, grace-ful full-arced casts things of rhythmic beauty against the boundless sea and skyline. For the striper angler, as with the salmon fisher, any day is a red-letter day when he has beached a fish.

Indeed, one beached fish is apt to fill a larder or feed a host. Is there any-thing better than stuffed baked striper for a summer supper?

POACHED WHOLE STRIPED BASS WITH CHEESE AND EGG SAUCE

If you have an elongated fish poacher, use it. I use an old porcelain refrigerator crisper (see page 241) and either place the fish in a bed of cheesecloth or on two or three layers of heavy foil that reach beyond the head and tail of the fish and can be used as handles. Ideally fish should be poached with the head and tail left on.

This recipe is fine also for snook, redfish, whitefish, pike, or big walleye.

SERVES 8

fish stock (the one for salmon
  on page 241 is fine)
6–8-lb. striper
2 Tb. butter
2 Tb. flour

1 cup milk, warmed
salt and pepper
½ cup grated Parmesan cheese
2 hard-boiled eggs, chopped

Bring to a boil enough fish stock to amply cover the fish, then turn down to a simmer.

Lay in the cheesecloth or foil, then the fish, and simmer, covered, according to the Canadian system (see page 248), 10 minutes per inch. To determine the cooking time, before immersing the fish lay it on the counter and with one edge of a ruler set flat against the counter, measure the depth or thickness of the fish.

While the striper is poaching, melt the butter over a low heat in a skillet or saucepan, stir in the flour and cook over low heat, stirring for 2½–3 minutes. Off heat, stir in the milk and then return to the heat and let the sauce simmer for 4 minutes or so, stirring occasionally. Add salt and pepper to taste.

When the sauce is almost done, stir in the cheese and the chopped eggs and serve hot over the poached striper.

JASON'S STRIPED BASS
BATHED IN OLIVE OIL, CILANTRO, AND LEMON

It is important that you find cilantro (or fresh coriander or Chinese parsley—whatever name it goes by) to get the full flavor of this delicate, aromatic dish. Chinese parsley is available nowadays in any Oriental vegetable place, or you can easily grow your own. Serve bass this way as a first course or as a luncheon dish with steamed new potatoes.

SERVES 4

1½ lb. striped bass fillets
about 2–3 cups court bouillon*
⅓ cup good fruity olive oil
¼ cup chopped cilantro

1 lemon
salt and freshly ground pepper
a dozen or so small black
  Mediterranean olives

Put the fillets in a shallow pan and cover with cold court bouillon (or you can use just water). Let the liquid come to a boil, then turn down the heat and simmer very gently, covered, for about 5 minutes or until the fish is opaque.

Remove the fillets and drain.

Break up the fish into bite-size pieces and put in a warm bowl. Pour olive oil over and gently fold in the cilantro. Squeeze enough fresh lemon juice over to get the right balance, and salt and pepper to taste.

Serve warm surrounded by small black olives.

* You can easily improvise your own court bouillon by adding the frame and heads of the bass to the recipe on page 241.

POACHED STRIPED BASS FILLETS WITH SHRIMP CREAM SAUCE

When the fish is filleted, save the heads, backbones, and tails for the stock.

SERVES 6

6 Tb. butter
1 carrot, chopped
1 rib celery with leaves, chopped
1 small onion, chopped
3 lb. striped bass fillets,
   cut in thirds (reserve
   bones and head)
3 sprigs of parsley
8 peppercorns

2 cloves
3 bay leaves
½ tsp. salt
3 cups water
1 cup white wine
1½ lb. shrimp in their shells
2 Tb. flour
½ cup heavy cream
¼ cup minced dill

Using half the butter, sauté the carrot, celery, and onion in a big saucepan for 3–4 minutes.

Add fish bones and head, and the parsley, peppercorns, cloves, bay leaves, salt, water, and wine.

Bring to a boil and add the shrimp. Cook for 3–5 minutes until the shrimp are pink, then remove them, but continue to simmer the broth for 30 minutes. When the shrimp have cooled, shell and devein them and reserve.

When ready to bake, lay the fillets in a shallow baking dish and pour over them about 2 cups of the strained stock. Cover with foil and in a preheated 350° oven bake for about 20 minutes.

Remove the fillets to a hot serving platter. In a saucepan melt the rest of the butter, and then add the flour, stirring gently for 2–3 minutes. Then, off heat, stir in about a cup of the stock; return to a low flame and simmer, stirring, until the sauce thickens. Add the shrimp.

Add the cream and dill, just enough to heat, and serve spooned over the fillets.

BAKED STRIPED BASS WITH OYSTER STUFFING

This fine fish is delicious poached, sautéed, grilled, or baked, so check other recipes utilizing one of the four methods for other species. For example, the recipe for poached salmon applies equally well for the striper. Here is a stuffed and baked dish from Cape Cod.

SERVES 6

5 shallots, chopped
½ cup chopped celery
¼ cup diced green pepper
3 Tb. butter
½ cup minced parsley
½ pint oysters and their liquor
½ cup bread crumbs

1 Tb. anchovy sauce
   (or 1½″ paste)
salt and pepper
¼ tsp. savory
¼ tsp. thyme
4–5-lb. dressed striper
5–6 slices of bacon

Preheat oven to 400°.

Sauté the shallots, celery, and green pepper in the butter until the pepper is soft.

Add the parsley, oysters and liquor, bread crumbs, anchovy sauce, salt, and pepper and cook for 3 minutes.

Stir in the herbs and stuff the fish with the mix.

Place the fish on buttered heavy foil, lay the bacon slices over the fish, and bake for 25–35 minutes or until fish flakes when prodded with a fork.

BARBECUED STRIPED BASS, SOUTHERN STYLE

Pauline Smith of Cheeha-Combahee Plantation, a bird shooter's haven near Green Pond, South Carolina, uses this recipe for stripers and weakfish. It would serve similarly for like-size fresh-water fish—lake trout, walleye, bass, etc.

SERVES 6

3–4-lb. striped bass
  (or flounder or trout)
½ tsp. salt
pepper to taste
2 Tb. chopped onions
1 Tb. lard
2 Tb. vinegar

2 Tb. brown sugar
3 Tb. Worcestershire sauce
1 cup tomato catsup
1 Tb. butter, melted
⅓ cup lemon juice
½ tsp. prepared mustard

Place fish in greased shallow pan and sprinkle with salt and pepper. Lightly brown onions in lard, then add remaining ingredients. Simmer 5 minutes, then pour over fish. Bake in hot oven (425°) 35–40 minutes. Baste fish with sauce while cooking.

Snook
Robalo, Spanish

When your southern angler friend first introduces you to snook fishing he will do so with such extravagant superlatives both as to this fish's fighting qualities and to its excellence on the table that you will tend to discount some of it. Don't do it! Snook are among the greatest of game fish, for they seem to have been spawned mad; they strike angrily and they fight the same way. Imagine a fish that fights and jumps like a smallmouth but that might weigh 8 to 40 pounds (over 50 in Costa Rican waters). *I was very* happy with 6- and 8-pounders. I prefer snook to pompano on the table anytime; it is a delicious and delicate white-meated fish.

———— BROILED FILLETS OF SNOOK ————
WITH BUTTER SAUCE

This fish is excellent prepared in almost any manner and can be prepared as most fish can with virtually any of the broiled, baked, and sautéed recipes in this book for other fish. The fillets of a 6-pound snook remind me most of walleyed pike fillets.

SERVES 4

salt and white pepper
2 fillets, unskinned,
  of 6-lb. snook
1 tsp. lemon juice
1 Tb. cooking oil
2 shallots, minced
  (scallions are fine)

3 Tb. wine vinegar
8 Tb. butter (¼ pound,
  cut in pats)
parsley sprigs

Salt and pepper the flesh side of the fillets, rub with lemon juice, then with oil, and broil, flesh side up, about 3 inches from flame for 10–12 minutes.

Test flesh with fork; when it breaks apart easily, it is done.

Just about 3 minutes before you serve, cook in a saucepan or small skillet the shallots and vinegar until the liquid is reduced by half.

Now begin to melt in the butter, one pat after another over low flame, stirring vigorously until you have a creamy sauce.

Pour over snook fillets and serve garnished with parsley sprigs.

═══ SAUTÉED FILLET OF SNOOK PROVOLONE ═══

This recipe is, of course, adaptable to fish steaks as well as to fillets of other species. It is a wonderful way to sauté fillets or steaks of both salt- and fresh-water fish; it's even good cold.

SERVES 4–5

four or five ½″ snook fillets
flour
1 egg
½ tsp. olive oil
¼ tsp. salt
⅓ cup flavored bread crumbs

⅓ cup grated provolone
(or Parmesan)
8 Tb. butter or margarine
3 Tb. minced parsley
1 Tb. lemon juice
parsley sprigs

Wipe the fillets almost dry, flour them on both sides, and then shake off excess flour.

Beat egg, oil, and salt and dip floured fillets in the mix (let fillets drain back into egg mixture; otherwise you need 2 eggs).

Mix crumbs and cheese in a dish and dredge both sides of the egged fillets.

Lay out the prepared fillets on waxed paper and let them stand for at least 30 minutes to dry out a bit.

Melt half the butter in a skillet over fairly high heat and just before the butter turns brown, lay in the coated fillets. Sauté one side until golden brown, turn fire down to medium, and brown the other side.

While the fillets are sautéing, melt the other half of the butter in a saucepan or small skillet. Add the minced parsley and lemon juice.

When the second side of the fillet is nicely brown place the fillets on a parsley-garnished platter. Pour the butter, parsley, and lemon sauce over them.

Bluefish

The flesh of this violent and ravenous gamester is delicious when quite fresh but tends to become soft if not cooked soon after it is taken. It freezes poorly because it is so oily, but I can vouch for it when smoked. I consider the smaller blues the tastier, 3- to 5-pounders being ideal. Snapper blues, the panfish-size blues, are also delicious. The flesh of the bluefish is quite oily and is strongly flavored. For this reason this fish, like mackerel, encourages more strongly flavored sauces than more lightly flavored fishes do. Blues run 2 to 6 pounds regularly, but get much larger—up to 25, even 30 pounds.

BAKED FILLETS OF BLUEFISH
IN MUSHROOMS AND ANCHOVY CREAM

SERVES 4

4–5 fillets of bluefish
flour
salt and white pepper
2 shallots or scallions, minced
⅓ lb. mushrooms, thinly sliced

½ tsp. tarragon
1 cup cream
2 tsp. anchovy sauce (or 1″ paste)
1 Tb. sherry (optional)

Dip the fillets in the salt and peppered flour and lay in shallow baking dish.

Sprinkle shallots or scallions, mushroom slices, and tarragon over top of fillets. Stir anchovy sauce into cream and pour it over fish. Bake 15–20 minutes at 450°. Stir in sherry if you wish.

BAKED BLUEFISH
IN SOUR CREAM AND PAPRIKA

This is a lusty dish which seems to me to call for beer with it. I serve it also with fried potatoes.

SERVES 6

4 slices bacon
salt and pepper
4–5-lb. bluefish,
  dressed and split
2 tsp. Hungarian paprika
½ tsp. marjoram
1 onion, chopped

1 green pepper, chopped
1 rib celery, chopped
¼ cup white wine
1 cup homemade
  or canned tomato sauce
⅔ cup sour cream

Lay the bacon slices in a shallow baking dish, then lay in salted and peppered fish.

Sprinkle fish with the paprika and marjoram, then distribute chopped vegetables over all.

Add wine and bake in a preheated 400° oven for 15 minutes.

Meantime stir the tomato sauce into the sour cream, then spread or pour over fish and bake 10–15 minutes more.

BLUEFISH BROILED ON A BED OF FENNEL

Fennel, that celerylike bulb that tastes faintly of anise and is so loved by Italian cooks, makes a delicious bed for fillets of strong-flavored fish like bluefish, mackerel, or shad.

SERVES 4

2 fennel bulbs
4 Tb. butter
salt
¾ cup water

4 fillets bluefish (about 2 lb.)
freshly ground pepper
½ tsp. fennel seeds
lemon wedges

Trim the long thin stalks and feathers from the fennel (saving a little of the feathery green) and slice away any part of the outer rib that is very coarse and fibrous. Cut into ¾-inch slices, cutting down from the tops of the bulbs toward the root ends.

Place the slices in a very large skillet so that they are pretty much in one layer with perhaps a little overlapping. Distribute 2 tablespoons of the butter around the slices, salt lightly, and add the water. Cover and cook slowly for about 10–15 minutes or until tender, checking to see that they are not burning on the bottom; if they are dry, add a little more water. When done the liquid should have evaporated.

Spread the fennel on the bottom of a large shallow pan and place bluefish fillets on top. Salt and pepper and dot with remaining butter.

Broil as close to the flame as you can for 10–12 minutes until lightly browned and opaque throughout. Sprinkle on the fennel seeds and broil another minute to toast them. Serve garnished with chopped feathery fennel greens and lemon wedges.

BLUEFISH BROILED WITH PESTO

SERVES 4

2 lb. bluefish fillets
about 6 Tb. pesto
  (without Parmesan; see page 367)

lemon wedges

Place bluefish fillets on an oiled broiler, skin side down.

Broil as close to the heat as your racks allow for 8–10 minutes, depending on thickness of fillets. Then brush the tops liberally with pesto and broil another minute—just enough to make the topping bubble but not to brown it.

Serve with lemon wedges.

GRILLED BLUEFISH
WITH ANCHOVY AND MUSTARD SAUCE

Use the recipe for Grilled Mackerel for a 2½–3-lb. bluefish (see page 307).

BAKED BLUEFISH IN TOMATO SAUCE

Bluefish responds well to dishes calling for tomatoes. Here's one with an Italian flavor.

SERVES 6

1 onion, chopped
1 rib celery, chopped
1 green pepper, chopped
2 cloves garlic, sliced
1½ cups canned tomatoes
½ cup dry white wine

2 bay leaves
½ tsp. oregano
½ tsp. fennel seed, crushed
2 cloves
3–4-lb. dressed bluefish
10 thin lemon slices

Put the vegetables, wine, bay leaves, oregano, fennel, and cloves in a saucepan, bring to a boil, and simmer for 30 minutes.

When done, put through a sieve, being sure to use a big spoon to press the vegetable pulp through.

Butter a baking dish and lay in the fish, cover with the lemon slices, and pour the tomato sauce over all.

Cover with foil and bake in a preheated 400° oven for 20–25 minutes.

Pompano

Both the common pompano and the round pompano (the former is the well-known commercial fish) range from North Carolina to the Gulf with a few straggling as far north as Cape Cod. This fish, famous for the excellence of its flesh, ranges in weight from 2 to 3 pounds. That other true pompano, also a member of the genus *Trachinotus*, is the permit. *This* gamester ranges up to 40 or 50 pounds. Some say the fillets of a 3–5-pound permit are as good as any pompano. Another rare visitor to the Florida Keys is the so-called African pomano (actually a member of the jack family), which gets to 30 pounds or more.

Except for the famous New Orleans dish, pomano en papillote, we give only one other recipe—a simple method of roasting—but pompano fillets respond to any fillet of fish dish in this book.

ROASTED POMPANO

This plump, silvery fish from the Gulf Coast tastes so good that it needs little embellishment. We like to roast it whole, just rubbing it first lightly with olive oil. A pompano of ¾–1 pound is just right for a single person; one 1½–2 pounds will feed two—and a little stuffing always makes it go further.

SERVES 2

1½–2-lb. pompano, cleaned
  (head left on)
1–2 tsp. olive oil
salt and freshly ground pepper

⅓ cup stuffing
  (optional; see pages 377–380)
lemon wedges

Rub the surface of the fish with olive oil, then salt and pepper it lightly inside and out. If using stuffing, spoon it into the cavity and skewer the opening together.

Roast in a baking pan in a preheated 375° oven for 40–50 minutes or until skin blisters and the flesh has turned opaque around the bone. Serve garnished with lemon wedges.

ANTOINE'S POMPANO EN PAPILLOTE

From Antoine's restaurant in New Orleans, where pompano is plentiful, comes this famous recipe for baking the fillets with embellishments in parchment heart-shaped packages. When the papillotes are brought to the table and the paper torn open, the heady scent of the baked seafood is irresistible—well worth trying at home if you have landed some delicious pompano.

SERVES 6

3 1½-lb. pompano
1 small carrot, chopped coarse
1 celery rib
1 small onion, chopped coarse
2 cups water
1¾ cups dry white wine
salt and freshly ground pepper
2 shallots or scallions (white
    part only), finely chopped

6 Tb. butter
3–4 drops Tabasco
2 cups cooked small shrimps
2 cups crabmeat
1 clove garlic, minced fine
pinch of dried thyme
1 bay leaf
2 Tb. flour
vegetable oil

Clean pompano and cut into 6 fillets. Use head and bones to make a fish stock, simmering them with carrot, celery, and onion in water and 1 cup wine for about 30 minutes, or until stock is somewhat reduced.

Strain stock and pour over fillets, seasoning them with salt and pepper and adding ½ cup of the wine. Let fish simmer very gently, covered, for about 8 minutes, then let them rest in the stock.

Meanwhile make the sauce: cook shallots or scallions in 3 tablespoons butter for a few minutes, then add Tabasco, shrimps, crabmeat, garlic, thyme, and bay leaf. In a separate pan melt remaining butter; blend in flour, and cook slowly, stirring constantly, for a minute or two, then blend in 1 cup of the warm stock and remaining ¼ cup wine. Combine with the shrimp and crabmeat mixture and correct the seasoning.

Now cut 6 pieces of parchment paper in the shape of hearts 8 × 12 inches and oil each piece well. Remove fillets from poaching liquid with a slotted spoon, saving remaining stock for another purpose. Place 1 fillet in the center of each piece of parchment, top with one-sixth of the seafood sauce, and fold the oiled paper over. Seal the edges by making a tight, firm rolled fold all around the open edge. Don't rub oil on the outside. Place parchment hearts on a baking sheet and bake in a preheated 450° oven for 15 minutes, or until the paper has browned. Serve immediately in the paper hearts, the papillotes.

Permit

Some fly fishermen I know consider taking a permit on a fly rod just about the ultimate achievement. This tough-mouthed bully boy of the deep is a member of the genus *Trachinotus* and is thus a big half-brother of the pompanos; indeed the permit is sometimes called the great pompano. Like its kin the permit makes excellent eating. In size permits can get to 50 pounds but average much smaller.

CRAB-STUFFED BAKED PERMIT

SERVES 6

3–5-lb. permit or pompano
1 tsp. lemon juice
¼ lb. mushrooms, sliced
2 Tb. butter
1 egg
½ cup cream
1½ cup cooked (or canned)
  crabmeat, shredded

½ cup bread crumbs
¼ tsp. tarragon
¼ tsp. chervil
salt and pepper
⅓ nutmeg, grated

Rub the dressed fish inside and out with lemon juice.

Sauté the mushrooms in butter for 3–4 minutes. Remove from heat.

Beat the egg with half the cream, then stir into mushrooms.

Add and mix into the mushrooms the crabmeat, bread crumbs, herbs, salt, pepper, and grated nutmeg.

Stuff the fish with the crabmeat and crumb mixture and skewer or sew the belly. Place in a shallow buttered baking dish, pour over the rest of the cream, and cover with foil.

Bake in the 400° oven for about 20 minutes, then remove foil and bake for another 10 minutes or so, basting occasionally.

Weakfish
Sea Trout

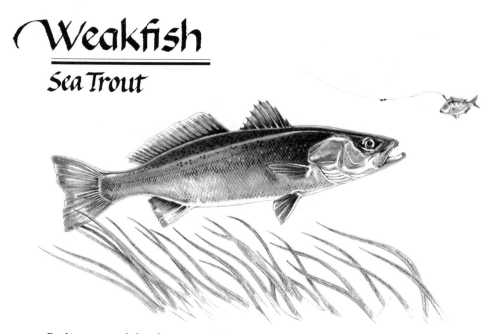

Both species of this fine game fish are sometimes called sea trout, and in the South *nebulases*, one of the two species of *Cynoscion*, is called *only* sea trout or spotted sea trout. *Regalis*, the northern variety, sometimes called squeteague there, probably does not range south as far as the Gulf. I have taken "sea trout" in the Gulf, fish of 1½–3 pounds, although this gamester reaches 16–17 pounds as the ultimate trophy size. The flesh of this fish is tender and moist and the flavor delicate. It should be eaten soon after capture, for it tends to soften quickly.

Recipes for trout, grayling, char, etc., do as well for weakfish.

WEAKFISH FILLETS
IN ROASTED PEPPERS AND ONIONS

By itself weakfish sometimes tastes bland, but when hearty flavors permeate its flesh, it can be a delicious fish.

SERVES 4

2 large red peppers
2 red onions, sliced
2–3 Tb. olive oil
2 cloves garlic, minced
2 lb. weakfish fillets
salt and freshly ground pepper

½ cup dry white wine
12 small black olives, pitted
1 Tb. fresh chopped basil
   or ½ tsp. dried
2 Tb. chopped parsley

Roast the peppers under a broiler or over a gas flame, turning as the skin blackens. Put them immediately into a paper bag, twist the top to close tight, and leave for about 5 minutes; then remove and pinch off the blackened skin. Slice in half, remove the seeds, and cut in strips.

Sauté the onions in the olive oil slowly. When wilted, add the garlic and pepper strips and sauté slowly 2–3 minutes.

Put the fillets in a large pan so they are in one layer. Salt and pepper them, then strew the onion-pepper mixture over. Pour white wine around, cover lightly with foil, and bake in a preheated 375° oven. Add olives after 20 minutes and bake another 5 minutes, uncovered.

Remove from the oven and sprinkle basil and parsley over the top.

Porgies to me seem more a fresh- than salt-water fish. I like them prepared as I sometimes prepare smallmouth bass.

FRIED PORGIE

SERVES 4

4 porgies, washed and patted dry
½ cup cornmeal
¼ cup flour
salt and pepper
2 Tb. oil

3 Tb. butter
2 shallots or scallions, minced
2 tsp. anchovy sauce
  (or 1″ of paste)
juice of ½ lemon

Dredge the porgies in the mix of cornmeal, flour, salt, and pepper.

Heat the oil and 2 tablespoons of the butter in a big skillet and fry the fish quickly over fairly high heat until they are brown on both sides.

Add the shallots around the edges of the skillet and over medium heat cook the fish for 15–20 minutes.

Remove fish to a warm platter. Melt remaining tablespoon of butter in the skillet, and stir in the anchovy sauce and lemon juice.

Dolphin
Dorado, Spanish

This fish (not the porpoise sometimes called dolphin) is to my taste one of the three most delicious salt-water fishes, and for a few moments after it is decked, one of the most beautifully colored of all fishes, salt or fresh. They go to 50, 60, or more pounds—to over 80 in Costa Rican waters. Treat dolphin as you would swordfish. Here are two recipes.

POACHED DOLPHIN IN WHITE WINE SAUCE

This recipe will also work well with albacore yellowfin tuna.

SERVES 4

2-lb. dolphin steak
1½ cups dry white wine
½ cup chicken broth
1 Tb. chopped parsley
1 rib celery
¼ tsp. basil
salt and pepper

6 shallots, diced
¼ lb. mushrooms, sliced
3 Tb. butter
1 Tb. flour
2 egg yolks
½ cup cream
¼ nutmeg, grated

In a skillet with a lid poach the steak at a simmer in the wine, broth, parsley, celery, basil, salt, and pepper. About 15 minutes should be enough, but test it after 10–12 minutes.

While the fish is poaching gently sauté the shallots and the mushrooms with butter until the latter are soft. Stir in the flour and set the pan mixture off the heat.

When the fish is poached, drain off the liquid mixture and stir 1 cup of it into the shallot and mushroom mixture. Cook, stirring well, until smooth, 4–5 minutes.

Meanwhile beat the egg yolks into the cream and spoon 2–3 tablespoons of the mushroom sauce into the cream and egg mixture. Then stir all into the mushroom sauce and let it heat without bubbling.

Grate in the nutmeg, arrange the fish on a serving platter, and pour the sauce over the steak.

BROILED DOLPHIN STEAK

This deliciously flavored fish may be best prepared broiled; at least it is so tasty that it needs little tending in the kitchen.

SERVES 4

5 Tb. butter	salt and pepper
1 Tb. lemon juice	2 lb. dolphin steak
1 Tb. minced parsley	lemon sections

Preheat the broiler and grease rack with cooking oil.

Melt the butter, then off heat stir in the lemon juice, parsley, salt, and pepper.

Broil the steak about 2 inches from the heat and baste it constantly on both sides as it broils—about 3–4 minutes for the first side and 5 for the second.

Serve with lemon sections after pouring parsley and lemon from the broiler over the steak.

Swordfish

All of us who have eaten but have never caught a broadbill envy those who have taken the great battler on rod and reel. But if we are doomed never to catch one, we can at least relish the savory, almost porklike flesh of this great species.

SWORDFISH STIMPIRATA

From Marcella Hazan, a Sicilian way of cooking swordfish, particularly good for thin steaks.

SERVES 4–6

¾ cup olive oil
⅔ cup flour
2 lb. swordfish, cut into
  steaks ½" thick
salt and freshly ground pepper

¼ cup finely chopped onions
⅓ cup finely chopped celery
2 Tb. capers, drained and chopped
¼ cup good-quality red wine
  vinegar

Heat the oil in a medium-size skillet. When it is quite hot, turn down to medium-high heat.

Flour the swordfish on both sides, salt and pepper them, then slip some of them into the hot oil. Do not crowd the pan. Cook briefly—about 1 minute on each side—then with a slotted spoon or spatula remove to a heated platter and continue with the rest.

Add the onions to the pan, lower heat, and, stirring frequently, cook until golden.

Add the celery and cook another few minutes until just tender.

Add the capers, and cook about ½ minute, stirring steadily.

Return all the fish to the pan. Pour the vinegar over them and cook for 2 minutes or so until the vinegar has evaporated. Turn the fish delicately to coat with the sauce, then transfer to a warm platter.

SWORDFISH CHOWDER

Good as swordfish is simply broiled, sometimes when you have a lot of meat you may want some variety (incidentally, this can also be made with mako shark if that's what you have on hand). An early American dish, this thick, delicious chowder will serve as a main course with some good crusty bread.

SERVES 4

1½ lb. swordfish, cut 2" thick
1 qt. fish stock, or half
  clam juice, half water
1 cup diced celery
2 tomatoes, peeled and chopped,
  or equivalent amount canned
  tomatoes, drained
1 Tb. tomato paste
½ green pepper, seeded and
  chopped

1 medium onion, chopped
½ cup chopped carrots
½ tsp. dried thyme
1 tsp. salt
freshly ground black pepper
4 bacon strips, cut into squares
2 small potatoes, diced
2 Tb. minced parsley

Wipe the fish and cut into 2-inch pieces.

Heat fish stock in a large pot and add celery, tomatoes and paste, green pepper, onion, carrots, thyme, salt, and several grinds of pepper. Let simmer for 30 minutes.

Meanwhile sauté bacon squares, drain fat, and when crisp, add the squares to the chowder. Add potatoes and continue cooking for 10 minutes.

Add swordfish chunks and cook for 20 minutes more or until potatoes are tender but still firm. Sprinkle parsley on before serving.

BROILED SWORDFISH

Fresh swordfish tastes so good that it needs almost no embellishment. It is best broiled, and the steaks should be cut about 1 inch thick; if they are thicker, the outside gets too dry while the inside remains uncooked, but you could use the method described for mako shark of broiling the steak in wine to ensure the steak is cooked through. If you have thinner steaks, it's better to sauté as in the Swordfish Stimpirata recipe opposite. Swordfish is wonderful cooked on an outdoor grill over good hot coals.

SERVES 4

2 lb. swordfish (1–2 steaks
  depending on size of fish,
  cut 1″ thick)

4 Tb. melted butter
salt and freshly ground pepper
lemon wedges

Preheat the broiler (or make a fire in the grill well ahead so you have hot coals).

Brush both sides of the swordfish with some of the melted butter and season with salt and pepper. Broil on the top rung of the broiler for 5 minutes, then turn, brush with butter, and broil 4–5 minutes more.

Pour on remaining butter and serve with lemon wedges.

Mako Shark

The mako shark, like its relatives the porkeagle shark and the white shark of evil reputation, is a warm-blooded creature. Also, it is ovoviviparous, for its eggs hatch inside the female and its young are born alive.

For our purposes it has one very important characteristic: it tastes like swordfish. Enough said?

MAKO SHARK MARINATED
AND GRILLED ON SKEWERS

The taste and texture of shark and swordfish are very similar, so this is equally good done with chunks of swordfish.

SERVES 4

2 cloves garlic
about ½ tsp. salt
2 lb. mako shark (or swordfish),
   cut in 1-inch cubes

juice of 2 limes
⅓ cup olive oil
freshly ground pepper
about 2 dozen bay leaves

Smash the garlic cloves and peel. Then chop fine and mash with the salt to make a paste. Rub this over the pieces of fish. Place in a bowl and pour the lime juice and olive oil over, then grind a liberal amount of pepper on top. Toss and let marinate at room temperature for 1 hour.

Thread chunks of fish alternately with bay leaves onto 4 skewers. Broil or grill over a fire close to the heat for 8–10 minutes, turning once and brushing with the marinade.

MAKO SHARK BROILED
WITH WHITE WINE

A simple, delicious recipe—equally good, of course, or better made with swordfish. You use a fair amount of white wine in the preparation, which isn't served with the fish, but there is no reason why it can't be recycled and frozen to use when you make this dish again or to add to any fish stew.

SERVES 4

2–2½-lb. mako shark (or
   swordfish) steak, at least 1″
   thick
about 2 cups dry white wine

salt
1 Tb. chopped fresh tarragon
   leaves (optional)

Place the shark steak in a shallow baking dish just a bit larger than its circumference. Pour in enough wine to come a good halfway up the side to gauge how much you'll need, then pour it off into a saucepan to heat as you preheat your broiler.

Salt the steak lightly, pour the hot wine around it, and broil as close to the heat as possible for about 12 minutes. Test to see that it is cooked through (it should be opaque). Sprinkle fresh tarragon on top, if you like and if it is available (the dried is too overpowering for this dish).

FLOUNDER

Sole, Halibut, and Flounder

The soles, halibuts, and flounder may not classify as game fish, but a lot of anglers fish for them nonetheless, for the flatfish make excellent fare. All cookbooks carry recipes for these fish, but here is one that should not be missed.

FILLET OF SOLE WITH WHITE GRAPES

This wonderful dish is made with sole in France, where it is called Sole Véronique. Here is a version that will be equally wonderful with fillets of walleye, whitefish, or snook, flounder, or other white-fleshed fish.

Here, as in many fish recipes, one makes the fish-flavored liquid for the sauce while one cooks the fish.

SERVES 3–4

2 lb. sole fillets
1 cup dry white wine
¼ cup water
2 shallots, sliced,
   or 2 Tb. diced onion
1 clove garlic, sliced
1 Tb. caper or lemon juice
6 peppercorns
1 Tb. minced parsley
¼ tsp. tarragon ⎤
½ tsp. basil   ⎟ tied together in a cheesecloth bundle
½ tsp. chervil   ⎟
½ bay leaf   ⎦

3 Tb. butter
2 Tb. flour
½ cup heavy cream
½ lb. seedless white
   or green grapes

Place the fillets in a buttered baking dish, pour in the white wine and water, then add the shallots, garlic, caper or lemon liquid, peppercorns, parsley, and herb bundle. Poach in a preheated 325° oven for 15 minutes.

Place the sole when done in a warm serving dish. Strain and reserve the liquid.

Melt the butter in a pan, stir in the flour, and on low heat cook for a minute or so. Off heat stir in about ¾ cup of the fish stock and returning to a low flame cook over medium heat, stirring until the sauce thickens. Stir in the cream and cook until it is just short of boiling.

Pour boiling water over the grapes and skin if you wish. I do not.

Place the grapes around the fillets and coat with some of the sauce, serving the remainder in a sauceboat.

FILLETS IN CREAM

This recipe is good with any fish fillets from salt or fresh water.

SERVES 4

1 tsp. lemon juice	1 Tb. chopped parsley
1 shallot or scallion, diced	6 Tb. butter
⅓ cup dry white wine	3 Tb. flour
5–6 fish fillets	½ cup milk
¼ lb. mushrooms, sliced	½ cup cream
1 clove garlic, minced	salt and pepper
¼ tsp. dry tarragon	⅓ cup grated Swiss cheese

Butter a shallow baking dish, add the lemon juice, shallot or scallion, and wine, lay in the fillets, and cover with foil or lid.

Steam-bake in a preheated 350° oven for about 12 minutes.

Remove fillets and keep warm. Strain the poaching liquid and retain it for later use.

Sauté the mushrooms, garlic, tarragon, and parsley in the butter for 3–4 minutes over medium heat. Stir in the flour and cook a minute. Then, off heat, stir in the milk, cream, and ½ cup of the fish broth.

Return to the heat and, stirring, cook until the sauce begins to thicken, adding fish stock, if needed. Add salt and pepper.

Stir in and melt the cheese; then pour the sauce over the fillets and brown under the broiler.

Red Drum
Redfish, Channel Bass

This fish, most often called redfish by my Florida friends, is both gamy and delicious (when 8–15-pound fish are used—called "rat reds" by the knowledgeable). In the Gulf off Texas this fish is one of the two top commercial species. They can range up to 70, 80, or even 90 pounds. Big ones are often taken off North Carolina.

FISH FILLETS VERACRUZ STYLE— PESCADO À LA VERACRUZANA

I am including this recipe from Elisabeth Ortiz's *The Book of Latin American Cooking* because Mrs. Ortiz calls it "Mexico's best-known fish dish" and because the jalapeño chilies called for are available in some supermarket fancy food sections. In both Venezuela and the Argentine this recipe is used in a very slightly varied form for striped bass.

Use as well for fillets of striped bass, or for fillets of great northern pike, walleyed pike, lake trout, or white fish.

SERVES 4

2 lb. redfish fillets
salt and freshly ground pepper
juice of 1 small lemon or lime
⅓ cup olive oil
2 medium onions, finely chopped
2 cloves garlic, chopped
6 medium tomatoes,
    peeled and chopped
3 Tb. capers

20 small pimento-stuffed
    green olives
2–3 canned jalapeño chilies,
    seeded and cut into strips
12 small new potatoes,
    freshly cooked, or 6 medium
    potatoes, halved
3 slices firm white bread
butter for frying

Season the fish with salt and pepper and the lemon or lime juice. Set aside. Heat the oil in a skillet and sauté the onions and garlic until the onions are soft. Reduce the tomatoes to a purée in a blender or food processor and add to the skillet with the capers, olives, jalapeño chilies, and the fish. Season with a little more salt and pepper and cook over very low heat until the fish is tender and the sauce slightly thickened, about 10 to 15 minutes. Transfer to a warmed platter and garnish with the potatoes. Cut the bread into 6 triangles, sauté in butter until golden, and arrange as a border around the edge of the platter.

BAKED REDFISH FILLETS
IN TARRAGON AND CHERVIL CREAM

This dish is just as good when made with the fillets of snook, pompano, or permit, or, for that matter, of the fillets of walleye or lake trout, or salmon.

SERVES 4

2½ lb. redfish fillets	½ tsp. tarragon
2 Tb. finely minced shallots	½ tsp. chervil
2 Tb. grated carrots	2 Tb. flour
4 Tb. butter	¾ cup heavy cream
salt and pepper	¾ cup dry white wine

Wash and dry the fillets.

Cook the shallots and carrots in the butter over low heat in a saucepan. When they have softened, stir in salt, pepper, the herbs, and the flour. Off heat stir in the cream and, back on low heat, stir in the wine to make a smooth sauce.

Butter a baking dish, spoon in a bed of sauce, and lay in the fillets. Cover with the remainder of the sauce.

Bake in a 400° oven until the sauce bubbles, perhaps 5–6 minutes, then turn oven down to 300° and bake another 10 minutes or until the fillets flake to the prodding of the fork.

(Albacore

This tuna is the "white meat tuna" of commercial parlance and is a game light-tackle salt-water fish seldom reaching 50 pounds, but off the Canary Islands reaching as much as 88 pounds. This is a delicious fish, most often coming to our tables in canned form, but a chunk of fresh albacore can be roasted and the steaks, of course, broiled.

The other tuna considered a delicacy is the yellowfin tuna. It is a larger fish than the albacore (record 308 pounds), and its meat, while not white like the albacore, is very light compared to that of other tunas.

These recipes serve bonito as well as the tunas.

BAKED ALBACORE OR YELLOWFIN TUNA

SERVES 8–10

2 cups dry vermouth or white wine
1 Tb. lemon juice
½ tsp. crushed marjoram
½ tsp. crumbled rosemary
1 chopped onion, large
1 rib celery, chopped

2 bay leaves
3 Tb. chopped parsley
4–5 lb. albacore
salt and pepper
3 Tb. butter
3 Tb. flour

Combine the vermouth or white wine, lemon juice, marjoram, rosemary, onion, celery, bay leaves, and parsley in a large bowl and marinate the albacore in the refrigerator overnight or for 5–6 hours.

When ready to roast, put the fish chunk or pieces in a casserole, add the marinade, salt and pepper, and bake covered at 400° for about 35 minutes or until the flesh flakes when prodded.

In a skillet melt the butter, stir in the flour, and cook a minute or two. Pour off the liquid from the casserole and, off heat, blend into the butter and flour. Return to the heat and cook for 5 minutes, stirring almost continuously, until thickened. Pour over fish in casserole.

BROILED ALBACORE STEAKS
WITH ROSEMARY AND ANCHOVY BUTTER

This recipe works fine for dolphin, swordfish, yellowfin tuna, or bonito. Cut the steaks thick—at least 1½ inches. Serve with baked potatoes and sour cream.

SERVES 1–3

1–2 albacore steaks,
  1½″ thick or more
1 tsp. lemon juice
1 tsp. dried rosemary,
  crumbled fine

4 Tb. butter
1½ tsp. anchovy sauce
  (or 1½″ anchovy paste)
salt and pepper

Preheat broiler. Grease grill, or place a layer of foil over it that has been buttered.

Brush the steaks with lemon juice, then press the rosemary onto each surface.

Melt the butter and off heat blend in the anchovy sauce.

Broil the steaks 2 inches from the heat for 6–8 minutes to the side brushing on the anchovy butter regularly during the process. Add salt and pepper to taste.

Mackerel

This fish, in several species, inhabits both the east and west coasts, but the king mackerel (kingfish) is most sought after by anglers. Because mackerel is commercially available, most general cookbooks give recipes for this firm-fleshed fish. They reach 20 pounds (the king, 80 or more pounds) but usually come much smaller. Mackerels are rich in oil and can take flavorful sauces or basting liquids.

See other fillets of fish recipes but especially bluefish recipes.

===== FILLETS OF MACKEREL, ITALIENNE =====

Here is a tomato sauce to match this strongly flavored fish.

SERVES 6

1 large onion, chopped
½ green pepper, chopped
3 cloves garlic, minced
4 Tb. cooking oil,
   preferably olive oil
2 Tb. capers
1 cup homemade or canned
   tomato sauce

1 tsp. oregano
½ tsp. cumin
3 dashes Worcestershire sauce
salt and pepper
2½ lb. mackerel
   (or bluefish) fillets

Sauté the onion, pepper, and garlic in oil, then add the capers, tomato sauce, oregano, cumin, Worcestershire, salt, and pepper and simmer for 20 minutes.

Into an ovenproof baking serving dish spoon a couple of tablespoons of sauce and lay fillets over.

Pour on remaining sauce and bake the fillets in a 450° oven for 7–9 minutes.

BAKED MACKEREL WITH MUSTARD

I think this mustard sauce is good with a variety of fishes. It is certainly excellent for bluefish, and it also enhances a 2- to 3-pound smallmouth bass.

SERVES 4

2-lb. fresh mackerel	2 Tb. flour
1 tsp. lemon juice	2 Tb. butter
salt and pepper	½ cup milk
½ cup dry white wine	½ cup cream
3 shallots or scallions,	2 tsp. or 1 Tb. Dijon mustard
finely minced	¼ tsp. thyme or rosemary

Preheat oven to 350°.

Rub fish inside and out with lemon juice. Salt and pepper it and lay into a shallow buttered baking dish.

Add the wine and the shallots or scallions and bake for 15–20 minutes.

While the fish is cooking melt the butter, stir in the flour, and cook slowly for a minute or two. Off heat, stir in the milk and cream. Return to a low heat and simmer for 4–5 minutes, stirring.

When done, remove the fish to a warm platter and quickly reduce the liquor in the baking dish to 4 tablespoons or less.

Stir into the cream sauce with the mustard and thyme or rosemary. Pour over fish and serve.

GRILLED MACKEREL WITH ANCHOVY-MUSTARD SAUCE AND SOUR CREAM

This recipe is rewarding when made with mackerel, but it also serves deliciously any strong-flavored fish like bluefish. If bluefish is used for this recipe, pick a 2½–3-pound bluefish.

SERVES 3–4

3 mackerel, cleaned and split	½ cup water
to lie flat (I skin this fish)	¼ cup white wine
1½ tsp. lemon juice	2 canned anchovies, finely diced,
1 tsp. caper juice	or 2 tsp. anchovy sauce
3 Tb. olive oil	1 Tb. Dijon mustard
2 Tb. finely chopped dill	2 tsp. crushed capers
or parsley	salt and pepper
2 Tb. butter	1 cup sour cream
2 Tb. flour	

Lay the cleaned mackerel in a flat dish and pour over them a marinade made of the lemon and caper juices, the oil, and the chopped dill or parsley. Let the fish lie in the marinade for a couple of hours before grilling, occasionally rubbing the marinade into each side of the fish.

Since grilling fish requires constant policing, I make the sauce next. First melt the butter and add flour, stirring and cooking gently 2–3 minutes. Then finish the white sauce by stirring in, off the heat, the water and wine. Return to low heat and cook for a minute or so to thicken before stirring in the anchovies and mustard.

Add the crushed capers with their juice last and continue cooking for another 2–3 minutes, stirring occasionally. Salt and pepper to taste.

When the fish have been grilled (see page 228), serve with the sauce, and pass the bowl of sour cream.

MACKEREL BAKED IN A TOMATO SAUCE

This is my version of a dish I once had in a quay-side restaurant on the south coast of Crete.

SERVES 4

two 1½-lb. mackerel
5 Tb. olive oil
2 cloves garlic, squashed
½ green pepper, diced
½ tsp. rosemary, crumbled fine
½ tsp. oregano
1 11 oz. can tomatoes, drained,
    or 3 fresh tomatoes,
    skinned and chopped

¼ cup white wine
salt and pepper
bread crumbs
2 Tb. chopped parsley

Place the dressed fish in baking dish oiled with 1 tablespoon of the olive oil.

In a skillet, sauté the garlic and green pepper in the remaining oil until just soft. Add the herbs, tomatoes, wine, salt, and pepper. Simmer until the tomatoes have softened (if fresh tomatoes are used).

Alternately pour sauce and sprinkle bread crumbs and parsley over the fish, ending with crumbs.

Bake in a preheated 450° oven for about 40 minutes, or slightly longer for larger mackerel.

COLD POACHED MACKEREL
WITH RÉMOULADE OR RAVIGOTE SAUCE

The fish stock given below will serve for poaching other fish.

SERVES 4

THE FISH STOCK
1 rib celery, sliced
1 onion, quartered
1 carrot, sliced
3 sprigs parsley
1 tsp. dried thyme
½ tsp. chervil
2 bay leaves
2 cloves garlic, sliced
2 cloves, stuck in 2 quarters
    of the onion

8 peppercorns
1 Tb. lemon juice
2 qt. water
1 cup white wine
2 tsp. salt
two 1–1½-lb. mackerel, cleaned
    and split to flatten
1 cup Rémoulade Sauce (page 369)
    or 1 cup Quick Ravigote Sauce
    (below)

Boil the fish stock ingredients in a large kettle for 15 minutes. Then lay the mackerel in a shallow glass or porcelain dish, pour in enough of the stock barely to cover, and bake in a preheated 325° oven for about 15–20 minutes. You can if you wish poach the fish over low heat, on top of the stove for 10 minutes.*

Let the fish cool in the bouillon. Then remove, garnish with parsley, and serve with sauce: rémoulade or ravigote is fine, but of course cold poached mackerel may be served with any other of your favorite sauces, such as tartare or a white wine sauce or cucumber and sour cream, etc.

Quick Ravigote Sauce (Green Mayonnaise)

This sauce is so good with poached fish and so easy to prepare that I often serve it with cold fish, or hot for that matter. It is really another green mayonnaise and can be made from scratch. For the quick sauce I use mayonnaise already prepared, preferably Hellmann's.

2 sprigs parsley	1 tsp. dried chervil
1 shallot or scallion, sliced	½ cup raw spinach
2 Tb. fresh or dried tarragon	1½ cups mayonnaise

In a blender or in a food processor using the steel blade, make a purée of all of the ingredients save the mayonnaise.

Remove and scrape the ingredients from the machine's receptacle and stir and thoroughly mix them into the mayonnaise.

* You may bottle the leftover stock for later use.

══════════ FISH CAKES FROM LEFTOVERS ══════════

Cod is not the only fish that makes delicious fish cakes; indeed any leftover fish will produce tasty fish cakes. The best ones I ever made (it seemed to me then) came from leftover Alaskan lake trout that had been poached in a fish broth and mixed with mashed potatoes made from Idahoan potato flakes and milk made from dried milk.

SERVES 3–4

2 cups mashed potatoes	1 small onion, grated
2 cups cooked fish, flaked small	½ tsp. nutmeg
2 egg yolks, beaten	⅓ cup yellow cornmeal
salt and freshly ground pepper	4 Tb. butter

I make the mashed potatoes rather thick, then stir in all of the ingredients above except the cornmeal and butter. If the mix seems a bit thin to handle as cakes, dust in a bit of flour until you can fashion the cakes.

Coat both sides with cornmeal and sauté the cakes in the butter rather slowly over a medium to low fire, turning once, until they are golden brown on both sides.

Fish Soups, Chowders, and a Stew

FISH CHOWDER

The best fish chowder I ever tasted was made by the mother of Fraser Mason and later by his wife, Ethel, successive chefs at Fraser's New Brunswick fishing and hunting camp. My method is basically theirs. If the chowder is made in camp, milk made from powdered milk (see p. 401) is fine without the cream.

SERVES 6

The Fish Stock

If you've kept, say, three smallmouths of 1½–2½ pounds, skin them and use the heads and tails of all three fish and half of the meat of the smallest one.

fish trimmings to make about a pound	1 chopped or thinly sliced carrot
3 cups water	¼ tsp. thyme
1 cup white wine	a clove or two
1 small onion, sliced	1 bay leaf
1 rib celery with the leaves, chopped	3–4 peppercorns salt

Combine the ingredients in a saucepan, bring to a boil, and simmer for 30 minutes.

Strain and set the stock aside. In camp you can make the stock one night and use it for the chowder the next to keep it from being too big a chore.

The Chowder

2½″ square salt pork, cut in ½″ cubes	2 bass, deboned, with the meat cut in chunks
1 medium onion, sliced thin	2 cups milk (at home make it half cream)
4 peeled potatoes, diced	salt and pepper
4 cups fish stock	

Try out the salt pork cubes over low heat in a skillet until the chitlins are crisp and brown. Set them aside.

Pour off all but 3 tablespoons of the salt pork fat, and in a soup pot sauté the onion in the fat. Stir in the potatoes. Add the fish stock and fish chunks to the pot, cover, and simmer until the fish is just tender, about 15–20 minutes.

Stir in the milk and bring to hot, but not to a boil. Check for salt and pepper.

Just before you serve, stir in the chitlins.

FISH CHOWDER FARNHAM

Ann Kessler, wife of Charles (L. L. Bean's director of product management), contributed this old-time New England chowder from the "receipt book" of her grandmother.

SERVES 6

"Try out salt pork (3 fat slabs).

"Chop 1 medium-size onion. Add to pork drippings, removing (but reserving) salt pork pieces for garnish. Lightly brown the onion.

"Then add to kettle with diced potatoes (about 4) and salted water to cover. (For quahaug chowder, do not add salt, but use quahaug liquor instead.)

"Cook until potato is barely cooked, about 20 minutes.

"Add about 4 lb. (large chowder) fish, previously boiled in salted water. Fish has been boned. Add fish when potato is done.

"Bring all to a boil; add thickening if necessary. Then add 1 quart milk—scald and set off stove. Can be warmed up."

NOTE: Salt and pepper to taste. Fresh basil added to this is a delicious variation.

FRESH-WATER BOUILLABAISSE

Just as bourguignon is a meat stew that is not called a stew, so bouillabaisse is a fish soup that is not called a soup. Each is so celebrated that to call it by a generic name would be lese majesty. But basically bouillabaisse is a quick fish soup, a potpourri, a potluck soup made up of a selection of whatever catch the fishermen brought to the quay.

Here is an American version of the "golden soup" made from fresh-water fish, but if a variety of fishes is difficult to achieve, one can provide it by using some salt-water species from the market.

Bouillabaisse is the dish nonpareil for the household that has a handsome soup tureen.

This golden soup may be served with fish pieces, crayfish tails, or shrimp. Add potato slices in soup bowls with the soup, or the soup may be served first in a bowl and later the fish, shellfish, and potatoes served on a plate.

The *rouille* may be passed in a sauceboat.

If you buy all of the fish at the market and want to be a purist about making the dish American, you may find lake trout, other smaller trouts (brook or rainbow), salmon, walleyed pike, and yellow or white perch on the market, although don't count on finding all of them necessarily at the same time.

A word about ingredients: Sometimes a Canadian fishing trip produced a mixed bag like bass, great northern pike, pickerel, walleye, and yellow perch (the latter two can often be bought in the market); other trips east and west might produce both salmon and trout and white perch. In any case, to serve eight, you'll need about 4 pounds of fish fillets and some kind of shellfish. Crabs and/or shrimp or lobster will do, of course, but if you are properly chauvinistic you will use the tail meat of fresh-water crayfish, the most sadly neglected, save in Louisiana and East Texas and environs, of all American river and lake resources. Crayfish, crawfish, or crawdads—as they are variously known in our country—taken from sweet-water rivers (there are some left) and lakes are surpassingly good, yet over vast stretches of our country they are caught only to use, alas, as fish bait.

One further note: When you serve your bouillabaisse to eight guests you may be sure that if all eight were cooks you would turn up eight different recipes for this soup. However, this American version preserves the essential ingredients, including *rouille,* the sauce (or cayenne-garlic-saffron mayonnaise) that is traditionally served with it.

Serve bouillabaisse with French rolls cut in half and toasted with garlic butter.

SERVES 8

4 lb. fish fillets
24 shrimp or crawfish tails,
    shelled and with the
    "black line" taken out

The basic fish broth

3 medium onions, chopped
3 cloves garlic, minced
2 ribs celery with leaves, chopped
2 carrots, sliced
5 Tb. oil
½ green pepper, diced
1 assortment fish bones
    and heads, plus shrimp
    or crawfish shells
7 large potatoes, sliced
    (use only 3 for the broth)
3 tomatoes, fresh (peeled)
    or canned
¾ tsp. thyme

½ tsp. rosemary
¼ tsp. crushed
    or ground fennel seed
4 bay leaves
3–4 sprigs parsley
backbones and heads
    from 4 lb. fillets
    (or 1–2 additional fillets)
3 curls of peel from
    ½ orange rind
salt and pepper
8 cups water
4 cups white wine
saffron threads (optional)

In a big skillet lightly sauté the onions, garlic, celery, and carrots for 3–4 minutes in the oil, then add the rest of the above ingredients (except the water, wine, and saffron) and continue to sauté for 5–6 minutes more. Put the sautéed ingredients into a saucepan large enough to hold them plus the liquid and, using some of the liquid to catch the residue in the skillet, add the water, wine, and optional saffron threads. Bring to a rapid boil, turn down heat, and simmer for 20–25 minutes (until potatoes and carrots are soft).

Take out the fish heads and bones, the bay leaves (if you can find them), the orange rind and the parsley, then over another saucepan put the liquid and vegetables through a food mill or, better yet, purée in a food processor. (In the latter case you won't have to use all of the liquid for this process but, of course, retain it and mix the purée into it.)

Put this liquid mix into a large kettle, add the fish fillets and the remaining 4 sliced potatoes, bring to a bubble, turn down the heat, and simmer very slowly for 25 minutes. Ten minutes before the soup is done add the shrimp or crawfish tails. Correct seasoning for salt.

If you are up to it, prepare the blender-made *rouille* (opposite) while the fish soup is simmering; if not make a quick *rouille* by using prepared mayonnaise (to me that means Hellmann's) as follows:

Quick Rouille

1½ cups mayonnaise
4 cloves garlic, put through
  a garlic press
½ tsp. cayenne pepper (or
  equivalent dashes of
  Tabasco). Better taste this as
  you add the cayenne or
  Tabasco so you achieve the
  hotness you prefer

½ tsp. saffron
salt and pepper

Mix and blend thoroughly.

Blender-Made Rouille

2 eggs
4 garlic cloves,
  mashed or put through
  garlic press
salt
1 cup oil, part olive,
  part vegetable oil

½ lemon of juice
½ tsp. saffron
¾ tsp. cayenne,
  or any part thereof

Blend the eggs for a minute at high speed. Add the garlic and a good pinch of salt. Now start adding oil, slowly at first, then more rapidly as sauce thickens. Add lemon juice. After the mayonnaise is made, put in a bowl and then stir in the saffron first, then the cayenne, ¼ teaspoon by ¼ teaspoon until it comes to the hotness you prefer. Tabasco can be substituted for cayenne but should be added in the same fashion, dash by dash. Adjust salt, if necessary.

═══ EARLY REPUBLIC CATFISH SOUP ═══

In giving this recipe Mary Randolph felt obliged to write "an excellent Dish for those who have not imbibed a needless prejudice against those delicious fish." Even then this catfish, surely in the first three of the most delicious American fresh-water game fish, was viewed askance by those prejudiced by its evil-looking, barbeled maw.

SERVES 3–4

8 strips bacon
  or ½ lb. salt pork, diced
1 large onion, diced
4 bullheads, skinned and
  cut into 4 chunks each
2 cups water

4 sprigs parsley, minced
salt and pepper
1 Tb. butter
2 Tb. flour
1 cup milk or cream
4 egg yolks

Try out the bacon or salt pork until crisp. Remove with a slotted spoon and drain on paper towel.

　　Sauté the onion in the fat.

　　In a cooking pot cover the fish pieces with the water, add parsley, salt, and pepper, and simmer until fish pieces are tender, about 20 minutes.

Melt the butter in a saucepan, stir in the flour, and cook 1 minute. Off heat, whisk in the milk or cream and stir this into the fish and liquid.

Beat the egg yolks, add 2 tablespoons of the hot liquid to the yolks, then stir all into the soup.

Simmer a few minutes, add the crisp bacon pieces (or salt pork chitlins) and serve.

═══════ CIOPPINO—FISH STEWED ═══════ WITH SHELLFISH

I first ran onto this famous California fish stew quite appropriately in *Helen Brown's West Coast Cook Book*. Since then I have seen it in at least two other cookbooks, each a variation. But it evidently originated with the fishermen of Mediterranean descent in California or was carried there from Portugal or Italy. My version uses any kind of firm-fleshed fish from fresh or salt water.

SERVES 8–10

½ cup cooking oil
2 onions, chopped
10 cloves garlic, diced
1 large green pepper, chopped
6–8 shallots, diced
½ lb. mushrooms, sliced
1-lb. 13-oz. can tomatoes
6-oz. can tomato paste
1 pint oysters with liquor
2 cups red wine
1½ tsp. salt
1 tsp. freshly ground pepper

½ tsp. basil
½ tsp. oregano
½ tsp. cumin
1 Tb. chili powder
3 medium potatoes, very thinly sliced
3 lb. fish, filleted and then cut in chunks
1 lb. crabmeat
1 lb. shrimps, raw and shelled
4 Tb. chopped parsley

In a deep pot (8 quarts), heat the oil and in it sauté the onions, garlic, green pepper, shallots, and mushrooms until the pepper is soft, 3–4 minutes.

Add the tomatoes, tomato paste, oyster liquor, and wine and bring to a simmer.

Add the salt, pepper, basil, oregano, cumin, chili powder, and potato slices and simmer for 25 minutes.

Now add the fish chunks and cook at a high simmer until almost done, perhaps 5 minutes.

Add the crabmeat, oysters, and shrimp and continue to simmer for another 3–5 minutes but not longer than it takes for the shrimps to turn pinkish.

Serve, sprinkled with minced parsley, in soup bowls with both spoons and forks and with thick slices of Italian garlic bread.

A Baker's Dozen
of Gameburger
Recipes

MOOSEBURGER DELUXE

1 cup red wine
1 medium onion, chopped fine
1 clove garlic, chopped
½ tsp. powdered thyme
  (or ½ tsp. rosemary, crumbled)
1 Tb. lemon juice

2 Tb. butter
2 tsp. chopped parsley
2 slices white bread
1½ lb. ground moose
6 hamburger rolls

Combine wine, onion, garlic, and thyme in saucepan, bring to boil, then simmer until liquid reduces by half.

Add lemon juice, butter, and parsley and let cool.

First soak and then whip with a fork 2 slices of bread into the sauce until it is uniform.

Using your fingers, knead and mix the wine and bread mixture into the ground moose until it is uniform.

Make into 6 patties and broil over coals or under broiler, or pan-fry.

While burgers are broiling, butter both halves of the six hamburger buns and toast the buttered halves, butter side down, in skillet over low flame.

GAMEBURGER AND ZUCCHINI

Here's a favorite way to have, say, venisonburger with zucchini. Serve it with French bread and a green salad.

4–5 medium zucchinis
1 lb. gameburger
2 Tb. oil
1 small onion, chopped fine
3 cloves garlic,
  minced or squashed
2 eggs, beaten

½ tsp. coriander
½ tsp. cumin
¼ tsp. thyme
½ cup grated Parmesan
  or provolone
salt and pepper
bread crumbs

Cover the zucchinis with boiling water and cook for 12 minutes. Remove, slice lengthwise, and allow to cool. Scoop out pulp and chop, setting the shells aside.

Sauté the burger in oil, cutting constantly with edge of a wooden spoon until brown and crumbly. Take burger out and set aside.

In same skillet sauté the onion and garlic, then add the zucchini pulp and simmer for 5–6 minutes. Remove from the heat, then cool the mix a bit.

Add and stir together gameburger, the beaten eggs, the herbs, and the cheese. Season with salt and pepper.

Fill zucchini shells with the mix, sprinkle with bread crumbs, and place in shallow baking dish.

Bake about 30 minutes in preheated 350° oven.

GAMEBURGER AND RICE SUPPER

SERVES 4–5

1 large onion, chopped
1 green pepper, diced
3 Tb. oil or lard
1 lb. ground venison, elk, etc.
1 tsp. salt
pepper

½ tsp. thyme
½ tsp. oregano
8-oz. can tomatoes
1½ cups beef broth
¾ cup uncooked white rice
⅓ cup grated Parmesan

Sauté the onion and green pepper in the oil or lard until soft. Add ground meat and sauté until it loses its color.

Stir in remainder of ingredients, save Parmesan, and heat to a boil. Turn down and simmer, covered, for 20–25 minutes. Sprinkle Parmesan over when you serve.

GAMEBURGER BOURGUIGNON

I believe this is my own favorite recipe for ground game meat. It makes gameburger into an elegant dish. Serve with noodles, French bread, and a tossed salad.

SERVES 6

¼ lb. salt pork,
  diced into ½" cubes
3 slices bacon
2 slices white bread moistened
  with milk
2½ lb. ground game meat
1 tsp. salt
¼ tsp. freshly ground pepper
1 beef kidney
3 Tb. brandy
½ lb. mushrooms, sliced
2 bouillon cubes

2 Tb. beach plum
  or currant jelly
1 Tb. Kitchen Bouquet
12–15 small white onions
4 carrots, thickly sliced
1 can mushroom soup, undiluted
2 cups burgundy
3 bay leaves
1½ tsp. thyme
2 Tb. tomato paste
3 sprigs parsley, chopped

In a Dutch oven try out the salt pork and bacon, then remove and set aside the bacon and cracklings.

Squeeze most of the milk from the moistened bread slices, break the bread up and mix thoroughly with the ground meat along with the salt and pepper. Form into 2-inch meatballs. Slice the kidney into thin strips and brown together with the meatballs in the fat. Do this in batches over a medium to low heat, taking your time, so the meatballs and kidney strips do not crowd and thus steam instead of browning. When all are brown, return them to the pan, pour on brandy, and flame it.

Remove meatballs and kidney and sauté the mushrooms. Remove and set aside.

Add fat if needed and stir in the bouillon cubes, jelly, and Kitchen Bouquet. Melt and blend. Cook the onions and carrots in this glaze, about 5 minutes, stirring to coat them all over.

Add the meats, mushrooms, and all of the remaining ingredients to the Dutch oven and simmer, covered, for about 30 minutes.

Stir in the crumbled bacon and the cracklings.

MOUSSAKA: A GROUND GAME AND EGGPLANT CASSEROLE

I find that ground venison goes very well in this classic Middle Eastern eggplant casserole. Recipes for moussaka (pronounced moose-ah-*kah*, accent on last sylla-ble) are legion; mine comes partly from my classics scholar friend, Arthur Kahn, and, lately, partly from Claudia Roden's fine book, *A Book of Middle Eastern Food.*

SERVES 8

3 medium eggplants
salt
about ½ cup oil
3 onions, chopped
2 lb. ground venison,
    moose, or elk
¼ tsp. allspice
¼ tsp. cinnamon
½ tsp. oregano
½ tsp. basil
salt and pepper

1 cup homemade or
    8-oz. can tomato sauce
2 Tb. minced parsley
2½ Tb. butter
2½ Tb. flour
1¾ cups milk
½ cup grated Swiss cheese
½ cup bread crumbs
    (about ½″ slices)
½ cup grated Parmesan cheese

Slice the eggplants into ½-inch slices and sprinkle each slice generously with salt. Place in colander and barely wet it down under the faucet. Let stand for 30 minutes to wilt out the initial bitterness of the juice. Rinse, press, rinse again, and then pat dry.

In a skillet brown the eggplant slices in some of the oil, then set aside on 2 thicknesses of paper towel to drain.

Add more oil to the skillet and sauté the onions just until soft, then add the ground meat and cook until the color disappears (4 minutes perhaps).

Stir in the allspice, cinnamon, oregano, basil, salt, pepper, tomato sauce, and parsley and let it simmer for 15 minutes or so or until the liquid has been absorbed.

Preheat the oven to 375°. While it's heating lay into a shallow baking dish an overlapping layer of eggplant slices. Spoon on some of the meat and onion mix, and then another layer of eggplant, etc., ending with a layer of eggplant on top.

Now for the topping sauce: melt the butter and stir in the flour. Off heat add the milk. After cooking the butter and flour for a couple of minutes stir in the milk. As it thickens stir in and melt the grated Swiss cheese.

Pour sauce over the eggplant, then mix the bread crumbs with the Parmesan, cover surface of the sauce, and bake for 45–60 minutes or until a crust has formed on top.

CARIBOUBURGER MARTHA

What Martha Helmericks says about the leanness of caribou sometimes applies to other game meats: "Caribou at times is quite lean; try adding cheese instead of fat for ground meat."

SERVES 2–3

1 lb. lean caribou meat,
  ground
6 Tb. butter

2 oz. blue cheese,
  crumbled
salt and pepper

Form meat in 2–3 patties. Melt butter in fry-pan; brown the patties on one side, turn, then add the blue cheese, salt, and pepper. Cook, and serve hot. Or cheese can be mixed into the meat before frying.

ANOTHER MOOSE OR GAMEBURGER

This recipe is an adaptation from one of the host of beef hamburgers I have tried over the years. When it is made from scratch, i.e., when you grind the meat yourself, try to use perfectly lean meat and then grind beef suet in with it (¼ pound suet to 1 pound lean meat). This is good with any big game meat, including that of the tame version of that early game animal, *Bos*.

SERVES 4

¼ lb. mushrooms, sliced
1 small onion, finely minced
3 cloves garlic, minced
3 Tb. butter or oil
1 egg, beaten
½ cup milk
1 slice bread, broken up
1 small potato, grated
2 Tb. chili sauce
2 tsp. anchovy sauce
  or 1 tsp. anchovy paste

1 tsp. capers, crushed,
  with some of the liquid
½ tsp. thyme
¼ tsp. savory
1 tsp. salt
½ tsp. freshly ground pepper
1 lb. gameburger
slices sharp Cheddar (optional)

Sauté the mushrooms, onion, and garlic, in the butter or oil.

In a bowl beat the egg with the milk, then add bread. Beat with a fork.

Next add the sautéed mushrooms, onion, and garlic. Stir in grated potato, egg mixture, and all the seasonings.

The mixing bowl's contents should be thoroughly mixed before you crumble in the ground meat. Complete the mixing with the fingers of both hands. Form hamburger-size patties.

The patties can be pan-broiled in a hot skillet for 3 minutes to the side or they can be broiled about 3–4 inches from the flame for 5 minutes for the first side and 3–4 minutes for the second.

Just before you serve the broiled gameburger (for the last minute of the broiling) you may melt a slice of sharp Cheddar on top of each patty.

Alternate as a Meatloaf

If you would rather serve the ground game as a meatloaf you may produce an excellent one by adding the below ingredients to all the ground meat mixture ingredients above (except Cheddar slices).

6 Tb. grated Parmesan	3 Tb. flour
1 can mushroom soup	
½ soup can of water	
or beef broth	

Mix the grated Parmesan with the ground meat mixture in the mixing bowl, then form into a loaf.

Dilute the mushroom soup by stirring in the water or broth. Blend the mixture and pour it around the flour-dusted ground meatloaf. Cover and bake in 350° oven for about 1 hour.

═══════ VENISON MEATBALLS À LA SHEILA ═══════

These meatballs make a hot hors d'oeuvre, or they can be served with spaghetti sauced with garlic butter.

SERVES 4 AS HORS D'OEUVRE

THE MEATBALLS
1 lb. chopped venison	1 tsp. oregano
½ lb. ground pork	½ tsp. basil
1 egg, beaten	salt and pepper
1 cup very finely chopped onion	7 Tb. grated Parmesan
1 clove garlic, crushed	½ cup bread crumbs
1 tsp. ground fennel seeds	butter and oil

THE SAUCE
2 Tb. flour	2 Tb. Madeira
2 cups venison or beef broth	

Using your fingers, mix the venison with the ground pork, beaten egg, onion, garlic, herbs, salt, pepper, and 4 tablespoons of the grated Parmesan. When thoroughly mixed, form into walnut-size balls and roll each in the bread crumbs mixed with the 3 remaining tablespoons of grated cheese. Let stand for an hour.

Sauté the meatballs in a mixture of butter and oil, making sure not to crowd the meatballs against one another. You do not want them steamed, but rather browned on the outside and rare inside. Remove the meatballs and set aside where they will keep warm. Reserve the skillet with the fat and dredgings still in it.

Add the flour to the fat and dredgings, and when the flour is brown, stir in broth and let it bubble. Turn down heat and simmer over a low flame for 5 minutes, stirring occasionally. Just before pouring the sauce over the meatballs, stir Madeira into the sauce.

CURRIED MEATBALLS OF GAME

SERVES 6

2½ lb. ground game meat
3 slices bread moistened
   with milk
1½ tsp. salt
4–5 Tb. curry powder
5 Tb. oil or lard
3 onions, diced
1 green pepper, diced
5 cloves garlic, squashed
2 Tb. flour
2 cups stock, or 1 cup stock
   and 1 cup red wine
juice of ½ lemon

rind of 1 orange, grated
2 apples, peeled, cored,
   and diced
2 Tb. chutney, the big
   pieces cut small
2 tsp. tomato sauce
   or catsup
¼ cup currants
¼ cup raisins
½ cup canned or freshly
   grated coconut
brown sugar (optional)

Put the meat in a big bowl, crumble and squash the moistened bread, and working with your fingers blend the meat, bread pulp, salt, and 1 tablespoon of the curry powder until the mix is uniform.

Fashion 1½-inch balls from the mix and, working in batches so as not to crowd the casserole, brown the meatballs in the oil or lard, removing and replacing as they brown.

When all of the browned meatballs have been set aside sauté the onions, pepper, and garlic until pepper is soft.

Stir in the flour and cook a moment, then, off heat, stir in the stock. Now

Making Your Own Curry

Whenever I make a curry I make my own curry powder first. One obvious advantage is that it is always fresh this way, and you can be your own judge as to how hot you want it, using more or less of the recommended amount of chili. Some of the spices like fenugreek and cumin are more readily found whole, but it is easy to grind them in a small electric coffee mill; they also stay much fresher when you are storing them if left whole.

MAKES ABOUT 6 TABLESPOONS

2 tsp. coriander
2 tsp. ground tumeric
2 tsp. ground fenugreek
2 tsp. black pepper
3 tsp. cumin
1½ tsp. cardamom
   (see note below)
½ tsp. dry mustard
½ tsp. ground ginger
1 tsp. ground cinnamon

1–2 tsp. crushed dried chilies
   (start with 1 tsp. and
   work up to hotness you
   like), or cayenne pepper
1 tsp. mace
¼ tsp. saffron
½ tsp. ground cloves
½ tsp. ground allspice
¼ tsp. ground nutmeg

Thoroughly mix all ingredients

add the remaining ingredients (except the brown sugar) plus another 2–3 table-spoons curry powder. Cook and stir until mixture bubbles, then cover, turn down heat, and simmer for 30–40 minutes.

Check the casserole from time to time; if it seems to cook down too much add stock or wine.

Also check the sauce to suit your taste; if it seems too sour, temper with some brown sugar.

If it needs more curry powder, add it.

Making Garam Masala

Curry dishes often called for an additional mixture of seasonings called *garam masala*. This can be bought in shops specializing in Indian foods but, again, it's easy to make your own.

20 cardamom pods	2 tsp. ground cinnamon
4 tsp. black peppercorns	3 tsp. caraway seeds
4 tsp. coriander seeds	1 tsp. ground cloves

Remove the cardamom seeds as described in note, and mix everything together. Grind to a powder in a small electric grinder or blend at high speed 2–3 minutes. The mixture will be a darkish, pungent, compost-brown.

NOTE: Cardamom seeds usually do not come as a powder but in the husk. Remove husk and pulverize the tiny clump of seeds inside in a mortar or put through a pepper grinder.

═══ SHEILA'S VENISON MEATLOAF ═══

This is one of the best of all possible ways to use venisonburger, or the ground meat of moose, elk, or caribou. Incidentally, whether or not this recipe is made with venison or moose (or even beef) the mix with veal and pork makes a better meatloaf than if all venison were used.

SERVES 6

4 slices bread	1½ tsp. finely ground pepper
moistened with milk	1 tsp. crushed fennel seed
1 egg, beaten	1 Tb. oregano
1½ lb. ground venison	1 Tb. basil
¾ lb. ground pork (with fat)	6 rounded Tb. grated Parmesan
¾ lb. ground veal	two 8-oz. cans cream of mushroom
1 medium onion, chopped	soup
½ green pepper, chopped	1 cup water or stock
2½ tsp. salt	6 potatoes, quartered

Squeeze most of the milk from the bread, fork or tear into pieces and whip the egg into it.

In a large bowl mix the three ground meats with your ten fingers. Add the egg-bread mixture and all the rest ot the ingredients save the mushroom soup, water or stock, and potatoes.

Turn into meat mix and again using your fingers make a uniform mix. Mold the loaf into an oblong, dust with flour, and place in roasting pan.

In one of the bowls stir the soup and water or stock into a uniform mix and pour over the loaf.

Cover and bake for about 1½ hours in a 350° oven. After about 30 minutes put the potato quarters around the loaf, re-cover the pan, and finish out the 1½ hours.

NOTE: If you don't like the pale look of the mushroom soup stir in 1 tablespoon Kitchen Bouquet before you pour soup and water mix over the loaf.

═══ GAMEBURGER AND WHISKEY STROGANOFF ═══

Roy Smith's trapping camp in Ontario had a meat grinder among its otherwise somewhat limited utensils. This is a fine way to use your game meat at home. Serve with rice, spaghetti, or noodles.

SERVES 3–4

1½ lb. ground game meat	¼ tsp. celery seed (optional)
1 egg, beaten	3 Tb. flour
1–2 slices bread,	3 Tb. lard or oil
moistened, then squeezed out	1 large onion, chopped
⅛ tsp. pepper	½ lb. mushrooms, sliced
1 tsp. salt	1 beef bouillon cube, dissolved in
½ tsp. savory	½ cup hot water
3 oz. bourbon	1 cup sour cream*

In a bowl mix with your fingers the first 8 ingredients until thoroughly blended. Then form into balls of 1-inch radius.

Roll meatballs in flour and brown them in the lard or oil (without crowding) well on all sides.

Add onion and mushrooms and cook 5 minutes.

Add bouillon dissolved in hot water, cover, and simmer for 20–25 minutes. (Let it cook down but not enough to stick.)

Stir in sour cream (or clabbered milk) and heat, but do not bubble.

*Or make clabbered milk by mixing ¼ cup dried milk with ¾ cup water and 2 tablespoons vinegar.

═══ GAMEBURGER SPAGHETTI SAUCE ═══

Sometimes I have been a bit disappointed in the hamburger the butcher makes up for me from the deer I've given him. Even when well-packaged gameburger frozen doesn't stay tasty as long as the frozen stew meat, chops, steaks, and roast retain their delicious flavors. So now I ask the processor to add both beef suet and pork fat (ground salt pork) to the fat-trimmed portions of the ground meat used for deerburger. This does improve the burger, but even so I often use ground game meat for spaghetti sauce and for meatloaf (see page 323).

Here is my own favorite spaghetti sauce recipe—it freezes happily.

SERVES 4

3 medium (or even large) onions, chopped
1 big green pepper, chopped
1 rib celery with leaves, minced small
2–3 Tb. bacon fat
1¼–1½ lb. deerburger
½ cup beef or chicken broth
¼ cup dry vermouth
1 large can tomatoes (15 oz.), plus one small (8 oz.) can tomato juice or V-8 if needed
1 Tb. dry basil

1 Tb. dry oregano
½ tsp. fennel seed, either ground in your pepper mill or crushed in a mortar and pestle
1 tsp. powdered cumin
1 dash Worcestershire sauce
2–3 shakes crushed red peppercorns
¼ tsp. savory, crumbled between thumb and finger
salt and pepper
3 cloves garlic, minced

Sauté the onions, green pepper, and celery in bacon fat until soft but not browned. Add the gameburger and chop and smash it with a wooden spoon until it is in small, pebbly bits. Sauté with the three vegetables until meat loses its red and turns an unappetizing gray. Never mind; it will taste good.

Add the broth, vermouth, and tomatoes and blend and mix with vegetables and meat. Have on hand a small extra can of V-8 juice or tomato juice for liquid to add if necessary as the sauce cooks down. Don't open it at once, for you may not need it.

Add all remaining ingredients save the garlic and simmer, stirring, mixing, and tasting occasionally, so the sauce pleases you. Maybe more oregano or cumin, or whatever, is needed to give *you* the blend *you* want.

Now as to the garlic. If you want the sauce to have a distinct garlicky bouquet, add the garlic 2–3 minutes before you serve it. On the other hand, if you want a less distinct garlic taste, add the garlic when you put in the other herbs. Garlic is highly volatile, and the *distinct* flavor cooks out if added early.

Simmer this sauce 12–15 minutes, which seems sufficient to blend the flavors.

RIGATONI WITH VENISONBURGER MEAT SAUCE, BOLOGNESE

After trying Marcella Hazan's masterly baked pasta dish made with hamburger from her *Classic Italian Cook Book*, I could scarcely wait to try it with gameburger. I give it with Mrs. Hazan's kind permission. If you happen to be cooking in camp and want to give your partners a stunning treat, as well as a substitute for spaghetti, try this dish. The recipe calls for those oversized and fluted pasta elbows called rigatoni, and this pasta should be used in your own kitchen, but macaroni or even spaghetti or egg noodles would do handsomely in camp.

SERVES 6

THE MEAT SAUCE (RAGÙ)
2 Tb. chopped yellow onion
3 Tb. olive oil
3 Tb. butter
2 Tb. chopped celery
2 Tb. chopped carrot
¾ lb. gameburger
salt

THE PASTA
1 lb. rigatoni
  or similar-cut pasta
salt
2 cups medium-thick
  white sauce (page 364)

1 cup dry white wine
½ cup milk
⅛ tsp. nutmeg
2 cups canned Italian
  tomatoes, roughly chopped,
  with their juice

6 Tb. freshly grated
  Parmesan cheese
2 Tb. butter

An earthenware pot should be your first choice for making ragù. If you don't have one available, use a heavy, enameled cast-iron casserole, the deepest one you have (to keep the ragù from reducing too quickly). Put in the chopped onion, with all the oil and butter, and sauté briefly over medium heat until just translucent. Add the celery and carrot and cook gently for 2 minutes.

Add the gameburger, crumbling it in the pot with a fork. Add 1 teaspoon salt, stir, and cook only until the meat has lost its raw, red color. Add the wine, turn the heat up to medium high, and cook, stirring occasionally, until all the wine has evaporated.

Turn the heat down to medium, add the milk and the nutmeg, and cook until the milk has evaporated. Stir frequently.

When the milk has evaporated, add the tomatoes and stir thoroughly. When the tomatoes have started to bubble, turn the heat down until the sauce cooks at the laziest simmer, just an occasional bubble. Cook, uncovered, for a minimum of 3½–4 hours, stirring occasionally. Taste and correct for salt. (If you cannot watch the sauce for such a long stretch, you can turn off the heat and resume its cooking later on. But do finish cooking it in one day.)

NOTE: Ragù can be kept in the refrigerator for up to 5 days, or frozen. Reheat until it simmers for about 15 minutes before using.

Now drop the pasta into 4 quarts of boiling salted water and cook until just al dente, firm to the bite. (It should be a shade firmer than you would ordinarily cook it because it will soften more as it bakes in the oven.) Drain and transfer to a large mixing bowl.

Add the ragù, white sauce, and 4 tablespoons of the grated cheese to the pasta. Mix thoroughly. Transfer to a butter-smeared bake-and-serve dish. Level the top with a spatula, sprinkle it with the remaining 2 tablespoons grated cheese, and dot with butter. Place in the uppermost level of a preheated 400° oven and bake for 10 minutes. Allow to settle a few minutes before serving.

Sausages, Pâtés, and Terrines

GAME SAUSAGE

These sausages are good warm served on toast with their own juices or cold with mustard and good bread.

1 small onion, chopped
2 cloves garlic, chopped
6 oz. pork fatback,
   cut in chunks
1 cup dry sherry
½ lb. red game flank
½ lb. venison stew meat
¼ cup chopped parsley
1 tsp. thyme

1 Tb. kosher salt
½ tsp. coarsely ground
   black pepper
1 Tb. Worcestershire sauce
2 tsp. fennel seed
2 tsp. caraway
pinch of saltpeter
sausage casings, soaked for
   30 minutes in warm water

Sauté the onion and garlic in the fatback slowly until limp and golden. Add the sherry and cook more rapidly 4–5 minutes.

Cut the two meats in rough chunks and then put into the food processor or through the medium blade of a grinder along with the onion-garlic mixture and the remaining ingredients (except casings). Fry a dab of this mixture and taste to see if it is highly seasoned enough; if not, correct.

If you don't have a sausage stuffer, use a pastry bag. Slide a length of the soaked casing up over the funnel. Tie a knot in the far end. Force the stuffing through the funnel. After the casing is about 2½ inches full, twist it and tie it up, then continue until the sausage meat is used up. Tie a knot at the end of the casing.

To cook: simmer the sausages in water to cover, lightly salted and peppered. They should be cooked through in 15 minutes.

PÂTÉ OF GAME MEAT, TONGUE, AND LIVER

approximately 1 lb. liver
   of venison, antelope,
   or other game, cut in
   ½" strips
4 Tb. butter
2 lb. venison or
   other red game meat
2 lb. pork with some fat
1 onion
2 eggs
4 cloves garlic
1 tsp. thyme
pinch of cloves

pinch of allspice
several gratings of nutmeg
2 tsp. salt
½ tsp. freshly ground pepper
½ cup bourbon or brandy
fatback, cut thin and
   flattened, or blanched bacon
   to line pan or terrine
approximately 1 lb. cooked
   tongue, cut in ½" strips
1 lb. pork fat cut
   in ½" strips
2 bay leaves

Sauté the strips of liver in the butter just for a minute. Set aside.

Cut the game meat, pork, and onion into rough chunks and spin in the food processor until minced; if you don't have a food processor put through a meat grinder.

Add the eggs, garlic, thyme, cloves, allspice, nutmeg, salt, pepper, and bourbon or brandy to the container of the processor and spin until everything is blended (or else mix together in a bowl).

Line a 2½-quart loaf pan or terrine with the fatback or blanched bacon. Pack a third of the ground meat mixture onto the bottom, then make alternating strips of half the tongue, sautéed liver, and pork fat. Cover with another third of the ground meat, then the rest of the strips, and finish with ground meat. Lay the bay leaves on top and place fatback on top.

Bake for 2½ hours in a 325° oven.

When done, refrigerate for 2–3 days before eating.

═══ TERRINE OF GAME ═══

Sometimes when you want to splurge at a game dinner make a terrine for the "poultry" course or as an appetizer. This dish comes in handy when your larder or freezer has some but not many items of game. The terrine does not have to be extensive; indeed the servings can be small, say, before a roast of venison. Prepare this dish the day or so before your dinner and refrigerate; it does take a bit of trouble, so get yourself into the self-indulgent frame of mind to give over the time for it.

These instructions are intentionally general, for one can never know what game may be on hand at any one time. If possible the pâté should be baked in one of those French earthenware terrines whose lid is a hare's head or a duck.

1 rabbit or squirrel	1 grouse or 3 chukars, skinned
2 cups white wine	(don't bother to pluck)
1 onion, sliced	1 pheasant, skinned
2 cloves garlic, chopped	1 wild duck or 1–2 supremes
2 cloves	from a wild goose breast,
¼ tsp. cinnamon	skinned
¼ tsp. ground ginger	4 lb. pork fat
½ bay leaf	salt and pepper
¼ tsp. tarragon	

Cut the rabbit or squirrel in serving pieces. Make a marinade of the wine, onion, garlic, cloves, cinnamon, ginger, bay leaf, and tarragon. Put rabbit or squirrel pieces down in the marinade for 3 hours or so, even overnight.

With a small sharp boning knife slice breasts and legs of birds into thin slices, making them as long as possible. Set these long bird slices aside.

Now cut, gouge, and hack carcasses of birds to collect small pieces and trimmings of remaining meat. Reserve the carcasses and set aside trimmings and liver.

Next take rabbit or squirrel pieces out of marinade (which reserve) and cut, gouge, and hack the meat off the bones in small pieces. Don't bother to try to accumulate neat slices, for all of the meat will be ground or processed.

Put the small pieces and trimmings of the game birds, their livers (or 4 chicken livers), plus the rabbit or squirrel pieces and the 4 pounds of pork fat through a meat grinder or, more easily, through a food processor and salt and pepper this. Mix well. Set aside.

1 batch bird carcasses	**2 cups water or chicken broth**
the marinade in which	**unflavored gelatin**
rabbit or squirrel was put	

Put carcasses with marinade and water or broth in saucepan, bring to a boil, turn down heat, and simmer for 45 minutes.

Drain and measure the hot liquid to determine how much gelatin to use; 1 tablespoon of gelatin to 2 cups of liquid is the rule. Soften the gelatin in a little *cold* water before stirring into hot liquid.

bacon slices	**3 cloves garlic, minced**
thyme	**1/4 lb. mushrooms, sliced thin**
nutmeg	**Madeira**
salt and pepper	**brandy**
1/4 lemon peel, grated	**several bay leaves**

Using 2 small or 1 large terrine, line bottoms (or bottom) with bacon slices and begin the assembling: first a layer of the processed meat mix, then a layer of the long bird slices that had been set aside in second paragraph of recipe.

Over the bird slices sprinkle sparsely powdered thyme, gratings of nutmeg, salt, pepper, pinches of grated lemon peel, garlic, and mushroom slices.

Continue in layers until terrine(s) are nearly full.

Pour in the gelatin liquid until nearly full, add 2 tablespoons Madeira or 1 tablespoon brandy to each terrine or 4 tablespoons Madeira and 2 tablespoons brandy if you use 1 terrine.

Lay five or six bay leaves over each top.

Place terrine, covered, in a shallow baking dish half full of hot water and bake for 2 hours.

Cool and place in refrigerator to set.

The pâté will shrink away from the terrine in setting and can be turned out onto a cold plate or platter for slicing if you wish. Or if you have a hare's head lidded terrine you can bring it to the table.

NOTE: Neither the delighted guests nor the chef will forget this dish. But the pleasure of your guests will be so great that you will determine to prepare it again. Maybe once a year?

LITTLE CANADA RABBIT TERRINE

From *American Food: The Gastronomic Story* by Evan Jones, a rabbit pâté of French Canadian origin.

SERVES ABOUT 12

MARINADE FOR RABBIT

1 1/2 cups red wine	**1 clove garlic, crushed**
3/4 cup wine vinegar	**1/2 tsp. dried dill weed**
1 onion, roughly chopped	**1/2 tsp. mustard seed**
1 carrot, cut in chunks	**1/2 tsp. coriander, bruised**
2 ribs celery, cut in short pieces	**1/2 tsp. peppercorns, bruised**

TERRINE

1 rabbit (3 lb.), cut in pieces	2–3 tsp. salt
1 lb. lean pork, ground	freshly ground pepper
1 lb. pork fat, ground	2 Tb. minced fresh parsley
2 medium-size onions, finely chopped	1 tsp. dried savory
3 Tb. lard	½ tsp. dried thyme
2 cloves garlic, finely minced	2–3 whole allspice, mulled
½ cup applejack or other brandy or Madeira	½ lb. salt pork, sliced thin
2 eggs beaten	½ lb. country ham, cut into ¾″ thick strips
	1 large bay leaf

Mix the marinade ingredients. After putting in the rabbit pieces, add about ¾ cup of water or enough to cover rabbit. Marinate 24 hours or more, turning occasionally.

Strip well-marinated rabbit meat from bones. Use best pieces (about half of total) to cut into long strips ½–⅓ inch thick. Grind less tender pieces and scraps of rabbit and mix with ground lean pork and ground pork fat.

Sauté onions in lard until translucent, then stir into ground meat; add garlic, applejack, eggs, and seasonings. Test flavor by frying a small sample of mixture; it should be heartily seasoned, but not oversalted if the country ham to be added later is as tangy as it should be.

Boil salt pork slices in 2 quarts water for two minutes; drain and pat dry, then use them to line 2-quart terrine, letting edges just meet.

Spread one-third of ground meat over bottom, then lay over it alternating strips of rabbit meat and country ham, using half of total. Repeat layer of ground meat and use remaining half of meat strips; cover with final layer of ground meat. Put bay leaf in the center, then cover top with salt-pork slices, tucking down into sides so mixture is well wrapped. Cover.

Set terrine in pan with hot water that comes about halfway up outside of terrine; bake for 2½ hours in a 450° oven. Remove to cool, weighting top surface with an old flatiron or other heavy object. When cool, chill for several days. Serve from the terrine.

GAME BIRD PÂTÉ

SERVES ABOUT 10

2 mallard ducks or 2 pheasants or other game birds	⅛ tsp. ground cloves
½ cup brandy	⅛ tsp. nutmeg
8–10 shallots, finely chopped	⅛ tsp. ground ginger
about 1 pound veal	6 juniper berries, crushed
½ pound pork fat	3–4 Tb. chopped parsley
1 Tb. kosher salt	3 eggs
½ tsp. freshly ground pepper	strips of fatback or blanched bacon
½ tsp. thyme	2 bay leaves

Bone the birds, leaving breast meat neatly intact. Cut this into strips and marinate overnight in ¼ cup of the brandy and 4 of the minced shallots. Be sure to extract every morsel of meat from the carcass; save the bones for stock. You should have about 11 ounces of breast meat and about 7 ounces of scraps. Set aside breast strips.

Grind (or use a food processor) the meat scraps with the veal—you'll want a total of 1¾ pounds; adjust accordingly, adding more or less veal. Grind again with the pork fat.

Mix the ground meats with the seasonings, juniper berries, parsley, eggs, the remaining brandy and shallots, and the juices from the marinade. (Again, this may all be mixed in a food processor.) This forcemeat should be highly seasoned, so to test gently fry a small piece in a nonstick pan and, when cool, taste. Adjust salt and other seasonings if necessary, remembering that flavors are less assertive when cold—and since pâtés are eaten cold, take this into account.

Line a 2-quart mold—a terrine or oval-shaped pâté form with cover—with fatback or blanched bacon. Spread one-third of the forcemeat on the bottom, then make a layer of breast strips. Repeat, ending with the last of the forcemeat. Place 2 bay leaves on the top and cover with fatback or bacon. Place aluminum foil on top, then cover so that the dish is well sealed.

Place the dish in a pan of boiling water (the water should come about halfway up the sides) and bake in a preheated 350° oven for 1½ hours.

Remove from the oven and take off lid, leaving the terrine in its pan of water. Place on top of the foil a weight or weights, distributing the weight as evenly as possible. Let cool in the pan a few hours, then place the dish, weights and all, in the refrigerator overnight. A pâté tastes better if it has the chance to mellow at least a day or two before you eat it.

Dishes Made with Cooked Game

GAME BIRD CASSOULET,
À LA LARRY KOLLER

We do not apologize for the length of this recipe, for to do so would be to apologize for the length of time it takes to prepare this wonderful dish. The time will be worth it, if not to you, then surely to your guests.

Game Bird Cassoulet should be served as an early Saturday dinner in the fall or winter to guests who deserve it and who have been warned to eat no lunch before coming. A green salad and French bread and, later, some cheese and fruit are all t' ' need go with it. A pheasant skin, if you have one, makes a nice centerp 'r this meal—otherwise a pressed-glass spoonholder with a bouquet of phe&   '^'s tail feathers. My version is a variation of the late Larry Koller's, wɪ˷   'ne was adapted from the classic recipe.

SERVES 10—12

2 lb. marrowfat or great northern
  beans
1 lb. pig skins
½ lb. salt pork
½ lb. ham butt
1½ cups chopped onions
1 bouquet garni (6 cloves garlic,
  6 sprigs parsley, 4 cloves,
  3 bay leaves, ½ tsp. thyme tied
  in cheesecloth)
2 lb. pork loin
1 wild duck or breast of wild goose
1 pheasant

1 grouse or partridge
2–4 woodcocks or quail
butter and oil
3 cups white wine
6-oz. can tomato paste
6 cloves garlic, crushed
½ tsp. thyme
2 bay leaves
1 qt. beef stock
1½ lb. Italian sausage
2 cups chopped onions
½ cup flavored bread crumbs
3 sprigs parsley, chopped

Soak the beans overnight in a 6–8-quart kettle.

Put half the pig skins in a large pot of water and bring to a boil. Drain, rinse, change water, bring to boil again, and simmer for 30 minutes. Remove and cut them in ½-inch strips and then into ½-inch squares.

Bring remainder of skins to boil, rinse and dry, and set aside separately for the morrow's continuation.

Drain the beans in the morning, replace in kettle, cover with boiling water, and add the pig skin squares, the salt pork (in one piece), the ham butt, chopped onions, and bouquet garni. Bring to a boil and skim once or twice, then simmer over low flame until the beans are just tender, about 1 hour. When the beans are just chewable set them aside with other ingredients in their liquor.

Just after you put on the beans put the pork loin and the duck or goose, uncovered, in the oven set at 400°. When it has browned, reduce heat to 350° and roast uncovered until done (40 minutes for the duck, 40 minutes to the pound for the pork). Set aside with juices.

Cut the pheasant into pieces (as you would a frying chicken), cut up or just quarter the grouse or partridge, and leave the woodcocks or quail whole. Brown the birds in butter and oil in a heavy skillet. Remove and keep warm.

Add white wine to the skillet and scrape loose the brown goodies. Pour this wine and drippings into a large container and add the tomato paste, crushed garlic, thyme, bay leaves, and beef stock.

Drain the beans (reserving the liquor) and add them to the above container to stand. Take out the salt pork and ham butt and let cool. If need be, cover beans with part of their reserve cooking liquor, and simmer beans, wine, tomato paste, garlic, thyme, bay leaves, and beef stock; simmer for 5 minutes, and let stand in this wine and herbed liquor.

Brown the sausage in a little oil, set aside the meat, and sauté the chopped onions in the sausage fat. Then stir into the skillet the reserved juices and pan scrapings from the roasted pork and duck. Reserve.

Line the bottom of a 7–8-quart casserole with the pig skins that were not cut into squares.

Slice the pork loin, duck, salt pork, and remaining ham butt.

Put in casserole a layer of beans, then some of the meats (the ham butt, the pig skin squares, pork loin, sausages) and the cut-up game birds (duck, pheasant pieces, grouse pieces), and alternate the layers until you finish with a layer of beans and sliced salt pork. Then garnish the top with woodcock or quail.

Add the herbed liquor the beans stood in and the onions with their meat juice until the beans are covered. Sprinkle with bread crumbs and parsley, and bring the cassoulet to a simmer on top of the stove. Then put the cassoulet into a 350° oven, covered, and after about 20 minutes check to see if a crust has formed. When it has formed, break through with a spoon and baste the crust with the juices. Repeat this 2–3 times while the cassoulet bakes (for about 3 hours). When it has been in the oven for 2 hours, remove the lid and let the crust brown. You may have to turn up the oven heat to accomplish this.

If, during the baking, it becomes necessary to add liquid, use the original, reserved bean-cooking liquid.

A lot of work for baked beans, but what baked beans!

VENISON HASH

When you have leftover gravy from venison or any other red-meat game roast, this recipe makes a savory quick meal. When you don't have leftover gravy, make your own via my favorite method (see page 356).

SERVES 4

1 medium onion, chopped	salt and pepper
1 clove garlic, minced	⅛ tsp. mace
½ green pepper, chopped	1 tsp. thyme
3 Tb. oil	chopped parsley
2 Tb. butter	1 Tb. catsup or tomato paste
4 medium potatoes, boiled, cooled, then diced	¼ cup heavy cream
	1 Tb. Worcestershire sauce
3 cups cold roast venison, diced	4 freshly poached eggs (optional)
½ cup venison gravy	

In an iron skillet sauté the onion, garlic, and pepper in hot oil and butter for a minute only, then add the potatoes and brown them without burning the onions.

Add the venison and continue cooking for a couple of minutes, then add the gravy and remaining ingredients (except eggs) and continue to cook, turning often until liquid of the gravy and cream cooks out some, leaving the bottom browned and crisp. Turn over and cook other side, in all about 12–15 minutes.

A poached egg with each helping is traditional, and I always serve chili sauce or catsup on the side.

GAME MEAT MIROTON

This is a good, quick, second-day dish to make with any boiled (or roast) game meat.

SERVES 6

1 large onion, chopped
2 cloves garlic, sliced
4 Tb. butter
1½ Tb. capers, crushed, with
   the liquor that dips out
   of the jar with them
1 Tb. wine vinegar
2 Tb. flour
1½ cup broth or beef bouillon
1 tsp. thyme
½ tsp. rosemary
1 tsp. catsup
salt and pepper

2 sprigs parsley
1 rib celery with leaves
2 bay leaves
4 Tb. butter
4 potatoes, boiled, cooled,
   then sliced
10–12 slices boiled moose or
   other game meat (see note
   at end of recipe)
½ cup bread crumbs
½ cup grated Parmesan
2 sprigs parsley, minced

Sauté the onion and garlic in the butter, then add the capers, caper liquor, and vinegar. Boil until the liquid just disappears.

Stir in the flour until it is evenly distributed to coat the onion pieces. Off heat, stir in the broth, thyme, rosemary, catsup, salt, pepper, parsley, celery, and bay leaves, and mix well, then return to the heat to simmer for 15–20 minutes, stirring occasionally and watching lest the sauce thickens too much. If it does, add broth or water.

While the sauce is cooking melt the butter and sprinkle it over the cold boiled potato slices.

Preheat oven to 450°.

When ready to assemble the dish, put a fourth of the sauce in the bottom of a shallow baking dish. Then add the moose slices arranged in a single layer but overlapping pattern. Add remainder of the sauce.

Make a border around the meat of the buttered potato slices, sprinkle on the bread crumbs mixed with the grated cheese, then bake in a 400° oven for 15 minutes or so.

Sprinkle with minced parsley and serve in the baking dish.

NOTE: If you'd like to give this dish a more "deviled" taste, spread the meat slices with Dijon mustard.

VENISON STROGANOFF

This can be made with leftover venison or other red-meat game steak. If it's been properly cooked in the first place, the meat should be rosy in the center.

2 cups venison cut in
  julienne strips
Madeira to marinate
1 medium onion, chopped, or
  3 Tb. chopped shallots
2 medium cloves garlic,
  crushed and minced
6 Tb. butter
¼ lb. (or more) mushrooms,
  sliced thin

2 Tb. flour
1½ cups stock
1 Tb. tomato paste or
  2 Tb. tomato sauce
1 tsp. lemon juice
3 Tb. finely chopped dill
¾ cup sour cream
salt
dash of cayenne
fresh dill or parsley, chopped

Marinate the strips of meat 1 hour or more in about ½ cup Madeira.

Sauté onion or shallots with garlic in half the butter for a minute or so, then add thinly sliced mushrooms and allow to just change color slightly. Add the remaining butter and, when melted, the flour; stirring, let it brown without burning. Pour in a little of the stock, letting it warm on the exposed surface of the pan, before stirring; repeat this process so that the butter-flour mixture absorbs stock smoothly. Add the tomato to make a rich, thick reddish brown sauce—it should in fact be too thick to drip off a spoon. Add lemon juice and stir in minced dill. The sauce may be prepared in advance to this point and set aside.

When you have prepared noodles or rice as accompaniment to Stroganoff, reheat sauce and turn into it the meat strips and any Madeira that has not been absorbed. Add sour cream and mix into sauce as it reheats, but don't let anything—meat particularly—cook. If you find sauce too thick add more cream and/or stock; it should be the consistency of a good cream sauce. Season with salt if necessary and a dash of cayenne—sometimes we use paprika for color and black pepper grindings to taste. Decorate top with chopped dill or parsley.

FRICADELLES

2 slices white bread
3 Tb. dry white wine
1½ cups cooked minced
  game meat
⅛ tsp. cinnamon
a grating or 2 of nutmeg
  (or a pinch of ground)
2 Tb. grated Parmesan

salt and pepper
1 egg yolk
3 Tb. flour
3 Tb. butter
3 Tb. tomato purée
¾ cup game or beef bouillon
2–3 sprigs rosemary or ¼ tsp.
  dried

Soak the bread in the wine until it is sopped through, then break it up with a fork. Mix in the meat, spices, Parmesan, salt and pepper to taste, and the egg yolk. Form into 8 patties.

Dust the patties with flour, then brown them in the butter on both sides.

Mix the tomato purée and bouillon together and pour it around the patties in the pan. Add rosemary and simmer very gently 30 minutes, covering if the sauce seems to evaporate.

═══════ GAME BIRD OR WILD-FOWL HASH ═══════

SERVES 4

1 onion, chopped
1 carrot, chopped
4 Tb. butter
1 cup game bird or chicken broth
1 rib celery, chopped
½ green bell pepper, chopped
2½ cups cooked game bird or
 wild-fowl meat, minced

salt
½ tsp. tarragon
pinch cayenne
¼ cup heavy cream (optional)
3 Tb. grated Swiss cheese
 (or Parmesan or combination)
3 Tb. chopped parsley

In a fairly large skillet sauté the onion and carrot in 3 tablespoons of the butter for a minute, then add ¾ cup of the broth, cover, and cook gently for about 6–7 minutes, at which point the liquid should have evaporated; watch carefully to see that it doesn't burn.

Now add the remaining butter and sauté the celery and green pepper with the onion and carrot for a minute. Add remaining broth, cover, and cook about 2 minutes. You want the celery and pepper to retain just a little crunch.

Stir in the minced fowl, and season with salt, tarragon, and cayenne. Poke a few holes on top of the hash and pour in the heavy cream, if you want to use it. Now pack down everything with the flat of your spatula and cook over medium heat about 3–4 minutes to form a crust. Again, watch your heat to see that the bottom doesn't burn.

Sprinkle the cheese over the top. To serve, you can slip the skilletful of hash under a hot broiler to brown the top, or you can loosen the hash from the pan and flip it over onto a warm serving platter or portions of it onto individual plates so the browned bottom is topside. Sprinkle with parsley.

With Mushrooms: Sauté ¼–½ pound sliced mushrooms in 2 tablespoons butter for 2–3 minutes, then add to the hash when you stir in the meat.

With Poached Eggs: Poach 4 eggs just before serving and place one on top of each serving.

═══════ GAME CROQUETTES ═══════

We love picking off all the last scraps of meat from any cooked game meat, and making well-seasoned, crisp-coated croquettes is one of the best ways of using it up. Serve these with Mushroom Sauce, page 365, or Tomato Sauce, page 365, or just plain with a squeeze of lemon.

SERVES 4–6

3½ cups ground cooked game meat
 or fowl
2 cups thick cream sauce*
1 small onion, minced fine, or
 about 6 scallions with part
 of the green
¼ tsp. each thyme and savory
 for red meat

¼ tsp. tarragon and a few
 gratings of nutmeg for fowl
2 Tb. chopped parsley
salt and freshly ground pepper
flour
2 eggs, lightly beaten
about 2 cups fresh bread crumbs
frying oil

Mix together the ground meat, cream sauce, onion or scallions, herbs, and salt and pepper to taste. Put the mixture in the refrigerator and chill thoroughly.

Form into 12 fat sausagelike shapes and dust each lightly with flour, then dip in egg all over, and finally roll in bread crumbs, making sure you cover the entire surface. Place on a platter lined with waxed paper and chill again for at least 30 minutes.

Fill a skillet (an electric one is good for frying) half full of oil and heat to 360°. Fry croquettes about 4 at a time so as not to crowd them (fewer if you're working in a quite small skillet). Cook until golden brown on both sides, turning once. Drain on paper.

* Follow the directions for making cream sauce on page 364, but use 6 tablespoons butter and 6 tablespoons flour to 2 cups milk to make it sufficiently thick for binding croquettes.

===== STUFFED PEPPERS WITH LEFTOVER GAME =====

SERVES 4

4 good-size bell peppers, green
   or red, or combination
2 onions, chopped
6 Tb. butter
2 cloves garlic, minced (optional)
¼ lb. mushrooms, chopped
2 cups cooked game meat,
   chopped
   fine
1 cup cooked rice
salt and freshly ground pepper
1 tsp. chopped fresh rosemary
   or ½ tsp. dried

1 Tb. chopped fresh basil
   or ½ Tb. dried
3–4 Tb. chopped parsley
about ½–¾ cups game or beef
   broth or leftover gravy
   or combination
1 cup canned tomatoes, crushed
   with juice, or tomato purée
½ cup bread crumbs

Either split the peppers in half lengthwise or cut ½ inch off the tops. Scrape out seeds and ribs. Parboil peppers in boiling salted water for 6 minutes. Remove and drain.

Meanwhile sauté the onions in 4 tablespoons of the butter until soft, then add optional garlic and chopped mushrooms, and sauté another 2–3 minutes.

Mix the sautéed vegetables with the meat and the rice. Add salt and pepper to taste, and mix in herbs. Add any gravy you may have and/or a little broth to moisten. Stuff the peppers with this mixture.

Place peppers upright in a shallow pan, add tomatoes and a little gravy or broth around them, top with bread crumbs, and dot with remaining butter.

Bake in a 350° oven for 40 minutes. Serve with a little of the tomato sauce poured around them.

Variations: Instead of mushrooms, add ¼ cup pine nuts and ¼ cup raisins and season with ½ teaspoon cinnamon in place of the basil.

Instead of rice use cooked barley and vary the seasonings—savory and thyme can be good.

PHEASANT TETRAZZINI

This recipe produces one of my favorite "leftover" game-bird dishes. It can be used, of course, for grouse, chukars, or quail, but when smaller birds are used one usually has to "prepare" this leftover dish when the original is prepared. For example, if you are roasting or broiling 4 chukars for a certain meal, add 2 or 4 additional with the intention of later preparing this dish. Here we will give the quantities for a leftover of pheasant where one can have 8–10 leftover slices of the bird or birds. A salad (or sliced tomatoes) is all you need to serve with this one-dish meal. Italian or French bread is not amiss, of course.

SERVES 4–6

½ lb. spaghetti
4 Tb. butter or chicken fat
3 Tb. flour
1 cup chicken or pheasant broth
salt and white pepper to taste
½ tsp. marjoram
½ tsp. crushed rosemary
¼ tsp. mace

½ cup heavy cream
1 large shallot or small onion, minced
½ lb. mushrooms, sliced thin
8–12 slices cooked pheasant
½ cup freshly grated Parmesan cheese

Cook the spaghetti for 9 minutes, drain, and spread in bottom of a buttered 2-quart casserole or baking dish.

Melt half the butter in a small saucepan, then add the flour, stirring. Cook for a minute or two. Off heat, stir in the chicken or pheasant broth. Back on medium heat, let the sauce thicken a bit as you stir it, then add the salt, pepper, marjoram, rosemary, and mace. Add and stir in over very low heat the heavy cream. Set this velouté sauce aside.

Now sauté the shallot and mushrooms in the remaining butter for 3–4 minutes.

Spoon one half of the velouté sauce over the spaghetti, then lay in the bird slices.

Cover the slices with the sautéed mushrooms and shallots, then cover with the other half of the velouté sauce.

Sprinkle the grated cheese over all and bake uncovered for 30 minutes.

GRATIN OF ROAST PHEASANT
OR OTHER GAME BIRDS

SERVES 4

4 Tb. butter
4 Tb. flour
1 cup chicken stock
¼ cup dry white wine
½–¾ cup heavy cream
1 tsp. chopped fresh tarragon or
    ½ tsp. dried

salt to taste
⅛ tsp. cayenne
1 tsp. Dijon mustard
3 Tb. grated Swiss cheese
4–6 substantial pieces of cold roast
    pheasant (or other game bird)
¼ cup bread crumbs

Melt 3 tablespoons of the butter and add the 4 tablespoons flour. Stir this roux over a low heat 2–3 minutes until it is smooth, then off heat pour in the chicken stock and wine. Beat together with a wire whisk, return the pan to the heat, and cook, whisking constantly, until the sauce thickens. Turn the heat down and let the sauce simmer as slowly as possible for about 5 minutes, stirring with a spoon every now and then. The sauce should be quite thick. Thin it with ½ cup or a little more of the heavy cream. Add the tarragon, salt, cayenne, mustard, and Swiss cheese and stir until well combined with the sauce. Taste and correct seasoning.

Spread a thin layer of the sauce on the bottom of a baking dish just large enough to accommodate the pheasant in one layer, and arrange the pieces on top. Salt lightly, then spoon the remaining sauce over them. Sprinkle the bread crumbs over the top and dot with the remaining butter. (If you don't intend to bake the chicken at once, cover the dish tightly with plastic wrap and refrigerate.)

Bake in a preheated 375° oven for about 20 minutes, or until the sauce begins to bubble, then slide under the broiler to brown.

═══════════ GAME MEAT SHEPHERD'S PIE ═══════════

Here is a grand way to use leftover braised or roast venison (or any other cooked game meat) or leftover roast pheasant or rebraised wild goose, or all three if you happen to have frozen leftovers in your freezer. This dish can be made just as easily in camp as in your own kitchen. I give a shortcut here for the "crust" of this hearty meat pie, but mashed potatoes can be made from scratch.

Since I am recommending the use of instant mashed potatoes in making this crust and bottom, I suggest that you follow the instructions on the can, for in my experience those instructions will make the mashed potatoes of just the right consistency for your purposes (if you are using such instant flakes for mashed potatoes as a side dish you should use more liquid).

SERVES 6

2 cups water
⅔ cup milk
¾ tsp. salt
1½ tsp. butter
2 Tb. *dry* onion flakes
2 cups Idahoan Instant Mashed
   Potatoes (flakes)
¼–½ cup grated Parmesan cheese
4 cups diced cooked game, red
   meat, and/or game bird
2 cups gravy from braised or
   roast dish (include the carrots)*
1 small onion, minced

1 small or ½ large green
   pepper, minced
1–2 cloves garlic, minced
2 tsp. tomato paste or catsup
1 Tb. vinegar
½ tsp. thyme
¼ tsp. oregano or marjoram
¼ tsp. savory
2 Tb. minced parsley
2 tsp. Worcestershire sauce or
   mushroom catsup
butter

Put water, milk, salt, butter, and onion flakes in saucepan and *just* bring to boil. Take off heat and stir in potato flakes gently, but do not whip. While it is still hot, but before it has set, stir in Parmesan. Set aside.

In a bowl mix diced meat, gravy, onion, green pepper, garlic, tomato paste or catsup, vinegar, herbs, and Worcestershire sauce. Then butter bottom and sides of a casserole, put in bottom a layer of the mashed potatoes, and pat down with a spoon. Add meat mixture, then cover with remaining mashed potatoes. Pat and smooth this top crust, but leave a hole in the middle. Dot with butter and bake, uncovered, in a 400° oven for 25–30 minutes or until top is lightly browned.

* If not enough leftover gravy, measure what you have and compensate with enough beef or chicken broth or stock, but keep the stock separate for the moment.

VENISON CURRY

SERVES 4

1 lb. leftover rare venison or other red game meat cut in bite-size chunks
1 pint plain yogurt
1 cup coarsely chopped onions
1 tsp. minced garlic
about 6 Tb. butter
1 Tb. flour
2–4 Tb. curry powder* (for homemade see Box, page 322)
2 Tb. garam masala (optional)* (for homemade see Box, page 323)

1 Tb. grated fresh ginger or 3 oz. crystallized (or about 1 Tb. powdered)
1 pint venison stock (see recipe)
¼ cup sun-dried shrimp (optional)
¼ cup vermouth (optional)
fruit condiments (see recipe)
1 tart green apple
3 medium tomatoes or 8 cherry tomatoes
sambals: see suggestions at the end of the recipe

The remains of a roast venison should be cut away from the ribs and backbone, trimmed of any fat, and cut into 1½-inch cubes before marinating, 1 hour or more, in the yogurt. If this is done at least 4–5 hours before cooking the curry, the bones may be used to make a stock by simmering with salt, 1 onion, 1 carrot, and a fair-sized bay leaf. Either beef or chicken bouillon may be used as a substitute or as an additive to the venison broth.

The longer a curry sauce is carefully and slowly simmered, the more it improves. Begin by gently sautéing the onions and garlic in at least 3 tablespoons of the butter for 4–5 minutes before adding flour. Stir this resulting paste at least one minute, then add the curry powder (and garam masala, if you are using it) and mix well. Add the grated fresh ginger, or if using crystallized, rinse off sugar and finely chop; if powdered ginger, be sure it is fresh enough to tantalize the nostrils, and stir in about 1 tablespoon. As these seasonings absorb the butter, add more—the mixture should be smooth, thick, and shinily lubricated before adding stock, a little at a time, to make at least a pint of thin sauce. Soak the shrimp (if you wish to use them) in the vermouth.

Now add fruit condiments, as desired: Mango chutney is not essential, but about 2 tablespoonfuls can be excellent; or the same of raisins, currants, and chopped dried dates are also very good. Or try a couple of tablespoons of a tart orange marmalade, or the same amount of apricot preserve. At this point tasting may indicate too much sweetness, but don't worry—the melding comes in the slow cooking. Now stir in optional shrimp and the wine in which they have been soaking. Not more than half an hour before the curry is to be served, add the green apple, peeled, cored, and cut in ½-inch wedges, along with the toma-

* If you are not using garam masala, you will want to use double the amount of curry powder. Taste is your best guide.

toes, peeled and chopped if normal size, or halved if very small. Add the meat and its yogurt marinade, being careful that it does not boil (which tends to toughen meat). Along with plain rice, a good curry dinner needs several sambals served on the side—hard-boiled eggs finely chopped, disks of fresh bananas or longitudinal slices lightly fried, crisp chopped bacon; a good chutney by all means; a mixture of chopped onion, green pepper, and cucumber, or the same combination mixed with yogurt. Chopped almonds are also very good.

Variation: Curried Venison Liver   Hunters generally prefer to cook and eat liver in the field—it's at its best when it is freshest. Yet if it is brought home and frozen, and used within three to five months, deer liver makes a curry to be remembered. Brought to room temperature, it needs no marination, and it can be cooked in a sauce like the one above, with the exception of apples and other sweeteners. Sauté onions and garlic; add curry powder and ½ teaspoon of chili powder if desired; cook 2–3 minutes, then add liver cut in cubes and simmer 25 minutes. Add tomatoes, cooking about 30 minutes before stirring in garam masala (if you have it available; otherwise use more curry) and 2 teaspoons lemon juice for 5 more minutes of cooking. Serve with a dish of quartered new potatoes which have been sautéed in butter and turmeric 15 minutes before mixing in chopped spinach to cook under cover another 15 minutes; add 1 teaspoon garam masala during the last couple minutes, mixing well.

CORNMEAL PANCAKES
STUFFED WITH GAME

A delicious dish made with leftover game—Canadian goose, mallard duck, teal, or any wild bird dinner of which enough might be left so that by assiduous picking the cook may have 2 cups of finely minced meat. Carcass and separate bones must be stewed several hours ahead.

SERVES 4

THE BIRD
1 game bird carcass
1 carrot
1 unpeeled onion

1 rib celery
salt and freshly ground pepper

Break and flatten carcass, put in pot with vegetables, and cover with at least 3 cups of water. Add seasoning after simmering 3 hours or more, during which stock is considerably reduced; it must be rich in flavor and make at least 1 cup game broth in quantity.

THE PANCAKES
½ cup yellow cornmeal
1 tsp. salt
½ cup boiling water
½ cup flour
3 tsp. baking powder

½ cup milk
¼ cup water
¼ cup corn oil
1 egg, well beaten

Mix the cornmeal, salt, and boiling water; beat well, then add flour, baking powder, milk, water, corn oil, and beaten egg, blending thoroughly.

THE FILLING

2 Tb. butter
¼ cup finely chopped shallots
   or scallions
1 cup coarsely chopped mushrooms
2 Tb. flour

1 cup game broth (as above)
2 Tb. Madeira
salt and freshly ground pepper
2 cups finely chopped game bird
   meat

Melt butter in skillet and sauté shallots 4–5 minutes. Add mushrooms and cook about 5 minutes. Stir in flour and let it brown slightly. Off heat, stir in broth, returning to heat when flour is absorbed; stir until it comes to boil, then add wine and the salt and pepper, simmer 5 minutes, and add meat, letting it heat up.

Preheat oven to 400°.

While this meat filling is simmering, start the pancakes: Brush 8-inch skillet with a little butter, heat until almost smoking, and pour in enough batter to thinly cover bottom of pan after it is tipped to spread batter evenly to edges. Cook over medium heat, turning when bubbles appear on surface; cook other side until lightly browned. Repeat, making 8 pancakes in all.

Reserve the skillet in which filling cooked. Divide filling into 8 portions. Spread one portion in a line down the middle of each pancake. Turn up the edge nearest and roll. Put the rolls, seam side down, in a buttered ovenproof dish just large enough to hold all 8 of them. Bake 15 minutes at 400°.

THE SAUCE

2 Tb. butter
2 Tb. flour
2 cups game bird broth, hot

salt and freshly ground pepper
3 Tb. chopped parsley

Melt the butter in skillet in which filling cooked, scraping up brown bits and letting butter turn almost brown without burning. Blend in flour, cooking 2–3 minutes, stirring. Add hot game broth. Cook, stirring constantly as sauce thickens, and add salt and pepper to taste. When stuffed pancakes are piping hot, spoon sauce over them and sprinkle with parsley.

GAME BIRD PASTIES

That delicious and formerly ubiquitous dish called pasties (little individual meat pies) that sounds so romantically appetizing in medieval literature has all but disappeared from modern cookery. This is a pity, for not only should pasties remain among our game dishes for traditional reasons, but they are also delicious, whether served hot or cold. A schnapps appetizer and cold ale served with the pasty can make even the most blasé eater feel as if he's feasting at some ancient thatched English inn. Pasties make excellent luncheon dishes or can be served cold at a late supper.

Steak and kidney pie and chicken pie and a few surviving game pies are all that are left from a vast assortment of pies and pasties in our past.

The meat ingredients of pasties have already been cooked before they are crusted and put in the oven. They can therefore be made from leftover roasts or grilled or "rotissed" meats and birds.

This particular recipe can also be made from scratch—i.e., from uncooked birds. Remember that doves, quail, or waterfowl can be substituted for the partridges, pheasant, or grouse.

SERVES 6

3 chukar partridges or 1 large
  pheasant or 2 or 3 grouse, cooked,
  or combination (enough to
  make 2½–3 cups)
3 Tb. butter
4 Tb. flour
1 cup chicken broth
¼ cup white wine
½ tsp. grated lemon rind
½ tsp. dry tarragon
½ tsp. savory
¼ tsp. powdered cloves
3 Tb. chopped parsley
2 tsp. mushroom catsup or
  Worcestershire sauce
salt, pepper
½ cup bread crumbs
½ cup cream
2 or 3 slices of cold boiled ham,
  cut into ½" squares
short pastry (page 433)

Dice the meat from the birds in ½-inch cubes, cover, and set aside.

Prepare the white sauce for a pasty so you can control its thickness after it has been simmered with its flavors. Melt the butter, but do not brown, and stir in the flour, cooking gently a minute or so. Remove from burner and stir in broth and wine until thoroughly mixed. Return the mix to the heat and, whisking constantly, let the sauce begin to thicken. Turn heat very low and cook for 4–5 minutes, stirring frequently.

Do not be alarmed if the sauce seems too thick, for you have the cream in reserve to thin it. Add lemon rind, tarragon, savory, cloves, parsley, mushroom catsup or Worcestershire, salt and pepper, and the bread crumbs, then stir in a bit of the cream and, still over low heat, mix the ingredients. Add a little more cream a tablespoon at a time until the sauce will just run off the spoon. Season to taste.

Add the cubed bird meat and ham and put in the refrigerator to cool. When you take it out later the meats and sauce should be of the proper thickness so that they hold together on the dough as you put together the pasties.

Have ready short pastry in the same quantity you would make for a 2-layer fruit pie. Roll it out on a floured board to ⅛-inch thickness and cut twelve 6-inch circles from it. Then, dividing the quantity evenly, put a dollop of the partridge-sauce mixture on each of the circles.

Lightly wet the exposed edges of these disks with water, then cover each with a dough disk and with thumb-and-finger crimp the edges together. Brush with butter, slice a vent or two in the top of each pasty to let steam escape, and place on a cookie sheet. I sometimes "draw" a rabbit on top of each pasty with punctures made by a toothpick.

Bake in a 450° oven for 20 minutes or until pasties have achieved your preferred degree of brownness.

VENISON PASTIES

Any red game meat—moose, elk, caribou—similarly treated produces a delicious pasty.

SERVES 2–3

THE VENISON
1½–2 cups cooked venison, diced
　into ½-inch cubes
1 small onion, diced fine and
　sautéed until soft
½ green pepper, diced and sautéed
　until soft
½ tsp. thyme
¼ tsp. fennel seeds, crushed

¼ tsp. savory
2 cloves garlic, minced
1 tsp. tomato paste
1 tsp. Harvey's mushroom catsup
　or Worcestershire sauce
¼ tsp. powdered cloves
¼ cup bread crumbs
salt and pepper

THE BROWN SAUCE
3 Tb. butter
4 Tb. flour
1 cup liquid: half meat stock,
　half red wine

½ cup cream
1 dash hot sauce
1–2 dashes Kitchen Bouquet

THE PASTY
short pastry (page 433) or Bisquick

After you have diced your meat, make a brown sauce using the same method called for in making the white sauce for game bird pasties and in the same proportions (see opposite). However, the ingredients are different.

Add onion, pepper, and other ingredients in "The Venison" listing above and proceed as in recipe for Game Bird Pasties.

For this pasty, as well as for others, you can, if you wish, use a biscuit crust either of your own making or with Bisquick, but you may prefer any short pastry crust.

NOTE: These pasties are also good cold. Aquavit as appetizer and ale with the pasties are good. If you want to have a bit of fun with your guests provide only a steak knife and a mug (plus a couple of paper napkins) as utensils, and remark that in the old days a belt knife and the fingers were the only utensils *they* had.

WILD FOWL SALAD:
PHEASANT, WILD DUCK, TURKEY

From a nineteenth-century cookbook, a recipe that is still good today.

"To cold prepared fowl cut in nice size pieces, add cold, well cooked wild rice. Serve with the following salad dressing:

"Whip cream very stiff. Add 3 teaspoons prepared mustard, 3 teaspoons white vinegar, dash each of salt, pepper, celery seed, and grains of sugar to taste. (The sugar is important.) Whip well again. Mix into the fowl and wild rice. Place into a suitable refrigerator pan and chill well before serving. The same procedure may be followed using cold dressing in place of rice. The tastiness of it is dependable, however, on a good spicy dressing."

Twentieth-Century Version

2 cups cooked pheasant, partridge, wild duck, turkey, or combination, cubed
¾ cup mayonnaise
½ cup chopped celery
2 Tb. chopped scallions, with some greens

salt and pepper to taste
3 Tb. chopped parsley
1 Tb. fresh herb if possible: tarragon or basil
lettuce
1 Tb. capers (optional)

Toss pieces of fowl with mayonnaise, celery, scallions, salt and pepper, parsley, and herb. Arrange over lettuce leaves and top with a few capers, if you wish.

Variation: Instead of celery, mix in ½ cup peeled green grapes (and don't include the capers).

Sauces

Sauces and Their Uses

While there is no gainsaying that hunger itself is the best sauce, the fact remains that there are hundreds of others that compete mightily, and some, indeed, that even stimulate and heighten hunger itself.

Most of the sauces included here are intended to be served with (or over) meats, birds, and fish that have been simply roasted, broiled, sautéed, poached, or boiled.

Thus broiled venison steaks can come to the hot plates of guests who prefer their game plain, while at the same board those who relish the additional flavors of a fine sauce may find them in the sauceboat.

Here we will make no attempt to start the reader who may wish it on a sauce career. But we do want to make one strong pitch, as it were: keep in your freezer a supply of brown stock from which brown sauce is made or, if not that, do consider making up a small batch of brown sauce for very special occasions.

Gravies and derivative sauces, such as sauce poivrade or venison great sauce, made from a brown-stock-into-brown-sauce base are so superior to shortcut gravies and sauces that it is a crime to deprive your guests (and yourself) of them.

Do not be intimidated by those who say "When I eat *game*, I want it to *taste* like game; I don't want it fancied up with French sauces." If you find a person like this you can simply serve your sauce *with* a roast or broiled steaks or chops, and let these purists pass up the sauce that other guests will relish. But, remember, you also have the option of inviting to your game dinner only those who deserve it.

Sometimes, of course, such opinion is expressed by one whose experience with good sauces is limited (the "good old meat 'n' potatoes" group). Even these can often be proselytized by a fine sauce.

From Brown Stock to Brown Sauce

This lovely sauce has three noble functions; it can be used for itself with broiled or roast meats; it can be used in salmi of game and meat pies and pastries (see steak and kidney pie, page 39); and, most important perhaps, it is used in making other game sauces, such as sauce poivrade, venison and jelly sauce, moscovite sauce, sauce au sang, sauce diable, Madeira, bordelaise, chasseur, chevreuil Robert, and brown tarragon sauce.

When you know you are going to be cooking red meat game regularly, and, more, expect to prepare a few meals where you won't mind *not* taking shortcuts, why not make up a supply of the broth or stock that so many recipes call for? To be sure, that "stock" can be bouillon cubes and water, but that liquid can be made ineluctably better without too much trouble. And the stock (brown stock), as we have already noted, can be stored or even frozen.

BROWN STOCK

MAKES ABOUT 5 CUPS

1½ lb. beef bones (or game bones)
1½ lb. veal bones
1 chicken or game bird carcass,
  if you have one on hand
  (optional)
1 cup game stew meat, cut into
  1″ cubes
4 Tb. diced boiled ham or Canadian
  bacon (optional)
1 carrot, sliced
2 onions, sliced

2 rib celery with leaves
10 cups water
8 peppercorns
2 tsp. salt
3 sprigs parsley
2 bay leaves
½ tsp. thyme
¼ tsp. savory
6 juniper berries, crushed
  (optional)

Put the bones, carcass (if you have it), stew meat, and ham in a shallow roasting pan, with the carrot and onions among them, and place in a 400°–450° oven. Let them brown, but watch them; they should "roast" to a dark brown in 30–45 minutes.

Put the richly browned bones, carcass, meat, ham, and vegetables in a kettle with the water, peppercorns, salt, and herbs. While bringing slowly to a boil, pour off all but a couple teaspoons of the fat in the pan in which the bones, etc., were roasted, add a bit of water, and, using a wooden spoon, stir the pan bottom over stove to scrape up the browned goodies in the bottom of the roasting pan. Add to the soup kettle.

Simmer for 3½–4 hours, skimming occasionally during the early stages of the cooking.

When reduced to about half, strain and store in the refrigerator or freezer to use as the base when you make brown sauce.

BROWN SAUCE FROM BROWN STOCK

If you are a purist you will prepare this "mother sauce" as Ray Sokolov instructs you to in his inimitable book *The Saucier's Apprentice*. If not, you can prepare a "quick" brown sauce that will be mighty fine with this recipe. I said "quick" brown sauce, but even this one must simmer for 2½ hours or so. It is worth it.

MAKES 2½ CUPS

four 3″ marrow bones (with
  marrow in them, no solid
  bones)
½ cup marrow fat
1 cup finely diced large onion
2 carrots, diced small
2 cloves garlic
1 rib celery with leaves, diced
  small
2 bay leaves
½ tsp. thyme

2 Tb. diced ham or bacon
2 Tb. flour
1 cup tomato purée or sauce
3 sprigs parsley
4 cups canned brown stock
  (preceding recipe) or
  beef broth
12 peppercorns
½ lb. game (or beef) stew meat
  cut into 1″ cubes

Vary the Commercial Cooking Sauces

That wonderful ingredient Worcestershire sauce, a stand-by sauce for steak and chops, an addition to a host of recipes, does have some English cousins that you might like to set alongside the fabulous Lee & Perrins sauce on your shelves.

Like Worcestershire itself, three of them include anchovies in their ingredients. Among others, George Watkins, London, makes them, and it is the products of this firm which we know best on our side of the Atlantic.

The first of these is anchovy sauce itself, a fine addition to any stew and an ingredient of a host of sauces you may make. It can substitute in any recipe for anchovy fillets or anchovy paste.

Almost as famous as Worcestershire sauce for steaks, chops, stews, and braises is Harvey's sauce, a veteran English sauce, that dates back at least to the eighteenth century. Colonel Hawker called for it in his wild duck sauce (see page 205).

The third is walnut sauce, also a sauce with a long tradition, including anchovies but derived also from English walnuts.

A fourth traditional sauce is, of course, mushroom catsup. Although this sauce is not anchovy-based, it was widely used by our ancestors here and in England.

Do you need them all? No, but it is fun to have them, just the same. I've both Harvey's sauce and walnut sauce in my own homemade barbecue sauce, for example, but Worcestershire alone does handsomely.

None of these sauces, save Worcestershire, is certain to be on super-market shelves, but they do turn up on shelves of exotic products occasionally. Bloomingdale's in New York City stocks all of them, and no doubt other similar stores across the country do likewise.

About an hour before you begin the sauce put the marrow bones in a pie pan and into a hot oven, 400°. Roast them until they begin to brown, reserving the tried-out marrow fat. Heat 1 tablespoon of the marrow fat in a skillet and sauté onion, carrots, garlic, celery, bay leaves, thyme, and ham or bacon until the vegetables are soft or translucent.

Put these with remainder of marrow fat into a heavy saucepan and stir in flour. Cook and stir until flour is brown.

Add tomato purée or sauce and parsley. Mix all by stirring and add the beef broth, peppercorns, marrow bones, and stew meat. Bring to boil, then turn down heat and simmer for an hour, skimming the fat off occasionally.

After about an hour, remove the stew meat and marrow bones (use the meat for another purpose) and continue the low simmer until the sauce has been reduced to about half. It should be of the consistency of cream. Strain and serve, or use as base for another sauce; in the case of venison (roast or steaks) use it for sauce poivrade or hunter's sauce (sauce chasseur) or bordelaise.

To Make a Supplement Game Meat Gravy

This little kitchen trick has two uses: (1) for making gravy when the roast seems to have left too skimpy a residue for the gravy to be sufficiently flavorful and (2) for those occasions when you have used all of the original gravy but have enough roast left over to make, say, hot venison sandwiches or a leftover dish calling for leftover gravy—if you had the gravy. The trick is to trim off the browned crust (both fat and flesh) and some of the gross, unbrowned fat and make your own dredgings and fat for a roux.

Trim out 2–3 tablespoon equivalents of *gross* fat, cube it, and melt it in a skillet as you would render out cubes of salt pork.

Also trim off some of the *browned* fat and with a scissors cut it fine and perhaps pulverize it in a mortar.

Do likewise with some of the meat itself, cutting it fine.

Add the browned fat and the meat particle dredgings to the fat and sauté together for 3–4 minutes.

Remove the unmelted lumps of *gross* fat.

Mix an equal amount of flour into the fat; stir and brown lightly over low heat. Then proceed to make gravy with beef broth or with water in which you have melted a bouillon cube.

This will be just as good as the original gravy you made from the roast's dredgings—in many cases, even better, for it is made with *authentic* meat essences although produced by deceit.

A SIMPLER BROWN SAUCE

YIELDS ABOUT 2½–3 CUPS

3½ cups beef bouillon, boiling
½ cup dry vermouth
2 Tb. tomato paste or catsup
2 sprigs parsley
1 bay leaf
¼ tsp. thyme
¼ tsp. rosemary

½ cup finely chopped onions
½ cup finely chopped carrots
½ cup finely chopped celery
2 Tb. diced boiled ham or salt pork
4 Tb. butter
3 Tb. flour

In a saucepan combine the bouillon, vermouth, tomato paste or catsup, and herbs, bring to a boil, and set aside.

In a saucepan sauté the vegetables and the diced meat in the butter for 6–8 minutes.

Blend in the flour and, stirring constantly over low heat, cook for 7–10 minutes or until flour *slowly* turns to nice, nutty brown. During this process bring liquid to a boil.

Take the browned vegetables and flour off heat, pour in the boiling bouillon, and with a wire whisk blend thoroughly.

Set on the lowest heat you can manage (use an asbestos simmering pad under the saucepan if your low heat boils the mixture in too lively a manner), cock a lid on it to allow steam to escape, and simmer for 2–2½ hours, skimming off scum 2–3 times in the early stages.

Watch the simmering sauce to be sure it does not thicken too much; if so, add liquid judiciously. You should end up with about 3 cups of brown sauce after straining it.

Cool, cover, and refrigerate. You can freeze the sauce if you wish.

Seasoned or Herb Butter

The blender and now the food processor have made the preparation of herb butters a breeze.

For broiled game birds I make it with sage, thyme, and tarragon, and in all herb butters I always use parsley and scallions (including some of the tops) or shallots (and sometimes garlic)—see proportions below.

A special mix can be made to substitute for the flavors found in béarnaise sauce—shallots, tarragon, and chervil.

HERB BUTTER FOR BASTING BROILING GAME BIRDS

SERVES 4

6 Tb. butter, cut in pieces
1½ tsp. dried tarragon
1 tsp. dried sage
½ tsp. dried thyme
1 Tb. fresh parsley

4–5 shallots, peeled and sliced,
   or 6 scallions, chopped
½ tsp. minced garlic or 1 small
   clove (optional)

In using a blender or the steel blade of a processor, bring butter to room temperature, cut it in several slices, and put butter and herbs and other seasonings (roughly chopped parsley, shallots, scallions, etc.) in the processor all at once.

Processing takes a matter of seconds, but be sure to stop processor a couple times to push down the butter-herb mix that accumulates on the sides of the processor.

The seasoned butter should then be put into a plastic container and firmed up in the refrigerator.

Green and dry herb equivalents: roughly, ⅓ teaspoon powdered herbs (like thyme) and ½ teaspoon dried herbs are the equivalent of 1 tablespoon fresh herbs.

Other Uses of Herb Butter

Herb butter may be melted and poured over broiled fish fillets, broiled salmon steaks, chops, other steaks, etc.

Or it may be melted, mixed with wine, and used as a baster while the fish or chops are broiling.

NOTE: In using dried herbs, as most of us do, two important ones lose their flavor rather quickly—sage and chervil. Dried tarragon or oregano, on the other hand, hold their pungency much longer. Always try to use fresh parsley and chives.

Bay Leaves and Other Real or So-Called
Fighting Herbs and Spices
(with comment on some herbs that are bashful)

Over the years I have discovered that either my taste buds are insensitive (actually I doubt this very much) or other cooks are too conservative in the use of bay leaves. One says, "Be careful to use no more than half a bay leaf, as this seasoning is very dominating." I find it just the opposite; most recipes use bay too sparingly. In our book we have tried to strike a happy medium, but each cook should decide for herself or himself how much to use. For me, when a stew recipe or a recipe for making a meat or bird stock calls for quantity, I usually double or treble such quantities when the herb is bay leaf.

Tarragon is a bully in the company of other herbs, and so is savory, and unless you wish the herb in question to *be* the dominating taste, then you must outnumber the dominating herb. Oregano is also a big-muscle herb, and one of the finest additions to a stew or a fricasse is ground fennel seed, but fennel is also an herb that is overeager to serve you and will overpower a bouquet garni. (Incidentally, if you find, as I do, that pulverizing fennel seed with a mortar and pestle is tedious, empty your pepper mill temporarily and grind the fennel seed. Then empty out the unground seed and put back the peppercorns, grinding a few times to eliminate the bits of fennel remaining in the mill.)

On the other hand, I find most cooks call for too little chili powder. Chili powder's bark is worse than its bite; its dark, strong-looking color belies its taste. The same goes for commercial curry powders, but then curry makers really should make up their own "curry powders" from a combination of the several herbs involved (see page 322).

Among the spices, powdered clove is a strong competitor, while nutmeg, it seems to me, is a bashful spice. I have never noticed that a "pinch of nutmeg" will even make its presence known. Incidentally if you use nutmeg, I urge you to buy whole nutmegs and grate them; ground nutmeg can turn to sawdust quickly on the shelf, but grating it only when called for will preserve its fine flavor. Ginger, like dry mustard, is a spice that brings a needed bite rather than a distinctive flavor to the combinations it is often used with. Cinnamon, on the other hand, can be used generously, as it is intended to dominate in sauerbraten, mincemeats, pumpkin or squash pies, and Indian pudding.

Many fine cooks add the herbs in a stew or sauce recipe for the last 15–20 minutes of the simmering. Personally, I don't do this usually except in cases where I want an ingredient like garlic to taste strong in the final dish—for further remarks about garlic, see page 35.

Do remember that salt is not the only ingredient that can be "corrected" in the late stages of a simmering stew or sauce. You can "correct the seasoning" in the case of herbs or spices too about 20–30 minutes before the dish is done, i.e., you can add herbs at that stage if you feel the sauce or gravy needs more herb taste.

SAGE MUSTARD À L'ELENA

My friend Elena Lorenzen gave me this recipe just as a change-of-pace mustard, but I think of it now as a fine substitute for Dijon in poultry recipes and especially good as a spread for broiled fish.

MAKES ABOUT 1¼ CUPS

½ cup Colman's Dry Mustard
⅛ cup sugar
½ tsp. salt
2 eggs

½ cup cider vinegar
½ cup water
2 Tb. butter
2 tsp. powdered sage

Combine the mustard, sugar, and salt.

Beat the eggs in the vinegar and water. Add to the mustard mixture in a thin stream, stirring the while.

Cook over moderate heat, stirring, until the mix is smoothly thickened. Stir in the butter and the sage.

For individual taste, two important controls are the sugar and the sage. Experiment to arrive at the balance between sugar and vinegar you prefer; also for the degree of sage flavor.

ANCHOVY AND CAPER SAUCE

This will be enough sauce for ½ pound dry spaghetti.

MAKES ABOUT ⅔ CUP

2-oz. can anchovy fillets
⅓ cup olive or salad oil
2 cloves garlic, quartered
¼ tsp. thyme
1½ Tb. capers

1 tsp. capers liquid or lemon
   juice
1 dash Tabasco
1½ Tb. minced parsley

First drain and then rinse anchovy fillets under faucet to reduce saltiness. Dry with paper towel and chop fine.

Heat oil in small saucepan and in it soak garlic until soft. Remove garlic and remove skillet from fire.

Stir into garlic-flavored oil the chopped anchovies and the rest of the ingredients.

BASTING LIQUID FOR BROILED GAME MEAT

This basting sauce is delicious for broiled meat.

MAKES ABOUT 1½ CUPS

½ cup olive or corn oil
1 cup red wine
1 tsp. rosemary

3 cloves garlic, crushed
½ tsp. Tabasco or pepper flakes
   to taste

Combine the oil and the wine. Crush the rosemary leaves and the garlic with a small mortar and pestle or chop very fine or spin in a food processor and add, with the Tabasco, to the mixture. Let stand a couple of hours.

GAME MEAT BARBECUE SAUCE

The fat ribs of game animals are usually braised, but they can also be barbecued to make a delicious fare. They should be sawed into 3–4-inch lengths and broiled under a low flame or over charcoal. The length of broiling time will vary according to the size and meatiness of the animal ribs, but one rule is basic: Have the ribs half done before brushing with the sauce, for you do not want the barbecue sauce to carbonize before the ribs are done.

There are a number of prepared barbecued sauces (Open Pit being in my opinion the best I know of), but a sauce prepared on your own stove will be even better. This one, my favorite, is an easy chore, as it is a one-step process: everything goes in at once. It goes without saying that this sauce is also delicious for barbecued pork spareribs or, for that matter, with poultry or game birds.

MAKES ABOUT 1½ CUPS

¾ cup red wine
¼ cup vinegar
2 cloves garlic, minced
1 onion, finely minced
1 Tb. cooking oil
2½ Tb. Worcestershire sauce
1 Tb. Harvey's sauce (or Heinz 57)
1 Tb. walnut sauce (optional)
a dash or two of Tabasco

1 Tb. brown sugar
⅓ cup catsup
1 tsp. dry mustard
½ tsp. powdered or dried thyme
½ tsp. oregano
1 tsp. salt
a few grinds of pepper
1 tsp. paprika
1 Tb. chili powder

Put all of these ingredients in a saucepan, heat to near-boil, then simmer for 15–20 minutes. Control the consistency with more wine if it gets too thick, but it should end up with about the same consistency as a slow-pouring catsup like Heinz's. Correct for taste.

CELERY SAUCE FOR TURKEY, PARTRIDGE, AND OTHER GAME

Here is the recipe, as Mrs. Randolph wrote it in *The Virginia Housewife:*

"Wash and pare a large bunch of celery very clean, cut it into little bits and boil it softly 'till it is tender; add a half pint of cream, some mace, nutmeg, and a small piece of butter rolled in flour—then boil it gently. This is a good sauce for roasted or boiled fowls, turkeys, partridges or any other game."

BREAD SAUCES

The bread sauces today are a characteristic part of British cookery, served usually with roasted birds or roasted game. They add a fillip of style to a game dinner not only because of their texture and wide variety of flavors, but because of their ancient tradition. British hunters and shooters have garnished their spit- and oven-roasted game with bread sauces since the Middle Ages.

To give the modern cook a notion of simple bread sauce base the following recipe will produce it. Of course, this basic recipe could include a variety of other ingredients to make sauces appropriate for game, game birds, wild fowl, or fish.

MAKES 1½ CUPS

1 cup water or milk
½ cup of onions, sautéed
1 Tb. butter

2 cloves
¼ cup bread crumbs
2 Tb. cream

Bring liquid, onions, butter, and cloves to a boil and add the bread crumbs. Remove the cloves if you wish after simmering over a very low heat for 15 minutes. Beat with a hand beater or in a blender, then stir in the cream.

Once you have made this basic base with the above proportions you can then decide whether the thickness is to your preference. If you want the mix thicker, use more bread crumbs.

Preparing Bread Crumbs for Bread Sauces

Bread sauces can be made from commercial bread crumbs, plain or flavored, but on occasion, you may want to prepare the crumbs yourself. As I have noted, any red meat game stew or braised dish is vastly improved if you include marrow bones. In the case of game dishes one sometimes uses the bones of the game animal itself, but when not available, beef marrow bones will do handsomely. And since these marrow bones should be browned darkly in the oven before they are put in the stew, one might as well use this step to make bread crumbs.

4–6 marrow bones (preferably cut so one sees marrow at both ends of the bone segments)

Put marrow bones in a pie pan and brown in a 400° oven. Remove marrow bones and save to use in a stew. Pour remaining marrow into skillet and fry two or three pieces of white bread in it until both sides of the bread are browned and the marrow fat absorbed.

You can also cut the bread into croutons for the top of the meat gravy or sauce or crumb the fried bread with a rolling pin and use it to thicken the stew. This is a much tastier way to thicken a meat stew than to use flour or cornstarch dissolved in water. And, of course, it produces a bread sauce in the process.

NOTE: Bread fried in marrow fat, or for that matter bread fried in bacon fat, served hot with salt and pepper atop, is delicious. Bread so prepared can be placed under the spit of a rotisserie to catch the essences of broiled birds and the bird served atop the bread slices.

CAMERON BREAD SAUCE

Because of a bit of Caledonian pride, I cannot resist including this bread sauce of the clove from Sara Walker's *The Highland Fling Cookbook*. Try it with roast or broiled game birds. It is stuffinglike in texture—and in purpose.

MAKES 2 CUPS

1 cup milk	2 Tb. butter
4 cloves	½ tsp. salt
1 medium onion, peeled	¼ tsp. white pepper
2 cups bread crumbs	¼ tsp. allspice

Put the milk in the top of a double boiler. Stick the cloves into the whole onion and add to the milk. Add the bread crumbs and simmer over medium heat for 30 minutes.

Remove the onion with the cloves and discard. Add the butter, salt, pepper, and allspice. Simmer for 10 minutes more. Serve in a sauceboat.

QUICK TARRAGON BREAD SAUCE FOR ROAST BIRDS (OR POACHED OR BAKED FISH)

MAKES ABOUT 1¼ CUPS

1 cup chicken broth and/or pan drippings, or 1 cup of water and 1 tsp. chicken bouillon, if powdered, or 2 cubes	½ tsp. dried tarragon
	a pinch of thyme
	4–5 grinds of fresh peppercorns
1 tsp. dried onion flakes	1–2 Tb. pan drippings from roasted bird (or butter)
¼ cup commercial bread crumbs (see page 361 for preparing your own crumbs)	2 Tb. medium or heavy cream

In saucepan bring cold broth or liquid with chicken bouillon and onion flakes to boil. Lower heat and stir in bread crumbs in which you have mixed tarragon, thyme, and pepper. Add pan drippings and/or butter, and simmer for 5 minutes or so, stirring occasionally.

Meanwhile *warm* the cream and stir into sauce. *Serve hym forth* with roast or grilled pheasant, grouse, quail, or poached fish.

HOLLANDAISE SAUCE

The method used here is quite different from the Béarnaise below, although the sauces are very similar. It is simply a matter of two different techniques to achieve the same end. Try each one and settle on the one that works best for you.

MAKES ABOUT ¾ CUP

2 egg yolks	salt
fresh lemon juice	pinch cayenne (optional)
¼ lb. cold butter, cut in 8 pieces	

In a double boiler or a very heavy pot set over a flame tamer, whisk the eggs until they are well blended, turn lemon-colored, and start to thicken. The top of the double boiler should not be directly on boiling water but set a little above it, and the water should just be simmering. If using a heavy pot, be sure the heat is low. Add 1 tablespoon lemon juice when thickening starts.

Start adding the butter one piece at a time, whisking each piece in until it is incorporated with the eggs. Continue doing this until all the butter is used up. It should take about 2 minutes, at which point the sauce will be thick. If at any point you sense that the sauce is about to separate, quickly add a teaspoon of cold milk or cream.

Now whisk in about 1 more teaspoon lemon juice, a pinch of salt, and optional cayenne. Taste to see that the sauce is lemony enough for your taste. You may leave it for a short while over hot, not boiling, water, and it will thicken even further; you may have to whisk in a little warm water before serving if it is too thick.

SAUCE MOUSSELLINE

This fish sauce enables the cook to "stretch" Hollandaise, for Sauce Mousseline is Hollandaise Sauce into which whipped cream has been folded. The proportion? About ½ cup of whipped cream to 1 cup of Hollandaise.

BÉARNAISE SAUCE

This is one of the very finest and perhaps *the* most versatile of the sauces for both game meat and fish. I have made this sauce "ten different ways," but I believe this is the best of them. Béarnaise sauce served beside a thick, rare broiled moose, elk, or venison steak seems made just for this luscious entrée; on the other hand, it provokes high praise always when served instead of a routine tartar sauce with a delicately flavored, sautéed salmon steak or with poached salmon or sautéed trout.

THE HERB-WINE LIQUID
⅔ cup white wine
3 shallots or scallions, finely
  minced

1½ tsp. dried tarragon
1½ tsp. dried chervil

Put all above ingredients together in a saucepan, bring to boil, and reduce until you have about 5 tablespoons left. Strain into another saucepan, but retain the shallots and herbs in the strainer.

MAKES ABOUT 1¼ cups

THE SAUCE
3 egg yolks
1 Tb. lemon juice, warmed
¼ lb. butter, melted and warm

⅛ tsp. cayenne pepper
¼ tsp. salt

You will need a smallish crock or thick bowl that can be set snugly, but shallowly, into the top of your double boiler base. Put 1½ inches of water in the double boiler base and bring it to a boil, then turn down heat and let it just simmer.

Meanwhile in a small saucepan just barely bubble the strained herb-wine liquid. (After straining, you will have about four tablespoons of liquid.)

Off heat beat up the 3 egg yolks with a wire whisk, place the crock onto the boiler base, and continue beating until the yolks begin to thicken. Then add 1 tablespoon of the bubbling strained herb-wine liquid, and beat again until the eggs again begin to thicken. Repeat the same drill until you have whisked in the remaining 3 tablespoons of the bubbling liquid. When the eggs begin to thicken after the fourth tablespoon, then beat in the tablespoon of warmed lemon juice. Beat again until the mix again thickens somewhat, then remove the crock from the fire and turn the fire off under the double boiler base.

Now slowly dribble in the melted butter, beating continuously, and add the cayenne and salt. Whip the sauce smooth and then taste it. If you feel you want more flavor scrape in some of the paste from the strainer.

By this time the steak should be broiling on its second side, but you can hold this sauce for a half hour or more by placing the crock over the boiler base and covering the sauce partially with a saucer or small plate.

If, delighted with your initial results, you discover the sauce has curdled, then whisk in slowly 1 tablespoon of cream.

THE ALL-PURPOSE WHITE SAUCE
(White Sauce, Cream Sauce, Sauce Béchamel)

This sauce, known variously by the three names above, dominates most kitchens where sauces are concerned. It is, or can be, the base for a variety of derivative sauces, but by itself white sauce has become a part of hundreds of appetizing dishes, including many in this book.

It can, of course, be made in various consistencies. This recipe is for a white sauce of medium thickness.

MAKES ABOUT 1 CUP

2 tablespoons butter or margarine
2 tablespoons flour

1 cup liquid (see below)
salt and freshly ground pepper

Melt the butter in a skillet or saucepan and stir in the flour. Cook over low heat for a couple of minutes stirring, then off heat, with a whisk, stir in the liquid. Return to heat and cook for 3–5 minutes over low flame. Whisk while the sauce thickens. Add salt and pepper to taste.

For a thinner sauce use 1 tablespoon each of butter and flour; for a thicker sauce 3 tablespoons each with the same 1 cup of liquid.

We say "liquid," for this sauce can be made with milk, cream, broth of all kinds, or a mixture of milk or cream and other liquids. It is often made with half broth and half wine.

When other ingredients are added to the basic white sauce it becomes, variously, sauces by other names, e.g.:

Mushroom cream sauce—when mushrooms sautéed in butter are added.

Mornay sauce—when grated Parmesan is stirred into the white sauce and then simmered 2–3 minutes (½ cup in the above recipe).

Au gratin sauce—when ¼–½ cup grated Swiss cheese with 1 teaspoon Dijon mustard is added.

Herb sauce—when to any of the above herbs are added (½ teaspoon of dry herb in the 1 cup of liquid above).

Garlic sauce—when a clove of garlic is minced into the basic sauce or into any of the above variations (shallots, scallions, too).

The number of sauces that can be derived from the basic white sauce is infinite, limited only by your own palate and ingenuity—for instance, Worcestershire, Harvey's, and walnut sauces (see page 355) as well as mushroom catsup and anchovy sauce can be good additions, often with other flavors.

TOMATO SAUCE

This recipe makes an ample amount of tomato sauce so you can freeze some and always have it on hand. Of course, when you have fresh tomatoes from your garden, you will want to substitute fresh ripe ones for the canned.

MAKES ABOUT 1½ QUARTS

2 medium onions, chopped
2 fat cloves garlic, chopped
⅓ cup olive oil
two 28-ounce cans whole
 (preferably Italian plum)
 tomatoes
about ⅓ cup parsley (preferably
 Italian), roughly chopped

2–3 sprigs fresh basil or
 ½ tsp. dried
½ tsp. thyme
¼ tsp. oregano
½ tsp. cumin
¼ cup tomato paste
1 cup beef or game broth
salt and freshly ground pepper

Sauté the onions and garlic in the olive oil in a large pot until limp and golden. Don't let them brown at all.

Add the tomatoes, the herbs, tomato paste, and broth, stirring to mix thoroughly. Salt lightly at this stage and pepper liberally. Bring to a boil, then lower the heat and simmer, partially covered, for about 1 hour.

Taste and correct the seasoning; it will probably need more salt.

Put the sauce through a food mill or a strainer and freeze what you're not using right away.

MUSHROOM SAUCE

MAKES ABOUT 1¾ CUPS

½ lb. mushrooms, sliced
3 shallots (or whites of scallions)
3 Tb. butter
2 Tb. flour
½ cup chicken or game bird stock

½ cup heavy cream
½ tsp. tarragon (1 Tb. fresh,
 if you have it)
2 Tb. dry sherry or Marsala
salt and freshly ground pepper

Sauté the mushrooms and shallots in the butter, tossing and stirring for 4–5 minutes.

Stir in the flour, blending well and cooking for another minute or so.

Off heat stir in the stock and cream, return to the heat, and stir until sauce thickens. Add tarragon, wine, and salt and pepper to taste. Let bubble gently a few minutes until it is the consistency you want; if too thick, add a little more broth; if too thin, cook down a little more.

Variation for Red Game Meats: Instead of chicken stock and cream, use 1 cup rich beef or game stock and season with ½ teaspoon thyme and ¼ teaspoon rosemary in place of tarragon. Add a few shakes of Worcestershire and use 1 tablespoon brandy in place of the wine (or stick with Marsala, if you prefer).

===== BEACH PLUM JELLY SAUCE =====

When some of your guests like their game served "plain," e.g., roasted goose, duck or pheasant or grilled game chops or steaks, you can please the remainder by serving this simple sauce on the side. This is a versatile and tangy sauce that always pleases. If you can't obtain beach plum jelly, then don't worry, for red currant or plum jelly is just as good.

MAKES 1¼ CUPS

1 cup beach plum jelly
  (or red currant or plum)
4 Tb. butter
½ tsp. mushroom catsup or
  Worcestershire sauce

1 Tb. horseradish
¼ tsp. powdered thyme

In a saucepan combine all of the ingredients and stir over simmering heat until the jelly and butter are melted and melded with the other ingredients.
  Serve hot in a sauceboat.

===== MUSHROOM CATSUP =====

Cross & Blackwell and Watkins both make this delicious addition to wild duck sauces, but you can make it yourself and doing so is simple.

MAKES 1 CUP

2 lb. mushrooms
2 Tb. salt
½ cup port wine
½ cup cider vinegar
½ tsp. ground allspice
¼ tsp. ground cloves

¼ tsp. ground mace
¼ tsp. ground nutmeg
¼ tsp. pepper
1″ squeeze of anchovy paste
2 dashes Angostura bitters

If you have a food processor or a blender whirl the mushrooms fine (but do not liquefy). Stir in the salt and put in a bowl or plastic refrigerator container for 2–3 days. Stir the salt and mushroom mix whenever you think of it.
  Drain and press the mushrooms (indeed after washing off salt keep the mushroom pulp to make minced mushrooms, called duxelles). Add remaining ingredients to the mushroom juice in a saucepan, bring to a boil, and simmer for 10–15 minutes. Cool, bottle, and keep in the refrigerator. You'll never regret it.

NOTE: Although recipes in this book will sometimes call for mushroom catsup specifically, remember that it can be used like Worcestershire or Harvey's sauce in a variety of stews, sauces, etc.

PESTO

This aromatic Italian sauce, used primarily for pasta, can add zest to a number of dishes. Make it in the summer when basil is abundant and freeze extra containers of it so that you can dip into it all winter long. Be sure to have a film of olive oil over the top when storing and cover tightly.

MAKES ABOUT 1¾ CUPS

3 cups loosely packed basil leaves
3 cloves garlic
¾ teaspoon salt

2 Tb. pine nuts or walnuts
½ cup olive oil
½ cup freshly grated Parmesan

Spin the basil, garlic, salt, and nuts in a food processor or blender until you have a paste. Add the olive oil, blending to make a smooth puree.

If you are going to use the pesto for pasta, stir in the Parmesan just before dressing the hot pasta. Do not add the cheese before freezing pesto. Also, when using pesto as a coating for game birds or fish, eliminate the cheese.

PESTO SAUCE FOR GAME

MAKES ABOUT 1¼ CUPS

livers from the birds plus
  2 chicken livers
3 Tb. butter
⅓ cup finely diced onions or
  shallots
½ cup sliced mushrooms

⅔ cup dry white wine or
  dry vermouth
½ tsp. dried mint or spearmint
3–4 Tb. Pesto
  (see preceding recipe)
½ cup cream

Sauté the livers in the butter until done but still pink in the middle. Reserve.
Sauté onions and mushrooms in skillet in which livers were sautéed.
Smash livers to paste and add with all of the other ingredients, save the cream, to the onions and mushrooms, cover, and simmer for 7 minutes.
Stir in cream and heat, but do not boil.

SAUCE VERTE

When you want to serve a quick luncheon dish and have leftover game roast that you can slice up and serve as cold cuts, try this sauce. It is also excellent when served in place of tartar sauce; it is excellent with cold poached fish. Its startling green color will cheer up the kind of guest who looks askance at a cold-cut lunch, as I confess I sometimes do. Incidentally it is wonderful, too, with cold sliced veal roast.

You can prepare this from scratch or with spinach that has been frozen, but in either case just *blanch* the spinach in boiling water and then drain and cool.

A friend tells me that sauce verte spread on salmon steaks and then broiled about 8 inches from the heat is also fine. I mean to try it the next time I can persuade myself that this sauce may not be better served with *cold* poached salmon. In any case, for whatever its use, don't fail to add this sauce to your repertoire.

MAKES ABOUT 1 CUP

½ lb. fresh spinach or
  ½ box frozen spinach
1 slice white bread,
  crusts removed
1 hard-boiled egg, quartered
one 4-inch squeeze of anchovy
  paste or 3–4 fillets of anchovies,
  chopped, or 1 Tb. anchovy sauce

½ cup olive oil or salad oil
juice of 1 lemon
1 clove garlic, sliced
½ tsp. Dijon mustard
½ tsp. dried chervil
1½ Tb. drained and coarsely
  chopped capers
freshly ground black pepper

Blanch the spinach by covering with boiling water and cooking 1 minute. Drain, and let cool. Set up blender or food processor. Put in the spinach from which you have squeezed all of the excess moisture (you can press it out with the bowl of a spoon in a strainer).

Moisten the bread slice with water and squeeze out the moisture; use enough to make about 2½ tablespoons of paste. Add bread paste, the egg, anchovy paste (or chopped fillets or anchovy sauce), the oil, lemon juice, garlic, mustard, and chervil to the spinach and blend quickly to a purée.

Scrape and pour the sauce into a bowl, mix in the chopped capers, grind in pepper, and taste. The anchovies may well have provided enough salt; if not, add salt and then set the sauce in the refrigerator to chill. If you are in a big hurry chill in the freezer compartment, but don't forget it.

SAUCE GALATINE

This sauce was among those served over meat fillets at Henry IV's great coronation feast. The recipes in the 1390 manuscripts often called for this sauce over meaty fowl as well as fish.

MAKES ABOUT ½ CUP

⅓ cup bread crumbs*
1 tsp. powdered galingale†
¼ tsp. powdered cinnamon
¼ tsp. powdered ginger

1 cup beef or fish stock
2 Tb. vinegar, or more to taste
salt

Mix crumbs with the three spices. Add stock, vinegar, and salt and simmer over low heat until thickened as desired.

   * Or fry bread in bacon grease until crisp. Crumb with rolling pin.
   † Powdered galingale may be obtained at some gourmet shops; it is an Indonesian herb.

HORSERADISH SAUCE

Here is a quick, simple horseradish sauce that goes especially well with sliced red meats or small furred game.

MAKES ABOUT ½ CUP

¼ cup mayonnaise
¼ cup sour cream
½ tsp. Dijon mustard

½ tsp. lemon juice
4 Tb. horseradish

Mix ingredients in a bowl and control thickness with sweet cream if need be.

MAYONNAISE

Mayonnaise is so simple to make in a food processor or a blender that the junior partner would seldom settle for store-bought mayonnaise. Even done by hand it is not a demanding task.

MAKES ABOUT 1½ CUPS

1 tsp. mustard, Dijon preferred
about ¾ tsp. salt
1 egg and 1 egg yolk
(for food processor) or 2 whole
eggs (for blender) or 2 egg yolks
(for handmade)

1–1¼ cups oil: peanut or
vegetable combined with some
good olive oil
2 tsp. lemon juice
about 2 tsp. wine vinegar

For the food processor, put the mustard, salt, and one whole egg plus one egg yolk into the container and process for a minute until lemony.

For the blender, put 2 whole eggs with the mustard and salt and blend for 1 minute.

For the hand method put 2 egg yolks (and be sure they are at room temperature) into a warm bowl with the mustard and salt and beat for about 2 minutes.

Start adding the oil rather slowly at first to the food processor bowl or the blender, then pour more quickly until the mayonnaise becomes nice and thick. By hand, pour very slowly at first, beating steadily, then as it begins to thicken you can pour the oil in a bit faster.

Now with the motor running pour in the lemon juice and most of the vinegar. Add more oil until you have the thickness you like, then adjust the seasonings, adding a little more salt and vinegar if you wish. By hand simply stir in the seasonings.

Store mayonnaise in the refrigerator in a clean jar with a top. It will keep about two weeks.

RÉMOULADE SAUCE

This is an accumulated, built-up recipe for my favorite fish sauce. I began with nine ingredients and now have fourteen. I believe I have this easy-to-make recipe perfected at last for my taste at least. I also use it for cold meats, tomatoes, and cucumbers.

MAKES 1 CUP

1 cup mayonnaise
1 Tb. anchovy sauce or
   2″ anchovy paste
2 medium or 1 large clove
   garlic, minced
1 Tb. chopped parsley
1 tsp. dried chervil
1 tsp. dried tarragon

1 Tb. minced capers and juice
1½ Tb. finely minced dill pickle
1½ Tb. Dijon mustard
2 tsp. prepared horseradish
1 tsp. paprika
½ tsp. Worcestershire sauce
1 dash Tabasco

To assemble the sauce merely mix the ingredients in a bowl, making sure that all are thoroughly distributed and blended.

Refrigerate, overnight preferably, for the sauce, though delicious when first made, is even better a few hours later.

YOGURT-DILL SAUCE

A simple, light, tart sauce for cold game birds and particularly for cold fish. You can vary the herbs, but try to use fresh.

MAKES ABOUT 1 CUP

½ cup mayonnaise (for
   homemade, see page 369)
½ cup yogurt
2 Tb. chopped fresh dill

3 scallions, chopped (including
   most of green part)
salt and freshly ground pepper
1 Tb. drained capers (optional)

Mix all but the last optional ingredient together, adding salt and pepper to taste. If you like, sprinkle capers over the top.

CUCUMBERS AND SOUR CREAM
FOR POACHED FISH

This is a side dish in a sense, but it can be thought of as a fish sauce as well. I usually serve this with cold poached salmon, and I think it delicious. Although I always wilt the sliced cucumbers first, you can use them just chilled and sliced if you prefer.

SERVES 4

2 cucumbers, peeled and chilled
⅓ cup salt
water and 3–4 ice cubes
3 Tb. olive oil or other
   cooking oil
1 Tb. wine vinegar or lemon juice

3 cloves garlic, squashed
¼ tsp. pepper
1 tsp. Dijon or other prepared
   mustard
1 Tb. capers, crushed or squashed
½ cup sour cream

Thinly slice the chilled cucumbers in a bowl. Add the salt, ice cubes, and enough water to cover about 30–45 minutes before you make the sauce.

While the cucumber slices are wilting, mix and shake up, in a covered jar or salad dressing shaker, all the rest of the ingredients except the sour cream.

When ready to serve, rinse the cucumber slices through two or three waters, squeeze out the limp slices, and mix into the vinaigrette.

Stir in the sour cream and serve with any fish dish.

SHRIMP SAUCE FOR FISH

This sauce can be served with poached or baked fish. It starts with a fish stock which you can make with head, tail, bones, and odd flesh chunks of your fish.

MAKES ABOUT 4 CUPS

THE FISH STOCK
(see page 284)
THE SHRIMP SAUCE
4 Tb. butter
1½ Tb. flour
2 cups fish stock (see above)
½ small onion or 2 shallots,
   minced

2 Tb. tomato sauce or catsup
2 Tb. brandy
½ cup raw, peeled shrimp

Strain the fish stock and set aside.

Melt the butter in a saucepan, stir in the flour, and mix and cook for a minute or two.

Off heat stir in the fish stock until blended and the remaining ingredients except the shrimp, and, covered, simmer for about 40 minutes.

Stir in the shrimp, chopped if the shrimps are large, and heat for another 10–15 minutes.

CUMBERLAND SAUCE

This sauce, famous as a game sauce, is often served with venison but just as often in my household as a sauce for wild fowl. I sometimes serve it as a substitute for Colonel Hawker's sauce. Cumberland sauce is usually made with red currant jelly, but I use beach plum jelly. Cumberland is also a fine sauce for ham, especially if raisins are added.

MAKES ABOUT ½ CUP

1 cup port wine
3 shallots or 3 scallions, finely
   chopped
1 Tb. brown sugar
1 tsp. Dijon mustard
¼ tsp. ground ginger
¼ tsp. salt
2 cloves
½ tsp. mace

⅛ tsp. cayenne
1½ tsp. cornstarch dissolved in 2
   Tb. cold water
⅓ cup red currant or beach plum
   jelly
1 Tb. grated orange rind
1 tsp. grated lemon rind
½ cup orange juice
2 Tb. lemon juice

Combine the first nine ingredients, bring to a boil, then cover and simmer for 10 minutes.

Stir in cornstarch dissolved in water and let it simmer to thicken somewhat.

Now stir in the jelly, the two rinds, and the orange and lemon juice, making sure the jelly dissolves.

NOTE: Leftover slices of red game meat warmed in this sauce make a fine second-day dish.

VENISON GREAT SAUCE

This sauce is the sauce to make when you are serving a heroic marinated game roast, such as a leg of venison or a moose rump or loin. It requires both the marinade and a brown sauce. Most cooks don't have a frozen supply of brown stock and must make up an individual batch. In this sauce the time this takes is amply justified. I make up the brown sauce the second day of the marinating. Your favorite marinade is fine, but see pages 5–6 and 46 for our red meat marinades. See page 354 for brown sauce.

The sauce is served in a sauceboat with plain roasted meats. See page 16 for roast leg of venison and under moose, elk, caribou, etc., for simple roasts of such game.

MAKES 1½ CUPS

2 Tb. oil
1 large onion, chopped
3 cloves garlic, sliced
2 medium or 1 large carrot, diced
2 bay leaves
½ tsp. powdered thyme
½ tsp. crumbled rosemary
1 Tb. minced parsley
¾ cup vinegar

½ cup dry white wine
1½ cups brown sauce (page 354)
3½ cups beef stock or game stock
1⅔ cups marinade, strained
18 peppercorns, coarsely crushed
1½ Tb. beach plum or red currant jelly
½ cup heaviest cream

In a skillet sauté in the oil the onion, garlic, carrot, bay leaves, dried herbs, and parsley until vegetables are lightly browned. Pour off oil and put mix in a granite, enamel, or stainless steel saucepan.

Add vinegar and wine and over a high heat reduce to a glaze.

Add the brown sauce, the beef or game stock, and the strained marinade and bring to a boil.

Cover, reduce heat as low as possible (use asbestos pad if need be), and barely simmer for about 4 hours. About 10 minutes or so before you take the sauce off, add the peppercorns.

Strain through a fine strainer into a clean saucepan and reduce it to about 1½ cups, skimming off the froth. Strain again, skim any fat off top, and reheat.

Meanwhile whip the beach plum jelly into the cream and stir this mixture into the hot sauce.

It should be hot enough if you serve at once, but if you have to reheat do it gently. To boil it will curdle the cream.

TWO MUSTARD SAUCES

There are lots of recipes for mustard sauce from a simple 1-to-1 mix of mayonnaise and prepared mustard to varieties prepared from a cooked butter-flour base. Over the years I have been struggling to imitate the one the Bistro in New York City used to serve with broiled pigs' feet. The recipe below is very good but somehow not as good as the one at Le Bistro. The second is a good basic mustard sauce for broiled meats or served cold with poached or baked fish.

MAKES ABOUT ½ CUP

1 Tb. butter, melted	1 Tb. vinegar
1 Tb. dry mustard	2½ Tb. dry white wine
1 Tb. flour	½ Tb. Worcestershire or
½ tsp. salt	Harvey's sauce
pepper	1 egg, beaten
½ tsp. powdered thyme	2 Tb. sweet or sour cream
1 tsp. sugar	

In the top of a double boiler mix butter, all the dry ingredients and the vinegar, and stir into a paste. Mix in the wine, Worcestershire, and beaten egg and cook over hot water until it thickens. Off heat thin with the cream.

This sauce spread on salmon steaks and put 6 inches under a broiler makes a fine dish. Spread on the ribs of game it makes a tasty broiled deviled ribs dish. With red meat ribs, be sure to broil both sides until almost done before smearing on the mustard sauce.

Some cooks may prefer this second sauce for fish:

MAKES ABOUT 1 ½ CUPS

1 cup heavy cream	¼ tsp. tarragon
2 eggs, beaten	¼ tsp. dillweed
6 Tb. Dijon mustard	1 tsp. anchovy sauce
1 Tb. vinegar	

Stir the cream into the beaten eggs and blend; then stir in the remaining ingredients.

Cook in a saucepan over very low heat, stirring the while, until it thickens to your taste; *don't* let it boil.

BASTING SAUCE FOR
GALLINACEOUS GAME BIRDS

I believe that the two herbs that distinguish a béarnaise sauce are especially suited to game birds like grouse, pheasant, partridge, or quail; I refer to tarragon and chervil. These herbs give a wonderful flavor to a basting sauce for spitted birds or distinguish a stuffing for any roasted bird. The two herbs with sage as a third addition are enhanced for either of the above purposes but especially in a bread stuffing.

MAKES ABOUT 1 ¾ CUPS

2–3 shallots or 1 scallion or	1 tsp. mushroom catsup (optional)
1 small onion, minced fine	1½ cups dry white wine or
¼ tsp. dried chervil	dry vermouth
¼ tsp. dried tarragon	3 Tb. butter
½ tsp. sage (optional)	

Bring all ingredients to boil, then simmer for 10 minutes over low heat. Strain and use for basting. It also makes a good liquid with a roux to make gravy.

══ OLD DOMINION OYSTER SAUCE FOR FISH ══

Here's a sauce from Colonial times that gives broiled fish, fish fillets, or steaks not only added savor, but makes any fish dish more appetizingly impressive to the eye.

SERVES 4–6

1 pint oysters and liquor
1 Tb. butter
1 Tb. flour
½ tsp. mace

¼ cup white wine
juice of ½ lemon
1 Tb. anchovy sauce
¼ lb. butter

Drain the oysters, retaining the liquor, and simmer in water ever so gently until their edges just curl. Remove from the hot water.

Melt the butter, stir in the flour and mace, and cook a minute over low heat. Off heat whisk in the wine, and the oyster liquor. Return to heat and cook, stirring, over low heat 2–3 minutes.

Add the lemon juice and the anchovy sauce, then over a low heat stir in and melt the remaining butter, pat by pat.

Add oysters and serve.

stuffings
and Game
Accompaniments

In this section we have included recipes for nine stuffings and twenty-six accompanying dishes with variations that go particularly well with game. We are being suggestive only, for there are many, many stuffings (incidentally, you will find scattered throughout the book other stuffings that go with a particular meat, fowl, or fish, so for the full spectrum of choice, check the Index) and virtually an infinite number of accompanying side dishes that would enhance a game dinner.

Among the stuffings, we have tried to give a sample of several *types;* each can be varied to your own taste, but you will find here fruit stuffings, fruit and nut, bread, and forcemeat stuffings. Of course, your own favorite stuffings for chicken and turkey will serve game birds equally well.

Among the accompaniment dishes we have included several vegetable purées which we feel are congenial to game and the sauces and gravies that come with it.

CELERY STUFFING

This celery stuffing has a very pronounced celery flavor, which is as it should be. If you use green celery, it will have a more pungent taste. This stuffing is nice with both fowl and fish.

MAKES 1 CUP

¾ cup (about 4 ribs)
  chopped celery
½ cup chopped onions
4 Tb. butter
¼ cup chopped green
  tops of celery

½ cup bread crumbs
salt and freshly ground pepper
¼ tsp. savory

Sauté the chopped celery and onions in butter in a small skillet for 15 minutes—until tender but still with a little bite.

Add the chopped celery tops and the bread crumbs. Season to taste with salt, pepper, and savory.

POTATO AND SAUSAGE STUFFING

This stuffing can be made quickly (using dried potato flakes to provide the mashed potatoes), is very tasty, and is a congenial carrier for sauces and gravies. This quantity will stuff 2 or 3 pheasants.

MAKES ABOUT 3 CUPS

1 cup sausage meat
1 Tb. butter
1 onion, chopped
1 rib celery, with leaves,
   chopped fine
2 cups mashed potatoes

¼ tsp. powdered thyme
1½ tsp. sage (rubbed
   Dalmatian sage is best)
2 Tb. chopped parsley
salt and pepper

Sauté the sausage in butter, stirring until the meat is pebbly and lightly browned.

Add and sauté onion and celery until onion is soft.

In a bowl mix above ingredients with the mashed potatoes, herbs, salt, and pepper.

Taste for sage and whip in more if you feel like it.

Variation: Potato and Liver Stuffing: Instead of sausage sauté ¾ cup livers after onions and celery are soft—3–4 minutes. Mash cooked livers with a fork until they are mushy, then mix (with onions, celery and 1 teaspoon marjoram instead of the sage) into the mashed potatoes. The liver should be just pink inside but still soft enough to mash up uniformly.

A FRUIT AND NUT STUFFING
FOR ROAST WILD FOWL

MAKES 3½ CUPS

1 cup chopped prunes, blanched
   for 5 minutes in boiling water
1 cup chopped apple
1 cup chopped walnuts,
   preferably black walnuts

½ cup chopped onion
1 tsp. paprika
½ tsp. pepper
½ tsp. salt
½ tsp. thyme

Mix ingredients and stuff bird.

JERUSALEM ARTICHOKE, HAZELNUT,
AND WILD RICE STUFFING

MAKES 2 CUPS

1½ cups peeled, chopped
   Jerusalem artichokes
1 medium onion, chopped
3 Tb. butter
⅔ cup cooked wild rice

⅓ cup toasted hazelnuts,
   chopped
4 Tb. chopped parsley
salt and freshly ground pepper
½ tsp. savory

Sauté the Jerusalem artichokes and onion in the butter slowly in a covered skillet for 15 minutes.

Mix together the Jerusalem artichoke mixture, which should be just tender,

Judging Stuffing Quantities for Various-sized Birds (and Fish)

I have heard a rule of thumb estimate that the cook should allow ½ cup of stuffing for each pound of bird. This is not a bad rule, but here are some more specific hints.

For a 4- to 5-pound bird. A goose or small turkey that dresses out at this weight will require about 2 cups of dressing. You can make an estimate of what 2 cups will be by the amount of the main stuffing ingredient you use, i.e., if the recipe calls for 2 cups of bread crumbs or chestnuts or sausage or a combination thereof, the yield with the other ingredients added—eggs, onions, etc.—will be about 2½ cups.

For an 8–12-pound wild turkey you need about 4–5 cups of stuffing. Five cups of stuffing will have about 4 cups of the basic ingredients in it (bread crumbs, cooked rice, etc.).

Quantity for Stuffing Pheasant, Grouse, and Partridge. A mature pheasant will hold about a cup of dressing. Use ½ cup for the smaller birds. In stuffing birds it is well to remember that the cavity should not be crammed but rather filled to about three-fourths capacity.

Quantity for Stuffing Fish. For a fish large enough to bake, 3½–6 pounds, 1–1½ cups dressing are sufficient.

not too soft, with the wild rice and hazelnuts. Toss in the parsley, season liberally with salt and pepper, and add savory. Taste and correct seasoning if necessary, then stuff the birds.

═══ PRUNE, APPLE, AND CHESTNUT STUFFING ═══

A rich stuffing that's particularly good with wild goose. Incidentally, the availability of imported, frozen chestnuts that have been peeled makes it much easier to use chestnuts in recipes now.

MAKES ABOUT 2 CUPS

1 dozen large dried prunes
½ cup Madeira
12 peeled chestnuts
2 Tb. butter
1 small tart apple,
   quartered and sliced

¾ cup fresh bread crumbs
1 sprig fresh rosemary,
   chopped (optional)

Let the prunes soak in the Madeira overnight. Remove the prunes, pit them, and cut up in large pieces.

    Pour the soaking liquid over the chestnuts in a small cooking pot and add just enough water to barely cover them. Cook gently until the chestnuts are tender—about 25 minutes—and the liquid is just about gone. Stir in the butter, then mix together with the apple, the prunes, and the bread crumbs. A touch of fresh rosemary is a good seasoner, if you have some; the dried is apt to be too overpowering.

===== APRICOT, NUT, AND BARLEY STUFFING =====

MAKES 2 CUPS

⅓ cup dried apricots
¼ cup raisins
⅓ cup roughly broken almonds
  or walnuts or combination
4 Tb. butter

½ tsp. ground cinnamon
¼ tsp. ground cloves
1 cup cooked barley
salt

Sauté the apricots, raisins, and nuts in the butter, stirring frequently, until the dried fruit has softened and the nuts are lightly browned. Sprinkle in the cinnamon and cloves, stir in the barley, and salt lightly. Stuff into wild duck or goose.

===== FENNEL SEED AND TARRAGON STUFFING =====

A subtle stuffing with a faint licorice aroma that's particularly compatible with delicate birds like quail. Also good for fish.

MAKES ABOUT 1½ CUPS

½ tsp. fennel seed
2 Tb. chopped fresh tarragon
  or 1 tsp. dried
6 Tb. butter, melted
about 1½ cups roughly torn
  fresh bread crumbs

2 Tb. chopped parsley
salt and freshly ground black
  pepper to taste

Mix all the ingredients together, tossing lightly.

===== BAKED RICE =====

SERVES 4

4 Tb. butter
1 onion, chopped
1 cup rice

2 cups chicken broth
salt and pepper

Melt the butter in a skillet (or use a flameproof baking dish) and sauté the onion until it begins to turn limp.

    Add the rice and stir to coat the grains.

    Heat the broth and pour over the rice. Bring to a boil and transfer to a baking dish, season with salt and pepper, cover, and bake in a preheated 325° oven for 30 minutes.

Baked Rice with Saffron: Crumble 3–6 threads of saffron into the hot broth and let steep for 5 minutes before pouring over rice.

Baked Rice with Mushrooms: Sauté ¼ pound chopped mushrooms with the onion before adding the rice and broth.

Baked Rice with Zucchini: Stir 1 cup grated raw zucchini plus 1–2 tablespoons chopped parsley combined with fresh basil, if available, into the rice before baking.

Baked Rice Mexican Style: Add 2 cloves minced garlic to the onion and sauté in oil instead of butter. Add 1 small fresh hot green pepper to the broth while cooking and discard when rice is cooked.

WILD RICE

Whether one uses wild rice as a side dish or as the base for stuffing, it must be cooked first. And one should use it occasionally in spite of its cost. This delectable grain of the northern marshes, coming as it does from the same wild places where wild fowl originated, seems eminently suited to accompany these birds at your board.

In timing your meal remember two things: wild rice *takes at least three times as long to cook* as white rice, and it must be thoroughly washed until the water runs clear.

SERVES 4

1 cup wild rice, washed
2 Tb. butter or margarine
   (the latter is lese majesty)
1 small onion, chopped small

2¼ cups hot game or chicken
   broth or water
salt

In metal casserole with lid, sauté the rice over low heat in 2 tablespoons butter for 2–3 minutes. Add onion and continue sautéing until onion is soft.

Pour hot broth into casserole, then add salt to taste. Cover, bring to boil, and simmer over low heat for 45 minutes. Check for doneness at this stage. If still moist, stir loosely with a fork and re-cover until all liquid has been absorbed.

Variation with Mushrooms: Sauté ½ pound sliced mushrooms in 2 tablespoons butter for 2–3 minutes, then add to the wild rice when you pour on the broth.

POTATO PANCAKES

These are so easy to prepare with the large-hole shredding disk of a food processor. Otherwise use the large holes of a grater, but work quickly because potato, once grated, discolors rapidly. For small individual pancakes use a 6–7-inch skillet, for a pancake for two use a 9–10-inch, and for four you can make a giant size in a 12–13-inch skillet. This recipe is for two, so halve or double ingredients as required. Serve as an accompaniment or place a roasted half of a game bird on top of individual pancakes or distribute them over a large one for a handsome presentation.

2 baking-size russet
  or Idaho potatoes
3 Tb. fat (preferably pork,
  goose, or chicken)

salt and freshly ground pepper

Peel and grate the potatoes coarsely. Have 2 tablespoons of the fat heating in a 9–10-inch skillet, swirl around to cover the bottom, then quickly spread the freshly grated potatoes evenly over the surface. Sprinkle salt and pepper on top and press down all over with a spatula.

Lower the heat and let the pancake cook 5–6 minutes. Check to see if the bottom is nicely brown by lifting the cake up with your spatula. When ready, drizzle the remaining fat into the pan as you've lifted the pancake, then flip it over (if you are making a large one you may find it easier to put a big plate over the skillet, turn the skillet over, dropping the pancake onto the plate, then slide the cake back into the regreased skillet to cook the other side). The second side will take 4–5 minutes. Serve immediately.

POTATOES ANNA

SERVES 4

2½ lb. russet
  or Idaho potatoes

12 Tb. sweet butter
salt and freshly ground pepper

Peel and cut the potatoes into ⅛-inch-thick even slices. Pat dry in paper towels.

Melt 3 tablespoons of the butter in a 7-inch heavy oven-proof skillet at least 1¾ inches deep (ideally it should be 2–2½ inches deep but they don't often come that way).

Lay overlapping slices of potato all around the bottom of the skillet. Salt and pepper lightly and dot generously with butter.

Continue making layers in this way until all the potato slices and butter are used up.

Find a heavy top or casserole that will fit inside your skillet and butter the bottom of it, placing it firmly on top of the potatoes, pressing down. Put the covered skillet on the lowest rack of a preheated 425° oven and bake for 20 minutes (it is advisable to lay foil on the floor of your oven under the skillet in case butter bubbles over).

After 20 minutes remove the top and bake uncovered 20 minutes more. Before taking the potatoes out press down on them firmly once again with the top and then give them another minute or two of baking.

Now take a warm round serving plate a little bigger than the skillet, place on top, then quickly flip the skillet over so that the crisp, golden potato cake unmolds all in one piece.

CASSEROLE OF MASHED POTATOES, SOUR CREAM, AND CHEESE

This can be served as a side dish, but it can double as a stuffing for pheasant, turkey, or wild goose, too.

SERVES 6

6 medium potatoes, peeled
½ cup sour cream
4 Tb. grated onion
4–5 Tb. grated provolone
  or Parmesan

salt and pepper
flavored bread crumbs
paprika
2 Tb. butter

Boil the potatoes until tender, about 20–30 minutes.

Mash or better, rice the potatoes, then stir in the sour cream, onion, cheese, and salt and pepper to taste.

Put in casserole and dust bread crumbs, then paprika over the top, dot with butter, and brown in 400° oven for 10–15 minutes.

CELERIAC-POTATOES GRATIN

SERVES 6

1 pound potatoes
1 pound celeriac
2–3 Tb. butter
salt and pepper
about 5–6 Tb. chopped parsley

1½ cups beef or chicken broth
  diluted with ½ water
1–2 Tb. Parmesan
  or sharp Cheddar (optional)

Peel the potatoes, cut in thin slices, and immediately drop into water. Do the same with the celeriac. Drain, then pat dry.

Butter a baking dish large enough to accommodate the vegetables and place alternate layers of potato and celeriac slices, dotting lightly with butter and sprinkling each layer with salt and pepper and parsley. Have the final layer potato slices. Pour in the diluted broth, drop remaining bits of butter on top, and bake in preheated 350° oven about 50 minutes.

Sprinkle with cheese and bake 10 minutes more. Vegetables should have absorbed all the moisture and be tender.

POLENTA OR CORNMEAL MUSH

The Italians would call it polenta; southerners, cornmeal mush. By either name it's delicious with a game stew or game birds, particularly when there's plenty of good sauce to mingle with the nutty-textured cornmeal. The easiest way to prepare it is in a double boiler; otherwise you have to stand over the cornmeal and stir and stir.

SERVES 6

1½ cups stone-ground cornmeal
4½ cups cold water

1 tsp. salt
3–4 Tb. butter

In the top of a double-boiler mix the cornmeal with 1 cup cold water.

Bring the rest of the water to a boil and then pour it over the cornmeal, stirring to mix thoroughly. Add the salt. Cook this over direct heat very slowly until it comes to a boil.

Put just enough boiling water into the bottom of the double boiler so that it barely reaches the top. Set the top in place, cover, and let the cornmeal cook over simmering water for 1 hour.

Stir in the butter, saving a little to float on the top of the serving dish.

Polenta with Sausages: Oil a baking dish and pour in the cooked cornmeal or polenta. Top with 1 pound game sausages (see page 329), cut in ½-inch slices. Bake in a 375° oven for 15 minutes, then spoon ¾ cup tomato sauce over the top and sprinkle with ¼ cup grated Parmesan cheese. Serve with an additional cup or so of tomato sauce and additional grated cheese.

KASHA

These buckwheat grains are lovely with game, particularly when there is a sour cream sauce to mingle with. They can be prepared plain or with the addition of sautéed onions and/or mushrooms. Let what you plan to serve them with be your guide.

SERVES 4

1 egg, lightly beaten
1 cup kasha
2 cups boiling chicken
  or game bird broth

salt and freshly ground pepper
2–3 Tb. butter

Stir the egg into the kasha, mixing thoroughly. This helps to keep the grains separate when the kasha cooks.

Put in a heavy saucepan, add boiling broth, cover, and simmer 10 minutes. Season with salt and pepper to taste and stir in the butter.

Variation: Sauté 1 chopped onion in a couple of tablespoons butter until limp. Add to the kasha before cooking. You can also stir ¼ cup sliced sautéed mushrooms into the cooked kasha. Sprinkle with a combination of chopped parsley and chives.

Purées

Assertive vegetables like turnips, parsnips, and celery root, particularly when combined with potatoes, make excellent purées and provide a very interesting foil for almost any kind of game. They are filling and creamy enough so that you don't need a starch accompaniment as well, and their earthy flavors mingle beautifully with the gamy juices of both meat and fowl. Certain legumes like chickpeas and lentils also make fine accompaniments, as does the traditional chestnut purée for venison.

PARSNIP AND POTATO PURÉE

SERVES 4

1 pound all-purpose potatoes
1 pound parsnips
salt and freshly ground pepper to
  taste

pinch of nutmeg
2–3 Tb. butter
sprinkling of finely chopped
  parsley

Peel the potatoes and cut in quarters. Peel the parsnips and cut in 1-inch pieces, splitting the larger ends in half. Set a large pot of salted water to boil and add the potatoes. After they've cooked about 15 minutes, add the parsnips. Continue to cook briskly until the vegetables are just soft but not mushy—about 10–15 minutes.

Drain and either put through a vegetable mill or spin in the food processor. Add salt, pepper, and nutmeg, and whip in the butter. Serve with chopped parsley sprinkled on top.

MASHED POTATOES AND TURNIPS WITH GARLIC GALORE

This is a super dish to serve with roasted red meat game as well as roasted wild goose. Don't let it intimidate you because of the seeming God-awful amount of garlic used. If it seems excessive, try the dish anyway and learn something about the "errant lily" (see page 35), for this dish is subtly and deliciously flavored.

SERVES 6

4–5 large potatoes
3 medium-sized turnips
25 garlic cloves
  (about 2 bulbs or heads)
¼ lb. butter
2 Tb. oil

2½ Tb. flour
1 cup milk
½ tsp. salt
freshly ground pepper
3 Tb. sour cream
4 Tb. minced parsley

Peel and quarter the potatoes and turnips and starting them in cold water, bring to a boil and continue to boil for 15–30 minutes or until tender.

At the same time, put 3 cups water in a saucepan, bring to a boil, and drop in the garlic. Boil the cloves for 2–3 minutes, drain, and peel. The inside will virtually squirt loose and free.

In a small skillet with a lid, melt 4 tablespoons of the butter and the oil. Add the peeled cloves of garlic, cover, and cook over low heat for about 20 minutes. Don't let the fat brown; if it threatens to do so, add a couple tablespoons of hot water.

Now blend in the flour and cook for a couple of minutes. Then, off heat, stir in the milk, salt, and pepper. Return to heat and stir until thickened.

Now either rub the sauce through a sieve or, better, put it in an electric blender for a few whirls.

If you arranged both cooking times to come out even, you can now drain the potatoes and turnips, put them through a ricer, and beat in the garlic sauce. However the sauce can be made, set aside, and reheated, and I usually leave the riced potatoes and turnips over a very low heat or in the center warming ring on my stove to dry out some and lose steam.

Now melt the last 4 tablespoons of the butter in the hot garlic sauce and beat the sauce into the whipped vegetables.

Lastly beat in the sour cream and the minced parsley.

RUTABAGA AND POTATO PURÉE

SERVES 4

1 lb. rutabagas
1 lb. all-purpose potatoes
salt

3 Tb. butter
nutmeg

Peel the rutabagas and the potatoes and cut in rough chunks. Cook in lightly salted water to cover for about 30 minutes or until tender but not mushy. Drain and put through a vegetable mill or ricer. Whip, beating in the butter while hot. Sprinkle a little nutmeg over, preferably freshly grated.

BEET AND CARROT PURÉE

It was James Beard who recently had the inspiration for this unusual combination of vegetables. It's particularly good with game—almost any kind—with its subtle, tantalizing flavor, and its bright color looks handsome encircling a platter of roasted birds.

SERVES 4

1 lb. beets
1 lb. carrots
2 Tb. butter

salt and freshly ground
pepper to taste

Cook the unpeeled beets with an inch or so of stem left on in plenty of boiling water until tender when pierced with a fork, which can take anywhere from 30 to 60 minutes or so depending on their age. Cool enough to peel, then halve or quarter them and put in the food processor (if you don't have one, use a vegetable mill).

Meanwhile peel the carrots, cut in chunks, and boil in salted water until tender—about 20 minutes. Drain and add them to the food processor. Process until you have a smooth purée. Mix in the butter, salt, and pepper to taste, and serve.

PURÉED CHESTNUTS

A rich and elegant accompaniment, particularly for venison.

SERVES 6

1 lb. chestnuts, peeled*
1⅓ cups light chicken stock
2 Tb. Madeira (optional)

2 Tb. cream
2 Tb. butter

Cover the chestnuts with the chicken stock and Madeira and simmer gently, covered, for about 40 minutes or until tender.

You should have about ⅓ cup liquid left with the chestnuts; if not, add a little more stock. Purée the chestnuts along with their liquid and the cream in a food processor. Or put through a vegetable mill and then add the cream. Whip in the butter.

    * Peeled chestnuts, frozen from Italy, are available today in some supermarkets. If you can't get them, you have a job ahead, but it is worth it. Some claim that if you have frozen the chestnuts first it makes the job of peeling them a little easier. With a sharp knife make a cross in each chestnut. Put them, frozen or not, into a pot and cover them with water. Bring them to a boil very, very slowly and when they have reached the boil, turn off the heat and let them stand in the water. When you can handle them, extract one or two chestnuts at a time and peel off the shell and membrane. Discard any chestnuts that have mold on them.

LENTILS

Lentils are good around a roast or braised game, picking up the meat, juices. They are also nice for a casserole of leftover game. Serve them whole, just strained from their juices, or purée them for a more elegant presentation.

SERVES 8

1½ cups lentils
3–3½ cups water
1 carrot, chopped
1 large onion, chopped
1 rib celery, chopped
1 small clove garlic, peeled

½ tsp. thyme
1 bay leaf
4–5 sprigs parsley
½ tsp. or more salt
3 Tb. butter (for purée)

Cover the lentils with the water and all the rest of the ingredients except butter. Use a heavy 2-quart pot because lentils expand to three or four times their size when cooked. Once the water has come to a boil, cover and simmer gently for about 40 minutes, add a little more water if they look too dry. Taste—the lentils should be soft but not mushy. If you are going to purée them, cook 10 minutes longer.
    Strain the lentils and serve as they are, removing the bay leaf and correcting the seasoning. Or drain and put through a vegetable mill; or mash in a food processor and then put through a strainer. Whip the butter into the purée and correct the seasoning.

FRIJOLES (FRIED BEANS)

Mexicans understand beans, and beans prepared in their style, fried, are delicious, especially somehow with barbecued game. To make fried beans in the classic Mexican fashion you *should* use the classic pink Mexican bean.

SERVES 8–10

1 lb. Mexican beans (or pinto
  beans or red kidney beans)
1½ qt. water

½ cup rendered salt pork fat,
  lard, or bacon fat
salt and pepper

Wash and pick the beans, then put them in a pot with the water and cook at a low simmer for 2 hours or so. Test them for doneness, bearing in mind that you want them tender, but not mushy.

When they are done, heat fat in a big, heavy skillet and begin "frying" by putting in a few beans. Then, mashing half of them with the back of a wooden spoon, adding a bit of the bean liquor each time, continue frying until you have used up all of the beans and the liquor they were boiled in and have them at the desired consistency. If they seem too watery when you mash half of each added batch of beans and water, smash a third of the beans.

NOTE: When I fix frijoles I simmer the beans with a quarter pound of salt pork and an onion cut in two with a clove bud stuck in each half.

CHICKPEA PURÉE

This is a delicious purée for sopping up good game meat juices. You can use canned chickpeas if you're in a hurry.

SERVES 6–8

1¼ cups dried chickpeas
  or three 15-oz. cans
½ tsp. baking soda
1 small clove garlic,
  minced very fine

¼–⅓ cup heavy cream
salt and pepper
2 Tb. butter

Soak the chickpeas, if you are using dried ones, overnight in water to cover.
    Drain and cook in 2½ quarts water to which you add the baking soda. It will take anywhere from 2½–3 hours, maybe a little more, until they are tender.
    Drain the cooked chickpeas, saving a little of the water; if you are using canned beans, drain and rinse in cold water.
    Purée the chickpeas in a food processor or put through a food mill along with the garlic, adding a little of the cooking liquid and/or cream to make a smooth purée. Salt and pepper to taste. Serve in a warm dish with lumps of butter stirred on top which you'll swirl around as you serve.

BRUSSELS SPROUTS WITH CHESTNUTS

Brussels sprouts still retaining a slight crunch and rolled in butter make a fine accompaniment for game, but they're even more special combined with chestnuts.

SERVES 4–5

1 pint or about 1 lb.
  Brussels sprouts
½ lb. chestnuts, shelled

½ cup chicken broth
2 Tb. Madeira
4–6 Tb. butter

Trim the sprouts and cut a cross in the root end (this makes for more even cooking). Bring to a boil a *large* pot of salted water—about 3 quarts; drop the sprouts in, and boil rapidly uncovered for about 10 minutes (if sprouts are very little, they may be done sooner—they should be just slightly crunchy). Drain and run cold water over to retain their green color.
    Cover the chestnuts with the broth, Madeira, and 1 tablespoon water. Bring to a boil and simmer gently, covered, until tender, about 20 minutes, adding a little water if they get dry.

In a largish shallow buttered baking dish, distribute sprouts, round side up, and chestnuts. Dot liberally with butter and pop into a hot oven to heat them just before serving.

STEAMED CABBAGE BEN MORE
FOR RED MEAT GAME OR WILD FOWL

I have found two vegetable dishes that seem to me and my guests to go especially well with game. This one I served first with wild duck. It came from the chef at Ben More Lodge in Sutherland.

SERVES 3–4

½ large cabbage, chopped
  or shredded
6–8 slices of bacon

1 onion, minced
½ cup heavy cream
nutmeg

Steam or boil the cabbage, being sure not to overcook—not more than 5 minutes.
    Fry the bacon until crisp. Set aside to drain.
    Sauté the onion in the bacon fat.
    When the cabbage has just softened, drain, add the crumbled bacon, the onion, and the cream and toss to mix uniformly.
    Grate on nutmeg to taste.

BRAISED CABBAGE

SERVES 6

1 medium head cabbage
  (about 2 lb.)
2 carrots, minced
1 medium onion, minced
2 Tb. butter

½–¾ cup chicken broth
½ cup water
salt and freshly ground pepper
2 Tb. chopped parsley

Quarter the cabbage, remove the hard core and any tough outer leaves, and cut each quarter into thin shreds.
    In a large, heavy skillet or a wok sauté the carrots and onion in the butter, adding a little of the broth if too dry. Stir so they don't stick, and after about 4 minutes, when nearly soft, throw in the shredded cabbage, stirring and tossing. Then add the broth and water, salt and pepper to taste, and cover.
    Cook gently for about 15 minutes until the cabbage is just tender. Stir occasionally to make sure there is enough moisture and add a little more broth if needed. Sprinkle with parsley.

RED CABBAGE WITH APPLES

SERVES 6

1 medium red cabbage
(about 2 lb.)
4 Tb. fat, goose or
duck preferred, or butter
1 large onion, chopped
½ cup red wine

½ cup water
¼ cup red wine vinegar
3 Tb. brown sugar
2 medium-size tart apples,
peeled, cored, and chunked

Quarter the cabbage, cut out the hard core, and remove any wilted outer leaves. Cut the cabbage into fine shreds.

In a heavy pot melt the fat and sauté the onion until translucent. Toss the shredded cabbage on top.

Mix the wine, water, vinegar, and brown sugar together, then pour over the cabbage. Add the apples. Cover and cook slowly for 1½–2½ hours, depending on freshness of cabbage. Check occasionally to make sure that all the liquid hasn't boiled away; if it gets too low add a little more red wine and water.

Toss before serving—the apples will have melted into the braised cabbage.

STEAMED KALE

SERVES 4

About 1–1½ lb. kale (or more
if you're removing stems)
1 large onion, chopped

3 Tb. bacon fat
salt
lemon wedges or vinegar

Remove the stems from the kale, pulling the center ribs off the leaves, if they seem tough or if you don't like them (I do when they're tender). Let soak in a big bowl of water.

In a large skillet or a wok slowly sauté the chopped onion in the bacon fat until limp.

Add the kale with water clinging to it. Stir-fry for a minute over quite high heat, then sprinkle with salt, lower heat, cover, and let steam for 15–20 minutes. It should be just tender, not mushy.

Serve with lemon wedges or a cruet of vinegar.

BAKED PARSNIPS WITH FRUIT

A wonderful recipe from *The Victory Garden Cookbook,* particularly recommended as an accompaniment to game birds.

SERVES 4

1 lb. parsnips
1 orange
3 Tb. melted butter

2 Tb. brown sugar
3 Tb. orange juice
2 apples

Peel the parsnips and cut into logs.

Slice the unpeeled orange in ¼-inch slices, cutting 4–5 of the larger slices in half.

Combine the butter, sugar, and orange juice and mix with the parsnips, apples, and orange. Put in a buttered baking dish, cover, and bake in a preheated 325° oven for 30 minutes. Uncover and bake 15 minutes longer to glaze. Baste with the juices and serve.

DUMPLINGS

Dumplings should be light and airy, and it's important for the liquid to simmer ever so gently; fast boiling will cause the egg in the dough to harden and you'll end up with a stodgy lump. (Dumplings are great for camp cooking when you're apt to have room for only one pot on the fire.) Wherever you're cooking, you can make a hearty soup or stew and bread at the same time by floating dumplings on top for the last 10 minutes of cooking.

SERVES 4

1 cup flour
2 tsp. baking powder
½ tsp. salt
1 egg
¼ cup milk

2 Tb. chopped parsley
1 Tb. finely minced scallions
1 Tb. chopped fresh dill,
  marjoram, or tarragon
  (optional)

Sift the dry ingredients together into a bowl. Lightly beat the egg and the milk together and stir into the dry ingredients along with the parsley, scallions, and optional herb.

Dip a teaspoon into the hot liquid in which you'll be cooking the dumplings—either soup or the juices of a stew—and then scoop up a rounded spoonful of the dough. Drop it onto the simmering liquid and continue with the remaining dough, distributing the dumplings on the top of your cooking pot a good 1½ inches apart to allow for swelling. Be sure that the pot remains just at a simmer, cover, cook 5 minutes on one side, then turn the dumplings carefully and cook another 5 minutes. Serve immediately, floating on soup or stew.

SPAETZLE

These little dumplings are so good when homemade and so easy to make when the little spaetzlemaker is used that I often make them as a substitute for potatoes, rice, etc. My spaetzlemaker is somewhat archly dubbed "Babsi's Noodlette" and is made by the Hirco Manufacturing Co. of Chicago. The spaetzlemaker you find will give instructions about how to use the little hand-cranked extruder, but normally, you would cook the spaetzle in boiling salted water. Spaetzle can be cooked and used immediately or can be dried and stored in the freezer and used later. These noodles taste better and are lighter than boiled dry commercial egg noodles.

SERVES 4

2¼ cups flour
½ tsp. salt
¼ tsp. baking powder

¼ tsp. nutmeg
2 eggs
1 cup milk

Sift flour, salt, baking powder, and nutmeg. Add eggs beaten into the milk. Crank the batter through the holes in your machine or push it through a colander into a large pot of boiling salted water.

Cook the spaetzle for 1–1½ minutes, until the little noodles rise to the surface, or just until tender. Drain, rinse with hot water, and serve.

Spaetzle with Sage, Parsley, or Other Herbs: Add to dry ingredients above 1 tablespoon sage or parsley or other herb of your choice. Rubbed Dalmatian is the best sage.

Spaetzle with Game Bird and/or Chicken Livers: Sauté 3 livers in butter until just pink, remove with the butter, and mash with a fork until you have a paste that you can stir into the batter. When you make liver spaetzle you should leave the miniature dumplings in the boiling water a minute longer than for plain spaetzle.

Cooking in Camp

Wood Range Cookery

Hunting and fishing camps that serve meals have their virtues, but with all the convenience of a camp with a regular chef, nothing quite matches living the hunting life in a remote cabin equipped with an old lumber camp wood range where one of the hunters does the cooking. Note that I say "where one of the *hunters* does the cooking." The emphasis is intended to convey a warning: "Don't let the guide cook the deer meat."

Guides usually know more about hunting than a campful of clients, but a knowledge of cooking is not usually one of their finest talents. Most guides can make a bannock and some can manage sourdough pancakes and even bread, but sautéing a venison steak usually means ½-inch thick slices fried gray on the inside and black outside.

But I have yet to spend a week or two with a guide, any guide, who did not relish good cooking done by one of his clients. Roy Smith, with whom I spent eight deer and moose hunting falls, used to say, "Now, Angus, if you could only shoot, you'd make a perfect hunting partner, for you sure as hell can cook." Roy's standards may not have been the highest, but there was something in it. Over the years, Roy taught me a lot about hunting and trapping, but his old friend, Didge Smith, used to say, "You notice, Angus, I always time my hunt with Roy when you and Mrs. Cameron are up here. That way I figure I have the best of it."

There are many advantages for the man who can do the camp cooking. In the first place, the hunter or angler who takes over the cooking usually likes to cook and finds the task no chore at all. Indeed, taking on the cooking reflects no credit for a martyr's role on him, for the good cook usually is a good, and maybe discriminating, eater, and prefers to do the job himself to assure some modicum at least of savory meals, and, besides, he knows that the work involved in the difference between poor meals and good is not all that great.

And, in addition, think of the other benefits that accrue to a decent camp cook. Like the cook in a lumber camp or the man who did the cooking on the open range in the West out of a chuck wagon, the hunting camp cook becomes a kind of privileged character (some of those old bush and range cooks were outright tyrants). He never bucks or splits or totes a stick of wood; he never washes or dries a dish or a cup; he carries no water sloshing icily on his stagged pants from the lake or spring. Usually, he never peels a potato or fills the Coleman lantern. If he's good enough, he instantly has a campful of willing hands and two or three cookees who are delighted to do second- or third-chef chores in exchange for savory, well-prepared meals.

In this section and the next we will discuss hunting and fishing camp cookery and will include a number of recipes that can be prepared under conditions that are not as ideal as those afforded in your own kitchen at home. But many recipes for dishes that can be prepared conveniently in camp have been scattered throughout the book and have been labeled with either of these two symbols.

We will also discuss wood range or bottle gas cookery in remote or wilderness camps that are permanent and tent cookery where the stove is a wood-burning Yukon stove (the sheet-metal box). In the latter section we will also offer a few words about cooking on a two-burner Coleman stove.

We will not discuss one-burner spirit-stove cookery in this book, i.e., backpack cookery, because neither author is experienced in hiking cuisine. However, for those who are interested we can recommend Gretchen McHugh's *The Hungry Hiker's Book of Good Cooking,* a remarkable book published in 1982 (Alfred A. Knopf) on how to eat well on a backpacking trip.

In writing this chapter, I am assuming that four hunting partners are off on a two-week trip to a cabin in the bush. I assume that it will take two days to get there and settle in and two days to get back. The quantities given here are for ten days in the woods. Lesser time or fewer (or more) hunters is just a matter of division or multiplication.

Four men can eat up a storm, so these quantities are figured as maximum. If there's plenty of game meat in camp there will be evenings when the men will be long on meat and short on other items. On other occasions, the company will be too tired to wait for the cook to prepare full fare, and on those occasions they might make do on leftovers or a pot of baked beans.

The basic assumptions are these: that breakfast will be hearty—eggs, bacon, toast or pancakes, fried mush or French bread; that lunches will basically be tea and two sandwiches each, one meat and one jelly or preserve; that supper will include meat (sautéed, or in stews or broiled), potatoes (or spaghetti or noodles), a canned vegetable, and canned fruit and cookies or pie for dessert.

The meat cookery can be as simple or elaborate as one wishes, once game is in camp. If it's a relaxed camp—where pressure is not so great that every man feels he *must* hunt from dark to dark to fill his license—then the cook is in for it: meals will be as important as license-filling. Then the camp cook will have time to show his prowess. But before he can manage that, he has yet to get the grub to camp.

The Grub List

The hunter or fisherman who is going to do the cooking for the camp, whether it be in a cabin back in the bush or in a tent camp in some wild country, should see to the grub list. Your mode of transportation determines to some extent at least what you *can* take in.

SMUGGLING IN THE INGREDIENTS

If you and your partner(s) are going into a permanent cabin camp by truck or jeep, grub logistics are simple; you can usually take in all you need, for there is room for it. But if you are flying in, the problem is different. I can't remember when I have flown into a wilderness cabin when something did not have to be bumped in order to get the floats up on the step. If you have bought your grub in a last outpost market it will be packed in paper bags that have probably been put into corrugated boxes. The pilot, eager to lighten the load, will grab a couple of bags that seem heavy and out they'll go. Now since these bags have been packed by the checker at the market, their contents will be a hodgepodge. For this reason you had better repack them and put in one or two of the heavy items that in a pinch you can do without.

A typical list of items that might be purchased but can be left behind:

the 2 extra #10 cans of tomatoes

the extra cans of peaches, pears, half of the potatoes (don't let them take out the big can of potato flakes)

2 of the 4 rutabagas you bought (don't let the pilot bump the 3 bunches of carrots)

1 of the 3 heads of cabbages

the 5 extra pounds of flour (but don't bump the baking powder), etc.

(A grub list for two is in the Appendix.)

But if you want to produce good meals be sure that you retain these items:

Herbs (they weigh close to nothing, especially if you put them in mixed combinations in plastic bottles)

Spices (as above)

Worcestershire sauce

Garlic bulbs

Red and white wine (make clear to your partners they are for cooking only)

Bouillon cubes

8-oz. cans tomato sauce

Since your last grub-assembling entrepot may not carry what you need, you may wish to buy at your home market the herbs and spices and repack them in 3-inch screw-top plastic bottles and throw them into your own duffel bag with your gear.

Here's the way I do it:

1 bottle crushed dry oregano and basil, mixed half and half

1 bottle crushed dry rosemary and marjoram, mixed half and half

1 small can celery seed

1 container grated Parmesan cheese

1 bottle bouillon cubes

1 bottle fresh sage

1 bottle powdered thyme

1 bottle ½ powdered cinnamon, ¼ ginger, ¼ cloves

1 bottle ¾ vanilla, ¼ almond extract (be sure cap is tight and maybe add foil under lid)

1 bottle dry mustard

paprika

onion powder or dried onions

These crucial ingredients together won't weigh half a pound, but they can turn hunter's stew into moose bourguignon.

A permanent camp in remote or wilderness areas can turn out to be a temporary home where you can literally live off the fat of the land. Venison, ruffed grouse, an occasional snowshoe hare, and fish may, with luck, grace your wilderness larder. If one of the guides does some trapping on the side, don't scorn the beaver and the muskrat that may be available. In the eastern woods the big lake trout will probably be on the surface during the hunting season and there is always some partner who has brought along a trolling rod and a few daredevils. (Wilderness cabins are usually located on a lake where a canoe or a boat is available.) Sometimes, if your guide is also a trapper he'll have a legal gill net for taking rough fish for cubby pen bait sets. He might even bring in an occasional nonrough fish like the delectable walleye. Fish prepared in various ways add a fillip of change to camp menus. See fish recipes marked.

In true wilderness areas throughout Canada and Alaska the larder may hold moose, caribou, sheep and elk, spruce grouse (they're good in the fall before winter forces them to feed on evergreen needles and have not become "sprucy"), ptarmigan, grayling, and trout. Often your stove will be under canvas, a sheet-metal Yukon stove that will challenge your ingenuity, for tent-stove cookery is a bit more difficult than cooking on a cabin wood range.

Vegetables in the Grub Box

Cooking in camp always creates a logistics problem, and especially so when you fly in. But always *try* to have the following in camp:
In order of magnitude

Garlic	Carrots
Onions	Potatoes
Celery	Mushrooms
Green peppers	

These above are musts. It would be nice, but not absolutely necessary, to have also:

Turnips (or rutabagas)	Parsnips
Cabbage	

Substitutes:

Garlic powder	Dried mushrooms
Celery salt	(or small cans of mushrooms)
Dried potato flakes	

Canned Goods in the Grub Box

Canned goods are a problem, for you are adding tin and water to the weight of the vegetables or fruits themselves. All bush pilots hate canned goods.
Insist on the following:

Canned tomatoes	Canned peas
Canned tomato sauce (or paste)	Canned fruit

Hope to smuggle in:

Canned green beans	Canned baked beans
Canned soups	Evaporated milk
Canned bouillon or chicken broth	

Substitutes:

You can use dried Knorr soups, bouillon cubes (beef and chicken), and if you bring dry navy beans and there is a bean pot in camp (and an oven) you can make your own baked beans. Dried apricots and/or dried peaches are good substitutes for canned fruit and they save weight.

Bottled Goods in the Grub Box

Bottles weigh and are fragile to bring in, but some are musts:

Dry red wine for coooking   *Worcestershire sauce*
Catsup   *Prepared mustard*
Pickles, your choice   *Vinegar*

Substitutes:

Dry mustard

Bulk Staples in the Grub Box

Flour   *Tea*
Baking powder   *Dry beans*
White sugar   *Pancake flour*
Brown (light) sugar   *Bisquick*
Dried milk powder   *Noodles*
Salt and pepper   *Cornmeal*
Spaghetti   *Cheese spreads*
Rice   *Canned meats*
Coffee   *Jams, jellies, and honey*

Fats
Two pounds cooking oil or 2 pounds lard or Crisco. By saving the bacon fat, one has a fine frying or cooking fat.

Quantities for Grub List

How much grub to take presents a difficult problem, for not only do appetites vary greatly but how much serious cooking is to be done also varies from camp to camp and cook to cook. What is prepared in camp varies also. For example, it is feasible on many occasions to take in enough bread to last four men for two weeks. In this case there won't be many bannocks or batches of biscuits made. On the other hand, if lunches are taken in the bush, each man will consume four slices of bread a day just for his lunch. In twelve days in the bush the lunches alone will consume sixteen slices a day or 192 slices (there are about eighteen slices in the average loaf of bread).

If the camp consumes at breakfast two pieces of toast per man, then that's another eight slices a day or ninety-six slices for twelve days.

How much bread do hungry hunters eat for the big meal at night? Probably at least two slices each—another eight per day or ninety-six for twelve days.

It's easy to see we're talking about 384 slices or about twenty-one loaves of bread. However, let's assume an ambitious cook made biscuits for breakfast five times and for supper twice. This would reduce the bread by about three loaves, but would consume fourteen to twenty cups of flour. This is four to five pounds of flour.

Pancakes? Figure 4 cups of flour each time you made a batch for four men; that's a pound each time.

And canned goods? Well, figure one can of fruit every time you serve it for dessert.

Six big cans of tomatoes won't be too much if you use the tomatoes just for cooking.

MEAT

Most hunters are optimistic, take in some bacon and ham, but figure to live off the game (and maybe a fish dinner or two). I once spent two weeks in the Ontario bush (the year of the great midwest storm and blizzard, 1940) and didn't taste red meat the whole time.

Fortunately, Roy Smith had an illegal gill net so we did have fish, walleyes mostly. We had a few cans of Spam, and the grouse happened to be numerous that year, but getting them was not like buying chickens at a supermarket.

About 10 pounds of bacon and half a ham will be about right—if you hang up game in the first two days or so. Bacon bought in 1-pound packages sliced gives about eighteen slices to the pound, but remember if you indulge yourself and bring in bulk bacon you won't get eighteen slices to the pound. Most men in camp like at least three slices of bacon with their eggs or pancakes. And, remember, the cook uses some bacon in his cooking.

SUNDRY ITEMS

Sugar presents a problem. It is useful to know that 2 measuring cups of sugar weigh 1 pound. One batch of mock maple syrup will use a pound of sugar. If you are really ambitious enough to try baking pies, you might bear in mind that one cherry pie made from canned cherries will require about 12 ounces of sugar.

As for sugaring coffee and tea, each man will consume about 6 cups of hot beverage a day and will use 6–12 teaspoons of sugar. Three teaspoons make a tablespoon, and 1 cup or ½ pound of sugar contains 16 tablespoons. If each man averages 1 teaspoon of sugar to a cup he will use 6 teaspoons or 2 tablespoons a day; 8 tablespoons a day for four; 96 tablespoons for four men for twelve days. This is 6 cups of sugar or 3 pounds.

If dry or hot cereal is sometimes served, figure just that much more.

Eight pounds of sugar for four men for twelve days will just do and still permit the cook to make up three batches of syrup (1 pound each time) and have enough left over for bannock and one pie.

As for other bulk items like spaghetti, one can estimate that ½ pound of spaghetti will serve four (if you have other food with the meal). The same goes for dry noodles.

Butter is a tricky item, for how much you use depends on so many variables, mostly on how ambitious the cook is. But figure roughly that you use ½ tablespoon butter every time you butter a slice of toast or bread. Looking back on our earlier figures for bread for four, for twelve days we are talking about 384 slices at ½ tablespoon per slice or 192 tablespoons. This comes to 6 pounds of butter. There are 8 tablespoons to a quarter-pound stick of butter, 32 to the pound. The cook will use at least 2 pounds more in his various dishes.

POTATOES

Most hunters eat hearty where potatoes are concerned and like them almost any way they are served: "fried" (either German- or cottage-fried), mashed, boiled, or lyonnaise. But most hunting camp cooks provide starch in other forms of food part of the time—spaghetti, noodles, etc.

But say you have potatoes for supper six times out of twelve. Most hearty eaters can eat 1½–2 medium potatoes each; that figures to 6–8 potatoes for each meal.

Boiled potatoes, cooled then cubed and browned in butter or bacon fat the next evening, are the simple way (cottage-fried). Sometimes I just take only potato flakes into camp and make mashed potatoes each time. Figure it takes 3 measuring cups of potato flakes to serve four hungry hunters their fill of mashed potatoes. Two pounds of potato flakes would be enough if you served only mashed potatoes during the twelve days in camp (along with 2 pounds of spaghetti and the same of noodles).

Eggs

I use the rough rule of thumb of two eggs per person a day. Four men in camp for twelve days = 8 dozen eggs. Most men will eat both eggs and pancakes at the same breakfast, while some will make a breakfast all of bacon and pancakes alone. But what if you have to eat eggs instead of venison? By the way, two eggs per man is about right if they are fried, but if they are scrambled eight eggs won't serve four men; for some reason when a man helps himself off a platter of scrambled eggs he will take more than the scrambled equivalent of two eggs every time.

Milk

A few cans of evaporated milk for coffee should be in the grub box, but I use dried milk, making up batches the night before according to the formula on the can.

One cup of dried milk will make one quart of "milk." I use the quotes to indicate that it doesn't taste like whole milk. Tip: It tastes better made up the night before and when prepared then and *served cold* later it's not bad. At least one out of four hunters will find it quite palatable as a beverage, and it certainly is quite fine for cooking pancakes, biscuits, etc.

Four men for twelve days will find it easy to use up 5 pounds of dried milk, especially if one or two of them drinks it straight.

When using dried milk powder figure about 4 tablespoons of dried milk to a measuring cup of water. In using dry milk in cooking I mix the milk powder with the dry ingredients.

Example: if you are making a batch of baking powder biscuits in a quantity that calls for 1 cup of milk, then put 4 tablespoons of dried milk right in with the flour, baking powder, and salt, sift together, then stir in 1 cup of water to make the dough.

You can, of course, use previously prepared liquid milk in the proper quantity as a liquid.

When using dried milk in soups or gravies (as in the recipe, say, for Chicken-Fried Rabbit, page 98), mix the dry milk in with the flour before you stir and cook the flour in with the fat and browned particles in the skillet. Some cooks say to use only 3 tablespoons dried milk to 1 cup water when making gravies and sauces that call for milk. The reason given: Dry milk tends to stick a bit over direct heat. In making a soup, one should use low heat anyway.

How to Make Buttermilk or Sour Milk in Camp

If you find yourself in camp with a recipe calling for sour milk, don't despair. Add a tablespoon of vinegar (distilled white vinegar preferred) to a cup of milk (or dry milk mix equivalent of a cup) and let stand 10 minutes until it starts to clabber. It will clabber completely if you let it stand for hours.

When the Grub Gets to Camp

The only hunting camp I ever cooked in whose storage and working spaces were convenient was a frame and tarpaper driver's camp on La Coote Lake in New Brunswick. That was the last year they drove logs on La Coote Brook. The lumber camp cook had a good wood range, there was plenty of shelving, and the big kitchen doubled as a "dining" room, for the single room had also a long trestle table with benches on each side. But most hunting camps or cabins have little shelf space (although always, some), so that much of the grub has to be stored under the oilcloth-covered table or under the bunks. The point is that the man who does the cooking should store the grub so he'll know where to find various categories of grub. Nothing worse than having to look for that last 1-pound 13-ounce can of peaches and finding it with the canned tomatoes, or even stuffed in between a bag of potatoes and the onions under the corner bunk.

There is no way that grub can be stored systematically, of course, but the cook, knowing his own habits, will create some order if he himself stores the grub. If you have come into a guide's camp that he uses as a trapper's shack, he'll have some staples there; those old-timers got practiced in storing staples like salt, sugar, or even flour left over from another season. But don't count on anything, and do check on the utensils.

Most trappers' camps used by the trapper who doubles as a guide for hunters or hunting camps that regularly cater to fall hunters, for example, usually have adequate utensils. Certainly housekeeping hunting camps that you can drive to will be reasonably well equipped. Don't depend on that in the case of permanent fishing or hunting camps that you have to fly to.

Most camps nowadays are run by outfitters who supply camps, guides, cook, and kitchen serving personnel. The cook in your party will never catch a glimpse of a stove unless he goes out of his way to see the kitchen under the guise of congratulating the chef.

Handling a Wood Range

Miss Fannie Farmer, of *Boston Cooking-School Cook Book* fame, included advice on how to cook on a wood range in the earliest editions of her famous book. We'll use her nineteenth-century advice from time to time, but let's begin by assuming the stove is a four- or six-lid stove with an oven. Such stoves usually have an unlidded surface on the right side as a warming area (or even simmering area if the fire is high). A camp cook who gets used to his stove soon learns that the lids over the firebox are hottest and that other lids would be called medium, medium-low, and simmer on the gauges of an electric stove. Of course how "medium" or how "low" will depend on the fire itself.

I usually cook over a big fire and depend on my knowledge of lid positions to give me the relative degrees of hotness (not forgetting the unlidded warming area).

Sautéing (or frying) and boiling are done over the firebox lids, of course, but shifting frying pans, kettles, and Dutch ovens to lids of lesser heat becomes automatic. For example, you may wish to bring a stew or soup to a fast boil over the firebox lids and then shift them to lids of lesser heat to simmer. I usually keep a kettle of water going at all times (for both cooking and washing), keeping it hot on lids of lesser heat or bringing it to a quick boil if need be by shifting it over the firebox lids or closer to them.

On wood ranges the oven is usually quite fickle, ranging from the heat intensity of a steel mill puddler to a "slow" that will scarcely "rise" baking powder biscuits.

You just have to experiment. My wife, who learns about wood range ovens instinctively, it seems to me, used to control oven heat by how much she kept the oven door open. A stick of kindling will crack the oven's opening to one degree of hotness. A larger piece of firewood to another. I've seen her bake cherry pies with the oven door wide open. As I say, ovens are fickle; sometimes they'll burn one side of a roast (or loaf) and leave the other half-baked. One turns the roasting pan around occasionally in such ovens.

Cooking with a big, constantly stoked fire in the firebox may mean living in a cabin with the door open. Your partners gabbing or playing cards around the oilcloth-covered table may beef about the heat, but can be counted on usually to adjust the cabin door. If the meal smells good enough they'll be willing to burn on one side and freeze on the other.

Stove-Pipe Drafts and Dampers

These two apertures, both adjustable, can become the friend or deadly enemy of the camp cook. If the range is in a cabin owned by your guide, or if it's his trapping camp on occasions, he'll know the permutations and combinations that achieve various effects, but since he may know little about cooking, you'll have to master the adjustments with his advice. The sliding cast-iron draft on the fire box door is usually fairly manageable; it should have a piece of tin nailed to the floor to catch hot coals, but you may have to learn about the damper on the stove pipe (such as remembering when it's open and when it's closed). You'll just have to hope that the flue is not choked with carbon. If the stove pipe is guy-wired by stove pipe wire you can tap the sections lightly to knock out carbon. But sometimes more serious ministrations are required, such as taking the pipe sections down when the fire is cold. But do ask the guide to do this before your party comes to camp. Also it's good to know ahead of time that there is an ample supply of firewood. In eastern Canada and the United States your range will usually be fed with birch or poplar (sometimes you'll have the luxury of hard maple).

A good guide will have firewood corded in the cabin yard and also nicely stacked stove-length pieces drying behind or at the end of the stove. See to it that this supply of dry or drying wood near the stove is kept replenished.

If the cook does not take care of his own fire, he should make sure that the kindling has been split small enough. Roy Smith used to say, "When splitting kindlin' fer a fire, split it till it looks small enough and then split it twice agin."

I usually have the sheep's-foot blade on my jackknife beveled on one side so I can the more easily shave a "beard" on the kindling to make it catch fire the more readily.

Most old bush guides will have a can of kerosene ("coal oil") standing outside the cabin door. The spout's cap will have been lost and replaced by a wrinkled potato pushed down on the aperture. Don't pour kerosene on a going fire, but it is permissible to hasten things before you start the fire by wetting the firewood. Don't do it if there are old live coals in the stove. Use the white gas *only* for the Coleman lantern and keep it also outside the camp door. Don't use white gas for any other purpose than its light-giving function.

Most busy cooks in their haste stoke the range by angling in the firewood through one or both of the opened lids rather than through the front firebox door. Make sure the firewood chunks are cut short enough to permit you to do this.

Wood Range Utensils

The most useful single utensil in my experience was an iron skillet. It had once graced the mass-production cook shack of a loggers' camp and it had a long wooden handle (for two hands) and was 18 inches from rim to rim. A man could "fry" a lot of venison round steaks or a couple of big, full-size moose steaks in that skillet; several partners could be served at the same time with hot, rare game steaks. You could make a lot of gravy in it, too. Lidded stew pots (I loved the old, flecked, blue-granite wear) are basic, for good stews are mainstays of a hunting camp. A big wide tall one with a lid is good to have for keeping a big supply of hot water on hand. I remember the blush on the face of Gordon Grant when he brought out from under a rude bunk in a tarpaper shack built especially for Mrs. Cameron and me in the New Brunswick bush a low, slightly urn-shaped, lidded blue-granite chamber pot to serve as a stew pot. He pointed out in some confusion that the manufacturer's sticker was still on it and it was all he could find in the general store at St. Croix to fill the bill in my letter asking for a "large stew pot." A tea kettle is handy but not necessary. Usually, most cabin camps will have a supply of skillets, tin pie plates, and other pots and maybe a low-sided roasting pan big enough for a leg of venison or a whole stuffed beaver.

The man who takes over the cooking does suffer under one handicap; if he's not careful he can lose a lot of hunting (or fishing) time. He has to start breakfast when it's dark out; he'll be the grateful beneficiary of the first light from the Coleman lantern and the first heat in a cold cabin from the wood range fire, both ample rewards for early rising. (He should have shaved "beards" on the kindling the night before.) Sometimes breakfast chores are divided with other early risers, and breakfasts are not too time-consuming anyhow. If it's pouring rain outside you'll probably have time for a batch of biscuits. Use Bisquick and make "drop" biscuits to save time. Scrambled eggs are quickest after the bacon is fried.

I always make "camp coffee," for it's both easiest to make and in my opinion the best of all coffees (see page 423). Wheat cakes are easy, too; their only disadvantages is that the cook usually eats them cold. Several hunters can consume prodigious amounts of syrup, so take your syrup in as sugar and save liquid weight of bottled syrup (especially if you fly in), and then make up your own syrup (see page 423).

The greatest saving of hunting time for the cook is achieved by preparing tomorrow's supper tonight. It is no trick, really, and a stew that has "set" a day is better-tasting anyway after it's warmed up.

In preparing stews and braised dishes the night before you will note that some recipes with the cabin symbol call for adding some of the vegetables during the last 45 minutes or so. While the poker game is going on, prepare your stew up to this point and then, the following night, heat it up, bring it to a simmer, and add those vegetables while drinks are served. A cookee (i.e., cook's helper) will peel the potatoes and scrape the carrots or quarter the cabbage.

Space is a consideration in most hunting cabins, and the cook may have to use one end of the poker table for his work on tomorrow's stew—such as cutting up and flouring meat chunks, etc. But a resourceful cook can use benches, chairs, the open oven door, or the washstand (with the wash basin) and a water bucket set outside for the time being for work space.

Meals based on sautéed game meats, chops and steaks, chicken-fried grouse, and various fish are easy to do after you come in from the day's hunt and can be accomplished quickly while your partners are having drinks. The trick is to come out even.

Basic Camp Cooking

The experienced camp cook, indeed the experienced cook at home, is marked by some skill at cooking logistics: that is, seeing to it that the various items on the menu are ready simultaneously or, at least, almost so. Nothing is more annoying than to discover that the eggs and bacon are ready, before the biscuits have even gone into the oven. So, a few words on the subject may be in order.

Coming Out Even at Breakfast

Since breakfasts tend to be hearty in camp, they may resemble old-time farm breakfasts more than they do the "coffee and Danish" or coffee and English muffin breakfasts of city people, e.g., potatoes often are on camp breakfast menus even when biscuits and bacon are also served.

Practiced camp cooks get used to boiling unpeeled potatoes every night, draining them, and then setting them out to cool and firm up, for (1) it is easier to scrape off the jackets than it is to peel them, and (2) it is easier to "cook" them quickly when they are already cooked, dicing and browning them for breakfast, or slicing and browning them for supper.

Logistics of a Breakfast of Bacon, Eggs, Potatoes, and Biscuits

Assuming that someone has got up and put on a hot fire for you (insist on this as routine), dragoon one of your cookees to scrape off the jackets and dice the potatoes.

While he is doing this, put on the bacon to fry and, between turnings, measure out the water and coffee and set the coffee pot on a back burner to begin to heat to a boil.

Break the eggs in a bowl and drop two half shells in the coffee pot.

Turn the bacon again and in a bowl mix the milk (best made the night before if you use dried milk) and the Bisquick.

When the bacon is done, fork it out onto a pie pan to drain on a paper towel, then scrape the diced potatoes into the hot fat and begin to brown on a hot plate. Let the potatoes brown, but slowly.

On the other equally hot plate set the coffee pot, appointing another cookee to watch it with instructions to set it off the moment it boils violently.

Turn and stir the potatoes, then beat the milk and Bisquick mixture and, making sure that the moisture is right, spoon out the thick biscuit batter onto a cookie sheet and shove it into the oven (camp biscuits should be drop biscuits rather than rolled out on a floured bread board because it's easier, and besides some guy will have found a way to use the table space needed for a bread board).

If the oven is as hot as I think it is the biscuits will be done in about 9–12 minutes.

Check on the coffee yourself in case your cookee has gone to the outhouse, then stir and turn the potatoes.

About 3–4 minutes before the biscuits are done, beat the eggs, and scramble them right in with the browned diced potatoes. Mix, stir, and later with a spatula turn over. If the biscuits are done before you scramble the eggs, open the oven door and pull the cookie sheet out onto the door to keep warm.

NOTE on individual cooking times:

    Biscuits: 9–12 minutes in a *hot* oven.

    Coffee: about 15 minutes to come to a boil over direct heat; if cooking on a wood range you may want to take the plate off and bring to a boil directly over the flames.

    Potatoes: done properly over medium heat (this should be a slow process) it can take up to 15 minutes or even more.

Coming Out Even with a Pancake Breakfast

No way! Unless you are willing to stack them up, thus assuring *soggy* pancakes, there is no way to come out even with this breakfast. The cook must face the fact that if the griddle cakes are to come to the table hot, he must fry them as they are being eaten by his partners; let *them* work out an equitable distribution of shares.

But some order can be got by the following procedure:

In a stew pan, bring the syrup water to boil (see page 423 for complete recipe), stir in the sugar, and set aside.

Start the bacon frying in the skillet.

Put on the water and coffee to boil and turn the bacon.

Put on another skillet when the bacon is done and share out into it part of the fat left in the bacon skillet, letting the second skillet come to heat while you quickly mix in a bowl the pancake flour and the liquid, preferably milk.

Begin to cook the pancakes (using both skillets) when the coffee is ready; serve them as they are done with the bacon. Have a cookee pour the coffee as the cakes get to individual plates.

NOTE: If you do try to make some of the cakes ahead of time, don't stack them, but put a cookie sheet on the open oven door and keep cakes warm by putting them, unstacked and separated, onto the sheet.

If your partners want eggs as well as hot cakes, fry the eggs after you have served the cakes, using the pancake skillets. Never mind that they'll have to eat the eggs on plates sweetened by the syrup.

If you are lucky enough to have a big pancake griddle in camp use it, but I have noticed that hungry partners do not mind—they, in fact, relish—hot cakes fried in more fat than one would normally use on a griddle. If a griddle is used, don't spoil the first batch of cakes by frying them on a griddle that is not hot enough. Besides, they'll stick on such a griddle. The griddle is hot enough when water sprinkled on it does not merely sizzle in wet puddles, but separates into discrete balls of water that scamper helter-skelter over the griddle's surface.

Coming Out Even on a Bacon and French Toast Breakfast

As above, prepare the syrup and put on the coffee.

Fry the bacon.

Using the recipe below in proper quantities for the company and their appetites, make up the batter.

3 eggs	2 tsp. sugar
1 cup milk	½ tsp. vanilla extract (optional)
¼ tsp. salt	6 slices bread

In a bowl beat the eggs, then beat in the milk and other ingredients (except bread), and pour into shallow dish or pie pan.

Dip both sides of bread slices in the batter (don't soak it to a mush) and brown in the bacon fat. (I keep fat from the bacon grease can, noting that most hunters or anglers like fat in their French toast.)

NOTE: It takes four or five times as long to fry French toast as it does to produce a hot cake.

Some guy will be used to eating *his* French toast with a couple of fried eggs rather than with butter and syrup. Serve him last.

If you have to fry French toast ahead, use the same method to keep hot as with pancakes, for French toast will get soggy if stacked, just as pancakes do.

Bacon, Eggs, and Fried Bread

Sometimes a nonhotcake and nonbiscuit breakfast may be relished. Here, using both the fat from the bacon and added fat for a second skillet, fry slices of bread to a golden brown on both sides, set aside to drain, and top each slice with a couple of fried eggs (and bacon) for each partner.

No matter how well the cook makes things come out even for his partners, he, himself, often eats alone at the second table. Never mind; your breakfast will be hot, and a little tone of martyrdom on the cook's part is good for morale; out of guilt your water-fetching, fire-tending partners, and your cookees and dishwasher, will go out of their ways with their chores to ensure that *you* continue to do the cooking.

Hot Cereals

Some people *always* want hot cereal for breakfast and most hunters welcome it in a bush camp. Oatmeal, Wheatena, cornmeal mush, and Cream of Wheat are obvious candidates. Somehow, when the camp is in Canada (or near the border), I always feel that Red River is the appropriate cereal. That was the cereal universally eaten in the logging camps in the Big North, and millions of board feet of white pine were cut with energy partly supplied by this ubiquitous porridge. To my taste Red River is the best of them, and you can still buy it in Canada. It is a mixed grain cereal with a fine nutty flavor. Loggers and other bushmen of days gone by sweetened this porridge with West Indian molasses, but those still under the influence of their Highland forebears took this cereal and the equally common oatmeal porridge just with a pinch of salt. I usually put on the cereal before I make the coffee.

Coming Out Even at Supper

The logistics and timing of the evening meal after a day's hunt are less trying for the cook; at breakfast the need for speed is greater if the company is to get into the woods or onto the stream or lake early. Conversely, at dinner, there is no rush, much relaxation, and conversation over drinks. The general hunger as a prod to the cook is about the same for both meals.

The meal at night is usually a bit more elaborate in preparation but not burdensomely so. However, timing is just as necessary. In the case of dinner, we can usually assume that the basic menu will be meat, potatoes (or noodles or spaghetti), and a vegetable. If game is on the gam stick and the meat course consists of pan-broiled steaks or chops, the meal is pretty straightforward. If embers are left in the stove, or even if not, the fire is usually attended to quickly, for it brings warmth as well as food, and sometimes the party is as grateful for the heat as for the coming meal.

A Pan-Broiled Steak, Potato, and Vegetable Supper

Let's face it: Most vegetables served in camp come out of cans. The exception, of course, is the one-dish meal, the stew in which *fresh* vegetables are used. But peas, string beans, corn, and spinach taste better out of cans if you drain their juices into a stew pan and boil the liquid down to half volume, then set the reduced liquid on a warming plate before pouring in the vegetables themselves. The hot liquid then merely warms the vegetable; after all, the vegetables are cooked when they are canned.

At supper, I usually make my partners eat bread, seldom baking biscuits save when grouse are served.

Potatoes take most time so, as I have suggested, I always have on hand boiled potatoes that can be sliced and browned in lard or fat. To vary the fare, and also to save time, I also serve mashed potatoes made from potato flakes, but I "doctor" them to improve their flavor.

As to the steaks, I serve them "pink," a compromise, for I like them rare; I have found that a number of hunters (and guides) when forced to eat medium-rare steaks discover the obvious for the first time—that they taste better than the well-done steaks they've "preferred" since boyhood. However, there is sometimes that finicky and benighted partner whose prejudice is ingrained; for him, I sauté a portion well done (this same man usually won't eat liver or kidneys, but will finally admit that moose heart soup is delicious).

Famished hunters, even those with sophisticated palates, never scorn plain old country-fried steaks or chops and the honest old pan gravy that is served with them. With fried potatoes this makes a meal fit for hungry hunters.

The Basic Procedure

Have a cookee strip off the potato jackets and dice the potatoes.

While he's doing this, put on a skillet to heat containing a dollop of lard or bacon fat.

Prepare the coffee pot with water and coffee (I've found that at least two out of three campers like their coffee with the meal) or have a cookee do this.

Stir up the fire, adding small sticks if necessary, for you'll want a hot stove with open draft and damper later for the steaks.

Put the potatoes in the skillet and try to find the second-hottest plate to brown them over. Turn them often with a spatula.

Put juice of canned vegetable in a saucepan and bring to a boil alongside the coffee pot on the hottest plate.

When the two have boiled, set them off on a warming plate, and ask a cookee to put the vegetables into the now reduced juice. Add 2 tablespoons butter.

By now, it has been about 15 minutes since you put on the potatoes, time to heat the fat for the steaks. Heat your biggest, heaviest skillet on the hottest plate, rub the skillet bottom with a piece of suet (add a tablespoon or so of lard or baking fat), and lay in the steaks.

Cock an eye at the potatoes; if they threaten to brown too much move the skillet over to a plate of lesser heat.

Pan broil the steaks' first side (remember the skillet must be very hot) for about a minute or two, or until the blood begins to ooze on the upper side, then turn and sear the other side 2 minutes. Move the skillet to a plate wtih less heat (close down partially both draft and damper) and cook for 8–10 minutes more for 1½-inch steaks. Don't hesitate to cut into a steak to check the sought-for degree of rareness; better to lose a little juice than to have the steak overdone.

Remove steaks to a platter that is warming on the open oven door.

Crush a garlic clove and a bouillon cube in the skillet, pour in ½ cup of red wine, stir, and let it bubble.

Just before you serve the steaks, pour off the juice that has come off the steaks into the sauce. Pour the sauce into a gravy boat—oops, into a tin cup—and serve steaks, potatoes, and vegetable.

General Comments on Handling Game Steaks and Chops in Camp

In this book there are several recipes for steaks, chops, gravies, and sauces, and most of these can be prepared in camp. But here is perhaps the place for some general comment on cooking steaks in a skillet on top of the stove. (Swiss steaks are sometimes prepared on top of the stove, but the following remarks exclude them.)

There are three ways to do it—pan broiled as above, fried, and *boiled*. The latter is anathema, but too often is the way steaks get cooked in camp if precautions are not taken.

The wet, boiled effect with the meat sickly steamed rather than seared, pan-broiled, or fried, comes from two errors or a combination: (1) using a skillet and fat that are not nearly hot enough, and (2) crowding the steaks in the skillet. Just as in browning meat cubes for a stew, steaks pan broiled or fried should be well separated in the skillet and seared violently on both sides before the rest of the cooking proceeds under somewhat lesser heat. To keep steaks apart, a big skillet is needed, and blessed is the cook who finds one of those 18-inch long-handled two-handed lumber camp cast-iron skillets among the utensils in camp.

One Further Note on Pan Broiling

If the chops or steaks have some marbling, as sometimes with moose, or have a suet rim, one can pan broil without any fat at all in the skillet. In this instance one replaces the fat with salt. I remember a moose steak pan broiled in salt at midnight (when high winds and heavy seas had prevented one canoeing home any earlier) that was delicious. Our old trapper friend, Roy Smith, happened to have rock salt in camp (rock salt is ideal) and I broiled a 1½-inch-thick steak from a fat dry cow (legal) on salt in that 18-inch skillet that was delicious beyond words.

Pile on the wood, open draft and damper, and sprinkle enough salt on the bottom of a skillet to make it white. Get your skillet and salt smoking hot.

Lay in the steak and follow directions for searing and cooking as for pan-broiled steak above.

While steak is searing move it around by shaking the skillet.

General Comment on Stews in Camp

There are two times to prepare stews in camp: on a blustery rainy day when not even you have the heart to venture forth and at night when you can cook or half-cook a stew for next night's dinner. It has to be a truly horrendous day to keep me out of the deer woods, for with most of us, some of the most successful still-hunting is done on drizzly days when the woods are quiet.

If the cook stays in camp he can prepare a fine stew at leisure from any of the stew or braised recipes in this book. But he can also make stew and hunt, too. I call the latter "Poker Game Cookery."

If you are a bad poker player you won't be able to do poker game cookery, for you will stay in every pot and lose your shirt in the process. But if you throw in when you should you will have plenty of time between hands or by dropping out for a hand or two to do the various steps. Take a look at the Cabin-Style Burgoo recipe, page 417, for the logistics of making a stew during a poker game, and then adapt any stew recipe marked with ⊟ to this system.

Baked Bean Strategy in Camp

There is no doubt that a big bean pot of baked beans saves the cook much "side dish" cookery and is always welcomed by hungry hunters when they see its comforting presence on the back of the stove.

The logistics of camp baked beans is easy. If you start them on Tuesday morning you can eat them Wednesay night without taking any time away from your hunting. Before you go to bed Monday night, wash and soak a pound of dry navy beans, put them in a stew pot in 2 quarts of cold water, cover, and set them aside. In the morning as you're putting on the coffee, add water (hot if you've got it) to cover the swelled-up beans and bring to boil on a hot lid out of the way and then set them back to simmer. Let them simmer for 30 minutes, then drain and reserve the liquid in another pot. Set the beans down on the floor out of the way, covered (otherwise you'll find a drowned whitefoot mouse in them later).

That night, after you come in from the hunt, commandeer one of your cookees and while you yourself are cooking supper, ask your cookee to assemble the beans and other ingredients in the bean pot. By now the wood range oven will be hot and the assembled bean pot can be put in with its lid slightly askew and to all intents and purposes forgotten save for periodic checking by you and/or your cookee. But during the evening you and he should check the beans several times (and dampen the stove if the oven gets raging hot) by digging and scraping up the bottom beans with a big spoon, adding liquid as it cooks down. I usually mix a small can of V-8 juice or plain tomato juice with the reserved drained liquor in which I've simmered the beans during breakfast and use this to keep the proper moisture in the bean pot.

If the bean pot went into the oven at 6:30 or 7:00 P.M. and if the poker or gin rummy game is still going at midnight, you probably can dole out a spoonful of sample as a midnight snack to those who are still up. Baked beans usually take about 5–6 hours of baking. They should be soft (but not a mush) and each bean thoroughly imbued with all of the delicious flavors in the recipe.

Next morning while you get breakfast you can set the bean pot on the corner of the warming section of the stove, putting in some liquid if the beans seem too dry, and maybe they'll still be slightly warm when you return from the hunt that night, or you can close the draft and damper and put the bean pot in the oven just before you leave for the day's hunt. They'll cook further there and stay warm for quite a while after the fire goes out during the day's hunt. If you went to bed at eleven the night before and took the bean pot out of the oven before you climbed into your sleeping bag, they will finish cooking during the morning before the oven cools out. Be sure there is enough hot liquid in the pot before you leave camp.

Game Cooking under Canvas

The logistics of camp cooking in a tent can be quite complex. Small space atop the Yukon stove and the minimum of utensils can sorely challenge the ingenuity of the cook. Yet, with practice and determination, one can prepare fine meals in a tent, and good meals go a long way toward making up for the inconvenience of the cramp and clutter of such temporary homes in the wild.

Nowadays one can get collapsible sheet-metal stoves cum detachable ovens (and even a water tank). The ones with an oven that hooks onto the long side of the stove itself are handy, although, again, one must learn how far to keep the oven door ajar to compensate for the inferno of heat that sometimes rages inside.

The top of a sheet-metal stove is capable of swift-changing areas of heat, for the whole box is a fire box. One must learn to pass the palm of the hand just over the surface to find which area is now hot enough to fry or sauté and which area is now the simmering area. The vagaries on the surface of a Yukon stove are wondrous to behold; its surface heat is as changeable as a sunset with clouds.

My wife and I once spent three weeks camped alone on the tundra on a cut-bank of the Alaskan Colville, a half mile upstream from where the Chandler joins the Arctic's greatest river. The meats in camp were moose, caribou, ptarmigan, and grayling, and when the spirit would move me, which was often, we dined like a medieval lady and lord. Two of the dishes prepared, Ptarmigan Tarragon and Bourguignon of Moose Fillets, represented two degrees of difficulty in cooking on a sheet-metal stove under canvas. On both occasions I kept a log in my journal, one of which I will reproduce verbatim below, for its record may be considered a lesson for the reader as it was for me.

As will be seen, the journal entry (unedited incidentally) reveals the intricacies of both fire-tending and cooking under the handicaps that do attend cooking on a sheet-metal stove.

But a brief word first about setting up a Yukon stove. The drill is to create a bed of gravel for the stove itself (under the asbestos stovepipe aperture in the tent's roof). This gravel bed will prevent the stove's heat from setting the sod afire, and, believe me, once afire that sod can burn like peat and spread laterally as a smolder under the surface. The gravel bed should be 3–4 inches deep, its surface made level with the tent's sod floor by removing some of the ancient sod before filling with gravel.

In windy country you may have to guy the portion of the chimney above the tent roof, and maybe experiment with the length of the chimney if you have, as you should, an extra section of stove pipe. The draft and damper of a sheet-metal stove can be fickle until you learn their almost animate personalities. Be sure to remember that the little handle on the sliding draft in the door is always hot, and the handle on the chimney damper may be hot too in a high fire. With its virtues of both heating and cooking, the Yukon stove in inexperienced hands can be dangerous. But then so can the rifles in your party. Later in this chapter we will speak of the precautions you must take in setting up a Yukon stove in a tent. If the tent camp is a summer camp, even with cool nights, a two-burner Coleman is safer, and it has an added virtue: it can be carried and used outside the tent if you wish.

Remember that the sheet-metal stove is a merciless and ravenous consumer of firewood; the stove size and door size make smaller sticks necessary and *they* burn quickly. So be sure to have plenty of wood at hand when cooking on a Yukon stove. Lay your sticks between the stove and the tent to dry if necessary.

When camped north of timber or beside a tundra river your tent site will be chosen for its proximity to willow flats, for willow will be your only firewood. Tundra rivers, like the Chandler, or the Colville, far north of timber, will nevertheless have flats of felt-leaf willows. These are not low-bush or prostrate Arctic willows, but are tree size, growing to heights of 15–25 feet or more. Moose will live on the tundra and feed on willow browse, following rivers with stands of felt-leaf willows or even low shrub willows (I once saw a moose cow and calf right out on the tundra not 15 miles from the Arctic Ocean).

Firewood (and moose meat) is easy here, for not only have the moose pushed over many such trees, but many 4–7-inch-thick willows will be dead and dry but still standing. One doesn't fell them but merely pushes them over, then limbs them out and drags them to camp for bucking and splitting. Willow burns hotly in a Yukon stove and is the stand-by firewood for cooking and heating in the far North.

When you lay down the sand and gravel bed on which to set up the Yukon stove, be certain that this bed extends well out in front of the slotted draft through which hot coals may fall. I once camped in a tent that was completely floored with a sewn-in ground sheet. We laid the gravel bed right over the canvas and let it extend enough beyond the stove's front to prevent such hot coals from burning holes in the ground sheet. We set the stove itself on four corners on flat stones (that stove was footed) on top of the gravel bed.

When the tent has no ground cloth, dig a 2–3-inch pit in which to "pour" your gravel and sand for the stove's flooring.

On the trip where it was at sun-up about 12° outside and 15° inside, I discovered that it took between 25 and 30 minutes after I got out of the sleeping bag to bring the tent's temperature (at folding table level) to 68°, the temperature at which my wife is willing to get up in any camp. (In camp, she is a tyrant on that one count.) She is, however, as interested as I in stoves and ovens. On this occasion, as always, she did the baking, and she soon learned all there was to learn about sheet-metal heat control, for she baked both yeast bread and delectable brown sugar and cinnamon yeast rolls in the infinitely variable temperatures of that oven. She did this partly by keeping the coals in the stove itself away from the side where the oven was attached, partly by manipulating the oven's door, and partly by shifting and turning the bread or roll pan. My journal records the step-by-step baking process too, but I'll leave the reader to learn baking for himself or herself.

Let the following record give a typical example of the steps in preparing a notable meal on a sheet-metal stove in a tent:

THURSDAY, SEPTEMBER 16, 1976, pp. 41–44, Vol. II, *"Hunting and Fishing, Alaska, 1976."*
—I figure to have moose heart broth with barley, chicken-fried ptarmigan in a tarragon cream sauce, cucumber pickles (some of the liquid leaked out in the plane as we flew in), camp-baked bread and butter, strawberry jam, and tea.

Sheila is putting water on to boil in the big saucepan and more in the pot for tea and I will put the blast on the stove—in the last 3 minutes I had the surface and 6 inches of the stove pipe red hot and had to dampen the pipe and close the draft at once—

Just came back with the last armful of willow. It is a fine feeling on this chill evening, with the ground fog now obscuring the bluffs across the river, to know that there is enough wood for tonight and tomorrow morning—

The teapot boiled earlier than the pot of water for potatoes (and, later, for dishes) so I set it aside on the oven (with a third of it sticking over onto the stove proper). I then dipped out 1½ cups of water into a smaller pan, added butter, salt and pepper, and dry milk and set it on the hottest place on the surface to boil. Set the pot with the remaining water back to keep hot.

While that was going on I cleaned up (I had picked them earlier) the birds and floured the bird breasts. Sheila had got out a pie pan for flour with enough for the birds and some left over for the roux—

Stoked the fire again and opened the draft, put on skillet when the potato water had boiled (and I could move it off to make space). Put margarine and butter in skillet (over hot spot located with a putting on of hand just above surface) and then stirred into the boiling "milk" 1 cup potato flakes and 2 tablespoons grated Parmesan, set them on serving surface. Then put in skillet the two floured breasts. By now the hot spot was toward back of stove, so I put skillet there and later moved it forward over a less hot place to cook more slowly under a lid—

While breasts were cooking (damper and draft off but more willow sticks put in on the deep coals), I mixed up a cup of cold water and dried milk for the "cream" gravy. My knees were getting sore again by now. I checked by cutting to see if the breasts were done, using the flashlight to see by in the dark, flap-closed side of the tent.

Sheila had put the teapot back on the hot spot (still at back of stove, but farther to the left) and it boiled quickly. She made tea and set it aside while I tended the stove. She handed me the flour pan after I had taken the breasts out of the skillet onto a tin plate (set on the oven top to keep warm), and I was gratified in stirring the flour into the fat and the bird crisps to note that there were ample makings for gravy. I found the tarragon cum basil plastic bottle, sprinkled in a heaping half teaspoon into the flour, and salted and peppered it. When flour had colored a bit I poured in the milk I had made. As it boiled and bubbled over the heat (closed draft) and as I stirred, Sheila added water as needed from a flagon of newly fetched water (the flagon was a cleaned-out syrup bottle).

Sheila had poured me a cup of heart soup [Ed. note: this soup had been made earlier that day and was heated in two tin cups set on a hot spot] which I drank as the gravy cooked. Meanwhile Sheila got out the pickles, gave me the breast pan *sans* one breast, now on her plate, served me the mashed potatoes and cream gravy, and then herself, cutting me a half pickle for salad.

When I got up to perk up the fire I served (myself, as I didn't want any more) up the last of the potatoes and gravy and took potato pot and gravy skillet outside and poured in some water to make washing easier, then came in and finished my meal—I got Sheila's compliments.

Sheila now poured tea, and while I sliced the bread, she produced the strawberry preserves. Sheila says I produced the meal in 25 minutes after the water boiled.

The menu had been, fancied up some:

SOUP: Broth of Moose Heart with Barley
ENTRÉE: Chicken-Fried Ptarmigan Breasts
       Cream Gravy with Tarragon
       Mashed Potatoes with Cheese
SALAD: Cucumbers Pickled in Dill
DESSERT: Camp-Baked Yeast Bread with Butter and Wild
       Strawberry Jam
BEVERAGE: Hot Tea

Most of the recipes in this book for stews and braises can be prepared on a sheet-metal stove in a tent; and, of course, any soup. Fish can be fried atop such a stove, of course, as can steaks and chops. Fish cookery is more difficult, for fish should cook slowly and gently, something hard to achieve on sheet metal. Usually we either sauté fish in butter, dipped in cornmeal, or poach them (or thick chunks of bigger fish) in a court bouillon (see page 241) and eat them with mayonnaise after cooling. (I sometimes make green mayonnaise by adding chervil and tarragon to Hellmann's wonderful base.)

When one cooks in a tent camp he must take in everything, including the utensils, and usually if one comes in by pack outfit or more likely by plane one has to go light. I can usually persuade a pilot that my much-used nested Bean cook kit represents the smallest package and lightest weight these items come in. The large and small kettle, the skillet, the four plates, four cups, salt and pepper shakers (lidded), and coffee pot will enable you to make it, but I sometimes smuggle in an extra skillet and stew pot if I can get them past the pilot's sharp eyes. In permanent cabin camps one seldom has to worry about utensils, for they are there when you arrive, usually as an accumulation of convenience from other hunting parties in the past.

In some wilderness areas, especially in pack-camp tarp lean-tos in the mountains, the cooking is done over an open fire. This is a special art, and the guide is apt to be better at it than you are. I have done it on occasion on four or five days of backpack hunts in Alaska, but the cooking is usually survival cooking. If you can manage, tie a wire grill with collapsible legs on the flat of your packboard. The grill, which can be kept level for a skillet or a pot far more easily than an arranged assortment of odd-size and shaped stones, will be a great convenience.

Cooking fires should be small, no wider than the grill, and you don't cook over leaping flames but over a bed of coals, the embers constantly pushed in under the utensils to keep up the heat. Sometimes it's a good idea to build two fires and push the nonflaming embers of one fire onto the grill's fire.

Of course, you can grill meat in the wilds using either the grill itself or an improvised spit. One of the most rewarding meals I ever ate was from a side of fat caribou ribs grilled on a green poplar pole turned over and sticks above alder coals. Bud Helmericks, the famous Alaskan guide and outfitter (author of *The Last of the Bush Pilots*), was cook on that occasion, and he did the same thing three years later with Dall sheep ribs over a willow fire.

But usually on such trips boiled or fried (sautéed) meat makes up the menu, supplemented sometimes with a tin cupful of tiny Arctic blueberries and a bit of sugar brought along for the tea. On those Alaskan hunts we always carried moose jerky, making lunch on slivers pared off thin with a jackknife and using larger pieces boiled for supper. I discovered on one of those trips that 8 pounds of moose jerky is the equivalent of about 32 pounds of the same meat when fresh.

Meals Afoot in the Bush

There is a full and varied cuisine of dried foods and one-dish meals for the man afoot in the bush, and hikers are skilled with the one-burner spirit lamp and its logistics in preparing decent meals. I have hunted and cooked in Alaska on four- or five-day jaunts afoot with sleeping bags, tarp for a lean-to, and the absolute minimum of food and gear. Bud Helmericks and I on a 1949 grizzly hunt in the Brooks Range in Alaska were away from our base cabin for four nights, and our grub consisted of sugar, tea, salt, and 8 pounds of moose jerky—period. For lunch we shaved off slivers of jerky like two sourdoughs (Bud was authentic), paring off a chaw of plug, and for supper we boiled chunks of jerky for a stew in one of the saucepans while we made tea in the other. And we had dessert, too, for we'd select a spot for camp where each of us could pick blueberries. Bud had brought enough sugar for the berries *and* the tea.

We had one grand repast on that hunt, for Bud had planned it so that we could shoot a caribou on our return trip close enough to the base camp to permit us to pack in all of the meat (two trips). It was darkish when we finished butchering that fat bull and I was so foot-weary and dog-tired that I got into my sack supperless. I slept like a baby and was awakened well into the morning by the most delicious odors I can remember: when fully conscious, and hungry as a wolf, I was greeted by the sight of a whole side of fat ribs on a green pole across a Y stick broiling over the embers of a willow fire. With hunger as the sauce, that meal was one of the two or three most memorably delicious meals I have ever eaten. Bud later gave me a picture he snapped of me. Peering through a slab of ribs, now denuded of meat, I looked for all the world like a disheveled unshaven vagrant peering through the jail bars of a drunk tank.

Quite elaborate dried-food meals are being prepared by seasoned hikers these days, but I have done little of this kind of cooking. My own campfire cooking has been of the simple one-skillet, one stew-pan, and one tea-pail variety that one does on a canoe and fishing cruise. This has been mostly survival cookery; trying to keep a skillet level on three stones over coals is not much fun for the cook. Nowadays on such jaunts I wouldn't even use a skillet for fish (see recipe, page 235, for fish in foil).

On Wilderness Lunches

The first year we hunted with Roy Smith out of his Horseshoe Lake trapping cabin, my wife and I learned a valuable lesson about preparing the next day's lunch. Supper was over, the dishes done, when I got out the bread, butter, and Spam can. Roy, his lips pursed as they always were when he was in momentary deep thought before bursting into violent action of some kind, the very next moment said philosophically, "Youse're making the lunch at the wrong time of day."

Startled at first, I then got, or thought I got, his meaning: "Oh, do you think they will be stale by morning?"

"No," said Roy, a bit wistfully. "It's just that if ye make up ye're lunch after ye'al had ye're supper youse will be a sandwich short on the morrow."

I've never forgotten that good bush advice: Always make the sandwiches for tomorrow's noon tea-fire while you are still hungry, i.e., *before* you eat your supper.

If you've got game in camp, sliced deer or moose heart or tongue cold with a bit of salt and catsup make delicious meat sandwiches, and you'd better also make up a jelly or preserve sandwich each for dessert, or at least put in hearty chunks of bannock, preferably containing raisins and/or apricots as well as brown sugar (see page 426).

We introduced into Roy's noon tea menu date cakes (squares of which we also carried in our pockets for quick energy). These confections Roy called Thousand Mile—"Eat one piece and a mon's good for a thousand miles in the bush," he said after first tasting one (see page 425).

Sliced roast game sandwiches (or sliced pot roast) are always welcome (and those little sandwich envelopes are fine for wrapping them).

My wife sticks to peanut butter and jelly sandwiches, getting both entrée and dessert in the same sandwich. Roy always baited her choice by saying, "Peanut butter sticks to the roof of me mouth—don't it yours?—and besides it's really fer baiting the camp mouse traps."

Take plenty of tea and sugar, and don't forget the old lard pail for a teapot. Roy always wrapped his in a piece of gunnysack to keep its sooty exterior "from dirtying me fine pack sack."

Remember, if you make the tea, be sure to cut a dip stick for lifting it and be sure there are plenty of tea leaves in it. Guides invariably like strong tea, as I once learned in New Brunswick. When the tea I had made caused old Henry Allen to give new expression to Ray's comment in a similar situation, Ray had said "Pale tea for pale people," but Mr. Allen answered my protest ("But I'd call that strong tea") by the rejoinder, "Why, Angus, a man could see to spear eels in thirty feet of that!"

I always prefer oranges as fruit at a noon tea, but bury the peels, for if you don't you'll be rebuked by their scarcely changed appearance when you pass by the dead coals of your tea site a full year later.

There is something about the ritual of the noon tea-fire that gilds the lily of pleasure on a hunt. Roy was once genuinely outraged when I, coming in from a lone hunt, confessed that I'd had a dry lunch. "Oh, you must never do that," said Roy. "A mon must have his hot tea at the noonin'." He is quite right, of course (and why is it that tea it must be, not coffee?).

Some General Camp Recipes

Although the previous sections include many recipes that can be prepared in camp (some are marked with this symbol ⌂), it seemed to us that more stand-by recipes might be useful for those who regularly cook in camp. Most of these are breads and pancakes; a couple are one-dish meals before the game is on the gam stick; others are useful miscellaneous recipes such as how to improve canned baked beans, how to improvise a delicious substitute for maple syrup, or how to make plain old camp coffee in a granite pot.

A CHANGE-OF-PACE
CAMP HAM DISH SUPPER

When you are still eating ham for supper, waiting for fresh meat, and if you have been able to smuggle in some sour cream here's a change-of-pace ham dish that will go well with some of your boiled potatoes sliced and browned.

SERVES 2

a big slice of ham ½" thick
2 Tb. bacon grease
¾ cup coffee

3 heaping Tb. sour cream
1 heaping tsp. prepared mustard
½ tsp. sugar, preferably brown

Fry the ham on both sides in the hot fat until it is well browned. Don't mind if it sticks a bit, for you want the brown dredgings.

Remove ham to a hot pie plate on the open oven door.

Stir in the coffee, being certain that you loosen all of the "greables." Let it simmer.

Just before you serve the ham, stir in and blend the sour cream, mustard, and sugar. Let it heat, but do not boil.

Serve in a mug or tin cup, doubling as a "gravy boat."

CABIN-STYLE BURGOO

Most wilderness or back country camps will manage (unless the hunters flew in) to have a variety of fresh vegetables in camp—potatoes, turnips, celery, carrots, cabbage, and onions—and in addition some canned goods. At the same time, if the luck has held, the gam stick will be hanging with game and someone will have supplied the larder with two or three grouse, and possibly a snowshoe rabbit.

During the poker game the night before while the fire in the wood range is good, put 4 pounds of red meat (deer, moose, elk) cut into two or three pieces, two or three grouse, and a rabbit (if you have it) in the big kettle in camp. Cover with cold water and add four or five onions, sliced, bay leaf, and a tablespoon of salt for each 2 quarts of water. Bring to a boil (you'll know where the hottest stove lid is by this time), skim a couple of times, then cover, and set the big pot on a lid where it will simmer. Go back to the poker game. Don't worry—some cold-blooded partner will keep the fire going. Two or three times when you've turned down your cards on a hand, check for doneness. When the meat and birds are tender, perhaps in an hour and a half to two hours (enough time to lose your shirt if the cards are running against you), take out the meats and put them to cool. (Use a covered receptacle; otherwise the whitefoot mice will get at it.) Set covered stock aside for the next night.

The next evening, after someone else has put on a fire, return the meats to the pot after first cutting the red meat into 1-inch cubes. Take the meat off the bones of the birds and cube also.

Bring to a boil on the hottest lid and add the vegetables in order of cooking time (potatoes, carrots, celery, and turnips cut into chunks), later the cabbage. Mince 3–4 cloves of garlic in at this stage.

Next have a look at the canned goods: there'll be a can of tomatoes (drain and put the tomatoes in); then add 1½ teaspoons thyme, 1 teaspoon oregano, and ¼ teaspoon savory, and simmer for 30 minutes or so. Now add a drained can of peas and a drained can of corn niblets; continue to simmer until the long-cooking trio are done.

I usually put 1–2 tablespoons of flour in some water, stir, add a couple of tablespoons of the hot stock, stir again, and then mix slowly into the pot to thicken the mix some.

As the meat, and later the meat cum vegetables simmer, you may have to add liquid. Water or water and wine will do if you have wine.

If you are an ambitious camp cook you will have made baking powder biscuits or better, corn bread, to go with the burgoo. The wood range oven will be free for baking. Figure about 20 minutes in a hot oven to bake corn bread (see pages 424–430 for recipes for breads). Of course unsweetened bannock goes well with this dish, too (see page 424).

Obviously this dish is prepared similarly at home, and perhaps more easily.

CROOKED KNIFE STEW

I once hunted with an old-time Maine woodsman named Didge Smith who carried jerky for his noon lunch. He'd dig into his pack basket and fetch out his jerky and an ancient crooked knife which he'd use to draw slivers off the edge of his jerky. When I twitted him about his crooked knife, he would counter, "A man never knows when he might need one to draw arrers [arrows]."

Crooked Knife Stew is any stew made when you're hard up for fresh meat—out of jerky.

SERVES 2

3–4 oz. jerky
1 onion, diced
2–3 potatoes, sliced
16-oz. can tomatoes
2 carrots

1–2 "of anything else you're a
    mind to put in, like turnips,
    say, or parsnips"
salt and pepper
2 Tb. flour

The game is to start the jerky in some water with the onion, bring it to a boil, and simmer until you're hungry. Then add the other ingredients (except flour) and continue cooking another 30 minutes.

Thicken by stirring in the flour mixed with 3 tablespoons water. Simmer a few minutes to cook out the flour taste.

— PAN-BROILED VENISON STEAK WITH BISCUITS — AND CAMP GRAVY WITH HERBS

Cut a 1½-inch round (or two) off the deer, put it in a pie pan, and save the blood that drains out.

Begin this basic camp meal about a half hour before you put on the steaks by mixing up a batch of biscuits, stoking up the fire and following the directions on the box for drop biscuits. Just before you flour the steaks put the biscuits in the wood range oven (450° if you are at home); they'll take 10 or so minutes to bake and brown.

After cutting a couple of deep gashes on one side of the steak, flour both sides and put it (gash side down) in a skillet with smoking grease (3 tablespoons, half lard and half butter).

Sauté quickly, turn, and sauté other side (about 3 minutes on each side), remove the rare steaks, and put on a hot platter.

Pour drained blood into the skillet and stir 2 tablespoons of flour and ½ teaspoon each thyme and rosemary into the fat drippings. Add half-cooked blood and cook over low heat for 2 minutes.

Now stir in 1 cup liquid, half water and half condensed milk or dried milk mix, and cook until it thickens. Simmer for 4–5 minutes, adding liquid to keep the thickening gravy at the right consistency.

While a partner is serving the steak, break a biscuit in half on each plate and cover with the hot cream gravy. Pass beach plum or red currant jelly.

════ EGGS HOPEFUL: ════

A Change-of-Pace Supper
When There's No Fresh Meat in Camp

When you've eaten the last of the ham and are saving the bacon for breakfasts and can't face another slice of those canned, pressed meats, here's a camp recipe that's easy to make and one that most hunters will appreciate while waiting for the luck to change.

I called it "Eggs Hopeful" once, and the name stuck. This one-dish meal will stick to the ribs and gives the illusion at least of good Italian cookery. Figure at least two eggs for each hunter. Be prepared to fix it again on a two-week trip, for your partners will probably suggest it again, even after someone has hung up a deer.

SERVES 4

2 medium to large onions, chopped
1 green pepper, chopped (optional)
2 Tb. lard or bacon fat
1 large can tomatoes
6 slices bread, crumbled
2 tsp. dry oregano and basil mix, or 1 tsp. of each herb

1 Tb. chili powder
1 tsp. Worcestershire sauce (optional)
¼–½ cup grated Parmesan or some sliced, diced rat cheese
2 cloves garlic, sliced thin or crushed
8 or more eggs

Sauté in a big skillet the onions and pepper in lard or bacon fat until soft, then add the tomatoes, crumbled bread slices, herbs, chili powder, and Worcestershire.

With a wooden spoon or big kitchen spoon smash up the tomatoes and stir the bread until the mix is more or less uniform in texture. Simmer until the mix thickens. Now stir in the cheese and garlic. When the cheese has melted, using the bowl of a big spoon, make indentations in the thickened mix and break an egg in each depression. Cover with a lid and simmer until the egg whites (or yolks too if you like) firm up.

═══ SPANISH RICE AS ANOTHER ONE-DISH ═══ MEAL BEFORE MEAT IS IN CAMP

The grub list for your hunting camp will certainly have, among your dry ingredients, rice, spaghetti, and noodles. The rice can be a box or two of precooked rice and, I'll admit, this is handy stuff to have around. But you can start from scratch. When I do so, I usually find the time some evening to cook up some rice, so I'll have it on hand. During long evenings over cards or beer (or both) you can find time to boil some rice for later use. That old wood range, always having to heat the cabin, can be used at any time for cooking.

SERVES 3–4

2 Tb. butter
1 cup uncooked rice
  (preferably long-grained
  Carolina)

salt and pepper
2 cups hot water

Melt butter in Dutch oven or lidded casserole and sauté rice until it becomes translucent and then lightly browned. Add salt, pepper, and hot water, cover tightly, and simmer for 16 minutes. After about 10 minutes stir once with a fork, but otherwise leave lid on. You can cool and keep for use a day or so later (or of course serve it for itself).

As to the Spanish rice dish, I'll give the recipe so you can use either boxed precooked rice or rice that you have cooked earlier yourself. In this version I am assuming that you brought along a couple of dozen frankfurters in your grub boxes. If you didn't, substitute any canned meat like Spam or corned beef that you did bring.

As we go along you'll see that you can improvise with Spanish rice; there is no such thing as a classic recipe, but this one I like very much—and so do a lot of hungry hunters.

Beer goes well with this hearty dish. Dessert? A big can of Elberta peach halves and fig newtons.

SERVES 4–6

6 slices bacon
6–8 frankfurters
2 onions, chopped
2 cloves garlic
1–2 green peppers, chopped
1 rib celery with leaves,
    chopped, or 1 tsp. celery salt
3 cups of your own cooked rice
    or 1½ cups (Uncle Ben's)
    precooked rice
1½ cups hot water
    (or stock if you have it)

8-oz. can tomatoes
2 Tb. chili powder
½ tsp. crushed fennel seed
    and/or basil and oregano
1 Tb. Worcestershire sauce
½ cup grated Parmesan
1 tsp. dry mustard
    or prepared mustard
1 chunk rat cheese
    or Cheddar, sliced thin

The rest is easy.

Cut up the bacon slices in 1-inch lengths and sauté until brown in a big skillet.

Add franks cut into 1-inch sections and brown.

Just before the frank chunks are brown, add and sauté onions, garlic, pepper(s), and celery until just soft.

Add all the rest of the ingredients, except the rat cheese, and stir well to mix. Cover and cook *slowly* for 15–20 minutes.

Just before ready to serve, thinly slice the rat cheese or Cheddar and spread over surface, replace lid, and cook until cheese has melted. Bring the skillet right to the table.

QUICK CAMP BAKED BEANS

Here's a way to improve on what comes out of a can of baked beans for a quick supper for a tired company. This is for three or four, and once the fire is going you can have it on their plates before your partners finish their second drink.

SERVES 3–4

6 frankfurters in 1″ slices
    (or a tin of Spam
    or even corned beef)
1 Tb. butter
1 onion, finely chopped
4 slices bacon, diced
28-oz. can baked beans
    (B&M are good)

2 tsp. prepared mustard
1 Tb. brown sugar, or,
    if you have it, substitute
1 Tb. blackstrap molasses
¼ cup catsup

In a skillet that you can put in the oven, sauté the frankfurter slices in butter. When they are half brown, add and sauté the onion and bacon until just softened.

Pour in the beans, stir in thoroughly the remainder of the ingredients, and bake in the now hot oven for 30 minutes. This will give *you* time for a drink.

L. L. BEAN'S CAMP POTATOES

I heartily endorse the late Mr. Bean's camp potatoes. This *is* the way to do it.

SERVES 4

¼ lb. salt pork
4 medium onions

8 medium potatoes
salt and freshly ground pepper

Fry the salt pork in frying pan until crisp. Remove the pork. Dice the onions and fry until soft. Dice the potatoes, add onions, and cook in covered pan until done. Remove the cover and brown. Add the cooked salt pork after chopping very fine. Do not stir. Turn when brown on the bottom. Salt and pepper to taste. Quantity enough for one meal for four hungry campers.

NOTE: When I make potatoes lyonnaise in camp, I dice the salt pork before trying it out.

JANET SIMON'S BARLEY AND KIDNEY BEANS

When you have marrow bones in camp, here is an ideal, easy-to-prepare rib-sticker of a dish. The deliciousness of this dish depends on long cooking and on excellent marrow bones. It could also be done with Kasha (see page 384).

SERVES 6–8

1½ cups barley
2 onions, chopped
3 ribs celery, chopped
4–6 cloves garlic, chopped

4 cans red kidney beans
marrow bones
¾ lb. fatback, cubed

Put barley, 3 cups boiling water, onions, celery, and garlic into pot until barley is almost done, about 30 minutes.

Add beans, bones, and fatback, stir and bake uncovered in 350° oven "for a long time"—meaning 3–4 hours—stirring occasionally. Add water from time to time.

Serve it with game or with barbecued spareribs.

THE CAMP SALAD

I always try to get into camp a cabbage or two so I can make slaw. Here's my camp slaw:

chopped and shredded cabbage
mayonnaise (I swear
  by Hellmann's)
evaporated milk or dried
  milk mix (to thin)

celery seed
salt and pepper
dry mustard (or prepared,
  if you have it)

Just mix all the above ingredients together thoroughly, using as much dressing as you like.

Sometimes, if I have managed to get a jar of dill pickles into camp I use a bit of the pickling liquid to add piquancy to the dressing.

If you wish you can add a bit of dry herbs, too.

This camp salad is always a nice touch to a meal. For those who want it served separately, make them use their coffee cups and rinse them out before the coffee is poured.

MOCK MAPLE SYRUP

I have never cared for syrup made with sugar, water, and maple extract, but when weight is important something can be said for bringing your "syrup" along as sugar and, happily, there is a quick camp syrup that is absolutely delicious. In fact, it is almost as good as maple syrup. Make it with *light* brown sugar (or even with ⅔ light brown sugar and ⅓ white sugar) and remember the simple formula: twice as much sugar as water.

MAKES ABOUT 1½ CUPS

⅔ cup light brown sugar
⅓ cup white sugar

½ cup water
2 Tb. butter

Put sugars into saucepan, add water, and stir to dissolve. Heat to a boil and let it bubble slowly for 3 minutes. Stir and melt in butter.

If you follow instructions, this syrup will keep for some time without crystallizing, but I usually make it up batch by batch each time we serve pancakes. If you make it at home, stir in a tablespoon of white corn syrup, for this will inhibit crystallization for certain. If you do make up a batch to keep on hand in camp or in the refrigerator don't stir in butter until you heat the syrup again before serving.

My late and much-missed Adirondack hunting partner, Leonard Pelkey of Upper Jay, New York, once painted the lily on this syrup on an occasion when I got fancy and made crêpes for breakfast by urging me to add a collop of rum. The next year I outdid him by bringing along a small plastic bottle of Armagnac just for this purpose.

CAMP COFFEE

Although coffee made by most any device is good (if there is enough coffee in it to begin with), coffee made camp style in an old blue-granite coffee pot is best. Sure, its superlative bouquet and taste may derive partly from the morning mood that the bush scene imparts, but, quite apart from that, it beats all to my taste. In giving this recipe I am assuming that the cup is one of those standard white mugs known to all. Such mugs when filled to the very brim hold one measuring cup of liquid, but when filled to normal serving heights these old mugs hold only a regular teacup of liquid. (If your service at home includes both coffee cups and saucers, as well as teacups and saucers, it's the quantity of the lesser size I am speaking of.) Just remember, filled-to-the-brim teacups—the old mugs hold the same amount—equal one measuring cup; filled to serving quantity, they each hold ¾ measuring cup. When "cup" is called for in this recipe, I mean ¾ measuring cup.

8 cups *cold* water   1 eggshell
9 slightly rounded Tb. coffee

Put the *cold* water and the coffee in the pot with two halves of an eggshell.
   Bring the mixture to a boil and then immediately set it off the fire to steep a
bit (but not get cold).
   Pour in ⅛ cup cold water to settle the grounds.

NOTE: *Don't* boil coffee and don't start camp coffee in warm water. Take the
water right out of that first morning bucket from the spring or lake.

Camp "Bread"—Bannocks and Scones

Some old-time trappers and guides baked sourdough bread on occasions, but
usually they made do with that old stand-by "bread of the bush," the bannock.
The bannock is right out of the Scottish Highlands and was "exported" from
there to Canada and U.S., when so many of the Highlanders themselves were
transported after The Clearances. A bannock is a baking powder bread that is
cooked on a griddle ("girdle" in Scotland) on top of the stove. In most Canadian
bush camps the bannock was simply cooked atop the wood range in the iron
skillet.
   My old friend Roy Smith had two basic recipes for bannock, one as a surrogate for bread, the other as a surrogate for cake. The latter he called "treacle-
bannock," which he often took along for his noon tea-fire and it was the original
"Thousand Mile" (see opposite).
   When this ½-inch-thick bread is cooked as a whole—i.e., in one round flat
cake—it is called a bannock; when the circle is cut into four to six wedges it is
called a scone. Each of the wedges in Scotland is called a "farl."

NOTE: "Scone" is pronounced to rhyme with "gone," not with "stone."

══════════ "BREAD" BANNOCK OR SCONE ══════════

When this bannock is made at home you can substitute buttermilk or a mix of
sour cream and milk for evaporated milk-and-water, in which case add ½ teaspoon of baking *soda* and reduce the 4 teaspoons baking *powder* to 2 teaspoons.
   Serve the bannock warm with butter and jelly or jam, or, if you are in
Maine, or certain other parts of New England or Canada, maybe with hot maple
syrup (see page 423 for Mock Maple Syrup).

SERVES 8–10

4 cups flour   4 Tb. butter or lard
4 tsp. baking powder   ½ cup evaporated milk*
½ tsp. salt   1 cup water*

Mix the dry ingredients together in a bowl. Then cut the butter or lard into the
mix (use your fingers, too, to crumble the mix until it is pebbly). Make a hole in
the center and pour the liquid in all at once. Mix it. "Gather" around the edges
of the bowl with a fork until it all comes together magically into one lump of
dough. Knead it five or six times quickly and turn out onto a floured board (or

the oilcloth top of the camp table). Shape and pat into a circle (be sure it is at least ½ inch thick) and bake in a lightly greased, medium-hot skillet or griddle on top of the range about 10 minutes to a side. (With a bit of practice or dexterity you can learn to flip it over.)

If it's scones you want, cut the circle into wedges and cook with wedges (or farls) put back into skillet to make a circle, their sides just barely touching. When baking scones you might wish to make two smaller circles and use two skillets.

＊ If you have powdered milk in camp make up the 1½ cups with water (see page 401).

CAKE- OR TREACLE-BANNOCK) OR SCONES (THOUSAND MILE)

This bannock is good cold at a tea-fire as a "dessert" with your tea or it is a fine pick-me-up along the trail. And why not? Flour, fat, sugar, fruit, molasses, spices, and milk—what more can you want to sustain you? And no wonder Roy Smith called it the original Thousand Mile.

SERVES 4–6

2 cups flour
1 Tb. baking powder
2 Tb. sugar
½ tsp. salt
½ tsp. powdered cinnamon
¼ tsp. powdered ginger
¼ tsp. powdered clove
3 Tb. butter or lard

1 egg, beaten with 60 strokes
 of the fork
½ cup milk
3 Tb. molasses
 preferably West Indian
¼–½ cup raisins, currants and/or
 finely chopped dried apricots

Combine and sift flour, baking powder, sugar, salt, and spices into a bowl.

As in previous recipe, blend with fork and rub in with fingers the butter or lard.

After the egg is well beaten, also beat in with it the milk and the molasses.

Make hole in center of dry mix, pour in liquid, and while mixing and gathering into a lump of dough, sprinkle on and then mix in the dried fruit.

Turn out on lightly floured surface. Knead a few times, pat out into ½-inch-thick circles, and bake on top of the stove in lightly greased skillet or on griddle as in previous recipe. When I make this recipe I usually produce scones, i.e., cut into wedges, in which case I divide the dough and make two ½-inch-thick cakes, then either bake them simultaneously in two skillets cut into farls, or make one batch and then a second. Treacle scones are handy on the trail because the individual farls or wedges can be packaged separately in little plastic envelopes and carried in jacket pockets for "piecing" along the portages or during a day's hunt in the woods (don't "piece" on them while inactive in camp, for they will surely spoil your appetite for supper).

SOURDOUGH PANCAKES

This section should be (and is) dedicated to Margaret Murie, great conservationist, native Alaskan, widow of the distinguished mammalogist Olaus Murie, and veteran of years of wilderness living. This starter and recipe for sourdough pancakes is "Mardie's." She makes no starter for herself, for hers has been "alive" since 1906; in the 1920s she brought it out from an Alaskan stock of that vintage.

The Starter

In a crockery bowl or pot (old-fashioned brown bean pot is best) mix

½ **envelope yeast**	**1 cup warm water**
1 tsp. sugar	**flour to make a thin batter**

Let stand, but not tightly covered, at room temperature for 3–4 days—until it smells like vinegar or alcohol.

2 cups flour	**1 Tb. molasses**
additional water	**½ tsp. salt**
1 egg	**½ tsp. soda**

The night before use: Into the starter in the crockery bowl or pot, stir *only* flour (about 2 cups for 4 persons) and water enough again to make a very thin batter (if you like thin cakes). Stir, but do not beat much. Leave it out of the refrigerator if you have it in storage.

In the morning: In a separate mixing bowl beat together 1 egg, 1 tablespoon molasses, ½ teaspoon salt. Into this pour the starter, as much as you think you need but always *leaving* in the pot at least a cup of batter. Stir the mixture in the bowl well, but do not beat. When griddle is hot and lightly greased, *not before,* fold gently into the bowl mixture ½ teaspoon of soda dissolved in a bit of water. The mixture will fluff about like whipped cream.

Ladle spoonfuls onto the griddle and bake on one side until lightly browned on the bottom and bubbles appear on the top. Turn and bake a minute on the other side. Eat quickly.

CAUTION. Never let anything but flour and water get into the starter pot. I use part whole wheat, Roman meal, bran, and any such in addition to the white flour, according to taste. Wheat germ may be added in the morning mix but should never be in the starter; it does something strange to it.

The starter in the pot can be kept in the refrigerator weeks at a time and still be good; you should feed it every 5 days or so with small equal amounts of flour and warm water; before using take out and into room temperature at least 24 hours. If there is a dark liquid on top, some of it may be drained off; it won't hurt anybody.

NOTE: In camp I usually make my starter with water from the boiled potatoes (as my grandmother did), but for this pot of potatoes I peel them. Many sourdough starter recipes specify warm potato water as the liquid. To me there is nothing—repeat, nothing—better than sourdough pancakes.

═══ SOURDOUGH TREACLE-BANNOCK ═══

When you have a starter in camp make your bannocks sourdough bannocks and make your batter half white flour and half cornmeal. You can put raisins in this bannock if you like, or, if *you* can afford it, bits of dried apricots.

SERVES 4–6

1 cup sourdough starter	4 Tb. light brown sugar
2 cups water	1 Tb. molasses
¾ cup cornmeal (all cornmeal	4 Tb. melted butter
for real is yellow to me)	raisins
¾ cup white flour	dried apricots, chopped
3 Tb. dried milk	½ tsp. salt
2 eggs	½ tsp. soda

The night before: Take a cup of starter from your starter pot; put it in a bowl with 1½ cups water, cornmeal, and flour. Stir but do not beat. Let stand overnight, partly covered.

In the morning: Make a paste of the dried milk and ½ cup water and stir into the mix. Then beat the eggs and stir them in the mix along with the sugar, molasses, and melted butter. Add the raisins or apricots if you have either.

Just before you ladle the batter into a well-greased hot cast-iron skillet, carefully stir in the salt and soda. Bake on top of the stove over a fairly hot plate for 10 minutes, shaking it after it sets to loosen it, then turn (flip it if you're sure of yourself) and bake the other side.

You *can* bake this bannock in the oven. Bake in a hot oven (450° at home) for about 30 minutes.

CORN PONE

From their performances in camp one might think breakfast was the favorite meal of a cabin full of hunters. For such lusty eaters toast seems a bit effete. In any case corn pone is always welcome as a base for the jams and jellies.

SERVES 6

1½ cups yellow cornmeal	1 cup milk
¼–½ cup white flour	1 egg, beaten
2 tsp. baking powder	3 Tb. melted bacon fat
1 tsp. salt	

Mix the dry ingredients.

Add the milk and beaten egg and stir to make the mix uniform. Stir in the bacon fat.

Heat a lightly greased griddle or skillet and drop the batter onto the surface, spreading it out with a kitchen spoon.

When one side is brown, turn and brown the other side. Both sides should brown in 2½–3 minutes.

SPOON BREAD

This is a good, dependable old southern spoon bread and is always sure to please a campful of hungry hunters or anglers.

SERVES 6–8

2 cups boiling water	1 tsp. salt
1 cup cornmeal (white preferred	2 cups milk
by some southerners)	2 eggs, beaten
1 Tb. butter	2 tsp. baking powder

Pour boiling water over the meal and cook for 5 minutes, stirring constantly. Off heat, add the butter, salt, and milk and mix well. Beat the eggs and add to the mixture, then sift in the baking powder and mix well.

Pour into a greased baking dish and bake 30 minutes in an oven of about 350°. Serve right out of the baking dish.

═══ SESAME SEED CHEESE CORN BREAD ═══
IN A SKILLET

This is bound to surprise and delight hungry campers—a wonderful change from the usual corn bread.

MAKES A 10-INCH ROUND

3 Tb. sesame seeds	¾ cup flour
4 Tb. butter	¾ cup yellow cornmeal
1 egg, beaten	1–2 Tb. baking powder
¾ cup milk	1 tsp. salt
1 cup grated Cheddar cheese	

Toast the sesame seeds in a dry 10-inch skillet over medium heat, shaking the pan frequently until they are lightly toasted (sometimes they will pop and splutter). Set aside. Melt the butter slowly in the skillet.

Meanwhile beat the egg well, then add the milk, 3 tablespoons of the melted butter, the cheese, and the toasted sesame seeds. Mix the remaining dry ingredients thoroughly and add them to the bowl, stirring enough to blend them well.

Rewarm the skillet with the remaining tablespoon of butter and pour the batter on top. Cover and cook over low heat for 20 minutes until firm on top. Serve hot directly from the pan in wedges or loosen the edges and slip onto a warm plate.

═══ SKILLET SCALLION BREAD ═══

If scallions aren't available, use finely chopped onion, about ¼ cup, which should be sautéed until limp in butter before adding.

SERVES 6–8

4 Tb. butter	5 scallions
1 tsp. sugar	1 package Bisquick

Put half the butter and the teaspoon of sugar in a 10-inch skillet, and heat and swirl the butter round. Remove from the heat.

Chop the scallions quite fine, using about two-thirds of the greens, and scatter half on the bottom of the skillet.

Prepare the Bisquick dough as directed on the package and cut into 1¾–2-inch rounds. Place the rounds on top of the butter-scallion mixture in an overlapping pattern to fill the whole skillet.

Cover and cook over medium-low heat 5–6 minutes, until golden on the bottom.

Put a large plate on top of the skillet and quickly flip the nest of biscuits over onto it. Melt the remaining butter in the skillet, sprinkle on remaining scallions, and slip the biscuits back into the skillet, uncooked side down. Cover and cook 5 minutes on this side. Remove to a warm serving plate.

HUSH PUPPIES

This is my favorite hush puppy recipe, and is, or course, traditional with fish. If you are making hush puppies in camp and don't have buttermilk, make your own as follows: make up a cup of milk from dried milk and water, and let it come to room temperature. In another cup put 1 tablespoon lemon juice, or white vinegar, pour in milk, and stir. Let stand for 10 minutes and you should have a nice clabber.

Hush puppies are normally fried in deep fat until they float, but when shy of lard or fat you can semideep-fry them in a plain old iron skillet.

SERVES 6

2 cups cornmeal
2 Tb. flour
½ tsp. baking soda
1 tsp. baking powder
1 tsp. salt

4 Tb. finely chopped onion
1 cup buttermilk
1 whole egg, beaten
deep fat

Mix all of the dry ingredients together.
Stir in the onions, the buttermilk, and last the egg.
Heat fat until a pinch of batter dropped in immediately sizzles and browns.
Drop batter by the spoonful into the deep fat and fry to nice brown or until the puppy floats. Drain on paper towels.

CORNMEAL MUSH

Hunters doing their own cooking always want a big breakfast and often forget fried mush, that breakfast dish that sticks to the ribs. Bacon, eggs, and fried mush with butter and syrup make a breakfast that will carry you through a light lunch. They also often forget that mush as a hot cereal is very good too.

Serve this with butter and syrup after you serve the bacon and eggs. Few hunters will fault this breakfast.

SERVES 4

1 cup yellow cornmeal
1 cup cold water

1 tsp. salt
4 cups boiling water

Stir together the cornmeal, cold water, and salt until thoroughly wet and smooth. Pour the boiling water over the cornmeal in top of a double boiler, stir, and set over 2 additional cups boiling water.

If you are cooking on a camp stove, push pan over area of less heat and cook for 3 minutes, stirring constantly. As it begins to thicken (don't let it stick), watch yourself, for when those thick, sullen bubbles explode they can burn hell out of you.

Cover, set the top of the double boiler over the bottom, and cook over water for 15 minutes (or longer if you have the time).

The mush could now be served as a hot cereal.

FRIED CORNMEAL MUSH

For fried mush, pour mush (see previous recipe) into a small cold loaf pan, cover with oiled paper or plastic wrap, and chill overnight.

In the morning before you make the coffee, turn the loaf pan over and drop out the mush mold. Slice into ¼–½-inch slices and spread slices out so they will dry out some. When ready to fry (in hot butter, lard, or bacon fat) coat both sides of slices in flour and brown slowly on both sides. Even with the flour coating, it always takes more time than you expect to "fry" the mush to a golden brown.

HAM, EGGS, RED-EYE GRAVY, AND HOT BISCUITS

This makes a nice camp breakfast, and I've seen times when it makes a good supper as well (when you haven't yet hung up a piece of fresh meat on the gam stick).

SERVES 4

coffee	milk
2 slices ham	Bisquick
1 Tb. lard or shortening	eggs

Make coffee, allowing 1½ cups extra for the red-eye gravy.

Put the ham on to brown in the melted fat and have one of your cookees watch it.

Make up your milk and Bisquick mix for drop biscuits, spoon them out on a baking sheet, and stick them in the oven.

Break the eggs in a bowl so you can pour them out all at once into a second skillet.

Make sure you are rendering out enough of the ham fat and getting some greables in the skillet.

When the biscuits are done, pull them out onto the open oven door, take up the ham on a pie pan, and set it alongside the biscuits.

While a cookee fries the eggs, you pour 1½ cups of coffee into the ham skillet, stir the drippings well, and let it come to a boil and bubble a minute or so.

Serve the ham, eggs, and biscuits, and the red-eye gravy in a "sauceboat," which is usually a small saucepan.

NOTE: Be sure to make enough biscuits so there will be some for the red-eye and some to be eaten later with butter and jam. At least one of your partners will say, "I didn't know red-eye gravy was made with coffee."

Camp Desserts

Standard camp desserts are canned fruit and cookies (until the latter run out) and such fruits as peaches, pears, pineapple, and plums are welcome. To add a fillip of flavor, I usually stir rum or brandy into the syrup when either is available, or in the case of canned peaches, ¼ teaspoon almond extract.

========== DATE CAKE (THOUSAND MILE II) ==========

Once the redoubtable Ivy Smith, lovely wife of our late friend John R. Smith, whose stony farm bordered the very edge of the bush back of Spanish Ontario, had given us this recipe, we made it for years on the first or second day of our two weeks to a month hunt out of Roy Smith's (John R.'s first cousin) trapping camp. Its function was the same as granola, a trail pick-me-up. Roy said, "It replaces the treacle-bannock as Thousand Mile" (see page 416 for Roy's explanation of Thousand Mile). We carried squares cut from it for noon tea-fire dessert and one in our pockets for a snack during the day's hunt.

THE "CRUST"
2 cups flour
2 cups oatmeal
1 cup brown sugar
½ tsp. salt

½ tsp. baking soda
½ lb. (2 sticks) butter,
  softened

Mix together all of the ingredients save the butter.

Cut pats of butter into the dry mixture, working and mixing with the fingers until you have a uniform "dough."

THE FILLING
1 lb. dates, pitted
1 cup brown sugar

1 cup hot water

Cook the filling ingredients in a saucepan or small skillet just until you have a uniform mixture. Cool this mixture.

Spread half the "dough" on the bottom of a pie pan. Cover with the cooled date filling, then spread remainder of the crumb "dough" on top.

Bake in a moderate oven for 25–30 minutes. Cool, then cut into squares like fudge or wedges.

========== BUSH ICE CREAM FOR FOUR ==========

When I have trudged back to camp in new-fallen snow I always plan Bush Ice Cream for dessert, and try to make it a surprise to new hunting partners. This ice cream, probably the ancestor of all ice creams, can be made with evaporated milk, but I usually use dried milk, which I make up thicker than normal by using more dried milk than the milk recipe calls for. Make up the milk as soon as you return to camp. Since you have made up milk before, no one will consider it as the makings of a dessert.

4 cups cold water	1½ cups dried milk

Mix thoroughly and set outside to keep cool. When you are ready after supper to make the ice cream and while your companions are gabbing about the day's hunt quickly collect:

6 Tb. sugar	1½ tsp. vanilla extract
4 eggs, beaten	

Stir and dissolve the sugar in the beaten eggs, then stir in the vanilla.

Take the egg mix outside the cabin and stir it thoroughly into the milk.

Hand your partners each an oatmeal mug or a soup bowl and ask each to fill it with snow. Tell them not to pack the snow (you don't want too much eventual liquid).

While they're out scooping snow, bring in the eggnog and when your partners return ladle it out into each bowl of snow.

Since the bowls (or cups) won't hold much snow you ought to have enough eggnog to make two helpings of ice cream for each partner. Even if the evening meal has been merely spaghetti and meat sauce, your partners will remember this bush meal for the surprise dessert.

Pies in Camp

If the cook wants to make a big hit with his partners let him bake a surprise pie. Pies are best done on those days when the cook alone stays in camp, perhaps to prepare a stew on the same day it is to be eaten. A pie is a breeze when the cook has the time and, best of course, when it's a surprise. My wife, Sheila, who would scorn the pumpkin pie recipe I'm about to give (because it calls for Bisquick), not only bakes crusts from scratch, but on more than one occasion has surprised the guide and me with a white cake with chocolate icing. I usually stick to one-crust pies, like pumpkin or butterscotch (because I'm lazy about crustmaking), but also because big cans of Elberta peaches and sour cherries are usually in the grub box for "desserts." I have, however, eaten my share of fruit pies in camp baked by Mrs. Cameron and occasionally by me.

═══════ PUMPKIN PIE ═══════

This pumpkin pie recipe is literally the kind my Hoosier grandmother baked. This recipe is for two pies because the canned pumpkin I have used comes out of a can holding 1 pound 13 ounces of tight-packed pumpkin.

1 box Biquick	2 tsp. nutmeg or mace
1-lb. 13-oz. can pumpkin	1 tsp. powdered ginger
2 cups sugar, preferably half white and half light brown	½ tsp. powdered cloves (if you have brought your cloves and allspice mixed, used ¾ tsp.)
4 eggs	
13-oz. can evaporated milk	¼ tsp. allspice
1 tsp. salt	
3 tsp. powdered cinnamon	

Prepare two unbaked pastry shells by following the instructions on a Bisquick box and line 9-inch pie pans with them. Fire the stove so the oven is very hot.

In a big bowl mix pumpkin and sugar thoroughly.

Separate the yolks from the whites. Beat the yolks well, then pour in the evaporated milk and stir to uniformity.

Stir in all the rest of the ingredients save the egg whites; mix these dry ingredients thoroughly into the liquid, breaking powdery lumps against side of the bowl, then pour and stir into the pumpkin-sugar mix.

Beat the egg whites stiff and fold them into the mix.

Put into the unbaked pie shells and bake for 15 minutes.

Now open the oven door and with your cap wave out the infernal 450°–500° heat until the oven is what you guess to be medium heat!

If you keep the fire up, put a stick of kindling in the oven door to keep the heat from raging back to 500°–600° and bake for another 35–40 minutes. If, when you look in, shortly after, the crust is browning too quickly damper the stove pipe and almost close the draft; also put a thicker piece of wood in the oven door.

The pies are done when a broom straw (upper end) stuck in comes out clean. Perhaps my strong opinion lacks modesty, but this is the best pumpkin pie I have ever tasted, bar none. By the way, it is ideal for camp where evaporated milk is always present; evaporated milk for some reason definitely turns out a better pie than whole milk or even half-and-half.

NOTE: If it is too much trouble to separate the eggs and beat and fold the whites, simply beat the eggs whole.

TWO-CRUST CHERRY PIES

Here I am going to give the superlative crust recipe my wife uses, inherited from her late aunt, Bernice Ferree. This recipe for one two-crust pie can also be used for two pumpkin pie crusts and is the crust I bragged about above. It is lusciously short. The cherry pie recipe is also Mrs. Ferree's.

1½ cups flour	8 Tb. lard
½ tsp. salt	¼ cup cold milk

Sift (and measure sifted) the flour. Resift with the salt.

With a hand pastry blender (a fork or 2 knives in camp) cut into the flour mixture half the lard until the mix has consistency of coarse cornmeal.

Cut in the remaining 4 tablespoons of lard until the crumbles are the size of large green peas.

Add ¼ cup cold milk and work with fork and fingers until the crumble holds together (if too dry, add 1 tablespoon more milk).

Divide dough in two parts, one half (the top crust) slightly larger than the other half, and set outside (in the bread box nailed on the outside wall of any working cabin) to cool for ten minutes or so.

two 17-oz. cans sour pitted cherries drained; retain juice	¼ tsp. salt
1½ cups sugar	¼ cup cherry juice (I drink the rest)
5 Tb. cake flour (in camp, 3 Tb. regular flour)	¼ tsp. almond extract
	1 Tb. butter

Sift sugar, flour, and salt into the cherries to which the ¼ cup cherry juice has been added. Stir in the almond extract.

On waxed paper (or the oilcloth top of the camp table) roll out the smaller "half" of the cold dough and line bottom of 9-inch pie pan. (Because the dough is short, you may have to fold over the crust into a half moon to handle; transfer it to the pan.)

Roll out larger half of crust and fold over to handle.

Pour cherry mix into the lined pie pan and dot with butter.

Lay on top crust, which should overlap bottom crust some and tuck under the slightly wetted lower crust edge. Crimp around with thumb and forefinger.

With fork make two decorative "flowers" so the steam can escape.

Bake 45 minutes in your hot oven (at home make it 400°; in camp watch, and if it seems too infernally hot, stick a piece of firewood between door and oven).

PEACH PIE

Here follow same dough instructions for cherry pie. For the peach filling:

1-lb. 13-oz. can Elberta peaches,
    drained
¼ cup peach juice
1 cup sugar
5 Tb. cake flour
    (3 Tb. regular flour)

¼ tsp. salt
¼ tsp. almond extract
1 Tb. butter

Mix as with cherry filling.

Appendix

Field Dressing Big Game

DEER

One man can hog-dress a deer in short order if he knows his business. The task looks formidable (and messy once the body cavity is opened), but it breaks down neatly into perfectly easy steps once you know the drill. All you need is a sharp knife (I use a jackknife with a 3½-inch blade) and a piece of binder twine or cod line. You should take off your jacket and roll up your shirt sleeves as high up the arm as possible.

If the problem were only to get the innards out, come what may, it would be easier, but what you want to do is to get them out without fouling the meat. Doing so is only slightly more difficult.

Turn the deer over on its back and turn the head so the antlers will help to prevent the animal from rolling over. Guarantee this by shoving a stick or stone under the side toward which the body tends to roll. Lying on its back will cause the innards to fall toward the backbone and away from the belly. Stand straddling the deer facing his rear end, find the sternum, and with the left hand seize the hair there and lift; then make the 3-inch cut through the hide and belly tissue toward the back with the knife in your right hand.

Now either get your partner to hold the deer's leg away from you while you use both hands or continue the slit with your right hand only. Slip fore and second fingers under the belly tissue, holding it away from the innards with your fingertips. Put the knife, sharp edge up, between the fingers and slit clear to the pelvic bridge from underneath the tissue and skin. This way there is no danger that you will cut into paunch or intestine.

At this juncture, if I am going to quarter the deer on the spot, I cut through the pelvic bridge (with my knife on young deer right down the softish suture, but with a bone saw on mature deer) and expose the rectal intestine and the bladder tube. Lifting them loose, I tie them off tightly.

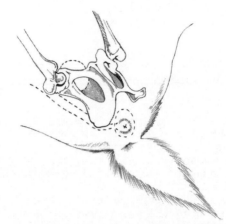

If, on the other hand, I am going to take the deer out whole I do not cut through the pelvic bridge at all. I learned from my old trapper friend Roy Smith in Ontario years ago that once the bony bridge is cut through "youse immediately have two deer to handle" said Roy. He meant that the two legs cut asunder at the bridge splay out wildly when the deer is dragged over rough ground.

The drill is to cut around the anus and loosen the rectum, for which the anus serves as outlet. It requires a sharp knife and a bit of persistence to cut around the aperture so you can finally draw it with the intestine out far enough to strip out the last pellets in the rectum, tie off the intestine, then cut off the anus and surrounding skin.

Time enough then to think about the bladder tube. Make a cut along the side of the pelvis to find the bladder tube (urethra). Lift it loose (it goes into the body cavity under the same bridge that houses the end of the rectal intestine), cut it off, and tie it off. You can cut the penis and scrotum off if you please (and if it is legal in your area), but this is not necessary.

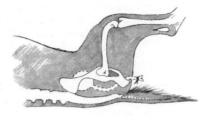

You are now ready to roll out the paunch and the intestines. Straddling the carcass, facing to the rear, reach in under the guts and locate the bladder. Feel for the exit tube and when you've got it pull it through under the bridge and then as you scoop out the innards press your left knee against the deer's left ham, at the same time pulling the left foot over with your left hand and rolling out the innards.

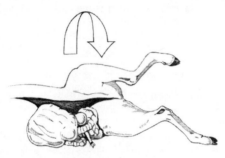

The paunch will be still attached to the gullet, which must be cut loose. Reach as far forward as you can and cut it off after first working any contents in it back into the paunch. Finish the job of rolling paunch and intestines over the opened flank and out onto the ground.

You have now removed everything behind the diaphragm except the liver and spleen, which lie against and just behind this membrane that separates the heart-lung area from the paunch and intestine. Unless this dividing membrane has been punctured either by bullet or, hopefully, by your knife, it will contain in the chest cavity most of the blood in the body (it is certain to if the fatal wound was through the ribcage).

When you remove the spleen and the liver by a couple of small cuts at the two organs you will have made a cut or two into the diaphragm as well. This will liberate the blood in the chest cavity which you can spill out after you have removed liver and spleen. You can then cut around the edge of and remove the diaphragm. Now you can remove the heart and with your fingertips by scratching along the ribs you can lift out the lungs. All that remains to be done is to reach into the throat and pull the gullet and windpipe out as far as you can and cut them off.

I usually take the kidneys out and put them with liver and heart in a rubber-lined cloth bag (I keep this bag rinsed off and clean and do not, of course, store the organs in it back at camp).

I hang a deer by the head and found years ago that the little Sportsmen's Block and Tackle was a godsend for this purpose.

If I am counting my chickens before they are hatched I carry in my day pack a dozen or more sheets of folded paper toweling to wipe out the cavity of the deer. Swab out the deer as soon as dry in the cavity, and with the belly opening propped wide with a stick the animal is soon cooled out as well.

Moose and Elk

Unlike deer, antelope, and sometimes bear, which are commonly brought home whole after being hog-dressed in the field, the meat of big animals like moose and elk and other animals like sheep is usually packed out in pieces, the former because of size and the latter because of the remoteness of the kill. Handling big animals, and especially moose in the wilds, is a big chore, but Alaskan outfitters like Bud Helmericks and men like Mark Wartes, one of Bud's guides, have turned the task into a high art, and as a result do a really simpler and infinitely neater and cleaner job. Their secret is that they never hog-dress a moose, messing up the locale of the kill with a near hogshead of innards; *they never remove the guts of a moose at all* but rather take the meat away from the contents of the body cavity.

In 1976 I assisted Mark Wartes in this big chore and wished fervently that I had known how to do it on a number of previous occasions. Further, I wrote up notes afterward, detailing the sequence of steps. Below are the results from my journal of September 1976, checked for accuracy by Mark himself.

ENTRY OF SEPTEMBER, 1976 *Hunting Journal*

. . . . Now I received a lesson on how one man can most easily dress out a moose, Arctic style. After we got back to the tent and Sheila, listening to my account of it, had asked at one juncture, "When did he take out the innards?" I had answered, "He never did, rather he took the meat away from the innards without ever touching them."

Here is how it is done. Although I helped in this case, the process described here can obviously be done by one man working alone.

Slitting the skin of the inner hind leg to the anus and from there to the belly line, we skinned out the top side of the animal as it lay on its side. This included the neck skin separated from the head by cutting the skin all the way around. We then laid the skin back on the ground. The upper side of the meat was now exposed.

Using a knife only, Mark then cut off the hind leg, cutting and probing until he found the hip joint. He then dragged it across the skin and onto the sod beyond.

Next he sliced off the foreshoulder and then removed the front leg and lay it alongside the hindquarter. Then he took out the backstrap from the exposed side of the backbone. Next, turning the moose up on the skin, he slit open the belly, then sawed off the exposed ribs, took out the heart and cut away the liver.

Now we shook out the innards by hoisting and jiggling the carcass. Then he turned the moose the rest of the way over and skinned out what had been the underside, now the upper side. The hind leg, then the front leg were cut off and dragged away, and the other backstrap was removed. It was at this stage that Mark mentioned that one of their hunter-clients, Jimmy Johnson from Arizona, always referred to the backstrap as "the buckin' muscle," in the jargon of bronc busting.

The ribs on this side were sawed off next, then the tenderloins were removed from the *under*side of the backbone. The head was now cut off and dragged away and the spine was cut in two just ahead of the pelvis leaving the neck still attached to the front section of the spine. The guts now lay on the skin, the meat all lying on the sod or draped over the dwarf willow. The last job was to cut out the tongue, and that was it—the best job of butchering a moose that I had ever seen, and the cleanest.

Butchering Your Deer

Read this once all the way through for best results. Many hunters nowadays leave the cutting up and packaging of deer meat for freezing to food processors (see page 445), and much can be said for this solution, but many hunters prefer to do this themselves. It is not a difficult task; my wife and I have done it many times. If on your first try you find yourself with a few odd pieces left over that do not seem to classify as classic cuts, don't worry; use these few odd pieces for deerburger or sausage or even stew. Generally, however, even a tyro will come out with identifiable steaks, chops, and roasts that will serve their purposes properly in the kitchen.

Let's assume that you have skinned out your deer, cut off his tail, and have him hanging on a solid crossbeam by the hocks on a gam stick with the legs

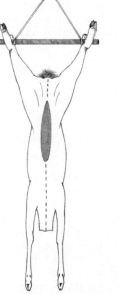

spread with a stick; let's assume further that you have at hand one or two *sharp* butcher's knives (or their equivalent), a stone or steel for touching them up, and a meat saw. If you don't own a meat saw, borrow one; and if that's not feasible use your regular carpenter's crosscut saw. One with ten teeth to the inch will do nicely. Your first task is to produce two "sides" that are bilaterally symmetrical.

Facing the cavity, first cut through with your knife the heavy muscle that lies over the pelvic arch. This will expose the center of the bone and will give you a sighting line. Then go around to the back of the carcass, and, again with your knife, cut through the meat from tail to nape along the center of the back. This not only gives you a line but fixes it so the saw will have to cut through a minimum of meat. Remember it is a bone saw. Your wife or friend can stand behind the carcass and tell you if and when you start to get off center on the far side. Now return to the cavity side and saw down through the center of the exposed backbone. Shortly you will have two sides, each hanging by a hock.

At this stage, place one of the "sides," cavity side down, on a table (covered with oilcloth is best, for paper sticks to the meat). Now you are ready to look at the cut charts again, either one that you can get from the Department of Agriculture or the one on page 442 in this book.

At this point, familiarize yourself with the bone structure so you'll know where and what you are cutting into.

I usually take off the *fore*quarter first, for it is not structurally anchored to the

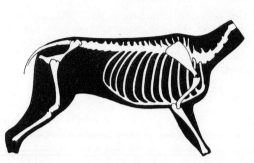

spine. Lift the leg away from the ribcage and slice and lift it off; it will separate neatly with a minimum use of the knife.

Next, cut and saw off the hindquarter. Begin just in front of the hump, or pin bone (see chart). Later you will cut and saw the leg proper from the rump roast or roasts on the top of the quarter (depends on size of the deer).

You now have three pieces, fore and hind quarters, and the ribcage. At this point you will have to make some basic decisions—chiefly, what proportions of the meat do you want as steaks or chops on the one hand, as against roasts on the other? While I'm thinking this over, I usually turn to the center section and cutting and sawing laterally take off the flank and shortrib section (see chart). Flank meat usually goes into hamburger or stew meat, but the delicious fat ribs I

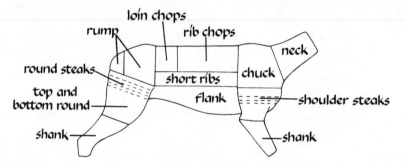

section across and braise for the next meal. What's left is the saddle made up of the rack (if we use lamb nomenclature) and the loin. Either makes a succulent roast, but both can be cut and sawed into chops; the rib chops (rack end) have the ribs to guide you, but in cutting loin chops you are on your own. A good rule of thumb? Don't cut and saw them too thin. Venison is tastiest when rare or pink, and it is difficult to achieve this with a thin chop (the same, by the way, goes for the round steaks).

I myself always find the forequarters less rewarding and more difficult to butcher than the hind. It is easy enough to slice off the foreleg, for you don't have to cope with any bones. Once the foreleg is off, I first cut off the shank at the "elbow" (the leg from the "knee" to hoof having been cut off earlier). To find the elbow joint it is easier to make your first cut from the front edge. The shank can be cut and sawed into two or three pieces for soup or stews. To cut up the remainder of the foreleg (see the drawing opposite) make a cross-cut to find the joint at the shoulder; the lower piece can be boned and rolled as a roast, or if you wish, two arm steaks can be cut off it and the remainder boned as stew meat. If you decide to bone this section out and use as a rolled roast, make your cut at either joint end, slice into the bone along its entire length, then cut the bone away by slicing parallel to it.

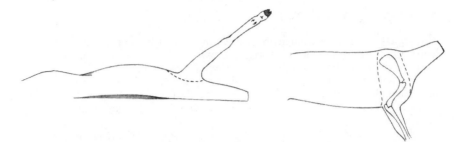

Here is perhaps the place to say that in making rolled and string-tied roasts, first trim off all of the deer's fat and replace it with slabs of beef suet which you can buy at a meat market.

Since I love venison stews I use the meat at the top of the forequarter around the shoulder blade and what's left in front of the rack *and* all of the neck meat cut into stew-meat chunks. The meat, not much, on the shank can be trimmed out for stew meat too.

If you decide to grind some of the stew meat for deerburger or sausage, don't make either at the time but freeze the chunks, then later thaw and grind. Ground meat does not hold its taste when frozen as well as the frozen stew chunks hold theirs. But remember here as well as with other cuts—trim off the fat. Deer fat is strong; beef suet or pork fatback will supply ground fat or larding fat for ground meat or roasts.

Butchering the hindquarters gives you one or two rump roasts, a number of top-round steaks, a leg of venison, and the rear shank. Again refer to the chart. First, cut off the leg, seeking to find the top of the big leg bone where it sockets in. Next cut and saw off the shank, reserving it for stew meat or ground meat. At this stage, unless the leg is thoroughly chilled, I put the leg in the freezer for a short time to chill while I do something else, for it is much easier to slice round steaks if the meat is cold. Slice the steaks at the very least an inch thick, thicker with a big deer. How stingy you are about the number of steaks you get will decide it for you. If you wish you can bone out this leg of venison, roll it, cover with bits and pieces of suet slab, and tie. For some reason, I never do this with this leg roast, as I feel the bone adds to the flavor.

Another Way to Cut Up the Hind Leg

I have two friends, one in Montana and the other who lives, hunts, and cooks in the Adirondacks, who never cut the round into steaks but rather handle the hind legs by separating the big muscles into the natural longitudinal strips. This is difficult to describe, but with the leg at hand one readily observes that the leg is not one big muscle, but several encased in tissue in discrete strips. With a knife and with one's fingers these can be easily located and separated. The muscles can be handled as a tenderloin, either roasted intact or cut crosswise into 2-inch-thick fillet steaks. These can be flattened with the flat side of a cleaver or handled as tournedos. The bigger muscle strips can also be sliced longitudinally. When frozen these muscle strips do not dry out as readily as sliced round steaks do. Save the bones for stock.

Big Game Dressed and Meat Weights

Although these figures are rough, one can estimate that if you butcher up your deer into cuts that include the bone, you will be able to freeze a total of about 60 percent of the weight of the hog-dressed animal.

On the other hand, if you yourself (or your butcher) bone out the meat, it will, of course, show less. Below are the weights of the various packages of *boned-out* meat from a buck that hog-dressed at 130 pounds.

BONED-OUT MEAT OF BUCK WEIGHED AT 130 POUNDS, HOG-DRESSED

	lb.	oz.
½ loin strip	2	3
" " "	2	3
" " "	2	8
" " "	2	9
Rolled shoulder	6	7
" "	6	8
Small steak roast	3	6
" " "	3	8
Large " "	6	7
" " "	6	10
Rump roast	3	6
" "	2	7
2 fillets	1	0
Neck meat	3	5
Ribs (with bone)	9	9

A 130-pound deer, hog-dressed, weighed alive about 160 to 165 pounds.

This boned-out meat represents about 40 percent of the hog-dressed weight.

In addition, there were 9½ pounds of ribs, but these, of course, had the bones in them.

The 150-pound hog-dressed buck referred to earlier could be expected to produce about 60 pounds of boned-out meat plus perhaps 12 pounds of ribs.

For the fun of it, how much meat would that ubiquitous 200-pound hog-dressed whitetail deer produce? This huge deer would have weighed about 250 pounds on the hoof, but would have produced about 120 pounds of venison with the bones in the cuts or about 80 pounds of boned-out meat plus, say, 15 pounds of ribs. It might be that the bigger the deer the higher proportion the boned-out meat might weigh, but I believe we can be reasonably sure that the 200-pound hog-dressed deer would produce no more than 90 pounds of *boned-out* meat. That's about 35 percent of the weight of the animal on the hoof.

If there is a moral, it is that one should not be optimistic in estimating how much actual meat he may expect to get from any deer.

Moose hunters, awed by the size of their prize, can usually be counted on to answer your question about how much the animal weighed with, "Well, the guide and I figure it weighed about twelve hundred pounds hog-dressed." No doubt the bull looked that big, but if he had been he would have weighed 1,500 live weight, which would have been a very, very big *Alaskan* moose, a strain that runs much bigger than the Canada moose.

A mature Canada bull weighs between 900 and 1,200 pounds usually, and the latter would be a very, very big one. The cows run roughly about 25 percent less. Few hunters outside of the Kenai peninsula in Alaska have ever seen a 1,300-pound bull, and that goes for most bulls shot in northern Alaska as well.

If the hog-dressed weight to live weight of hoofed animals is roughly comparable, a 1,000-pound bull on the hoof would weigh about 800 pounds hog-
dressed. It would produce perhaps 450–500 pounds of unboned meat—in any
case, a lot of meat.

As to elk, most hunters overestimate their weights also. But a mature bull
elk is a big animal, and Olaus Murie reported the *average live* weight of 30
mature bulls from the Jackson Hole–Yellowstone areas as 631 pounds, while 38
cows averaged 521 pounds. Mr. Murie weighed one huge bull in August, when
he says they are at their best, that tipped the scales at 1,032 pounds. This animal
weighed 657 pounds dressed—I take it he meant not hog-dressed but with head
and antlers, hide, legs, feet, and hooves as well as innards removed. This would
tally fairly well with our rule of thumb for deer similarly dressing at about 60
percent of their live weight (see below).

Caribou vary considerably by areas in live weight, but mature bulls have
been known to weigh as much as a small bull elk. Their outsized antlers, huge for
the actual size of the animals, make the caribou bull appear much heavier to the
average hunter, averaging perhaps 275 pounds. Cows are 30 percent smaller.

Most big rams among the wild sheep seldom weigh much over 200 pounds,
although they do sometimes go as much as 250 or even more with a very fat ram.

Nomenclature of Hog-Dressed and Dressed Weights

Although there are regional differences in nomenclature, generally speaking in the U.S., a "hog-dressed" game animal is one that has been bled
and gralloched, i.e., gutted, period.

In some areas the term "dressed" is used to mean a hog-dressed animal
that has also been skinned and from which the head and antlers, hooves,
lower legs (from the "knees" down) and damaged meat have been removed.

Among hoofed game a hog-dressed animal in the first sense weighs
about 80 percent of what it weighed on the hoof; a dressed animal weighs
about 80 percent of its hog-dressed weight and about 60–70 percent of its
weight on the hoof.

Two small deer that weighed 100 and 116 pounds hog-dressed (say 120
and 145 pounds on the hoof) produced 76 pounds of steaks, chops, roasts,
and burger. This weight did not include the ribs, and presumably the
butcher was honest. But the loss from two deer might be expected to be
greater proportionately than from one, i.e. I would expect that a big buck
weighing 216 pounds hog-dressed having only one head and one hide
would produce a greater percentage of freezer meat than two deer whose
combined weights equaled his.

When You Deliver a Deer to the Food Processor

Although the cuts of a deer are standardized by the nature of the beast and the
practices of butchers, there is ample leeway for choice. If you don't exert it, you
may find yourself without roasts, brisket ribs, or boned breast, and overwhelmed
by a plethora of venisonburger and stew meat. Furthermore, unless you give

specific instructions, the ground meat will leave something to be desired. There is nothing wrong with loin chops, but you just might have preferred one of the loins as a roast. Similarly, you might wish that one ham be made into two roasts, a rump roast and a leg of venison, reserving the other ham for a rump roast and round steaks.

Butchers will invariably cut both loin and round steaks too thin; you must instruct specifically that you want 1½–2-inch steaks if such thickness is your preference.

If you are going to have the venison burger-ground, it will be much better if you ask the processor to add pork fat when he grinds the burger. He will charge extra for this, but it will be worth it, for venison is lean (and you do not want venison fat ground into your burger; it is strong and becomes rancid in the freezer).

When you open the frozen packages for later use, you will have some tissue and fat trimming to do yourself when the meat has thawed. For example, you will need to trim the stew chunks for both fat and membrane, and the steaks should be trimmed of fat also.

Most all processors date and mark the packages for content, and some mark the weight of each package as well. When the weights are not marked, I weigh each package and mark it myself. Later you will need to know to be sure you have the proper quantities for the number of diners at the board.

Usually when you pick up the freezer-packaged meat, you'll wonder where the ribs have gone. Some processors trim the ribs for burger meat; others discard the ribcages. This is too bad, for braised shortribs of venison are delicious.

CARVING A LEG OF VENISON

There are two schools of leg-of-venison carvers: one cuts crosswise and worries out the underside of slice from the encountered bone; the other carves as suggested here. A flexible carver is recommended. Do the job on a hot platter (or on a platter resting on a warming tray) and do it with dispatch, for venison fat (what remains of it) congeals quickly and is unappetizing in texture.

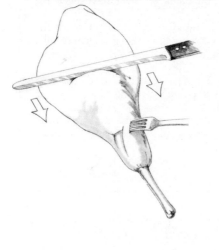

Lay the leg on a big platter or carving board, bone down and shank end to the left.

Start carving partway up the leg, right to left and with the grain.

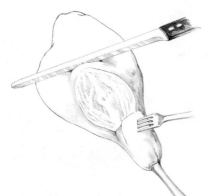

When you have sliced the meat off the top, then slice off the two sides, again with the grain.

The Nomenclature of Carving

So preoccupied were our forebears with the niceties of the etiquette of hunting and feasting on their kills that a bewildering vocabulary of terms evolved to describe the highly formalized procedures of carving game. As if the differentiating terms used in the serving of game were required to match the infinite number and variety of the dishes themselves, a pheasant was "allayed" by these medieval folk; but they "unbraced" a mallard and "dismembered" a heron; similarly they "winged" a quail, "minced" a plover, and "thyed" a pigeon. When you sit down at your table to carve game you "breke" the venison, "rere" the goose, "sauce" a capon, and alas, "disfigure" a peacock (see page 239 for what you do to a salmon or a trout.)

These terms are from the 15th-century *Boke of Kervinge* printed by Wynkyn de Worde. This is the same man who printed the second edition of the famous *The Boke of St. Albans* (1496) that includes a section on hunting attributed by the publisher to the abbess Dame Juliana Berners, who may or may not have contributed also the unsigned section on fishing (the first printed in English, *Treatyse of fisshynge wyth an Angle*) in the same edition.

The material on hawking and hunting was partially plagiarized from an earlier illuminated manuscript, in the Boke of St. Albans, *Venerie de Twety*, written down in the early 1300s.

CARVING A SADDLE OF VENISON

If you have butchered your deer to provide a saddle roast—that is, if you have not had the loin split and each side cut into chops—you will have a big, solid piece of meat that can be sliced lengthwise, with the grain of the loin instead of crosscut.

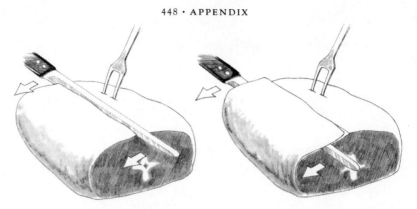

Simply arrange the saddle bone side down and carve toward the bone with the knife slicing parallel to the spinal column. These lengthwise slices should be thin. Needless to say they will be succulent.

Field Dressing and Storing Birds and Waterfowl

I suppose I have handled game birds and waterfowl in just about every way that it is possible to handle them from the field, woods, and marsh to the table. Some of the various ways have been pure opportunism, but as we shall see later some have been experimental. I have carried birds stuffed in the game pocket of an old canvas hunting coat, but I don't recommend it. I have carried them (or on reserves the dog handler has carried them) on a game strap, which is a better way. And I have toted them around both drawn and undrawn by these two methods. Nowadays, I carry a Bean Bird Knife with a gut-hook "blade" and draw the birds in the field or very shortly after coming in.

Similarly, I have hung birds in that "cool, airy place," both drawn and undrawn and for varying lengths of time. On other occasions I have "hung" or aged them by storing them loosely in the refrigerator for a few days before dressing and freezing. I have eaten many a grouse or pheasant the same day it was killed, just as we used to eat chickens the same day we wrung their necks.

As to freezing methods I have also handled them in a variety of ways. When really ambitious, I dry-pluck the birds as soon as I get home, clean them, package them, and freeze them at once. But on other occasions, I have hung them for two or three days before performing these chores.

On a number of occasions I have frozen the birds in the feathers, usually after they had hung for a day or two. The first time I did this involved a dozen doves that were given to me frozen in the feathers and undrawn. My benefactor said simply, "Just take them home as they are (frozen and undrawn) and package them in twos or threes and don't touch them until you are ready to cook them. Then thaw them, pluck them, and dress them just as you would normally do." I took the advice, and all of those doves were simply delicious—and some were not dressed and eaten for several months.

Recently I froze 22 chukars in the feathers; half of them were drawn first, the other half was undrawn. Since then I have cooked birds from both categories, and to me (and our guests) they were delicious.

Birds frozen in the feathers (stored in airtight plastic bags) do not freezer-burn even after several months.

Dry- vs. Wet-Plucking Upland Birds

I must admit that for years I fell under the thralldom of the familiar rule: "Always dry-pluck game birds." I have spent a lot of hours at this and have been plagued with the tediousness of the method. On a few occasions I have skinned game birds, too, and this is perfectly all right for certain cooking methods such as fricassees, stews, etc.

But recently I rebelled, and felt justified in doing so, when I learned from my friend Jim Campbell that he wet-plucked wild turkeys. "Don't douse them in *boiling* water," he advised, "but in hot water of about 195 degrees." The first time, I used some of the chukars mentioned above (frozen in the feathers); I first let them thaw and dunked them three or four times in water whose hotness I had measured with a candy thermometer. I had let the water temperature rise to 185°, figuring to use water less hot for small birds. The feathers of course came off easily, (incidentally, generally speaking, pluck with the grain) and by the time the birds were finished the skin was again cold from the inner temperature of the birds. There had been no cooking of the skin whatever.

Jim advises first wetting down the bird under a lukewarm faucet (against the grain of the feathers); I agree that this is a good opener for hot water dunking, as the bird's feathers are quickly affected by the heat and wetness. I'll never dry-pluck another upland bird.

Trussing a Bird

Set the bird on its back, tail facing you.

Place the center of a long piece of string under the tail, cross it on top, then loop the strands over the ends of the drumsticks and cross them again to hold the legs firmly together above the tail.

Now run the strands along either side of the breast toward the head, then turn the bird, secure the wings flat against the body with the string, and tie the ends together at the back.

Carving Game Birds and Waterfowl

Carving, whether it be a leg of venison or a pheasant or partridge is unduly intimidating to many servers. If at first you are one of these, remember two things: the chances are that no one else at your board knows any more about it than you do, and, second, also remember that your guests have not only an affectionate tolerance "for him who has to carve," but they deserve to view the process, for the ritual adds to your guests' appetites. Nothing stimulates salivation like the appearance of the platter with the garnished roast or bird, and with "mine host" presiding with his carving utensils.

I always bring a steel to the board and give the blade a few professional flourishes before beginning the carving. All instructions are given for a right-hand carver.

Carving Pheasant

This bird is of sufficient size to carve just as you would a roast chicken, and eventually you will be able to do it with just the two-tined fork and the knife, i.e., without touching the bird with your fingers. The joints on the pheasant are easy to find (as we shall see later, this is less true of a wild duck or goose). But don't worry if you have to take hold of a wing with thumb and fingers; the point is to get on with it.

Place the bird on its back with the legs pointing toward you, your fork holding the bird down, and slice down through the skin between the body and the leg's second joint.

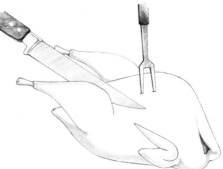

Turn your wrist to the right and press the leg down with the flat of your blade. This will expose the joint at the hip.

You can now easily cut through between the joint and remove the leg. Lay it on a plate.

Separate drumstick from the second joint with the tip of your knife. You won't have any trouble finding the knee joint. Remove other leg in same fashion.

Turn the bird with the tail pointing away from you and, cutting close to the body, remove the wing. Again by slicing and juggling, you will find the wing joint easily. Do the same for the other side.

Now lay the bird on its side, breastbone to your right. Hold it down with your fork and carve from the thick side toward the breastbone, in slices or by taking off the whole breast in one piece. Repeat process on the other side.

Serve the stuffing if you have stuffed the bird, for now the carcass is only a handy receptacle for these goodies.

Carving a Mallard

In carving a wild duck you may find a third utensil, the poultry shears, a useful tool; and you can, if you wish, carve the duck in the kitchen. The point is that you are going to serve it in six pieces, for starters a half of bird to each guest (breast with wing attached and a whole leg). You can, if you wish, serve a whole half, with wing and leg attached, but this forces the guest to be his own carver. (If you do serve in this fashion, do the crude job with the shears in the kitchen by shearing from vent to neck, breast side up, then by turning the bird over and cutting through or alongside the backbone.)

To Carve at Table With legs facing you, cut through the skin between leg and body until you feel the joint.

Holding the bird firmly with your fork, turn your wrist and with the flat of your blade press the leg over. This tussle can be done with two forks or the finger and one fork. Don't expect the joint magically to reveal itself as a pheasant joint does at this stage, for the hip joint of a duck or goose lies more underneath the bird. You can find it with your knife but a poultry shears will be easier. Cut through the joint.

Lay the severed leg on another plate and separate the two joints. This time you won't have any trouble finding the joint, although the cartilage will be tougher.

The breast can be removed by slicing from the vent end to the neck and right through the bone at the neck, then by pulling off the breast (wing still attached) with two forks, or you can do this with the poultry shears.

Carving a Wild Goose

What has been said about leg joints of the wild duck also applies to the goose, but with the goose, a larger bird, it seems a bit easier to find the hip joint. The same applies to the wing. With a goose you may wish to slice the meat off the two leg joints. The breast, being robust, slices easily.

Carving the Partridge or Grouse

With roasted or spitted chukars, for example, the drill is to serve the bird by halves.

With neck end toward you, breast down, hold the bird with the fork (on the thigh) and cut the bird in half longitudinally, cutting just to the side of the breastbone keel. You may, if you wish, do this job in the kitchen, making use of the poultry shears, which brutally eliminate the vexing problem.

Carving the Wild Turkey

Most American hosts and hostesses have carved a Thanksgiving turkey and will not be surprised to know that carving the wild one is basically the same job. There are a couple differences that might be noted, however. While the wild turkey breast is large, it does not serve as much white meat as a butterball does; second, old hands usually discard the drumstick because of tendons that harden into stiletto and rapierlike "bones" under roasting (see page 146 for removing tendons of gallinaceous birds before cooking).

Place the platter so that the drumsticks point to your right. With your fork press the leg away from the ribcage, and slice through skin. As you press and slice the leg will come away, revealing the joint.

Slice the cartilage between the ball and cup joint and remove the leg to another platter.

With the drumstick tip held by the fingers, cut through the angle between drumstick and thigh. You will have no trouble finding the joint.

Still holding the drumstick, slice downward to remove what meat you can get; also slice meat off the thigh.

With the fork, pull the wing away from the body and cut in and down to find the wing joint; the more you pull the wing away from the body, the easier to find the joint.

Cut off the dried-out wing tip.

To facilitate the slicing of the breast meat, make a long, horizontal cut under the thick part of the breast, end to end, so the slices will fall away.

Slice breast at an angle and, as the slices become larger, take a slice off the neck end of the bird, then another off the tail end, alternately.

Later, after you have similarly sliced the other side, the pulley-bone or wishbone can be cut and pried off, for there will be meat still left on it after the breast has been carved. And besides, the wishbone of a wild turkey should be pulled for luck.

Supplementary Reading

Harold F. Blaisdell. *The Art of Fishing with Worms and Other Live Bait.* Alfred A. Knopf, New York (1977). Photographs and clearly written text show just how to dress and fillet various game fish.

Robert Candy. *Getting the Most from Your Fish and Game.* Garden Way Publishing, Charlotte, Vermont (1978). An eminently useful little book on handling game and fish that includes illuminating drawings on almost every process relating to dressing, skinning, and butchering big and small game and gamebirds plus expert advice on handling, filleting, and freezing fish as well.

Editors of *House and Garden*, Introduction by James Beard. *The Art of Carving.* Simon and Schuster, New York (1963).

Jack Sleight. *The Smoked-Foods Recipe Book.* Stackpole Books, Harrisburg, Pennsylvania (1973).

————. *The Home Book of Smoke-Cooking Meat, Fish and Game.* Stackpole Books, Harrisburg, Pennsylvania (1971).

Gretchen McHugh. *The Hungry Hiker's Book of Good Cooking.* Alfred A. Knopf, New York (1982).

Index

About the Authors

ANGUS CAMERON was born in Indianapolis and educated at DePauw University. In his distinguished career in publishing, spanning nearly fifty years, Mr. Cameron has worked at Bobbs-Merrill, at Little, Brown & Company where he was editor-in-chief, and from 1959 to 1980 at Alfred A. Knopf as senior editor and vice president. There he edited a wide range of books in history, natural history and the social sciences, and many classic hunting and fishing books by such authors as Ray Bergman, Jack O'Connor, and Arnold Gingrich. He is the author of a book on owls, *The Nightwatchers* (1971), and his many articles, derived from his extensive camping and hunting throughout North America, have appeared in *Field & Stream, Outdoor Life, Sports Afield,* and *Fly Fisherman.* He lives with his wife, Sheila, in Connecticut.

JUDITH JONES was born in New York, and has spent her summers in northern Vermont. She was educated at the Brearley School in New York and at Bennington College. She is a senior editor and vice president at Alfred A. Knopf, where for more than twenty-five years she has worked with many distinguished authors and has specialized in cookbooks, including those by Julia Child and James Beard. Recently she was responsible for the newly revised edition of *The Fannie Farmer Cookbook.* She is the author, with her husband, Evan Jones, of *The Book of Bread,* and *Knead It, Punch It, Bake It,* a children's baking book, and collaborated with him on the recipes for *American Food: The Gastronomic Story.*